Economic Costs and Consequences of Environmental Regulation

International Library of Environmental Economics and Policy
General Editors: Tom Tietenberg and Wendy Morrison

Titles in the Series

Fisheries Economics, Volumes I and II
Lee G. Anderson

Green Accounting
Peter Bartelmus and Eberhard K. Seifert

The Economics of International Environmental Agreements
Amitrajeet A. Batabyal

Agro-Environmental Policy
Sandra S. Batie and Rick Horan

Direct Environmental Valuation Methods, Volumes I and II
Richard T. Carson

International Trade and the Environment
Judith M. Dean

Economic Costs and Consequences of Environmental Regulation
Wayne B. Gray

The Theory and Practice of Command and Control Regulation
Gloria E. Helfand and Peter Berck

The Economics of Residential Solid Waste Management
Thomas C. Kinnaman

Property Rights and Environmental Problems, Volume I and II
Bruce Larson

Indirect Valuation Methods
Robert Mendelsohn

The Economics of Land Use
Peter J. Parks and Ian W. Hardie

The Economics of Sustainability
John C.V. Pezzey and Michael A. Toman

The Economics of Biodiversity Conservation
Stephen Polasky

The Economics of Environmental Monitoring and Enforcement
Clifford S. Russell

Discounting and Environmental Policy
Joel D. Scheraga

Economics of Forestry
Roger A. Sedjo

Economics and Liability for Environmental Problems
Kathleen Segerson

Experiments in Environmental Economics, Volumes I and II
Jason F. Shogren

Emissions Trading Programs, Volumes I and II
Tom Tietenberg

Economic Costs and Consequences of Environmental Regulation

Edited by

Wayne B. Gray

Clark University, USA

LONDON AND NEW YORK

First published 2002 by Dartmouth Publishing Company and Ashgate Publishing

Reissued 2018 by Routledge
2 Park Square, Milton Park, Abingdon, Oxon OX14 4RN
711 Third Avenue, New York, NY 10017, USA

Routledge is an imprint of the Taylor & Francis Group, an informa business

Copyright © Wayne B. Gray 2002.
For copyright of individual articles please refer to the Acknowledgements.

All rights reserved. No part of this book may be reprinted or reproduced or utilised in any form or by any electronic, mechanical, or other means, now known or hereafter invented, including photocopying and recording, or in any information storage or retrieval system, without permission in writing from the publishers.

Notice:
Product or corporate names may be trademarks or registered trademarks, and are used only for identification and explanation without intent to infringe.

Publisher's Note
The publisher has gone to great lengths to ensure the quality of this reprint but points out that some imperfections in the original copies may be apparent.

Disclaimer
The publisher has made every effort to trace copyright holders and welcomes correspondence from those they have been unable to contact.

A Library of Congress record exists under LC control number: 2001022939

ISBN 13: 978-1-138-73114-1 (hbk)
ISBN 13: 978-1-138-73111-0 (pbk)
ISBN 13: 978-1-315-18801-0 (ebk)

Contents

Acknowledgements ix
Series Preface xi
Introduction xiii

PART I   PRODUCTIVITY AND PRODUCTION FUNCTIONS

1. Edward F. Denison (1978), 'Effects of Selected Changes in the Institutional and Human Environment Upon Output Per Unit of Input', *Survey of Current Business*, **58**, pp. 21–44. — 3
2. Gregory B. Christainsen and Robert H. Haveman (1981), 'Public Regulations and the Slowdown in Productivity Growth', *American Economic Review*, **71**, pp. 320–25. — 27
3. Wayne B. Gray (1987), 'The Cost of Regulation: OSHA, EPA and the Productivity Slowdown', *American Economic Review*, **77**, pp. 998–1006. — 33
4. Frank M. Gollop and Mark J. Roberts (1983), 'Environmental Regulations and Productivity Growth: The Case of Fossil-fueled Electric Power Generation', *Journal of Political Economy*, **91**, pp. 654–74. — 43
5. Wayne B. Gray and Ronald J. Shadbegian (1995), 'Pollution Abatement Costs, Regulation, and Plant-Level Productivity', *NBER Working Paper 4994*, pp. i, 1–30. — 65
6. Klaus Conrad and Catherine J. Morrison (1989), 'The Impact of Pollution Abatement Investment on Productivity Change: An Empirical Comparison of the U.S., Germany, and Canada', *Southern Economic Journal*, **55**, pp. 684–98. — 97
7. Runar Brännlund, Rolf Färe and Shawna Grosskopf (1995), 'Environmental Regulation and Profitability: An Application to Swedish Pulp and Paper Mills', *Environmental and Resource Economics*, **6**, pp. 23–36. — 113

PART II   PLANT LOCATION

8. Timothy J. Bartik (1988), 'The Effects of Environmental Regulation on Business Location in the United States', *Growth and Change*, **9**, pp. 22–44. — 129
9. Arik Levinson (1996), 'Environmental Regulations and Manufacturers' Location Choices: Evidence from the Census of Manufactures', *Journal of Public Economics*, **62**, pp. 5–29. — 153
10. Randy Becker and Vernon Henderson (2000), 'Effects of Air Quality Regulations on Polluting Industries', *Journal of Political Economy*, **108**, pp. 379–421. — 179

PART III MACROECONOMIC AND GENERAL EQUILIBRIUM EFFECTS

11 Dale W. Jorgenson and Peter J. Wilcoxen (1990), 'Environmental Regulation and U.S. Economic Growth', *Rand Journal of Economics*, **21**, pp. 314–40. 225
12 Michael Hazilla and Raymond J. Kopp (1990), 'Social Cost of Environmental Quality Regulations: A General Equilibrium Analysis', *Journal of Political Economy*, **98**, pp. 853–73. 253

PART IV TRADE AND COMPETITIVENESS

13 Carlo Carraro and Marzio Galeotti (1997), 'Economic Growth, International Competitiveness and Environmental Protection: R & D and Innovation Strategies with the WARM Model', *Energy Economics*, **19**, pp. 2–28. 277
14 Xinpeng Xu (1999), 'Do Stringent Environmental Regulations Reduce the International Competitiveness of Environmentally Sensitive Goods? A Global Perspective', *World Development*, **27**, pp. 1215–26. 305
15 H. David Robison (1988), 'Industrial Pollution Abatement: The Impact on Balance of Trade', *Canadian Journal of Economics*, **21**, pp. 187–99. 317

PART V MISCELLANEOUS EFFECTS

Plant Closures
16 Mary E. Deily and Wayne B. Gray (1991), 'Enforcement of Pollution Regulations in a Declining Industry', *Journal of Environmental Economics and Management*, **21**, pp. 260–74. 335

Investment
17 Wayne B. Gray and Ronald J. Shadbegian (1998), 'Environmental Regulation, Investment Timing, and Technology Choice', *Journal of Industrial Economics*, **46**, pp. 235–56. 353

Capital Turnover
18 Randy A. Nelson, Tom Tietenberg and Michael R. Donihue (1993), 'Differential Environmental Regulation: Effects on Electric Utility Capital Turnover and Emissions', *Review of Economics and Statistics*, **75**, pp. 368–73. 377
19 B. Peter Pashigian (1984), 'The Effect of Environmental Regulation on Optimal Plant Size and Factor Shares', *Journal of Law & Economics*, **27**, pp. 1–28. 383

PART VI THE PORTER HYPOTHESIS

20 Michael E. Porter and Claas van der Linde (1995), 'Toward a New Conception of the Environment-Competitiveness Relationship', *Journal of Economic Perspectives*, **9**, pp. 97–118. 413

21 Karen Palmer, Wallace E. Oates and Paul R. Portney (1995), 'Tightening Environmental Standards: The Benefit-Cost or the No-Cost Paradigm?', *Journal of Economic Perspectives*, **9**, pp. 119–32. 435

Name Index 449

Acknowledgements

The editor and publishers wish to thank the following for permission to use copyright material.

Academic Press for the essay: Mary E. Deily and Wayne B. Gray (1991), 'Enforcement of Pollution Regulations in a Declining Industry', *Journal of Environmental Economics and Management*, **21**, pp. 260–74. Copyright © 1991, Elsevier Science USA.

American Economic Association for the essays: Gregory B. Christainsen and Robert H. Haveman (1981), 'Public Regulations and the Slowdown in Productivity Growth', *American Economic Review*, **71**, pp. 320–25; Wayne B. Gray (1987), 'The Cost of Regulation: OSHA, EPA and the Productivity Slowdown', *American Economic Review*, **77**, pp. 998–1006; Michael E. Porter and Claas van der Linde (1995), 'Toward a New Conception of the Environment-Competitiveness Relationship', *Journal of Economic Perspectives*, **9**, pp. 97–118; Karen Palmer, Wallace E. Oates and Paul R. Portney (1995), 'Tightening Environmental Standards: The Benefit-Cost or the No-Cost Paradigm?', *Journal of Economic Perspectives*, **9**, pp. 119–32.

Blackwell Publishers Ltd for the essays: H. David Robison (1988), 'Industrial Pollution Abatement: The Impact on Balance of Trade', *Canadian Journal of Economics*, **21**, pp. 187–99. Copyright © 1988 Canadian Economics Association; Timothy J. Bartik (1988), 'The Effects of Environmental Regulation on Business Location in the United States', *Growth and Change*, **9**, pp. 22–44; Wayne B. Gray and Ronald J. Shadbegian (1998), 'Environmental Regulation, Investment Timing, and Technology Choice', *Journal of Industrial Economics*, **46**, pp. 235–56. Copyright © 1998 Blackwell Publishers Ltd.

Elsevier Science Ltd for the essays: Arik Levinson (1996), 'Environmental Regulations and Manufacturers' Location Choices: Evidence from the Census of Manufactures', *Journal of Public Economics*, **62**, pp. 5–29. Copyright © 1996 Elsevier Science SA; Carlo Carraro and Marzio Galeotti (1997), 'Economic Growth, International Competitiveness and Environmental Protection: R & D and Innovation Strategies with the WARM Model', *Energy Economics*, **19**, pp. 2–28. Copyright © 1997 Elsevier Science B.V.; Xinpeng Xu (1999), 'Do Stringent Environmental Regulations Reduce the International Competitiveness of Environmentally Sensitive Goods? A Global Perspective', *World Development*, **27**, pp. 1215–26.

Wayne B. Gray and Ronald J. Shadbegian (1995), 'Pollution Abatement Costs, Regulation, and Plant-Level Productivity', *NBER Working Paper 4994*, pp. i, 1–30. Copyright © 1995 Wayne B. Gray and Ronald J. Shadbegian.

Journal of Law & Economics for the essay: B. Peter Pashigian (1984), 'The Effect of Environmental Regulation on Optimal Plant Size and Factor Shares', *Journal of Law & Economics*, **27**, pp. 1–28. Copyright © 1984 The University of Chicago. All rights reserved.

Kluwer Academic Publishers for the essay: Runar Brännlund, Rolf Färe and Shawna Grosskopf (1995), 'Environmental Regulation and Profitability: An Application to Swedish Pulp and Paper Mills', *Environmental and Resource Economics*, **6**, pp. 23–36. Copyright © 1995 Kluwer Academic Publishers.

MIT Press Journals for the essay: Randy A. Nelson, Tom Tietenberg and Michael R. Donihue (1993), 'Differential Environmental Regulation: Effects on Electric Utility Capital Turnover and Emissions', *Review of Economics and Statistics*, **75**, pp. 368–73. Copyright © 1993 The President and Fellows of Harvard College.

Rand Journal of Economics for the essay: Dale W. Jorgenson and Peter J. Wilcoxen (1990), 'Environmental Regulation and U.S. Economic Growth', *Rand Journal of Economics*, **21**, pp. 314–40.

Southern Economic Association for the essay: Klaus Conrad and Catherine J. Morrison (1989), 'The Impact of Pollution Abatement Investment on Productivity Change: An Empirical Comparison of the U.S., Germany, and Canada', *Southern Economic Journal*, **55**, pp. 684–98.

University of Chicago Press for the essays: Frank M. Gollop and Mark J. Roberts (1983), 'Environmental Regulations and Productivity Growth: The Case of Fossil-fueled Electric Power Generation', *Journal of Political Economy*, **91**, pp. 654–74. Copyright © 1983 University of Chicago Press; Randy Becker and Vernon Henderson (2000), 'Effects of Air Quality Regulations on Polluting Industries', *Journal of Political Economy*, **108**, pp. 379–421. Copyright © 2000 University of Chicago Press; Michael Hazilla and Raymond J. Kopp (1990), 'Social Cost of Environmental Quality Regulations: A General Equilibrium Analysis', *Journal of Political Economy*, **98**, pp. 853–73.

Every effort has been made to trace all the copyright holders, but if any have been inadvertently overlooked the publishers will be pleased to make the necessary arrangement at the first opportunity.

Series Preface

The *International Library of Environmental Economics and Policy* explores the influence of economics on the development of environmental and natural resource policy. In a series of twenty five volumes, the most significant journal essays in key areas of contemporary environmental and resource policy are collected. Scholars who are recognized for their expertise and contribution to the literature in the various research areas serve as volume editors and write an introductory essay that provides the context for the collection.

Volumes in the series reflect the broad strands of economic research including 1) Natural and Environmental Resources, 2) Policy Instruments and Institutions and 3) Methodology. The editors, in their introduction to each volume, provide a state-of-the-art overview of the topic and explain the influence and relevance of the collected papers on the development of policy. This reference series provides access to the economic literature that has made an enduring contribution to contemporary and natural resource policy.

TOM TIETENBERG
WENDY MORRISON
General Editors

Introduction

How expensive is environmental regulation, and how does it affect the economy? These questions have been around since the significant increase in government regulation of environmental pollution which began in the early 1970s in most industrialized nations and has spread to developing countries more recently. Regulation has been credited with substantial improvements in environmental quality. At the same time, it has aroused criticism for increasing costs, particularly from businesses which face higher production costs on account of the required pollution abatement expenditures.

A proper understanding of the costs imposed by environmental regulation is important for policy-makers and others concerned with optimal regulatory design. At the simplest level, an accurate estimate of costs is needed to compare with the expected regulatory benefits when deciding whether to implement new regulation, or when evaluating existing regulation. More sophisticated analyses of costs examine the marginal costs of increased stringency in order to identify the optimal level of pollution abatement. If firms respond to higher regulatory costs by closing plants or reducing employment, this may also influence political decisions about whether to tighten or relax environmental standards.

This book focuses on empirical studies of the impact of environmental regulation on the economy, exposing the reader to a variety of estimation methodologies and data sets that have been used in this area. Most of the studies done in this field have used data from the United States, because of greater data availability, but an effort has been made to include studies using data from other countries, including Sweden, Germany and Canada. The more recent studies examined here have generally had access to more detailed data, and are thus able to derive more precise estimates of regulation's impact. Earlier studies have been included as well, to give a sense of the progress made in this research area over time and to provide examples of what can be accomplished within the data limitations currently relevant for most countries.

The book explicitly excludes studies which focus on quantifying the benefits that arise from environmental regulation, or on doing a cost–benefit analysis of regulation (such an analysis can be found in US EPA (1997)). This is not intended to suggest that no benefits come from environmental regulation, or that the costs of regulation always outweigh the benefits – it's just outside the scope of this volume. The relative costs and benefits of environmental regulation also appear to vary substantially across different pollutants. Studies of US regulation (see Freeman, 1982 as well as US EPA, 1997) find that some regulatory programmes have benefits that far exceed their costs – most notably the reduction of particulate concentrations through reduced industrial emissions – whilst others have costs exceeding their benefits.

Measuring Costs: An Overview

Three basic sources provide information on the costs of environmental regulation: surveys, engineering studies, and econometric analyses. The simplest way to collect cost information is to ask the businesses affected by regulation how much they spent for pollution abatement. For the US manufacturing sector the Pollution Abatement Costs and Expenditures (PACE) Survey, carried out annually by the Census Bureau between 1973 and 1994 (and resumed in 1999), provides detailed information on air, water and solid waste pollution abatement spending, both for capital investment and operating costs. This can be supplemented with pollution abatement capital investment data collected for selected non-manufacturing industries, and specific pollution abatement costs such as emissions controls on motor vehicles. A major concern with survey data is its reliance on respondents to correctly allocate costs between abatement and production – for example, investment in new capital that is both cleaner and more productive.

Engineering analyses can be used to predict the costs of particular environmental standards, based on the expert opinion of engineers about what equipment would be needed for compliance. This method is most commonly applied to the prospective analysis of a newly proposed regulation, during the process of preparing supporting documentation comparing its benefits and costs. The major criticism of the engineering approach is its tendency to focus on existing abatement methods and not to allow for improvements in technology that could reduce abatement costs.

Econometric analyses can be used to measure the costs of environmental regulation, if data are available on the cost of production and the extent of regulation faced by the unit of observation, whether plant, firm, industry or economy. This is the approach used by nearly all the studies collected here, although they differ greatly with respect to their unit of observation and data sources. Some of the more recent studies have had access to plant-level information for the US manufacturing sector, combining production cost data with pollution abatement cost survey data, and providing a test of the accuracy of the survey data.

Econometric analyses have the advantage over the other two methods in that they 'let the data speak' regarding the impact of regulation on production costs, and the estimated coefficients provide a direct measure of the size of that impact. However, econometric analyses are subject to biases of their own. Errors in measuring regulation can lead to understatements of regulation's impact, while omitting key variables from the regression can lead to overstatements. These issues are discussed in more detail below.

Productivity and Production Functions

Part I of the book consists of a set of studies that measure the impact of regulatory costs on business through productivity. Productivity is defined as output per unit of input; many different productivity measures are available, using the same output measure but varying in their definition of inputs. Total factor productivity measures include all the plant's inputs (labour, capital and materials), while single factor productivity measures, such as labour productivity (output per worker hour), focus on only one input. Productivity growth happens when a plant increases its output faster than its measured inputs. A plant facing environmental regulation spends money on pollution abatement, increasing its measured inputs, but the result of that spending – improved environmental quality – is not counted as an output of the plant, decreasing the plant's measured productivity.

As noted by Denison (Chapter 1) and elsewhere, this reduction in productivity should be roughly equivalent to the share of pollution abatement costs in the plant's total costs. A plant which spends 2 per cent of its total costs on abatement will have a 2 per cent lower level of productivity, all else being equal. If its abatement costs increase from 1 per cent to 2 per cent of total costs in one year, the plant's annual productivity growth rate would be 1 per cent lower. In this simple approach based on a productivity measurement technique called growth accounting, existing information on abatement costs, expressed as the share of abatement costs in total costs of production, give the expected impact of environmental regulation on total factor productivity. Over time, small changes in productivity *growth rates* add up, resulting in significant changes in productivity *levels*: a 0.5 per cent decline in a plant's annual productivity growth rate, if it persisted for two decades, would result in the plant having a 10 per cent lower productivity level at the end of the period, producing 10 per cent less output than it would otherwise have done with the same inputs.

The technique of growth accounting derives from an essay by Solow (1957), who shows that an aggregate production function can be used to decompose the growth in output into three components: growth in labour, growth in capital and a residual. This residual is identified as technical change, presumably due to improved knowledge about the production process or various technological improvements made over time that are not already captured by the measured growth in capital. Solow demonstrates, using annual US data from 1909–49, that this technical change is an important contributor to economic growth, playing a larger role than capital per worker in explaining the growth in output per worker over that period.

During the 1950s and 1960s the United States continued to enjoy sustained growth in productivity, and associated benefits in terms of steadily growing income and output levels. Denison (1974) applies the growth accounting method to detailed US data for this period. Again, the data show a sizeable positive rate of total factor productivity growth, indicating that the growth rate of output exceeded that of measured inputs.

In the 1970s aggregate measures of total factor productivity growth in the United States began to turn negative, as measured output grew more slowly than measured inputs. This led to some awkwardness regarding the interpretation of the productivity residual – did negative values represent decreasing knowledge about the production process or signs of technological regress? It also led to a search for significant changes in the economy that might help explain the productivity growth decline. Besides increases in government regulation, particularly for environmental regulation, the increase in energy prices during the 1970s and the deterioration in the macroeconomic climate stood out as potential explanations of the decline.

How can fluctuations in energy prices or the business cycle affect a total factor productivity calculation that, in principle, accounts for all the inputs used in production? The answer lies in the capital input, which is measured in terms of the stock of available capital rather than the capital that is actually being used for production. In a recession, factories may operate on reduced shifts, or not at all, but the capital stock that makes up those factories is still being counted as if it were producing output, overstating capital inputs and reducing measured productivity in much the same way as described above for pollution abatement costs. To minimize this problem, calculations of productivity growth rates tend to be averaged over an entire business cycle, and regression analyses of productivity tend to include year dummies, to control for differences between recession and boom years.

High energy prices may raise the cost of operating old, energy-inefficient machinery to the point where it is temporarily (or permanently) taken out of service, although it is likely to remain counted in the capital stock. High energy prices may also discourage the use of capital, as indicated by the finding of Berndt and Wood (1975) that capital and energy are complements in production. Although in principle the capital input accounts for the contribution of new capital to production, in practice new investments provide the mechanism by which the latest technological advances are incorporated into production. In fact, similar arguments provide an explanation for the considerable impact of environmental regulation on productivity: some of the capital stock is now too polluting to be operated, but is still included in measured capital inputs, and pollution regulators focus on large, capital-intensive plants with highly visible pollution, raising the costs of capital relative to other inputs. In any event, it could be difficult to disentangle the impacts of energy prices from regulatory stringency: both increased during the 1970s, and energy-intensive plants and industries often operate their own power plants, generating sizeable amounts of air pollution.

In Chapter 1 Denison provides one of the earliest attempts to quantify the contribution of different factors to the productivity slowdown. He uses the same methodology as in his 1974 book, but focuses on changes in the business environment that might have reduced productivity: environmental regulation, health and safety regulation and criminal activity. He examines US productivity growth between 1967 and 1975 – the very beginning of the productivity slowdown. A particular strength of his essay is his painstaking attention to detail in describing the sources of regulatory cost data, along with the distinctions he makes between the different types of cost which belong in the abatement cost calculations. He estimates that environmental regulation had an increasing impact on productivity growth over the period, slowing annual total factor productivity growth by 0.23 per cent in 1975.

Other early studies use multiple regression analysis on aggregate or industry-level data to estimate the impact of environmental regulation on productivity. Christainsen and Haveman (Chapter 2) use annual data for the US manufacturing sector for 1958–77 to estimate a relationship between regulation and labour productivity, controlling for cyclical fluctuations and a time trend. They test a variety of measures of regulatory intensity by the federal government, including regulatory expenditures and full-time regulatory employees. They conclude that federal regulations are responsible for slowing annual productivity growth by about 0.3 per cent, representing about one-fifth of the slowdown in labour productivity growth in the 1970s.

Gray (Chapter 3 and 1986) uses data for 1958–78 to measure the total factor productivity performance of 450 US manufacturing industries and finds that industries which faced higher regulation had slower productivity growth and a greater productivity slowdown during the 1970s. Measures of both environmental and worker health and safety regulation are included in the analysis. Environmental regulation accounts for a slowdown of between 0.17 and 0.28 per cent in the average industry's annual total factor productivity growth rate, up to one-fifth of the average industry's slowdown. The estimates of regulation's impact are smallest in analyses which control for each industry's energy costs, confirming the notion that energy-intensive industries are also pollution-intensive.

Conrad and Morrison (Chapter 6) use time series data for the manufacturing sectors in the United States, Canada and Germany to compare the impact on measured productivity growth of increases in environmental regulation which began around 1970 in all three countries. In traditional productivity measures, all the capital stock is assumed to contribute to production – even the capital being used for pollution abatement. They adjust the productivity calculations for this mismeasurement, and find that the rapid growth of pollution abatement capital had its strongest impact in the United States, accounting for a 0.23 understatement in annual total factor productivity growth rates during the 1973–80 period – about one-fifth of the overall slowdown in traditionally measured productivity growth. The comparable numbers for Germany and Canada are 0.12 and 0.05 per cent, respectively.

Norsworthy, Harper and Kunze (1979) also studied regulation's impact on the productivity slowdown, using growth accounting to calculate the contribution of various components of the capital stock, including mismeasurement due to pollution abatement capital. They report results for the private business, private non-farm business and manufacturing sectors. Not surprisingly, they find that pollution abatement capital expenditures had the largest impact in the manufacturing sector, since that sector had the largest abatement costs. They estimate that annual labour productivity growth in manufacturing was about 0.16 per cent lower than it would have been without regulation – about one-tenth of the slowdown in measured productivity.

Scherer (1982) focuses primarily on the relationship between productivity growth and spending for research and development for 87 industries, mostly in manufacturing, but he also tests for an impact of environmental regulation, measured as the share of investment devoted to meeting environmental, health and safety regulations. He finds that higher abatement spending is associated with lower labour productivity growth, with an implied reduction of up to 0.27 per cent per year. The results were not statistically significant, perhaps due to the small sample size in the regressions.

Table 1 shows the estimated contribution of environmental regulation towards the productivity slowdown for these studies, focusing on results for the US manufacturing sector. Note that the actual magnitude of the reduction in productivity growth is similar across the studies, although the analytical methodology and data sets used vary widely. It appears that environmental regulations contributed slightly more than 0.2 per cent to the slowdown in annual productivity growth during the 1970s. The fraction of the total slowdown explained by environmental regulation is also similar across the studies – about 20 per cent.

Table 1 Environmental regulation and productivity slowdown, US manufacturing sector: comparison of results

	Annual reduction %	Slowdown %	LP/ TFP	Method	Data	Time period
Denison (Chapter 1)	0.23	NA	TFP	Growth account	Aggregate	1975
Christainsen and Haveman (Chapter 2)	0.27	21	LP	OLS	Aggregate	1973–77
Gray (Chapter 3)	0.17–0.28	12–19	TFP	OLS	Industries	1973–78
Conrad and Morrison (Chapter 6)	0.23	18	TFP	Index	Aggregate	1973–80
Norsworthy et al. (1979)	0.16	11	LP	Growth account	Aggregate	1973–78
Scherer (1982)[1]	0.19–0.27	24–35	LP	OLS	Industries	1973–78

[1] Scherer (1982) includes 81 manufacturing and six non-manufacturing industries.

Other studies have examined differences in regulatory impacts across industries. Barbera and McConnell (1986) look at four US industries (paper, chemicals, primary metals and stone, clay and glass). Using annual data on production and pollution abatement capital expenditures between 1960 and 1980, they run separate analyses for each industry and find that abatement expenditures significantly reduced productivity growth for three of the four industries, paper being the exception, whose abatement expenditures are not significantly related to productivity growth. The estimated reductions in annual productivity growth rates range from 0.28 to 0.38 per cent, and account for a large part of the productivity slowdown for those industries whose productivity fell in the 1970s.

In a study examining ten German industries from 1975–91, Conrad and Wastel (1995) find much smaller effects than studies using US data. They find significant differences across industries, with reductions in annual productivity growth rates ranging from 0.03 to 0.15 per cent. They also find that environmental regulation affected measured productivity significantly more in the 1986–91 period than it had in the 1976–85 period.

A more recent set of studies has used plant-specific data to examine the impact of environmental regulation on productivity. Gray and Shadbegian (Chapter 5) use 1979–90 Census Bureau data on US manufacturing plants in the steel, oil and paper industries, comparing pollution abatement operating costs from the PACE survey at each plant with the plant's productivity performance. They find that productivity levels are significantly lower at plants which have higher abatement costs. This impact of regulation on productivity is noticeably larger than would have been predicted from a standard growth accounting calculation, with a $1.00 increase in abatement costs being associated with reductions in productivity of $1.74, $1.35 and $3.28 for paper, oil and steel plants respectively. These results are consistent with a substantial understatement of abatement costs in the PACE survey, at least for the paper and steel industries.

One caveat regarding the Gray and Shadbegian results is that they are based on ordinary regression results, and derive most of their explanatory power from variation across plants in productivity levels and abatement costs. If some relevant variables have been omitted from the analysis, the results could be biased. For example, suppose that plants with inept managers spend more than they need to for both pollution abatement and production. The econometric analysis will associate high abatement costs with low productivity across plants, even though increasing the abatement costs at a given plant might not have any direct effect on that plant's productivity.

The usual econometric solution, given a panel data set including multiple years of data for each plant, is to eliminate all plant-specific fixed factors from the analysis in a fixed-effects model. Unfortunately, this results in another source of bias if there is measurement error, as noted in Griliches and Mairesse (1995). Since fixed-effects models eliminate much of the real cross-plant variation in abatement costs while retaining the random measurement errors, measurement errors become a relatively larger part of the variation in regulation. This tends to push the estimated impact of regulation towards zero. In fact, Gray and Shadbegian find that the estimated impact of regulation on productivity is substantially reduced when they include fixed effects in the analysis. Unfortunately, they cannot distinguish whether this reduced impact is due to eliminating biases from omitted variables, or due to increasing measurement error.

Recently, other studies have taken advantage of the plant-level Census Bureau data on productivity and abatement costs. Like Gray and Shadbegian, Morgenstern et al. (1997) find much smaller effects of regulation on productivity when fixed-effect analyses are used, and also find sizeable variation in effects across industries. Becker and Henderson (1999) use data on county non-attainment status to identify plants which face more stringent air pollution regulations. These plants have significantly higher costs, and hence lower productivity levels. In contrast, Berman and Bui (2001) focus on oil refineries, using detailed measures of local regulatory stringency in the Los Angeles area, and find no evidence that productivity was falling during a period in the early 1990s when regulatory stringency and abatement costs were increasing substantially. Part of this variation across studies may be attributable to differences across industries, as Gray and Shadbegian find their smallest impacts for oil refineries.

Other studies of regulation's impact on costs use more detailed production function models to see how the entire production process responds to environmental regulation. Gollop and Roberts (Chapter 4) use data from 1973–79 for the electric power industry, measuring regulatory intensity by comparing firm-specific data on actual emissions with permitted emissions and desired unconstrained emissions. This allows them to identify which firms were actually constrained by regulation, and they find that the firms without regulatory constraints had significantly faster productivity growth, with regulation reducing annual productivity growth at regulated firms by 0.59 per cent. Their use of a production function model, rather than a simple productivity regression, allows them to examine the impact of regulation on specific inputs. For example, since utilities often reduce emissions by switching fuels, the model includes low-sulphur and high-sulphur fuels as separate inputs, along with capital and labour, and finds that regulation increases the demand for low-sulphur fuels while decreasing the demand for high-sulphur fuels. Much of the increase in production costs due to regulation can be attributed to the use of more expensive low-sulphur fuels.

Brännlund *et al.* (Chapter 7) use data from 1989–90 for a set of Swedish pulp and paper mills, incorporating production and input data along with data on discharges of specific water pollutants. A non-parametric production function is estimated, with plants assumed to maximize their output, subject to the constraints on pollution emissions imposed by regulations. The results of the estimation indicate that a majority of plants are not constrained by the pollution regulations. This may be related to the short-term nature of the analysis, which does not include information on pollution abatement capital and only includes two years of discharge data, with hardly any plants facing changes in permitted emissions.

Plant Location

Part II turns to studies of the economic consequences of environmental regulation as firms respond to cost differences. The first area of firm response considered is the plant location decision. Here the presumption is that a firm's location decision is based on a number of factors, including factor prices and availability, as well as the costs of complying with environmental regulation. One often-expressed concern is that more stringent environmental regulations discourage firms from opening new plants. This is incorporated in theoretical models such as Markusen *et al.* (1993) which shows the possibility of a 'race to the bottom' in environmental stringency: when one jurisdiction relaxes its standards in order to attract new investment, neighbouring jurisdictions reduce their standards, with serious consequences for overall environmental quality. This outcome is especially likely for pollutants whose damages are dispersed over a wide area. The models can yield the opposite prediction, with a 'race to the top' or 'Not In My Back Yard' outcome, if the damages from a pollutant are concentrated in a smaller area than the benefits derived from new jobs.

A concern about states competing for new investment was one of the initial justifications given in the United States for establishing federal control over environmental standards; it would reduce the temptation for individual states to relax their standards for competitive reasons. Similar concerns were also used later to justify regulatory initiatives such as the New Source Performance Standards and Prevention of Significant Deterioration programmes. Both these programmes increased the stringency faced by new plants, even in locations where air pollution was a relatively minor problem so that the applicable standards would have been relatively weak. However, in analyses of the political support for these regulatory initiatives, both Navarro (1981) and Crandall (1983) find that the principle beneficiaries were eastern industrial and coal industries, and Congressional voting on the 1977 Clean Air Act Amendments paralleled these economic interests.

Given the political interest in plant location, along with some data sources that show where new plants arise, it is not surprising that many studies have tested whether the location of new plants is influenced by local environmental stringency. The studies have varied substantially in terms of the data used, with some focusing on specific industries and others using broader measures, although all the studies included here (and all large-scale published studies) use data for plants in the US manufacturing sector for reasons of data availability. Since part of the federal regulatory structure is designed to equalize compliance costs across states, the magnitude of compliance cost differences in US data may be quite small, at least when compared to international differences in compliance costs.

In Chapter 8 Bartik uses data for 1607 plants owned by Fortune 500 firms, which opened between 1972 and 1978. He estimates a model predicting the state in which the plant will open, using a variety of control variables and several regulatory measures, including spending for pollution abatement by firms and spending for pollution regulation by the state – separately for air and water pollution and direct measures of the stringency of the regulation of particulate emissions. He finds no significant effects of regulation on plant location; the particulate emissions stringency measure is negative, and larger for plants in high-polluting industries, but its effect is quite small and statistically insignificant. He interprets the results as supporting the conventional wisdom that environmental regulation imposes only small cost disadvantages on high-regulation states, so that location decisions should not be greatly affected.

Levinson (Chapter 9) uses data for 3880 plants which opened between 1982 and 1987, and considers, in particular, 2060 plants which were owned by large, multi-plant companies. He uses a model similar to Bartik's, predicting in which state the plant will open, using a variety of control variables and a slightly different set of regulatory measures. He finds some statistically significant effects for regulation, but the impacts are quite small, with a one standard deviation increase in regulation being associated with a 1.2–1.7 per cent decline in the probability of a plant locating in that state. He examines data for individual industries, but does not find consistently larger results for high-regulation industries, and concludes that environmental regulation has had little impact on plant location.

Becker and Henderson (Chapter 10) use a longer span of data, covering plants which opened between 1963 and 1992, and use county-level data, because their regulation measure is ozone non-attainment status at the county level. They look at four specific manufacturing industries that are high emitters of volatile organic compounds, major precursors of ozone, and are therefore likely to be targets of regulatory agencies seeking to improve ozone quality. They find large and statistically significant decreases of new plant openings in non-attainment counties, ranging from 26–45 per cent. On examining the timing of these impacts, they discover that plants opened by larger, multi-plant firms were affected sooner (1972–77) than those owned by single-plant firms (1977–82), consistent with the larger firms having an earlier understanding of the regulatory process.

In addition to the impact on new plants, their analysis shows that regulation raises survival rates at existing plants, perhaps due to those plants gaining a competitive advantage from being grandfathered. They also find that new plants in non-attainment areas tend to be larger initially and then grow more slowly, consistent with their facing stricter regulations on facility expansions. The overall impact is to spread out emissions of volatile organic compounds, with fewer emissions in the initially high-ozone counties and more in the initially low-ozone counties. This may be optimal, since it reduces peak ozone exposures in high-population areas, but also represents an unintended consequence of the regulation whose authors did not recognize the incentives it provided to locate new plants in formerly clean areas.

Macroeconomic and General Equilibrium Effects

The previously described studies examined the costs of environmental regulation from the perspective of the regulated businesses, measured in terms of the costs they incurred for pollution abatement, and the effects of such costs on decisions concerning plant location. Part III moves on to studies which focus attention on the interactions between different sectors of the economy as the entire economy responds to the costs induced by higher levels of environmental regulation. These studies can find either larger or smaller impacts of regulation, depending on the types of interactions being considered.

Jorgenson and Wilcoxen (Chapter 11) use a detailed sectoral model of the US economy, quantifying the impact of pollution controls on production costs in specific industries for the 1974–85 period, looking separately at operating costs and capital expenditures associated with pollution abatement, along with motor vehicle emissions control equipment. They find that investment in pollution abatement capital has the largest impact on the economy, having increased the cost of capital equipment and reduced investment in productive equipment throughout the economy, not just in those sectors which made large investments in pollution abatement capital. The overall impact of environmental regulation was to reduce US output growth by 0.19 per cent annually during the period.

In Chapter 12 Hazilla and Kopp also use a multi-sectoral model of the US economy, with 36 production sectors. Their focus is on comparing the private and social costs of pollution abatement, and they find substantial general equilibrium effects on this comparison. Given competitive product markets, sectors experiencing high pollution abatement costs raise their prices substantially. This reduces demand for their output and shrinks their importance in the economy as a whole, so the general equilibrium effect of abatement costs on the overall economy is less than a partial equilibrium analysis would suggest. Even more important, the general equilibrium model allows substitution between labour and leisure by consumers. As nearly all goods become more expensive, consumers choose to work less, earn less income, and consume more leisure.

On the investment side of their model, lower income means lower savings and less investment, which substantially reduces economic growth over the long run. They analyse compliance costs over the 1975–90 period, and compare traditional partial equilibrium costs (as calculated by EPA) with general equilibrium measures for both 1981 and 1990. In 1981, the benefits to consumers from increased leisure dominates the calculation, with social costs being one-third lower than private costs ($28.3 billion versus $42.5 billion). However, by 1990 the reductions in investment slow down growth, and the price level rises substantially, so the nominal dollar comparison shows greater costs in the general equilibrium model ($977.0 billion versus $648.0 billion).

The bottom line to be gained from these general equilibrium models is that, while environmental regulation imposes significant direct costs on only a few industries, many other industries face substantial indirect costs as a result of higher costs for their inputs. These indirect effects are especially likely to operate through the prices of electricity and capital equipment. Some less-regulated industries might benefit from increases in demand for their output if consumers substitute between goods, but not if consumers substitute leisure for consumption. Modelling the determinants of technology change is especially important for long-run projections, and could provide a mechanism for relatively inexpensive improvements in environmental performance (bearing in mind the caveats expressed in Palmer *et al.* (Chapter 21) about the opportunity cost of firms' research activity being directed towards a particular environmental goal).

Another active research area tests whether the interactions between environmental regulation and the existing tax system might affect the welfare implications of the regulation. Early work in this area speculated that using the revenues from an environmental tax to reduce other taxes might provide a 'double dividend' to the economy – removing the environmental externality while also reducing the economic distortion caused by other taxes. Bovenberg and de Mooij (1994) show that, instead, environmental taxes tend to interact with other tax distortions, resulting in a smaller optimal pollution tax. Despite this negative conclusion, recycling pollution tax revenue to reduce other taxes is still a good idea when compared to alternative policies which return revenue in a less efficient way, such as with a lump-sum rebate, or policies which generate no revenue, such as a pollution permit system in which permits are allocated freely to existing producers. In fact, Parry *et al.* (1999) show that a permit system to reduce carbon dioxide emissions cannot be welfare-improving, given generally accepted values for the benefits of carbon abatement, while a tax system with appropriate revenue recycling can improve welfare.

Trade and Competitiveness

Differences in compliance costs could also influence trade flows between countries from existing plants. Higher production costs could put one country at a competitive disadvantage relative to other countries. In particular, debates about increasing regulatory stringency in developed countries have been coloured by concerns that developing countries with less stringent regulations will gain a trade advantage. A number of studies have used varying methodologies to examine impacts on trade – as with other areas, the greater availability of data for the United States has tended to attract most of the studies.

Part IV opens with Carraro's and Galeotti's examination of the cost of environmental regulation in European countries. Their focus is on modelling technology adoption, particularly the possibility of using policy instruments designed to increase the use of clean, energy-saving technologies. They consider two policy instruments: subsidizing R & D spending to encourage the development of these technologies, or subsidizing investment in new capital equipment to encourage the adoption of new technologies. They apply a general equilibrium model designed to deal with environmental issues (called WARM, for World Assessment of Resource Management) to six European countries, estimating the model parameters for each country using 1978–89 data and then forecasting the results of different policy scenarios for the 1995–2015 period. They find that subsidizing either the development or the adoption of new technologies would be effective in reducing carbon dioxide emissions, by increasing the energy-efficiency of production. Their model also predicts that five of the six countries could achieve both higher economic growth and improved competitiveness over the 1995–2015 period if they adopted these clean-technology policies.

Xu (Chapter 14) uses data on trade flows of environmentally sensitive goods for 34 countries over the 1965–95 period to test whether stricter environmental regulations in some countries led to a shift in production towards less strictly regulated countries. The study compares the export specialization of countries in the 1960s and the 1990s, and finds little evidence of production shifting. The pattern of export performance is quite persistent in the sample period, including for a set of six high-regulation countries. The study concludes that no obvious evidence exists to support the claim that higher environmental standards reduce the international competitiveness of 'dirty' industries.

Mani and Wheeler (1998) examine the shift in location of high-pollution industries across countries over the 1960–95 period. They note that apparel assembly industries have been shifting towards progressively poorer countries over time, to take advantage of low-wage workforces, and hypothesize that polluting industries might exhibit a similar shift towards pollution havens, countries with weak environmental regulations. They find some evidence that such shifts have occurred – with a growing share of pollution-intensive output in developing countries, relative to developed countries. However, these shifts seem to have been driven more by growing domestic demand for basic industrial products in developing countries than by production for export to richer countries, contrary to the notion that world production might become concentrated in a few nations with lax environmental standards. In any event, the cross-country shifts in polluting industries seem to be as transient as the shifts in apparel assembly industries: as economic growth continues in a country, its environmental regulation increases in stringency, reducing its appeal as a pollution haven.

Finally in Chapter 15, Robison uses US pollution abatement operating cost data to examine the 'abatement content' of US imports, exports and total output over the 1973–82 period. All three categories had increasing abatement content over the period, but imports showed larger growth, starting out smaller than total output and ending up slightly larger. The abatement cost ratio between imports and exports increases substantially between 1977 and 1982. He also looks at US trade flows with Canada and finds no such increase, presumably due to the United States and Canada having similarly strict environmental regulations. Calculations of the impact of product prices on trade flows indicate that increasing US abatement costs would tend to reduce the US balance of trade.

Miscellaneous Effects

Plant Closures

Higher costs and lower profits due to environmental regulation may persist over time, affecting the long-run decisions of firms. Firms could invest less in production capital at plants which face greater pollution abatement requirements, for (at least) two reasons. First, strict regulations are likely to raise the marginal cost of production at the plant, inducing the firm to shift production towards other plants – possibly even closing the high-cost plant altogether, if it faces especially high regulatory costs or if the industry is in decline, requiring that some plants be closed anyway. Second, stringent regulations may require substantial investments in abatement capital at the plant, reducing the capital funding available for investments in production capital, especially if the firm follows a rule of thumb, such as a pre-set capital budget for each plant, to allocate routine capital expenditures across plants.

Deily and Gray (Chapter 16) examine the impact of environmental regulation on plant closure decisions in the US steel industry between 1977 and 1986. They measure regulation by the number of enforcement actions directed at the steel mill, and include a number of other factors in modelling whether or not a given mill was closed. They find that plants which face relatively high expected enforcement are significantly more likely to close, although the effect is small: a 12 per cent increase in enforcement increases the probability of plant closing by 1 per cent.

Investment

The production technology in use at the plants may also be influenced by environmental regulation. If there are different technologies to choose from, with different environmental consequences, firms are likely to choose cleaner technologies in plants facing more stringent regulation. More importantly, the very existence of regulation may affect the types of production technology that are in use, by providing incentives to develop and utilize cleaner technologies – recall the importance of this effect in the Carraro and Galeotti analysis reprinted as Chapter 13 of this book. In some cases, this encouragement of technology is done explicitly, through 'technology-forcing' regulations. Such regulations impose an 'impossibly strict' standard (one which no existing technology can meet), in the expectation that research on cleaner production will make it possible to meet the standard by the time it takes effect. A major goal of such regulations is to encourage research in production process changes, especially those geared towards cleaner production.

In Chapter 17 Gray and Shadbegian examine the impact of environmental regulation on both production technology and investment spending decisions, using plant-level data for the pulp and paper industry. Paper mills can employ several different production techniques, and new plants in high-regulation states are more likely to choose a low-pollution technology; choices between technologies with a different mix of air and water pollution are sensitive to the state regulatory agencies' relative stringencies on air and water pollution. Finally, investment in production capital appears to be 'crowded out' by investment in abatement capital, with high-abatement-capital plants doing significantly less investment in non-abatement capital.

On the broader question of whether environmental regulation induces more research effort and quicker technological advance, Jaffe and Palmer (1997) examine industry-level data for manufacturing firms. They find that increasing regulatory stringency, as measured by increasing pollution abatement costs, is associated with higher research and development expenditures in the following year, although the effect is small. On the other hand, they find that the number of successful patent applications in an industry is not related to abatement costs. The overall impression is that while the allocation of research inputs seems to respond to environmental regulation, the outputs from that research effort are not as sensitive.

Capital Turnover

Environmental regulations tend to impose different costs on different regulated parties. Sometimes these cost differences are explicit, as in the common case of grandfathering regulations – not requiring existing plants to meet new standards. This exemption may arguably be necessary, as it is often extremely costly to retrofit an existing plant to meet strict new standards, but it does place new plants at a cost disadvantage. Even when the same regulations are being applied to all plants, larger firms may enjoy substantial economies of scale in compliance, having more plants across which to spread the costs of understanding the regulations and planning an optimal response. Scale economies in pollution abatement equipment are also likely to benefit larger plants, although small plants might benefit from less strict enforcement, as noted in Chapter 10 by Becker and Henderson, if they are presumed to be less capable of compliance, or are simply too small to be noticed by the regulator.

One of the clearest examples of regulatory grandfathering and its potential drawbacks comes in automobile emissions standards. As Gruenspecht (1982) shows with a model simulating owners' decisions, tighter emissions standards on new cars raise their prices, inducing current owners to delay purchasing a new car. This raises the average age of the fleet, and actually increases aggregate emissions in the short run. Alternative regulatory approaches, such as paying a bounty to owners who scrap older vehicles, are predicted to be more effective in reducing overall emissions.

Nelson, Tietenberg and Donihue (Chapter 18) examine a similar issue for private electric utilities over the 1969–83 period. They test whether stricter environmental regulations on new generating plants, combined with the grandfathering of old plants, encouraged firms to maintain their existing plants rather than investing in new plants. They use state air pollution regulation expenditures, the firm's air pollution abatement capital stock, the firm's total abatement capital stock, and an indicator for sulphur dioxide non-attainment status to measure regulatory pressures faced by the firm. They find evidence that environmental regulation has reduced the turnover of capital in the industry, increasing average plant age by over three years, or 22.6 per cent. However, this increased age did not seem to increase sulphur dioxide emissions significantly.

As noted above, regulation is likely to have differential impacts on different sized firms and plants. Pashigian (Chapter 19) examines changes in the number and size distribution of plants in high and low abatement cost manufacturing industries over the 1972–77 period, and compares this to prior changes, going back to 1958. He finds declining numbers of plants and increasing average plant size in high abatement cost industries during the 1970s. This contrasts with the experience of the same industries during the 1960s, and of low abatement cost industries during the 1970s, both of which had decreasing average plant size. These results suggest that the costs imposed by environmental regulation have been a greater burden for small plants, and that regulation has given a competitive advantage to large plants – another potentially unexpected impact of the costs of environmental regulation.

Bartel and Thomas (1987) examine the potential for differential impacts of regulation, both environmental and worker health and safety, on profitability. They find that older and larger plants in declining regions of the country face much less of a burden than new, small plants in growing regions. Regulation may even have caused old and large plants to become more profitable, by exploiting the competitive advantages which the differential impacts of regulation provided to them.

The Porter Hypothesis

Finally, some controversy has arisen about whether environmental regulation could be suitably structured to reduce or eliminate the net costs of compliance, through incentives for innovation and development of new production processes. Mainstream economic analysis has been sceptical, reasoning that if firms could earn higher profits by reducing pollution, they would have done so without government intervention. Unexploited profitable opportunities are like 'unclaimed $10 bills on the ground' – one would expect them to have already been picked up, if they were genuine.

One of the strongest challenges to the mainstream view has been the work of Michael Porter, who developed what has become known as the 'Porter Hypothesis'. Briefly, Porter argues that properly designed environmental regulation can provide net benefits to the regulated firms, by encouraging innovation in clean technologies and by giving domestic firms a head-start on foreign competitors who will eventually be required to develop similarly clean technologies in their own countries. He doesn't suggest that all programmes of strict environmental regulation have net benefits, and he is critical of past implementation of regulation that encourages reliance on a fixed set of end-of-pipe abatement technologies to achieve compliance.

The contrast between the two viewpoints is nicely illustrated in Part VI by the exchange in the *Journal of Economic Perspectives* between Porter and van der Linde (Chapter 20) and Palmer *et al.* (Chapter 21). The former lays out the Porter Hypothesis and provides empirical evidence on its behalf. The evidence consists of many examples of situations in which companies were forced to change their production process for regulatory reasons, and found significant benefits (called pollution offsets) that resulted in higher profitability for the firm, as well as reduced pollution. Porter uses these offsets as evidence that most companies tend to operate with a 'business as usual' approach, not considering significant changes to their production process, so that they often fail to recognize and implement profitable changes in production. The existence of such pervasive opportunities may be an inconvenience for economic models of optimizing firms, but it allows environmental regulation to have a beneficial impact on the economy.

The response of the economists is twofold. First, Palmer *et al.* note that Porter's examples represent only a small, and non-representative, fraction of situations in which firms are affected by environmental regulation. The firms identified by Porter as benefiting from pollution offsets were contacted, and asserted that, despite the cited cases of cost-saving regulation, the overall impact of environmental regulation was to raise their costs of production. Broader evidence comes from questions in the Census Bureau's PACE survey which asks firms to identify pollution offsets. In 1992 these offsets totalled only $1.7 billion, compared to $102 billion in abatement expenditures. This suggests that the overall impact of existing regulation on production costs in the economy is positive, and that the possibility for offsets cancelling out any sizable fraction of abatement costs is remote.

Second, Palmer *et al.* express a concern that the Porter Hypothesis has been used as an argument that environmental regulation does not impose any costs on the economy, removing the need for careful benefit–cost analysis to determine the advisability of increasing regulatory stringency. If strict regulations encourage innovation and raise profits, then regulations should become stricter still – without any obvious limit to the process of increasing stringency. They also express doubts whether environmental regulators are well equipped to identify profitable areas for private research activity and conclude that environmental regulations should not be relied on as a major source of technology enhancement for the economy.

The Policy Impacts of Research

The essays included in this book, and others referenced in this Introduction, represent a sizeable investment of researcher time, spread over the past quarter-century. In recent years more sources of plant-specific microdata have become available, both in the United States and abroad. This provides a rich source of information for testing whether differences in regulation across plants matter, in terms either of production costs or the decisions which firms make based on costs. It seems likely that the research will continue – but what have we learned so far, and how useful has it been for the policy-making process?

The largest single question which policy-makers need to answer is the size of the pollution abatement costs imposed on business by environmental regulation. Estimates of these costs exist, based primarily on surveys of affected firms. These surveys are clearly difficult to answer: among other things, it is difficult to identify precisely the 'pollution abatement' part of a major investment project that reduces pollution and raises production. It is entirely possible that these survey responses are systematically biased, overstating or understating the costs of pollution abatement.

The essay by Gray and Shadbegian (Chapter 5) suggests that pollution abatement costs are substantially understated, to different degrees across the three industries being examined, although (as noted earlier) this is primarily based on cross-plant comparisons. Morgenstern, *et al.* (1997), focusing on fixed-effects results, conclude that abatement costs are overstated. Berman and Bui (2001) find no evidence of understated costs, although they focus on the oil refinery industry which had the smallest degree of understatement in the Gray and Shadbegian study.

How have these abatement cost measurement studies fared in the policy-making arena? Perhaps not surprisingly, given the variety of results, individual studies have been cited in support of pre-existing positions: those who want stronger regulation cite studies suggest little or no cost; those who want weaker regulation cite other studies suggest larger-than-expected costs. This may provide a ready audience for research conclusions, but it's difficult to argue that the research on mismeasured abatement costs has been influential in changing many positions on the desirability of regulation.

One area of environmental policy in which economists have been influential is the use of tradeable permits rather than fixed emissions standards. The strongest arguments for the advantages of flexible regulation may have come from simple, theory-based arguments, but the supporting empirical work was important. Gollop and Roberts (1985) use their earlier estimates of differences in abatement costs across electric utilities from their 1983 study to estimate the cost of reducing sulphur dioxide emissions at 56 electric utilities around the United States. They find that the current abatement expenditures are 47 per cent higher than the cost-minimizing levels, amounting to nearly $2 billion in unnecessary costs. Another essay by Seskin, Anderson and Reid (1983) considers nitrogen oxide emissions in the Chicago area, finding that the current regulatory approach is more than ten times as expensive as the least costly way of achieving the same emission reductions.

These arguments helped convince many participants in the debate over the 1990 Clean Air Act Amendments that emissions trading could lower abatement costs. A political deal was struck, imposing relatively strict overall reductions in sulphur dioxide emissions but allowing for emissions trading among electric utilities to reduce the costs of pollution abatement. Once trading began, the actual emission allowance prices have been far below the pre-trading estimates of marginal abatement costs. This has suggested to many that allowing trading of emissions greatly reduced abatement costs – a clear victory for the economists. However, detailed studies of this market such as Ellerman et al. (2000) and Carlson et al. (2000) find that most of the reduction in abatement costs is due to falling prices for low-sulphur coal and improvements in boiler technology that have allowed more utilities to use low-sulphur coal. The existence of emissions trading may have made firms quicker to switch to low-sulphur coal, compared to traditional command and control regulation, but the lower abatement costs cannot be completely attributed to emissions trading.

Other economic studies of the consequences of environmental regulation could potentially be important for policy-making. For example, in policy debates a common response to calls for stricter regulation is that it would cost jobs, reduce competitiveness or otherwise disadvantage the local economy. Jaffe et al. (1995) extensively review the literature on competitiveness, finding relatively little evidence for large negative economic consequences from environmental regulation – but that message has had little impact on the policy-making process.

Economists can contribute more generally to the design of policy in cases where environmental regulations change the incentives for decision-makers, with possibly unintended consequences. Stricter regulations in dirty areas can lead pollution to spread to once-clean areas (see Becker and Henderson, Chapter 10). Stricter regulations on new plants can lead to delays in replacing old capital, possibly lowering productivity (Nelson, Tietenberg and Donihue, Chapter 18). Making these consequences of regulations more clear – preferably before the regulations are adopted! – could be a valuable contribution to policy-making.

It is important that we have reasonable expectations for the impact of economic research on the making of environmental policy: it may occasionally achieve a major breakthrough in some policy arena, but will most often be used as a source of supporting evidence, marginally bolstering one side or the other of the policy debate. Economists and their empirically-based research are likely to be most effective when their work is based on reasonably straightforward economic theory, when they have large and diverse datasets to work with, when the results are consistent enough across different studies to provide a 'preponderance of evidence' within the policy debate – and when they go to the trouble to explain their results to those who make policy.

References

Barbera, Anthony J. and McConnell, Virginia D. (1986), 'Effects of Pollution Control on Industry Productivity: A Factor Demand Approach', *Journal of Industrial Economics*, **35** (2), December, pp. 161–72.
Bartel, Ann P. and Thomas, Lacy Glenn (1987), 'Predation Through Regulation: The Wage and Profit Effects of the Occupational Safety and Health Administration and the Environmental Protection Agency', *Journal of Law and Economics*, **30**, October, pp. 239–64.
Becker, Randy A. and Henderson, J. Vernon (1999), 'Costs of Air Quality Regulation', *NBER Working Paper 7308*, August.
Berman, Eli and Bui, Linda (2001), 'Economic Regulation and Productivity: Evidence from Oil Refineries', *Review of Economics and Statistics*, **83** (3), August, pp. 498–510.
Berndt, Ernst R. and Wood, David O. (1975), 'Technology, Prices, and the Derived Demand for Energy', *The Review of Economics and Statistics*, **57** (3), August, pp. 259–68.
Bovenberg, A. Lans and de Mooij, Ruud A. (1994), 'Environmental Levies and Distortionary Taxation', *American Economic Review*, **94** (4), September, pp. 1085–89.
Carlson, Curtis, Burtraw, Dallas, Cropper, Maureen and Palmer, Karen L. (2000), 'Sulfur Dioxide Control by Electric Utilities: What Are the Gains from Trade?', *Journal of Political Economy*, **108** (6), December, pp. 1292–1326.
Conrad, Klaus and Wastel, Dieter (1995), 'The Impact of Environmental Regulation on Productivity in German Industries', *Empirical Economics*, **20**, pp. 615–33.
Crandall, Robert W. (1983), *Controlling Industrial Pollution*, Washington, DC: The Brookings Institution.
Denison, Edward F. (1974), *Accounting for United States Economic Growth 1929–1969*, Washington, DC: The Brookings Institution.
Ellerman, A. Denny, Joskow, Paul L., Schmalensee, Richard, Montero, Juan-Pablo and Bailey, Elizabeth M. (2000), *Markets for Clean Air: The U.S. Acid Rain Program*, Cambridge: Cambridge University Press.
Freeman, A. Myrick (1982), *Air and Water Pollution Control: A Benefit-Cost Assessment*, New York: John Wiley & Sons.
Gollop, Frank M. and Roberts, Mark J. (1985), 'Cost Minimizing Regulation of Sulfur Emissions: Regional Gains in Electric Power', *Review of Economics and Statistics*, **67**, February, pp. 81–90.
Gray, Wayne B. (1986), *Productivity vs. OSHA and EPA Regulations*, Ann Arbor, MI: UMI Research Press.
Griliches, Zvi and Mairesse, Jacques (1995), 'Production Functions: The Search for Identification', *NBER Working Paper 5067*, March.
Gruenspecht, Howard K. (1982), 'Differentiated Regulation: The Case of Auto Emissions Standards', *American Economic Review*, **72** (2), May, pp. 328–31.
Jaffe, Adam B. and Palmer, Karen (1997), 'Environmental Regulation and Innovation: A Panel Data Study', *Review of Economics and Statistics*, **79** (4), November, pp. 610–19.
Jaffe, Adam B., Peterson, Steven R., Portney, Paul R. and Stavins, Robert N. (1995), 'Environmental Regulation and International Competitiveness: What Does the Evidence Tell Us?', *Journal of Economic Literature*, **33** (3), March, pp. 132–63.
Mani, Muthukumara and Wheeler, David (1998), 'In Search of Pollution Havens? Dirty Industry in the World Economy, 1960–1995', *The Journal of Environment and Development*, **7** (3), September.
Markusen, James R., Olewiler, Edward R. and Olewiler, Nancy (1993), 'Environmental Policy When Market Structure and Plant Locations are Endogenous', *Journal of Environmental Economics and Management*, **24**, pp. 69–86.
Morgenstern, Richard D., Pizer, William A. and Shih, Jhih-Shyang (1997), 'Are We Overstating the Real Economic Costs of Environmental Protection?', *Resources For the Future Discussion Paper 97/36R*, June.
Navarro, Peter (1981), 'The 1977 Clean Air Act Amendments: Energy, Environmental, Economic, and Distributional Impacts', *Public Policy*, **29** (2), Spring, pp. 121–46.
Norsworthy, J.R., Harper, Michael J. and Kunze, Kent (1979), 'The Slowdown in Productivity Growth: Analysis of Some Contributing Factors', *Brookings Papers on Economic Activity*, **2**, pp. 387–421.

Parry, Ian W.H., Williams III, Roberton C. and Goulder, Lawrence H. (1999), 'When Can Carbon Abatement Policies Increase Welfare? The Fundamental Role of Distorted Factor Markets', *Journal of Environmental Economics and Management*, **37** (1), January, pp. 52–84.

Scherer, Frank M. (1982), 'Inter-industry Technology Flows and Productivity Growth', *Review of Economics and Statistics*, **64** (4), pp. 627–34.

Seskin, Eugene P., Anderson jr, Robert J. and Reid, Robert O. (1983), 'An Empirical Analysis of Economic Strategies for Controlling Air Pollution', *Journal of Environmental Economics and Management*, **10**, pp. 112–24.

Solow, Robert M. (1957), 'Technical Change and the Aggregate Production Function', *Review of Economics and Statistics*, **39** (3), August, pp. 312–20.

US Environmental Protection Agency (1997), *The Benefits and Costs of the Clean Air Act, 1970–1990*, Washington DC: Government Printing Office.

Part I
Productivity and Production Functions

By EDWARD F. DENISON

[1]

Effects of Selected Changes in the Institutional and Human Environment Upon Output Per Unit of Input

CONTENTS

	Page
Summary	21
Part 1: Introduction	22
Part 2: Costs Incurred To Protect The Physical Environment	23
A General Explanation of the Estimating Procedure	23
The proportion of inputs diverted from production of measured output	23
Use of incremental costs	24
Numerical illustration of effects on output per unit of input	24
Derivation of Cost Estimates	25
1. Current costs: motor vehicle emission abatement	26
2. Current costs: air and water pollution abatement except motor vehicle emissions	26
3. Current costs: payments to use public sewer systems	27
4. Current costs: solid waste disposal	27
5. Depreciation: motor vehicle emission abatement	28
6. Depreciation: air and water pollution abatement except motor vehicle emissions	28
7. Depreciation: solid waste disposal	28
8. Net opportunity cost of invested capital: motor vehicle emission abatement	28
9. Net opportunity cost of invested capital: air and water pollution abatement except motor vehicle emissions	30
10. Net opportunity cost of invested capital: solid waste disposal	30
11. Value of materials and energy reclaimed	31

	Page
Omitted Items	31
Land and inventories	31
Noise, radiation, and pesticide pollution abatement	31
Agriculture, real estate operators, and independent professional practitioners	31
Research and development expenditures	32
Index of Effect of Pollution Abatement Costs Upon Output Per Unit of Input	32
Part 3: Costs Incurred To Protect the Safety and Health of Workers	32
Safety Requirements for Motor Vehicles	33
Automobiles	33
Trucks	33
Total incremental cost	34
Mining Industries	34
Industries Other Than Mining	36
Index of Effect of Costs of Protecting Worker Safety and Health Upon Output Per Unit of Input	37
Part 4: Costs of Dishonesty and Crime	37
Costs of Protection	38
Protection that firms provide for themselves	39
Protection purchased from specialized firms	40
Index of effects of costs of protection	40
Thefts of Merchandise and Damage to Property	40
Part 5: Combined Effects	42

Summary

IN the last decade, the institutional and human environment within which business must operate has changed in several ways that adversely affect output per unit of input. This article examines the effects of three such changes: (1) New requirements to protect the physical environment against pollution; (2) increased requirements to protect the safety and health of employed persons; (3) a rise in dishonesty and crime. The common characteristic of these changes is that they have reduced the measured output that is produced by any given amount of input. By "measured" output, I mean national income or net national product as defined by the Bureau of Economic Analysis.

By 1975, the last year for which this article provides estimates, output per unit of input in the nonresidential business sector of the economy was 1.8 percent smaller than it would have been if business had operated under 1967 conditions. Of this amount, 1.0 percent is ascribable to pollution abatement and 0.4 percent each to employee safety and health programs and to the increase in dishonesty and crime. The reductions had been small in 1968–70 but were rising rapidly in the 1970's. The increase in their size cut the annual change in output per unit

(See footnotes at end of article)

Mr. Denison is a Senior Fellow of The Brookings Institution. Estimates described in this article are part of a comprehensive study of U.S. economic growth in which he is engaged. Financial support for the study was provided in part by National Science Foundation Grant 75-23131 to the Institution. Views expressed are the author's and should not be ascribed to the trustees, officers, or other staff members of the Institution or to the Foundation or to the U.S. Department of Commerce.

The author is greatly indebted to Frank W. Segel, Gary L. Rutledge, and Frederick J. Dreiling of the Abatement and Control Expenditures Branch, Bureau of Economic Analysis, not only for information concerning costs of environmental protection but also for a number of suggestions that led to improvement in both his estimates and their presentation. Henry M. Peskin and Leonard Gianessi of the staff of Resources for the Future provided very helpful advice in the initial stage of estimation, and valuable comments on a preliminary draft of this article. Jack Alterman, Carol S. Carson, George Jaszi, Sharon Roach, and Billy L. Wayson are among others who provided particularly useful comments. Assistance in the project by Genevieve B. Wimsatt is gratefully acknowledged.

of input from 1972 to 1973 by 0.2 percentage points, the change from 1973 to 1974 by 0.4 percentage points, and the change from 1974 to 1975 by 0.5 percentage points.

A reduction of 0.5 percentage points in the annual growth rate, the reduction reached by 1975, is equal to a large fraction of the growth rates that have been achieved in the past. For example, it is equal to nearly one-fourth of the annual growth rate of output per unit of input from 1948 to 1969 (2.1 percent) and nearly one-fifth of the growth rate of output per person employed during that timespan (2.6 percent). The fractions are even larger if comparisons are made with more recent growth rates, which are lower for other reasons besides the impact of pollution abatement, employee safety programs, and crime.

The purpose of this article is to aid analysis of growth and productivity; it is not to judge the wisdom of government programs, which have benefits as well as costs. It must also be stressed that, as the article explains, many of the costs occasioned by pollution abatement, employee safety and health programs, and dishonesty and crime do not reduce output per unit of input and therefore are not included in cost estimates cited. In particular, costs imposed directly upon governmental units and consumers do not have this effect. A major part of the estimating process was the division of costs between those that change output per unit of input and those that do not.

Part 1: Introduction

This article presents estimates of the effect upon output per unit of input in the nonresidential business sector of three changes in the institutional and human environment within which business operates. It is part of a comprehensive study of the sources of economic growth. That broader study will revise and update series developed in my previous publication, *Accounting for United States Economic Growth 1929–1969* (hereafter cited as *Accounting*).[1] I begin with a short explanation of how this article fits into the broader framework.

The size of any nation's output is governed by many determinants. They include the number, composition, and skills of persons engaged in production, and the capital and land that workers use—that is to say, all of the "inputs" used in production. They also include the existing state of knowledge as to how to produce at low cost, the size of markets served, the efficiency with which resources are allocated among uses, and many other conditions that may affect the amount of output that is obtained from a given amount of input.

In *Accounting*, the growth rate of output in nonresidential business was divided between changes in input and changes in output per unit of input. Changes in output per unit of input were then allocated among seven determinants, or groups of determinants.[2] Examples are changes in the extent to which labor was overallocated to agriculture, and economies of scale made possible by the growth of markets. For each determinant, an index was computed that measured the course that output per unit of input would have taken if nothing had changed except that determinant. Six indexes were estimated directly; the seventh index, labeled "advances in knowledge and all other determinants," was obtained by dividing the index of output per unit of input by the first six indexes. Consequently, the seventh index captures the effects of all output determinants that were not separately estimated; it may be described as the residual in the analysis of the sources of growth. It had a growth rate of 1.4 percent a year from 1948 to 1969 and rose at a fairly steady rate during this period.

This residual index was defined as a measure of the joint effects of the incorporation of knowledge into production and of changes in a variety of miscellaneous determinants. In *Accounting*, I expressed a tentative judgment (which still seems correct) that in the period covered changes in miscellaneous determinants had only a small net effect on the residual index, so that its growth rate provided an approximation to the contribution that the incorporation of knowledge into production had made to the growth rate of output. But I continued as follows:

"Let me stress that this judgment does not necessarily extend to the period since 1969 or the years immediately ahead. Several changes that do or may affect measured productivity adversely (which is not a criterion by which to assess their desirability) are now taking place, simultaneously and over a brief timespan. Most prominent are major and far-reaching controls for environmental protection which require firms to use labor and capital for protection of the environment that could otherwise be used to provide measured output. The cost of the required measures is higher in the short run than it is likely to be in the long run because of the need to develop appropriate new technology and different sources of supply; because of immobility; and because delays in securing approval for new plants threaten to cause shortages of some products, especially fuels and power, that are used by other firms.

"Major new legislation to promote employee and consumer safety is a second source of increased costs. A third source has been a rise in the incidence of crime, particularly holdups of business establishments, thefts of their merchandise (including shoplifting), and embezzlement. Wage and price controls—introduced in 1971, relaxed in 1972, and subsequently reimposed and again liberalized—are a possible fourth source. If long continued they may raise overhead costs, distort resource allocation, and introduce uneconomic labor turnover."[3]

To interpret the recent behavior of the residual, or indeed of any productivity measure, one needs estimates of the amount by which it has been affected by such changes. Estimates are provided here for three that seemed especially likely to be important. One is the imposition of government controls to protect and improve the physical environment. The second is the controls to protect the safety and health of workers.[4] The third is the increase in dishonesty and crime among employees, customers, and the public. The effects of other changes in the environment within which business must operate are not examined here.[5]

The series reported for the effects of the three changes upon productivity rest on less adequate information than one would like, and are by no means precise. Nevertheless, they are believed sufficient to add appreciably to understanding of recent productivity experience.

Part 2: Costs Incurred To Protect the Physical Environment

Legislation relating to pollution passed prior to the mid-1960's—the Water Pollution Control Act of 1948, with amendments in 1956; the Air Pollution Control Act of 1955; and the Clean Air Act of 1963—expressed governmental concern about pollution but did not importantly affect business costs. Subsequent legislation did. At the Federal level, this legislation included the Water Quality Act of 1965 and the 1972 Water Pollution Act Amendments, the Motor Vehicle Air Pollution Control Act of 1965, the Air Quality Act of 1967, the Clean Air Amendments of 1970, numerous amendments to these basic air and water pollution laws, and provisions affecting other types of pollution. State and local governments have also introduced new laws and regulations and more vigorous enforcement of existing provisions. The effect of the new environmental controls was not immediate and their impact upon business costs and productivity can be ignored through 1967. I attempt annual estimates beginning with 1968; they are meant to cover controls imposed by all levels of government.

A General Explanation of the Estimating Procedure

Some of the expenditures made to protect the environment reduce measured output per unit of input. The reason is that the labor and capital whose services they purchase provide no measured output whereas they would have done so if not diverted to environmental protection. Measured output refers to products that are counted as final products in the national income and product accounts (NIPA's). My objective is to calculate the effect of changes in environmental expenditures upon an index of output per unit of input. To do this for any period, one must know the percentages by which environmental expenditures reduced measured output per unit of input at both the beginning and end of the period, or at least the amount by which the percentage changed during the period. This section provides a general explanation of the estimating procedure. It is followed by a detailed description of sources and methods, and the actual estimates.

The proportion of inputs diverted from production of measured output

The estimates rely on the presumption, common in economic analysis, that if purchases of any commodity represent a certain percentage of the value of the Nation's output, then the percentage of the Nation's total factor input that is used to produce that commodity is about the same. Consequently, percentage distributions of output and input are similar. In this formulation total factor input refers to a combined measure of labor, capital, and land. To calculate total factor input, these three factors of production, and the various types of each factor, are combined by using their earnings as weights.

The percentage distribution of total factor input corresponds to the percentage distribution of output more closely if output is valued at factor cost—that is to say, as the sum of the earnings, including profit, of labor and property—than if it is valued at market prices, which also include indirect business taxes. When measured net of depreciation, the factor cost measure is called national income (NI) and the market price measure, net national product (NNP).

Measured output per unit of total factor input (henceforth, simply "input") is reduced if there is an increase in the proportion of input that is used in activities that do not contribute to the production of products counted as final products. This occurs when certain types of purchases for pollution abatement and control (PAC) increase relative to purchases of goods and services that are counted as final products.

Because only certain types of expenditures for PAC divert input from production of measured output, and thus reduce output per unit of input, environmental expenditures must be divided between those that have this effect and those that do not.

When the costs of environmental protection are borne by government or by consumers, diversion of expenditures and inputs to environmental protection does not reduce measured output per unit of input. This is so because purchases of goods and services for environmental protection by government and consumers, like all their other purchases, are counted as final products. Consequently, such purchases merely replace other final products that could have been produced by the inputs absorbed by environmental protection.

In contrast, costs of environmental protection that are incurred by business on current account, whether for purchases from other enterprises or for the direct hiring of labor, are not counted as purchases of final products. Because they absorb inputs that would otherwise be used to produce final products, the diversion of inputs to environmental protection lowers output per unit of input below what it would have been in the absence of the diversion. The dollar cost of the environmental expenditures, when expressed as a percentage of measured output plus these expenditures themselves, measures both the percentage of input diverted to unmeasured production and the percentage reduction in measured output per unit of input that they cause.

Capital goods acquired by business for pollution abatement are counted as final products when they are purchased, so their production in place of other final products does not immediately reduce measured output per unit of input. What does reduce measured output per unit of input is the use of part of the stock of capital for pollution abatement, because the proportion of the stock of capital goods present at any date that business devotes to pollution abatement is not available to produce products that are counted as final. Given the total stock of capital, measured output is reduced by the value of the services that this capital would have provided if used to produce final products.

This value is measured as the sum of depreciation on pollution abatement capital and an imputed net return on this capital. It represents the opportunity cost of using capital for pollution abatement. Depreciation is calculated directly for pollution abatement capital, using a formula (the straight-line method), service lives, and procedures as consistent as practical with those used in the NIPA's. The imputed net return, which I call the net opportunity cost of using capital for pollution abatement, is calculated as the product of the net stock of pollution abatement capital and the ratio of earnings net of depreciation to the net capital stock that is observed for capital in general.

The business sector in the NIPA's can be divided between the services of dwellings and nonresidential business. This article is confined to nonresidential business so environmental expenditures associated with dwellings, chiefly for trash collection and sewage disposal, must be omitted from the aggregate used.

I now summarize the discussion to this point. PAC costs incurred by government and consumers, and PAC costs arising from the use of dwellings, must be omitted in appraising the effect of programs for environmental protection on output per unit of input in nonresidential business; only PAC costs incurred by nonresidential business enterprises need to be considered. Viewed from the standpoint of a pollution-abating enterprise, PAC costs are the cost of the labor it hires directly for PAC, depreciation on the capital it uses for PAC and the net opportunity cost of this capital, and payments to other firms for materials and services that are purchased for PAC (which represent returns to the labor and capital used by such suppliers).[6] Summed for all enterprises, these PAC costs provide an estimate of the amount by which the value of measured output is reduced by outlays for environmental protection.

Classification of costs between government and consumers, on the one hand, and business, on the other, usually is clearcut and can be based on who makes the expenditure in the first instance. But this is not necessarily so in exceptional cases when, as the result of the initial business expenditure, there is a recognizable change in a final product. Pollution abatement devices installed in motor vehicles (autos and trucks) are the outstanding example. Such devices add to the unit values of motor vehicles but they do not raise motor vehicle prices as measured by the Bureau of Labor Statistics (BLS) and the Bureau of Economic Analysis (BEA). This is so because these agencies consider that the difference in unit value between vehicles with and without these devices represents a difference in real product rather than in price. The outcome is the same as if purchasers bought the pollution abatement devices separately from vehicles. Consequently, the devices on vehicles bought by consumers and government must be classified in the category of PAC purchases by these groups (and omitted from expenditures that reduce output per unit of input) while devices on vehicles bought by business must be classified as capital outlay for pollution abatement equipment by business (and included in the stock of pollution abatement capital against which depreciation and net opportunity cost are charged).

Use of incremental costs

Business incurred costs for disposal of sewage and solid wastes and to limit air, water, and other forms of pollution before 1967 and would have continued to do so in the absence of new environmental controls. Consequently, the total cost of pollution abatement must be distinguished from the incremental cost.

Total cost, as I shall use the term, refers to the concept that BEA uses when it provides estimates of national expenditures for PAC. It is, in brief, the difference between costs with techniques actually used and costs that would be incurred with the minimum cost method that business would choose if it were indifferent to pollution.[7]

By incremental cost, I mean the excess of total cost over a baseline cost that may be defined either as (1) the cost that would have been incurred in the absence of an increase in the stringency of environmental requirements since 1967, or (2) the cost that would have been incurred if the 1967 level of abatement costs had continued unchanged after allowance for growth and price level changes. These two alternative definitions, it may be noted, are not precisely synonymous, but data are not sufficiently refined to permit any distinction between them to be drawn in practice.

To obtain the effect of increased pollution controls upon an index of output per unit of input, one must know incremental costs. In this article, these are sometimes calculated by measuring directly the incremental costs that were occasioned by changes in requirements and sometimes by estimating both total costs and baseline costs and subtracting to obtain incremental costs.

Numerical illustration of effects on output per unit of input

Use of the incremental cost estimates will now be illustrated with some hypothetical numbers. As a preliminary, I note that—as in the broader study of which this is a part—output is measured by NI, which is the same as net national product valued at factor cost. Use of NI rather than some other output measure, such as gross or net national product at market price, influences my procedures to a minor degree.

Suppose now that incremental costs incurred for environmental protection of types that must be counted, which were zero by definition in 1967, reached $3 billion in 1972 and $10 billion in 1975. Suppose also that measured NI originating in nonresidential business was $597 billion in 1972 and $990 billion in 1975. In the absence of a diversion of resources to environmental protection, the sector's measured NI would have been the sum of these amounts, $600 billion in 1972 and $1,000 billion in 1975. Therefore, the change in environmental protection conditions after 1967 reduced output per unit of input in nonresidential business 0.5 percent in 1972 and 1.0 percent in 1975. The same statement can be made about total output in the sector only if the change in provision for environmental protection did not change the amount of total input.[8] But such a qualification is not needed when the percentages are used, as I do use them, to measure effects on output per unit of input, because an induced change in total input would change total output rather than output per unit of input.[9]

Since output is valued at factor cost, costs of environmental protection must also be valued at factor cost if the percentages are to be correct. If, instead, environmental costs are valued at market price, which is normally higher, the percentages will be too high unless NNP is substituted for NI when the percentages are computed.

The percentages should be based on data in current (as distinguished from constant) prices, as is usually the case in resource-allocation calculations. The reason is that relative prices of products each year should reflect the relative quantities of inputs required for their production in the same year, not in some earlier or later year.

Subtraction of the illustrative percentages from 100 percent provides an index that is similar in form and meaning to those I derived for components of output per unit of input in *Accounting*. With $1967=100$, its value is 99.5 in 1972 and 99.0 in 1975. Its meaning is that measured output per unit of input would have been equal to these percentages of its 1967 amount if nothing had changed except provision for environmental protection. The growth rate of the index—minus 0.13 percent in 1967–75—provides the amount in percentage points by which provision for environmental protection reduced the growth rate of output per unit of input.

The index for effects of environmental costs on output per unit of input would be approximately the same whether output is measured by NI or NNP. However, if gross national product were used, the decline in the index would be reduced—in practice by about one-tenth. The appropriate dollar figure for the incremental cost of environmental protection is the same whether it is related to net or gross product. But the value of gross product is larger, by an average of 11 percent in nonresidential business in the 1972–75 period. If this were also true in the illustrative example, gross product would have been $663 billion in 1972 and $1,099 billion in 1975. The percentage reductions would have been 0.45 $(3/663+3)$ in 1972 and 0.9 $(10/1,099+10)$ in 1975.

Derivation of Cost Estimates

My series for the incremental cost of pollution abatement to nonresidential business is the sum of 10 component series, less the value of materials and fuel reclaimed as a result of the incremental outlays for pollution abatement. Table 1 shows these components and total incremental cost, which rose from zero in 1967 to $9,549 million in 1975. The estimates for each year are expressed in current prices of that year. The series had to be pieced together from various sources. Some guessing was also required. A general review of sources will be followed by a line-by-line description of the series.

The most important source of information is the Abatement and Control Expenditures Branch (ACEB) of the Environmental and Nonmarket Economics Division, BEA. Two articles in the SURVEY OF CURRENT BUSINESS report 1973, 1974, and 1975 plant and equipment expenditures by U.S. business for the abatement of air, water, and (except for 1973) solid waste pollution abatement; a third provides detailed estimates of national expenditures for PAC in 1972, 1973, and 1974.[10] These figures refer to total rather than incremental expenditures. ACEB also provided unpublished detail and, very importantly, annual series for the net stock of pollution abatement structures and equipment that it prepared for this study by use of the perpetual inventory method. Depreciation estimates consistent with these capital stock estimates were also prepared and made available, and I have used them in preference to lower estimates, published in the February 1977 SURVEY, that were secured by adjusting estimates valued at historical cost so as to reflect current prices. ACEB furnished additional estimates, which are described below, and advice on the use of its information.

Annual reports of the Council on Environmental Quality (CEQ) contain estimates of total and incremental pollution control expenditures; however, each report contains estimates for only a single year. Because procedures are constantly changed and underlying data revised, estimates for most components are not comparable from year to year and time series cannot be obtained. Nevertheless, estimates for 1974 and 1975 were used as checks on estimates for some components of business costs and, occasionally, other use was made of the data.

BLS reports annually the value of changes in automobiles that result from environmental regulations (as well as from safety regulations and other causes).

The Bureau of the Census, U.S. Department of Commerce, has collected and published a variety of data for the pollution abatement costs and expenditures of manufacturing establishments in 1973, 1974, and 1975.[11]

I now turn to the line-by-line description of the estimates in table 1. The reader will follow the description more readily if he appreciates that, both in table 1 and in the BEA estimates of national expenditures for PAC, costs are classified from the standpoint of the enterprise whose pollution is being abated.

1. Current costs: motor vehicle emission abatement

The cost of additional maintenance and gasoline consumption that was incurred on business-owned motor vehicles as a result of environmental requirements in 1972–74 is taken directly from the SURVEY, February 1977, p. 15, table 2. Incremental cost and total cost, as the latter is defined and measured by BEA, are synonymous for this component. Nearly all of the cost was incurred on automobiles, as distinguished from trucks.

The 1972 estimate was extrapolated back to 1968, and the 1974 estimate forward to 1975, by a preliminary series that was constructed in the following way. (a) Annual pollution abatement costs in the form of additional gasoline (the "fuel penalty") and additional maintenance, valued in 1974 dollars, in 1968–74 were obtained for *all* automobiles from CEQ's *6th Annual Report*, December 1975, figure 8, p. 525.[12] The percentage increase from 1974 to 1975 was calculated from the series for projected costs attributable to light-duty vehicle emission controls (total costs less equipment costs) shown in Environmental Protection Agency (EPA), *The Cost of Clean Air*, April 1974, table III–10, p. III–22. (b) To secure business expenditures in constant prices, each year's estimate for all automobiles, obtained in (a), was multiplied by the ratio of the new automobile component of producers' durable equipment to the sum of this series and the new automobile components of personal consumption expenditures and government purchases. Data are from NIPA table 1.17. Each year's allocation was based on the value, in 1972 prices, of car purchases during the preceding 5 years, excluding years before 1967. (c) A price index with 1972=100 was constructed by combining the implicit price deflators (1972=100) for personal consumption expenditures for gasoline and oil (weighted 5) and for user-operated transportation services (weighted 3) from NIPA table 7.12. The weights were based on relative expenditures for the fuel penalty and for additional maintenance in 1972, as shown in the CEQ figure 8 cited in (a). (d) The constant-price series was multiplied by this price index to secure the series for business costs in current prices that was used to extrapolate the 1972–74 BEA data.

2. Current costs: air and water pollution abatement except motor vehicle emissions

Total nonresidential business expenditures on current account for air and water pollution abatement, other than motor vehicle emission abatement, in 1972–74 were obtained from the SURVEY, February 1977, p. 15, table 2, by combining eight series: expenditures for air pollution abatement by private manufacturing establishments, privately owned electric utility establishments, other private nonmanufacturing establishments, and publicly owned electric utilities, and expenditures for water pollution abatement by the same four groups. This is the series that is conceptually desired except that it is for total rather than incremental expenditures.[13]

In the absence of similar data for other years, 1972 current expenditures were extrapolated back to 1967, and the 1974 figure forward to 1975, by a series for the stock of capital for air and water pollution abatement; it seemed reasonable to suppose that the two series would rise in a fairly similar pattern, and they actually did so from 1972 to 1974.[14] The capital stock series has the same industrial coverage as the series for current expenditures except that, for lack of data, it excludes outlays by publicly owned electric utilities. (Such utilities account for only 2 percent of current expenditures.) The

Table 2.—Incremental Pollution Abatement Capital of Nonresidential Business, Average for Year
[Billions of dollars]

	1967	1968	1969	1970	1971	1972	1973	1974	1975
Motor vehicle emission abatement [1]		0.0	0.1	0.1	0.2	0.3	0.4	0.7	1.0
Air and water pollution abatement except motor vehicle emissions		.5	1.3	3.1	5.4	8.1	11.9	18.2	26.0
Solid waste disposal		.0	.0	.1	.1	.2	.3	.5	.6
Total incremental net stock		.5	1.4	3.2	5.7	8.6	12.6	19.4	27.6
Addendum: Total net stock, air and water pollution abatement except motor vehicle emissions	5.0	6.0	7.2	9.2	11.9	15.3	19.8	26.6	35.0

1. Business vehicles only.

Table 1.—Incremental Pollution Abatement Costs That Reduce National Income Per Unit of Input in Nonresidential Business
[Millions of dollars]

	1967	1968	1969	1970	1971	1972	1973	1974	1975
Current costs:									
1. Motor vehicle emission abatement [1]	0	86	180	257	396	558	867	1,409	1,831
2. Air and water pollution abatement except motor vehicle emissions.	0	71	180	431	742	1,115	1,521	2,221	3,217
a) Direct labor cost	0	24	61	147	252	379	517	686	933
b) Equipment leasing, materials, supplies, services, and other.	0	47	119	284	490	736	1,004	1,535	2,284
3. Payments to use public sewer systems	0	20	40	60	100	139	179	218	242
4. Solid waste disposal	0	26	56	87	127	167	225	289	362
Depreciation:									
5. Motor vehicle emission abatement [1]	0	3	10	19	31	48	72	111	174
6. Air and water pollution abatement except motor vehicle emissions.	0	17	50	116	198	295	426	660	976
7. Solid waste disposal	0	1	2	5	9	14	24	37	53
Net opportunity cost of invested capital:									
8. Motor vehicle emission abatement [1]	0	3	10	17	28	42	60	89	136
9. Air and water pollution abatement except motor vehicle emissions.	0	56	144	341	589	883	1,285	1,947	2,756
10. Solid waste disposal	0	1	3	7	13	23	33	51	68
Less:									
11. Value of materials and energy reclaimed.	0	8	17	27	48	74	93	136	266
Total incremental cost	0	276	658	1,313	2,185	3,210	4,599	6,895	9,549

1. Business vehicles only.

capital stock series (which is unofficial and was prepared by ACEB) measures net stock in current prices as of July 1. It is shown in the addendum line of table 2.

The baseline value of current expenditures for air and water pollution abatement, like the baseline value of most other types of pollution abatement costs, was calculated on the assumption that expenditures would have moved like output in nonfarm nonresidential business in the absence of changes in environmental requirements. (Farm output is excluded because the expenditures exclude those made in farming—which were, in any case, small.) Consequently, to obtain an annual series for baseline current expenditures, the figure of $687 million, which had been obtained for actual expenditures in 1967, was extrapolated to all later years by NNP originating in nonfarm nonresidential business. Baseline current expenditures were then deducted from total current expenditures to secure incremental expenditures.

My estimates for 1974 and 1975 can be compared with CEQ estimates. With values expressed in billions of dollars, the comparison is as follows.[15]

	Total cost	Baseline cost	Incremental cost
1974: Denison	3.4	1.2	2.2
CEQ	3.0	1.3	1.7
1975: Denison	4.4	1.2	3.2
CEQ	5.6	2.1	3.5

In 1974, the two estimates of baseline cost are fairly similar while the estimates of incremental cost diverge, whereas in 1975, the opposite is the case. Such different results for the 2 years are possible because CEQ's estimates for 1974 are not comparable with its estimates for 1975.

For subsequent calculations, it is desirable to divide the series for incremental expenditures between direct labor costs and other current costs. The Census Bureau reports already cited provide such data for total environmental expenditures by manufacturing establishments: labor costs were 34.0 percent of the total in 1973, 30.9 percent in 1974, and 29.0 percent in 1975. Lines 2a and 2b of table 1 were calculated on the assumption that direct labor cost constituted the same percentage of the incremental cost in all industries combined as it did of the total cost in manufacturing. The 1973 percentage was used for earlier years.

3. Current costs: payments to use public sewer systems

Payments to use public sewer systems are not counted in water pollution expenditures of private business in line 2 of table 1, so there is no duplication between lines 2 and 3. The incremental cost to be counted in line 3 is not large, however, even though public sewer systems are in the business sector (they are classified as government enterprises) and their current expenditures are large ($1.6 billion in 1974 according to the February 1977 SURVEY, p. 15, table 1). Most costs of public sewer systems are excluded from incremental cost, both because they are allocated to dwellings rather than nonresidential business and because they cover ordinary sewage disposal and treatment no different from practices already customary in 1967.

There were no new Federal controls in the period covered by this study. The cost that is to be counted arises in part because new local environmental regulations sometimes required secondary and tertiary treatment of sewage from nonresidential business firms, which entailed higher charges to the firms, and in part because the raising of standards for primary treatment itself increased charges to nonresidential business along with other users.

Manufacturers paid $178 million in 1973, $203 million in 1974, and $228 million in 1975 to governmental units (all levels) for "public sewage use," according to the Bureau of the Census.[16] ACEB analysts suggested that two-thirds of the 1973 outlay may have been attributable to new environmental requirements. Thus, the 1973 payments of $178 million divide into $59 million of baseline cost and $119 million of incremental cost. The 1973 baseline cost was extrapolated to 1974 and 1975 by NNP originating in nonfarm nonresidential business; the resulting series was then subtracted from total payments to secure incremental costs for manufacturers in 1974 and 1975. To allow for nonmanufacturing industries, for which not even figures for total payments are available, the incremental cost for manufacturers was raised one-half.

No usable data for years before 1973 were located. Incremental cost was set at zero in 1967, and the intervening years were estimated on the assumption that the absolute annual increase from 1970 to 1973 was double that from 1967 to 1970.

4. Current costs: solid waste disposal

Trash collection and disposition, and other solid waste disposal, may be performed by governments or privately. Unlike sewerage, solid waste disposal by governments is not considered a government enterprise in the NIPA's (see NIPA tables 3.13 and 3.14) but, instead, an activity of government. As a result, government purchases for solid waste disposal are final products. Consequently, diversion of resources to solid waste disposal by government does not reduce measured output, and costs incurred by government must not be counted in table 1—not even when governments impose a charge for their services. BEA and CEQ use classifications to report environmental statistics that distinguish government from private solid waste disposal so government expenditures are readily omitted.

BEA provided unpublished estimates of the nonresidential portion of the series for total private current expenditures for solid waste disposal that is shown for 1972–74 in the February 1977 SURVEY, p. 15, table 1. BEA also divided the nonresidential expenditures among manufacturing ($476 million in 1974), commercial nonmanufacturing (consisting of retail trade, finance, and services, and amounting to $974 million in 1974), and other nonmanufacturing ($932 million in 1974). The commercial nonmanufacturing series was provided for 1970–71 as well as for 1972–74.

Of the three components, only the manufacturing series rose appreciably faster during the period for which it was available than did nonfarm nonresidential business NNP. The absence of a sharp increase in the other components suggests that the incremental cost of pollution abatement was not a large part of total cost except in manufacturing. ACEB analysts suggested that it would be reasonable to assume that about 14 percent of the total 1975 private cost was incremental cost in nonresidential business as a whole, and about 30 percent in manufacturing. These percentages, which implied about 10.1 percent for nonmanufacturing industries, were incorporated into the estimates.

The exact procedure for securing the series for incremental cost shown in table 1, line 4, will now be described. It is the sum of series for manufacturing and nonmanufacturing.

The 1972-74 series for total expenditures by manufacturers was first extended to 1975 on the assumption that the ratio of such expenditures to nonfarm nonresidential business NNP increased the same amount in 1975 as in 1974. The 1975 incremental cost in manufacturing was taken as 30 percent of total cost (or $157 million). The percentage was assumed to have increased a constant 3.75 points a year, from zero in 1967. These data and assumptions yielded 1972-75 estimates of incremental cost. To secure estimates for 1968-71, when total manufacturing costs were not available, the ratio of incremental cost to nonresidential business NNP was assumed to have increased the same amount each year from 1968 to 1972.

To complete a 1967-75 series for total expenditures by nonmanufacturing industries, the 1972-74 estimates were extrapolated back to 1970 by the "commercial" component. The resulting 1970 figure was extrapolated back to 1967, and the 1974 figure to 1975, by NNP originating in nonfarm nonresidential business. (It may be noted that the percentage change from 1973 to 1974 was the same in the two series.) Incremental expenditures of all nonresidential business in 1975, computed as already stated at 14 percent of total expenditures, came to $362 million.[17] Subtraction of the estimate of $157 million for manufacturing left $205 million as the incremental cost in nonmanufacturing industries, equal as already stated to 10.1 percent of the total cost in these industries. To secure incremental costs in earlier years, this percentage was estimated to have increased linearly from zero in 1967.

5. Depreciation: motor vehicle emission abatement

See description of line 8.

6. Depreciation: air and water pollution abatement except motor vehicle emissions

Estimates of total depreciation in current prices for the years 1967-74 were provided by ACEB. ACEB derived them as part of the calculations to obtain the estimates of capital stock provided for this study. The estimates rise from $223 million in 1967 ($173 million in manufacturing and $50 million in nonmanufacturing, including electric utilities) to $1,036 million in 1974 ($721 million in manufacturing and $315 million in nonmanufacturing).[18] A preliminary estimate was made for 1975 on the basis of the previous pattern of increase in constant-price depreciation and the rise in the BEA implicit price deflator for fixed nonresidential investment (NIPA table 7.1).

Baseline depreciation was estimated by extrapolating 1967 depreciation by NNP of nonfarm nonresidential business. Incremental depreciation is equal to total depreciation minus baseline depreciation.

7. Depreciation: solid waste disposal

See description of line 10.

8. Net opportunity cost of invested capital: motor vehicle emission abatement

This line and line 5 (depreciation), which is also described here, are the sum of series for automobiles and trucks. The automobile component is the larger by far.

Automobiles.—Series for gross and net capital stock and depreciation were compiled in the following steps.

(a) The dollar increase in average retail value of automobiles that resulted from pollution abatement devices that were added in each model year was assembled from BLS releases titled "Report on Quality Changes for (year) Model Passenger Cars." There were increases in every model year from 1968 through 1977, except in 1969; much the biggest increase was in 1975.

(b) The series was converted to a calendar-year basis on the assumption that each model year's addition applied to one-fourth of the previous calendar year's cars.

(c) The calendar-year series was converted to 1967 prices by deflating the current-price series by the BLS Consumer Price Index for new cars. The constant-price series was then cumulated to secure the increment to the price per car due to additions to pollution control costs since 1967, valued in 1967 prices. The cumulated increments were then multiplied by the passenger car price index to place them in current prices.

(d) Average prices of new cars in current dollars were obtained from annual issues of *Automobile Facts and Figures* (published by the Motor Vehicle Manufacturers Association of the United States, Inc. [MVMA], Detroit).[19]

(e) The ratio of the cumulated incremental pollution abatement cost per car (computed in step c) to the price per car (described in step d) was computed for each year.

(f) This ratio (which reached 5 percent in 1975) was multiplied by the "new autos" component of BEA's series for producers' durable equipment in 1972 prices (NIPA table 1.17) to obtain the value in 1972 prices of pollution abatement devices included in new business automobiles.

(g) The undepreciated value of the pollution abatement devices contained in used automobiles sold by business to consumers (minus devices sold by consumers to business) was subtracted from the value of devices in automobiles newly purchased by business to secure gross capital formation in the form of antipollution devices.[20] (All of these data were in 1972 prices.)

(h) Gross capital stock in 1972 prices was computed from the series for gross capital formation by use of the 10-year average service life for cars used by BEA in computing capital stock and depreciation in the NIPA's.[21] (The Winfrey distribution was not introduced.) Because the period since capital formation began was less than 10 years, pollution abatement devices in all cars that were not sold remained in the business stock throughout the period. Gross capital stock in 1972 prices at yearend was obtained by cumulating past investment, and a yearly average of the values at the beginning and end of the year was calculated.

(i) Depreciation in 1972 prices was calculated as 10 percent of this gross stock series. Depreciation was converted to current prices (as shown in table 1, line 5) by use of the BLS price index for new automobiles.

(j) Net capital stock in 1972 prices at yearend was obtained by deducting the depreciation in 1972 prices accumulated during the previous and current years from yearend gross stock in 1972 prices. Values at the start and end of each year were averaged. This constant-price series was multiplied by the BLS price index for new automobiles, shifted to a 1972 base, to obtain the value of the net stock in current prices. This series represents the incremental net stock.

To secure the opportunity cost of invested capital, the incremental net capital stock was multiplied by an estimate of the ratio of earnings to net stock in alternative uses for capital. For the latter series, I used the ratio of nonlabor earnings in nonfarm corporations to the value of the net stock of capital and land in such corporations. This series is described in *Accounting*, appendix J; revisions in NIPA's and other data entering into its calculation were incorporated.

The actual ratio for nonfarm corporations is strongly affected by the business cycle, and collapsed in 1974–75 after falling sharply earlier in the 1970's. However, I wish to use a series from which the effects of business cycle swings have been removed in order to prevent the adverse effect of pollution abatement costs on output per unit of input from diminishing in recessions because of cyclical drops in the general ratio of earnings to capital stock.

To do this, I substituted trend values for the actual ratios. Two periods from which least squares trends might reasonably be computed are 1947–69 and 1947–73. The former yields trend percentages that decline slowly from 11.6 percent in 1969 to 11.4 percent in 1975. The latter yields percentages that are lower and fall more sharply, from 10.5 percent in 1969 to 9.8 percent in 1975. Use of either period implies that the 1974–75 figures were greatly reduced by recession. For the pollution abatement calculation, I have averaged the values from these two trend lines, securing a cyclically adjusted series that drops from 0.112 in 1967 to 0.111 in 1969 and to 0.106 in 1975.

The ratios of earnings to asset values, actual and cyclically adjusted, from 1967 to 1975 are shown in table 3. The estimate of net opportunity cost is the product of net stock and the cyclically adjusted ratio.

Trucks.—The estimated cost of pollution abatement devices in new trucks purchased by business each year is the sum of estimates for gasoline-fueled trucks with a gross vehicle weight (GVW) of 6,000 pounds or less and those with a GVW of 6,001 pounds or more.[22] This division was necessary because these classes were subject to different controls.

(a) The first step was to obtain the number of trucks in each category in each calendar year. The National Income and Wealth Division of BEA provided annual estimates of the number of new trucks purchased by private buyers, divided between consumer and business purchases, with each category divided between trucks of 10,000 pounds or less GVW and heavier trucks. It was necessary to estimate the number of gasoline-fueled trucks purchased by business and their division between trucks of 6,000 pounds or less GVW and heavier trucks.

Private purchases of all trucks of 10,000 pounds or less GVW were allocated between the 6,000 or less and 6,001–10,000 pound classes in proportion to domestic factory sales in these size classes, as reported by MVMA. Business purchases of gasoline-fueled trucks in the 6,000 pounds or less size class were then estimated on two assumptions: (1) the ratio of business purchases to total private purchases was one-third lower in the 0–6,000 pounds size class than in the 6,001–10,000 size class and (2) all trucks in the former class were gasoline fueled. Business purchases of gasoline-fueled trucks of 6,001 pounds or more GVW were then approximated by eliminating from total business purchases of trucks those of 6,000 pounds or less GVW, as well as domestic factory sales of diesel trucks as reported by MVMA.

(b) The next step was to obtain the value in 1967 prices of pollution abatement equipment included in business purchases of new trucks each year. The two size classes were estimated separately.

Trucks in the 0–6,000 pounds size class were subject to the same requirements as automobiles and requirements were met with the same devices.[23] The number of trucks purchased by business was therefore multiplied by the calendar-year cost per automobile, in 1967 prices (see paragraph c under automobiles), to secure capital outlays for pollution abatement devices in 1967 prices.[24]

Gasoline-fueled trucks of more than 6,000 pounds GVW were subject to less stringent standards than automobiles. EPA put the cumulated cost per truck at $21.50 in 1970 prices in 1970–73, and at $45.50 in 1974 prices in 1974–75. These amounts were converted to 1967 prices and multiplied by the number of trucks to obtain total outlays in 1967 prices. I used the cost per vehicle for lighter trucks in the 1968 and 1969 model years; little money is involved in this decision.

(c) Trucks leave the gross capital stock of business by sale to consumers or by retirement. Based on BEA data for business purchases and resales of trucks, I estimated that one-ninth of the pollution abatement devices on trucks acquired by business eventually leave the stock by sale to consumers and eight-ninths by retirement. For purposes of the calculation, one-half those sold were assumed to be 4 years old and one-half 5 years old. All retirements were assumed to be at 9 years, the average service life that BEA uses for trucks in computing its capital stock series. Consequently, the estimate of retirements is zero in the period, which ends at 1975, that is covered by my estimates.

(d) The gross stock of pollution abatement equipment in trucks at yearend, valued in 1967 prices, was calculated by cumulating business investment in such devices in new trucks each year and deducting the undepreciated value of those sold. (As stated, there were no retirements in the period covered.)

(e) Remaining estimation procedures were the same as for automobiles, except that depreciation was computed at one-ninth of gross stock.

9. Net opportunity cost of invested capital: air and water pollution abatement except motor vehicle emissions

ACEB provided estimates of the net stock of nonresidential business capital acquired for air and water pollution abatement, valued in current prices, annually (as of July 1) from 1967 to 1975. The capital stock estimates have the same coverage as the BEA surveys of plant and equipment expenditures for air and water pollution abatement. The estimates, prepared by the perpetual inventory method, are the sum of six components: stocks for air and water pollution abatement, separately, in manufacturing, electric utilities, and other nonmanufacturing industries.

The principal sources that ACEB used for capital outlays were the BEA surveys of expenditures for pollution abatement plant and equipment, available annually from 1973, and the similar surveys by the McGraw-Hill Publications Company, available annually from 1967, and capital outlays from the Census Bureau surveys of pollution abatement expenditures by manufacturing establishments. Other sources were also used. The estimates were constructed by use of straight-line depreciation, BEA deflators for business fixed nonresidential investment, and expected useful lives that were suggested for water pollution controls by EPA in the Federal Register of September 10, 1973, and for air pollution controls by the Bureau of Internal Revenue in its Bulletin F. (ACEB used 85 percent of Bulletin F lives.)

The net capital stock rises from $5.0 billion in 1967 to $35.0 billion in 1975. A series for the value of the baseline stock was obtained by extrapolating the 1967 figure by the net domestic product of nonfarm nonresidential business. Subtraction from the total stock yielded a series for the value of the incremental stock ($26.0 billion in 1975). Both total and incremental stock are shown in table 2.

The value of the incremental stock each year was multiplied by the cyclically adjusted ratio of nonlabor earnings to asset values in nonfarm corporations (table 3) to secure net opportunity cost of invested capital (table 1, line 9).

10. Net opportunity cost of invested capital: solid waste disposal

CEQ estimated that incremental private capital costs ("depreciation and interest," including imputed interest) of solid waste disposal were $0.1 billion in 1975 (7th Annual Report, p. 145). This estimate is comparable to the sum of my estimates for depreciation and net opportunity cost, but was not used directly because of the absence of comparable data for other years. However, it agrees with the estimate of $121 million that I obtain as the sum of depreciation and net opportunity cost in 1975.

BEA (SURVEY, February 1977, p. 15, table 1) estimates capital outlays by nonresidential business for solid waste disposal at $315 million in 1972, $403 million in 1973, and $424 million in 1974. A 1975 estimate of $422 million is obtained by assuming the same percentage change as in plant and equipment expenditures for solid waste disposal, as reported in the SURVEY, July

Table 3.—Nonfarm Corporations: Ratios of Nonlabor Earnings to Asset Values

	Ratios	
	Actual	Cyclically adjusted
1967	0.123	0.112
1968	.122	.111
1969	.107	.111
1970	.085	.110
1971	.087	.109
1972	.094	.109
1973	.088	.108
1974	.084	.107
1975	.069	.106

1976, p. 14, table 1. The latter source provides an industrial distribution of plant and equipment expenditures for solid waste disposal. For 1974 and 1975, combined, electric utilities accounted for 23 percent, petroleum 20, primary metals 10, chemicals 9, paper 7, and all other industries 33. Discussion with ACEB staff elicited an opinion that the portion of such spending that was due to strengthened requirements for pollution abatement (that is, the portion that was incremental) was perhaps 35 percent in 1974, having risen gradually until about 1970 and more rapidly thereafter. (From 1973 to 1976 outlays for solid waste disposal did not increase in real terms and their share of capital outlays did not rise.)

A series for incremental capital outlay for pollution abatement was constructed as follows. I assigned 35 percent ($148 million) of the 1974 total to the incremental outlay and 65 percent ($276 million) to baseline capital outlay. The baseline outlay in other years from 1972 through 1975 was assumed to be the same percentage as in 1974 (0.246) of total expenditures for new plant and equipment by U.S. business for all purposes (as reported in the SURVEY, March 1977, p. 31, and earlier issues). Incremental outlays in these years were obtained by subtraction. For earlier years, they were estimated on the assumption that the annual increase from 1967 (when they were zero) to 1970 was one-half that from 1970 to 1972.

From this series, and two assumptions, series for gross stock, net stock, and depreciation in current and constant prices were calculated by the perpetual inventory method, using straight-line depreciation. The assumptions are (1) that the capital included had an average service life of 15 years (a sheer guess, but the importance of trucks in capital suggests a fairly short life) and (2) that the BEA implicit price deflator for gross private domestic nonresidential fixed investment (NIPA table 7.1) is applicable to solid waste disposal capital.

A check on the depreciation estimate is provided by engineering data which, ACEB analysts inform me, suggest that depreciation equals about 15 percent of current cost in an ongoing situation. My 1975 estimate is $53 million; 15 percent of current cost would be $54 million.

The net opportunity cost is the product of the net stock in current prices (average of values at the beginning and end of the year), which is shown in table 2, and the cyclically adjusted ratio of earnings to asset values in nonfarm corporations shown in table 3.

11. Value of materials and energy reclaimed

Against incremental costs incurred by business must be set the value of materials and energy reclaimed as a result of the incremental expenditures.

BEA estimates the *total* value of materials and energy reclaimed at $415 million in 1972, $470 million in 1973, and $538 million in 1974.[25] The 1974 estimate compares with a total for manufacturing of $534 million reported by the Census Bureau; the $4 million difference is BEA's allowance for public utilities.[26] The 1974 BEA estimate was extrapolated to 1975 by the Census Bureau series for manufacturing, yielding an estimate of $693 million.

The BEA estimates for materials and energy reclaimed equaled 0.05254 percent of nonfarm nonresidential business NNP in 1972 and 0.05811 percent in 1974, an increase of 0.00279 percentage points a year. Ratios for earlier years were estimated on the assumption that the yearly increase in the ratio from 1970 to 1972 was the same as the average increase from 1972 to 1974, and that from 1967 to 1970 it was half that big. The ratio was multiplied by nonfarm nonresidential business NNP to secure an estimate of the total value of materials and energy reclaimed for each year from 1967 to 1971.

The 1967 ratio so derived, 0.04278 percent, was multiplied by nonfarm nonresidential business NNP each year to secure a baseline series for materials and energy reclaimed. The baseline value was deducted from the total value to obtain the series for the incremental value of materials and energy reclaimed. The results imply that the incremental value comprised 38 percent of the total value in 1975. This conforms to my general impression that the larger part of the value of materials and energy reclaimed, which is widely dispersed by industry, would have been reclaimed under practices prevailing before the new legislation and is not an appropriate deduction from incremental costs.

Omitted Items

Four types of incremental business costs are omitted because of lack of information or because their inclusion would be conceptually questionable.

Land and inventories

An opportunity cost estimate for land and inventories required for pollution abatement should be included. It would be the product of the value of such land and inventories and the ratio of earnings to assets that was used to secure net opportunity cost estimates for fixed capital. Information concerning incremental stocks of land and inventories devoted to pollution abatement has not been located.

Noise, radiation, and pesticide pollution abatement

BEA estimates of national expenditures for PAC include noise, radiation, and pesticide control; however, none of the expenditures that appear in its accounting are made by business (SURVEY, February 1977, p. 15, table 1). CEQ shows only an estimate for nuclear power plants, put at $0.0 billion—i.e., less than $50 million—in 1975 (*7th Annual Report*, pp. 145, 167). This omission clearly is of no importance.

Agriculture, real estate operators, and independent professional practitioners

BEA data for business do not cover agriculture, real estate operators, and independent professional practitioners in legal and medical services (including proprietary hospitals). The total omission from incremental expenditures for nonresidential business is believed negligible. (Expenditures by owners of large cattle feeding lots may be the largest component.)

Table 4.—Pollution Abatement Costs: Calculation of Effect Upon Output Per Unit of Input in Nonresidential Business

	Nonresidential business output (billions of dollars)		Incremental pollution abatement costs (millions of dollars)		Ratios of input diverted to pollution abatement to input not so diverted			Ratios of input diverted to pollution abatement to total input	Ratios of input not diverted to pollution abatement to total input	Index of effect of pollution abatement costs upon output per unit of input
	Measured by:		Direct labor and net opportunity costs of invested capital	Other costs including depreciation	Col. 3 ÷ col. 1	Col. 4 ÷ col. 2	Col. 5 ÷ col. 6	Col. 7 ÷ (one + col. 7)	One − col. 8	From col. 9 (1972=100)
	National income	Net national product								
	(1)	(2)	(3)	(4)	(5)	(6)	(7)	(8)	(9)	(10)
1967	509.1	566.7	0	0	0.00000	0.00000	0.00000	0.00000	1.00000	100.41
1968	554.5	619.7	84	192	.00015	.00031	.00046	.00046	.99954	100.37
1969	595.5	666.4	218	440	.00037	.00066	.00103	.00103	.99897	100.31
1970	610.3	685.8	512	801	.00084	.00117	.00201	.00201	.99799	100.21
1971	650.9	734.7	882	1,303	.00136	.00177	.00313	.00312	.99688	100.10
1972	724.6	814.5	1,327	1,883	.00183	.00231	.00414	.00412	.99588	100.00
1973	817.3	914.9	1,895	2,704	.00232	.00296	.00528	.00525	.99475	99.89
1974	862.2	970.1	2,773	4,123	.00322	.00425	.00747	.00741	.99259	99.67
1975	916.5	1,032.6	3,894	5,685	.00425	.00551	.00976	.00967	.99033	99.44

Research and development expenditures

Incremental research and development (R. & D.) expenditures for pollution abatement probably should not be regarded as subtracting from output per unit of input and I have deliberately omitted them from the incremental pollution abatement costs that affect it. The reason is that R. & D. by business is not counted as a final product regardless of its purpose, so that R. & D. expenditures by business reduce productivity when they are made whether or not the R. & D. is for pollution abatement. Diversion of resources to pollution abatement R. & D. from other R. & D. thus has no immediate effect on productivity.[27] Output per unit of input is adversely affected by an increase in R. & D. expenditures for pollution abatement at the time it occurs only if the resources are diverted from uses other than R. & D. (If resources added to R. & D. were previously unemployed, their addition will reduce output per unit of input whether they are allocated to R. & D. for pollution abatement or for other purposes.)

Even if incremental R. & D. costs are included, they have no appreciable effect on the growth rate of output per unit of input. BEA reports that R. & D. expenditures by business for PAC amounted to $518 million in 1972, $568 million in 1973, and $594 million in 1974; four-fifths was concerned with air pollution (SURVEY, February 1977, p. 15, table 1; its source is the National Science Foundation). Earlier data are absent. Even if there were no R. & D. expenditures for pollution abatement in 1969, so that incremental expenditures in 1974 were the same as total expenditures, and if none of the 1974 R. & D. expenditures used for pollution abatement was diverted from other R. & D., the reduction in the 1969–74 growth rate of output per unit of input in nonresidential business would have been only 0.01 percentage points.

Index of Effect of Pollution Abatement Costs Upon Output Per Unit of Input

The percentage that incremental costs of pollution abatement represented each year of the value of output plus these costs was next computed. As explained earlier, this is the percentage by which measured output per unit of input was reduced by the diversion of inputs to pollution abatement as a result of changes occurring after 1967. The following paragraphs describe the calculations; table 4 shows them in detail.

To refine the calculation slightly, incremental costs were first divided into two parts, one of which is compared with NI and the other with NNP. The direct labor component of the incremental current cost of air and water pollution abatement and the net opportunity cost of invested capital (lines 2a, 8, 9, and 10 of table 1) represent direct factor costs. To calculate the ratio of these costs to net output, net output is also valued at factor cost. Other current costs are business purchases from other enterprises and are therefore valued at their market price, i.e., they include indirect taxes in their value. Depreciation is also at market price, because it is based on capital stock data that are derived from gross capital formation at market price. To calculate the ratio of incremental cost in these categories to net output in the nonresidential business sector, net output is also valued at market price. The sum of the two ratios is shown in table 4, column 7.[28] In 1975, it was 0.00976 or 0.976 percent. If environmental protection in 1975 had been as it was in 1967, the resources used in production in 1975 would have provided a measured net product 0.976 percent larger than they actually provided. This is equivalent to saying that 1975 resources provided a measured net product 0.967 percent smaller than if environmental protection had been as it was in 1967 (table 4, column 8). Thus, by 1975 changes in environmental constraints since 1967 had diverted nearly 1 percent of the total input in nonresidential business to pollution abatement that is not counted as measured output.

The ratio of input not so diverted to total input, shown in table 4, column 9, is converted to index form in column 10. This is an index of the course that measured output per unit of input in nonresidential business would have followed if nothing had changed except pollution abatement. The index is expressed with 1972 equal to 100 to conform to the broader study of which this is a part.[29]

The index shows that the increasing diversion of labor and capital to pollution abatement was impairing the growth of measured output per unit of input importantly by the mid-1970's and that the amount was growing. From zero before 1967, the amount of impairment increased to an annual average of one-twentieth of a percentage point from 1967 to 1969, one-tenth of a point from 1969 to 1973, and nearly one-fourth of a point from 1973 to 1975.

Part 3: Costs Incurred To Protect the Safety and Health of Workers

Major changes in legislation, regulations, and other provisions controlling the protection of the safety and health of workers have become effective since 1967. In the measurement of national income and product, expenditures made to conform with the new requirements are treated in the same way as expenditures to conform with requirements to protect the physical environment. As in the environmental case, to obtain the effect on output per unit of input it is necessary to estimate the proportion of input in nonresidential business that has been diverted from the production of measured NI and NNP. This requires knowledge of the incremental costs that business has incurred to conform to the new provisions. The costs that must be counted are, as before, current costs (labor and purchases from other enterprises), depreciation, and the net opportunity cost of invested capital. The proportion of output diverted to protect employee safety and health is estimated as the sum of three major components. The first component consists of new safety features on motor vehicles. Price and output measures treat these features, like antipollution devices, as additions to real product. As a result, only safety features added to vehicles that are sold to business need to be considered here. Safety features on business vehicles may, of course, protect the general public as well as employees who drive and ride in them, but the effect on output per unit of input is the same.

The second component consists of the incremental costs of protecting employee safety and health in coal, metal, and nonmetal mining. These costs arise largely as a result of legislation that applies only to mining. Safety and health costs have been much larger in mining than in other industries.

The last component consists of the costs incurred by business in all industries except the three mining industries. They have arisen as a result of the Occupational Safety and Health Act. According to the estimates derived in this section, measured output per unit of input in 1975 was reduced 0.42 percent by the diversion of inputs after 1967 to protect the safety and health of workers. Of this amount, 0.09 percentage points were attributable to safety features on motor vehicles, 0.24 points to programs in mining, and 0.09 points to programs in other industries, which began to have an impact only toward the end of the 1967–75 period.

Safety Requirements for Motor Vehicles

New safety features on automobiles and trucks affect output per unit of input in just the same way as do features required to reduce pollution: only when the vehicles are sold to business users is output per unit of input affected.

Computations of costs were confined to capital costs: depreciation and the net opportunity cost of invested capital. Current expenses may be affected either favorably or unfavorably by safety requirements. For example, better bumpers may reduce damage sustained in collisions and hence repair costs but increased weight may reduce gas mileage; moreover, some devices require maintenance, repair, or replacement. In the absence of information, favorable and unfavorable effects are assumed to be offsetting, and no allowance is made for changes in current costs.

Capital cost estimates were made separately for automobiles and trucks. Automobiles accounted for three-fourths of their combined cost to business in 1975 and more in earlier years.

Automobiles

From the 1968 model year on, changes in automobiles have been made every year to meet actual and anticipated Federal safety standards. BLS provides an annual release (already cited) that enumerates each of the changes adopted in the latest model year and its estimated retail value. Column 1 of table 5 shows the costs of each model year's improvements, in that year's prices.

Starting with these data, I derived gross and net stock, depreciation, and the net opportunity cost of invested capital in just the same way as the corresponding estimates for abatement of air pollution by automobiles, which are fully described above. The estimates imply that by 1975, some 8.9 percent of the price of new cars represented incremental safety equipment compared with 5.0 percent for pollution abatement. Table 5, column 2 shows the net stock of incremental safety equipment, expressed in current prices, based on an average of values at the beginning and end of each year. Columns 4 and 6 show the cost estimates.

Trucks

Safety improvements on trucks, like those on automobiles, are treated as additions to real product rather than price increases in the NIPA's, so the conceptually correct treatment of costs is the same.

Trucks have long been subject to safety regulations by various agencies, but the cost of changes that correspond to those counted for automobiles or that were required to meet orders of the National Highway Traffic Safety Administration (NHTSA) may properly be counted as incremental cost. Estimation is difficult, in part because of lack of information on the number of business trucks affected by any regulation.

The estimates are the sum of two series.

One, covering trucks, bought by business, that had a gross vehicle weight of 10,000 pounds or less, assumes that in this weight class the cost per truck was the same as the cost per automobile.

Table 5.—Incremental Costs of Safety Equipment on Business Motor Vehicles

[Millions of dollars]

	Costs of new provisions for safety, automobiles, model year	Net capital stock of incremental safety equipment, average for year, current prices		Depreciation, current prices		Net opportunity cost of invested capital, current prices		Total incremental cost of safety equipment	
	Dollars	Autos	Trucks	Autos	Trucks	Autos	Trucks	Millions of dollars (Cols. 4+5+6+7)	Percentage of nonresidential business NNP
	(1)	(2)	(3)	(4)	(5)	(6)	(7)	(8)	(9)
1967									
1968	42.00	81	20	9	2	9	2	22	0.00
1969	14.00	238	60	26	7	26	7	66	.01
1970	26.50	437	114	50	15	48	13	126	.02
1971	10.00	665	173	80	23	72	19	194	.03
1972	12.00	907	215	113	31	99	23	266	.03
1973	85.60	1,313	292	168	44	142	32	386	.04
1974	107.80	1,973	485	238	72	211	52	593	.06
1975	10.70	2,701	921	368	134	286	98	886	.09
1976	13.40								

Note.—Except for column 1, estimates refer to calendar years. Estimates for 1967 ignore small amounts deriving from 1968 cars bought in 1967.

The second covers trucks, bought by business, with a GVW of more than 10,000 pounds. The only significant cost of compliance resulted from an amendment to the NHTSA Standard No. 121, which required expensive improvements to air brake systems on trucks produced after March 1, 1975. BLS estimates of the additional cost, at wholesale, for various kinds of trucks were mainly in the range of $500 to $1,200. The Planning and Evaluation Division of the U.S. Department of Transportation informally estimated the average cost per vehicle at $1,000 to $1,500. I have used $1,000 as an estimate of the average cost of compliance per vehicle with GVW of more than 10,000 pounds for vehicles produced under the Standard in 1975. My estimates assume that two-thirds of 1975 business purchases of such trucks, by number, consisted of vehicles produced in accordance with the Standard.

Once the cost of safety equipment in new trucks purchased by business was established, the procedure was the same as for pollution abatement devices in trucks. Columns 3, 5, and 7 of table 5 show resulting estimates for net stock, depreciation, and the net opportunity cost of invested capital.

Total incremental cost

The total incremental cost for automobiles and trucks is shown in table 5, column 8. (It will be recalled that nothing is included for current costs.) Cost is expressed as a percentage of nonresidential business NNP in column 9.

Mining Industries

This section covers mining of coal, metal, and nonmetallic minerals, but not oil and gas extraction. In the mining industries, recent actions affecting the safety and health of workers have involved Federal and State governments and unions. The major Federal laws were the Federal Metal and Nonmetallic Mine Safety Act of 1966 (the "Metal Nonmetal Act") and the Federal Coal Mine Health and Safety Act of 1969. Enforcement responsibility was originally placed in the Bureau of Mines, U.S. Department of Interior, but dissatisfaction with the vigor of enforcement led in 1973 to creation of the Mining Enforcement and Safety Administration (MESA), which was formed from the pertinent organizational components of the Bureau of Mines. MESA employs a large inspection staff. Tightening of State regulation often accompanied or preceded Federal actions. Under the Metal Nonmetal Act, six States currently operate inspection systems in accordance with Federal standards and under MESA's supervision. In coal, the United Mine Workers of America (UMW) has its own safety department, which was strengthened in 1973. The union itself inspects for safety. Union locals may shut down mines until violations are corrected.

Information is insufficient to estimate the effect of these developments by the methodology used up to this point in the article. Instead, the estimate is based upon the amounts by which productivity trends have deteriorated and the opinion of informed persons that the change in trends resulted from stronger controls for the protection of safety and health.

Productivity in all three mining industries has declined in recent years after long periods of strong advance.[30] Output per person employed peaked in 1968 in coal mining, even though descriptive evidence suggests that technology has continued to advance, and even though earlier trends in the composition of mining by type of mine and process and degree of mechanization, continued uninterrupted. Peaks in output per person employed were reached in 1970 in both copper mining and iron mining, which together account for about seven-tenths of employment in metal mining.[31] The peak was reached in 1973 in nonmetallic minerals.

Individuals familiar with mining consider that controls imposed to promote safety were responsible for the sudden reversals of productivity trends in these industries. Coal mining, the largest mining industry, has been discussed most. For example, Harold Davis, editor-in-chief of *Coal Age* began an article in the February 1973 issue (p. 111) with the sentence: "The coal industry looks back upon three years of declining productivity that stems from stringent new safety regulations which must be lived with."

In its July 1975 issue (p. 98), *Coal Age* "posed a series of questions" on productivity to officials of UMW and summarized the interchange as follows:

"*Coal Age*: The decline in productivity that is affecting the coal industry has resulted largely from the requirements specified in the 1969 Coal Mine Health and Safety Act. How does the leadership of the United Mine Workers relate the need for improved safety to the need for improved productivity?

Table 6.—Coal Mining: Derivation of Employment Required by Strengthened Controls for Worker Safety and Health

	Index of output per employee (1967=100)		Col. 1+col. 2	Employment in coal mining [1] (thousands)		
	Actual	If growth rate were 6.5 percent after 1968		Actual	Without strengthened controls Col. 3×col. 4	Required by strengthened controls Col. 4−col. 5
	(1)	(2)	(3)	(4)	(5)	(6)
1968	101.3	[2] 101.3	1.000	133	133	0
1969	99.6	107.9	.923	136	126	10
1970	97.5	114.9	.849	146	124	22
1971	87.4	122.4	.714	148	106	42
1972	83.3	130.3	.639	161	103	58
1973	81.9	138.8	.590	161	95	66
1974	76.9	147.8	.520	180	94	87
1975	70.9	157.4	.450	214	96	118

1. Full-time and part-time employment.
2. Set equal to column 1.

Sources: Column 1, U.S. Department of Labor, Bureau of Labor Statistics, Bulletin 1938, table 11. Column 4, U.S. Department of Commerce, Bureau of Economic Analysis, NIPA, table 6.7.

Economic Costs and Consequences of Environmental Regulation

"*UMW:* We believe that until recently, productivity in the United States was artificially inflated because of safety risks that coal companies were willing and able to take in their efforts to mine more coal with less men. . . .

"It is our opinion that over the years, operators have cut back on work crews beyond the limit where it is safe. They have not allowed enough men to man equipment, and they've cut back on maintenance, ventilation, and dust control teams.

". . . when we talk about 'productivity,' we should be meaning 'productivity consistent with safety.'"

Clearly, *Coal Age* and UMW officials agree that safety legislation was responsible for the reversal of the former upward trend in coal output per worker or man-hour.

Business executives and the Bureau of Mines also regard safety regulations as the obvious and main reason for the reversal of the productivity trend.[32] Other factors, particularly an influx of inexperienced workers, wildcat strikes, and increased absenteeism, are mentioned but regarded as secondary influences.[33] I shall base my estimate for mining on the opinion that failure to continue the past trends in output per worker was due, through 1975, to the strengthened controls to protect workers' safety and health. I shall estimate the amount by which the actual number employed in mining exceeds the number that would have been required to obtain the same output if the former trends in output per worker had continued. When this amount is expressed as a percentage of total employment in nonresidential business, an estimate is secured of the percentage by which output per unit of labor input in nonresidential business was reduced by the strengthening of safety and health controls in mining. The same percentage is used for the reduction of output per unit of input, the main justification being that labor is a large percentage of gross factor cost. (The assumption implies that the ratio of depreciation and the net opportunity cost of invested capital to labor cost in mining was not altered by the controls.)

For coal mining, I start the calculation of the effect of strengthened safety and health controls from 1968 (when they are assumed to have had no effect) and, based on the 1957-68 period, use 6.5 percent as the past annual growth rate of output per person employed. Rates for some possible alternative periods are 5.8 percent for 1948-68, 7.0 percent for 1953-68, and 7.1 percent for 1960-68. All these rates are higher if the period is ended in 1967; the 1957-67 rate was 7.0 percent as against the 6.5 percent rate for 1957-68. Actual coal mining employment increased from 1968 to 1973, then more sharply from 1973 to 1975. My calculation implies that in the absence of strengthened controls, employment would have declined until 1973 and then stabilized. By 1975, actual employment was 214,000. The calculation implies that only 96,000 would have been needed to obtain the same output in the absence of strengthened safety and health controls. Table 6 shows the calculation.

For nonmetallic minerals, the calculation starts from the 1973 productivity peak, and as the past growth rate of output per person employed I used 3.5 percent, based on the 1955-73 period. Rates for some other reasonable periods were 3.6 percent for 1957-73, and 3.5 percent for 1964-73. The rate was 3.7 percent from 1955 to 1969 and 3.0 percent from 1969 to 1973. By 1975 actual employment was 116,000, and the calculation implies that it would have been 97,000 in the absence of strengthened safety and health controls.

For iron and copper mining, the calculation starts from a 1970 productivity peak. In both these small industries, in which annual changes in productivity tend to be erratic, the past growth rate of output per person employed was based on the change from the 1952-56 average to the 1966-70 average: 2.2 percent in iron mining and 2.8 percent in copper mining. To obtain estimates for "other" metal mining, I assumed that the ratio of employment in the absence of strengthened safety and health controls to actual employment would have been the same as in iron and copper mining combined. It is estimated for metal mining as a whole that actual employment was 95,000 and that it would have been only 72,000 in the absence of new safety legislation.

Columns 1 to 6 of table 7 show the annual estimates of the additional employment that stronger safety and health controls necessitated, given the actual output of the mining industries. The estimate for 1975 is 160,000, which is equal to 0.24 percent of total employment in all nonresidential business (as shown in column 7 of table 7). As stated earlier, the same figure is used as the percentage of total input in nonresidential business that was diverted from production of final products to protection of safety and health in mining. The percentage is remarkably large for the effect of strengthened controls in such small industries. It may, of course, be an overestimate if safety and health controls were not the only cause of the productivity turnaround.

The recession, by lowering output, contributed to poor productivity performance in the economy as a whole in 1974 and 1975. If the recession also contributed to poor performances in the mining industries, the effect of

Table 7.—Mining (Except Oil and Gas): Employment Required by Strengthened Controls for Worker Safety and Health

	Employment required by strengthened controls, by type of mining (thousands)						Col. 6 as a percentage of nonresidential business employment
	Coal	Nonmetal	Iron	Copper	Other metal	Total mining	
	(1)	(2)	(3)	(4)	(5)	(6)	(7)
1968							
1969	10					10	0.02
1970	22					22	.04
1971	42		2	3	3	50	.08
1972	58		4	5	4	71	.11
1973	66		4	7	4	80	.12
1974	87	6	3	13	7	116	.17
1975	118	19	3	12	8	160	.24

Table 8.—Plant and Equipment Expenditures for Safety and Health, Business Except Mining

	Expenditures in current prices		Expenditures in constant (1972) prices
	Millions of dollars	Percentage of nonfarm nonresidential business NNP	Millions of dollars
	(1)	(2)	(3)
1972	2,425	0.306	2,425
1973	2,485	.286	2,443
1974	2,922	.315	2,656
1975	2,608	.263	2,047

Source: Column 1: Economics Department, McGraw-Hill Publications Company.

safety and health controls is overestimated in these years. This may be so in metal and nonmetal mining, but seems unlikely in coal, the biggest industry, because, as measured by BLS, output actually rose 8 percent, and employment 24 percent, from 1973 to 1975.

Industries Other Than Mining

The Williams-Steiger Occupational Safety and Health Act, effective April 28, 1971, covers business in general. This section is confined to the effects of this law, which is administered by the Occupational Safety and Health Administration (OSHA) of the Department of Labor.

Through 1975, the last year covered by the estimates in this article, only moderate costs seem to have been imposed upon business by this legislation. This was partly because OSHA regulation consisted mainly of the codification of existing standards in the field of safety, and safety (as distinguished from health) has been promoted by business for many years both on its own volition and under the prodding of State agencies and insurers. OSHA, in accordance with the law, began its work by issuing as its own regulations a book of "consensus" standards—safety standards that had previously been adopted by trade associations and professional societies. This initial package was effective August 27, 1971, and most subsequent standards were similar in character.

Through 1975, relatively little OSHA regulation had been imposed in the area of health.[34] Health regulation is likely to be much more costly because it is new and will require greater changes in existing practices. Costs will be especially large if OSHA adheres to the principle that personal protective equipment, such as earplugs and earmuffs to reduce noise, should not be relied upon to meet standards.

Enforcement policy was based on belief that business would comply voluntarily if it understood OSHA standards, an approach that could be expected to secure compliance only gradually and after a lapse of time. Firms were never or rarely cited for violating the majority of OSHA standards; violations were concentrated in only a few standards. Penalties were small. As of the end of 1975, nonserious violations discovered (98.7 percent of the total) drew fines averaging $16 and serious violations (the remainder) fines averaging $648.[35]

The McGraw-Hill Publications Company, which regularly surveys plant and equipment expenditures by U.S. business, has collected capital outlays for employee safety and health for years beginning with 1972. Table 8, columns 1 and 2, shows expenditures by industries other than mining in millions of dollars and as a percentage of nonfarm nonresidential business NNP. Column 3 shows the series in constant prices that is obtained when current-dollar outlays are divided by the NIPA implicit price deflator for producers' durable equipment. These data refer to total, rather than incremental, capital outlays; the amounts that stem from OSHA's requirements are not reported separately.

It appears to be the general view that OSHA is responsible for a substantial fraction of the total. Thus, McGraw-Hill states in its annual releases: "Investment in job health and safety is related, in part, to the present enforcement of the 1970 Occupational Safety and Health Act (OSHA). This is still a relatively new area of large-scale capital expenditures. . . ."[36] Also, Murray L. Weidenbaum, after noting difficulties of reporting and interpretation, says the data "should be taken mainly as illustrative of the substantial costs involved in meeting federally mandated requirements."[37]

However, the trend of capital outlays from 1972 to 1975 suggests a different interpretation: that nearly all of the reported expenditure would have been made in the absence of new legislation. In this period, capital outlays for safety and health showed no uptrend relative to output or, when measured in constant prices, even in absolute value. The absence of an increase after 1972 suggests that capital outlays resulting from OSHA regulations could not have been large unless capital outlays in 1972 were already raised substantially by OSHA regulations. But it is not likely that OSHA could have had a substantial impact fast enough to raise outlays to a substantially higher plateau as early as 1972. The law became effective only April 28, 1971, the first standards did not go into effect until August 27, 1971, and the early standards were not regarded as stringent. Weidenbaum regards 1973 as "the first year of operation" of OSHA and to assess the effectiveness of the new safety legislation, examines changes in accidents from 1972 to 1973.[38]

Table 9.—Incremental Costs of Protecting Worker Safety and Health, Nonresidential Business Except Mining

	Incremental costs (millions of dollars)				Total incremental costs as percentage of nonresidential business NNP plus incremental costs
	Current costs	Depreciation	Net opportunity cost of invested capital	Total	
	(1)	(2)	(3)	(4)	(5)
1970	0	0	0	0	0.00
1971	26	14	14	54	.01
1972	113	59	60	232	.03
1973	197	117	105	419	.05
1974	319	197	177	693	.07
1975	450	285	237	972	.09

I compromise the opposing views in the following way. First, I carry the series for capital expenditures for safety and health shown in table 8 back to 1970 by assuming that in 1970 the ratio of such expenditures to nonfarm nonresidential business NNP was three-fourths of the 1972 ratio, or 0.231 percent, and that in 1971 it was midway between the 1972 and assumed 1970 ratios. Second, I assume that in the absence of OSHA the 1970 ratio would have continued until 1975. This ratio, 0.231 percent, was multiplied by nonfarm nonresidential business NNP to obtain baseline capital expenditures. Baseline capital expenditures were deducted from total expenditures to secure a 1971-75 series for incremental capital expenditures. The incremental capital expenditures series was then used to construct series for the gross and net stock of safety and health capital, and of depreciation. A service life of 10 years for capital goods bought with these outlays and the straight-line formula for computing depreciation were used, and the BEA implicit deflator for fixed nonresidential investment was adopted as a price series in the calculations.

Depreciation in 1975, calculated as 10 percent of the average gross stock value at the start and end of 1975, was $285 million in current prices (table 9, column 2). The net stock averaged $2,232 million in 1975. The cyclically adjusted ratio of earnings to asset values of 10.6 percent (table 3) was multiplied by this value to secure the net opportunity cost of the incremental stock, $237 million in 1975 (table 9, column 3). Total capital cost, then, was $522 million in 1975 ($285 million plus $237 million).

Data for current-account expenditures are unavailable and little is known even qualitatively about their importance. Complaints about needs to keep track of regulations, maintain records, and report were widespread during the period up to 1975, but whether current costs for other purposes—such as hiring additional safety and health personnel, testing, cleaning, diverting worktime to safety instruction, adopting more costly work layout, and so on—represented an appreciable burden is not known.

Even the few published projections of future costs usually do not separate current costs, if they count them at all. Three analyses that do make a separation, suggest current costs at least as large as annual capital costs but may not be representative.[39]

To complete the estimates, I assume that current costs bear the same ratio to annual capital costs (depreciation plus net opportunity cost of invested capital) as they do for air and water pollution abatement (excluding motor vehicles). This ratio was 0.86 in 1975 (table 1, ratio of row 2 to the sum of rows 6 and 9). Column 1 of table 9 shows the resulting estimates of current costs, and column 4 shows incremental cost of all types.

Total incremental cost is shown in column 5 of table 9 as a percentage of nonresidential business NNP.[40] This is an estimate of the percentage by which net output (NI or NNP) per unit of input in nonresidential business would have been higher if there had been no costs imposed by the Occupational Safety and Health Act. The percentage had reached only 0.09 by 1975. The incremental cost imposed by the act was reducing the growth rate by about 0.02 percent a year after 1971.

Index of Effect of Costs of Protecting Worker Safety and Health Upon Output Per Unit of Input

Table 10 brings together the ratios of incremental cost to net output that were computed for three types of programs to protect the safety and health of employed persons. The sum of the ratios is 0.42 percent in 1975 (column 4), and the figure is unchanged to this degree of rounding if incremental cost is stated as a percentage of the sum of measured product and the incremental cost (0.0042/1.0042=0.0042). As in the case of pollution abatement, this calculation yields the effect upon output per unit of input so the diversion of resources to protection of the safety and health of employed persons reduced measured output per unit of input by 0.42 percent in 1975. Ratios for all years are shown in column 5. Column 6 measures the ratio of input not so diverted to the total, and column 7 presents the same series in index form.

This index measures the course that output per unit of input in the nonresidential business sector would have followed if nothing had changed except provisions for the safety and health of workers (including regulations concerning motor vehicle safety). From 1967 to 1975, the index fell 0.42 percent, a growth rate of −0.05 percent. Mining was responsible for nearly three-fifths of the drop. The decline was accelerating throughout the period and by 1975 the rate had reached −0.12 percent. These growth rates are also the amounts, expressed in percentage points, by which the changes described were reducing the growth rate of output per unit of input in nonresidential business.

Part 4: Costs of Dishonesty and Crime

The number and costs of criminal acts, including those committed against business, have increased in the United States. There is no need to decide whether this results from changes in the governmental system of criminal justice or from changes in individuals' attitudes toward dishonesty and crime. Regardless of its cause, the increase in crime, and the apparent decline in the ability to rely upon the honesty of other people, is an important change in the human environment within which business must operate.

Business is affected by an increase in dishonesty and crime among the public in general—and among customers, employees, and suppliers in particular—in two ways, both of which reduce measured output per unit of input. First, in an effort to limit its losses, business may

Table 10.—Costs of Protecting Worker Safety and Health: Calculation of Effects Upon Output Per Unit of Input in Nonresidential Business

	Ratios of incremental costs to net output in nonresidential business			Ratio of input diverted to protection to total input Col. 4÷one + Col. 4	Ratio of input not diverted to protection to total input One−Col. 5	Index of effect of protection costs upon output per unit of input From Col. 6 (1972=100)
	Safety equipment on motor vehicles [1]	Mining [2]	Other industries [2]	Total			
	(1)	(2)	(3)	(4)	(5)	(6)	(7)
1967					0.0000	1.0000	100.17
1968	0.0000			0.0000	.0003	1.0000	100.17
1969	.0001	0.0002		.0003	.0003	.9997	100.14
1970	.0002	.0004		.0006	.0006	.9994	100.11
1971	.0003	.0008	0.0001	.0012	.0012	.9988	100.05
1972	.0003	.0011	.0003	.0017	.0017	.9983	100.00
1973	.0004	.0012	.0005	.0021	.0021	.9979	99.96
1974	.0006	.0017	.0007	.0030	.0030	.9970	99.87
1975	.0009	.0024	.0009	.0042	.0042	.9958	99.75

1. Business vehicles only.
2. Excludes safety features on cars and trucks.

Table 11.—Industries Providing Protective Services Against Crime: Receipts and Employment Based Upon the *Census of Business*

	Receipts (millions of dollars)				Wage and salary workers employed in March (thousands)			
	Detective agencies and protective services	Armored car services	Burglar and fire alarm systems	Total, three industries	Detective agencies and protective services	Armored car services	Burglar and fire alarm systems	Total, three industries
	(1)	(2)	(3)	(4)	(5)	(6)	(7)	(8)
1954	60	n.a.	n.a.	[3] 93	[3] 17	n.a.	n.a.	n.a.
1958	177	n.a.	n.a.	[3] 272	[3] 42	n.a.	n.a.	n.a.
1963	289	67	n.a.	[3] 443	67	8	n.a.	[3] 80
1967	[1] 444	[1] 91	n.a.	[3] 658	92	9	n.a.	[3] 109
1972	[1] 938	[1] 233	[1] 283	1,453	176	21	14	212

n.a. Not available.
1. Receipts of firms with no employees are estimated.
2. Includes estimates for components not shown.
3. Week ended nearest November 15.
Source: U.S. Department of Commerce, Bureau of the Census, *Census of Business*.

Table 12.—Industries Providing Protective Services Against Crime, and Selected Occupations: Employment and Wage Data Based on Various Sources

	Detective and protective service industry: data from *County Business Patterns*		Guards and watchmen employed in business service industries: data from *Census of Population*	Private wage and salary workers: data from *Current Population Survey* (yearly average, in thousands)	
	March employment (thousands)	First-quarter taxable wages (millions of dollars)	March employment (thousands)	Private policemen and detectives	Private guards and watchmen
	(1)	(2)	(3)	(4)	(5)
1959	[1] 21	[1] 12	n.a.	n.a.	n.a.
1960	n.a.	n.a.	[1] 24	n.a.	n.a.
1964	62	48	n.a.	n.a.	n.a.
1967	97	79	n.a.	n.a.	n.a.
1969	133	123	n.a.	n.a.	n.a.
1970	152	144	[1] 61	n.a.	n.a.
1971	164	163	n.a.	20	239
1972	183	193	n.a.	20	281
1973	203	220	n.a.	21	272
1974	250	288	n.a.	21	311
1975	253	320	n.a.	19	332
1976	n.a.	n.a.	n.a.	21	352

n.a. Not available.
1. Private detective agencies only.
2. Proprietors and unpaid family workers are included. Estimation was required to include persons not reporting occupation and/or industry, to include females in 1960, and to exclude persons employed by nonprofit organizations.

Sources: U.S. Department of Commerce, Bureau of the Census, *County Business Patterns* (columns 1 and 2) and *Census of Population* (column 3). U.S. Department of Labor, Bureau of Labor Statistics (columns 4 and 5).

divert resources from the production of measured output to protection against criminal and dishonest acts. A highly visible example has been the appearance of guards in many drug and grocery stores. In comparison with the period before crime increased, input in these stores is raised but output is not. From the standpoint of the economy, labor that could otherwise be used to produce measured output is no longer available for that purpose. Second, business sustains increased costs as a result of criminal acts that nevertheless occur. Theft of merchandise is the main example. The production of merchandise that is stolen from inventories before it reaches a final buyer absorbs inputs that are measured but the merchandise stolen is not counted as output. Costs resulting from various other types of crime, such as the cost of repairing property damaged by vandalism, also reduce output per unit of input.

Some costs of protection are so indirect that measurement seems nearly impossible, and it was not attempted. For example, extensive dishonesty among the public completely bars self-service at retail stores in some areas, and high crime rates may prevent placing businesses in cities or neighborhoods that would otherwise provide the most advantageous locations.

I shall, with one exception, initially measure the total rather than the incremental cost of crime.[41] But to judge the effect of crime on the course of output per unit of input, attention must, of course, be directed to changes in the cost burden, that is, to the incremental cost.

Data for crime costs are inadequate. They are increasingly so as one moves back in time. However, it is clear that the increase in crime started much before 1967, the starting point for the estimates presented in parts 2 and 3 of this article. To avoid a discontinuity, I have carried the series back to 1957.

Costs of Protection

The costs of protection against dishonesty and crime can be divided between the protection that firms provide for themselves, particularly the direct hiring of guards and detectives, and the purchase of protective services from firms specializing in this activity.

The former is probably the larger; it occupies most of the persons engaged in these activities. But the increase in protective activity during the past two decades, in excess of that associated with growth of the economy, seems to have been confined to the purchase of protective services from specialized firms. To measure the increase in the cost of protection, therefore, direct hiring of protective service workers can be disregarded. The estimates of the cost of purchased services were based on the receipts of the specialized firms. Two tables providing data used in the analysis will be introduced at this point. I shall then describe, first, the statistical basis for the judgment that direct hiring could be disregarded and, second, the derivation of the estimates for purchased services.

Table 11 shows receipts and employment of firms specializing in protection against crime, based on the *Census of Business*.[42] Receipts of such firms are an approximation to expenditures by business firms although they include some receipts from individuals and others. These receipts represent the following percentages of NI originating in nonresidential business.

Year	Percent
1954	0.038
1958	.093
1963	.117
1967	.131
1972	.201

Social Security (Old Age and Survivors' Insurance) data reported in *County Business Patterns* (CBP) provide March employment for detective and protective services in a number of years. The series (table 12, column 1) appears tolerably consistent with *Census of Business* data (table 11, column 5) although it runs slightly higher. This series and corresponding data for taxable payrolls (table 12, column 2) can be used to interpolate and extrapolate *Census of Business* data. Other data in table 12 will be mentioned shortly.

Protection that firms provide for themselves

Statistical information related to the provision that business makes directly for its own protection consists chiefly of the numbers employed in business in two occupations, "policemen and detectives" and "guards and watchmen," and the division of the number in the latter occupation between business service and other industries. Practically all guards and watchmen in the business service industry are employed in protective service components so "business service" and "protective services" can be used interchangeably in this context. From the 1960 and 1970 *Censuses of Population*, the following approximations were obtained to the total numbers in the two occupations employed by all private business and, for guards and watchmen, the distribution between business service and other industries (data in thousands):

	March 1960			March 1970		
	Policemen and detectives	Guards and watchmen	Both	Policemen and detectives	Guards and watchmen	Both
Total private business	17	176	193	17	224	241
Business service	n.a.	24	n.a.	n.a.	61	n.a.
Other industries	n.a.	152	n.a.	n.a.	163	n.a.

n.a. Not available.

The increase from 1960 to 1970 in employment of private guards and watchmen was concentrated in the business service industry. The number employed directly in the rest of the business sector did not increase more than total employment. The number of private policemen and detectives is too small to permit this finding to be altered by their inclusion.[43] I conclude that from 1960 to 1970, the ratio of directly hired protective service workers to total business employment did not change much.

What happened after 1970? The *Current Population Survey* (CPS) provides annual averages of the numbers of private wage and salary workers employed in the two occupations. The data appear in table 12, columns 4 and 5. Because the number of private policemen and detectives is both small and stable, attention can be confined to guards and watchmen. The number shown for 1971, the first year available, probably is not indicative of the level around that time. This is inferred from the CPS series for the total number of guards and watchmen, which is available without a division between private and government workers for a longer time period. In this series, the 1971 figure is erratically low, probably as a result of a sampling fluctuation. Stated in thousands, the numbers were 377 in 1969, 373 in 1970, 350 in 1971, 412 in 1972, and 420 in 1973. It is reasonable to infer that the private component, which represented 68 percent of the total in both 1971 and 1972, was also erratically low in 1971. Extrapolation of the number of private guards and watchmen backwards from 1971 by the series that includes government workers yields 255,000 as the estimated 1970 number that is comparable to the 332,000 in 1975 and the figures for other years shown in table 12, column 5.

Estimates based on the *Census of Population* for 1970, already provided, showed that 27 percent of 244,000 private guards and watchmen in nonresidential business were employed in business service and 73 percent in other industries. When the 255,000 estimated to be comparable to the CPS series for later years are similarly divided, 69,000 fall in business service, which is to say in the three protective service industries, and 186,000 in other industries.

From 1970 to 1975, CBP data for employment in protective service industries (table 12, column 1) rose 66.45 percent. If the number of private guards and watchmen in these industries rose by the same percentage, they increased from 69,000 in 1970 to 115,000 in 1975. Since the total number of private guards and watchmen is estimated to have increased from 255,000 to 332,000, the number in other industries can be estimated by subtraction to have increased from 186,000 in 1970 to 217,000 in 1975. This would represent a minor increase in the percentage of total nonresidential business employment in this category, but it is too small a change to suggest a diversion of inputs sufficient to affect output per unit of input perceptibly.

I conclude that the costs to business of policemen, detectives, guards, and watchmen who are employed directly by the enterprises they protect did not change enough to affect output per unit of input either before or after 1970. It can be inferred that this was also true of related costs, such as those for supervision or uniforms. I therefore simply omit all these costs from the totals analyzed.[44]

Protection purchased from specialized firms

Receipts of the protective service industries in *Census of Business* years (table 11, column 4) were interpolated and extrapolated by first-quarter taxable wages (table 12, column 2) to obtain a series covering 1954, 1958, 1963, 1967, and all years from 1969 to 1975. The ratio of these receipts—regarded as payments by business for protection—to NI originating in nonresidential business was computed for all these years to supplement the ratios presented earlier for census years. Ratios for years that were needed but still missing (1957, 1959–62, 1964–66, and 1968) were estimated by geometric interpolation.

Index of effects of costs of protection

To secure an index of the effects of costs of protection on output per unit of input, these percentages were deducted from 100 percent, and the remainders converted to an index with 1972 equal to 100 (table 13, column 1). For example, costs of protection provided by business service firms were 0.117 percent of NI in 1963 and 0.201 percent in 1972; the remainders were therefore 99.883 in 1963 and 99.799 in 1972; and the indexes 100.08 in 1963 and 100.00 in 1972.[45] The meaning is that if no determinant of output per unit of input except costs of protection had changed, output per unit of input would have been 0.08 percent higher in 1963 than in 1972.

This estimate covers only payments to the protective service industries and costs of direct hiring of police, guards, and watchmen. Other costs of protection include special design of buildings (notably banks), shutters and locks, safes, closed-circuit TV, alarm signals purchased independently of services, bookkeeping safeguards, packaging small consumer items in large containers (to discourage shoplifting), and procedures for validating checks and credit cards, among others, but I have no information as to whether the sum of these costs has changed relative to the value of output. It is unlikely that it has changed enough to affect the course of productivity appreciably.

Thefts of Merchandise and Damage to Property

The value of measured output is reduced by the value of goods, including those in transit, that are stolen from business inventories or are destroyed by arson or vandalism. This is so whether the value of output is derived from the NIPA's as the sum of national product components or as the sum of "charges" against national product. In the former case, this outcome results because goods stolen reduce the change in business inventories without raising any component of final sales. In the latter case, the outcome is the same because the value of goods stolen reduces corporate profits or proprietors' income and is not included in business transfer payments nor any other charge against national product. Since inputs used to produce goods stolen from inventory are counted in total input, thefts of merchandise from business reduce output per unit of input. When repairs to structures, equipment, and goods in inventory become necessary because of damage sustained from vandalism or arson, they too absorb input without providing final product, and thus reduce output per unit of input. To measure the effect on output per unit of input, losses sustained by business must be estimated.

The Bureau of Domestic Commerce (BDC) of the U.S. Department of Commerce has the only time series of which I am aware for the costs that crime has imposed upon business. Its estimates cover 1971, 1973, 1974, and 1975. BDC has sought to provide

Table 13.—Effects of Changes in Costs of Dishonesty and Crime Upon Output Per Unit of Input in Nonresidential Business

	Type of cost		
	Protection	Losses	Total
	(1)	(2)	(3)
1957	100.13	100.20	100.33
1958	100.11	100.16	100.27
1959	100.10	100.18	100.28
1960	100.10	100.12	100.22
1961	100.09	100.11	100.20
1962	100.09	100.11	100.20
1963	100.08	100.09	100.17
1964	100.08	100.07	100.15
1965	100.08	100.08	100.16
1966	100.07	100.07	100.14
1967	100.07	100.02	100.09
1968	100.05	99.99	100.04
1969	100.03	99.95	99.98
1970	100.01	99.90	99.91
1971	100.01	99.88	99.89
1972	100.00	100.00	100.00
1973	100.00	99.95	99.95
1974	99.95	99.88	99.83
1975	99.94	99.73	99.67

Table 14.—Bureau of Domestic Commerce Estimates of the Cost of Crime Against Business

	Costs of crime (billions of dollars)			Nonresidential business national income	Costs of crime as percentages of nonresidential business national income		
	Preventive	All other	Total		Preventive	All other	Total
1971	3.3	12.4	15.7	650.9	0.51	1.91	2.41
1972	n.a.	n.a.	n.a.	724.6	n.a.	n.a.	n.a.
1973	3.5	14.8	18.3	817.3	.43	1.81	2.24
1974	3.9	16.4	20.3	862.2	.45	1.90	2.35
1975	4.5	19.1	23.6	916.5	.49	2.08	2.58

n.a. Not available.
Source: Costs of crime from U.S. Department of Commerce, Bureau of Domestic Commerce, *The Cost of Crimes Against Business*, p. 7.

comparable data for the 4 years. The estimates are shown, with a two-way breakdown, in table 14. Costs of prevention are those discussed in the previous section. The definition of other costs differs from that which is desired mainly in that it covers not only losses of tangible property but also unrecovered losses of money—by theft, fraud (including passing of bad checks), forgery, embezzlement, and so on. The data exclude some costs that BDC does not regard as "ordinary." For example, the costs of special measures by the airlines to prevent highjacking are excluded from protection costs.

The BDC estimates are admittedly based on fragmentary information, and the Bureau makes no claim as to their accuracy. BDC describes them as follows:

"To gather current information, a review of articles in the trade press on crime problems within particular industries was conducted, while many industry associations supplied information and estimates based on the experiences of their memberships. Various Federal Government agencies also provided statistics on crimes.

"This report, therefore, presents a detailed summary of the available knowledge of both the industries themselves and the Federal Government on the extent of the dollar loss of American business to crime in the period since 1971. In almost every case the estimates are conservatively stated. The report also demonstrates that accurate data with which to quantify the economic impact of crimes against business are either scarce or, as is most likely, not available."[46]

The BDC estimates for components that can be compared seem higher, after allowance for differences in dates, than those derivable from earlier reports by the Task Force on Assessment of The President's Commission on Law Enforcement and Administration of Justice and the Small Business Administration.[47] Much of the difference stems from higher estimates by BDC of the value of employee thefts. Personnel of the office now believe that even their higher estimates of inventory losses in retail trade from employee thefts and shoplifting are too low.

No direct use is made here of the BDC series for costs of protection, which implies that the rise in such costs subtracted 0.01 percentage points from the 1971–75 growth rate. My series, derived in the preceding section, yields the same result for this period.

I reduced the BDC series for "all other" costs by 20 percent ($3.8 billion in 1975). The intent was to eliminate unrecovered losses of money because they do not reduce measured output, at least in principle.[48]

The ratio of the remaining costs to NI was calculated for each of the years for which BDC provides data. The first column of the text table below shows these ratios in percentage form. They represent the percentages by which output per unit of input was reduced by losses from crime.

To test the plausibility of the movement of this series, an independent measure of the prevalence of crime is needed. The Federal Bureau of Investigation (FBI) selects certain types of crimes for inclusion in its crime index and classifies three of these types as property crimes. They are burglary, larceny-theft, and motor vehicle theft.[49] I calculated the ratio of the number of FBI "index" property crimes to NI originating in nonresidential business—measured in constant prices because the number of crimes does not rise with the price level. The ratio is expressed as thousands of FBI "index" property crimes per billion dollars of NI, measured in 1972 prices.

The two ratios are as follows:

	Costs (except protection and cash losses) as a percentage of NI (current prices)	Thousands of FBI index property crimes per billion dollars of NI in 1972 prices
1971	1.524	11.49
1972	n.a.	10.23
1973	1.449	10.22
1974	1.522	12.51
1975	1.567	14.32

n.a. Not available.

Table 15.—Indexes of the Effects of Changes in Three Aspects of the Institutional and Human Environment Upon Output Per Unit of Input in Nonresidential Business

	Indexes, 1972=100				Percentage change in indexes from previous year			
	Pollution abatement (table 4)	Worker safety and health (table 10)	Dishonesty and crime (table 13)	Total	Pollution abatement	Worker safety and health	Dishonesty and crime	Total
	(1)	(2)	(3)	(4)	(5)	(6)	(7)	(8)
1957	100.41	100.17	100.33	100.91				
1958	100.41	100.17	100.27	100.85			−0.06	−0.06
1959	100.41	100.17	100.28	100.86			.01	.01
1960	100.41	100.17	100.22	100.80			−.06	−.06
1961	100.41	100.17	100.20	100.78			−.02	−.02
1962	100.41	100.17	100.20	100.78			.00	.00
1963	100.41	100.17	100.17	100.75			−.03	−.03
1964	100.41	100.17	100.15	100.73			−.02	−.02
1965	100.41	100.17	100.16	100.74			.01	.01
1966	100.41	100.17	100.14	100.72			−.02	−.02
1967	100.41	100.17	100.09	100.67			−.05	−.05
1968	100.37	100.17	100.04	100.58	−0.04	0.00	−.05	−.09
1969	100.31	100.14	99.98	100.43	−.06	−.03	−.06	−.15
1970	100.21	100.11	99.91	100.23	−.10	−.03	−.07	−.20
1971	100.10	100.05	99.89	100.04	−.11	−.06	−.02	−.19
1972	100.00	100.00	100.00	100.00	−.10	−.05	.11	−.04
1973	99.89	99.96	99.95	99.80	−.11	−.04	−.05	−.20
1974	99.67	99.87	99.83	99.37	−.22	−.09	−.12	−.43
1975	99.44	99.75	99.67	98.86	−.23	−.12	−.16	−.51

The FBI series is introduced only as a general indicator of crime prevalence; it does not count most crimes against business and does count many crimes against others. But it does tend to confirm the dip from 1971 to 1973 in the cost ratio based on BDC data, which I would regard with skepticism in the absence of some independent confirmation.

Percentages comparable to the first column of the text table were needed for other years. A percentage for 1972, 1.404 percent, was obtained by interpolating the first column of the text table by the second column. To serve as a basis to estimate similar cost percentages for earlier years, the second column was carried back to 1957.[50] However, a simple extrapolation of the first column by the second would not have been satisfactory, because the amplitude of fluctuation in the two columns is not the same. Instead, it was assumed that the value of the first column in each year before 1971 differed from its value in 1971 by 0.0506 of the difference between the 2 years in column 2. The ratio is based on the differences between 1971 and 1975 in the preceding text table: $0.0506 = (1.667 - 1.524) \div (14.316 - 11.490)$.

From the series of cost percentages obtained by thus extending the first column of the text table, an index of the effect of losses on output per unit of input (table 13, column 2) was computed by the procedure used for costs of protection.[51] The product of these two series, shown in column 3, measures the course that output per unit of input in nonresidential business would have followed if nothing had changed except costs incurred as a consequence of changes in the prevalence of crime and dishonesty.

Part 5: Combined Effects

The indexes of the effects of changes in the three conditions discussed in this article upon output per unit of input in nonresidential business are repeated in the first three columns of table 15. An index of their combined effect, the product of the first three columns, is shown in column 4. This index is a measure of the course that output per unit of input in nonresidential business would have followed if there had been no change in the provisions adopted by business to protect the physical environment and the safety and health of employed persons, and no change in the prevalence of dishonesty and crime. Costs of pollution abatement increased annually after 1967 and costs of employee safety and health after 1968, while costs of dishonesty and crime fluctuated about an upward trend. The 1967 indexes for pollution abatement and worker safety and health are used for all earlier years because there is believed to have been no significant change in them until that time.

The last four columns of table 15 show the annual percentage changes in the indexes. By the mid-1970's, the three determinants were importantly retarding the growth of output per unit of input in nonresidential business. Together, they subtracted 0.2 percentage points from the percentage change in output per unit of input in 1973, 0.4 points in 1974, and 0.5 points in 1975.

Over the 6 years from 1969 to 1975, the three determinants subtracted 0.26 percentage points from the growth rate of output per unit of input. Costs of pollution abatement subtracted 0.15 points, costs of protecting safety and health of workers 0.07 points, and costs imposed by dishonesty and crime 0.05 points. From 1973 to 1975, the subtraction from the growth rate had reached 0.47 percentage points, with half the deduction due to pollution abatement. Estimates of this type are subject to substantial error, but it is not possible to appraise recent growth experience without them. The data base for their computation needs to be strengthened.

These estimates refer to output per unit of input when output is measured by NI or NNP. The effects on the growth rate of output per unit of input would be about one-tenth smaller if output were measured gross of depreciation, that is, by gross national income or GNP.[52] Although dollar costs of pollution abatement, protection of employee safety and health, and dishonesty and crime are the same in absolute terms, the percentage of gross output lost from diversion of resources is smaller because the value of gross output, the denominator in the percentage calculation, is larger by the value of depreciation.

Annual growth rates in 1948-69 were derived in *Accounting* for total output (measured by NI) in nonresidential business and for a number of related series. These rates included 3.7 percent for total output, 2.6 percent for output per person employed, 3.1 percent for output per hour worked, 2.1 percent for output per unit of input, and 1.4 percent for the index that measures the contribution of advances in knowledge and miscellaneous determinants to these growth rates. In the 1948-69 period, the reduction in all these rates that resulted from the effect on output per unit of input of changes in the three determinants examined in this article had been only 0.02 percentage points.[53] The transition to a situation in which, by 1975, the same determinants were deducting 0.5 percentage points has been a large drag upon the recent growth rate of all these measures—large, that is to say, when compared with their growth rates in the past. Thus, costs arising from protection of the physical environment, protection of employee safety and health, and crime help to explain why all these rates have fallen in recent years. It is likely that costs imposed by other new governmental controls, including those intended to protect the health and pocketbooks of consumers and to minimize fuel imports, are responsible for an additional portion of the drop in growth rates, but estimates for these determinants are yet to be attempted.

Footnotes

1. Edward F. Denison, *Accounting for United States Economic Growth 1929–1969*, The Brookings Institution, Washington, D.C., 1974.

2. *Accounting*, p. 62, table 6-1. Additional possible determinants were specifically estimated to have had no effect (p. 76).

3. *Accounting*, pp. 78–79.

4. The first two estimates cover the entire effect upon measured output per unit of input of changes in motor vehicles that were introduced to reduce air pollution and to make vehicles safer. As is explained later, this results in part because costly changes in vehicles reduce output per unit of input only if the vehicles are used by business, and in part because all of the costs of safety improvement on business-owned vehicles is included in the estimates for worker safety and health even though the public as well as worker-occupants of the vehicles may benefit.

5. Among the more important are probably legislation intended to protect consumers against dangerous products and deceptive practices, and controls intended to reduce dependence on foreign energy sources.

6. Complications caused by the difference between market price and factor cost values of output are discussed later.

7. For further explanation, see John E. Cremeans and Frank W. Segel, "National Expenditures for Pollution Abatement and Control, 1972," SURVEY OF CURRENT BUSINESS, February 1975.

8. Total input might change, for example, if provision for environmental protection raised total investment, and thereby the capital stock, by raising total capital needs of business, or if it lowered total investment by lowering profits. It could have increased total hours worked by improving health or reduced them by worsening real wages. If profits or investment were affected, this might in turn have changed the gap between actual and potential employment. None of these possible effects seem likely to be amenable to confirmation and measurement.

9. This statement needs expansion to cover one minor point. If the economy operates under increasing returns to scale, as the estimates in my broader study imply, a change in input changes output more than proportionally. The difference appears in output per unit of input in my main classification of growth sources, though not in an alternative classification. (See *Accounting*, pp. 113–114.) For those interested in relating this article to my broader study, I note that in neither classification are gains from economies of scale included in the residual series for "advances in knowledge and all other determinants" from which I seek to isolate the effects of pollution abatement.

10. Frank W. Segel and Gary L. Rutledge, "Capital Expenditures by Business for Air, Water, and Solid Waste Pollution Abatement, 1975 and Planned 1976," SURVEY, July 1976, pp. 14–17. Frank W. Segel, Gary L. Rutledge, and Frederick J. Dreiling, "Pollution Abatement and Control Expenditures, 1974," SURVEY, February 1977, pp. 14–16. Earlier articles describe concepts and some of the series more fully, but do not provide additional data; see SURVEY, July 1974, July 1975, February 1975, and February 1976. The June 1977 issue provides later data for capital outlays.

11. U.S. Department of Commerce, Bureau of the Census, *Pollution Abatement Costs and Expenditures 1973*, *Pollution Abatement Costs and Expenditures 1974*, and *Pollution Abatement Costs and Expenditures 1975*.

12. The same figures are variously described as in December 1974 dollars and in 1974 dollars.

13. One other qualification is needed. As explained later, all the BEA data for environmental expenditures exclude farming, real estate operators, and independent professional practitioners.

14. From 1972 to 1974 current-account expenditures increased 17 percent a year and the capital stock 20 percent. If a bias adjustment based on this experience were introduced and carried back to 1967, a reasonable alternative to simple extrapolation, the net result would be to raise the incremental cost estimates about $200 million a year in the period from 1972 to 1974.

15. The CEQ data cited are for operating and maintenance costs for air and water pollution control in the private "industrial" and "utilities" categories. They are from CEQ's *6th Annual Report*, pp. 534 and 564, and *7th Annual Report*, pp. 145 and 167.

16. Source: table 3A of the 1973, 1974, and 1975 issues of the Census Bureau report, *Pollution Abatement Costs and Expenditures*. Census Bureau instructions informed respondents to its surveys that the item refers to "all payments to governmental units for sewerage service. Include payments to government for overstrength effluent charges, sewer district tax assessments, etc. Include sewage payments which are included in your local tax bill. Estimate if necessary."

17. The 1975 estimate for nonresidential business, $362 million, compares with CEQ's published estimate of $0.3 billion. CEQ *7th Annual Report*, p. 145.

18. This estimate of $1,036 million in 1974 compares with a figure of $784 million for the same components that had been obtained earlier by the ACEB by adjustment of book depreciation, and that was included in the capital consumption allowance estimate of $1,566 million shown in the February 1977 SURVEY, p. 15, table 1.

19. An estimate for 1975, not available from MVMA, was based on the change from 1974 in the price index and adjustments for costs of safety improvements and pollution controls.

20. The deduction was estimated as follows. The depreciated value in 1972 prices of used automobiles sold by business to consumers, after deduction of automobiles sold by consumers to business, was obtained from NIPA table 1.17. It was divided by 0.55 to secure an estimate of the value in 1972 prices before depreciation. The ratio of 0.55 is based on a 10-year service life and straight-line depreciation and an estimated average age of 4½ years when sold. To obtain the undepreciated value in 1972 prices of the pollution abatement devices in these cars, the undepreciated value of the cars was multiplied by the average, during the preceding 8 years, of the ratios (step e) of the value of the devices to the value of the cars. This would be the correct ratio if the cars sold were equally divided over the age range of 1 to 8 years.

21. U.S. Department of Commerce, Bureau of Economic Analysis, *Fixed Nonresidential Business and Residential Capital in the United States, 1925–1975*, June 1976, p. T-6.

22. No estimate was included for diesel-fueled trucks, for which the pollution abatement problem is quite different. EPA considers that costs of equipment for pollution abatement were nominal. EPA, *The Cost of Clean Air*, p. III-31.

23. EPA, *The Cost of Clean Air*, pp. III-15, 28. This was literally true only through 1974. Starting in 1975, standards were lower for trucks but I have been unable to find an estimate of the cost differential, if any, on 1975 models. See *Ibid.*, pp. III-8 to 9.

24. To maintain uniformity with the automobile estimates, the automobile price index is assumed to be appropriate for abatement costs of trucks, and was used to convert devices in trucks from one price level to another.

25. SURVEY, February 1977, p. 15, table 1.

26. Census Bureau data are from *Pollution Abatement Costs and Expenditures*, (1973, 1974, and 1975 editions), table 3-A. Census Bureau instructions to respondents read as follows: "The estimate of costs recovered through abatement activities may have two parts: (1) The value of reclaimed materials or energy reclaimed . . . that were reused in production, and (2) revenue that was obtained from the sale of materials or energy reclaimed. . . . Heat is an example of reclaimed energy. Value and revenue are net of any additional cost incurred for additional processing of materials or energy to make them reusable or salable." The Census Bureau did not report a 1972 figure. Its 1973 figure for manufacturing was only $376 million but ACEB considered this too small relative to 1972 and 1974 on the basis of technical information and the impact of legislation in force at the time.

27. R. & D. not for pollution abatement would provide new knowledge of a different kind. Insofar as it would otherwise be of a type that would raise measured output per unit of input, productivity growth will eventually be adversely affected by diversion to pollution abatement R. & D., but the retardation will be in some future period.

28. The division of incremental costs between those valued at factor cost and those valued at market price is, obviously, an approximation but the combined ratio is not very sensitive to errors in this division. It would rise only to 1.045 percent even if all costs were compared with NI and fall only to 0.928 percent if all costs were compared with NNP.

29. This difference from the illustration in which 1967 was taken as 100 does not affect the definition or movement of the series.

30. Data are from U.S. Department of Labor, Bureau of Labor Statistics, *Productivity Indexes for Selected Industries*, 1976 Edition, Bulletin 1938, 1977.

31. For copper, I use the series in which output is measured by copper ore and, for iron, the series in which output is measured by usable ore.

32. See *Business Week*, January 27, 1975, p. 130; *Coal Age*, February 1973, p. 88; and U.S. Department of the Interior, Bureau of Mines, *Mineral Facts and Problems*, 1975 Edition, Bulletin 667, preprint "Bituminous Coal and Lignite," p. 10.

33. The influx of inexperienced workers was itself due indirectly to safety legislation because, with output increasing only modestly, only the adverse behavior of productivity resulting from the legislation made rapid employment expansion necessary. The need to hire new workers was intensified by requirements to replace experienced supervisors and miners who were hired as government safety inspectors. The new young workers were also active in wildcat strikes and were the cause of higher absenteeism. The cost of hiring new workers was itself raised by regulations that imposed safety training course requirements for new and reassigned workers.

34. A standard for asbestos fibers in the atmosphere was introduced in December 1971; standards for 14 carcinogens and for pesticides (the standard for the latter was promptly voided by the courts) in April and May 1973; for vinyl chloride in May 1974; and for a series of toxic substances during fiscal 1976.

35. Based on Robert Stewart Smith, *The Occupational Safety and Health Act, Its Goals and Its Achievements*, American Enterprise Institute for Public Policy Research, Washington, 1976, pp. 60–64.

36. Economics Department, McGraw-Hill Publications Company, *4th Annual McGraw-Hill Survey Investment in Employee Safety and Health*, May 28, 1976, p. 4.

37. Murray L. Weidenbaum, *Government-Mandated Price Increases*, American Enterprise Institute for Public Policy Research, 1975, p. 51.

38. "Reducing Inflationary Pressures by Reforming Government Regulation," in William Fellner, Editor, *Contemporary Economic Problems*, American Enterprise Institute for Public Policy Research, 1976, p. 277.

39. These examples are cited by the Regulatory Policy Committee of the U.S. Department of Commerce in *Toward Regulatory Reasonableness*, January 13, 1977, p. 61.

40. In deriving such percentages for pollution abatement, it may be recalled, costs were divided between those best related to NNP and those best related to NI. This refinement was not attempted for safety and health, for which estimates are smaller and cruder, nor was it for dishonesty and crime, which is considered in part 4. Instead, all incremental costs were related to the measure that seemed more appropriate: NNP for safety and health (except the large mining component, for which the percentage was based on employment), and NI for dishonesty and crime.

41. The exception is costs of protection that firms provide for themselves.

42. Numbers shown are partly estimated, as footnotes to the table indicate. Estimated receipts of industries not separately reported amounted to one-fifth of the total in 1963 and 1967, and about one-third in 1954 and 1958. Receipts of component industries not separately reported in the earlier censuses were assumed to have moved like receipts of industries that were reported.

43. For example, if one-third of them were employed outside business service in both years, employment outside business service in the two occupations combined increased from 158,000 to 169,000. This is an increase of only 9 percent, which is less than the 16-percent increase in total business employment. Even an assumption that the percentage of policemen and detectives who were employed outside business service increased sharply would not do more than close the gap between the two percentages.

44. The series shown in the preceding table and the alternative series show irregular fluctuations that could be incorporated into the estimates. But I think they are more likely to reflect errors of estimate than reality and therefore ignore them.

45. Examination of the ratios suggests that the 1954 census may have understated receipts of detectives agencies. If so, my estimate of protection cost in 1957 is understated about one-fourth as much. Other years are unaffected.

46. U.S. Department of Commerce, Bureau of Domestic Commerce, *The Cost of Crimes Against Business*, January 1976, p. 2.

47. The President's Commission on Law Enforcement and Administration of Justice, *Crime and Its Impact—An Assessment*, U.S. Government Printing Office, 1967. U.S. Small Business Administration, *Crime Against Small Business*, Senate Document 91-14, 1969, p. 3.
48. When, as in my estimates, the value of output is measured as the sum of charges against national product, the inclusion of unrecovered cash losses in business transfer payments offsets the reduction that the losses cause in business profits. However, only $121 million, less than 1 percent of the BDC figure for "all other" costs, is included in the NIPA transfer payment series in 1975. The BDC series surely implies a larger amount.
49. The weights of the three types, which simply reflect the numbers of crimes, have been fairly stable. They were, respectively, 29 percent, 60 percent, and 11 percent in 1960 and 32, 58, and 10 in 1975.
50. The number of index property crimes from 1960 onward is from Federal Bureau of Investigation, *Crime in the United States 1975, Uniform Crime Reports*, p. 49. The 1960 figure was extrapolated back to 1957 by an earlier series for the number of property crimes reported in the FBI's uniform crime reports. The source is U.S. Department of Commerce, Bureau of the Census, *Historical Statistics of the United States Colonial Times to 1970*, Series 958.
51. One check on a small segment of the index is provided by statistics from Underwriters' Laboratories (UL). From 1963 to 1967, the number of burglary attempts against UL-certificated business installations of alarms increased from 6.1 per 100 protected properties to 8.8, with more than one-half of the 4-year increase occurring from 1966 to 1967. (*Crime Against Small Business*, p. 23). My series shows an even greater concentration of the 1963–67 increase in costs occurring in 1966–67. (The 44-percent increase in attempts over the 4 years is much larger than the increase in my series for costs of crime, but burglaries are only part of crime costs.)
52. From 1972 to 1975, the ratio of NNP to GNP averaged 0.001 at market prices.
53. This calculation uses the 1957 index in table 15 for 1948. This seems reasonable, and it is unlikely that any different plausible assumption about crime costs would raise the figure above 0.03.

Sales and sales prices

Manufacturers expect their sales to increase 10 percent in 1978 (table 3). The actual increase in 1977 was 13 percent, compared with an expected increase of 10½ percent. Trade firms expect an increase of 10½ percent; last year, they had a 10-percent increase, compared with an expected 9 percent. The corresponding figures for public utilities are 11, 19, and 14½ percent.

Information on price changes of goods and services sold by manufacturers and public utilities is shown in table 4. Manufacturers expect a larger sales price increase this year than last; utilities expect a smaller increase.

ERRATA

Corrections are shown here for certain items in the National Income and Product Tables published in the July 1977 SURVEY OF CURRENT BUSINESS. Additional corrections were published in the August and September SURVEYS.

Gross Nonfarm Business Product

Period	Fixed-weighted price index, 1972=100 (Table 7.2, line 22)		Percent change from preceding period, fixed-weighted price index (Table 8.9, line 100)		Percent change from preceding period, chain price index (Table 8.9, line 99)	
	Published	Correct	Published	Correct	Published	Correct
1973	104.1	104.0	4.1	4.0	4.1	4.0
1974	116.4	115.5	11.9	11.1	11.4	10.6
1975	127.7	127.4	9.7	10.3	(*)	(*)
1976	134.7	134.5	5.5	5.6	(*)	(*)
1973:IV	106.6	106.8	9.8	9.5	(*)	(*)
1974:I	110.5	109.5	15.5	10.5	15.5	10.2
1974:II	114.4	113.7	14.8	16.4	(*)	(*)
1974:III	118.1	117.3	13.7	13.3	(*)	(*)
1974:IV	121.8	120.8	12.9	12.2	(*)	(*)
1975:I	124.7	124.2	9.8	11.8	(*)	(*)
1975:II	126.3	126.0	5.4	5.9	(*)	(*)
1975:III	128.4	128.1	6.7	6.9	(*)	(*)
1975:IV	130.2	130.0	5.7	6.1	(*)	(*)
1976:I	131.7	131.6	(*)	(*)	(*)	(*)
1976:II	133.3	133.0	5.0	4.4	(*)	(*)
1976:III	135.2	134.9	5.5	5.9	(*)	(*)
1976:IV	137.2	137.1	6.2	6.7	(*)	(*)
1977:I	139.4	139.0	6.5	5.8	(*)	(*)
1977:II	141.9	141.6	7.2	7.5	(*)	(*)

*Correct as published.

[2]
Public Regulations and the Slowdown in Productivity Growth

By GREGORY B. CHRISTAINSEN AND ROBERT H. HAVEMAN*

Since 1965, indices of labor productivity have had a disappointing and largely unexplained performance. Not only is the rate of productivity growth over the post-1965 period lower than in preceding postwar years, but its upward trend has been broken at least twice. Since 1978, productivity growth has been effectively zero. If the trend of labor productivity from 1946-65 had continued until 1980, the current index would be about 15 percent above its actual level. Table 1 summarizes the postwar behavior of four alternative measures of productivity.

While productivity growth has slowed in nearly all sectors, there is a large variance in the distribution of post-1965 sectoral productivity growth rates. The most dramatic slowdowns have been recorded for the mining, utilities, and construction sectors. The manufacturing sector has experienced a much milder slowdown, and since 1967 its productivity index has risen over 12 percentage points more than that for the entire nonfarm sector.

Many phenomena have contributed to poor productivity performance. They range from subtle changes in worker motivation to the propensity to innovate in both products and processes to exogenous shocks to the production process (due, for example, to unexpected energy price changes) to alterations in output mix, the demographic characteristics of the labor force, or the ratio of labor to capital to the nature and intensity of regulatory policy. Not only are these effects numerous, but they interact in complex and dynamic ways. Numerous assertions have been made regarding the contribution of each of these factors, and studies seeking to identify their relative contributions have been undertaken. At present, the contribution of public regulations to both the productivity slowdown and to poor economic performance generally is both widely debated and little understood. It is this relationship that is the focus of this paper. In Sections I and II, the direct and indirect ways in which regulations can adversely affect productivity are distinguished, and the existing studies of this relationship are described. Sections III and IV describe our attempts to model and estimate the contribution of regulation to the slowdown. Some preliminary results are presented.

I. Public Regulations as a Source of the Productivity Slowdown

By definition, public regulations are interventions into market processes. Because of them, the utility and profit-maximizing decisions of individual decision makers are altered. In a smoothly functioning market economy (without externalities), such interventions ensure deviation from the private sector production frontier. Holding output composition constant, this deviation means that additional inputs are required to produce any given level of output. Under these conditions, increases in the intensity of public regulations will be associated with larger deviations from the private output frontier, and equivalently, reduced rates of growth of output per unit of input—productivity. In a dynamic setting, increased regulatory intensity, through its alteration of private optimizing decisions, is likely to induce reductions in the measured rate of productivity growth.

The channels by which public regulations are likely to affect either the output numera-

---

*Assistant professor of economics, Colby College, and professor of economics, University of Wisconsin-Madison, respectively. Helpful comments on an earlier draft by John Bishop, Laurits Christensen, Sheldon Danziger, Donald Nichols, Eugene Smolensky, and Barbara Wolfe are gratefully acknowledged.

TABLE 1—POSTWAR ANNUAL PRODUCTIVITY GROWTH RATES IN THE UNITED STATES,
VARIOUS MEASURES OF PRODUCTIVITY
(Shown in Percent per Year)

	Output per Person-Hour, Private Sector	Output per Person-Hour, Nonfarm Private Sector	Nonresidential Business Income per Person Employed	Total Factor Productivity in Domestic Private Business
1947-66	3.44	2.83	2.9	2.9[a]
1966-73	2.15	1.87	1.3	1.4[b]
1973-78	1.15	1.02	−.1	−
1979	−.9	−1.2	−	−

Source: Figures for output per person-hour, private sector and output per person-hour, nonfarm private sector were taken from Jerome Mark, p. 486. Figures for nonresidential business income per person employed were taken from Denison (1979c), p. 21. Figures for total factor productivity in domestic private business were taken from Kendrick, p. 511.

[a] For years 1948-66.
[b] For years 1966-76.

tor or input denominator of productivity indices are complex. Each channel involves some aspect of policy-induced business behavior entailing a reduction in the ratio of output to input. To illustrate these channels, we will deal with environmental regulations; analogous channels of impact exist for other forms of regulation.

By their nature, environmental regulations require investments to reduce residual flows. To the extent that these investments compete with standard plant and equipment investments, the ratio of labor to conventional capital will be increased. Moreover, because these regulations are typically based on engineering standards, the activities which they generate tend to be excessively capital intensive. Because these regulations fall especially heavily on new pollution sources, incentive is given for uneconomic retention of existing—and lower productivity—plant and equipment. These regulations have also tended to be more heavily imposed on sectors with high postwar rates of productivity growth (for example, utilities), and in low pollution regions attractive for plant location. And, because pollution control equipment requires manpower to operate it, employment levels rise with no addition to marketable output. Finally, complying with these regulations requires the information-gathering, administrative, and legal activities which require inputs yielding no saleable output. Meeting these requirements may also require time— causing delay in expansion and modernization plans and the stretching-out of construction periods.

II. Public regulations and the Productivity Slowdown: Some Estimates

No comprehensive study of the effect of public regulations on the slowdown in productivity growth has been undertaken. A few studies of the contribution of environmental and health/safety regulations have been made, however.

The most influential of these is that of Edward Denison (1979a, b, c) who uses his growth accounting framework to derive an estimate of the contribution of these regulations to the retardation of growth in his productivity measure—final output valued at factor cost per unit of labor, capital, and land inputs. Denison's index suggests that the average annual impact of post-1967 environmental regulations on the rate of productivity growth was .05 percentage points from 1967–69, .1 percentage points from 1969–73, .22 percentage points from 1973–75, and .08 percentage points from 1975–78. Robert Crandall has also studied the environmental regulation-productivity interaction, using both cross-section and time-series regression approaches. While the results from these estimates vary substantially, he finds that the index of manufacturing in 1976 is about 1.5 percent below what it would be in the absence of mandated pollution control expenditures, and that those manufacturing sectors heavily impacted by environmental regulations showed a greater slowdown in productivity growth after 1970 than manufacturing as a whole. Finally, Robin Siegel has attempted to account for the slowdown in the private nonfarm labor productivity trend by regressing this quarterly time-series variable on variables designed to account for changes in output due to the business cycle, output and labor force composition, relative energy prices, pollution control expenditures, and capital investment, among other potential factors. Pollution control expenditures were estimated to have caused a 0.5 percentage-point reduction in the rate of productivity growth from 1965–73, but no significant effect after 1975.

These studies have focused on pollution control (as opposed to the full set of public) regulations. They have not been based on a rigorous theoretical or estimation framework, and omitted variable and other data and statistical problems plague the estimates. Elsewhere, we have critiqued these and other studies and the estimates which they have yielded, concluding that between 8–12 percent of the post–1973 slowdown in the growth rate of labor productivity is attributable to environmental regulations (see our paper with Frank Gollop).

III. The Productivity Impact of Regulation: An Empirical Framework

To provide a preliminary evaluation of the contribution of public regulations to the slowdown in productivity growth, we employ a simple time-series regression model for the U.S. manufacturing sector. We assume that there is a differentiable aggregate production function underlying economic activity in the manufacturing sector which relates the flow of output (Q) to the flow of total factor input (TFI). The function shifts over time (T) and also in response to what we refer to as "regulatory intensity" (R).

Assuming constant returns to scale, a simple first-order form is

$$(1) \quad Q = A(TFI) \cdot e^{\alpha R + \beta T}$$

where A, α, and β are parameters. Taking the natural logarithm of both sides of (1):

$$(2) \quad \ln Q = \ln A + \ln(TFI) + \alpha R + \beta T$$

If $\ln(TFI)$ is subtracted from both sides of (2), an equation for the level of total factor productivity (TFP) is obtained:

$$(3) \quad \ln(TFP) = \ln A + \alpha R + \beta T$$

That is, to the extent that economic activity follows the hypothesized production function, the level of total factor productivity is a function of a constant, regulatory intensity, and time.

We assume that production in the U.S. manufacturing sector can be approximated by (1) except during periods in which the sector is "shocked" by business-cycle effects. Accordingly, in addition to an additive disturbance term (v), we add two terms to (3) designed to capture cyclical effects on total factor productivity. Following William Nordhaus, who has justified this procedure in a more rigorous setting, the additional variables are current and lagged values of $\ln(Q/Q^*)$, where Q is actual output and Q^* is a measure of the level of output which would have been produced in the absence of cyclical influences.[1]

Thus, our equation for the level of total factor productivity is

$$(4) \quad \ln(TFP) = \ln A + \alpha R + \beta T + \gamma \ln\left(\frac{Q}{Q^*}\right) + \delta \ln\left(\frac{Q}{Q^*}\right)_{-1} + v$$

---

[1] Assume that the actual level of output (Q) depends on the level of demand which, in turn, depends on a constant, the price level of sector output relative to the general price level, the deviation of the actual from the "natural" rate of unemployment ($U - U^*$), and "natural" real GNP (GNP^*). The Q^* is estimated by regressing Q on its determinants and imputing values of Q assuming $U = U^*$. (The U^* and GNP^* are from Robert Gordon.)

where γ and δ are parameters, and R enters the equation with an as yet unspecified lag distribution. As is well known, *TFP* differs from *labor* productivity by a factor reflecting the influence of the ratio of nonlabor to labor inputs (K/L).

We have estimated (4) for the U.S. manufacturing sector from 1958-77 using unpublished annual data on the quantities and proportions of total cost accounted for by labor, capital, energy, and materials, and price and quantity data pertaining to output.[2] In order to reduce the presence of multicollinearity, these inputs were combined into a measure of *TFI* by using their respective shares in total cost as weights. Because of this comprehensive set of inputs, the effect of some factors often assigned responsibility for the productivity slowdown (for example, the energy crisis) is filtered out of the *TFI* measure.

"Regulatory intensity" is a difficult concept to define, let alone quantify. As noted, our definition of this concept is based on the view that public regulatory agencies distort optimizing private sector decisions which would, *ceteris paribus*, maximize the measured rate of productivity growth. We have constructed three alternative indices of this variable for the postwar period. The first is based on an estimate of the cumulative number of "major" pieces of regulatory legislation in effect during any of the years in question (R_1).[3] The second and third indices are based on the volume of real federal expenditures on regulatory activities for the years in question (R_2) and the number of full-time federal personnel engaged in regulatory activities (R_3).[4] For our measures, that portion of each agency's activities devoted to the manufacturing sector was

[2] We wish to thank J. R. Norsworthy and Michael Harper of the U.S. Bureau of Labor Statistics for these data.

[3] This series was calculated from data presented in Center for the Study of American Business.

[4] R_2 and R_3 were estimated from agency data published in the *Budget of the United States Government*. For large, diverse agencies such as the Environmental Protection Agency, data on regulatory functions are separable from other agency functions. For smaller regulatory agencies, we have used expenditure and staffing data for the agency as a whole.

the average of the judgments of several recognized students of regulation.[5] Though crude proxies for regulatory intensity, we believe these indices provide a reasonable characterization of postwar trends in the regulation of the manufacturing sector; indeed, the only characterization available without a major research effort.

Each of the R indices imply only a gradual increase in regulatory intensity until the mid-1960s. Then, all three measures accelerate, with R_2 increasing at a more rapid rate than R_3 which in turn shows a greater acceleration than R_1. All of the measures show a further acceleration during the 1970's, though the acceleration is again least pronounced in the case of R_1. Setting each index equal to 100 in 1947, R_1 attains a level of 402.88 in 1977, while R_2 and R_3 read 1003.77 and 668.03 respectively. While there are exceptions, the indices generally imply a monotonic increase in regulatory intensity during the 1947-77 period.

Alternative estimates of equation (4) were obtained using R_1, R_2, and R_3, with lag specifications chosen on the basis of the Bayesian estimation criterion proposed by John Geweke and Richard Meese. A simple one-year lag was chosen for R_2 and R_3; two-years for R_1. So lagged, the simple correlation coefficients among the alternative measures are: .85 (R_1, R_2), .86 (R_1, R_3), and .94 (R_2, R_3). Pseudo-generalized least squares estimates of the equation were made by using Takeshi Amemiya's procedure for prefiltering the data.

IV. The Productivity Impact of Regulation: Preliminary Results

Combining our regression estimates with estimates of the impact of K/L accounted for by differences in the growth rates of *TFP* and labor productivity, we obtain the results in Table 2.

[5] Each individual was asked to estimate the percentage of each agency's activities which are devoted to the manufacturing sector, and how this percentage had changed over time. In each case, the highest and lowest estimates were discarded, and the mean of the remaining estimates was used in constructing these indices.

TABLE 2—CONTRIBUTIONS TO THE RATE OF GROWTH OF LABOR PRODUCTIVITY
IN U.S. MANUFACTURING, 1958–77: PRELIMINARY RESULTS

Source	1958-65	Contribution during: 1965-73	1973-77
R	0 to −.1	−.1 to −.3	−.2 to −.3
T	.9 to 1.0	.9 to 1.0	.9 to 1.0
Q/Q^*	0 to .1	0	0 to −.1
Unexplained	.4 to .5	−.1 to −.2	−.3 to −.4
Average Growth Rate of Total Factor Productivity	1.4	.6	.3
K/L	1.6	1.9	1.4
Average Growth Rate of Labor Productivity	3.0	2.5	1.7

These numbers are derived by simply taking the parameter estimates for equation (4) and then multiplying them by the average annual changes in the associated variables. In the case of R, the estimated regression coefficients for α are .011 (R_1), .005 (R_2), and .006 (R_3). Lagged appropriately, the average annual changes in R for the three periods of Table 2 are 6.66, 13.48, and 20.44 (R_1), 6.09, 65.90, and 61.32 (R_2), and 5.05, 33.61, and 49.80 (R_3). The average percentage point contributions of regulation to the rate of growth of total factor productivity are then calculated to be −.073, −.148, and −.224 (R_1), −.030, −.330, and −.301 (R_2), and −.030, −.202, and −.299 (R_3).

Neither R_1 nor R_3 was statistically significant at either a .01 or a .05 level, but both were significant at a .10 level. The estimated coefficient for R_2 was significant at the .05 level. In all cases, neither the estimated coefficient on the lagged cyclical variable nor an interaction term for R and T were significant at the .10 level. The same was true of an interaction term for R and K/L in an equation for the level of labor productivity. All other estimated coefficients were significant at the .05 level.

The ranges indicated in Table 2 thus stem from the alternative measures of R. Of the alternatives, R_2 (which shows the greatest acceleration in regulatory intensity over time) implies the most negative impact on the rate of productivity growth. It also implies the greatest rate of "technical change" and the smallest average cyclical impact. These conclusions are reversed for R_1, with those for R_3 being intermediate to the other two.

V. Summary and Caveats

These results suggest that federal regulations are responsible for from 12 to 21 percent of the slowdown in the growth of labor productivity in U.S. manufacturing during 1973–77 as compared to 1958–65.[6] They are consistent with previous research noted in section II. Reductions in the ratio of nonlabor to labor inputs (K/L) are responsible for about 15 percent of the slowdown. The contribution of the average cyclical impact could fall anywhere in the 0–15 percent range. The unexplained portion of the slowdown in the rate of productivity growth —often attributed to changes in labor force composition, R&D expenditures, or sectoral output shifts—remains substantial.

These results on the impact of regulation are, in certain important respects, sensitive to the manner in which the model is specified. For example, with alternative lag specifications, estimated coefficients for R may be insignificant. Also, if a separate trend variable for each of the three periods in Table 2 is entered into the model, or if time enters in second-order form, multicollinearity among the explanatory variables causes the coefficients for both regulatory intensity and time to be insignificant. Moreover, the R variables may be capturing other exogenous forces inducing contemporaneous productivity growth reductions, in

---

[6]This conclusion is derived by taking the difference between the percentage point contributions of each regulatory intensity variable during 1958–65 and 1973–77, and dividing this difference by the difference between the rates of growth of labor productivity during the two periods. These values are all shown in Table 2.

which case improved specifications may reduce the estimated R impacts. While we believe that our 12–21 percent estimated contribution of regulatory intensity to the slowdown in the growth of labor productivity will prove to be robust with respect to improved data and more sophisticated models,[7] we recognize the uncertainties surrounding this estimate caused by less-than-ideal data and the possible recent impact on productivity growth of many other factors —factors which may be difficult to measure or capture in any simple model. It should be noted, however, that the procedure employed is more robust with respect to assumptions than those used in widely quoted studies which estimate the response of investment spending to taxation, private savings to Social Security wealth, or productivity growth to $R\&D$ spending.

Finally, our study focuses on the contribution of public regulations to *measured* productivity. Such regulations are typically undertaken in the belief that they will yield contributions to economic welfare not fully reflected in measured output (for example, improved health and safety; an improved environment). If such gains are forthcoming, growth in "true" economic productivity would exceed its measured counterpart. Our results have little implication for the contribution of public regulations to true productivity growth.

[7]The impact of R was also estimated using 1947–71 data on prices, quantities, and proportions of total cost accounted for by labor, capital energy, and materials compiled by Ernst Berndt and David Wood. This series was extended to 1977 by applying estimated percentage changes in each variable indicated by the *BLS* data, and normalizing cost shares. Because the variable definitions in the two data sets are not identical this exercise, taken by itself, would be of dubious value. This estimation implied an impact on *BLS*-defined labor productivity in the 12–25 percent range, however.

REFERENCES

T. Amemiya, "Generalized Least-Squares with an Estimated Autocovariance Martix," *Econometrica*, July 1973, *41*, 723–32.

E. R. Berndt and D. O. Wood, "Technology, Prices, and the Derived Demand for Energy," *Rev. Econ. Statist.*, Aug. 1975, *62*, 259–68.

G. Christainsen, F. Gollop, and R. Haveman, "Environmental and Health-Safety Regulations, Productivity Growth, and Economic Performance: An Assessment," Joint Economic Committee, U.S. Congress, 1980.

R. Crandall, "Pollution Controls and Productivity Growth in Basic Industries," in Thomas G. Cowing and Rodney Stevenson, eds., *Productivity Measurements in Regulated Industries*, New York forthcoming.

Edward F. Denison, (1979a) "Pollution Abatement Programs: Estimates of Their Effect Upon Output Per Unit of Input, 1975–1978," *Surv. Curr. Bus.*, Part I, Aug. 1979, *59*, 58–59.

_____, (1979b) "Explanations of Declining Productivity Growth," *Surv. Curr. Bus.*, Part II, Aug. 1979, *59*, 1–24.

_____, (1979c) *Accounting for Slower Economic Growth*, Washington 1979.

J. Geweke and R. Meese, "Estimating Regression Models of Finite But Unknown Order," SSRI Paper no. 7925, Univ. Wisconsin-Madison, 1979.

Robert J. Gordon, *Macroeconomics*, Boston 1978.

J. Kendrick, Testimony before the Congressional Joint Economic Committee, in *Special Study on Economic Change: Hearings before the Joint Economic Committee, Congress of the United States*, Part 2, Washington 1978, 616–36.

J. Mark, Testimony before the Congressional Joint Economic Committee, in *Special Study on Economic Change: Hearings before the Joint Economic Committee, Congress of the United States*, Part 2, Washington 1978, 476–86.

W. O. Nordhaus, "The Recent Productivity Slowdown," *Brookings Papers*, Washington 1972, *3*, 473–546.

R. Siegel, "Why Has Productivity Slowed Down?," *Data Resources Rev.*, Mar. 1979, *1*, 1.59–1.65.

Center for the Study of American Business, *Directory of Federal Agencies*, Formal Publication No. 31, St. Louis 1980.

The Cost of Regulation: OSHA, EPA and the Productivity Slowdown

By Wayne B. Gray*

The slowdown in productivity growth in the U.S. economy during the 1970's has been a matter of great concern to policymakers, associated as it is with inflation, unemployment, and declining real wage growth. This paper examines the impact on productivity growth of government regulation, specifically worker health and safety regulation by the Occupational Safety and Health Administration (OSHA) and environmental regulation by the Environmental Protection Agency (EPA). Looking at data for 450 manufacturing industries between 1958 and 1978, the study finds a large, negative relationship between such regulation and productivity growth. Using these results, about 30 percent of the decline in productivity growth in manufacturing during the 1970's may be attributed to such regulation.

Several previous studies have looked at the contribution of regulation to the productivity slowdown. Many of these have inferred that the contribution must be small, on the basis of the relatively small amount spent on complying with such regulations. Edward Denison (1979) estimates that only about 16 percent of the productivity slowdown in the 1972–75 period was due to regulation (.35 percentage points out of a slowdown of 2.17 percentage points). Paul Portney (1981) notes that little of GNP is spent on pollution control (under 2 percent), concluding that therefore pollution regulations could have little effect on productivity growth. Norsworthy et al. (1979) also find a small impact of pollution-abatement capital expenditures on productivity growth.

Studies based on econometric estimation of the regulation-productivity relationship have found a wide range of results. Gregory Christainsen and Robert Haveman (1981) find regulation reduced labor productivity growth by .27 percentage points, using time-series data and measures of total federal regulation. Robert Crandall (1981) finds a strong relationship between pollution-abatement capital and productivity growth, but this relationship disappears when a measure of energy intensity is included. Robin Siegel (1979) observes a significant contribution (.5 percentage points) from pollution control expenditures to the productivity slowdown for 1965–73, but not for later years. Finally, Frank Gollop and Mark Roberts (1983) examine data for a set of electric utilities and find that regulation of emissions had a large impact on total factor productivity growth, lowering it for regulated firms by .59 percentage points.

Many other factors might help to explain the productivity slowdown, including the rise in energy prices, the long and severe recession, and declines in research and development expenditures. There have been a variety of studies examining the contributions of each factor to the slowdown. They generally conclude that many factors contributed to the slowdown, but that a sizable fraction of the slowdown remains unexplained by the estimated contributions of all the factors considered.[1]

---

*Department of Economics, Clark University, Worcester, MA 01610. This research was partially supported by the Sloan Foundation and the National Bureau of Economic Research. I thank seminar participants at the National Bureau and anonymous referees for helpful comments. I also thank various individuals in OSHA, EPA, and the Commerce Department for providing data.

[1] Exceptions to this tendency are not uncommon, with several studies (such as Michael Darby, 1984, and Thomas Weisskopf et al., 1983) finding that the particular factor under consideration explains nearly all (or even more than 100 percent of) the productivity slowdown.

I. The Model

This paper concentrates on total factor productivity (TFP) measures of productivity growth, which consider the contribution of all productive inputs to output growth. Given a simple production function,

(1) $\quad Y = T * F(X_1, \ldots, X_N),$

where output Y depends on the level of productivity T (assumed to be Hicks-neutral) and inputs X_i, we can calculate TFP growth (τ) as

(2) $\quad \tau = dy - \sum \alpha_i dx_i,$

where α_i is the share of input i in total cost, and dy and dx_i are the growth rates of Y and X_i. This method of calculating productivity growth, known as growth accounting, requires no estimation of the production function, but cannot test for changes in the productivity of different inputs over time.

Regulation could affect measured productivity growth by requiring firms to use some inputs for compliance. If a firm uses R_i of each input to comply with regulations, but TFP is calculated without recognizing this, X_i, α_i, and τ will be mismeasured as X_i', α_i' and τ':

(3) $\quad X_i' = X_i + R_i, \quad \alpha_i' = p_i X_i'/p_y Y,$

and $\quad \tau' = dy - \sum \alpha_i' dx_i'.$

If the fraction of each input used in compliance is $\theta_i (= R_i / X_i')$ we have the following relationship between measured (τ') and true (τ) TFP growth:

(4) $\quad \tau' - \tau = \sum \alpha_i x_i - \sum \alpha_i' x_i'$

$\cong \sum \alpha_i'(x_i - x_i') \cong -\sum \alpha_i' \theta_i,$

where the quality of the approximation depends on θ_i being close to 0.[2] This "measurement effect" (so called because the inputs actually contributing to output are being mismeasured) leads a growth accounting measure to understate true productivity growth. We can further simplify this:

(5) $\quad \sum \alpha_i' \theta_i = \sum (p_i X_i'/p_y Y)(R_i / X_i')$

$= (\sum p_i R_i)/p_y Y = \theta,$

showing that it is not necessary to know how much of each input is used for compliance; the share of compliance costs in total cost (θ) is enough.

In addition to the "measurement effect," regulation might have a "real effect" on productivity. It could impose constraints on the firm's choice of production processes, make it harder to take advantage of new innovations, cause firms to lower new investment by increasing uncertainty, or otherwise reduce the productivity of other (noncompliance) inputs.[3] If we measure productivity growth without (0) and with (1) regulation imposed, we get

(6) $\quad d\tau' = \tau_1' - \tau_0' = \tau_1 - \tau_0 - \theta,$

where $\tau_1 - \tau_0$ is the real effect and θ is the measurement effect.

If we observe $d\tau'$ and θ for many different firms, indexed by j, we could estimate an equation like the following:

(7) $\quad d\tau_j' = \mu - \beta(\theta_j) + \varepsilon_j.$

Here μ and ε_j allow for influences other than regulation to affect productivity growth (economywide and firm-specific, respectively). If regulation had only a measurement effect, the regression suggested by (7) would yield $\beta = 1$. If regulation does have a real effect, we would get $\beta > 1$, as firms facing greater regulation would have lower true productivity growth. If a measure of compliance costs were not available for a particular

---

[2] This ensures the α_i' is close to α_i and that $x_i - x_i'$ is close to $-\theta_i$.

[3] Nicholas Ashford and George Heaton (1983) and Fred Hoerger et al. (1983) examine these issues for the chemical industry. Kip Viscusi (1983) develops a model of how regulation could affect investment.

type of regulation, some alternative measure of regulation could be used (replacing θ_j), but the effect on productivity could not be separated into real and measurement components.

All of the foregoing discussion has been in terms of individual firms' productivity growth. Unfortunately, firm-specific information linking productivity growth with measures of regulation is not available. Instead, I use industry-level data on output and inputs in a growth accounting calculation of TFP growth for each industry. This is then related to measures of the amount of regulation faced by each industry, as in equation (7), with controls for other factors that might affect industry productivity growth.

Some previous studies have estimated industry production or cost functions to look at productivity growth, rather than simply calculating TFP. An example of this is found in Dale Jorgenson (1984), which looks at the relation between energy usage and productivity growth. This allows the investigation of the effect of regulation on the productivity of different inputs, but is not done here for a number of reasons. First, the amount of regulation faced by an industry is not determined by the industry, but by the regulatory agency, so it can properly be treated as exogenous to the industry (unlike energy usage). Also, a proper model of the response by an industry to regulation would be quite complicated, depending on past and expected future costs of compliance, penalties for noncompliance, and enforcement efforts (much of which cannot be measured here). Finally, the goal here is to examine how much of the productivity slowdown might be attributed to regulation, so the first-order relation between regulation and productivity seems to be the appropriate level of analysis.

II. Data Description

The data set I created for this analysis is the first to combine extensive information on both productivity growth and regulation. The data cover the entire U.S. manufacturing sector, divided into 450 separate industries. Annual productivity growth for each industry is calculated from 1958 to 1978, based on a growth accounting model with five inputs (see the Data Appendix for data sources). TFP growth is calculated as real output growth minus real input growth (the real growth of each input, weighted by its cost share):

$$(8) \quad \tau_t = (\log Y_t - \log Y_{t-1})$$
$$- \Sigma \left[(\alpha_{it} + \alpha_{it-1})/2 \right.$$
$$\left. \times (\log X_{it} - \log X_{it-1}) \right].$$

The measure of EPA regulation of each industry is the industry's annual operating cost associated with pollution control. The data are based on the Pollution Abatement Costs and Expenditures survey of about 20,000 establishments, taken annually by the Bureau of the Census since 1973. Following equation (5), the compliance costs are divided by the value of shipments for the industry, yielding θ_j.

There is no usable data on costs to individual industries of complying with OSHA regulation.[4] Instead, a measure of the enforcement effort directed by OSHA toward each industry is used. OSHA's Management Information System, which tracks OSHA inspections for agency review purposes, identifies the industry and number of employees for each inspected establishment. The number of workers inspected is aggregated each year by industry and divided by total industry employment, yielding the fraction of industry employment in plants inspected by OSHA that year.

The use of an enforcement measure does not allow us to separate OSHA's effect on productivity into real and measurement components. However, enforcement effort is likely to be positively correlated across in-

---

[4] There is an annual McGraw-Hill survey on capital spending that asks what fraction of total capital spending is allocated to worker safety and health. Unfortunately, it has little industry detail, covers only a few hundred firms, and shows little correlation with either productivity growth or other measures of OSHA regulation.

dustries with compliance cost (establishments in industries without serious health and safety risks have no need to expend resources improving performance, and are less likely to be inspected). Also, enforcement may itself impose costs on establishments (for example, OSHA inspections disrupting the normal production routine). Thus differences in enforcement effort across industries should measure differences in the impact of OSHA regulation on those industries.

III. Results

The basic variables used in the analysis are presented in Table 1. To reduce the impact of strong cyclical fluctuations in productivity, average TFP growth is calculated for periods covering several years, chosen to match the cycle of productivity fluctuations from peak to peak. The measure of the productivity slowdown for each industry is the change in average annual TFP growth between the 1959–69 period and the 1973–78 period ($TFPCHG$).[5] The earlier period was chosen to end before the regulatory agencies studied here began operating, to ensure that the measures of levels of regulation in the later period would also measure changes in regulation from the earlier period.[6] The level of productivity growth in the later period ($TFP7378$) is also examined, to see whether results for the TFP slowdown are due to faster TFP growth in the earlier period or slower TFP growth in the later period.

TABLE 1—DESCRIPTIVE STATISTICS
(Full Sample, 450 industries)

Variable	Mean	Description
TFPCHG	−.0146 (.032)	Change in annual TFP growth rate: 1959–69 to 1973–78
TFP7378	−.0054 (.029)	Annual TFP growth rate: 1973–78
OSHINS	.5404 (.665)	Average OSHA employee inspection rate: 1974–78
PAOC	.0029 (.005)	Average pollution-abatement operating costs as share of total cost: 1974–78
SHEN	.0164 (.022)	Average cost share of energy: 1969–73
SHCAP	.2630 (.078)	Average cost share of capital: 1969–73
GPLCHG	−.0216 (.053)	Change in growth rate of production worker hours: 1959–69 to 1973–78
TFPCHGX	.0032 (.035)	Change in annual TFP growth rate: 1959–63 to 1963–69

Note: Standard deviations are shown in parentheses.

The explanatory variables measure both regulation and other factors that might affect productivity growth.[7] The regulation measures, $OSHINS$ and $PAOC$, are averaged over five years of data in the later period. Two input cost shares, $SHEN$ and $SHCAP$, are used to test the possibility that industries which are energy- or capital-intensive suffered greater productivity slowdowns than average. Industries that experienced faster employment growth in the 1970's than in the 1960's (measured by $GPLCHG$) might have experienced less of a productivity slowdown. Finally, industries with declining productivity growth in the 1960's (measured by $TFPCHGX$) might have continued declining in the 1970's.

---

[5] The results are not materially affected by extending the later time period to 1980 or changing the earlier period, but are somewhat sensitive to the choice of 1973 as the starting year.

[6] There certainly was some such regulation before OSHA and EPA, but most of it was administered by state agencies that (with few exceptions) had little enforcement power. As long as the regulation in the earlier and later periods is similarly distributed across industries, it will not affect the estimated impact of regulation. To see this, suppose that each industry faced half as much regulation in the earlier period as it did in the later one. The regulation measure (which purports to measure the change in regulation) will be twice as big as it should be, but its coefficient will therefore be cut in half, exactly canceling out.

[7] Several other regulation measures were tested, but not presented, as they did not affect the basic results. They included capital expenditures on pollution abatement (taken from the same PACE survey that was the source for the $PAOC$ variable) and EPA inspections of establishments for violation of air-quality standards (based on information from EPA's Compliance Data System, similar to the OSHA data). Both were negatively correlated with productivity growth (in levels and changes), but are not included because they are less comprehensive than $PAOC$.

TABLE 2—CORRELATIONS

	TFPCHG	TFP7378	OSHINS	PAOC	SHEN	SHCAP	GPLCHG	TFPCHGX
TFPCHG	1.0	.86	−.14	−.17	−.15	−.15	.15	.17
TFP7378		1.0	−.16	−.20	−.17	−.09	.09	.14
OSHINS			1.0	.33	.18	−.08	.01	−.09
PAOC				1.0	.66	.09	.03	−.03
SHEN					1.0	.18	.07	.02
SHCAP						1.0	.11	.03
GPLCHG							1.0	.08
TFPCHGX								1.0

TABLE 3—INITIAL REGRESSION RESULTS (Full sample, $n = 450$)

Model	Constant	OSHINS	PAOC	SHEN	SHCAP	GPLCHG	TFPCHGX	R^2(SSE)
Dependent Variable = TFPCHG								
A1	−.0110 (.0019)	−.0068 (.0018)	−	−	−	−	−	.020 (.445)
A2	−.0113 (.0017)	−	−1.17 (.40)	−	−	−	−	.029 (.441)
A3	−.0094 (.0020)	−.0046 (.0017)	−0.95 (.42)	−	−	−	−	.037 (.437)
A4	.0100 (.0053)	−.0050 (.0015)	−0.60 (.55)	−.078 (.093)	−.066 (.019)	.100 (.028)	.135 (.049)	.111 (.403)
Dependent Variable = TFP7378								
B1	−.0015 (.0018)	−.0072 (.0017)	−	−	−	−	−	.027 (.374)
B2	−.0035 (.0015)	−	−1.28 (.30)	−	−	−	−	.041 (.368)
B3	.0002 (.0018)	−.0048 (.0015)	−1.05 (.31)	−	−	−	−	.052 (.364)
B4	.0102 (.0050)	−.0049 (.0015)	−0.69 (.45)	−.100 (.080)	−.032 (.018)	.055 (.030)	.101 (.048)	.086 (.351)

Contribution of Regulation to TFP Slowdown between 1958–69 and 1973–78

	Contribution to Slowdown[a]			Fraction of Slowdown[b]		
	OSHINS	PAOC	Total	OSHINS	PAOC	Total
A1	−.36	−	−.36	.25	−	.25
A2	−	−.34	−.34	−	.23	.23
A3	−.25	−.28	−.53	.17	.19	.36
A4	−.27	−.17	−.44	.19	.12	.31

Note: Standard errors are shown in parentheses.

[a] The predicted impact of the mean value of each regulation measure (.54 for OSHINS and .0029 for PAOC) on TFPCHG, measured in percentage points per year.

[b] Calculated as (contribution to slowdown)/(mean slowdown = −1.46).

Several things can be learned from the correlations in Table 2. The regulation measures are negatively correlated with the productivity measures (as expected). They are positively correlated with each other, so analyzing only one measure would overstate its effect on productivity. Finally, they are correlated with some of the other factors that might affect productivity growth, so that omission of these factors could bias the estimated effect of regulation on productivity. Of course, any remaining factors (regulatory or otherwise) that have not been included here could also bias the results.

The regression results found in Table 3 show the connection between the regulation measures and the productivity slowdown.[8] When analyzed alone, each regulation measure has a significant negative coefficient. When both regulation measures are included, their coefficients fall (as expected from the correlations earlier), but generally remain significant. With all of the other factors included, the effect of *PAOC* falls by about 40 percent (and is no longer significant), but *OSHINS* remains strong.

One feature of these results is the similarity between the coefficients on the regulation measures in the regressions explaining the change in the rate of productivity growth (A) and those explaining the rate of productivity growth (B). This means that the regulation measures are not correlated with the earlier period's (1959–69) productivity growth: more highly regulated industries had a greater productivity slowdown than average because they did worse than average during the 1970's, not because they did better than average during the 1960's. Also, the coefficient on *PAOC* is generally smaller than 1 in magnitude, suggesting, in terms of equation (7), only a measurement effect on TFP calculation, without a real effect on productivity of noncompliance inputs.

Given some evidence for a regulation-productivity link, can we tell how important it is quantitatively? The R^2s from the regressions indicate what fraction of the variation in productivity growth across industries can be explained by the regulation measures. They tend to be small, indicating that regulation measures alone can only explain 4–5 percent of the variation across industries in TFP growth. Even with other factors included, only slightly over 10 percent of TFP variation is explained. This is due in large measure to the calculation of productivity as a residual: Input growth accounts for most of the variation in output growth rates, so the majority of the remaining variation in output growth is due to random disturbances.[9]

The estimated impact of regulation on productivity growth for the average industry is found by multiplying each regulation coefficient by the mean value of the regulation measure. In Table 3, model A4, the *OSHINS* coefficient ($-.005$) times the *OSHINS* mean (.54) yields a contribution to the TFP slowdown of .27 percentage points per year. This is 19 percent of the total slowdown of 1.46 percentage points. These measures are presented at the bottom of Table 3, where it can be seen that the regulation measures together account for a slowdown of .44 percentage points, somewhat over 30 percent of the average industry's productivity slowdown. The standard error of this total effect is only .15, so it is significant (due primarily to *OSHINS*).

There are a number of potential objections to these results, of which three will be treated here. First, the measures of regulation might themselves be affected by the industry's productivity growth, with this relationship being misinterpreted as an effect of regulation on productivity. Second, the linear regression model might be giving excessive weight to a few outlying industries with high regulation and poor productivity performance. Third, there could be some other explanation for the slowdown, not included in the current set of controls, whose omission biases the regulation coefficients.

---

[8] All of the standard errors are corrected for arbitrary heteroskedasticity, using the procedure suggested by Halbert White (1980). These corrections generally increased the standard errors of *PAOC* and decreased those of *OSHINS*.

[9] We can use equation (8) to represent TFP growth as the difference between output growth and aggregate input growth. Then *TFPCHG* is the difference between the change in output growth from the earlier to the later period (*OUTCHG*) and the change in aggregate input growth (*INCHG*). Regressing *OUTCHG* on *INCHG* along with the regulation measures and the other factors, we get

$$OUTCHG = .0082 \quad + .864^*INCHG$$
$$\quad\quad\quad (.0051) \quad\quad\quad (.074)$$

$$\quad\quad\quad -.0055^*OSHINS - .66^*PAOC,$$
$$\quad\quad\quad (.0016) \quad\quad\quad (.52)$$

with an R^2 of .76 and standard errors in parentheses.

TABLE 4—REGRESSIONS RESULTS EXCLUDING OUTLIERS
(Subsample, $n = 439$)

Dependent Variable	Const.[a]	OSHINS	PAOC	SHEN	SHCAP	GPLCHG	TFPCHGX	R^2(SSE)
TFPCHG	.0100 (.0054)	−.0086 (.0029)	−0.70 (.71)	−.063 (.104)	−.060 (.019)	.103 (.028)	.133 (.050)	.113 (.397)
TFP7378	.0102 (.0050)	−.0077 (.0026)	−0.83 (.55)	−.084 (.089)	−.028 (.018)	.055 (.030)	.101 (.049)	.084 (.346)

Note: Standard errors are shown in parentheses.
[a] Subsample excludes 7 industries with $OSHINS > 3.0$ and 4 with $PAOC > .025$.

TABLE 5—REGRESSION RESULTS INCLUDING NONLINEARITY TEST
(Full sample, $n = 450$)

Dep. Var.	Const.[a]	OSHINS	PAOC	OSH*PAOC	$OSHINS^2$	$PAOC^2$	R^2(SSE)
TFPCHG	.0118 (.0055)	−.0136 (.0047)	−1.06 (1.23)	.053 (.260)	.0023 (.0012)	18.88 (38.9)	.120 (.400)
TFP7378	.0113 (.0051)	−.0090 (.0044)	−1.33 (1.00)	−.017 (.217)	.0012 (.0011)	29.05 (32.2)	.090 (.350)

Note: Standard errors are shown in parentheses.
[a] Both regressions also include SHEN, SHCAP, GPLCHG, and TFPCHGX.

The reverse causality argument, that industry productivity affects the regulation measures, could bias the results in either direction. Industries that were doing poorly (in productivity terms) might choose to reduce their spending on pollution abatement, leading PAOC to be underestimated.[10] On the other hand, if OSHA responded to diminished compliance expenditures by stepping up enforcement activities, the OSHINS coefficient would be overstated. Redoing all the equations using the 1973 values of OSHINS and PAOC (which should not be affected by post-1973 productivity growth) leaves the regression coefficients essentially unchanged. In a more formal test suggested by Hausman (1978), the predicted values of OSHINS and PAOC are insignificant when included in the regression, supporting the treatment of the regulation measures as exogenous.[11]

Possible failings of the linear regression model are examined next. Table 4 shows that when a few industries with exceptionally high regulation values are excluded from the regression, the coefficients on PAOC are almost unchanged, while the coefficients on OSHINS nearly double. This suggests that the marginal effect of OSHA regulation declines as regulation increases.[12] Table 5 tests directly for such nonlinear effects, showing that marginal impact declines (though not significantly) for both regulation measures. Table 6 presents a simple, nonparametric

---

[10] In terms of equation (7), θ_j is positively correlated with ε_j, biasing the estimate of β downward (in absolute magnitude).

[11] The variables used to explain PAOC and OSHINS are the cost share of labor, industry concentration and measures of establishment size within the industry, the 1973 regulation variables, the other four exogenous variables from Table 3, model A4, and for OSHINS the industry injury rate and an index of worker exposure to hazardous substances. These variables explain about 40 percent of the variation in OSHINS and 80 percent of the variation in PAOC. The results are available from the author.

[12] This result would seem to indicate that OSHA should do more inspections, since the inspections have declining marginal cost to the establishments inspected. This need not be true, since the marginal benefit of further inspections is also likely to decline as the number of inspections increases.

TABLE 6—MEAN TFP VALUES FOR INDUSTRY QUARTILES, RANKED
BY EACH REGULATION MEASURE
(1 = lowest regulation, 4 = highest regulation)

| | Ranked by OSHINS | | | | Ranked by PAOC | | |
| | Mean Values of: | | | | Mean Values of: | | |
Q	OSHINS	TFPCHG	TFP7378	Q	PAOC	TFPCHG	TFP7378
1	.122	−.0072	.0009	1	.0004	−.0058	.0016
2	.256	−.0087	.0002	2	.0010	−.0133	−.0031
3	.461	−.0204	−.0104	3	.0019	−.0206	−.0106
4	1.325	−.0223	−.0125	4	.0082	−.0188	−.0095

examination of the regulation-productivity connection. Industries with high values for the regulation measures have slower productivity growth and a greater slowdown. In another nonparametric test, the Spearman rank correlations between $TFPCHG$ and the regulation measures are negative and significant ($-.19$ for $OSHINS$ and $-.16$ for $PAOC$). These tests do not suggest that the initial results are an artifact of the linear model.

The third objection, of omitted explanatory factors, is more difficult to address. A number of possible explanatory factors, including other input cost shares, the fraction of nonproduction workers in the work force, and changes in the use of various inputs, were tested and found not to affect regulation or productivity growth (these results, and all others referred to but not presented, are available from the author). When the four factors tested here are added to the regressions separately, the only one that affects the regulation coefficients noticeably is the energy cost share ($SHEN$), whose inclusion reduces the $PAOC$ coefficient to -0.65. This could be due in part to multicollinearity, given the high correlation between $SHEN$ and $PAOC$. The coefficient on $OSHINS$ appears to be quite robust, although one cannot rule out the possibility of some other factor (as yet untested) being involved.

IV. Conclusions and Future Work

This study has found evidence that OSHA and EPA regulation reduced productivity growth in the average manufacturing industry by .44 percentage points per year, over 30 percent of the slowdown in the 1970's. This effect is larger than that found by most previous studies, which could be due to the focus on manufacturing, which faces relatively high OSHA and EPA regulation. The major surprise is that the effect of OSHA is quite strong, while that of EPA is comparatively weak. The prevailing opinion (that EPA has had more effect on productivity) may be due in part to the lack of good measures of compliance costs for OSHA regulation. There is also some evidence to indicate that pollution-abatement spending only affected the measurement of productivity growth, with no real effect on the productivity of inputs actually used in production. This result may be sensitive to the assumption of negligible regulation before 1970 and the strong ties between pollution-abatement spending and energy intensity. Further research is needed to resolve these issues.

I see two main areas for future research: collecting additional data and developing a more detailed model. Collecting more years of data will allow testing the effect of changing regulation over time, especially in recent years when the growth of regulation may have been reversed. Collecting variables measuring other factors such as research and development spending, labor quality, and market structure may help explain more of the slowdown. Finally, a model of the effects of regulation on productivity that explicitly incorporates a production or cost function will provide tests for whether the effect of regulation on productivity differs across inputs, and will allow a more complete explanation of why regulation affects productivity.

DATA APPENDIX

To calculate TFP growth, we need the real growth rate of output (measured here by the value of industry shipments) and the real growth rate and cost shares of each of five inputs: production workers, nonproduction workers, nonenergy materials, energy, and capital. The *Annual Survey of Manufactures* and the *Census of Manufactures*, published by the Census Bureau, provide data for each industry from 1958 to 1978 on the number of production worker hours, the number of nonproduction workers, and nominal measures of the value of shipments and expenditures on each input except capital. This enabled calculation of the cost shares for each input (capital's share is assumed to be 1 minus the sum of the other four inputs' shares).

Deflators for the value of shipments were provided by the Bureau of Industrial Economics in the Commerce Department. Various price indices from the Bureau of Labor Statistics were combined to create deflators for expenditures on energy and non-energy materials, with weights for energy based on 1976 expenditures on six types of energy, and weights for other materials based on the 1972 Input-Output tables.

The growth in the capital input for each industry is measured by the growth in the industry's real, depreciated capital stock. The capital stocks were initially calculated for the 1958–76 period by a joint project of the University of Pennsylvania, the Census Bureau, and SRI, Inc. They were extended by the author to 1978, based on data from the Bureau of Industrial Economics.

Further details on the procedures used can be found in my book (1986), and the data set itself is available upon request.

REFERENCES

Ashford, Nicholas A. and Heaton, George R., "Regulation and Technological Innovation in the Chemical Industry," *Law and Contemporary Problems*, Summer 1983, 46, 109–57.

Christainsen, Gregory B. and Haveman, Robert H., "Public Regulations and the Slowdown in Productivity Growth," *American Economic Review Proceedings*, May 1981, 71, 320–25.

Crandall, Robert W., "Pollution Controls and Productivity Growth in Basic Industries," in Thomas G. Cowing and Rodney E. Stevenson, *Productivity Measurement in Regulated Industries*, New York: Academic Press, 1981.

Darby, Michael R., "The U.S. Productivity Slowdown: A Case of Statistical Myopia," *American Economic Review*, June 1984, 74, 301–22.

Denison, Edward P., *Accounting for Slower Economic Growth: The United States in the 1970s*, Washington: The Brookings Institution, 1979.

Gollop, Frank M. and Roberts, Mark J., "Environmental Regulations and Productivity Growth: The Case of Fossil-fueled Electric Power Generation," *Journal of Political Economy*, August 1983, 91, 654–74.

Gray, Wayne B., *Productivity versus OSHA and EPA Regulations*, Ann Arbor: UMI Research Press, 1986.

Hoerger, Fred, Beamer, William H. and Hanson, James S., "The Cumulative Impact of Health, Environmental, and Safety Concerns on the Chemical Industry During the Seventies," *Law and Contemporary Problems*, Summer 1983, 46, 109–57.

Hausman, Jerry A., "Specification Tests in Econometrics," *Econometrica*, November 1978, 46, 1251–71.

Jorgenson, Dale W., "The Role of Energy in Productivity Growth," *American Economic Review Proceedings*, May 1984, 74, 26–30.

Norsworthy, J. R., Harper, Michael J. and Kunze, Kent, "The Slowdown in Productivity Growth: Analysis of Some Contributing Factors," *Brookings Papers on Economic Activity*, 2:1979, 387–421.

Portney, Paul R., "The Macroeconomic Impacts of Federal Environmental Regulation," in Henry M. Peskin, Paul R. Portney, and Allen V. Kneese, *Environmental Regulation and the U.S. Economy*, Baltimore: Johns Hopkins University Press, 1981.

Siegel, Robin, "Why Has Productivity Slowed Down?," *Data Resources Review*, March 1979, 1, 1.59–1.65.

Viscusi, W. Kip, "Frameworks for Analyzing the Effects of Risk and Environmental Regulations on Productivity," *American Economic Review*, September 1983, 73, 793–801.

Weisskopf, Thomas E., Bowles, Samuel and Gordon, David M., "Hearts and Minds: A Social Model of U.S. Productivity Growth," *Brookings Papers on Economic Activity*, 2:1983, 381–450.

White, Halbert, "A Heteroskedasticity-Consistent Covariance Matrix Estimator and a Direct Test for Heteroskedasticity," *Econometrica*, May 1980, 48, 817–38.

[4]
Environmental Regulations and Productivity Growth: The Case of Fossil-fueled Electric Power Generation

Frank M. Gollop
Boston College

Mark J. Roberts
Pennsylvania State University

> This paper measures and analyzes the effect of sulfur dioxide emission restrictions on the rate of productivity growth in the electric power industry over the 1973–79 business cycle. A firm-specific measure of regulatory intensity is developed which depends on the severity of the emission standard, the extent of enforcement, and the unconstrained emission rate relevant to each utility. The results indicate that emission regulations result in significantly higher generating costs, primarily from the increased use of low-sulfur fuels. The average rate of productivity growth was reduced by 0.59 percentage points per year for constrained utilities.

The Clean Air Act Amendments of 1970 set national air quality standards for major pollutants and established a framework for state regulation.[1] Since 1970 individual states have placed emission restrictions on an increasing number of industries and pollutants. It has been argued that these emission standards have adversely affected

---

An earlier version of this paper was presented at the winter 1981 meetings of the Econometric Society in Washington, D.C. We are grateful to Robert Halvorsen and Jon Nelson for helpful comments and to Elizabeth Hall and Linda Wang for research assistance.

[1] The Clean Air Act Amendments of 1970 modify the Clean Air Act of 1963 and the Air Quality Act of 1967. For the complete text of the 1970 amendments, see *U.S. Code Annotated: Congressional and Administrative News* (1971), pp. 1954–2001.

the performance of American industry, particularly its productivity growth, by diverting resources from the production of marketable output to the satisfaction of emission constraints.[2] This paper analyzes and quantifies the effect of sulfur dioxide emission restrictions on productivity growth in one of the earliest and most widely affected industries, electric power generation.

Identifying the productivity impact of emission regulations during the seventies is complicated by coincident changes in market conditions, the unprecedented increase in fuel prices, and the dramatic decline in output growth for electric power. The annual increase in the average price per million Btu of fuel consumed by utilities was less than 0.3 percent between 1958 and 1969, 18 percent from 1969 to 1979, and nearly 30 percent between 1973 and 1976 (U.S. Federal Energy Regulatory Commission 1959f, p. xii; 1973f, p. xix; 1977a, table 3; 1980a, table 3). If electric power generation is fuel using, rising fuel prices have contributed to the industry's declining rate of technical change.[3] In addition, kilowatt-hour sales by privately owned utilities increased at average annual rates of 7.6 percent between 1958 and 1969 and 4.6 percent between 1969 and 1979 while falling to 1.8 percent between 1973 and 1976 (U.S. Federal Energy Regulatory Commission 1959d; 1973d, table 23; 1980d, table 31). If there are scale economies in production, then declining output growth has reduced the contribution of a traditional source of the industry's productivity growth.[4]

Concurrently, the introduction of emission standards in the seventies encouraged utilities to switch from lower cost high-sulfur fuels to more expensive low-sulfur fuels. An important empirical objective of this research is to disentangle the regulatory and pure market determinants of the decline in productivity performance in electric power, a decline that has been substantial. Among the 45 sectors examined by Fraumeni and Jorgenson (1980), electric power ranked third in terms of average annual rates of productivity growth in the 1948–69 period but fell to thirty-fifth in the 1969–76 period.

The underlying framework for this paper is a model of the industry's technology which isolates the components of productivity growth associated with scale economies, environmental regulations, and technical change. The model treats low-sulfur and high-sulfur fuels as

---

[2] Denison (1978) argues that as much as 0.35 percentage points of the growth in total factor productivity in 1975 were lost due to environmental and safety regulation. See also Denison (1979), pp. 58–59, 65–71, and 111.

[3] Stevenson (1980), Gollop and Roberts (1981), and Fraumeni and Jorgenson (1982) find that the technology in the electric power industry is fuel using.

[4] See Christensen and Greene (1976) and Gollop and Roberts (1981) for a description of scale economies in electric utilities.

distinct inputs in order to separate the productivity effects of increasing fuel prices from regulation-induced fuel switching. To measure the productivity impact of regulation, a regulatory intensity variable is developed. It accounts for the applicable statutory emission rates and the degree of compliance by each firm.

The model is applied to a sample of 56 electric utilities over the 1973–79 period. The main conclusion to be drawn is that environmental regulations have had a significant negative impact on the rate of productivity growth in the industry over the 1974–79 period. On average, effective air pollution regulations reduced firm-level productivity growth by 0.59 percentage points per year. Environmental regulations primarily have resulted in the increased use of low-sulfur fuels and capital with the main cost impact arising from the substitution from high-sulfur to low-sulfur fuels. Economies of scale are present in electric power generation, but these have not made a large contribution to productivity growth because of low output growth rates over the period. Finally, an upward trend in the rate of technical change is responsible for most of the improvement in productivity growth in this industry during the late 1970s.

I. The Clean Air Act Amendments and Electric Utilities

With the goal of protecting public health, the Clean Air Act Amendments were passed by Congress in December 1970. As required by the Act, the Environmental Protection Agency (EPA) established uniform national standards for six major pollutants, including sulfur oxides. Each state then submitted a state implementation plan (SIP) that outlined how existing pollution sources would be regulated so that the national ambient air standards would be achieved by July 1975.[5] The majority of SIPs were approved by the EPA during 1972.

In 1970 coal-fired power plants were the source of more than 50 percent of the nation's sulfur dioxide emissions and as a result were one of the first pollution sources to be regulated (see Randle 1979, p. 1722). Now, as then, the state plans vary greatly in both the stringency of the regulations and the method of regulation. Approximately one-third of the states restrict the percentage of sulfur in the fuel that each plant can burn. These states tend to be concentrated in the Northeast and West. The remaining states focus on emission levels either by limiting the pounds of sulfur dioxide per million Btu which each plant can emit or by restricting the concentration of sulfur dioxide in the exhaust gas. In approximately one-third of the states, the size of the generating source affects the allowed emission rate with

---

[5] See Roberts and Farrell (1978) for a discussion of the SIP process and its effectiveness.

larger sources generally being regulated more tightly. The type of fuel burned also affects allowed emissions in approximately one-third of the states. Oil-fired generators usually are controlled more strictly.

Generating plants built or modified after August 1971 face a uniform national emission standard of 1.2 pounds of sulfur dioxide per million Btu of fuel input for coal-fired generators and 0.8 pounds per million Btu for oil-fired generators. These new source performance standards allow plants to meet the emission restrictions by burning low-sulfur fuels. This was amended in 1978 so that new plants now also are required to install some type of emission desulfurization system.[6]

Enforcement of the SIPs is the responsibility of the states. The diversity of regulations and enforcement levels has resulted in varying degrees of compliance and different emission rates across plants.

Understanding the response of utilities to these air pollution restrictions is important in analyzing potential productivity effects.[7] In general, utilities have lowered sulfur dioxide emissions by switching to higher priced, lower sulfur fuels. The price effect can be substantial. In 1980, for example, low-sulfur fuel oil commanded a 35 percent price premium per million Btu over high-sulfur oil.[8] If regulation-induced fuel switching results in higher costs with no corresponding increase in productive inputs, then measured rates of productivity growth fall.

A smaller number of utilities have responded to environmental regulations by installing flue gas desulfurization systems, known as scrubbers, to clean the exhaust gases. By the end of 1980, scrubbers had been installed on all or part of the generating capacity of 47 plants. This compares with seven plants operating scrubbers at the end of 1975 (U.S. Federal Energy Regulatory Commission 1975a, 1980a). If the installation of scrubbers results in increased capital input with no corresponding increase in kwh production, there is a negative impact on productivity growth.[9]

---

[6] The development of these 1978 new source standards and their impact on utilities are detailed in Ackerman and Hassler (1981).

[7] A detailed case study of how six utilities have responded to environmental restrictions is presented in Roberts and Bluhm (1981).

[8] U.S. Federal Energy Regulatory Commission (1980a, table 15). In addition, 66 percent of the total number of barrels of oil purchased was low-sulfur oil.

[9] Other industry responses have been blocked. For example, the industry has argued for the use of higher stacks as a method of dispersing pollutants over a wider area, but this control method has been rejected by the EPA because it does not reduce emissions. In addition, the industry has argued for the use of intermittent controls such as burning low-sulfur fuels only when weather conditions are apt to aggravate pollution problems. This method also has been rejected by the EPA in favor of continuous controls on pollution emissions. The EPA decisions on these questions have been upheld in court. For a discussion of the legal implications of the Clean Air Amendments on electric utilities see Raffle (1978) and Randle (1979).

The utilities' method of pollution control has an important implication for the model of firm technology developed in the next section. Specifically, fuel input is divided into low- and high-sulfur components not only to capture the productivity effect of regulation-induced fuel switching but also to distinguish this regulatory effect from the pure market effect of rising fuel prices.

II. Productivity Growth

The model of total factor productivity developed in this paper is based on a factor-minimal cost function for an electric utility. Production cost (C) is assumed to be a twice-differentiable function of the input prices of labor (p_L), capital (p_K), low-sulfur fuel ($p_{F_{ls}}$), and high-sulfur fuel ($p_{F_{hs}}$), the output of kilowatt hours (Q), regulatory intensity (R), and time (T):

$$C = C(p_L, p_K, p_{F_{ls}}, p_{F_{hs}}, R, Q, T). \tag{1}$$

The model maintains that factor markets are competitive and that each utility must supply all electricity demanded at any given price. The arguments of the cost function are exogenous variables and input levels are endogenous.

Logarithmically differentiating the cost function with respect to time identifies the sources of growth in total cost:[10]

$$\frac{d \ln C}{dT} = \sum_i v_i \frac{d \ln p_i}{dT} + v_R \frac{dR}{dT} + v_Q \frac{d \ln Q}{dT} - v_T, \tag{2}$$

where

$$v_i \equiv \frac{\partial \ln C}{\partial \ln p_i} = \frac{p_i X_i}{C}$$

by Shephard's lemma ($i = L, K, F_{ls}, F_{hs}$),

$$v_R \equiv \frac{\partial \ln C}{\partial R}, \quad v_Q \equiv \frac{\partial \ln C}{\partial \ln Q}, \quad -v_T \equiv \frac{\partial \ln C}{\partial T}.$$

The conventional dual Divisia index of productivity growth (see Gollop and Jorgenson 1980) is

$$v_G = -\left(\frac{d \ln C}{dT} - \frac{d \ln Q}{dT}\right) + \sum_i v_i \frac{d \ln p_i}{dT}. \tag{3}$$

---

[10] Regulatory intensity equals zero when the utility is not constrained by an emission standard. Consequently, derivatives involving R are stated in semilogarithmic form. Stated precisely, the cost function (1) is assumed to be $C(p_L, p_K, p_{F_{ls}}, p_{F_{hs}}, e^R, Q, e^T)$.

ENVIRONMENTAL REGULATIONS

Substituting (2) into (3) identifies the sources of growth of the productivity index:

$$v_G = -v_R \frac{dR}{dT} + (1 - v_Q)\frac{d \ln Q}{dT} + v_T. \qquad (4)$$

The first term in (4) represents the direct productivity effect of environmental regulations. It is the product of the marginal cost of increased regulation ($\partial \ln C/\partial R$) and the extent of the change in regulatory intensity (dR/dT). This direct productivity effect is characterized by a vertical displacement of the average cost curve. The second term equals the scale effect. It is a function of scale economies ($\partial \ln C/\partial \ln Q$) and output growth ($d \ln Q/dT$). Productivity growth through the scale effect is characterized by a movement along the average cost curve. The third term measures the productivity contribution of technical change. It too results in a shift of the average cost curve. An important objective of this paper is to estimate these three sources of productivity growth.

Application of this model requires estimates of v_R, v_Q, and v_T. This is accomplished by selecting a functional form for the cost function (1) and estimating its parameters. We consider the translog cost function:[11]

$$\begin{aligned}C = \exp[&\beta_0 + \sum_i \beta_i \ln p_i + \beta_Q \ln Q + \beta_R R + \beta_T T \\ &+ \tfrac{1}{2}\sum_i \sum_j \gamma_{ij} \ln p_i \ln p_j + \sum_i \gamma_{iQ} \ln p_i \ln Q + \sum_i \gamma_{iR} \ln p_i R \\ &+ \sum_i \gamma_{iT} \ln p_i T + \tfrac{1}{2}\gamma_{QQ}(\ln Q)^2 + \gamma_{QR} \ln QR + \gamma_{QT} \ln QT \\ &+ \tfrac{1}{2}\gamma_{RR}R^2 + \gamma_{RT}RT + \tfrac{1}{2}\gamma_{TT}T^2]. \end{aligned} \qquad (5)$$

This form allows the partial derivatives v_R, v_Q, and v_T to be functions of the input prices, output level, degree of regulation, and time. The estimated sources of productivity growth vary with the economic and regulatory environment of the firm.

Regulatory Impact

Changing environmental regulations are hypothesized to have productivity consequences. If $v_R = 0$, then emission standards have no productivity effect. The parameter restrictions to test this hypothesis are

$$\beta_R = \gamma_{LR} = \gamma_{KR} = \gamma_{F_lR} = \gamma_{F_hR} = \gamma_{QR} = \gamma_{RR} = \gamma_{RT} = 0.$$

---

[11] The cost function must be linearly homogeneous in input prices. The estimated translog cost function will satisfy this condition at all data points if and only if $\Sigma_i \beta_i = 1$ and $\Sigma_j \gamma_{ij} = \Sigma_j \gamma_{jQ} = \Sigma_j \gamma_{jR} = \Sigma_j \gamma_{jT} = 0$, $i, j = L, K, F_{ls}, F_{hs}$.

If this zero effect hypothesis is rejected, the parameters γ_{LR}, γ_{KR}, γ_{F_lR}, and γ_{F_hR} reveal the factor-using/factor-saving nature of environmental regulations. Each parameter represents the partial derivative of the corresponding input cost share with respect to the regulatory intensity variable. A positive (negative) value for γ_{iR} implies that environmental regulations are ith factor using (saving).

The hypothesis of input neutral regulation is tested by restricting $\gamma_{LR} = \gamma_{KR} = \gamma_{F_lR} = \gamma_{F_hR} = 0$. If this hypothesis is rejected, the parameters γ_{F_lR} and γ_{F_hR} are of particular interest. The expectation is that γ_{F_lR} will be positive and γ_{F_hR} will be negative; environmental regulations are low-sulfur fuel using and high-sulfur fuel saving. The important empirical issue is the extent of this fuel shift effect on productivity growth.

Scale Effects

The most important scale hypothesis is whether production exhibits constant returns to scale, $v_Q = 1$. The parametric restrictions to test this hypothesis are $\beta_Q = 1$, $\gamma_{LQ} = \gamma_{KQ} = \gamma_{F_lQ} = \gamma_{F_hQ} = \gamma_{QQ} = \gamma_{QR} = \gamma_{QT} = 0$. If this hypothesis cannot be rejected, then the scale effect, $(1 - v_Q)d \ln Q/dT$ defined in (4), equals zero regardless of the extent of market growth. Given a horizontal average cost curve, changes in production levels ($d \ln Q/dT$) have no effect on average cost and therefore productivity growth. If constant returns to scale is rejected, then the productivity consequences of market growth can be determined from (4).

Technical Change

The basic technical change hypothesis is $v_T = 0$, which requires $\beta_T = \gamma_{LT} = \gamma_{KT} = \gamma_{F_lT} = \gamma_{F_hT} = \gamma_{QT} = \gamma_{RT} = \gamma_{TT} = 0$. If this hypothesis cannot be rejected, then technical change makes no contribution to the rate of productivity growth.

The results of all hypothesis tests as well as the decomposition of a representative utility's productivity growth into its source components are reported in Section IV.

III. The Data

If emission standards affect productivity growth in the electric power industry, they are expected to affect the productivity of fossil-fueled generation, the precise target of environmental regulation. Consequently, this study abstracts from all transmission and distribution activity as well as all nuclear and hydroelectric generating capacity.

The necessary data on generation cost, input expenditures, output, input prices, and environmental regulations are available for the 1973–79 period for 56 privately owned utilities. The analysis begins with 1973 since detailed fuel transaction data, including sulfur content by transaction, are first reported in that year; 1979 is the most recent year for which all necessary data are available. The sample years not only span the period when environmental regulations became increasingly important but also represent a complete business cycle.

Output, Inputs, and Input Prices

Annual output for each utility is measured as net steam generation (kwh) reported in the annual editions of *Statistics of Privately Owned Electric Utilities in the United States* (hereafter, *Statistics*). Total expenditures for labor input are defined as the sum of production payroll for steam generation plus pensions and benefits accruing to those laborers. Labor input is the number of employees in steam generation. The price of labor input in each utility is measured as the average annual labor expenditure per steam generation employee.

Utility expenditures for capital input and capital's service price are constructed according to methods originally described in Christensen and Jorgenson (1969). Expenditures are defined as the product of the capital stock of steam production plant and its service price. The capital stock in each period is constructed according to the perpetual inventory method of capital accumulation. The service price is a function of capital gains, the service life of the asset, tax policy, and the firm's opportunity cost of capital.[12]

Price, quantity, and expenditure data for low-sulfur and high-sulfur fuels are constructed from transaction-specific data found in the *Monthly Report of Cost and Quality of Fuels for Electric Plants* (hereafter, *Monthly Report*). The *Monthly Report* records the physical quantity, Btu content, delivered cost, and sulfur content of each fuel transaction at each electric plant. A sulfur emission boundary of 1.5 pounds of sulfur dioxide per million Btu when burned was used to distinguish high-sulfur and low-sulfur fuel transactions.[13] Each utili-

---

[12] For additional detail concerning the output, labor, and capital data, see Gollop and Roberts (1982).

[13] This figure was developed after consultation with staff personnel in the Department of Energy's Office of Coal and Electric Utility Statistics and the Policy Planning Division of the EPA. It corresponds to a sulfur content of approximately 0.70–1 percent by weight for coal and 1.25–1.4 percent for oil. The exact conversion depends on the Btu content of the fuel. Conversion formulas are given in U.S. Federal Energy Regulatory Commission (1969e). In order to judge the sensitivity of the results to this assumption, all estimation and hypothesis testing is carried out using fuel expenditure

ty's expenditures for low-sulfur (high-sulfur) fuels are defined as the sum over all transactions of the delivered cost of low-sulfur (high-sulfur) fuels purchased by any of its plants.[14] The average price per million Btu is defined as the ratio of total low-sulfur (high-sulfur) fuel expenditures to total Btu of low-sulfur (high-sulfur) fuel purchased.

Regulatory Intensity

The final data series involves the measure of regulatory intensity, R. Modeling R as a dummy variable that takes the unit value when an emission standard exists and zero otherwise is inadequate because the severity of environmental regulations varies considerably over time and across firms. While an improvement, measuring R solely in terms of the legal emission standard is still deficient because it fails to account for permitted variances, a firm's simple failure to comply with the standard, and, most important, the extent to which the standard actually constrains the utility. What affects producer behavior, and therefore cost and productivity, is the actual impact of the standard on each utility's operation. An appropriate measure of R must reflect the emission constraint due to environmental regulation as perceived by each utility.

This research defines R for each utility as a function of the legally mandated reduction in emissions and the effective enforcement imposed on the utility. At year t,

$$R_t \equiv \left(\frac{E_t^* - S_t}{E_t^*}\right)\left(\sum_{i=t-1}^{t} \frac{1}{2} \frac{E_i^* - E_i}{E_i^* - S_i}\right), \tag{6}$$

where S_t, E_t, and E_t^* are all expressed as emission rates (pounds of SO_2 per million Btu) and are, respectively, the legal standard constructed from the relevant state implementation plan (SIP), the utility's actual emission rate, and the utility's desired or unconstrained emission rate.

The first term in (6) is the proportional reduction in unconstrained emissions required by the SIP and captures the extent to which the legally allowed emission rate constrains the firm. It has an upper bound of unity which would occur if the SIP mandated no emissions ($S_t = 0$). In practice this upper bound is never reached. The ratio is bounded from below by zero. This occurs whenever the legal stan-

---

and price data based on sulfur boundaries of 1.2 and 1.8 as well as the 1.5 pounds of SO_2 per million Btu level. The results of all hypothesis tests, reported below, were unchanged when a dividing line of 1.2 or 1.8 pounds of SO_2 per million Btu was used.

[14] Fuel purchased by jointly owned plants is allocated to the fuel accounts of parent firms on the basis of the parent firm's ownership shares.

dard is greater than or equal to the firm's unconstrained emission rate ($S_t \geq E_t^*$), implying that the standard is of no importance to the firm.[15]

The second term in (6) serves as an enforcement scalar and reflects the degree to which a firm's actual emission reduction corresponds to the required emission reduction. Under the assumption that actual emission rates, for firms which face legal standards, are reasonable indicators of the emission rates actually permitted by state enforcement agencies, enforcement is defined as a 2-year moving average of the ratio of the actual reduction to the legally required reduction in emission rates.[16] The enforcement scalar also is bounded in the zero-to-one interval. It is set equal to unity anytime $E_t < S_t$, the actual emission rate is less than the legal standard, to reflect complete enforcement of the standard. It is bounded from below by zero whenever the actual emission rate equals the unconstrained emission rate ($E_t = E_t^*$).[17]

Each of the two components of R is measured and bounded before being multiplied together. Consequently, the regulatory intensity variable R is bounded between zero and unity.

The legal emission limit, S_t, is constructed for each plant using state SIPs. Plant standards are aggregated to the firm level using the plants' shares in total firm Btu as weights.[18]

The firm's actual emission rate, E_t, is calculated by constructing total sulfur emissions and total Btu use for each plant using data in the *Monthly Report* and conversion formulas in *Steam Electric Plant Air and Water Quality Control Data* (1969). Sulfur emissions for plants with installed scrubber systems are adjusted based on the design efficiency of the scrubbers and the proportion of plant capacity on which the

---

[15] Given our measure of the unconstrained emission rate, described below, 11 of the 56 sample firms never face an effective emission standard during 1973–79. This usually occurs in states which did not have serious air pollution problems and therefore did not build strict emission limits into their SIP.

[16] The 2-year average recognizes that the firm cannot tell at each point in time whether or not it will be allowed to violate the emission standard. Instead it looks to recent past experience to establish perceived enforcement levels. Violations of the SIP standards can occur for many reasons, including delays and extensions granted to the utility in order to allow it to phase in regulations slowly, legal disputes over the SIP standards, or poor enforcement. In any of these cases the enforcement component of (6) will scale down the value of the regulation variable to recognize that the regulation constraint on the firm is less than that implied by the SIP.

[17] Given our definition of the unconstrained emission rate (see below), E_t cannot be greater than E_t^*.

[18] Plant level emission standards were constructed from the relevant states' SIP and the EPA publication *State Implementation Plan Emission Regulations for Sulfur Oxides* (2d ed.). The most recent version of each SIP is published in *The Environment Reporter—State Air Laws*. Conversations with staff at state environmental protection agencies were used to verify the laws and resolve discrepancies between sources.

scrubber is installed.[19] Finally, the plant totals are summed to the firm level and a firm-level emission rate is constructed.

The firm's desired or unconstrained emission rate, E_t^*, is calculated using the sulfur and Btu contents of all its fuel purchases in the high-sulfur fuel category. It is the average emission rate for all fuel purchases which would result in emission rates greater than 1.5 pounds of SO_2 per million Btu. The main advantage of this measure is that it acknowledges that utilities, even if unconstrained by environmental regulations, still would purchase fuels with differing sulfur contents. Based on the actual mix of high-sulfur fuels purchased by the utility, E_t^* recognizes that the firm normally would adjust its unconstrained purchases in response to changing sulfur premiums, transportation rates, and supply constraints. The main disadvantage of E_t^* is that it results in a conservative estimate of the regulatory intensity variable in the later years of the sample because it does not attribute any of the reduction in the average emission rate of the high-sulfur fuel category to regulation. This average high-sulfur fuel emission rate has fallen in our sample from a high of 4.18 pounds of SO_2 per million Btu in 1974 to a low of 3.78 pounds of SO_2 per million Btu in 1979.[20]

The average yearly values of the regulatory intensity variable and its components are reported in table 1. Over time, S_t, E_t^*, and E_t reveal the expected downward trend. The mean value of S_t falls primarily because a larger proportion of firms became subject to regulations and not because existing standards were tightened. Actual emission rates decline steadily after 1975, the first year in which the national ambient air quality standards were supposed to be satisfied. The proportional reduction in unconstrained emissions required by law, reported in column 4, rises from 1973 to 1976 as emission standards were phased in. It falls slightly after 1976 because of the decline in E_t^*. The average enforcement scalar, reported in column 5, increases from 0.188 in 1973 to 0.521 in 1979. Together, columns 4 and 5 reveal that although state standards had mandated an average reduc-

---

[19] Design efficiencies for scrubbers are listed in U.S. Federal Energy Regulatory Commission (1980a). Actual operating efficiencies are not available. In our sample 15 firms had scrubbers installed on at least part of one plant for at least 1 year. However, with the exception of four firms, scrubbers do not play a large role in reducing firm-level emissions in our sample.

[20] Two alternatives for the unconstrained emission rate are possible but are less desirable. One method would be to use the emission rate for the least expensive fuel type purchased by the firm. This assumes the unconstrained firm would purchase all one type of fuel. This ignores supply constraints and violates the observation that unconstrained firms buy a mix of different fuels. A second alternative is to use emission rates from a preregulation period such as 1970. This fails to account for changes in the market for fuel including changes in relative fuel prices and the establishment of new supply sources that would affect an unconstrained firm's fuel choice and thus its emission rate.

TABLE 1
REGULATORY INTENSITY VARIABLE
(Mean Values over All Firms, Standard Error of the Mean in Parentheses)

Year	S_t	E_t^*	E_t	$\dfrac{E_t^* - S_t}{E_t^*}$	$\dfrac{E_t^* - E_t}{E_t^* - S_t}$	R_t
1973	3.31 (.256)	4.08 (.246)	3.27 (.229)	.172 (.039)	.188 (.047)	.090 (.027)
1974	3.29 (.258)	4.18 (.248)	3.27 (.225)	.195 (.040)	.226 (.049)	.095 (.025)
1975	2.89 (.227)	4.11 (.254)	3.27 (.236)	.253 (.039)	.377 (.056)	.115 (.025)
1976	2.82 (.216)	4.03 (.239)	3.14 (.230)	.256 (.038)	.423 (.057)	.141 (.027)
1977	2.87 (.206)	4.04 (.251)	3.03 (.218)	.245 (.037)	.414 (.057)	.144 (.028)
1978	2.82 (.205)	3.83 (.232)	2.79 (.191)	.240 (.034)	.478 (.059)	.153 (.024)
1979	2.79 (.212)	3.78 (.238)	2.72 (.193)	.233 (.035)	.521 (.060)	.159 (.026)

Note.—If the firm did not face an emission standard, then S_t is set equal to E_t^* when calculating the average yearly value of S_t.

tion in unconstrained emissions of approximately 25 percent, only slightly over half of this reduction had been achieved by 1979. The upward trend in the regulatory intensity variable, reported in column 6, does not result from further tightening of existing legal standards. Instead, it is due to the increase in the enforcement scalar as firms adjusted to the new restrictions and emission rates fell toward the legally mandated rates. Overall, the regulatory intensity variable is included in the cost function to measure the severity of emission constraints on the cost of the utility's operations.

Estimating Model

The estimating model consists of the cost function (5) and four factor share equations derived by applying Shephard's lemma. Symmetry and linear homogeneity restrictions are imposed. In addition, we use a procedure, developed by Lau (1978) and recently implemented by Fraumeni and Jorgenson (1982), to ensure that the estimated cost function is concave in factor prices. The stochastic disturbances in the estimating equations for any observation are assumed to be correlated across equations. Iterative-Zellner estimation is used after one share equation is deleted to avoid singularity of the estimated variance-covariance matrix across equations. The resulting estimates are maximum likelihood. All hypothesis tests are evaluated using the likelihood ratio test statistic.

IV. Empirical Results

Parameter estimates for the translog cost function are reported in table 2. Each of the three possible sources of productivity growth is derived from these estimates and discussed in a separate subsection.

TABLE 2

Cost Function Parameter Estimates
(Standard Errors in Parentheses)

Parameter	Estimate	Parameter	Estimate
β_0	11.9980 (.0314)	γ_{LQ}	−.0082 (.0172)
β_L	.0819 (.0335)	γ_{KQ}	−.0224 (.0050)
β_K	.3676 (.0111)	γ_{F_lQ}	.0358 (.0076)
β_{F_l}	.1225 (.0169)	γ_{F_hQ}	−.0052 (.0082)
β_{F_h}	.4280 (.0181)	γ_{QQ}	.0412 (.0151)
β_Q	.9817 (.0196)	γ_{QR}	.1389 (.0469)
β_R	.1783 (.1442)	γ_{QT}	−.0105 (.0038)
β_T	.0537 (.0169)	γ_{LR}	.0331 (.0846)
γ_{LL}	−.0001 (.0002)	γ_{KR}	−.0653 (.0249)
γ_{LK}	−.0002 (.0101)	γ_{F_lR}	.6128 (.0382)
γ_{LF_l}	.0028 (.0047)	γ_{F_hR}	−.5806 (.0415)
γ_{LF_h}	−.0025 (.0117)	γ_{RR}	.7917 (.3511)
γ_{KK}	−.0009 (.0017)	γ_{RT}	.0136 (.0190)
γ_{KF_l}	.0115 (.0106)	γ_{LT}	−.0029 (.0082)
γ_{KF_h}	−.0104 (.0088)	γ_{KT}	−.0131 (.0024)
$\gamma_{F_lF_l}$	−.1412 (.0212)	γ_{F_lT}	.0054 (.0037)
$\gamma_{F_lF_h}$	.1269 (.0204)	γ_{F_hT}	.0106 (.0039)
$\gamma_{F_hF_h}$	−.1140 (.0212)	γ_{TT}	−.0120 (.0041)

Regulation

The impact of changes in regulatory intensity on cost is measured as v_R, defined in (2). As reported in table 3, the hypothesis that $v_R = 0$ at all observations is rejected at the .01 significance level, which implies that changes in regulatory intensity will impact productivity growth. Average annual values of v_R, reported in table 4, have the expected positive sign in every year. Moreover, except for 1978, the estimates increase steadily from a low of 0.119 in 1973 to a high of 0.371 in

TABLE 3

Test Statistics for Hypothesis Tests

Hypothesis	Test Statistic	χ^2 Critical Value ($\alpha = .01$)
Regulation:		
No regulatory effect ($v_R = 0$)	299.65	18.48
No input bias	225.44	11.35
Scale:		
Constant returns ($v_Q = 1$)	138.57	18.48
Technical change:		
No technical change ($v_T = 0$)	61.86	18.48

TABLE 4

ESTIMATED PARTIAL EFFECTS OF REGULATION, SCALE, AND TIME ON COST
(Mean Values over All Firms)

Year	v_R	v_Q	$-v_T$
1973	.119	.943	.037
1974	.206	.951	.034
1975	.233	.945	.023
1976	.265	.941	.011
1977	.327	.938	.001
1978	.296	.927	−.011
1979	.371	.918	−.026

1979, implying that a given increase in the intensity of regulation has become more costly over time.[21]

The estimates of v_R can be converted to elasticity form by multiplying $\hat{v}_R$ at each observation by the corresponding value of R. The average annual estimates of these elasticities vary from a low of 0.051 in 1973 to a high of 0.098 in 1979. On average, a 1 percent increase in R during 1979 would have resulted in a 0.098 percent increase in total generating cost. If the analysis is restricted to firms which had non-zero values for the regulatory intensity variable, the average yearly cost elasticities vary from a low of 0.089 in 1975 to a high of 0.134 in 1979. In dollar terms, a 1 percent increase in regulatory intensity in 1979 would have raised the average level of total cost for firms which faced effective regulation by $478,000. The average cost per million kwh would have risen by $41.[22]

This regulatory cost effect is due primarily to the input biasing character of environmental regulations. As reported in table 3, the hypothesis of no input bias is rejected at the .01 significance level. The fuel input bias parameter estimates $\hat{\gamma}_{F_h R}$ and $\hat{\gamma}_{F_l R}$ presented in table 2 suggest that environmental regulation is low-sulfur fuel using and high-sulfur fuel saving. Both coefficients are statistically significant. In addition, the parameter estimates $\hat{\gamma}_{LR}$ and $\hat{\gamma}_{KR}$ indicate that regulation has had a positive but insignificant effect on the cost share of labor and a significant negative effect on the cost share of capital.

The γ_{iR} parameters are also important in estimating the impact of regulation on input demands. The elasticity of input demand with

---

[21] Virtually all of the movement in v_R from 1977 to 1979 is due to a decline in the average price of low-sulfur fuel between 1977 and 1978 followed by a large increase from 1978 to 1979.

[22] The average level of total cost in 1979 for all firms that faced effective regulation was $358.05 million in our sample. The average output level for these firms was 11.65 billion kwh.

respect to regulation can be derived, in terms of the translog parameters, by logarithmically differentiating the equation $X_i = (C/p_i)v_i$ with respect to R:

$$\frac{\partial \ln X_i}{\partial \ln R} = R\left(v_R + \frac{\gamma_{iR}}{v_i}\right), \quad i = L, K, F_{ls}, F_{hs}. \tag{7}$$

The mean values of these elasticities over the complete sample are 0.126, 0.037, 0.493, and −0.551 for labor, capital, low-sulfur fuel, and high-sulfur fuel, respectively. Environmental regulations have increased the representative electric utility's demand for labor, capital, and low-sulfur fuel and reduced the demand for high-sulfur fuel.

It is important to note that, although regulation has reduced the cost share of capital ($\gamma_{KR} < 0$), it has increased the demand for capital ($\partial \ln K / \partial \ln R > 0$) in every sample year. The capital elasticities vary from a low of 0.022 in 1973 to a high of 0.064 in 1979. This trend is consistent with the increased use of exhaust gas scrubbers over this period.

Finally, the total cost elasticity $\partial \ln C / \partial \ln R$ can be decomposed into its input-specific components by weighting each input demand elasticity (7) by its cost share. The average values for labor, capital, high-sulfur fuel, and low-sulfur fuel are 0.010, 0.010, −0.056, and 0.103, respectively. The cost effect of environmental regulations has resulted primarily from switching from lower priced high-sulfur to higher priced low-sulfur fuels.

Scale

The important scale hypothesis of constant returns to scale is rejected at the .01 significance level as reported in table 3. This implies that output growth will be an important determinant of productivity growth.

Mean annual average estimates of the elasticity of cost with respect to output are reported in table 4. The estimates of v_Q indicate that the average utility in each year 1973–79 operated in a region of scale economies, $\hat{v}_Q < 1$. The cost elasticity in any year varies from approximately 0.82 to 1.07, implying that the smallest firms still faced substantial scale economies while the largest sample firms were producing in a region of scale diseconomies.[23]

Two additional scale parameters are of interest. The effect of increased output on the share of low-sulfur fuel, $\hat{\gamma}_{F_l Q}$, is positive and significant, indicating that larger generating units have larger de-

---

[23] The estimates of scale economies, particularly for the early years of our sample, are very similar to those found by Christensen and Greene (1976) using 1970 data.

mands for low-sulfur fuels. The parameter $\hat{\gamma}_{QR}$ is positive and significant, indicating that increased regulatory intensity reduces the level of scale economies or, equivalently, reduces the cost benefits of larger-scale operations. Both of these results are consistent with the observation that larger generating units generally face stricter emission standards than smaller units.

Technical Change

As reported in table 3, the hypothesis of no technical change is rejected at the .01 significance level. This implies that technical change will act as a contributing factor to the rate of productivity growth.[24] As utilities adjusted to rising fuel prices, the estimates of $\hat{v}_T$ reported in table 4 reveal a strong upward trend over time from a low value of -3.7 percent per year in 1973 to a high of 2.6 percent per year in 1979. Over the years 1973–77, technical regression resulted in reduced rates of productivity growth. Technical change acted as a positive source of productivity growth for the years 1978 and 1979.

Sources of Productivity Growth

The sources of productivity growth are defined in continuous time in (4). Using Diewert's (1976) quadratic approximation lemma, we define a discrete time Tornqvist index of productivity growth from (4) as the average rate of productivity growth between two points in time, $(T - 1)$ and T:

$$\bar{v}_G \equiv -\bar{v}_R[R(T) - R(T - 1)] \\ + (1 - \bar{v}_Q)[\ln Q(T) - \ln Q(T - 1)] + \bar{v}_T, \quad (8)$$

where $\bar{v}_R \equiv \frac{1}{2}[v_R(T) + v_R(T - 1)]$, $\bar{v}_Q \equiv \frac{1}{2}[v_Q(T) + v_Q(T - 1)]$, and $\bar{v}_T \equiv \frac{1}{2}[v_T(T) + v_T(T - 1)]$.

Estimates of the average annual sources of productivity growth are reported in table 5. They are calculated separately for firms which faced binding sulfur dioxide emission constraints ($R \neq 0$) in at least one of the 2 years over which the average is calculated and for firms which did not face effective emission restrictions ($R = 0$) in either year. Three descriptive statistics are worthy of note. The number of

---

[24] In addition, we reject the hypothesis of Hicks's neutral technical change. The γ_{iT} parameters reported in table 2 reveal that technical change is fuel using and capital and labor saving. This implies that rising fuel prices in the 1970s reduced the rate of technical change. Stevenson (1980), Gollop and Roberts (1981), and Fraumeni and Jorgenson (1982) all report the same pattern of technical change biases.

TABLE 5

SOURCES OF PRODUCTIVITY GROWTH: AVERAGE ANNUAL RATES OF GROWTH
(Means over All Firms)

Period	Number of Firms	Productivity Growth $\bar{v}_G$	Regulation $-\bar{v}_R \cdot [R(T) - R(T-1)]$	Scale $(1 - \bar{v}_Q) \cdot [\ln Q(T) - \ln Q(T-1)]$	Technical Change $\bar{v}_T$
Firms facing binding emission constraints:					
1973–74	24	−.0327	.0050	−.0002	−.0375
1974–75	36	−.0295	−.0038	.0024	−.0282
1975–76	39	−.0271	−.0196	.0088	−.0164
1976–77	39	−.0072	−.0063	.0041	−.0051
1977–78	38	.0017	−.0054	.0011	.0060
1978–79	41	.0139	−.0055	.0010	.0183
Average	...	−.0135	−.0059	.0029	−.0105
Firms not facing binding emission constraints:					
1973–74	32	−.0348	0	−.0011	−.0337
1974–75	20	−.0297	0	−.0008	−.0289
1975–76	17	−.0134	0	.0057	−.0191
1976–77	17	−.0090	0	−.0008	−.0083
1977–78	18	.0076	0	.0039	.0036
1978–79	15	.0273	0	.0083	.0190
Average	...	−.0087	0	.0025	−.0112

firms whose emissions were constrained by regulations increased from 24 to 41 over the sample period. Fifteen of the sample firms were not effectively constrained by sulfur dioxide regulations in 1979; 11 of these were never constrained during the complete sample period.

The overall trend in productivity growth is similar for both groups of firms. Negative rates of productivity growth of more than 3 percent per year at the beginning of the sample period increase steadily and become positive after 1977. However, the average annual rate of productivity growth over the 1973–79 period for the constrained firms is −1.35 percent, which is almost half a percentage point lower than the −0.87 percent average rate for the unconstrained firms.

Most of the difference occurs over the 1975–79 period. During those years the constrained firms have an average annual productivity growth rate of −0.46 percent compared to 0.31 percent for the unregulated firms. The reason for this large difference can be seen by examining the separate productivity contributions of regulation, scale, and technical change.

The contribution of environmental regulation to productivity growth is summarized in table 5. On average, it reduced the annual rate of productivity growth for regulated firms by 0.59 percentage points. After 1975, this annual average reduction increases to 0.88 percentage points. The largest impact of regulation occurs in 1976, the first full year in which the EPA's ambient air quality standards were supposed to be met. During that year, productivity growth fell by almost two percentage points as a result of increased regulatory intensity. Since then the yearly regulatory impact has been much smaller, varying from -0.54 to -0.63 percentage points. The overall conclusion is clear. In recent years, environmental regulation has resulted in a 0.5–0.6 percentage point decline in the annual rate of productivity growth for constrained firms in the electric utility industry.

Scale economies in production have not played a large role as a contributing source of productivity growth over this period for either group of firms. In general this is due to the low rate of output growth over the period and not the exhaustion of scale economies in production. Average output growth rates during 1973–79 were 2.3 percent per year for constrained firms and 2.1 percent for unconstrained firms. On average, the scale contribution to productivity growth was less than 0.3 percentage points per year for both groups. While there still may be unexploited economies of scale available to the average size firm in this industry, the contribution of scale effects to productivity growth will continue to be extremely small unless output growth rates increase significantly.

The importance of technical change to productivity growth is summarized in the last column of table 5. Like the scale contribution, annual rates of technical change do not differ greatly between the two groups of firms. On average, productivity growth has fallen by 1.05 percentage points per year for the constrained firms as a result of technical regression and 1.12 percentage points for the unconstrained firms. While this average contribution has been negative, the trend over time has been positive. Large negative rates of technical change in the early years of the sample fell in magnitude and became positive in the 1977–79 period. Importantly, the positive rates in the 1977–79 period were sufficient to overcome the negative effect of environmental regulations in those years, thereby restoring positive productivity growth to the industry.

V. Conclusion

Environmental regulations are popularly blamed for the disappointing productivity performance of electric utilities in the seventies. In spite of this issue's provocative nature, little quantitative evidence has surfaced in the economics literature. We suspect this is due, in part, to the difficulty of transforming the notion of environmental regulation into a meaningful and measurable variable.

This paper attempts to fill this gap by introducing an index of regulatory intensity that is used to disentangle the competing determinants of the industry's performance during the 1973–79 business cycle. The index R developed for this research is a function of the severity of the emission standard, the extent of enforcement, and the unconstrained emission rate relevant to each utility. The principal conclusion is that sulfur dioxide emission regulations have resulted in both significantly higher generating costs and markedly lower rates of productivity growth. Among utilities facing effective regulation, the elasticity of cost with respect to regulation rose from 0.089 in 1975 to 0.134 in 1979. The evidence makes clear that this cost impact results primarily from regulation-induced input bias, particularly an increased reliance on expensive low-sulfur fuels. For a representative utility in 1979, a 1 percent increase in regulatory intensity would have increased generating costs by $478,000 or by $41 per million kwh.

The actual impact on industry performance is best viewed through the effect of emission regulations on productivity growth. Compared to unconstrained firms, the average rate of productivity growth for environmentally constrained utilities was reduced by 0.59 percentage points per year during 1973–79. Stated equivalently, annual average productivity growth for these firms would have been 44 percent higher had it not been for sulfur dioxide regulations. By raising the average yearly generating cost per million kwh by $122, this decline in productivity performance cost the average regulated utility and its ratepayers $1.35 million each year.

The productivity effects were considerably larger over 1975–79, precisely the period (beginning July 1975) when the EPA ambient air standards were scheduled to be met. Environmental regulations reduced the annual productivity growth rate of constrained utilities by 0.88 percentage points. This more than accounted for the full difference in annual productivity growth rates of unconstrained and constrained utilities. The 1975–79 average rate of productivity growth for the former was 0.31 percent while for the latter it was −0.46 percent.

Finally, it is important to note what we hope is obvious: Society presumably benefits from cleaner air. Any discussion of the desirability of environmental regulation must weigh these benefits against the costs of regulation. This paper does not measure these benefits. Rather, it is an attempt to identify the effects of emission constraints on average generating cost and productivity growth defined in terms of marketable output.

References

Ackerman, Bruce A., and Hassler, William T. *Clean Coal/Dirty Air.* New Haven, Conn.: Yale Univ. Press, 1981.
Bureau of National Affairs. *Environment Reporter—State Air Laws.* Washington: Bur. Nat. Affairs, 1982.
Christensen, Laurits R., and Greene, William H. "Economies of Scale in U.S. Electric Power Generation." *J.P.E.* 84, no. 4, pt. 1 (August 1976): 655–76.
Christensen, Laurits R., and Jorgenson, Dale W. "The Measurement of U.S. Real Capital Input, 1929–1967." *Rev. Income and Wealth* 15 (December 1969): 293–320.
Denison, Edward F. "Effects of Selected Changes in the Institutional and Human Environment upon Output per Unit of Input." *Survey Current Bus.* 58 (January 1978): 21–44.
———. *Accounting for Slower Economic Growth: The United States in the 1970s.* Washington: Brookings Inst., 1979.
Diewert, W. E. "Exact and Superlative Index Numbers." *J. Econometrics* 4 (May 1976): 115–45.
Fraumeni, Barbara M., and Jorgenson, Dale W. "The Role of Capital in U.S. Economic Growth, 1948–1976." In *Capital, Efficiency and Growth*, edited by George M. von Furstenberg. Cambridge, Mass.: Ballinger, 1980.
———. "Substitution and Technical Change in Production." In *The Economics of Substitution in Production*, edited by Ernst R. Berndt and Barry C. Field. Cambridge, Mass.: MIT Press, 1982.
Gollop, Frank M., and Jorgenson, Dale W. "U.S. Productivity Growth by Industry, 1947–73." In *New Developments in Productivity Measurement and Analysis*, edited by John W. Kendrick and Beatrice N. Vaccara. Chicago: Univ. Chicago Press (for Nat. Bur. Econ. Res.), 1980.
Gollop, Frank M., and Roberts, Mark J. "The Sources of Growth in the U.S. Electric Power Industry." In *Productivity Measurement in Regulated Industries*, edited by Thomas G. Cowing and Rodney E. Stevenson. New York: Academic Press, 1981.
———. "Environmental Regulations and Productivity Growth: The Case of Fossil Fueled Electric Power Generation." Working Paper no. 3-82-2. Pennsylvania State Univ., Dept. Econ., 1982.
Lau, Lawrence J. "Testing and Imposing Monotonicity, Convexity, and Quasi Convexity Constraints." In *Production Economics: A Dual Approach to Theory and Applications*, vol. 1, edited by Melvyn Fuss and Daniel McFadden. Amsterdam: North-Holland, 1978.
Raffle, Bradley I. "The New Clean Air Act—Getting Clean and Staying Clean." *Environment Reporter Monograph* no. 47, vol. 8 (May 1978).
Randle, Russell V. "Forcing Technology—the Clean Air Act Experience." *Yale Law J.* 88 (July 1979): 1713–34.
Roberts, Marc J., and Bluhm, Jeremy S. *The Choices of Power—Utilities Face the Environmental Challenge.* Cambridge, Mass.: Harvard Univ. Press, 1981.
Roberts, Marc J., and Farrell, Susan O. "The Political Economy of Implementation: The Clean Air Act and Stationary Sources." In *Approaches to Controlling Air Pollution*, edited by Ann F. Friedlaender. Cambridge, Mass.: MIT Press, 1978.
Stevenson, Rodney. "Measuring Technological Bias." *A.E.R.* 70 (March 1980): 162–73.
U.S. Code Annotated: Congressional and Administrative News. 91st Cong., 2d sess., 1970, vol. 3. St. Paul: West, 1971.

U.S. Environmental Protection Agency. *State Implementation Plan Emission Regulations for Sulphur Oxides: Fuel Combustion.* 2d ed. Research Triangle Park, N.C.: Office of Air Quality Planning and Standards, 1977.

U.S. Federal Energy Regulatory Commission. *Cost and Quality of Fuels for Electric Utility Plants.* Washington: Government Printing Office, 1975–80. (a)

———. *Hydroelectric Plant Construction Costs and Annual Production Expenses.* Washington: Government Printing Office, 1973–79. (b)

———. *Monthly Report of Cost and Quality of Fuels for Electric Plants.* Computer tape compiled by the Office of Coal and Electric Utility Statistics from utility responses to FPC Form 423, 1981. (c)

———. *Statistics of Privately-Owned Electric Utilities in the United States.* Washington: Government Printing Office, 1958, 1969–79. (d)

———. *Steam-Electric Plant Air and Water Quality Control Data.* Washington: Government Printing Office, 1969, 1973–76. (e)

———. *Steam-Electric Plant Construction Costs and Annual Production Expenses.* Washington: Government Printing Office, 1958, 1969–79. (f)

[5]
POLLUTION ABATEMENT COSTS, REGULATION, AND PLANT-LEVEL PRODUCTIVITY

ABSTRACT

We analyze the connection between productivity, pollution abatement expenditures, and other measures of environmental regulation for plants in three industries (paper, oil, and steel). We examine data from 1979 to 1990, considering both total factor productivity levels and growth rates. Plants with higher abatement cost levels have significantly lower productivity levels. The magnitude of the impact is somewhat larger than expected: $1 greater abatement costs appears to be associated with the equivalent of $1.74 in lower productivity for paper mills, $1.35 for oil refineries, and $3.28 for steel mills. However, these results apply only to variation across plants in productivity levels. Estimates looking at productivity variation within plants over time, or estimates using productivity growth rates show a smaller (and insignificant) relationship between abatement costs and productivity. Other measures of environmental regulation faced by the plants (compliance status, enforcement activity, and emissions) are not significantly related to productivity.

Wayne B. Gray
Department of Economics
Clark University
Worcester, MA 01610
and NBER

Ronald J. Shadbegian
Department of Economics
University of Massachusetts, Dartmouth
North Dartmouth, MA 02747

I. Introduction

Environmental regulations have often been criticized for imposing excessive costs and reducing the competitiveness of U.S. firms. In 1990 the U.S. manufacturing sector reported over $17 billion in operating costs and $6 billion in capital expenditures for pollution abatement, based on a Census Bureau survey. However, abatement costs may be difficult to measure (design costs for a new production process) or not covered by the survey (managerial attention absorbed by required paperwork), leading to an understatement of true abatement costs. Alternatively, forcing firms to pursue cleaner technologies could encourage innovation and lead to gains in competitiveness, so regulation might raise productivity (associated with the 'Porter hypothesis' - Porter (1990;1991)).

Instead of relying exclusively on survey evidence, it may be possible to measure abatement costs indirectly, through their impact on productivity. Productivity is defined as output per unit of inputs, so pollution abatement spending should reduce productivity: increasing inputs without creating more output. In fact, the quantitative impact of abatement costs on productivity should be equal to their share in the firm's total cost (Gray (1987)). A greater than expected effect of abatement costs on productivity indicates that abatement costs are understated; a smaller than expected effect on productivity indicates an overstatement of abatement costs (or some offsetting benefits from regulation).

Several studies have examined the impact of environmental regulation on productivity. Some use estimates of compliance costs to calculate productivity effects (e.g. the 'growth accounting' work of Denison (1979)). Others use econometric analysis with plant-level (Gollop and Roberts (1983)) or industry-level (Gray (1986; 1987), Barbera and McConnell

(1986)) data to test for regulation's impact on productivity. The latter studies tend to find that regulation significantly affects productivity, with more regulated plants or industries having lower productivity levels and slower productivity growth. The former tend to stress that compliance costs are a small part of total cost, so that the impact on productivity is likely to be small. Of course, both views could be correct: the impact could be small, but statistically significant. Little is known about the magnitude of regulation's impact during the 1980s, and prior studies have not combined productivity and compliance cost data at the plant-level.

In this paper, we analyze plant-level productivity data for three industries, taken from the Longitudinal Research Database (LRD). This data was developed by the Center for Economic Studies in the Census Bureau, and we are using the data at the Census's Boston Research Data Center. Our data includes 117 pulp and paper mills (SIC 2611 and 2621), 101 oil refineries (SIC 2911), and 51 steel mills (SIC 3312). We have information on pollution abatement expenditures, along with enforcement, compliance, and emissions data for the 1979-1990 period. We focus on total factor productivity (TFP), examining both productivity levels and growth rates for each plant, and their relationship to the regulatory measures.

We find that plants which spend more on pollution abatement, one measure of regulatory impact, are significantly less productive. A plant with $1 higher abatement costs tends to have the equivalent of $1.74 lower productivity in paper, $1.35 lower in oil, and $3.28 lower in steel. These coefficients suggest that the survey estimates of abatement costs are understated. However, we find smaller and less significant results when we look at changes in abatement costs over time. Other regulatory measures (enforcement, compliance, and emissions) are not significantly related to productivity, and their impacts vary across industries, though their signs tend to point in the same direction (more regulation is associated with lower productivity).

In earlier work (Gray and Shadbegian, 1993) we found larger productivity impacts of differences in abatement costs across plants, with $1 of abatement costs reducing productivity by $2.26 for paper, $2.38 for oil, and $4.19 for steel. Perhaps more importantly, the earlier paper found that plants with growing abatement costs had significantly lower productivity growth, so those results were consistent, whether for levels or for changes. Our earlier work used fewer years of data (1979-1985), and a different measurement procedure which may have biased the coefficient estimates (see Section 3 below).

Properly interpreting our current results is tricky, since the results for productivity levels and productivity changes are different. One possibility is that abatement costs affect productivity, but that measurement error on abatement costs affects the productivity change estimation, biassing down those coefficients. Another interpretation is that there are 'good' and 'bad' plants: good plants are more productive, more likely to comply with regulations, and more clever about discovering low-cost means of compliance. Since most of the variation in abatement costs comes across plants, it is difficult to separately identify the impact of unmeasured (and persistent) plant quality. Including lagged productivity levels in our regressions yields strong evidence for persistence in plant productivity, but reduces the estimated impact of abatement costs on productivity by only about one-quarter in each industry.

4

In section II we discuss various reasons why regulation might affect a plant's productivity. We address the data sources used and various econometric issues in section III. The results are presented in section IV, with conclusions in section V.

II. Does Regulation Hurt (or Help) Productivity?

According to standard economic analysis, government regulation ought to reduce productivity. With firms assumed to choose the best (profit-maximizing) combinations, regulations that constrain these choices will tend to force plants away from the optimum production decisions. Increases in regulation could also lead firms to become more uncertain about future regulatory demands. This may lead them to postpone investment (Viscusi 1983), the development of new products (Hoerger, Beamer, and Hanson 1983), or research on new production processes. Similar effects could result if firms had a limited budget for research and development, and regulation required them to investigate cleaner technologies rather than more productive ones. New plants generally face more stringent rules, and current regulations tend to be written for existing technologies, which further discourages the building of new plants or development of new technologies.

In addition to these constraints, most regulations force firms to use inputs directly for regulatory compliance: a scrubber on a smokestack, a water treatment plant, or clerks to fill out government forms. Existing measures of productivity do not distinguish between inputs used for production and inputs used for regulatory compliance, so inputs are overstated and productivity is understated. This 'mismeasurement' effect, added to the constraints described above, drive the prevailing view that plants facing more regulation should have lower productivity.

The opposing view, that regulation can increase productivity, is necessarily based on the notion that firms were not really behaving optimally (in productivity terms) before the regulation was imposed. One possibility is the presence of 'X-inefficiency' (Leibenstein 1960), where workers and managers don't bother to work their hardest unless prodded by an outside stimulus such as regulation (see Clark (1980) for a similar effect following the unionization of cement plants). New, cleaner equipment may also be more productive than the old equipment it replaces, although for this to represent a productivity gain from regulation we have to assume that the plant would not have installed the new equipment without the regulatory pressures.

Recent suggestions that regulation could have a beneficial impact on the economy are based on anecdotal observations that some firms, forced to modify their production processes for environmental reasons, later found that the new process was also superior in strictly economic terms.[1] The savings often come from redesigning processes to eliminate waste and recycle production by-products (so-called 'closed loop' production methods). Supporters of stricter regulation often point to such examples, but fail to consider the costs of making these innovations: if firms had been free to innovate in any direction they chose, they might have achieved even greater improvements in productivity. Regulation can only improve a firm's innovation if the firm is making some systematic errors. This could be due to X-

---

[1] Oates, Palmer, and Portney (1994) discuss several issues associated with the argument that stringent regulation can provide economic benefits.

inefficiency in technology choice, if firms complacently accept current production methods rather than aggressively seeking new ones.

Some advantages attributed to regulation would not show up for many years, and are unlikely to be captured in our data. Porter (1990; 1991) argues that the demand for 'clean' production technologies will greatly increase in the future, and that firms (or countries) which develop the technology first will have competitive advantages in later years. Again, this argument assumes that firms fail to recognize, or have difficulty appropriating, the gains from the technology, so that regulation is needed to induce the development. Some proponents of economic benefits arising from regulation also argue for more incentive-based regulation, encouraging innovation and developing new markets. Since our data is based on existing regulation, we may find higher costs (and less scope for productivity benefits) than would arise from some future, more efficiently designed regulatory system.

III. Data and Estimation Issues

Our major source of plant-level data is the Longitudinal Research Database (LRD) maintained by the Center for Economic Studies at the Census Bureau.[2] The LRD contains annual data for U.S. manufacturing plants from the Annual Surveys and Censuses of

---

[2] For a detailed description of the LRD data, see McGuckin and Pascoe (1988). Several published studies have examined productivity issues using the LRD, including Lichtenberg and Siegel (1990a and 1990b) and Nguyen and Kokkelenberg (1992).

Manufactures from 1972 through 1990. Using these data, we calculate productivity levels and growth rates for the three industries in our sample (paper, oil, and steel). We selected plants with continuous LRD data through the period, and with adequate data to construct a capital stock measure, dropping a few plants with implausible values for key variables. Our plants tend to be very large, since these are more likely to have continuous LRD data, so our sample includes 60 percent of total industry shipments for paper, 70 percent for oil, and 65 percent for steel.

We also have plant-level data on compliance costs from the Census Bureau's Pollution Abatement Costs and Expenditures (PACE) survey, done annually since 1973.[3] We work with the PACE surveys beginning from 1979 (the oldest available year of data) through 1990. The PACE survey samples about 20,000 plants each year, concentrating on large plants in heavily polluting manufacturing industries. The plants are asked about both new capital expenditures and total annual operating costs for pollution abatement. We measure compliance costs as the plant's annual operating cost for pollution abatement.

We concentrate on operating costs rather than new capital expenditures for both theoretical and practical reasons. First, we would expect current production to be affected by the entire stock of existing pollution abatement capital, not just this year's capital expenditures. Much of these industries' investment in pollution abatement capital occurred before 1979 (when our data begins), so we cannot calculate accurate pollution abatement capital stocks for our plants. In addition, the operating cost measure is already a 'total cost'

---

[3] The survey was not done in 1987, due to budget difficulties. We interpolated the 1987 values, based on information from the 1986 and 1988 surveys.

measure, because it includes depreciation and amortization of existing pollution abatement capital. Finally, we are able to impute pollution abatement operating costs for years in which the plant was missing from the PACE sample, based on the plant's data in other years.[4] Since capital expenditures exhibit larger year-to-year fluctuations, a similar imputation procedure would be more problematic.

We also use information from EPA's own regulatory datasets. We collected plant-level data from the Compliance Data System (CDS) on air pollution inspections (both federal and state), as well as total enforcement actions. This serves as a proxy for the intensity of regulatory enforcement faced by the plant, and is expected to be negatively related to productivity.[5] If a plant did not appear in the CDS, we assume that it did not receive any enforcement (only a few plants were missing from the CDS data). The CDS data also provides annual information on the plant's compliance with air pollution regulations. Data from the National Emissions Data System (NEDS) gives the plant's emissions of common air pollutants, with periodic updates to reflect changes in the emissions over time. We concentrate on air pollution data because the EPA's water pollution data is not fully available until the late 1980s.

We use the value of shipments (adjusted for inventory changes and deflated by the industry price of shipments) to measure a plant's output. To calculate total factor

---

[4] In each year some plants are missing from the sample, so requiring plants to be present every year from 1979 to 1990 would reduce our sample sizes by more than one-third.

[5] Deily and Gray (1991) find that steel mills facing more enforcement were more likely to be closed; Gray (1987) finds that industries facing more enforcement had a greater productivity slowdown.

productivity (TFP), we calculate the difference between output (Q) and the weighted average of three inputs: labor (L), materials and energy expenditures (M) and capital stock (K):[6]

(1) $\text{TFP} = \log(Q) - a_L \log(L) - a_M \log(M) - a_K \log(K)$.

We obtain the factor weights (a_L, a_M, and a_K) for the TFP calculation by regressing $\log(Q)$ on $\log(L)$, $\log(M)$, $\log(K)$ and year dummies for each of the three industries, using the 1979 to 1990 LRD data. The results of these regressions are as follows:[7]

(2)
paper: $\log(Q) = 1.255 + 0.20*\log(L) + 0.65*\log(M) + 0.14*\log(K)$ $R^2=.94$
       $(.089)$ $(.01)$ $(.02)$ $(.01)$ $N=1414$,

oil: $\log(Q) = 0.886 + 0.036*\log(L) + 0.90*\log(M) + 0.04*\log(K)$ $R^2=.98$
     $(.078)$ $(.011)$ $(.01)$ $(.01)$ $N=1212$,

steel: $\log(Q) = 1.650 + 0.31*\log(L) + 0.64*\log(M) + 0.04*\log(K)$ $R^2=.96$
       $(.108)$ $(.01)$ $(.02)$ $(.02)$ $N=612$.

Note that these production functions do quite well in explaining the variation of output across plants and over time, leaving only 2-6% of output variation to be explaining by other factors (such as regulation).

These productivity calculations assume that all of the measured inputs are used to produce output. When some inputs are used for compliance with regulation (such as

---

[6] This is equivalent to assuming a three-input Cobb-Douglas production function:
$$Q = A * L^{a_L} * M^{a_M} * K^{a_K},$$
where A is a 'productivity index' (and TFP = $\log(A)$ in equation (1)).

[7] The factor weights derived from these regressions are similar to those that would be obtained if we used ex-post cost shares to calculate weights.

pollution abatement expenditures), the measured inputs will overstate the amounts of inputs actually used in production, understating 'true' productivity. This 'mismeasurement' effect of regulation on measured TFP can be approximated by the share of compliance costs in total costs, as shown in Gray (1987). Using '*' to represent 'true' TFP and 'true' inputs (excluding compliance costs), we have:

$$
\begin{aligned}
(3) \quad TFP^* &= \log(Q) - a_L \log(L^*) - a_M \log(M^*) - a_K \log(K^*) \\
&= \log(Q) - a_L \log(L-L_R) - a_M \log(M-M_R) - a_K \log(K-K_R) \\
&= TFP + a_R,
\end{aligned}
$$

where the R subscript refers to inputs used for regulatory compliance, and a_R indicates the share of compliance costs in total costs.

Since our TFP measure is already in logarithmic form, differences across plants in compliance cost shares translate into percentage differences across plants in measured TFP. If plant A spends one percent of its total cost on compliance and plant B spends three percent, the level of measured TFP at plant A should be two percentage points higher than at plant B. Regressing TFP levels on compliance cost shares would lead to a coefficient of minus one. A similar relationship, with expected coefficients of minus one, holds between productivity growth rates and changes in compliance costs.

Several problems arise which may bias the regression coefficient away from minus one. The first is the issue of properly 'scaling' the compliance costs to allow for differences in plant size. The same dollar amount of pollution abatement expenditures could be huge for one plant and tiny for another plant, relative to their production. If one paper mill produces $200 million of paper each year and another produces only $20 million, $1 million of pollution abatement spending would be 5 percent of output for the smaller plant, but only 0.5 percent for the larger - the difference between a very heavily regulated plant and a lightly regulated one. Thus we need to divide pollution abatement costs by a measure of the plant's size.

In our earlier paper, we divided each year's pollution abatement spending by the value of the plant's output in that year. This seems a natural way to account for plant size, but it can cause problems, especially for analyses looking at productivity changes over time. When a plant's output increases substantially (moving from a recession to a boom, for example), its productivity also tends to increase substantially. Pollution abatement expenditures tend not to change as quickly, so abatement costs divided by output tends to fall in these years. This seems to have influenced our earlier results, leading to a negative connection between changes in productivity and changes in the 'scaled' abatement cost measure.

In our current paper, we divide pollution abatement costs by a fixed measure of the plant's capacity (based on the plant's top two years of output). Because this capacity measure does not change from year to year, no negative connection with productivity changes is generated by the scaling factor. This helps explain why our current results do not find a significant effect of abatement costs on productivity changes.

A second issue is the exogeneity of our regulatory measures: does high abatement spending 'cause' low productivity, or does low productivity 'cause' high abatement spending? To test this, we can model the determinants of abatement costs, using variables which are clearly exogenous (not determined by either current productivity or current regulation). We then calculate unexplained (actual-predicted) abatement costs and enter this along with actual abatement costs in a second-stage regression of productivity on abatement costs. A significant coefficient on the unexplained abatement costs raises the possibility that productivity is directly affecting regulation (through the part of regulation not captured by the predicted value).

A third possible complication is that both regulation and productivity may be affected by other unmeasured factors. One likely candidate is the quality of the plant's management: good managers might run things more efficiently for both production and compliance, raising productivity and lowering pollution abatement costs. This would tend to create a negative correlation between abatement costs and productivity. We test for this bias by including the plant's past productivity in a regression of productivity on abatement costs, to see whether the coefficient on abatement costs is greatly reduced (a sign of omitted variable bias).

A fourth and final factor that might influence the estimated coefficient is the presence of measurement error, especially in the abatement cost variable. Because it is difficult to measure abatement costs, and because the survey considers primarily the capital side of abatement costs (the maintenance and operation of pollution control equipment), the survey results may give only an approximate picture of true abatement costs. If a large part of the variation in abatement costs is due to mismeasurement, the coefficient on abatement costs in our regression will be biassed towards zero. If two different analyses have different amounts of 'true' variability in abatement costs but similar amounts of 'error' variability, the analysis with less 'true' variability will have larger bias.

In general, we need to pay attention to the source of variation in abatement costs across plants and over time, and how this corresponds with the policy questions to be addressed. If we are interested in how plants would respond to increased regulation, it would be helpful to observe variation in regulation within plants over time. If most of our variability in regulation is across plants, with relatively small variation at a specific plant over time, it will be harder to generate precise estimates of regulation's impact on productivity, and our predictions about the impact of changing regulation will have to be more tentative.

IV. Results

The variables used in the analysis are described in Table 1, with means and standard deviations presented in Table 2. Table 2 also presents the fraction of the variable's total variation which is cross-sectional (explained by plant dummies), addressing the issue of the sources of variation for the variables we consider. Note that the annual growth rate variables (GTFP and GPAOC) are defined for only eleven, rather than twelve, years, starting with the 1979-1980 growth rates.

Comparing productivity growth rates for the three industries, we see that paper shows a substantial productivity decline (due to a poor performance in the late 1980s), with TFP declining by 2 percent per year. Steel's productivity rises during the period by 0.5 percent per year, while oil's productivity is rising by 2.4 percent per year. Since the productivity levels are calculated based on each industry's production function, they cannot be meaningfully compared across industries.

The average paper mill spends 1.5 percent of its output on pollution abatement, while oil refineries spend only about half as much (0.8 percent). Steel is intermediate, spending about 1.2 percent. Steel has declining PAOC (shrinking by .04 per year) due to the contracting nature of the industry, while both oil and paper have increasing PAOC (by .02 and .07 per year, respectively). Paper shows the highest compliance rate (75 percent), while steel is markedly lower (64 percent) and oil is in between (70 percent). The average paper mill is more often in compliance, faces less regulatory activity and emits fewer total tons of air pollution (due to its smaller size), but has higher air pollution emissions relative to output. Steel mills are least often in compliance, face the most enforcement and emit the most pollutants in absolute terms.

The basic regression results for compliance costs are given in Table 3. The first line gives the simplest model for each industry, an ordinary regression of productivity levels on abatement cost levels. The next three models show different ways to control for differences across plants in regulation or abatement costs. Some include individual controls for plant-specific fixed effects: any part of productivity or abatement cost which remains fixed for the plant is removed from the analysis, with only variations at a given plant over time being considered in the estimation. Still others use changes in productivity and abatement costs, which also 'differences out' any fixed characteristics of the plants. The final two lines for each industry consider the possibility that plants facing more regulation might face constraints on their adoption of new productive technology, so that the level of abatement cost could be associated with the growth rate of productivity at the plant.

The results are similar in a broad sense across the three industries: plants with high compliance expenditures tend to have lower total factor productivity levels; plants with growing compliance expenditures tend to have slower productivity growth rates (except for steel). The coefficients for the oil industry are somewhat smaller than those for paper, while the steel industry has noticeably larger coefficients. We also find a small negative connection between pollution abatement levels and productivity growth rates.

We can use the magnitude of the pollution abatement cost coefficients in the productivity equations in Table 3 to distinguish between the 'mismeasurement' of productivity (which would lead to a PAOC coefficient of -1.0) and any other impacts of regulation on productivity, either positive or negative. In the simplest regressions of productivity levels on abatement costs in Table 3, the PAOC coefficient exceeds unity in magnitude, with the coefficient for steel being substantially larger than the other two. This suggests the presence of additional costs due to regulation. However, because of the imprecision in the estimated coefficients, while the coefficients are significantly different from zero we cannot reject the 'pure mismeasurement' hypothesis of -1 at the usual 5% significance level.

The other estimates in Table 3 (using growth rates of productivity, or fixed-effects) tend to show coefficients somewhat smaller in magnitude than -1, and not significant. This could be explained by the presence of measurement error in the abatement cost variables. Since most of the variation in abatement costs is across plants, when we examine changes in abatement costs we throw away the across-plant variation (the biggest part of the total variation). Thus any measurement error is a larger part of the remaining variation, and hence exerts a stronger bias towards zero in the coefficient. However, it could also be interpreted as indicating some beneficial effect of regulation on productivity (though not large enough to outweigh the direct costs of compliance). Thus our evidence on the existence of additional benefits or costs due to regulation is mixed: the results could be interpreted as indicating some additional costs, but other explanations are possible.

We now turn to a two-stage analysis, allowing for the possibility that abatement costs are endogenous. Table 4 describes the variables used in the first stage analysis where we model the compliance cost variable, with regression results in Table 5. The explanatory variables in the first stage are designed to capture some of the different factors expected to increase a plant's level of compliance spending. Plants in states with especially active enforcement might face more pressure to comply, though little impact is found on abatement costs. Plants that consume more fuel tend to produce more air pollution, and both oil and paper have the expected positive signs. Plants located in non-attainment areas (where air quality fails to meet national standards) face tougher regulations than plants in cleaner areas, and these plants have higher compliance costs for all three industries.

For each industry we also include one or two dummy variables to represent aspects of the plant's technology that influence the difficulty of meeting pollution standards. For paper mills, we observe whether or not the plant uses the chemical-based Kraft technology for processing pulp, whether or not the plant operates its own water pollution treatment plant, and whether or not the plant bleaches its pulp (all factors expected to be associated with higher compliance costs). For oil refineries, we observe whether or not the plant uses catalytic cracking, a process where it is especially difficult to contain the resulting pollution: the plant's relative use of the technology (CATF2) is associated with significantly higher compliance costs. For steel mills, we observe whether or not the plant uses electric arc furnaces (rather than blast furnaces); electric arc is a much cleaner technology, so these plants have lower abatement costs.

Although these variables do tend to have the expected relationship with abatement costs, we find that they explain only about 20 percent of the variability in costs. This could cause problems in the second stage of the analysis, since only the predicted variability is being used in that regression. Therefore we also try including the lagged value for the plant's compliance costs in the first stage. Not surprisingly, this had substantial explanatory power, raising the R-square to .7 or .8 and generally rendering the other explanatory variables insignificant. Since lagged PAOC is predetermined it cannot be directly influenced by this period's productivity, and lagged values are commonly used as explanatory variables in first stage regressions, although lagged PAOC is obviously less 'purely' exogenous than the other explanatory variables (due to the possibility of intertemporal correlation in the determinants of PAOC).

Table 6 presents the second-stage regressions, using the predicted values of PAOC generated from the first stage regressions. Note that we do not consider the growth rate or fixed-effect versions of the regressions (as we did in Table 3). This is because all of the explanatory variables for the plants (except for lagged PAOC) are invariant over time. This means that (except for the year dummies, which are also included in the second-stage regression) there is no within-plant variation for such regressions to pick up. As expected from the low R-squares on the first-stage regressions without lagged PAOC, these predicted PAOC coefficients have little explanatory power, with standard errors nearly three times as large as those in Table 3 (though the coefficients are positive). When we include the lagged PAOC variable, the second-stage estimates are similar to those we found in Table 3 (with slightly larger standard errors). The magnitude of the PAOC coefficient is somewhat smaller for oil, slightly larger for paper, and noticeably larger for steel.

We also used the predicted values from the first-stage regressions to generate Hausman tests for the exogeneity of PAOC in the regressions. This involves calculating the residual value of PAOC (actual minus predicted values) and including it along with actual PAOC in a second stage regression. We present the t-statistic associated with the residual coefficients in the bottom line of Table 6. A significant coefficient on the residual indicates potential problems, but in all cases we find the residual's coefficient to be insignificant. This indicates little evidence for causality running from productivity to compliance costs, at least in a contemporaneous sense.

Another concern was the possibility of long-term quality differences across plants, correlated with both productivity and abatement costs. Table 7 shows the results of including five-year-lagged productivity levels in our basic regression of productivity levels on abatement costs. As expected, lagged productivity levels are positively (and significantly) related to current productivity. The abatement cost coefficient does fall slightly: by one-quarter for oil and steel and by one-eighth for paper, although these reductions are enough to reduce the significance of the oil and steel results (with the oil coefficient being almost exactly the expected minus one). Plant quality appears to play a relatively small role in the observed connection between abatement costs and productivity. [8]

Although our focus is on the relationship between compliance costs and productivity, the other regulatory measures we gathered may be useful in obtaining a more complete picture. This is especially true because most of the variation in compliance costs is across plants, so that other plant-specific characteristics may be driving both compliance costs and productivity. The regression results for these other variables are presented in Table 8. The results are not very strong, and rarely consistent across industries. We usually find that higher enforcement, higher emissions, and lower compliance are associated with lower productivity, but the results are not consistent in sign across industries (in fact, in each case one industry has an unexpected sign) and tend to be insignificant. Our earlier study (Gray and Shadbegian, 1993) also found insignificant results, using cross-section regressions based on average values for the regulation measures.

V. Summary and Future Work

Using plant-level data for three manufacturing industries, we have found a negative relationship between a plant's pollution abatement costs and its total factor productivity level. The magnitudes of the estimated coefficients suggest an impact of regulation on productivity that is somewhat larger than existing compliance cost data would suggest, but these results

---

[8] The reduction in the abatement cost coefficient could also arise if lagged abatement costs matter. In that case, the lagged productivity term picks up part of the effect of lagged abatement costs, reducing the estimated impact of current abatement costs (and possibly underestimating the total impact of abatement costs).

depend on the specification used. Point estimates suggest that steel costs might be three times as large as expected, with oil and paper about one and a half times as large as expected, but the estimates are sufficiently imprecise that we cannot reject the hypothesis that existing estimates of compliance costs (based on abatement cost surveys) are about right. It does not appear that regulation imposes productivity <u>benefits</u> large enought to outweigh the measured compliance costs, but even this cannot be rejected if we focus on the analysis of productivity changes over time, or otherwise control for unobserved differences across plants. Our results for other measures of regulation, such as enforcement, compliance, and emissions, show little significant relationships with productivity. More often than not, plants with higher enforcement, lower compliance, or more emissions tend to have lower productivity levels, but the results are neither significant nor consistent.

Several avenues of research remain to be pursued. We are looking at other environmental areas with more limited data (water and toxic waste pollution) and at OSHA regulation, to provide a broader coverage for the enforcement and compliance measures for the plant. We are considering MIMIC models which would allow us to combine several indicators of the regulation faced by a plant into an overall index of regulation, to see whether that index does a better job explaining productivity than the individual indicators do. Finally, we are working on more detailed models of the production function, allowing the influence of regulation to affect labor and capital differently, estimating the effect of regulation on employment and investment, and testing possible explanations of why regulation affects productivity.

21
REFERENCES

Barbera, Anthony J., and Virginia D. McConnell, "Effects of Pollution Control on Industry Productivity: A Factor Demand Approach," Journal of Industrial Economics, V. 35 n. 2 (December 1986), pp. 161-172.

Clark, Kim B., "The Impact of Unionization on Productivity: A Case Study," Industrial and Labor Relations Review, v. 33 (1980), pp. 451-69.

Deily, Mary E. and Wayne B. Gray, "Enforcement of Pollution Regulations in a Declining Industry," Journal of Environmental Economics and Management, v. 21 (Fall 1991), pp. 260-274.

Denison, Edward P., Accounting for Slower Economic Growth: The U.S. in the 1970s, (Washington: The Brookings Institution) 1979.

Gollop, Frank M., and Mark J. Roberts, "Environmental Regulations and Productivity Growth: The Case of Fossil-Fueled Electric Power Generation," Journal of Political Economy, v. 91 (August 1983), pp. 654-674.

Gray, Wayne B., "The Cost of Regulation: OSHA, EPA and the Productivity Slowdown", American Economic Review, v. 77 (December 1987), pp. 998-1006.

_____, Productivity versus OSHA and EPA Regulations, (Ann Arbor: UMI Research Press), 1986.

_____ and Ronald J. Shadbegian, "Environmental Regulation and Manufacturing Productivity at the Plant Level," CES Discussion Paper 93-6, March 1993.

Hoerger, Fred, William H. Beamer, and James S. Hanson, "The Cumulative Impact of Health, Environmental, and Safety Concerns on the Chemical Industry During the Seventies," Law and Contemporary Problems, v. 46 (Summer 1983), pp. 59-107.

Leibenstein, Harvey, "Allocative Efficiency versus X-Efficiency", American Economic Review, v. 56 (June 1966), pp. 392-415.

Lichtenberg, Frank R., and Donald Siegel, "The Impact of R&D Investment on Productivity - New Evidence Using Linked R&D-LRD Data," Economic Inquiry, v. 29 (1990), pp. 2-13.

_____, "The Effects of Leveraged Buyouts on Productivity and Related Aspects of Firm Behavior," Journal of Finance and Economics, v. 27 (1990), pp. 165-194.

McGuckin, Robert H., and George A. Pascoe, "The Longitudinal Research Database: Status and Research Possibilities," Survey of Current Business, 1988.

Nguyen, Sang V. and Edward C. Kokkelenberg, "Measuring Total Factor Productivity, Technical Change, and the Rate of Returns to Research and Development," Journal of Productivity Analysis, v. 2 (1992), pp. 269-282.

Oates, Wallace E., Karen Palmer, and Paul R. Portney, "Environmental Regulation and International Competitiveness: Thinking about the Porter Hypothesis," Resources for the Future Discussion Paper 94-02, November 1993.

Porter, Michael E., "America's Green Strategy," Scientific American, April 1991, p. 168.

_____, The Competitive Advantage of Nations (New York: The Free Press) 1990.

U.S. Bureau of the Census, Pollution Abatement Costs and Expenditures, 1990 MA200(90)-1 Washington: U.S. Government Printing Office, 1992.

Viscusi, W. Kip, "Frameworks for Analyzing the Effects of Risk and Environmental Regulation on Productivity," American Economic Review, v. 73 (September 1983), pp. 793-801.

Table 1

Variable Descriptions

Variable	Description
LTFP	Total factor productivity level (based on equation 1 and coefficients for each industry from equation 2)
GTFP	Annual growth rate of LTFP
PAOC	Pollution abatement operating cost, divided by plant 'capacity' (top two years of shipments in period)
GPAOC	Annual growth rate of PAOC
EMIT	Total emissions (thousand tons/year) of five 'criteria' air pollutants (particulates, SO_2, NOX, CO, and hydrocarbons)
REMIT	EMIT per dollar of plant 'capacity' <used in regressions>
COMP	Compliance status with air pollution regulations (0 if in violation during any month of the year, 1 if not)
ACT	Number of air pollution enforcement actions in year (from EPA's Compliance Data System)
LACT	log(ACT) <used in regressions>
INSP	Number of air pollution inspections in year (from EPA's Compliance Data System)
LINSP	log(INSP) <used in regressions>

Table 2

Descriptive Statistics
(1979-1990 Annual Data)

Variable	Paper (N=1404) mean	(sd)	% plant[2]	Oil (N=1212) mean	(sd)	% plant[2]	Steel (N=612) mean	(sd)	% plant[2]
LTFP	101.840	(23.6)	32%	79.250	(20.0)	26%	147.600	(22.8)	29%
GTFP[1]	-2.040	(16.7)	1%	2.440	(15.8)	2%	0.538	(24.8)	1%
PAOC	1.509	(1.18)	81%	0.802	(0.89)	70%	1.249	(0.78)	51%
GPAOC[1]	0.015	(0.53)	2%	0.072	(0.36)	6%	-0.042	(0.52)	2%
EMIT	7.901	(11.0)	76%	21.663	(45.7)	57%	26.573	(50.1)	6%
REMIT	0.146	(0.27)	56%	0.121	(0.31)	53%	0.082	(0.09)	69%
COMP	0.747	(0.43)	32%	0.697	(0.45)	29%	0.644	(0.47)	54%
ACT	3.846	(5.61)	53%	7.245	(12.6)	53%	11.930	(22.2)	55%
LACT	1.180	(0.84)	52%	1.623	(0.93)	58%	1.868	(1.11)	55%
INSP	1.345	(1.37)	39%	1.952	(1.90)	38%	3.843	(6.33)	48%
LINSP	0.723	(0.50)	34%	0.916	(0.57)	36%	1.190	(0.80)	47%

[1] GTFP and GPAOC are growth rates, so they are only available for 11 years rather than 12. The first observation is the 1979-80 growth rate, with correspondingly smaller sample sizes.

[2] %plant is the percentage of the variance explained by the identity of the plant (the R-squared obtained by regressing the variable on a complete set of plant dummies)

TABLE 3

Basic Regressions

Industry	Dep Var	PAOC	Controls GPAOC	Year	Plant	R^2	N
Paper	LTFP	-1.737 (0.437)		X		.354	1404
	LTFP	-0.546 (0.809)		X	X	.666	1404
	GTFP		-0.756 (0.712)	X		.433	1287
	GTFP		-0.855 (0.745)	X	X	.447	1287
	GTFP	-0.196 (0.305)		X		.433	1287
	GTFP	-0.609 (0.798)		X	X	.447	1287
Oil	LTFP	-1.350 (0.553)		X		.357	1212
	LTFP	-0.972 (0.945)		X	X	.618	1212
	GTFP		-0.569 (1.267)	X		.155	1111
	GTFP		-0.493 (1.358)	X	X	.173	1111
	GTFP	-0.067 (0.513)		X		.155	1111
	GTFP	-0.579 (1.155)		X	X	.173	1111
Steel	LTFP	-3.280 (1.181)		X		.082	612
	LTFP	-2.755 (1.520)		X	X	.368	612
	GTFP		0.264 (2.109)	X		.047	561
	GTFP		0.349 (2.230)	X	X	.054	561
	GTFP	-0.648 (1.406)		X		.047	561
	GTFP	-1.497 (2.196)		X	X	.055	561

Table 4

Exogenous Variables
(used to explain PAOC in two-stage model)

STENF - air pollution enforcement actions per plant reported in
    EPA's Compliance Data System for the state (1984-1987)
ENETVS - energy spending / total value of shipments (1972)
DIRTY - plant is located in a county which fails to meet air
    EPA quality standards (dummy variable)

KRAFT - (paper) uses Kraft technology for paper-making
BLEACH - (paper) bleaches pulp
TREAT - (paper) has water treatment plant on site

CATF1 - (oil) uses catalytic cracking technique
CATF2 - (oil) ratio of catalytic cracking capacity to other
    capacity

EARC - (steel) uses electric arc furnaces

Descriptive Statistics

	Paper	Oil	Steel
STENF	4.09 (1.91)	4.92 (1.62)	4.44 (2.13)
ENETVS	.06 (.02)	.02 (.02)	.14 (.05)
DIRTY	.48 (.50)	.65 (.48)	.80 (.40)
KRAFT	.39 (.49)		
BLEACH	.41 (.49)		
TREAT	.56 (.50)		
CATF1		.74 (.44)	
CATF2		1.22 (1.62)	
EARC			.49 (.50)
N	1404	1212	612

Table 5

First-Stage Regressions
(dep var=PAOC)

	Paper		Oil		Steel	
CONST	0.7754 (0.1690)	-0.1111 (0.0805)	0.4791 (0.1247)	-0.0859 (0.0564)	1.5764 (0.1522)	0.3640 (0.1073)
LPAOC	-	0.8919 (0.0130)	-	0.9637 (0.0139)	-	0.733 (0.0264)
STENF	0.0092 (0.0167)	-0.0030 (0.0080)	-0.0585 (0.0154)	-0.0016 (0.0071)	0.0082 (0.0147)	0.0044 (0.0097)
ENETVS	2.9460 (1.3130)	0.5242 (0.6302)	6.0727 (1.3750)	0.4711 (0.6338)	-0.6651 (0.5672)	-0.0847 (0.3751)
DIRTY	0.3732 (0.0628)	0.0252 (0.0305)	0.1885 (0.0528)	0.0020 (0.0243)	0.1399 (0.0753)	0.0678 (0.0498)
KRAFT	0.1236 (0.0846)	0.0351 (0.0406)				
BLEACH	-0.0289 (0.0883)	0.0495 (0.0423)				
TREAT	0.6462 (0.0789)	0.0479 (0.0387)				
CATF1			-0.0325 (0.0599)	-0.0049 (0.0274)		
CATF2			0.1164 (0.0167)	0.0163 (0.0078)		
EARC					-0.4766 (0.0606)	-0.0567 (0.0421)
R^2	.206	.832	.210	.854	.173	.655
N	1404	1287	1212	1111	612	561

All regressions include year dummies.

Table 6

Second-Stage Regressions
(dep var=LTFP)

1st stage w/LPAOC	Paper		Oil		Steel	
	no	yes	no	yes	no	yes
Predicted PAOC	-0.075 (1.024)	-2.086 (0.463)	0.126 (1.612)	-1.095 (0.539)	0.722 (3.520)	-5.019 (1.647)
R2	.347	.372	.353	.356	.064	.076
N	1404	1287	1212	1111	612	561

The above regressions involve regressing LTFP on the predicted PAOC values generated by the first-stage regressions presented in Table 5. For each industry two different predicted PAOC values are used: one includes LPAOC in the first-stage model and the other doesn't.

Exogeneity Tests

Paper		Oil		Steel	
-1.81	-0.23	0.96	-0.86	1.39	1.65

The above exogeneity tests involve regressing LTFP on both actual and residual PAOC. Each industry has two test values reported, corresponding to the two different first-stage regressions (excluding or including LPAOC). The statistics given are t-statistics on the residual PAOC measure (based on the first-stage regressions). A significant t-statistic indicates possible endogeneity of PAOC (or at least the rejection of the null hypothesis which includes exogenous PAOC).

All sets of regressions include year dummies.

Table 7

Regressions including lagged TFP
(dep var=LTFP)

	Paper	Oil	Steel
PAOC	-1.51	-1.04	-2.36
	(0.434)	(0.537)	(1.38)
5-year lagged LTFP	0.384	0.347	0.257
	(0.027)	(0.027)	(0.047)
N	1404	1212	612
R2	.437	.434	.123

Each regression also includes year dummies.

Table 8

Other Regulatory Variables
(dep var=LTFP)

	Paper	Oil	Steel
REMIT	-0.0086	-0.0228	0.2413
	(0.0191)	(0.0149)	(0.1041)
COMP	0.0018	0.0115	-0.0061
	(0.0120)	(0.0104)	(0.0460)
LACT	-0.0002	0.0087	-0.0128
	(0.0062)	(0.0051)	(0.0084)
LINSP	0.0114	-0.0027	-0.0152
	(0.0105)	(0.0085)	(0.0117)
N	1404	1212	612

Each pair of numbers above comes from a separate regression of LTFP on year dummies and that particular regulatory variable (along with year dummies).

The numbers presented in the table are the coefficient and standard error for the regulatory variable.

[6]
The Impact of Pollution Abatement Investment on Productivity Change: An Empirical Comparison of the U.S., Germany, and Canada*

KLAUS CONRAD
University of Mannheim
Mannheim, West Germany

CATHERINE J. MORRISON
Tufts University,
and National Bureau of Economic Research
Medford, Massachusetts

I. Introduction

Since environmental quality became an important focus of government regulations in most industrialized countries in the early 1970s, many researchers have assessed the impact of these regulations on economic performance. For example, Leontief and Ford [11] and Pasurka [15] investigated the impact that environmental protection costs had on prices in the U.S.; Walter [24] calculated the effect of pollution abatement expenditures on U.S. trade; and Robinson [19] measured the distributional impact of the burden of industrial pollution abatement. A related issue involves the productivity consequences of environmental regulations. In this paper we address this issue by considering the impact of pollution abatement investment on productivity growth measures.

The imposition of environmental regulations has often been suggested as a partial explanation for the productivity growth slowdown experienced by most industrialized countries in the early 1970s. The contention is that investments are foregone because resources that otherwise would be productive must be used to satisfy the regulations, and the goal of the regulations—pollution abatement—has no marketable and therefore quantifiable effect in terms of productivity. This hypothesis has been explored by researchers such as Denison [6]. He attempted to determine the effects of environmental regulation by first estimating the incremental costs of production due to environmental regulations, and then using these estimates to impute the percentage reduction in output per unit of input attributable to regulation. Similarly, Norsworthy, Harper, and Kunze [13] assessed the impact of environmental regulations by removing the pollution abatement capital component of total capital input to purge the capital measure of "unproductive" capital. Pittman [17] instead derived a productivity index which includes measures of "undesirable" as well as

---

*Catherine J. Morrison acknowledges the support of the Deutsche Forschungsgemeinschaft and Resources for the Future.

"desirable" outputs where undesirable outputs (pollution) are valued by their shadow prices. Gollop and Roberts [7] included regulation in a long run total cost function and used econometric estimates of the production technology to determine the biases resulting from regulations. Some researchers including Crandall [4] and Christainsen and Haveman [2] emphasized the impact of more indirect and difficult to quantify impacts of regulations, including discouraging otherwise productive investments and technological innovations.

It has also been asserted that environmental regulation may instead facilitate economic growth. This hypothesis has been suggested by Meyers and Nakamura [12] who use a putty-clay model to show that it is possible for increasingly stringent environmental regulation to cause more capital turnover, and therefore modernization, so that the net effect may be increased productivity growth.

Finally, some researchers have recently focused on the impacts on international competitiveness of environmental regulations and resulting low productivity growth in the U.S. An important example of this is Kalt [8] who asserts that the U.S. is at an extreme disadvantage in international markets because of the depressing impacts of environmental regulations, especially since regulations in the U.S. are so cost-ineffective.

It is clear that there is a wide range of methods and focuses in studies about the impact of environmental regulations on productivity, and no clear consensus of the magnitude—or even direction—of the impacts, how to quantify these impacts, or what the international effects of the regulations may be. In addition, the impact of these regulations has not generally been motivated within an explicit model of the behavior of firms when faced with regulations on a resource which, without regulation, is a free good to the firm. Most of the existing models which consider the impacts of regulation on productivity growth calculations either adjust output or input in an ad-hoc manner, or simply consider regulation to be an additional input into the production process and use an econometric model. Other studies are not based on a theoretical model but instead assess as many costs of regulation as are quantifiable given available data.

In this paper we develop a model of the decisions of a firm facing a standard for pollution emissions which explicitly recognizes the effects of environmental standards and resulting pollution abatement capital investments. This model permits consideration of the explicit and implicit costs of purchasing pollution abatement capital to satisfy these regulations, and the values to the firm of compliance with the regulation. The framework incorporates the notion that the pollution abatement capital is not productive in the usual sense; it is unproductive in terms of measured output and therefore should not be treated like a productive input for productivity calculations.

The implications for measurement of productivity growth from the theoretical model incorporating pollution abatement capital investment are interpretable and straightforward to implement nonparametrically, and are therefore useful for applied researchers. The signs of the biases are, however, theoretically ambiguous.

The costs incurred from pollution abatement capital purchases are separated from production capital costs, so any upward surge in capital growth from sudden increases in pollution abatement capital investment is purged. The benefits accruing to expenditures on pollution abatement capital are implicitly also taken into account. They are represented by a shadow value characterizing the value of the standard at the margin which is equivalent to the cost of pollution abatement capital if the actual and regulator's efficient choice of pollution abatement capital coincide.[1] The resulting

---

1. Theoretically this value could be interpreted as an implicit measure of some of the indirect costs of regulations including regulation-induced inefficiency from discouraging technological innovation or other more productive investment which would have a higher shadow value.

bias term which shows the difference between our measure and the traditional less precise measure can be interpreted as an adjustment to marginal cost of output and depends on the difference between the growth rates of output and pollution abatement capital. A second bias term which partially reflects the impact of the existence of pollution abatement capital regulations is based simply on purging pollution abatement capital from the capital data, and depends on the difference in the growth rates of output and productive capital.

Computation of these biases allows interesting comparisons between the manufacturing sectors of three important industrial countries, the U.S., Canada, and Germany. Productivity growth rates as correctly measured are compared with traditionally measured rates to determine whether differences in productivity growth rates between countries can be attributed to irrelevant treatment of pollution abatement capital expenditures. They are also compared to rates implied by constraining pollution abatement capital investment to zero. This allows some assessment of the comparative impact of the productivity growth harm resulting from the existence of regulations, and therefore, in this particular sense, of the impact on international competitiveness of these regulations.

Note that the methods here, as for any productivity measurement studies which explicitly are based on a model of the production process, do not recognize pollution abatement as a beneficial output. It is clear that if environmental impacts were marketable, returns to abatement would compensate—to a greater or lesser extent—for the decrease in marketed output. Production-oriented studies cannot assess the social benefits from abatement. The theoretical framework for this study, through the shadow valuation of the capital investment required for abatement, does provide however an implication about how to assess the value society has imputed to environmental protection by imposing standards. This information could be used, if benefit data were available, to determine whether the standards imposed on the industry were at the appropriate level to facilitate social optimization.

II. Model Specification

The model of firm behavior including environmental standards is in the spirit of Conrad [3] and Dasgupta [5]. The firm's production decision is assumed to be based on the maximization of profits by the choice of output (x), variable inputs (v_j), and investment in both productive capital (I, with stock level K) and pollution abatement capital (IPA and KPA). This problem can be written as:

$$\max_{x_t, I_t, IPA_t} \sum e^{-rt}\{p_t x_t - G(x_t, K_t, q_t) - PI(I_t + IPA_t)\} \tag{1}$$

subject to

$$K_{t+1} = K_t + I_t - \delta \cdot K_t \tag{1a}$$

$$KPA_{t+1} = KPA_t + IPA_t - \delta \cdot KPA_t \tag{1b}$$

$$TE_t = \xi \cdot x_t \tag{1c}$$

$$\overline{NE}_t - f(KPA) \cdot TE \geq 0. \tag{1d}$$

The maximization process represented by (1) is standard, where p_t is the price of output at time t so $p_t x_t$ is equal to revenue, $G(\cdot)$ is the variable cost function representing the optimized choice of variable inputs for any given x_t, K_t vector and input prices q_j, and PI is the common asset price of investment goods so $PI(I_t + IPA_t)$ is the expenditure on investment in both types of capital. (1a) and (1b) also are typical definitions. (1c) and (1d), however, require some explanation.

Note that the variable cost function is assumed to depend on K but not KPA since KPA is not productive. This results because KPA is not in the production function for output and thus not in the dual cost function. KPA is instead included in total costs as a fixed cost. The interpretation of this is that if output changes, even if this causes greater fixed costs from greater required KPA, these costs are not in the form of greater variable input use but instead are "rental" costs. This is similar to the distinction between costs that are external to the production process rather than internal.

(1c) represents the flow of pollution from the production process without regulation. TE stands for total emissions, in this sense the unabated total rate of discharge of pollutants. ξ is an emission to output parameter which represents the constant proportional relationship between pollutant discharge and production when no standards and therefore no pollution abatement capital exist. The reduction of emissions requires additional costs associated only with pollution abatement. This reduction therefore is a function of the level of pollution abatement capital, KPA, and is represented by $f(KPA)$. The resulting level of emissions, denoted non-abated emissions (NE) is characterized by (1d), where $\overline{NE}$ is the standard set for allowable emissions.

$f(KPA)$ is a positive but decreasing function since increasing the pollution abatement capital stock causes the amount of emissions to decline; $f'(KPA) < 0$. In addition, the second derivative of this function should be positive so that the contribution of incremental units of KPA diminishes as the stock of KPA increases, and $f(\infty) = 0$ so that if $KPA \to 0$, $NE = 0$. In other words, $f(KPA)$ is the percentage of potential emissions actually released.

Note that this model does not require knowledge of the stock of pollutants because regulation is assumed to be on emissions. This can be adapted to apply to regulations about the existing stock instead of flow of emissions as developed by Dasgupta [5]. Note also that this approach does not require a damage function because valuation of the damage is implicitly incorporated in the specification of the standard. The balance of the (private and social) benefits received from production and the costs imposed by the pollution are therefore captured by the profit function and the constraint and corresponding shadow value, respectively.

The constrained maximization problem facing the firm from (1) can therefore be written as:

$$\max_{x_t, J_t, JPA_t} \sum e^{-rt} \{p_t x_t - G(x_t, K_t, q_t) - PI(I_t + IPA_t)\} - \bar{\tau} \cdot (f(KPA) \cdot \xi x_t - \overline{NE}, \quad (2)$$

subject to (1a) and (1b).

We assume both K and KPA, the state variables, as well as output, x_t, are chosen by the firm in each time period to optimize (1). The first order conditions for the control variable x_t and the state variables K_t and KPA_t which capture the investment paths I_t and IPA_t can therefore be written as:

$$p - G_x - \tau \cdot f(KPA)\xi = 0,$$

so

$$p_t - \tau \cdot f(KPA)\xi = G_x, \quad (3a)$$

so
$$-PI(r+\delta) - G_K = 0,$$
$$q_K = -G_K, \tag{3b}$$

and,

so
$$-PI(r+\delta) - \tau \cdot f'(KPA)\xi x = 0,$$
$$q_K = -\tau \cdot f'(KPA)\xi x, \tag{3c}$$

where $\tau = \bar{\tau} \cdot (1+r)^t$ is the current (undiscounted) shadow value of non-abated emissions, and q_k is the rental price of capital goods which is assumed the same for both KPA and K because PI, r, and δ are assumed the same.[2]

These first order conditions provide interesting inferences. (3a), for example, captures the typical assertion in the pollution literature that additional revenue with a change in output must cover both the change in production costs and the extra required costs of abatement on the margin. "Extra" profit must be made to pay for pollution abatement capital expenses associated with production. τ is positive because it represents a cost to the firm—an emission charge reflecting the undesirable effects of pollution. The firm will therefore reduce production from that level which it would choose without regulation; it will try to maximize, not simply profit from production, but profit net of emission charges. (3b) says that $q_k = -G_K$ is the value of having more capital in terms of using less inputs to produce a given output—the shadow value of capital discussed by Lau [10]. (3c) is the corresponding shadow value determination equation for KPA, including the recognition of (i) the social valuation of pollution—or the damage resulting from the pollution—represented by the standard, and (ii) the nonproductive nature of the pollution abatement capital stock represented by the lack of a G_{KPA} term.

In order to see the connection between τ, society's valuation of abatement expenditure and the standard, we may assume that a regulatory authority runs the firm. With $D(NE)$ as a damage function of emissions released ($D' > 0, D'' > 0$), the regulator pursues optimal resource allocation and maximizes social profits. He therefore has to solve the problem:

$$\max_{x_t, I_t, IPA_t} \sum e^{-rt}\{p_t x_t - G(x_t, K_t, q_t) - PI(I_t + IPA_t) - D(NE_t)\} \tag{4}$$

subject to (1a) and (1b), where $NE_t = f(KPA_t)\xi x_t$. First order conditions are the same as given in (3), but with $D'(NE)$ instead of τ. The resulting optimal net emission NE_t should be the standard $\overline{NE}$ in (1d).[3] The level of τ corresponds in this case exactly to $D'(NE)$, society's marginal disutility of non-abated emissions. If abatement were performed efficiently, there will be no difference between society's valuation of the benefits to abatement expenditure (τ) and that implied by the regulator's choice of emission standards.[4]

(3a,b,c) can be rewritten to facilitate consideration of the homogeneity properties of the functions as:

---

2. This assumption is not necessary for the analysis, and in some cases it may not be justified. In principle the return to productive capital could be determined in the typical manner while the return to KPA is the fees or penalties avoided.

3. Dasgupta [5] outlines an approach including a damage function as compared to a standard. If the damage function is a threshold type of function where the marginal damage is very large in the neighborhood of a given level of emissions (in the Dasgupta framework, the stock) these two approaches are equivalent.

4. Note that if τ can be identified, which is possible with an econometric investigation, it will therefore capture the implied valuation by society of the damage on the margin and can be used to assess the implications of the standard. Pittman [16] seeks to estimate econometrically this sort of shadow price.

$$p \cdot x/G - \tau \cdot f(KPA)\xi x/G = p \cdot x/G - \tau \cdot NE/G = \partial \ln G/\partial \ln x, \quad (5a)$$

$$-q_K \cdot K/G = \partial \ln G/\partial \ln K, \quad \text{and}, \quad (5b)$$

$$q_K KPA/G = -\tau \cdot f'(KPA) \cdot KPA \cdot \xi x/G = \tau \cdot NE/G. \quad (5c)$$

Note that the last equality, (5c), requires the $f(KPA)$ function to be homogeneous of degree (-1). This assumption is not necessary to impose for the analysis but is a useful simplifying assumption. It is not possible in general to determine the degree of homogeneity of $f(KPA)$.

The expressions in (5) can be employed to motivate the definition of the total cost function, C, and define homogeneity properties of G and C. Homogeneity of degree one in output (constant returns to scale) of G implies that $\partial \ln G/\partial \ln x + \partial \ln G/\partial \ln K = 1$ [10]. From (5), this implies that $p \cdot x/G - \tau \cdot NE/G - q_K \cdot K/G = 1$ for each time period t. Rewriting this equality results in $p \cdot x = G + \tau \cdot NE + q_K \cdot K$, which, using (5c), is equivalent to $p \cdot x = G + q_K \cdot KPA + q_K \cdot K$—the firm's total costs, C. More specifically, the firm pays variable plus capital costs for production and $q_K \cdot KPA$ for the corresponding required pollution abatement. This regulatory cost is equivalent on the margin to the valuation of emitted pollutants to society, so the cost function can be written in terms of either cost. The $\tau \cdot NE$ cost component, however, is implicit. Thus the expression based on this component is not very useful for empirical analysis. It is easy to show[5] that this implies homogeneity of degree one also for the total cost function defined as $C = G + q_K K + q_K KPA$.

The specification of the cost function above can be used to derive a cost-side productivity measure, capturing $\partial \ln C/\partial t$, similar to traditional accounting productivity growth measures but adjusting for the fact that KPA is not a productive input. This measure is[6]

$$\epsilon_{C_t}' = -\partial \ln C/\partial t = (p \cdot x - q_K \cdot KPA/C) \cdot \dot{x}/x - \sum_j (q_j v_j/C) \cdot \dot{v}_j/v_j - (q_K K/C) \cdot \dot{K}/K. \quad (6)$$

Note that $\epsilon_{C_t}' = -\partial \ln C/\partial t$ is a positive number because cost diminution is equivalent to an increase in productivity.

The adjustment to this theoretically based expression from the traditional expression is based on purging the effect of pollution abatement capital from the output value measure to capture marginal costs correctly, and removing the KPA component from the total capital stock. The correction is measured on the cost side (in terms of marginal costs) because productivity growth is measured in terms of costs.

More specifically, the traditional expression may be decomposed into the corrected expression (6) and a bias term,

$$\epsilon_{C_t} = -\partial \ln C/\partial t = \dot{x}/x - \sum_j (q_j v_j/C) \cdot \dot{v}_j/v_j - q_K\{(K+KPA)/C\} \cdot (\dot{K}+\dot{KPA})/(K+KPA)$$

$$= (\{p \cdot x - q_K \cdot KPA\}/C) \cdot \dot{x}/x - \sum_j (q_j v_j/C) \cdot \dot{v}_j/v_j - (q_K K/C) \cdot \dot{K}/K$$

$$- q_K(KPA/C) \cdot \{(\dot{KPA}/KPA) - (\dot{x}/x)\}$$

$$= \epsilon_{C_t}' - b[6,7], \quad (7)$$

where the bias $b[6,7]$ simply reflects the difference between the correct and traditional measure

---

5. For a proof see the Appendix.
6. A proof is given in the Appendix.

of productivity growth in the face of pollution abatement capital regulation, or the "error" in traditional computations from assuming KPA is used to produce output instead of a cleaner environment. Thus a positive value of $b[6, 7]$ implies that the true measure of productivity growth (6) is greater than the traditional measure (7).

Interpretation of this bias relies on returning to the first order conditions of the original maximization problem of the firm and developing the concept of measuring actual marginal costs. (3a) says that with pollution abatement capital regulations the price of output must cover not only marginal input costs but also the costs of satisfying the regulations; extra "rents" must be generated to pay for use of the environment. However, for correct representation of productivity output must be evaluated at the actual level of marginal costs rather than at the observed output price which includes the returns to the environment. Thus in (6) as compared to (7) the weight on the $d \ln x/dt$ term is lower (one minus a positive number instead of one), the weight on the $d \ln K/dt$ term (which has a negative sign) is lower, and $d \ln K/dt$ is calculated as the change only in productive rather than total capital.

Although both (6) and (7) may show a decline in multifactor productivity growth in response to environmental regulations, the error in (7) arises from treating abatement capital as conventional capital, thus attributing the returns to use of the environment to capital. The error thus depends on the relative growth rates of output, which should be devalued to account for negative environmental impacts or rents to use of the environment, and the pollution abatement capital stock, which was included in the incorrect measurement of capital returns.

The sign of the bias is therefore theoretically ambiguous. When growth of pollution abatement capital exceeds growth of output, as would be expected when regulations initially are put into place or suddenly increase, the traditional expression underestimates productivity change. If KPA and x grow by the same rate, however, which may be the case in a steady state, the bias is zero. In this case the downward correction of the weight of output growth by the cost share of abatement capital equals the upward correction by not subtracting in the adjusted measure the weighted growth of pollution abatement capital.

It is also possible to compute a bias term which represents the impact on productivity growth arising from the existence of pollution abatement capital regulations. This can be accomplished by simulating a situation with no regulation at all, i.e., $KPA = 0$, and comparing it to the correct productivity measure when environmental regulations exist. The resulting bias can be interpreted as an indicator of the productivity impact of environmental regulations. Some qualifications and adaptations of the framework are necessary, however, in order to apply this concept, since the nonparametric model is not capable of true simulation of a situation with no KPA requirements.

First, it should be noted that a correct measure of the impact of pollution abatement regulation on productivity growth requires consideration of what investment and output would have been in the absence of environmental regulation. This is not possible in the nonparametric framework; all that can be measured is the impact of removing all pollution abatement equipment from the total capital stock. In this case the KPA term must be deleted from (6). The measure of marginal cost is thus based on the equivalence of price and marginal cost without the wedge resulting from KPA requirements. In addition, the computation of K must be adapted since the return to capital depends on the existence of pollution abatement capital. In particular, once the marginal cost used to evaluate productivity growth is increased to equal price, this cost must be imputed to an input, which in the constant returns to scale case becomes the residual capital return. Thus we must assume a higher ex-post rate of return on capital, included in the ex-post price of capital $\bar{q}_K$ without regulation. Then from $\bar{q}_K K = q_K(K + KPA)$ we obtain $\bar{q}_K = q_K(K + KPA)/K$.

The resulting productivity growth measure with no regulations is

$$-\partial \ln C/\partial t = \dot{x}/x - \sum_j (q_j v_j/C) \cdot \dot{v}_j/v_j - (\bar{q}_K K/C) \cdot \dot{K}/K$$

$$= (\{p \cdot x - q_K \cdot KPA\}/C) \cdot \dot{x}/x - \sum_j (q_j v_j/C) \cdot \dot{v}_j/v_j - (q_K K/C) \cdot \dot{K}/K$$

$$- q_K (KPA/C)\{(\dot{K}/K) - (\dot{x}/x)\}$$

$$= \epsilon_{Ct}{}' - b[6,8], \tag{8}$$

where the new bias term reflects the productivity difference between the no regulation and existing regulation cases. This bias depends on the difference between output growth and capital growth since without regulation the "rents" to pollution abatement capital or regulation expenditures which were counted as before tax revenues are now attributed to capital returns. If $b[6,8]$ is negative, productivity growth under (6) is less than productivity growth (8) under no regulation.

III. Empirical Results

Data

The U.S. and Canadian manufacturing data for capital, labor and output prices and quantities respectively were provided by Berndt and Wood [1] and G. Campbell Watkins [25]. The corresponding German data were provided by Unger [23]. Output is net output, i.e., total output minus materials and energy expenditures.

The pollution abatement capital data for the U.S. is based on data on capital stocks and expenditure (constant and current) for pollution abatement capital equipment presented by Kappler and Rutledge [9]. This data was used to determine a beginning capital stock and investment over the period in pollution abatement capital. The price of capital was calculated from the zero profit condition as the ex-post price of the total capital stock, including K and KPA. The Canadian pollution abatement capital data is more sparse. The data used is from the Statistics Canada publication *Water and Air Pollution Abatement Expenditures* [20], which provides information on air and water pollution expenditures only for 1970–75. This data is, however, based on the Class 24 and 27 CCA claims available in the Revenue Canada publication *Corporation Taxation Statistics* [18]. The data from this publication was therefore used to extrapolate the 1970–75 expenditure numbers forward and backward.

For the German data, data collection on the costs of environmental protection regulations began in 1970 with the proclamation of an environmental protection program by the German government. The data on net investment for pollution abatement equipment for the years 1971–75 have been developed by the *Umweltbundesamt* (Federal Office for the Environment) [22] in Berlin. Since 1975 these data have been published yearly by the *Statistisches Bundesamt* [21]. To determine a capital stock series we calculated from the U.S. ratio of pollution abatement capital to total capital in 1970 the beginning capital stock in 1970 and cumulated the investment data according to the perpetual inventory method. Due to the problem of finding consistent data for several industries in each country we had to deal with aggregate numbers in this study. Standards on pollution abatement capital may be assumed to be the motivating regulatory force for environmental control over this aggregate, especially for Canada and Germany which rely

Table I. Value-Added Productivity Growth Indexes (percent) for U.S. Manufacturing, Traditional and *KPA*-adjusted Indexes and Differences

Year	Productivity			Biases	
	Traditional	*KPA*-Adjusted	*KPA* = 0	$b[6,7]$	$b[6,8]$
1960	6.462	6.445	6.474	−0.017	−0.029
1961	0.826	0.840	0.835	0.014	0.005
1962	10.950	10.842	10.932	−0.108	−0.018
1963	−1.318	−1.316	−1.335	0.002	0.019
1964	7.970	7.936	7.975	−0.034	−0.039
1965	2.026	2.000	2.004	−0.026	−0.004
1966	−5.501	−5.426	−5.471	0.075	0.045
1967	1.562	1.596	1.612	0.034	−0.016
1968	2.878	2.941	2.937	0.063	0.004
1969	0.555	0.677	0.662	0.122	0.015
1970	−4.865	−4.599	−4.708	0.266	0.109
1971	4.700	4.724	4.742	0.024	−0.018
1972	7.046	7.028	7.137	−0.018	−0.109
1973	6.754	6.836	6.934	0.082	−0.098
1974	−4.057	−3.554	−3.677	0.503	0.123
1975	−0.231	−0.128	−0.200	0.103	0.072
1976	5.471	5.400	5.527	−0.071	−0.121
1977	5.128	5.007	5.146	−0.121	−0.139
1978	1.263	1.382	1.412	0.119	−0.030
1979	0.176	0.513	0.441	0.337	0.072
1980	−1.987	−1.155	−1.486	0.832	0.331
Averages					
1960–67	2.872	2.865	2.878	−0.008	−0.001
1967–72	1.979	2.061	2.064	0.082	−0.002
1967–73	2.661	2.743	2.759	0.082	−0.016
1972–80	2.174	2.370	2.359	0.196	0.011
1973–80	1.565	1.788	1.762	0.223	0.026

heavily on standards. The U.S. system too is in principle based on a system of standards imposed by the Environmental Protection Agency (EPA), although in practice the regulation is often in terms of specification of control techniques.

Results

The productivity indexes calculated for the empirical comparison include indexes computed using traditional accounting methods (7), corrected indexes (6) and *KPA*-free indexes (8). Only one "variable" input was considered, labor, so the indexes represent multifactor productivity growth for net output. The differences between the traditional and corrected measures $b[6,7]$, and when *KPA* is or is not required $b[6,8]$ were also estimated. These indexes and biases were computed for the U.S. for 1960–80 (Table I), Canada for 1967–80 (Table II) and Germany for 1972–81 (Table III). Summary information in terms of averages over selected time periods are reported at the bottom of the tables.

The first point to note is that in all of these countries, especially the U.S. and Canada, response to regulations is spread out and often delayed as long as possible because penalties for non-compliance are usually not very effective. This makes it very difficult to identify a particular year in which environmental regulations should begin to have an impact on productivity measures. In both North American countries purposive environmental regulation at the Federal level really commenced at the end of the 1960s; one would therefore not expect a large impact of environmental regulations on productivity measurements before this. In Germany the timing is similar; in 1971 the government became an active participant in environmental control. The impacts of environmental regulation for the three countries should therefore take place approximately during the same time period and are closely comparable.

The U.S. indexes in Table I show that productivity growth was quite large on average throughout the 1960s, and, as would be expected, the difference from incorporating the impact of pollution abatement capital expenditures is small. On average this impact becomes larger in the late 1960s. In periods of high KPA growth the traditional measures underestimates productivity growth. The impact in 1969 of purging the productivity measure of the KPA-effect, for example, is an increase in measured productivity of .122 percentage points. This caused measured productivity growth in that year to increase from .555 percent to .677 percent, approximately a 20 percent change in the growth rate. The strongest impact of KPA adjustment is in those years when productivity growth is catastrophic and there were strong increases in KPA, for example in 1974 and 1980.

As hypothesized by most researchers, the standard practice of including pollution abatement capital in productivity growth calculations appears overall to have a depressing effect on the evidence of productivity growth. This is evident from the positive averages of $b[6,7]$ after the late 1960s. The only post-1965 years in which this impact has the opposite sign are 1972, 1976 and 1977, all years of higher than average productivity growth. In these years the impact of strongly increasing output growth overwhelms the small changes in KPA. This is consistent with the interpretation of the bias $b[6,7]$, above. When output growth is strong, lowering the valuation of output to its marginal cost has a large impact relative to the increase in KPA.

For the case of no regulation, (8), reported in column three, would be one measure for the potential change in multifactor productivity growth. As expected by the expression for this bias, in periods of high growth rates of output and little investment (such as 1971–73 and 1976–78) $b[6,8]$ is negative and regulation has a depressing effect on the change in multifactor productivity.

Additional information on overall trends may be obtained from the summary statistics on average productivity growth rates provided at the end of the table. For the U.S., productivity growth dropped from an average of 2.872 percent per year for the traditional measure (7) from 1960 to 1967 to 2.661 percent from 1967 to 1973 and 1.565 percent from 1973 to 1980. The adjusted U.S. measures do "smooth" the productivity decline somewhat; the corresponding growth rates for (6) are 2.865 percent, 2.743 percent and 1.788 percent. Overall the upward trend in the average biases indicate this smoothing but show that the downward bias in the traditionally measured productivity growth indexes is small.

Somewhat different patterns appear in the productivity growth indexes for Canada reported in Table II. Overall both the productivity growth fluctuations and impacts of adjustment for KPA are stronger for Canada than for the U.S. The annual averages of productivity for Canada summarize evidence of a strong productivity growth decline over time; the average annual percentage growth rates for 1967–73 and 1973–80 for the traditional productivity calculations are 3.239 percent and .229 percent. This decline is, however, exacerbated rather than attenuated by the correction for KPA, which is evident from the declining (and sometimes negative toward the end of the sample) bias $b[6,7]$. By contrast, the adjustment does tend to smooth the yearly changes; the worst productivity years, especially 1975, have the largest positive biases. This is consistent

Table II. Value-Added Productivity Growth Indexes (percent) for Canadian Manufacturing, Traditional and KPA-adjusted Indexes and Differences

Year	Productivity			Biases	
	Traditional	KPA-Adjusted	KPA = 0	$b[6,7]$	$b[6,8]$
1967	−3.599	−3.478	−3.514	0.121	0.036
1968	4.052	4.158	4.152	0.106	0.006
1969	1.534	1.598	1.588	0.064	0.010
1970	−8.973	−8.806	−8.669	0.167	0.137
1971	12.003	12.124	12.268	0.121	−0.144
1972	5.891	6.039	6.129	0.148	−0.090
1973	11.762	11.884	12.200	0.122	−0.316
1974	−3.045	−2.883	−3.072	0.162	0.189
1975	−12.729	−12.152	−12.695	0.577	0.543
1976	4.213	4.267	4.353	0.054	−0.086
1977	3.870	3.836	3.932	−0.034	−0.096
1978	3.730	3.443	3.585	−0.287	−0.142
1979	3.003	2.643	2.730	−0.360	−0.087
1980	−8.969	−8.838	−9.078	0.131	0.240
Averages					
1967–72	1.818	1.939	1.992	0.121	−0.008
1967–73	3.239	3.360	3.451	0.121	−0.052
1972–80	0.858	0.918	0.898	0.057	0.017
1973–80	0.229	0.278	0.244	0.046	0.031

with the interpretation of the bias term $b[6,7]$; in these recession years $\dot{x}/x$ (and $\dot{K}/K$) became increasingly smaller than $K\dot{P}A/KPA$. Similarly, if the economy were not regulated, as $b[6,8]$ indicates especially for the years 1971–73 and 1976–79, in years of healthy growth of output the regulated economy shows lower growth in multifactor productivity.

The German productivity growth indexes in Table III provide evidence of much stronger and consistent productivity growth than in the U.S. and Canada, although the trends are similar. The KPA-adjusted measure indicates even higher multifactor productivity growth than traditionally estimated for all years except 1979. The depressing effect of KPA investment on traditional productivity measurements is quite substantial in the beginning, approximately .2 percent to .3 percent for each year from 1972–75, even though 1972 to 1974 otherwise were years of healthy productivity gains. After this period investment in KPA has much less effect on multifactor productivity measurement. Apparently initial investments to satisfy the standards were completed and growth of output and KPA were closer to the same size. An unregulated economy would have experienced even higher multifactor productivity growth in the highest growth years (1973, 1976, 1977); the bias $b[6,8]$ is negative in these years.

Finally, the averages for Germany highlight the relatively high and consistent productivity growth patterns reflected by the indexes. The traditionally measured 1973–80 average annual productivity growth rate is 2.855 percent, as compared to 1.565 percent and .229 percent for the U.S. and Canada. The corrected 1973–80 growth rate measure for Germany is 3.0 percent, compared to 1.788 percent for the U.S. and .278 percent for Canada, all showing greater average annual productivity growth with the depressing impacts of pollution abatement capital purchases removed. The percentage magnitudes are different, however; the bias $b[6,7]$ is largest for the U.S., with an average of .22 percentage points added to the productivity measure with the KPA

Table III. Value-Added Productivity Growth Indexes (percent) for German Manufacturing, Traditional and KPA-adjusted Indexes and Differences

Year	Productivity			Biases	
	Traditional	KPA-Adjusted	KPA = 0	$b[6,7]$	$b[6,8]$
1972	2.617	2.876	2.617	0.259	0.043
1973	3.502	3.711	3.740	0.209	−0.029
1974	2.552	2.767	2.745	0.215	0.022
1975	−1.774	−1.488	−1.616	0.286	0.128
1976	6.041	6.136	6.307	0.095	−0.165
1977	4.042	4.125	4.205	0.083	−0.080
1978	2.892	2.960	2.880	0.068	0.080
1979	5.011	4.996	4.916	−0.015	0.080
1980	0.573	0.588	0.584	0.015	0.004
1981	0.152	0.258	0.176	0.106	0.082
Averages					
1972–80	2.828	2.963	2.939	0.135	0.009
1973–80	2.855	2.974	2.970	0.120	0.005
1972–81	2.564	2.693	2.655	0.132	0.165
1973–81	2.555	2.673	2.660	0.118	0.014

adjustment, second for Germany with approximately .12 percentage points, and smallest for Canada which already exhibited the poorest productivity growth performance, with about a .05 percent difference. The error in traditional measures therefore has for this period the greatest impact on evidence of poor U.S. productivity performance.

In the case of no regulations the patterns are quite different. On average, in Germany, $b[6,8]$ is positive and increasing because of high investment rates. Thus productivity growth in the absence of environmental regulations would likely have been worse, especially in the later years of the sample. The same type of time trend is evident from the averages in the U.S. and Canada, although at least initially the impact would have been better productivity growth without environmental regulations. In the 1973–80 time period, without environmental regulation U.S. and Canadian productivity growth would have been about .03 percentage points worse per year, whereas Germany would have been only .005 percent worse on average. However, for both Canada and the U.S. this relatively large positive value arises because of the large 1980 value; because of sluggish investment productivity growth would have been .24 to .33 percentage points worse in 1980. Without the impact of this year, both Canada and the U.S. appear to have been worse off in general with environmental regulation whereas Germany is slightly better off.[7]

One interpretation of these results might be in the context of international competitiveness. In particular, the country with the larger (positive) $b[6,8]$ term has experienced the least productivity decline, and thus the least harm to competitiveness, from the impact of environmental regulations. This suggests that the reported productivity growth indexes provide some evidence of declining international competitiveness in the U.S. and Canada relative to Germany because of environmental regulations. This is implied from the generally negative values for $b[6,8]$ in the U.S. and Canada and positive in Germany, although, especially in Canada, poor productivity growth years would have been even worse without environmental regulation.

---

7. This is consistent with Meyers and Nakamura [12].

IV. Concluding Remarks

In this paper we have considered the often proposed suggestion that compliance with environmental regulations in the form of investment in "unproductive" capital, pollution abatement capital, KPA, has caused part of the observed "productivity slowdown" since the early 1970s in industrial countries. In particular, we have considered the effects of emission or discharge standards, and resulting investment in KPA to satisfy these standards, on the measurement of productivity growth for the manufacturing sectors of the U.S., Canada and Germany. The overall conclusion is that treating KPA incorrectly in productivity computations has biased productivity measures downward, particularly for later years in the sample and for poor productivity growth years. Thus investment to correct for this smooths some of the cyclical behavior and the downward time trend in conventional productivity growth measures. In addition, some evidence has been presented that KPA investment has depressed productivity growth for these countries on average, with the greatest impact in the North American countries.

Although the framework developed here is useful and provides theoretical justification for some assertions made in the literature, other hypotheses about the structure within which environmental legislation affects productivity growth may not be modeled and quantified using the type of nonparametric approach utilized here. For example, the measure of the impact of the existence of regulation here does not take the impact of corresponding output and investment changes into account. In addition, there are important indirect effects from control of pollution abatement technology which some authors have argued causes environmental regulation to be inefficient or cost-ineffective because of distortion of technical change and investment patterns. In reverse, incentives stemming from financial assistance for purchases of pollution abatement capital as compared to productive capital may distort investment decisions toward capital which may be classified as pollution abatement capital. Direct assessment of the associated costs and benefits of environmental regulation requires determination of a shadow value of pollution abatement capital which differs from that for productive capital. This, however, cannot be accomplished with the available data and a nonparametric framework since the ex-post returns only to total capital can be determined; the individual components cannot be separated. Further research along these lines may therefore be beneficial.

Appendix

a) To show $\partial \ln C/\partial \ln x + \partial \ln C/\partial \ln K + \partial \ln C/\partial \ln KPA = 1$—$C$ has long run constant returns to scale over x, K and KPA—note that this expression is equal to:

$$(\partial G/\partial x) \cdot x/C + (\partial G/\partial K + q_K) \cdot K/C + q_K \cdot KPA/C = (p_t - \tau f(KPA)\xi) \cdot x/C + q_K \cdot KPA/C$$

$$= p \cdot x/C - \tau \cdot NE/C + q_K \cdot KPA/C. \tag{a1}$$

Since $p \cdot x/C$ is equal to one by definition and $\tau \cdot NE = q_K \cdot KPA$, this is clearly equal to one. Q.E.D.

b) To prove (6), it is first necessary to determine the total derivative of C with respect to time:

$$d \ln C/dt = (1/C) \cdot (dG/dt + dq_K K/dt + dq_K KPA/dt)$$

$$= (1/C) \cdot (\partial G/\partial x) \cdot dx/dt + (\partial G/\partial K) \cdot dK/dt + \sum_j (\partial G/\partial q_j) \cdot dq_j/dt$$

$$+ K \cdot dq_K/dt + q_K \cdot dK/dt + KPA \cdot dq_K/dt + q_K \cdot dKPA/dt). \tag{b1}$$

following Ohta [14] the primal output-side measure of productivity—$\partial \ln x/\partial t$ as contrasted to the cost measure $\partial \ln C/\partial t$—is equivalent to the cost measure with constant returns to scale and can be calculated from (b1) by calculating $d \ln C/dt$ directly from total cost $C = \sum_j q_j v_j + q_K \cdot K + q_K \cdot KPA$ to equate to (b1):

$$d \ln C/dt = \dot{C}/C = \sum_j (q_j v_j/C) \cdot \dot{q}_j/q_j + \sum_j (q_j v_j/C) \cdot \dot{v}_j/v_j + (q_K K/C) \cdot \dot{q}_K/q_K$$
$$+ (q_K KPA/C) \cdot \dot{q}_K/q_K + (q_K K/C) \cdot \dot{K}/K + (q_K KPA/C) \cdot \dot{KPA}/KPA. \quad \text{(b2)}$$

Setting these two expressions for $d \ln C/dt$ equal, solving for $\partial \ln C/\partial t$, and using Shephard's lemma results in:

$$-\partial \ln C/\partial t = (G_x \cdot x/C) \cdot \dot{x}/x - \sum_j (q_j v_j/C) \cdot \dot{v}_j/v_j - (q_K K/C) \cdot \dot{K}/K, \quad \text{(b3)}$$

where $G_x \cdot x = p \cdot x - \tau \cdot NE$ by the first order conditions, so,

$$-\partial \ln C/\partial t = (\{p \cdot x - \tau \cdot NE\}/C) \cdot \dot{x}/x - \sum_j (q_j v_j/C) \cdot \dot{v}_j/v_j - (q_K K/C) \cdot \dot{K}/K. \quad \text{(b4)}$$

Q.E.D.

References

1. Berndt, Ernst R. and David O. Wood. "Energy Price Changes and the Induced Revaluation of Durable Capital in U.S. Manufacturing During the OPEC Decade." Manuscript, MIT Center for Energy Policy Research, January, 1984.
2. Christainsen, G. B. and R. H. Haveman, "The Contribution of Environmental Regulations to the Slowdown in Productivity Growth." *Journal of Environmental Economics and Management*, December 1981, 381–90.
3. Conrad, Klaus, "An Incentive Scheme for Optimal Pricing and Environmental Protection." Forthcoming in the *Journal of Institutional and Theoretical Economics*.
4. Crandall, R. W., "Pollution Controls and Productivity Growth in Basic Industries", in *Productivity Measurement in Regulated Industries*, edited by T. G. Cowing and R. E. Stevenson. New York: Academic Press, 1981, pp. 347–68.
5. Dasgupta, Partha. *The Control of Resources*. Cambridge, Massachusetts: Harvard University Press, 1982.
6. Denison, Edward F. *Accounting for Slower Economic Growth: The United States in the 1970s*. Washington D.C.: The Brookings Institution, 1979.
7. Gollop, F. M. and Mark J. Roberts, "Environmental Regulations and Productivity Growth: The Case of Fossil-fueled Electric Power Generation." *Journal of Political Economy*, August 1983, 654–73.
8. Kalt, J. P. "The Impact of Domestic Environmental Regulatory Policies on U.S. International Competitiveness." John F. Kennedy School of Government Energy and Environmental Policy Center Discussion Paper No. E-85-02, 1985.
9. Kappler, Frederick G. and Gary L. Rutledge, "Stock of Plant and Equipment for Air and Water Pollution Abatement in the United States, 1960–81." *Survey of Current Business*, November 1982.
10. Lau, Lawrence J., "Applications of Profit Functions", in *Production Economics: A Dual Approach to Theory and Applications*, edited M. A. Fuss and D. McFadden. Amsterdam: North-Holland, 1978.
11. Leontief, W. and D. Ford. "Air Pollution and the Economic Structure: Empirical Results of Input-Output Computations," in *Input-Output Techniques*, edited by A. Brody and A. P. Carter. Amsterdam: North-Holland, 1972.
12. Meyers, J. G. and L. Nakamura. "Energy and Pollution Effects on Productivity: A Putty-Clay Approach," in *New Developments in Productivity Measurement and Analysis*, edited by John W. Kendrick. Chicago: The University of Chicago Press for National Bureau of Economic Research, 1980.
13. Norsworthy, J. R., M. J. Harper and K. Kunze, "The Slowdown in Productivity Growth": Analysis of Some Contributing Factors." *Brookings Papers on Economic Activity*, 2: 1979, 387–421.
14. Ohta, M., "A Note on the Duality Between Production and Cost Functions: Rate of Returns to Scale and Technical Progress." *Economic Studies Quarterly*, March 1975, 63–65.
15. Pasurka, C. A., "The Short-Run Impact of Environmental Protection Costs on U.S. Product Prices." *Journal of Environmental Economics and Management*, December 1984, 380–90.
16. Pittman, R. W., "Issues in Pollution Control: Interplant Cost Differences and Economies of Scale." *Land Economics*, February 1981, 1–17.

17. ———, "Multilateral Productivity Comparisons with Undesirable Output." *The Economic Journal*, December, 1983, 883–91.

18. Revenue Canada. "Corporation Taxation Statistics." Corporate Statistics Division, Ottawa, various years.

19. Robinson, D. H., "Who Pays for Industrial Pollution Abatement?" *The Review of Economics and Statistics*, November 1985, 702–5.

20. Statistics Canada. "Water and Air Pollution Abatement Expenditures 1970–75." Business Finance Division, Financial, Taxation and General Research Section, Ottawa, August 1978.

21. Statistisches Bundesamt, Fachserie 19, Reihe 3. *Investitionen für Umweltschutz im Produzieren den Gewerbe*. Various issues since 1975.

22. Umweltbundesamt, Berichte 9/83, "Struktur and Entwicklung der Umweltschutzindustrie in der Bundesrepublik Deutschland." Berlin, 1983.

23. Unger, Rolf. "Theorie und Messung der totalen Faktorproduktivität, 1960–1981." Ph.D. Thesis, University of Mannheim, 1985.

24. Walter, J., "The Pollution Content of American Trade." *Western Economic Journal*, March 1973, 61–70.

25. Watkins, G. C. "The Relationship Between Energy and Other Production Inputs in Canadian Manufacturing Revisited." Prepared for Energy, Mines and Resources, Canada, by DataMetrics Ltd., March, 1985.

[7]

Environmental Regulation and Profitability: An Application to Swedish Pulp and Paper Mills

RUNAR BRÄNNLUND[1], ROLF FÄRE[2] and SHAWNA GROSSKOPF[2]
[1] *Department of Economics, University of Umeå, S-901 87 Umeå, Sweden;* [2] *Department of Economics, Southern Illinois University at Carbondale, Carbondale, IL 62901-4515, U.S.A.*

Abstract. In this paper we analyze the impact on firm profits of the environmental regulations in the Swedish pulp and paper industry. The approach taken is a non-parametric programming model of the technology. A feature of this industry is that environmental regulations are determined individually for each mill. A question, then, is if these individual regulations have a similar impact on firm profits. The approach in this paper allows us to calculate both the regulated and unregulated profits, which means that the severity of the regulations, in terms of foregone profits, can be calculated for each mill. The empirical result shows that the impact on the mills varies substantially, and that the burden from the regulations is less severe in 1990 than in 1989.

Key words. Environmental regulation, pulp and paper, profit.

1. Introduction

Industrial activity is in most cases characterized by some kind of negative externality. By negative externalities we mean technological externalities, i.e., negative side effects from a particular firm's (or individual's) activity which reduces the production possibility set (feasible consumption set) for other firms (individuals). Well known from the literature is that these kinds of externalities, or production of "bads", will be excessive in the absence of corrective measures. Such corrective measure include Pigovian taxes, permit markets, and direct regulation. In Sweden it is stipulated that environmental policy should be based on individual permits, or direct regulation on each source, and investment in best-practice technology.[1] Economic instruments, such as taxes, which have been used infrequently, have only been viewed as complements to the standards approach.

The Swedish pulp and paper industry is a sector which is subject to individual permits, i.e., each plant is allowed to discharge a specific amount of pollutants. In this paper, the aim is to analyze the impact on this industry, and especially the effect on firm profits, of the environmental regulations imposed on the Swedish pulp and paper industry. The approach we take to accomplish this is a non-parametric programming model of the technology in this industry.

The empirical work in this area has employed a variety of approaches. One of the earliest attempts to estimate the effects of environmental regulations in the pulp and paper industry is a study by Pittman (1981). Using econometric methods, he estimates the shadow price of emissions from the pulp and paper industry in the US using a restricted profit maximizing approach. In Barbera and McConnel (1986) and (1990), the idea is that environmental protection regulations force the firm to invest in abatement capital, which has a crowding out effect on productive investments. To test this idea they use a cost minimization approach, and they estimate the cost function parameters econometrically. Gollop and Roberts (1983) take another point of departure which, at least implicitly, takes uncertainty into account. In order to estimate the effect of sulphur dioxide emission restrictions on the rate of productivity growth in the electric power industry, they develop a variable measuring regulatory intensity. The idea is that an increase in the regulatory intensity shifts the cost function upwards, implying a change in the input mix. The cost function in this case is also estimated with econometric methods. Brännlund and Liljas (1993) use the idea proposed by Gollop and Roberts and a restricted profit maximization approach to estimate the shadow prices of the waste load from the Swedish pulp industry. Färe *et al.* (1993) and Hetemäki (1994) calculate the shadow prices of undesirable outputs from the US and Finnish pulp and paper industry, respectively, using a distance function approach. In Färe *et al.* a linear programming approach is adopted (deterministic), while Hetemäki uses an econometric approach.

The remainder of the paper is structured as follows. Some institutional facts, as well as a short description of the environmental impact of the pulp and paper industry complete this introductory section. In Section 2 we introduce the theory on which the empirical investigation rests. Section 3 is devoted to a description of the data, while Section 4 contains the empirical results. We conclude with some remarks and a possible extension of the model in Section 5.

It is well known that the Swedish Pulp and Paper industry is an important part of the Swedish economy. It employs 54,000 people and provides 15% of manufacturing exports each year. However, while providing welcome income opportunities for the population, the pulp and paper industry places a heavy burden on the environment. For instance, the industry accounts for more than fifty percent of the total discharge of biological oxygen demand (BOD) and virtually all the discharge of chlorinated compounds (AOX) in Sweden. Since most of the pulp and paper mills are located along the Swedish east coast, the emissions end up in the Gulf of Bothnia, the Bothnian Sea and the Baltic Sea.

The discharge of suspended solids (fibre) affects both the behaviour of fish and their ability to grow and breathe. It can also create mud banks which change the structure of the sea bed and, thereby, affect fish and other creatures in the sea. When oxygen demanding substances, such as BOD and COD, are discharged into water, the level of oxygen is reduced. Some of these effluents also affect photosynthesis. How fast these substances break down depends both on the temperature and on the amount of oxygen in the water. The warmer the water is, the faster these substances break down. BOD (biochemical oxygen demand) and COD (chemical oxygen demand) are measures of how much oxygen is needed to break down the substances. If the amount of oxygen in the water changes, it affects the marine life (salmon are the most sensitive fish to low oxygen concentration), especially fish-spawn. The firms use chlorine in the bleaching process. As many as 300 different types of chlorine substances are discharged into the sea. It takes a long time for these substances to break down and when they do so, some may become even more poisonous than before! Since the composition of bleached pulp mill effluents is very complex, it is almost impossible to characterise the impact of every substance on the environment. It is clear, though, that the effects are greater close to the factory, but effects can appear as far away as up to 50 km from the source. The biological effects of the discharge of chlorine are injuries to fish spines and changes in their vertebrae. There are also serious physiological effects, such as damage to fish livers and immune systems. Some of these effects, especially lowered reproduction capability, constitute a serious threat to the survival of the population of some species.

Because of these various impacts on the environment, the pulp and paper industry is subject to regulation. The substances which are regulated, apart from the already mentioned emissions of BOD and AOX, include chemical oxygen demand (COD), suspended solids (SS), and nutritive salts such as nitrogen. The emission standard applying to all of these substances is a plant-specific, absolute pollution standard, which means that each firm is allowed to discharge a specific amount of pollutants. The standard, or permit, is set by the "Environmental Protection Agency" (Koncessionsnämnden för Miljöskydd), which consists of two lawyers and two engineers, one from the industry and one from the Swedish Environmental Protection Board. The agency's decision concerning the pollution permit has, typically, been contested, either by the firm or by the monitoring authority (The Swedish Environmental Protection Board). The final decision, which is made by the government, has in most cases been against the industry. According to the law concerning environmental protection, every firm that discharges environmentally dangerous substances has to ensure that its emissions do not exceed the limitations set specifically for it. Ensuring compliance is achieved by running checks, and issuing an annual report. So far, no penalties have been levied on any company.

2. Short-Run Profit Maximization

In this section we develop a short-run profit maximization model. This model is used in the evaluation of the cost of regulation. In particular we compute the ratio of short-run profit with and without regulation and use the ratio as a measure of regulatory "costs".

The technology is modelled as an output correspondence, mapping input vectors $x \in R_+^N$ into subsets of outputs $P(x)$, where $P(x) = \{(y, z): x \text{ can produce } (y, z)\}$. The subvector $y \in R_+^M$ denotes the desirable or good outputs, while $z \in R_+^Q$ denotes the undesirable or bad outputs. It is assumed that $P(x)$ is a compact set and that outputs (y, z) are weakly disposable, i.e., if $(y, z) \in P(x)$ and $0 \leq \theta \leq 1$ then $(\theta y, \theta z) \in P(x)$. This assumption models the idea that disposing of the bads is not a free activity, but it requires giving up some of the good outputs. In addition to imposing weak disposability, we assume that the desirable outputs are freely disposable, i.e., $(y, z) \in P(x)$ and $\hat{y} \leq y \Rightarrow (\hat{y}, z) \in P(x)$. The disposability assumptions are illustrated in Figure 1.

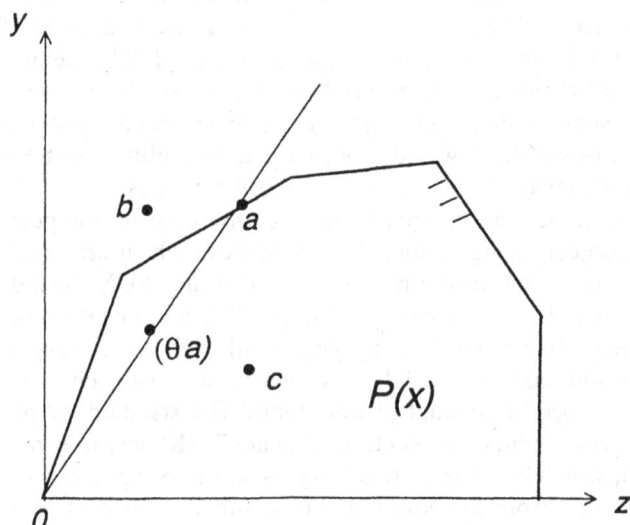

Fig. 1. The output set.

The output set in Figure 1 illustrates the conditions that the two outputs (y, z) are weakly disposable and that the desirable output y is in addition freely disposable. For example, point a is feasible and so is its proportional contraction (θa). Free disposability of y is verified for points a and c. However, b is not feasible showing that the undesirable output is not freely disposable.

The regulatory constraints facing the firms are quantitative in nature, i.e., each of the undesirable outputs is restricted in quantity. For say z_q, it cannot exceed a given bound $\bar{z}_q$, thus $z_q \leq \bar{z}_q$, $q = 1, \ldots, Q$. We denote these constraints as

$$Z(\bar{z}) = \{(y, z): z_q \leq \bar{z}_q, q = 1, \ldots, Q, y \in R_+^M\}. \tag{1}$$

The quantitative constraints in (1) are similar to rationing, familiar from consumer theory, see e.g. Deaton (1981). The regulated output set, i.e., the intersection between $P(x)$ and $Z(\bar{z})$ is illustrated in Figure 2. The regulated output set consists of the intersection $P(x) \cap Z(\bar{z})$, and it is bounded by the line segments ($0A\bar{z}0$). In our example the constraints are binding in the sense that $P(x)$ is not a proper subset of $Z(\bar{z})$.

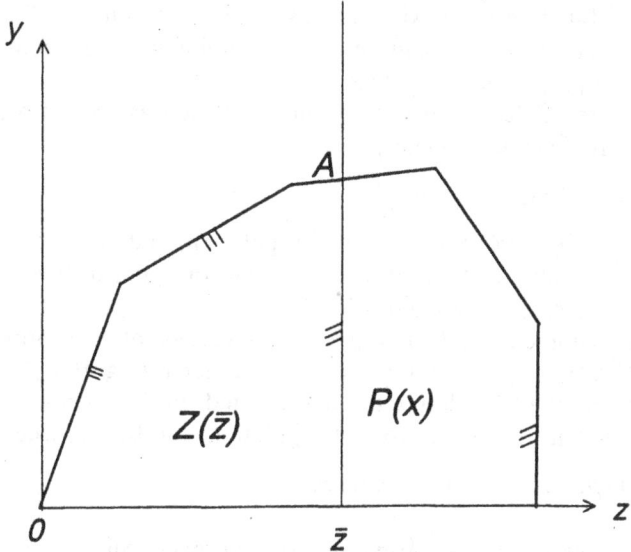

Fig. 2. The regulated output set.

In order to introduce the short-run profit function, we assume that the prices of the desirable goods are known. We denote them by $p \in R_+^M$. Prices of the bads, on the other hand, are not known. Finally, we denote the prices of the variable inputs by $\tilde{w} \in R_+^{\tilde{N}}$, where $\tilde{N} < N$, i.e., we assume that the last $(N - \tilde{N})$ inputs are fixed. Under these conditions we define the short-run quantity constrained profit function as

$$\tilde{\pi}(p, \tilde{w}, \hat{x}, \bar{z}) = \max \sum_{M=1}^{M} p_m y_m - \sum_{N=1}^{\tilde{N}} \tilde{w}_n \tilde{x}_n \qquad (2)$$

$$\text{s.t.} \quad (y, z) \in P(x) \cap Z(\bar{z}),$$

where $x = (\tilde{x}, \hat{x})$ with $\hat{x}$ denoting the subvector of fixed inputs, and $\tilde{x} = (x_1, \ldots, x_{\tilde{N}})$ denoting the variable inputs. The short-run unregulated profit function is

$$\pi(p, \tilde{w}, \hat{x}) = \max \sum_{M=1}^{M} p_m y_m - \sum_{N=1}^{\tilde{N}} \tilde{w}_n \tilde{x}_n \qquad (3)$$

$$\text{s.t.} \quad (y, z) \in P(x).$$

Following the argument by Deaton (1981) or Färe and Logan (1983) one can show the following relationship between the two profit functions

$$\pi(p, \tilde{w}, \hat{x}) = \max_{\bar{z}} \hat{\pi}(p, \tilde{w}, \hat{x}, \bar{z}) \tag{4}$$

This shows that the unregulated short-run profit functions can be retrieved from the regulated function by maximizing over the constraints, $\bar{z}$. Recall Figure 2, the maximization over, $\bar{z}$ can be seen as "unbinding" the constraints and making $P(x)$ a proper subset of $Z(\bar{z})$.

Our measure of "cost" of regulation is defined as the ratio of the two short-run profit functions, namely

$$\hat{\pi}(p, \tilde{w}, \hat{x}, \bar{z})/\pi(p, \tilde{w}, \hat{x}). \tag{5}$$

This measures the "profit loss" due to regulation, and since $\hat{\pi}(p, \tilde{w}, \hat{x}, \bar{z}) \le \pi(p, \tilde{w}, \hat{x})$, the value of this ratio is less than or equal to one; it takes the value one if the regulation is not binding.

There is a parametric and a non-parametric method of calculating the profit ratio (5). The first approach consists of parameterizing $\hat{\pi}(p, \tilde{w}, \hat{x}, \bar{z})$, then making the use of (4) to derive the unregulated profit function (3). In other words, the ratio in (5), or the cost of regulation, can be constructed as

$$\hat{\pi}(p, \tilde{w}, \hat{x}, \bar{z})/\max_{\bar{z}} \hat{\pi}(p, \tilde{w}, \hat{x}, \bar{z}) \tag{6}$$

In this paper we choose a non-parametric approach. Suppose there are $k = 1, \ldots, K$ observations of inputs $x^k \in R_+^N$, good and bad outputs $y^k \in R_+^M$, $z^k \in R_+^Q$, respectively. The technology generated from these data that satisfies the previously discussed disposability assumptions may be written as

$$\begin{aligned}
P(x) = \{(y, z); & \sum_{k=1}^{K} \lambda_k y_{km} \ge y_m, \, m = 1, \ldots, M, \\
& \sum_{k=1}^{K} \lambda_k z_{kq} = z_q, \, q = 1, \ldots, Q, \\
& \sum_{k=1}^{K} \lambda_k x_{kn} \le x_n, \, n = 1, \ldots, N, \\
& \lambda_k \ge 0 \qquad , k = 1, \ldots, K, \sum_{k=1}^{K} \lambda_k \le 1\}.
\end{aligned} \tag{7}$$

To verify that (7) satisfies weak disposability, let $(y^\circ, z^\circ) \in P(x^\circ)$ and let $0 < \theta \le 1$. We need to show that $(\theta y^\circ, \theta z^\circ) \in P(x^\circ)$.

$(y^\circ, z^\circ) \in P(x^\circ)$ is equivalent to

$$\sum_{k=1}^{K} \lambda_k^\circ y_{km} \ge y_k^\circ, \, m = 1, \ldots, M,$$
$$\sum_{k=1}^{K} \lambda_k^\circ z_{kq} = z_q^\circ, \, q = 1, \ldots, Q,$$
$$\sum_{k=1}^{K} \lambda_k^\circ x_{kn} \le x_n^\circ, \, n = 1, \ldots, N,$$

for some $\lambda_k^\circ \ge 0$, $k = 1, \ldots, K$, with $\sum_{k=1}^{K} \lambda_k^\circ \le 1$. Since $0 < \theta \le 1$, we have

$$\sum_{k=1}^{K} \theta \lambda_k^\circ y_{km} \ge \theta y_m^\circ, \, m = 1, \ldots, M,$$
$$\sum_{k=1}^{K} \theta \lambda_k^\circ z_{kq} = \theta z_q^\circ, \, q = 1, \ldots, Q,$$
$$\sum_{k=1}^{K} \theta \lambda_k^\circ x_{kn} \le \theta x_n^\circ, \, n = 1, \ldots, N,$$

where $(\lambda_k^o) \geq 0$, and $\sum_{k=1}^{K} \theta\lambda_k^o \leq 1$.

Moreover, $\theta x_n^o \leq x_n^o$, $n = 1, \ldots, N$, thus take $\hat{\lambda}_k = \theta\lambda_k^o$ and we have shown that $(\theta y^o, \theta z^o) \in P(x^o)$.

The desirable outputs $(y_1, \ldots, y_M)$ are also freely disposable, which can be seen from the relevant inequalities.[2] Moreover, we note that (7) satisfies Non-Increasing Returns to Scale (NIRS), i.e.,

$$P(kx) \subseteq kP(x), \ k \geq 1. \tag{8}$$

See Grosskopf (1986) for a discussion of how the restriction on λ, i.e., $\sum \lambda_k \leq 1$ implies NIRS.

Whenever the prices of outputs and variable inputs are known, we can calculate the unregulated short run profit function for firm k' as

$$\pi(p^{k'}, \tilde{w}^{k'}, \hat{x}^{k'}) = \max \sum_{M=1}^{M} p_{k'm} y_m - \sum_{N=1}^{\tilde{N}} \tilde{w}_{k'n} x_n \tag{9}$$

s.t. $\sum_{k=1}^{K} \lambda_k y_{km} \geq y_m$, $m = 1, \ldots, M$,
$\sum_{k=1}^{K} \lambda_k z_{kq} = z_q$, $q = 1, \ldots, Q$,
$\sum_{k=1}^{K} \lambda_k x_{kn} \leq x_n$, $n = 1, \ldots, \tilde{N}$,
$\sum_{k=1}^{K} \lambda_k x_{kn} \leq \hat{x}_{k'n}$, $n = \tilde{N} + 1, \ldots, \tilde{N}$,
$\lambda_k \geq 0$, $k = 1, \ldots, K$, $\sum_{k=1}^{K} \lambda_k \leq 1$.

Note that since there are no prices or restrictions on the undesirable outputs $(z_1, \ldots, z_Q)$, these play no role in (9) and could have been omitted. The case is different though under regulation. Recall that for k', $z_q \leq \bar{z}_{k'q}$, $q = 1, \ldots, Q$. Thus the regulated short run profit function can be written for k', as

$$\hat{\pi}(p^{k'}, \tilde{w}^{k'}, \hat{x}^{k'}, \bar{z}^{k'}) = \max \sum_{M=1}^{M} p_{k'm} y_m - \sum_{N=1}^{\tilde{N}} \tilde{w}_{k'n} x_n \tag{10}$$

s.t. $\sum_{k=1}^{K} \lambda_k y_{km} \geq y_m$, $m = 1, \ldots, M$,
$\sum_{k=1}^{K} \lambda_k z_{kq} \leq \bar{z}_{k'q}$, $q = 1, \ldots, Q$,
$\sum_{k=1}^{K} \lambda_k x_{kn} \leq x_n$, $n = 1, \ldots, \tilde{N}$,
$\sum_{k=1}^{K} \lambda_k x_{kn} \leq \hat{x}_{k'n}$, $n = \tilde{N} + 1, \ldots, \tilde{N}$,
$\lambda_k \geq 0$, $k = 1, \ldots, K$, $\sum_{k=1}^{K} \lambda_k \leq 1$.

3. The Empirical Model and Data

In order to produce pulp, y, we assume that three variable inputs are used; labor, x_l, wood fibre, x_f, and energy, x_e, and one fixed factor, capital $\hat{x}$. The respective prices on the desirable output and the variable inputs are denoted p, w_l, w_f, and w_e.

The data we use is a panel data set for the Swedish pulp and paper industry.

The data sources are primary data for the pulp and paper industry gathered by Statistics Sweden and the Swedish Environmental Protection Board.

The part of the data set used here contains annual information from 41 pulp mills for the period 1986–90. It includes information on quantities, both in physical and monetary terms, of sulphate pulp, sulphite pulp and mechanical pulp. Data on emissions of BOD, COD and suspended soils as well as factor inputs of labor, capital, electricity, and materials (fibre), both in physical and monetary terms are also provided. The emission data are the sum of daily emissions, divided by the number of production days, i.e., the daily average level. Prices of the output as well as all variable inputs, labor, energy and materials, are calculated by dividing the production and input values by the respective quantities. Also included in the data set is information on firm specific regulations of emission of BOD, COD and SS (suspended solids). A problem though, is that these data are only available for 1989 and 1990. Unfortunately this means that the model can be estimated only for the period 1989–1990. Another problem is that no data on investment in abatement capital exists. For this reason we view this model as a short run model where all capital is fixed.

Descriptive statistics for the data are presented in Table A.1 (1989) and Table A.2 (1990) in the Appendix.

4. Results

The maximization problems in (9) and (10) are solved by using linear programming techniques (see Färe *et al.* (1990)). The solutions for each observation are then used in (5) to obtain the cost of regulation in terms of the ratio of the regulated and unregulated profits.

The average ratios for different processing categories and different years, and for the whole sample, are presented in Table I.

One interesting result is that the profit ratio increases between 1989 and 1990 for all processing categories, implying that the regulations have become less severe. One explanation for this may be that the regulations, or permits, are fixed for quite long periods. In fact, almost every firm has an unchanged

Table I. Average ratio between regulated and unregulated profits for the whole sample and for different processing categories. Standard deviation in parentheses.

Sample	1989	1990
All	0.83 (0.23)	0.96 (0.15)
Bleached sulphate	0.98 (0.05)	0.99 (0.02)
Unbleached sulphate	0.83 (0.23)	0.98 (0.05)
Bleached sulphite	0.62 (0.41)	0.81 (0.43)
Unbleached sulphite	0.62 (0.32)	0.96 (0.08)
Mechanical	0.80 (0.17)	0.99 (0.03)

permit level between 1989 and 1990. This, combined with technological progress (or the tuning of the production process), may be one explanation.[3] This result is emphasized by the figures in Table A.3 in the appendix, which shows that in 1989 27 out of 41 firms (66%) have a profit ratio that equals unity, implying that they are unaffected by the regulations, while in 1990 36 out of 41 (88%) are unaffected.

A notable result is that the producers using unbleached sulphite and mechanical processes are hurt more by the regulations than the others.

These results are based on average values. In order to formally test whether the size of the firm, or the type of pulp produced, have any significant effect on the profit ratio, we run the following regression:[4]

$$\left(\frac{\hat{\pi}}{\pi}\right)_{kt} = \left[1 + \exp\left(\alpha_0 + \alpha_1 y_{kt} + \sum_i \beta_i D_{ikt} + \delta I_{kt} + \varepsilon_t\right)\right]^{-1},$$

where k denotes firm k and t is the time subscript. D is a dummy variable which takes the value of one if the firm belongs to the ith processing category. The processing categories are bleached sulphate ($i = 1$), unbleached sulphate ($i = 2$), and unbleached sulphite ($i = 3$). The fourth group, mechanical pulp, is thus the reference group, captured by the overall constant α_0. The variable I is a dummy variable which takes the value of one if pulp production is integrated with paper production. Hence, if α_1 and β_i, $i = 1, \ldots, 3$, are jointly zero, we cannot reject the hypothesis that the profit ratio is independent of firm characteristics. The choice of functional form forces the residuals to be such that the fitted ratio stays between zero and one.

The results from the regression are presented in Table II.

The most striking result in Table II is that most of the estimated parameters are not significantly different from zero. A tentative conclusion would then be that the severity of the prevailing regulation is independent on which processing category the firm employs. Firm size, however, seems to matter; large firms seems to be worse off than small ones. Holding firm size constant we see that firms producing unbleached sulphate and sulphite are affected most

Table II. Regression results. Dependent variable is $\hat{\pi}/\pi$.

	Parameter	t-ratio
α_0	−9.97	−2.10
α_1	0.000012	2.13
β_1	−12.50	−0.02
β_2	4.97	1.20
β_3	3.79	0.97
δ	−0.39	−0.44
R^2	0.14	
logl	110.4	
NOBS	82	

by the environmental regulations, compared to mechanical pulp. The negative sign of β_1 implies that environmental regulations are less severe for producers of unbleached sulphate. In addition, pulp producers that are integrated with paper production seem to be less affected by the regulation that non-integrated firms.

To test whether there are any differences between different firms, in terms of size and processing category, we use the likelihood ratio test. In the first test the null hypothesis is that all firms are affected to the same extent by the regulations, i.e., we estimate the model with a constant term only. In the second test the null hypothesis is that the effects from regulations are independent of processing category, i.e., we estimate the model with a constant term and a parameter representing firm size (α_1). The results are presented in Table III.

Table III. Likelihood ratio test.

Test	Test Statistic	Critical value $\alpha = 0.05$
L_1	13.0	11.07
L_2	11.8	7.81

The results from the first test yield a rejection of the null hypothesis, i.e., firms seem to be affected differently by the regulations. The second test also yields a rejection of the null hypothesis. In other words, the effects of environmental regulations also depend on the process employed. The result that different firms face different costs from the regulations may indicate that the prevailing regulation scheme is ineffective. To be more precise one can state that, given that some firms' profits seem to be unaffected by the regulations it must be profitable to lower the allowable permit marginally for these firms, and increase the permits marginally for those firms facing a high cost.

5. Conclusions

In this paper we have tried to calculate the cost of environmental regulation imposed on the Swedish wood pulp industry. The approach we have taken can be viewed as a semi-parametric approach. A programming non-parametric approach is used to calculate the cost of environmental regulation in terms of the ratio between regulated and unregulated profits. This ratio is then used as the dependent variable in a parametric regression model where the independent variables are firm size and dummy variables representing different kinds of production processes.

To summarize the empirical results we have found that some firms do, which we should expect, encounter a cost, or loss in profit, due to the environmental regulations imposed on them. It should also be stressed that for 27 out of 41 firms in 1989, and 36 out of 41 in 1990 the ratio between regulated and unregulated profits is equal to unity, which implies that they are unaffected by the regulations. From a policy point of view this latter result indicates that the prevailing regulations system may be ineffective in the sense that some firms bear a relatively heavy burden. From the regression analysis it was found that large firms suffered more from the regulations than small firms.

There are, of course, problems connected with an analysis like this. One objection with respect to the model is that we *assume* weak disposability, which means that we cannot really verify, or test, this assumption.[5] Another weakness with the model is that the regulatory constraints are in the form of absolute limits, meaning that constraints are never violated, and that firms which pollute less than the allowed level in this model are unconstrained. However, if the discharges of the bads are subject to random fluctuations we may find firms which actually discharge more than the allowed level, and some firms which discharge less than the allowed level but still are constrained (see Brännlund and Liljas (1993)). A possible extension of the model would then be to assume that production of bads (and/or goods) are subject to random fluctuations. Then, given that a firm decides to not violate the constraint by a given probability, they must on average pollute less than the allowed level. In a deterministic model like the present one, this behavior would be interpreted as if regulations were non-binding, while they in fact are affecting the firm.

Acknowledgements

We acknowledge research grants from the STORA foundation and the Swedish Council of Forest and Agricultural Research (SJFR).

Appendix

Table A.1. Descriptive statistics, 1989.

	Mean	Std Dev	Minimum	Maximum
y	257732.7	189073.7	30720.0	872615.0
z_{BOD}	7.90	7.68	0.34	31.0
z_{COD}	33.20	33.23	0.73	140.0
z_{SS}	4.86	7.61	0.12	42.0
x_l	826589.4	512932.6	106924.7	2267972.0
x_f	1060928.7	726275.6	82000.0	2543000.0
x_e	4.14 + 08	4.11D + 08	6.32D + 07	1.59D + 09
Capital	412.16	293.56	51.28	1368.5
p	3813.4	626.21	2751.3	4659.8
w_l	94.40	10.60	65.77	111.9
w_f	355.81	56.18	224.20	450.68
w_e	0.193	0.032	0.118	0.263
π	4.91D + 08	5.12D + 08	−2.87D + 07	2.69D + 09
NOBS = 41				

Note:
y = production of pulp, tons; z_{BOD} = emissions of BOD, tons/day; z_{COD} = emissions of COD, tons/day; z_{SS} = emissions of SS, tons/day; x_l = input of labor, hours; x_f = input of fibre, m^3; x_e = input of electricity, kwh; Capital, million of SEK; p = price of pulp, SEK/ton; w_l = price of labor, SEK/hour; w_f = price of fibre, SEK/m^3; w_e = price of electricity, SEK/kwh; π = observed short run profit, SEK.

Table A.2. Descriptive statistics, 1990.

	Mean	Std Dev	Minimum	Maximum
y	251116.5	175917.8	29199.0	855076.0
z_{BOD}	6.88	6.31	0.32	28.00
z_{COD}	29.18	27.73	0.73	120.00
z_{SS}	4.64	7.22	0.15	36.00
x_l	808736.2	497891.2	95932.7	2201970.0
x_f	1011433.1	687839.3	75000.0	2255600.0
x_e	4.03D08	4.07D + 08	6.03D + 07	1.51D + 09
Capital	407.49	287.12	51.32	1325.6
p	3538.1	370.8	2508.5	4001.1
w_l	105.21305	13.22128	77.80	139.59
w_f	373.26	63.31	232.76	510.81
w_e	0.21	0.039	0.139	0.332
π	3.67D + 08	4.01D + 08	−1.29D + 08	2.10D + 09
NOBS = 41				

Environmental Regulation and Profitability

Table A.3. Processing category and firm size for firms with profit ratio equal to unity (T = year, $r = \hat{\pi}/\pi$, y_1 = prod.bleached sulphate (dummy variable), y_2 = prod.unbleached sulphate (dummy variable), $y/\bar{y}$ = production of pulp divided by average production).

T	r	y_1	y_2	$y/\bar{y}$	T	r	y_1	y_2	$y/\bar{y}$
89	1	1	0	1.62	90	1	1	0	1.54
89	1	1	0	1.31	90	1	1	1	1.53
89	1	1	1	1.73	90	1	1	0	1.21
89	1	1	1	3.42	90	1	0	0	1.28
89	1	1	1	2.16	90	1	0	0	0.30
89	1	1	0	1.46	90	1	1	1	1.76
89	1	1	1	2.30	90	1	1	1	3.36
89	1	1	0	1.29	90	1	0	0	0.46
89	1	0	0	1.10	90	1	1	1	0.44
89	1	1	0	1.07	90	1	0	0	0.17
89	1	1	0	1.08	90	1	0	0	2.00
89	1	0	0	1.60	90	1	0	0	0.35
					90	1	1	0	1.18
					90	1	0	1	0.29
					90	1	1	0	0.94
					90	1	1	0	0.50
					90	1	0	0	0.12
					90	1	0	0	1.85
					90	1	1	0	1.40
					90	1	0	0	0.49
					90	1	0	1	0.66
					90	1	0	0	0.84
					90	1	1	1	2.03
					90	1	0	0	0.28
					90	1	0	1	0.95
					90	1	0	0	0.27
					90	1	0	1	0.85
					90	1	1	0	0.94
					90	1	1	0	1.10
					90	1	0	0	1.06
					90	1	1	0	1.12
					90	1	1	0	0.90
					90	1	0	0	1.53

Notes

[1] See Kriström and Wibe (1992).
[2] Note that the constraint for the undesirable outputs, z, is a strict equality rather than an inequality. This prevents the bads from being freely disposable.
[3] This result is in line with the findings in Brännlund and Liljas (1993), in which the shadow price of the constraint decreased between 1989 and 1990.
[4] In the regression analysis bleached and unbleached sulphite are merged into one category. The reason is that there are no variations in the profit ratio for bleached sulphite.
[5] According to Porter (1990) it is possible that tighter regulations, resulting in investment in abatement capital, may lead to productivity gains in general. Hence, reductions of emissions are observed simultaneously with increased production of the good.

References

Barbera, A. J. and D. McConnell (1986), 'Effects of Pollution Control on Industry Productivity: A Factor Demand Approach', *The Journal of Industrial Economics* **35**, 161–172.

Barbera, A. J. and D. McConnell (1990), 'The Impact of Environmental Regulations on Industry Productivity: Direct and Indirect Effects', *Journal of Environmental Economics and Management* **18**, 50–65.

Brännlund, R. and B. Liljas (1993), The Effects of Emission Standards. Umeå Economic Studies, No. 320, University of Umeå.

Deaton, A. S. (1981), 'Theoretical and Empirical Approaches to Consumer Demand under Rationing', in A. S. Deaton, ed., *Essays in the Theory and Measurement of Consumer Behavior*, Cambridge: Cambridge University Press.

Färe, R., S. Grosskopf and H. Lee (1990), 'A Nonparametric Approach to Expenditure-Constrained Profit Maximization', *American Journal of Agricultural Economics*, Aug., 574–581.

Färe, R., S. Grosskopf, C. A. K. Lovell and S. Yaisawarng (1993), 'Derivation of Shadow Prices for Undesirable Outputs: A Distance Function Approach', *Review of Economics and Statistics* **75**, 374–380.

Färe, R. and L. Logan (1983), 'The Rate of Return Regulated Firm: Cost and Production Duality', *The Bell Journal of Economics* **14**, 405–414.

Gollop, F. M. and M. J. Roberts (1983), 'Environmental Regulations and Productivity Growth: The Case of Fossil-fueled Electric Power Generation', *Journal of Political Economy* **91**, 654–673.

Grosskopf, S. (1986), 'The Role of the Reference Technology in Measuring Productive Efficiency', *Economic Journal* **96**, 499–513.

Hetemäki, L. (1994), 'The Impact of Pollution Control on Firm's Production Technology and Efficiency: A Stochastic Distance Function Approach', in R. Brännlund, B. Kriström and K. G. Löfgren, eds., *Environmental Economics*, Proceedings of the International Conference held at Ulvön, Sweden, June 10–13.

Kriström, B. and S. Wibe (1992), *En Effektiv Miljöpolitik*. Bilaga 6 till Långtidsutredningen 1992. Allmänna förlaget, Stockholm.

Pittman, R. W. (1981), 'Issue in Pollution Control: Interplant Cost Differences and Economies of Scale', *Land Economics* **57**, 1–17.

Porter, M. (1990), *The Competitive Advantage of Nations*, MacMillan, London.

Part II
Plant Location

[8]
The Effects of Environmental Regulation on Business Location in the United States

TIMOTHY J. BARTIK

ABSTRACT This article empirically examines whether variations in state environmental regulations have affected the location of manufacturing branch plants by the Fortune 500 companies. Using several measures of environmental regulation, no statistically significant effects of environmental regulation on business location are found. For most manufacturing industries, the estimates are precise enough to rule out the possibility of large effects of environmental regulation on business location. For highly polluting industries, however, the variance in the estimates is quite large. We cannot rule out the possibility of effects of environmental regulation on the location of highly polluting industries that are large enough to be important to policymakers.

THE UNITED STATES HAS EVOLVED a complex system of intermingled federal and state responsibility for environmental regulation. A common argument for strengthening federal authority within this regulatory system is that business would migrate to states with weak environmental controls. This result, it is argued, puts unfair pressure on states to weaken their environmental regulations.

Industrial migration in response to state environmental regulation can also be used as an argument for less federal intervention. If state environmental regulations are based on a reasoned weighing of the costs and benefits to state residents, then industrial migration in response to state regulations is economically efficient.[1] Uniform federal regulations would tend to shift polluting industries from states where marginal pollution damages are low to states where these damages are high. The greater the industrial migration in response to varying state regulations, the greater the inefficiency caused by federal preemption.

Timothy J. Bartik is an assistant professor of economics at Vanderbilt University.

Whichever view one takes, an important issue is whether business location decisions are substantially affected by state environmental regulations. The conventional wisdom is that this effect is probably small. The usual argument is that regulatory costs are quite small compared to other business costs, such as labor costs, and hence do not play an important role in business location. However, this theoretical argument, while persuasive, has not yet been tested in the literature by an empirical examination of the relationship of observed business location decisions to the stringency of state environmental regulations. This article seeks to fill this gap in the literature.[2]

Specifically, this article empirically examines the effects of state environmental regulations on the location of new manufacturing branch plants owned by the Fortune 500 companies during the 1970s. I use a data set on individual plant location decisions, originally developed by Roger Schmenner, that is more accurate than those used by previous researchers. The use of microdata, rather than aggregate data, allows a specific focus on new branch plants.

This focus on new branch plants has both benefits and costs for research on environmental regulation's effects on business location. Focusing on one type of location decision allows the empirical specification to be based on the usual microeconomic model of profit maximization. Changes in aggregate employment or value added in an area reflect so many different business location decisions (expansions, contractions, closings, and openings of both branch plants and small business) that it is difficult to develop a theory-based empirical specification. Focusing on new branch plants is better than focusing on existing plants because we are more likely to detect even small effects of state characteristics; new branches are probably more responsive to differentials in state characteristics than are existing plants whose mobility is limited by their extensive existing investments. Furthermore, environmental regulations in the U.S. are applied more stringently to new plants than existing plants.

On the other hand, this study's focus on new branch plants ignores possible effects of environmental regulation on small business. It is often asserted that there are economies of scale in business compliance with environmental regulation, and one would ideally like to examine both small business and branch plant location decisions. However, the data set used in this current study only contains information on branch plants, so an examination of small business is impossible in this study. While there are other publicly available business microdata, none is as accurate as the Schmenner data base.[3]

The results do not show any statistically significant effect of current variations in state environmental regulations upon business location. In most specifications and for most industries, the results are precise enough that we can rule out a substantively "large" negative effect of stricter state environmental regulations on business location. However, for a few specifications and a few highly polluting industries, the statistical estimates are not precise enough to rule out a negative regulatory effect on business location that might be large enough to concern some state policymakers.[4]

The plan of the article is as follows. The next section briefly outlines the post-1970 history of federal and state roles in environmental regulation, and attempts to show that federal concern over states using lax regulations to compete for business helped rationalize a stronger federal role. The section after that explains the data and theoretical model, and emphasizes the efforts made in this study to find the best possible measure of state environmental regulations. Then the empirical results are presented and interpreted. The concluding section suggests avenues for future research that might lead to more precise empirical results.

Historical Background on Federal-State Roles in Environmental Regulation

The Clean Air Act (CAA) of 1970 and the Federal Water Pollution Control Act Amendments (FWPCAA) of 1972 significantly strengthened federal authority over environmental regulation through such means as federal regulation of major new sources of pollution. An important rationale for federal intervention was that states were incapable of effective environmental regulation because of their need to compete for new business. The House Committee Report on the 1970 Clean Air Act stated this rationale as follows:

> The promulgation of Federal emission standards for new sources . . . will preclude efforts on the part of States to compete with each other in trying to attract new plants and facilities without assuming adequate control of large scale emissions therefrom. (H. Report No. 91-1146, in *Legislative History of the Clean Air Act* [1979], p. 3)

Although federal authority was strengtened by the 1970 and 1972 Acts, significant state disparities in environmental regulation of business were still possible. Under the CAA, regulatory standards for all existing plants—and the many new plants not in the few categories considered "major" by EPA— continued to be set by the states. Under the FWPCAA, the federal government set general standards for industries, but states were usually delegated the task of issuing the permits for allowable water pollution from a specific plant. Under both acts, states had primary responsibility for enforcement of both federal and state standards.

In the 1977 Clean Air Act Amendments and 1977 Clean Water Act Amendments, Congress sought to further reduce differences between states in environmental regulation. The 1977 CAA Amendments legislated a policy of "Prevention of Significant Deterioration" that required strict air pollution controls even in areas that already met federal air quality standards. The House Committee report stated the purpose of the PSD policy as follows:

> Abandonment of a policy of prevention of significant deterioration will encourage flight of industry—and jobs—from areas where pollution levels are approaching or exceed the minimum Federal standards to cleaner areas requiring less controls on industry. (H. Report 95-294, in *Legislative History of the Clean Air Act*, p. 133)

The 1977 CAA Amendments also required EPA to regulate additional types of major new pollution sources. The text of the amendments requires that EPA, in setting priorities for which new sources to regulate, should consider "the mobility and competitive nature of each such category of sources and the consequent need for nationally applicable new source standards of performance." The EPA was also required to consider petitions from state governors for categories of new sources to be federally regulated. The House Committee report stated that one of the purposes of these provisions was "to assure that industries do not play off states with weak or no environmental controls against states with stronger controls in decisions to locate new sources" (H. Report 95-294, *Legislative History*).

Concern over differing state environmental regulations played less of a role in the 1977 Clean Water Act Amendments. The CWA Amendments did strengthen EPA's authority to issue its own water pollution permit in lieu of a state's permit if EPA felt the permit was incorrect. The Senate committee criticized EPA for lax oversight of states which had been delegated responsibility for issuing permits.

> EPA has been much too hesitant to take any actions where states have [federally-] approved permit programs. The result might well be the creation of "pollution havens" in some of those states which have approved permit programs. This result is exactly what the 1972 amendments are designed to avoid. (S. Report 95-370, in *Legislative History of the Clean Water Act 1978*, p. 73)

The historical evidence thus suggests that concern over states using weak environmental standards to compete for business has played a major role in federal environmental policy. I turn in the next section to empirical examination of whether state differences in environmental regulation have actually affected business location.

Description of the Data and Models

The Data Base on Industrial Location. This study uses data on the new manufacturing plants opened by the Fortune 500 companies between 1972 and 1978 in the United States. This data base was originally developed by Roger Schmenner (see Schmenner 1982) using data from the Dun and Bradstreet Corporation. Dun and Bradstreet collects information on the location, employment, and Standard Industrial Classification (SIC) codes of manufacturing plants in the U.S. Schmenner purchased this data for the Fortune 500 companies for 1972 and 1978, matched the two years to determine possible openings and closings, and then cross-checked the data with the companies to obtain a corrected data base.

Schmenner's data base is particularly attractive for the current study for three reasons. First, the time period covered (1972-78) is clearly a period during which some federal policymakers felt that states were using lax environmental regulations to compete for business. As discussed above, this concern led to some strengthening of the federal role in the 1977 legislation, although considerable state regulatory authority continues today.

Second, using business microdata allows us to look at a specific type of business location decision, in this case the new branch plant location decision, and this narrower focus allows a more theoretically grounded empirical specification. Many business location studies use data on aggregate employment, capital, or value added in a region. (Several excellent recent aggregate studies include Newman 1983, Plaut and Pluta 1983, and Helms 1985.) But aggregate measures of regional economic activity reflect a number of different types of decisions: small business start-up decisions, branch plant location decisions, decisions about expanding or contracting production at an existing small business or branch plant, and plant closing decisions. These different types of decisions presumably are made in quite different ways, which makes it difficult to produce an empirical model of aggregate business activity in a region that is based on the microeconomic theory of the firm. A focus on a specific type of location decision, such as the new branch plant location decision, makes it easier to come up with a theory-based empirical specification.

For example, a longstanding controversy in business location research is whether growth in business activity in a region should be seen as a function of levels of relevant state characteristics affecting profitability, changes in state characteristics, or both levels and changes. (See Sullivan and Newman 1988 for a discussion of this issue.) A disequilibrium view of regional economic structure would assume that profit level differences exist among regions, and that business growth responds to these profit level differences, and indirectly to these differences in the levels of state characteristics affecting profits. A simplistic equilibrium view assumes that profits are initially equal across regions, and that only changes in a region's characteristics can cause changes in a region's economic activity. A more sophisticated equilibrium view would allow for the possibility that national or international economic forces may lead to expansions in certain industries, and that this expansion need not be distributed equally across all regions. It is difficult to decide a priori whether to focus on changes or levels or both changes and levels in modeling aggregate regional economic activity. But a focus on branch plant location decisions allows a much cleaner, more plausible model. I assume that some change, such as an increase in national demand for the corporation's products, or a drop in costs at some location, leads to a decision to open a new branch plant. Conditional on the decision to open a new plant, however, the probability of opening the plant at a particular location can be plausibly assumed to depend on the level of profits and hence levels of characteristics of that location compared to other locations. These conditional probabilities are what is empirically modeled in this article, and so the levels of location characteristics are used as the independent variables. This type of theoretical model is consistent with Schmenner's (1982) finding, based on interviews with corporate decision-makers, that large corporations first decide whether a new branch is needed and then decide where it should be located.

Finally, Schmenner's data base is attractive for empirical research because it is more accurate than most other publicly available business microdata bases. Many other business microdata bases, such as the Small Business Data Base (SBDB) of the U.S. Small Business Adminsitration, are derived, like Schmenner's data base, from Dun and Bradstreet data. But Schmenner's is one of the few Dun-and-Bradstreet-derived data bases that correct the data using individual contacts with the companies. Schmenner's cross-check with the companies corrected for significant errors in the raw Dun and Bradstreet data files. For example, the Dun and Bradstreet files missed 34 percent of all plants opened or acquired by the Fortune 500 companies between 1972 and 1978, and 12 percent of the supposed new plants that existed in 1972.

The Model of the New Branch Plant Location Decision. As mentioned above, this study focuses on the conditional probability, given that a branch plant will be opened, of a corporation choosing a particular state as a site for that branch plant. This conditional probability is modeled using the conditional logit model, following the precedent of my previous study (Bartik 1985).

To develop the model, suppose that profits of new branch plant i at location j are a function of a vector X_{ij} of observed characteristics of that site (where X_{ij} may vary from one industry to another as well as over sites), or

(1) $\pi_{ij} = B'X_{ij} + e_{ij}$

I assume the corporation chooses the location for its branch plant where profits are maximized. If the disturbance term e_{ij} is distributed according to the Weibull distribution, then it has been shown (McFadden 1974) that the probability of new branch plant i choosing site k will be given by

(2) $\Pr(ik) = \dfrac{\exp(B'x_{ik})}{\sum_j \exp(B'X_{ij})}$

This equation can be estimated by maximum likelihood.

To make the conditional logit model more applicable to the business location decision, I modify the model in two ways. First, I add a vector of dummy variables for regions (the South, West, and Northeast regions of the U.S., with the Midwest region the excluded dummy variable). The conditional logit model requires that the disturbance term be independent across the choices. This is implausible in the present case unless regional dummy variables are used to capture the likely intraregional correlation of unobserved state characteristics. This is a variant of the "nested logit" model suggested by McFadden (1978a) to allow for some inter-choice correlation in the disturbance terms.

Second, I include a variable for the area of the state. This variable is intended as a rough proxy for the number of potential industrial sites within a state. These industrial sites, not the state, are the ultimate objects of choice for a corporation locating a new branch plant. Other things being equal, it would seem reasonable that a state with more sites should have a higher probability of being chosen. Intuitively, if there is some random variation across sites in profitability or in corporate information about the site, then a state with more sites has a higher probability of having a site that has a larger positive disturbance term, and hence the highest profits. This procedure is based on previous research by McFadden (1978a) and Lerman (1979). McFadden and Lerman show that the probability of choosing some group (here, the state) of alternative (here, the actual sites) can be modeled by using the average characteristics of the group (the state) and the number of alternatives within the group (the number of sites in the state).

Variables Measuring State Environmental Regulations. The key variables in this study are those measuring state environmental regulations. Because there is no obvious way to measure state environmental regulations, this study experiments with alternative variables. In fairness to the reader, results are reported for the several alternatives used, rather than only reporting the "best" results.

Specifically, this study uses two measures of state water pollution regulation and four measures of state air pollution regulation. The specific definitions and sources of all environmental variables are in Appendix A. Two variables, one for air and one for water pollution, are based on state spending on air and water pollution control divided by state manufacturing employment.[5] The rationale for this variable is that state air (water) pollution spending per manufacturing employee should affect the probability of an air (water) polluter facing inspections and other enforcement action.[6] In addition, this spending level may proxy for general public concern in the state about pollution, and hence the strictness of state pollution regulations. On the other hand, there are several reasons why this variable might not negatively affect business location. For example, businesses might prefer a state with sufficient personnel to explain regulations and quickly process applications for environmental permits. In addition, perhaps states that have more polluting industries must spend more on pollution control without obtaining better enforcement.

Two other variables for air and water pollution regulations are based on industry costs for complying with pollution regulation in the state, compared to the national average. Data are available on costs of complying with air and water pollution regulation, by two-digit SIC code and state, along with data on value of shipments by SIC code and state. Using this data, one can calculate how great total air (water) pollution compliance costs would be in each state if all state industries had the nationwide average for their industry of compliance costs per dollar of product shipped. The compliance cost measure used in this study is the percentage by which the compliance costs in the state exceed those predicted based on nationwide averages for each industry. Although this variable might seem an ideal measure, it suffers from serious problems. In particular, this measure does not control for the mix of new versus existing plants in a state. Because new plants face stiffer environmental regulation than existing plants, states that attract more new plants will have higher average compliance costs. This may lead to a positive correlation between compliance costs and new plant locations.

For air pollution, because states regulate most new pollution sources, one can obtain measures of the actual stringency of state regulations. The difficulty of defining a variable in this case is the variety of state regulations. Regulations are often industry-specific, and states without a particular industry may not have any specific pollution regulation for that industry. To develop a variable, I tried to find an air pollution regulation that most states use, and one that is important to a wide variety of industries. I chose state air pollution regulations of industrial boilers. Industrial boilers provide heat and steam for a variety of industrial processes, and sometime space heating as well. In the 1972-78 period, industrial boilers that produced less than 250 million BTU/hour (about 83 percent of all boiler capacity) were not covered by any federal new source standard. Furthermore, air pollution regulation of industrial boilers was a major cost for industry, about $5.6 billion/year or about 33 percent of all private business costs of complying with air pollution regulations. Finally, industrial boilers are one of the additional source categories that the 1977 Amendments required to be covered by federal standards to minimize state competiion for new business, although the actual federal regulation was not issued until 1984.

The most important air pollutants emitted by industrial boilers are particulates and SO_2. State SO_2 regulations generally can be met by burning low sulfur fuels. The cost to industry of this regulation is the premium for purchasing low-sulfur fuel. Hence, the stingency of state SO_2 regulations is already reflected in the price of energy in the state, a variable which is separately included in the estimation. In contrast, state particulate regulations generally require the installation of pollution control equipment. I focus, therefore, on the particulate regulations applied to industrial boilers.

Two alternative measures of particulate regulations are used in this study. The first is the logarithm of the actual particulate regulation, expressed in permitted pounds of particulates emitted per million BTUs of heat input per hour. The problem with this variable is that the difficulty of complying with particulate regulations depends on the state's fuel mix. Uncontrolled particulate emissions from coal and residual oil are much higher than those from distillate oil and natural gas. Emissions also increase with a higher ash content of coal, or with a higher sulfur content of residual oil. Industrial plants in Midwest states where high-ash coal is plentiful have a harder time satisyfing particulate regulation than plants in regions where clean fuels are plentiful (the West, Louisiana, Texas, etc.).

To incorporate the effects of fuel mix on the effective stringency of the regulation, I constructed a second particulate variable. The first step in constructing this variable was to calculate the percentage reductions from uncontrolled emissions required by the state regulation for each type of fuel used in the state, given the average ash and sulfur content of each fuel type in the state. I then calculated the weighted average percentage reduction required, using as weights the percentage used in that state of each fuel type. This calculation dramatically changes the relative position of states. For example, Texas had particulate regulations in the 1970s of .30 pounds per million BTUs. Michigan's regulations were seemingly much less stringent, at .65 pounds per million BTUs for coal, and higher for oil. But because Michigan's industrial plants generally burn dirty fuel, whereas Texas industrial plants can burn natural gas and other clean fuels, the Michigan regulations require a weighted average percentage reduction in emissions of 47 percent, while the Texas regulations only require about 2 percent.

In comparing all these variables, I contend that the second particulate variable is the best available measure of environmental regulation. This variable is the closest to a direct measure of the pollution cutbacks required for a new plant. However, with this variable, as with all other environmental variables in this study, we still do not have a direct measure of what specific pollution reductions were actually enforced for a particular plant in a given state, compared to what reductions would have been enforced for that plant in another state. This ideal direct measure is unobtainable at present, and is likely to be unobtainable in the future, given the reluctance of both firms and state regulators to publicize the differences between the official regulations and what is enforced. This study uses the best obtainable indicators of environmental regulatory costs across states, but it must be admitted that these indicators may vary in accuracy from state to state, which limits the cross-state comparability of the data and hence the accuracy of the results.

Applying the Model

The model is estimated in two types of specifications. In the first type, the location decisions of all industries are assumed to respond similarly to state characteristics. In the second type of specification, variation across industries is allowed. Within both types of specifications, all eight possible combinations of the two water pollution and four air pollution variables are estimated.[7,8]

In addition to the environmental variables, all specifications include many other state characteristics that affect corporate profits and hence should affect business location.[9] The variables included are state land area, average wage, percent of labor force unionized, corporate income tax rate, business property tax rate, unemployment insurance tax rate, workers' compensation insurance rate, highway miles, level of existing manufacturing activity, education level of population, construction costs, population density, energy prices, and dummy variables for the region of the U.S. (East, South, Midwest, or West).

In the second type of specification, variation across industries is allowed in two respects. First, all the variables that represent input prices (wages, property taxes, UI taxes, workers' compensation, energy prices) are weighted by the factor share of that input in the industry, i.e, the effect of an input-price variable on location is assumed to be proportional to the factor share of that input. This restriction can be shown to hold as a first-order approximation for any profit function (Bartik 1986).

Second, for each environmental regulation measure, two variables are included in estimation: the measure itself, and the measure mutliplied by an indicator of the importance of that regulation to the industry. This allows the coefficient of each environmental regulation measure to vary across industries according to how strongly environmental regulations affect costs. For the state air pollution spending and state air pollution compliance costs variables, the weight used is the national average ratio of air pollution compliance costs to shipments in that industry. An analogous weight is used for the state water pollution spending and water pollution compliance costs variables. For the two particulate variables, the weight used is the ratio of BTUs produced by boilers in that industry to the industry's value of shipments.

Empirical Results

The empirical results for the environmental regulation variables are presented in this section. The results for the non-environmental variables are similar to those obtained before in specifications without environmental variables (Bartik 1985) and hence will not be discussed here. A sample of the results for the other variables is shown in Appendix B.

Table 1 presents coefficient estimates that do not allow for industry variation in business location determinants. Because the original units of the environmental variables are not of particular interest, and in order to roughly compare the effects of different variables, the environmental variables have been rescaled so that a one standard deviation increase in each variable is defined as a one unit increase. To further aid in interpretation, note that a conditional logit specification implies that any coefficient B on a variable x is equal to $[\partial \ln(p/1-p)/\partial x]$, where p is the probability of locating in that state. In a sample with 48 states, (1-p) is close to 1, and hence B is approximately equal to $\partial \ln p/\partial x$, or the percentage change in the probability of a new plant locating in that state. If the number of new branch plants nationwide is fixed, this percentage change in probability is simply the percentage change in numbers of new branch plants choosing the state. The coefficients in Table 1 can, therefore, be interpreted as showing, for a one standard deviation increase in the stringency of environmental regulation in a state, the percentage effect (in decimal form) on the number of new branch plants choosing the state. This effect would be predicted to be negative.

As can be seen in Table 1, none of the estimated environmental coefficients is statistically significant at conventional levels of significance. Furthermore, many of the coefficients have unexpected signs. Given that we cannot reject the hypothesis that all the coefficients in Table 1 are zero, we should not place too much stress on explaining the pattern of variation in coefficients across different measures of environmental regulation. However, it should be noted that the point estimates indicate that state pollution spending generally has coefficients of the unexpected (positive) sign, while the coefficients on other environmental regulatory measures generally have the expected negative sign. Perhaps state pollution spending is too far removed from what pollution cutbacks firms actually undertake, while the other measures are more directly related to actual pollution cutbacks. Furthermore, for the particulate regulation variables, the measures that reflect the state's fuel mix, and hence the effective cutback required (specifications 1.7 and 1.8) have the expected negative coefficient, while the particulate regulation measures that do not control for fuel mix (specification 1.5 and 1.6) have an unexpected positive sign.

While Table 1 indicates that there is no statistically significant negative effect of environmental regulation on business location, further interpretation of the coefficients and standard errors is required to see whether, as a practical matter, state policymakers can reject the possibility that a politically feasible change in state environmental regulations would have a "large" effect on business location. This interpretation, of course, requires some judgment as to what is a politically feasible regulatory change, and what is a large business location effect.

I would regard a one standard deviation increase in stringency of a state's environmental regulation as the maximum feasible political change. Such a change would, for example, move a state from the national average to the top third of all states. According to the point estimates in Table 1, this type of "large" change in environmental regulations would at most reduce the number of new plants choosing a state by 3.3 percent (specification 1.8, the percent reduction in particulates variable). Even if we increase this coef-

TABLE 1. EFFECTS OF ENVIRONMENTAL REGULATION VARIABLES ON BUSINESS LOCATION, NO VARIATION ALLOWED ACROSS INDUSTRIES

Variable	Specification Number							
	1.1	1.2	1.3	1.4	1.5	1.6	1.7	1.8
State Air Pollution Spending	.150 (.088)		.150 (.090)					
Average Air Compliance Costs in State		−.009 (.062)		−.016 (.059)				
Allowable Particulate Emissions x(−1)					.063 (.038)	.063 (.039)		
% Reduction Required in Particulates							−.032 (.048)	−.033 (.048)
State Water Pollution Spending	.007 (.085)			−.005 (.096)	−.011 (.095)		.010 (.095)	
Average Water Compliance Costs in State		−.015 (.056)	−.001 (.053)			−.003 (.054)		−.019 (.052)

Number of observations: 1607

Standard errors of estimates are in parentheses below the coefficients. All variables are measured in standard deviation units. Allowable particulate emissions variable is multiplied by (−1) so that predicted sign will be same as other variables (negative).

ficient estimate by one standard error, the negative effect only becomes an 8.1 percent reduction in the number of new plants.

In my judgment, a 3 or 8 percent effect is fairly small for so large a change in environmental regulations. Perhaps some state officials would disagree. This effect is certainly much smaller than that produced by one standard deviation changes in many of the non-environmental variables. For example, a one standard deviation increase (about 8.5 percent) in the percentage of a state's labor force unionized results, in most specifications, in a 30-40 percent reduction in the number of new plants locating in a state (Bartik 1985).

Although the Table 1 specifications suggest that environmental regulations do not have large effects on business location for the average industry, there remains the possibility that these effects are large for heavily polluting industries. To test this possibility, I estimated specifications in which the effects of the environmental regulations are allowed to be greater for heavily polluting industries, and these results are presented in Table 2.

As in Table 1, the environmental variables in Table 2 are scaled in standard deviation units. To further aid in interpretation, the industry pollution weights are scaled so that the least polluting industry has a weight of zero, and the most polluting industry a weight of one. As a result, the coefficient on the unweighted environmental variable is the effect of regulation on business location decisions of the least polluting industry; the sum of the coefficients on the unweighted and weighted variables is regulation's effect on the most polluting industry. One would expect the coefficient on the weighted variable to be negative, implying that more polluting industries are more sensitive to state environmental regulations. The coefficient on the unweighted variable is of uncertain sign. If enough polluting industries avoid states with stricter environmental regulations, industrial land prices may drop (a variable not included, because not available, in any specification) and low-polluting industries could actually be attracted to states with strong environmental regulations.

The results in Table 2 again show that none of the environmental regulation variables has a statistically significant effect on business location decisions. Furthermore, many of the point estimates not only indicate a positive effect of stricter regulations on business location, but a positive effect that is greater for more polluting industries, which is totally contrary to expectations. It is even more difficult than in Table 1 to detect any pattern in Table 2's point estimates of coefficients, which perhaps merely reflects the problems inherent in attempting to interpret coefficients which are not statistically significantly different from zero. The air pollution spending variable, and the particulate variable (with no adjustment for fuel mix) perform poorly in Table 2 as in Table 1. However, the compliance costs variables, whose point estimates were sensible in Table 1, tend to have point estimates with unexpected signs in Table 2, while the water pollution spending variable does better in Table 2. The variable whose coefficent estimates most closely meet expectations is again the particulative reduction variable (adjusted for fuel mix). The point estimates suggest that this

TABLE 2: EFFECTS OF ENVIRONMENTAL REGULATION VARIABLES ON BUSINESS LOCATION, WITH EFFECT VARYING ACROSS INDUSTRIES

Variable	Specification Number							
	2.1	2.2	2.3	2.4	2.5	2.6	2.7	2.8
State Air Pollution Spending	.024 (.094)		.059 (.091)					
Air Pollution Spending x Industry Air Weight	.207 (.154)		.174 (.108)					
Average Air Compliance Costs in State		.013 (.069)		.009 (.066)				
Air Compliance Costs x Industry Air Weight		.078 (.160)		.077 (.160)				
Allowable Particulate Emissions x(−1)					−.004 (.039)	.009 (.043)		
Emissions x Industry Boiler Weight x(−1)					.168 (.095)	.158 (.096)		
Percent Reduction Required in Particulate							.010 (.051)	.015 (.050)
Percent Reduction x Industry Boiler Weight							−.111 (.098)	−.091 (.092)
State Water Pollution Spending	.056 (.092)			.060 (.092)	.062 (.093)		.063 (.091)	

Water Spending x Industry Water Weight	−.123 (.156)	−.069 (.148)	−.102 (.146)	−.114 (.159)
Average Water Compliance Costs	.048 (.057)	.060 (.056)	.046 (.057)	.048 (.055)
Water Compliance Costs x Industry Water Weight	−.017 (.102)	.005 (.099)	.031 (.104)	−.007 (.104)

Standard errors are in parentheses below coefficient estimates. All environmental variables are measured in standard deviation units. Weights are measured so that the lowest polluting industry has a weight of zero and the highest polluting industry has a weight of one. According to the air weight variable, the most polluting industry is primary metals (SIC 33), with petroleum and stone, clay and glass close behind. According to the boiler weight variable, the most polluting industry is paper (SIC 26) with chemicals close behind. According to the water weight variable, chemicals (SIC 28) is the most polluting industry, and paper is close behind. In the units used, the average polluting industry has a weight of .18 for the air variable, .23 for the water variable, and .16 for the boiler variable.

variable has an effect on business location that is close to zero for the least polluting industry, but a negative effect on the most highly polluting industry, with the estimated negative effect having a T-statistic close to one, higher than for the other coefficients for the weight variables in Table 2. This result is consistent with my argument above that the fuel-adjusted particulate reduction variable comes closest to measuring the true stringency of environmental regulations.

As with Table 1, Table 2 requires interpretation to see if policymakers should be concerned that politically feasible increases in state regulatory stringency might discourage business location, at least for some industries. I focus my interpretation on the two specifications (2.7 and 2.8) that included the fuel-adjusted particulate reduction variable, which seemed to have the most sensible and precisely estimated effects. To aid in interpreting specification 2.7 and 2.8, I constructed Table 3, which calculates, using specifications 2.7 and 2.8, the effects of the environmental variables on business location for the most polluting industry, the least polluting industry, and an imaginary "average" industry. For the average industry, the pollution weight is a weighted average—using the number of new plants in each 2-digit SIC as weights—of the pollution weights for each individual industry.

For the average industry, Table 3 leads to conclusions similar to those gained from Table 1: the location effects of environmental regulation are probably not large. A one standard deviation increase in state environmental regulation seems to have an effect on the number of plants choosing a state in the ±5 percent range. For highly-polluting industries, the magnitude of these effects is much more uncertain. For example, in specification 2.7 the air pollution variable has an estimated negative effect on highly-polluting industries of 10 percent with a standard error close to 10 percent, while the water pollution variable has a negative effect on highly-polluting industries of 5 percent, with a standard error of 15 per-

TABLE 3. EFFECT OF ENVIRONMENTAL VARIABLES ON BUSINESS LOCATION, LOW-POLLUTING INDUSTRIES, AVERAGE INDUSTRIES, AND HIGH-POLLUTING INDUSTRIES, FROM SPECIFICATIONS 2.7 and 2.8

	Specification 2.7		Specification 2.8	
	% Reduction in Particulates	State Water Spending	% Reduction in Particulates	Average Water Compliance Costs
Low Polluting Industries	.010 (.043)	.063 (.091)	.015 (.049)	.048 (.055)
Average Polluting Industries	−.008 (.048)	.036 (.086)	.001 (.047)	.046 (.050)
High Polluting Industries	−.101 (.097)	−.051 (.151)	−.076 (.092)	.040 (.094)

Standard errors are in parentheses below estimated effects.

cent. These estimates for highly-polluting industries are quite imprecise, and we clearly cannot reject the possibility of effects in the 20 percent or greater range. For states that are particularly interested in attracting a highly-polluting industry, these effects could well be important.

Conclusion

Using the best data available on business location and environmental regulation, this study does not find any statistically significant effect of state environmental regulations on the location of new branch plants. The point estimates suggest that even sizable increases in the stringency of state environmental regulation are unlikely to have a large effect on the location decisions of the average industry. But the point estimates are not precise enough to rule out large regulatory effects on the location decisions of highly polluting industries. On the other hand, even for highly polluting industries, we cannot statistically reject the hypothesis of a zero effect of state regulation on business location.

What implications do these results have for policy? This depends on how strong one's prior beliefs are about the likely magnitude of the effects of environmental regulation on business location. In my opinion, the conventional wisdom among economists, that environmental regulation's effect on business location should be small, is well-founded in economic theory. It is straightforward to show that, to a first-order log-linear approximation, the percentage effect of some input variable on profits is proportional to that input's factor share (Bartik 1986). If business location decisions are based solely or primarily on profitability, then the effect of a variable on business location should also depend on what proportion of costs is accounted for by that variable. Environmental regulation's share of costs is quite small compared to other inputs for most industries, so theory indicates that environmental regulation's effects on location should be small compared to variables such as wages.

Because I find this theoretical argument convincing, I would generally put the burden of proof on anyone claiming that environmental regulations do have sizable effects on business location. This study does not provide any strong evidence of sizable location effects, so I believe state policymakers would be best advised to regard environmental regulations as having only very small location effects on most industries. A reader with different prior beliefs could perhaps come up with a different interpretation of these results.

It would thus be fair to say that this study, after great effort to collect data and construct a model, largely just reaffirms the prevailing wisdom that environmental regulations have only small effects on business locations. But I would argue that there is value in testing the prevailing wisdom and one would certainly expect the prevailing wisdom to sometimes be correct.

How could future research come up with more precise estimates of environmental regulation's effects on business location? One conventional suggestion is better data, and that clearly could help in this case. Ideally, one would like data on an industry that is subject to only one very well-defined regulation, with a great deal of geographical variation in that regulation. Furthermore, there would need to be a sufficient volume of location decisions to allow for precision in the estimates (the present study did not have a sufficient number of new plants in any one industry to allow for a statistical analysis of only one industry). Finally, the researcher would want to have some evidence that the actual enforced regulations in each location were closely correlated with the stated regulations. Developing data of such high quality is likely to be difficult.

An alternative approach to future research on business location and environmental regulation would be to impose more constraints on the estimation based on economic theory. Business location studies traditionally have used a wide variety of variables, selected and defined in a relatively ad hoc manner; it is perhaps not surprising that business location studies often have reached contradictory conclusions about relative effects of wages, taxes, energy prices and other variables. (See Wasylenko and McGuire 1985, McGuire 1986, or Sullivan and Newman 1988, for literature reviews.) One way to make further progress in business location research, and particularly in looking at environmental regulations, would be to arrive at some consensus as to appropriate theoretical constraints to be imposed on business location estimates, thus reducing the parameters to be estimated, and encouraging greater commonality of empirical specifications among researchers.

I have argued here, and elsewhere (Bartik 1986), that the effects of variables on business location should be proportional to their share in business costs. If this is true, then effects of regulatory-imposed costs on business location may be inferred from the effects on business location of other costs that are easier to measure or vary more across states (taxes, wages, etc.). Researchers can impose appropriate constraints across these different costs and possibily get better estimates. If a researcher has good data on all cost variables, and there was no measurement error or omitted variables biasing the estimates, one would prefer not to impose these constraints. But in the presence of these sources of biases, constrained estimation may be necessary to increase precision and avoid bias. These constrained estimates may not be particularly convincing to observers skeptical of economic theory. But constrained estimation may be the best we can do at present, while continuing the research needed to improve our measurement of business location determinants.

Finally, one issue that should be addressed in future business location research is the possible endogeneity of state environmental regulation and other policy choices of state and local government. This endogeneity may help explain the imprecision of the estimates here. Ideally, one would like to specify a model with several structural equations, and with state policy choices and business location decisions as endogenous variables. Estimation of such a model would require finding appropriate instruments for the environmental regulation variables and other state policy variables, a difficult task. Instruments would perhaps be easier to find if the theoretical constraints mentioned above were imposed. In that case, all cost variables would be aggregated into one variable, and we would only have to find an instrument that exogenously shifts any business cost variable to consistently estimate the business location structural equation. Economic theory may thus help provide better estimates until data on more plausible instruments can be obtained.

NOTES

1. This assumes that pollution in one state does not affect other states. In cases where there are pollution spillovers (e.g., acid rain), a rational state serving the interests of its residents will tend to underregulate.
2. There has been some research which has surveyed firms to determine how important the firms say environmental regulations are relative to other location factors. (See, for example, Stafford 1985.) This research generally finds that environmental regulation is not rated by most firms as a highly important location factor. While I believe this survey research is valuable evidence, an examination of actual business location decisions provides evidence of a different sort on the importance of such business location factors as environmental regulation. The two types of research should be seen as complementary, each with its own strengths and weaknesses.
3. The other business microdata available include the raw Dun and Bradstreet data files, the Small Business Data Base (SBDB) of the U.S. SBA, and the Longitudinal Establishment Data (LED) file of the Census Bureau. As numerous researchers have pointed out, the raw Dun and Bradstreet data suffer from numerous reporting errors. As explained in this paper, Schmenner's data base was developed from Dun and Bradstreet data, but incorporated numerous corrections after checking with the individual companies. The SBDB also is based on the Dun and Bradstreet data, and does attempt to correct for errors, but only through statistical checks for the internal consistency of the data base, not through contacting companies. Finally, the Census-based LED file is only available under very restrictive conditions to researchers outside the Census Bureau. Thus, if one is most concerned with the accuracy rather than the breadth of the data, the Schmenner data base is probably the best publicly available business microdata.
4. McCloskey (1986) has recently argued that economists focus too much on statistical significance. McCloskey argues that economists need to make some value judgments about what is meant by a "large" coefficient. My approach is in the spirit of McCloskey's argument.
5. It should be noted that because manufacturing employment is already in the specification as a possible explanatory variable (see Appendix B), this division by manufacturing employment does not affect the coefficient on the pollution variable. The coefficient on a ln (pollution spending) variable, without the division by manufacturing employment, would reflect the effects on business location of pollution spending, holding other independent variables constant, including the ln (manufacturing employment). Defining the pollution variable as ln (pollution spending/manufacturing employment) instead affects the coefficient on the ln (manufacturing employment) variable, which now holds pollution spending per employee constant, not pollution spending. Once one recalls that the coefficient on the pollution spending variable implicitly holds the other

independent variables constant, it becomes a little less important exactly how one scales the pollution spending variable. The other independent variables in the specification include population, state land area, the education level of the population, and the manufacturing wage rate, and several other variables which may affect the demand for or cost of supplying environmental regulation in the state. By holding these variables constant, we are implicitly examining the effects of pollution spending variation which is independent of these possible explanatory variables, and hopefully explained by exogenous taste factors in the state population. Ideally, one would, of course, like to include state pollution spending as an endogenous variable in a more complex model, a point I return to in the conclusion.

6. One referee was concerned that variation in state unemployment rates would affect the results obtained by using the pollution spending per employee variable. As noted in Note 5, this scaling does not affect the coefficient compared to no scaling, or scaling using one of the other independent variables (e.g., population). Furthermore, one would expect pollution spending in a state to vary with the business cycle in a manner similar to employment, although probably not as much. Finally, other research (Marston 1985) suggests that the overwhelming proportion of variation in unemployment across different areas in the U.S. was quite persistent during the 1970s. Based on this finding, although the average value of ln (pollution spending/employee) would vary over the nationwide business cycle, as unemployment varied nationwide, the interstate pattern of variation in ln (pollution spending/employee) would not be expected to vary much from one year to another due to the business cycle, as state unemployment rates tended (from Marston's findings) to move up or down together during the 1970s.

7. A referee has suggested that one alternative to examining all of these variables in separate specifications would be to use some kind of factor analysis of the separate variables to develop two indexes of state regulation, one for air, and one for water. I have rejected this alternative for several reasons. First, I believe that the second particulate variable is clearly the best measure of state regulation of the six alternatives explored. As argued above, the other measures probably suffer from various biases, and in particular, are probably correlated with unobservable variables affecting business location. This reduces the attractiveness of using some weighted average of the alternative measures produced by factor analysis, such as those produced by "MIMIC" models such as LISREL (Goldberger 1974). These models work best when the unobservable "index" that one is trying to obtain is measured by several alternative variables, with the measurement errors uncorrelated with each other or with unobservables in the primary equation of interest, here the probability of business location in the state. These assumptions are unlikely to hold here.

Second, MIMIC models such as LISREL have generally been developed only for cases where the dependent variable in all equations is continuous. Here, the dependent variable is a multinomial discrete variable, i.e., whether plant j chooses state i. It would be a daunting statistical and computational task to extend MIMIC models to this situation.

8. One referee suggested looking separately at air quality regulation or water quality regulation. I rejected this alternative because of the likely possibility that the stringency of these two types of regulations would be correlated, leading to omitted variable bias.

9. One referee asked whether these independent variables were systematically drop-

ped and entered to see what would happen to the coefficients on the environmental variables. I chose not to do this for two reasons. First, I believe the independent variables included here could all plausibly affect business location. If dropping some of these variables resulted in statistically "significant" coefficients on the environmental variables, I would have little trust in this result, since this restricted equation would be misspecified. Second, given the eight different combinations of environmental variables, dropping some of the independent variables would require eight additional computer runs each time a variable was dropped. While this is no problem for the computer, the resulting voluminous computer output would be difficult to digest, and impossible to fully present in a paper.

APPENDIX A: Definitions of Environmental Variables and Weights

1. State Spending on Water Pollution Control:
    The average of 1972-78 water quality control expenditures (current operation) divided by manufacturing employment. Source: *Environmental Quality Control*, State and Local Government Special Studies, U.S. Department of Commerce, Bureau of the Census.
2. State Spending on Air Pollution Control:
    The average of 1972-78 air quality control expenditures (current operations) divided by manufacturing employment. Source: *Environmental Quality Control*, State and Local Government Special Studies, U.S. Department of Commerce, Bureau of the Census.
3. Water Pollution Compliance Costs:
    The log of actual divided by expected water pollution abatement costs (less public sewerage) for 1978. Expected values were calculated by applying national costs per $ of value shipped to values shipped for each state for each two-digit SIC and then summing to get a total expected cost for each state. Source: *Pollution Abatement Costs and Expenditures*, Current Industrial Reports, U.S. Department of Commerce, Bureau of the Census.
4. Air Pollution Compliance Costs:
    Same as water compliance costs but for air pollution.
5. Water Weight:
    Water pollution abatement costs in industry nationwide divided by value of shipments for 1978. Source: *Pollution Abatement Costs and Expenditures*, Current Industrial Reports, U.S. Department of Commerce, Bureau of the Census.
6. Air Weight:
    Same as water weight only for air pollution.
7. Boiler Weight:
    10^6 BTU per $ value of shipment, for each two-digit SIC. Source: Table 9-1, page 9-5, *Fossil Fuel Fired Industrial Boilers: Background Information*, U.S. Environmental Protection Agency, March 1982, EPA-450/3-82-006a.
8. Particulate Regulations:
    The primary source for state particulate regulations was *National Summary of State Implementation Plan Reviews* (July 1975), with some reference also to *Fossil Fuel Fired Industrial Boilers: Background Information* (1982), *Analysis of Final State Implementation Plans* (1971), and *Analysis of State and Federal Particulate and Visible Emission Regulations for Combustion Sources* (1981). Data on proportions of each energy type used in each state

are taken from the 1972 Census of Manufacturers. Data on average ash and sulfur content of different fuels in various states were taken from *Steam-Electric Plant Air and Water Quality Control Data, 1970* (1973). Formulas for converting these ash and sulfur contents into uncontrolled emission levels are given in *Fossil Fuel Fired Industrial Boilers: Background Information*. The particulate emissions variable was defined as ln(E), where E is the regulation expressed in pounds of particulates per 10^6 BTU per hour for a boiler that produces 100×10^6 BTU/hour. The percent cutback in particulate emission was defined as

$$\sum_i S_i \left(\frac{1.4U_i - E_i}{1.4U_i} \right)$$

where i indicates different fuel types, S_i is the percentage share that fuel type has in a particular state, U_i is the uncontrolled emissions rate for that fuel type given the average ash/sulfur content in that state, and E_i is the particulate emissions regulation or $1.4U_i$, whichever is smaller. The 1.4 is included to allow for some variation in uncontrolled emission rates within a state. On the other hand, E_i was set equal to the lesser of $1.4U_i$ or E_i because at some point an increase in E_i will make no difference to polluters.

APPENDIX B: An Example of Results for All Variables

Below are the full results for specification 1.1. Most variables are measured in logarithmic terms, and hence can be interpreted as the percentage change in the number of new plants for a percentage change in the independent variable. The corporate income tax variable is measured as ln(1-tax rate). The other tax variables are measured as ln(1 + tax rate). The unionization variable is measured as percentage unionized, not the logarithm of the percentage. The environmental variables

Variable	Coefficient Estimate	T-Statistic
Land Area	1.02	15.57
Unionization Percent	−4.10	5.16
1 - Corporate Tax Rate	6.21	3.29
Property Tax Rate	−.578	1.53
Unemployment Insurance Tax Rate	5.14	.37
Workers' Compensation Rate	.992	.42
Road Miles	.566	2.80
Existing Manufacturing	.956	5.29
Wage Rate	−.161	.46
Education Level of Population	−1.21	1.21
Construction Costs	3.11	2.92
Population Density	−.303	1.48
Energy Prices	−.208	.82
Northeast Dummy Variable	−.047	.38
South Dummy Variable	.297	1.58
West Dummy Varible	.621	3.08
State Air Pollution Spending	.150	1.71
State Water Pollution Spending	.007	.08

are measured in standard deviation units. More details on the variables are presented in Bartik (1985). The results for specification 1.1 are similar to those for the other specifications and those in Bartik (1985).

REFERENCES

Bartik, T. 1985. Business location decisions in the United States: Estimates of the effects of unionization, taxes, and other characteristics of states. *Journal of Business and Economic Statistics*. 3:14-22.

―――――. 1986. Tax effects on the location of new branch plants in the United States. Vanderbilt University working paper.

Goldberger, Arthur. 1974. Unobservable variables in econometrics. In *Frontiers in Econometrics*, ed. P. Zarembka. New York: Academic Press.

Helms, L. Jay. 1985. The effect of state and local taxes on economic growth: A time series-cross section approach. *Review of Economics and Statistics* 67:574-82.

Lerman, S. 1979. Neighborhood choice and transportation services. In *The Economics of Neighborhood*, ed. D. Degal. New York: Academic Press.

Marston, Stephen. 1985. Two views of the geographic distribution of unemployment. *Quarterly Journal of Economics* 100:57-79.

McCloskey, Donald. 1986. *The rhetoric of economics*. Madison: University of Wisconsin Press.

McFadden, D. 1974. Conditional logit analysis of qualitative choice behavior. In *Frontiers in Econometrics*, ed. P. Zarembka. New York: Academic Press.

―――――. 1978a. Cost, revenue, and profit functions. In *Production Economics: A Dual Approach to Theory and Applications*. Vol. 1, ed. D. McFadden and M. Fuss. Amsterdam: North-Holland.

―――――. 1978b. Modelling the choice of residential location. In *Spatial interaction theory and residential location*, ed. A. Karlquist. Amsterdam: North-Holland.

McGuire, Therese. 1986. Interstate tax differentials, tax competition, and tax policy. *National Tax Journal* 39:367-73.

Newman, Robert. 1983. Industry migration and growth in the South. *Review of Economics and Statistics* 65:76-86.

Plaut, Thomas, and Joseph Pluta. 1983. Business climate, taxes and expenditures, and state industrial growth in the United States. *Southern Economic Journal* 50:99-119.

Schmenner, R. 1982. *Making business location decisions*. Englewood Cliffs, NJ: Prentice-Hall.

Stafford, Howard. 1985. Environmental protection and industrial location. *Annals of the Association of American Geographers* 75 2:227-40.

Sullivan, Dennis, and Robert Newman. 1988. Econometric analysis of business tax impacts on industrial location: What do we know, and how do we know it? *Journal of Urban Economics* 23:215-34.

U.S. Department of Commerce, Bureau of the Census. 1972-78. *Environmental quality control*. State and Local Government Special Studies. Washington, DC: U.S. Government Printing Office (GPO).

―――――. 1978. *Pollution abatement costs and expenditures*. Current industrial Reports Series. Washington, DC: U.S. GPO.

―――――. 1974. *1972 Census of manufacturers*. Washington, DC: U.S. GPO.

U.S. Environmental Protection Agency. *Analysis of final state implementation plans.* Washington, DC: U.S. GPO.

―――――. 1975. *National summary of state implementation plan reviews.* Washington, DC: U.S. GPO.

―――――. 1979. *Population and characteristics of industrial/commercial boilers in the U.S.* Washington, DC: U.S. GPO.

―――――. 1981. *Analysis of state and federal particulate and visible emission regulations for combustion sources.* Washington, DC: U.S. GPO.

―――――. 1982. *Fossil fuel fired industrial boilers: Background information.* Washington, DC: U.S. GPO.

―――――. 1984. *Final report to Congress: The cost of clean air and water.* Washington, DC: U.S. GPO.

U.S. Federal Power Commission. 1973. *Steam electric plant air and water quality control data, 1970.* Washington, DC: U.S. GPO.

U.S. Senate, Committee on Environmental and Public Works. 1978. *Legislative History of the Clean Water Act.* Washington, DC: U.S. GPO.

―――――. 1979. *Legislative History of the Clean Air Act.* Washington, DC: U.S. GPO.

Wasylenko, Michael, and Therese McGuire. 1985. Jobs and taxes: The effect of business climate on states' employment growth rates. *National Tax Journal* 38:497-512.

[9]

Environmental regulations and manufacturers' location choices: Evidence from the Census of Manufactures

Arik Levinson

Department of Economics, University of Wisconsin, 1180 Observatory Drive, Madison, WI 53706, USA

Abstract

This paper uses establishment-level data from the Census of Manufactures and the Survey of Pollution Abatement Costs and Expenditures to examine the effect of differences in the stringency of state environmental regulations on establishment location choice. Unlike previous work in this area, which has focused on particular industries or sets of plants and on one or two measures of environmental regulatory stringency, this study explores the relationship between site choice and environmental regulations using a broad range of industries and measures of stringency. It uses a conditional logit model of plant location choice to show that interstate differences in environmental regulations do not systematically affect the location choices of most manufacturing plants.

Keywords: Industry location; Environmental regulations; Interjurisdictional competition

JEL classification: H73; R38; Q28

1. Introduction

The question of whether manufacturers' choices of locations are responsive to environmental standards has an intuitive answer. Profit-maximizing producers should take into account the compliance costs of local regulations, along with local factor availability and prices, when deciding where to locate a new plant. This intuition is supported by the behavior of national and local legislators and industry representatives, and by anecdotal evidence from the popular press. While the intuition is clear, the few empirical studies of manufacturer sensitivity to environmental regulations have mostly concentrated on particular industries or sets of plants, focusing on one or two environmental standards or measures of stringency. In general, they have found weak or insignificant effects. This study examines manufacturer location choice across most manufacturing industries and employs a wide array of measures of environmental standard stringency in an attempt to explore systematically the gap between what intuition suggests and what economists have found.

The results reported here show that the locations of branch plants of large firms are more sensitive to state characteristics than are plants in general, and that these branch plants appear to be deterred by stringent environmental regulations, as measured by a variety of different proxies for state environmental stringency. However, only a few of the coefficients on the measures of environmental stringency are statistically significant and none is large. Furthermore, the degree of aversion to stringent states does not seem to increase for pollution-intensive industries, which suggests either that the stringency proxies used are capturing some other state characteristic, or that pollution intensity is inversely correlated with an omitted variable such as geographic footlooseness.

Previous studies of industrial location choice have taken several forms. Surveys of manufacturing executives involved in plant location decisions generally conclude that environmental regulations are not a major determinant of site choice,[1] but these results are difficult to interpret. Some surveys ask open-ended questions about factors potentially influencing location, while others ask respondents to rank a preselected list of factors. Even consistently conducted surveys may be of little value if the respondents, through intent or ignorance, misrepresent the true effects of environmental regulations on location choice.

Empirical studies using data on state characteristics are potentially more useful. However, because of the limited availability of establishment-level data on new plant locations, most such work has used aggregate data on economic activity such as employment growth and net investment. The conclusions drawn using aggregate data generally support the survey evidence: environmental regulations do not appear to influence industry growth, employment, foreign direct investment, or cross-border trade. Duerksen (1983) presents the results of a study examining changes in industrial employment among states during the 1970s. States that gained employment relative to the national average had more lax environmental

---

[1] See, for example, Epping (1986), Schmenner (1982), Duerksen (1983), Wintner (1982), Stafford (1985), and Lyne (1990).

standards than states that lost employment, though this difference was statistically insignificant.[2] Duffy-Deno (1992) regresses employment and earnings for all manufacturing industries on a set of regional characteristics, including total pollution abatement costs for 63 metropolitan areas from 1974 to 1982. He finds that the coefficient on total pollution abatement costs per dollar of value added has statistically and economically insignificant coefficients. Most recently, Crandall (1993) finds that environmental compliance costs, as measured by the Census Bureau, do not have a "measurable effect on the regional distribution of manufacturing employment."

Many of the studies of the aggregate effects of environmental regulations have focused on the discrepancy between US environmental regulations and those found overseas. After examining trends in US direct investment abroad and US imports from pollution-intensive industries, Leonard (1988) finds no evidence that establishments in robust domestic industries have moved abroad in order to avoid US pollution regulations. Similarly, Grossman and Krueger (1991) conclude that differences between the US and Mexico's environmental regulations "play at most a minor role in guiding intersectoral resource allocations" (p. 36). Low and Yeats (1992) show that developing countries have gained a greater share of total world exports of pollution-intensive products, but that industrialized countries continue to be by far the largest exporters of these goods. They judge that the observed changes are "unlikely to be adequately explained by environmental policy" alone. Only Tobey (1990) attempts to control for other national characteristics and to include a quantitative measure of national environmental stringency. He uses a 1976 UN study that rates the environmental policies of about 40 countries on a scale from 1 (strict) to 7 (tolerant), and finds that this index does not have a statistically significant effect on net exports.

A problem faced by all domestic and international studies is that they use aggregate data, which cannot distinguish among changes caused by births of new plants, expansions of existing plants, contractions of existing plants, and plant closures, each of which will be affected differently by state characteristics. Many state environmental regulations, for example, consist of 'new source performance standards' that are more stringent for new firms. These standards effectively raise barriers to entry that protect existing older, often more labor-intensive plants. Using data that include all employment in a study of the consequences of regulations may conceal effects that work in opposite directions. Consequently, to isolate the effects of regulation on location it is necessary to use establishment-level data.

The primary obstacle to studying plant location decisions has been the inaccessibility of establishment-level data. Crandall (1993) uses data from

---

[2] Oddly, the difference was even smaller for pollution-intensive industries.

Dun and Bradstreet[3] to disaggregate employment changes due to plant openings, expansions, contractions, and closings. As a measure of regulatory stringency, Crandall uses total state-wide pollution abatement operating costs, divided by gross state manufacturing output. He finds that plant openings and closings are unresponsive to this measure of compliance costs, but warns against the conclusion that environmental policy does not affect plant openings because compliance costs from plants that are deterred from opening are by definition zero. In other words, Crandall is concerned about the nature of his proxy for environmental stringency: states may have low pollution abatement costs because they have stringent regulations and polluting industries choose to locate elsewhere.

Bartik (1988) and McConnell and Schwab (1990) use subsets of the Dun and Bradstreet data and an empirical specification following McFadden's (1974) conditional logit model. Bartik examines the locations chosen by branch plants of Fortune 500 companies between 1972 and 1978. The results lead him to support "the prevailing wisdom that environmental variables have only small effects on business locations." McConnell and Schwab examine data from the 1970s on SIC code 3711, vehicle assembly. These plants, in the process of painting cars and trucks, emit volatile organic compounds that contribute to urban ozone (smog). As a measure of regional environmental stringency, McConnell and Schwab use a series of dummy variables for whether or not the county chosen is in compliance with federal ambient ozone standards.[4] They find significant coefficients only for those counties that were extremely far out of compliance (Houston, Los Angeles, and Milwaukee).[5] Friedman et al. (1992) use the conditional logit model and establishment-level data on the planned locations of foreign firms within the United States. In one specification they include a variable similar to that used by Crandall (1993), i.e. total state-wide pollution abatement capital expenditures per dollar of gross state product from manufacturing. The resulting coefficient is statistically insignificant, though this may be due to the fact that the abatement expenditures variable measures statutory incidence, includes only direct capital expenditures, and does not control for the states' industrial compositions.

---

[3] There are many acknowledged problems with these data. Both Schmenner (1982) and McConnell and Schwab (1990) cross-checked their extracts of the Dun and Bradstreet data carefully, and found problems with many of the observations. Crandall (1993) notes that the Dun and Bradstreet data have difficulty distinguishing plant births and deaths from sales and acquisitions.

[4] Their interpretation of this regulatory stringency variable is that out-of-compliance counties will enforce stricter standards in an effort to comply. It is possible, of course, that the effect works in the other direction, i.e. that cities with lax regulations exceed federal ambient air quality standards.

[5] McConnell and Schwab note in their conclusion that these results may not reveal much about location choice in general if vehicle assembly plants are not geographically footloose.

All three studies (Bartik, 1988; McConnell and Schwab, 1990; and Friedman et al., 1992) use McFadden's conditional logit model and establishment-level data to study the effect of environmental regulations on plant site choice. However, they are not directly comparable, because they use different samples of new plants, different measures of environmental stringency, and different sets of other independent variables. This paper attempts to examine this issue systematically by testing different subsets of plants from different industries, and by testing a wide variety of measures of state environmental standard stringency.

2. The data

I use the establishment-level Census of Manufactures data to examine the effect of environmental regulations on the number of new plants that locate in each state.[6] 'Establishments' constitute the unit of observation for the Census, and are defined as single physical locations engaged in one of the manufacturing industry categories of the SIC.[7] Manufacturing establishments that appeared in the 1987 quinquennial Census but were not in the 1982 Census are designated as 'new plants' here and constitute the dependent variables in the models that follow. There are several arguments in favor of using new plant openings, rather than plant closings, as a measure of sensitivity to variations in state environmental standard stringency. The first, and most obvious, involves the fixed cost of building a manufacturing facility. If the facility is a viable economic enterprise, but because of high local environmental compliance costs is incurring losses or would be more profitable elsewhere, then the facility should shut down and move to another location only if the savings in environmental compliance costs exceed the cost of the move. The locations of existing plants will thus appear insensitive to all but large differences in state regulations. This apparently inertial behavior in the face of compliance cost differentials is avoided by examining the location decisions of new plants. New plants with no fixed costs can, in theory, make location decisions on the basis of even tiny differences in compliance costs, all else being equal.

Other reasons for studying the locations of new plants involve the

---

[6] Previous work has emphasized that establishment-level microeconomic data are necessary to study location choice. In particular, Schmenner (1982), Bartik (1988), and Crandall (1993) have noted the suitability of the Census of Manufactures, but were prevented from using it by confidentiality restrictions. For this study, I have gained access to the Census data through the Census Bureau's Center for Economic Studies, which has available both the Census of Manufactures and the Pollution Abatement Costs and Expenditures (PACE) Survey.

[7] I have excluded plants with fewer than 20 employees because data for many of these small plants are imputed by the Census Bureau. They accounted for only 2.2% of the total value added in 1987.

structure of existing regulations. Many environmental regulations, both state and federal, apply only to new plants, or are more stringent for new plants than for old plants. By protecting existing plants, these 'grandfather' regulations provide a reason to expect plant births to be more sensitive to environmental regulations than plant deaths. Finally, state versions of the federal Superfund law, and the federal law itself, impose stringent cleanup and liability costs on manufacturers that dismantle and sell industrial sites. To avoid these costs, many manufacturers claim that they maintain existing sites with skeletal work crews, without manufacturing any product, merely to avoid the regulatory costs of shutting down (Lyne, 1985). On the books these facilities appear as open factories, while in practice they have closed. To avoid the complications posed by these liability regulations and grandfather regulations, and to avoid inertial behavior driven by moving costs, this study focuses solely on the locations of new manufacturing plants.

A critical problem faced by all studies that examine the economic effects of environmental regulations has been quantifying those regulations in a meaningful way. Attempts have taken three broad directions: qualitative indices of regulatory stringency, quantitative measures of enforcement effort on the part of states, and measures of compliance costs incurred by plants. In the empirical results that follow, I explore six environmental regulatory measures drawn from these categories. The descriptive statistics for these measures and the other independent variables used are presented in Table 1.

The Conservation Foundation Index. In 1983 the Conservation Foundation constructed a qualitative index to attempt to measure each state's "effort to provide a quality environment for its citizens" (Duerksen, 1983). The 23 components of this index include environmental and land-use characteristics such as the League of Conservation Voters' assessment of the congressional delegation's voting record, the existence of state environmental impact statement processes, and the existence of language specifically protecting the environment in state land-use statutes. These were assigned point values on the basis of their importance, as judged by the Conservation Foundation staff, and aggregated into an index ranging from 0 to 63. For this study the components containing the dollar amount of state spending on various environmental programs were dropped, leaving a total of 19 components.[8]

The FREE Index. The Fund for Renewable Energy and the Environment

---

[8] The qualitative indices of regulatory stringency are negatively correlated with the quantitative measure of regulatory effort (given by Monitoring Employment). The unmodified Conservation Foundation Index thus contains offsetting components from different types of these stringency proxies. To separate clearly the different stringency measures, I removed the dollar spending by regulatory agencies from the rest of the Conservation Foundation Index.

Table 1
Descriptive statistics

Variable	Mean	Median	Minimum	Maximum	Standard deviation	Source
Conservation Foundation	23.6	22.0	9	39	7.3	Duerksen (1983)
FREE Index	30.3	29.5	14	49	9.5	FREE (1987)
Green Index	10.1	10.0	3	18	3.4	Hall and Kerr (1991)
Monitoring Employment	0.06	0.04	0.01	0.20	0.04	NGA (1982)
Aggregate Abatement Cost	0.77	0.54	0.12	3.56	0.73	PACE Survey and Census of Manufactures
Industry Abatement Cost	−0.12	−0.11	−0.57	0.27	0.18	Author's calculations from merged PACE and Census data (Table 2)
Business Tax	0.067	0.062	0.031	0.126	0.024	Wheaton (1983)
Wages	8.55	8.61	6.54	11.47	1.21	1982 Census of Manufactures
Unionization	0.21	0.18	0.04	0.52	0.13	Troy and Sheflin (1985)
Roads	3.20	2.90	1.00	8.71	1.55	Statistical Abstract of the United States
Energy Cost	4.92	4.68	2.77	8.40	1.35	Alexander Grant & Co. (1985)

(FREE, 1987) published as index of the strength of state environmental programs. The components of the index include state laws regarding air quality, hazardous waste, and groundwater pollution for the early 1980s.

The Green Index. Hall and Kerr (1991) compiled the widely cited 'Green Index' of state environmental standards by simply adding up the number of statutes each state had from a list of 50 common environmental laws. For this paper I have excluded statutes pertaining to consumer recycling programs, agriculture, and transportation that appear unlikely to affect manufacturing costs. The remaining 21 statutes include state superfund laws, air toxics programs, air emissions fees, and water permit programs.

Monitoring Employment. The above three qualitative indices attempt to capture state regulatory stringency as reflected by the states' statutes. To measure the states' effort and ability to enforce these statutes, I use the number of employees at state environmental agencies in 1982, divided by the number of existing manufacturing plants (National Governors' Association, 1982).

Aggregate Abatement Cost. This is the first of two compliance cost measures used in the empirical work that follows. It is essentially the variable used by Crandall (1993) and Friedman et al. (1992). I use the gross aggregate pollution abatement operating costs (across all plants in all industries) from the published PACE data, divided by the number of production workers in the state in 1982.[9] A major problem with this variable is that it aggregates abatement costs across industries that self-select into states for many unobservable reasons. A state that attracts polluting industries will naturally have high abatement costs, regardless of that state's environmental standards.

Industry Abatement Cost. This last variable attempts to eliminate the industry aggregation problem from the previous measure of compliance costs. The goal of this variable is to estimate how much manufacturers are required to pay for pollution abatement in each state, holding constant the characteristics of the manufacturer, including its industry. Using the raw, establishment-level PACE data, I regressed the log of gross pollution abatement operating costs on the log of the book value of capital, the log of

---

[9] An immediate question arises: How do we normalize gross abatement costs by the size of each state? Dividing by the number of production workers implies that such costs vary linearly with plant size, whereas dividing by the number of plants would imply that these costs are fixed and that there are large returns to scale in pollution abatement. (Crandall, 1993, and Friedman et al., 1992, normalize abatement costs by gross state manufacturing output.) To address this issue I ran a simple test using raw data from the PACE survey. I regressed establishment-level gross abatement costs on the number of production workers, and that number squared. The squared term has a negative and significant but tiny coefficient, indicating that abatement costs over the relevant range of plant sizes is most closely approximated by a linear function of the number of production workers.

the number of production workers, the log of value added, a dummy for new plants, dummies for four-digit SIC codes, and individual state dummies.[10] The results are reported in Table 2. A high point estimate for a state dummy coefficient indicates that, all else equal, plants in that state spend more on pollution abatement operating costs. The omitted state, New York, appears to have high environmental costs by this measure, and as a result all of the statistically significant coefficients are negative, indicating that plants in most states incur lower compliance costs than similar plants in New York. These state dummy coefficients are interpreted as measures of state stringency, and are included as independent variables in the location choice models that follow.[11]

There are several remaining problems with this final measure of state-specific compliance costs. First, respondents to the PACE survey presumably provide direct dollar amounts spent on pollution abatement. It would be impossible for them to assess the true economic costs of pollution abatement, including inefficiencies resulting from input substitution or altered production processes. Thus the plant-specific abatement operating costs may overstate or understate true compliance costs. Second, the coefficient on the state dummy variable measures how much more a plant would have to spend on pollution abatement if it located in that state rather than in the omitted state, holding constant capital, labor, value added, and industry. But it is unlikely that plants locating in two different states would hold all of those other factors constant. Given that manufacturers can respond to regulations in ways aside from spending more on pollution abatement, this measure may overstate true compliance cost differences.

Table 3 presents the correlations among the six variables. The three qualitative variables (the Conservation Foundation, FREE, and Green indices) are strongly positively correlated with each other, suggesting that the three may measure the same phenomenon. The measure of state regulatory effort (Monitoring Employment) is positively correlated with aggregate abatement costs, but negatively correlated with the qualitative variables. Finally, my measure of industry-specific abatement costs from the first-stage regression of abatement costs on state dummies (Industry Abatement Cost) is positively correlated with all of the other environment variables except state Monitoring Employment. It is positively, but not

---

[10] Implicit in this specification is a Cobb–Douglas production function in which output (value added) is estimated as a function of capital (K), labor (L), and pollution (P), with dummy variables for new plants, industries, and states: $Y = A \cdot K^{\beta_1} \cdot L^{\beta_2} \cdot P^{\beta_3}$. The model estimated here substitutes pollution abatement, which is observable, for pollution, takes the logarithm of both sides, and inverts the function to estimate abatement as a function of the other variables.

[11] Note that the asterisks in Table 2 reflect only the fact that the relevant coefficients are statistically different from zero. More important is the fact that many coefficients are statistically different from each other.

Table 2
First-stage regression for industry-specific compliance costs
Dependent variable: ln(gross pollution abatement operating costs)

Variable	Coefficient	Std. error
ln(capital)	0.545*	0.016
ln(production workers)	0.439*	0.022
ln(value added)	0.084*	0.016
New plant dummy	0.060	0.061
AL	−0.035	0.094
AR	−0.072	0.103
AZ	−0.232	0.155
CA	−0.150*	0.064
CO	−0.384*	0.140
CT	−0.001	0.097
DE	0.273	0.194
FL	0.022	0.095
GA	−0.194*	0.084
IA	−0.034	0.104
ID	−0.004	0.190
IL	0.055	0.067
IN	0.013	0.078
KS	−0.330*	0.115
KY	0.065	0.101
LA	−0.102	0.107
MA	−0.109	0.086
MD	0.148	0.108
ME	−0.041	0.163
MI	0.084	0.076
MN	−0.209*	0.091
MO	−0.195*	0.091
MS	−0.255*	0.123
MT	0.110	0.273
NC	−0.144	0.080
ND	−0.566	0.384
NE	−0.196	0.144
NH	−0.276	0.178
NJ	0.117	0.077
NM	−0.500	0.322
NV	−0.239	0.348
NY	na	na
OH	0.056	0.067
OK	−0.396*	0.120
OR	0.122	0.110
PA	0.022	0.067
RI	−0.247	0.148
SC	−0.184	0.096
SD	−0.020	0.264
TN	−0.078	0.088

Table 2 (continued)

Variable	Coefficient	Std. error
TX	−0.151*	0.071
UT	−0.494*	0.177
VA	−0.097	0.093
VT	−0.111	0.220
WA	−0.182	0.107
WI	−0.186*	0.078
WV	−0.115	0.143
WY	−0.412	0.365

$n = 11\,034$, d.f. = 10 565, $R^2 = 0.74$.
* Statistically significantly at 5%.
Uses PACE data without sample weights.
Includes dummy variables for four-digit SIC codes.

perfectly, correlated with Aggregate Abatement Costs. There are two possible conclusions from the pattern of correlations in Table 3. If environmental stringency is a one-dimensional phenomenon, then it would seem that these cannot all be correctly measuring stringency, and that studies of the economic effects of environmental regulations that examine only one or two proxies for the strength of such regulations run the risk of mismeasuring stringency. Alternatively, if environmental stringency has several dimensions, such as the strength of the laws, the strength of states' enforcement, and compliance costs, then these variables may simply be measuring those different dimensions.

Other variables included in the models that follow are typical of those found in other studies of industrial location: measures of, or proxies for, business taxes, labor market conditions, market size and accessibility, and energy costs. The measure of business taxes used is taken from Wheaton (1983), and was also used by McConnell and Schwab. A problem common to all of these studies has been defining the pertinent average effective tax rate. Wheaton's business tax rates are among the most carefully developed, although they use data from 1977, several years before the time period studied here.[12] Labor costs are captured by the average production worker wage in the state, as calculated from the 1982 Census of Manufactures. The models also control for the percentage of the work force that was unionized in 1984 (Troy and Sheflin, 1985). The proxy for infrastructure used here is the number of highway miles per 1000 acres of non-federal land in each state. Energy costs are the average cost of energy for manufacturers per million BTUs as reported by Alexander Grant & Co. (1985).

---

[12] I developed a similar tax rate using 1988 data from the Advisory Commission on Intergovernmental Relations (ACIR), and the results below do not depend on which set of rates are used. The reported results use the Wheaton rates.

Table 3
Correlation of environmental stringency measures across states

$N = 48$ states	Conservation Foundation	FREE Index	Green Index	Monitoring Employment	Aggregate Abatement Cost	Industry Abatement Cost
Conservation Foundation	1.00					
FREE Index	0.68	1.00				
Green Index	0.66	0.71	1.00			
Monitoring Employment	−0.22	−0.45	−0.28	1.00		
Aggregate Abatement Cost	−0.09	−0.30	−0.21	0.48	1.00	
Industry Abatement Cost	0.39	0.38	0.30	−0.01	0.32	1.00

Finally, I include data on the number of existing plants in each state (by industry for the disaggregate specifications). This variable has three interpretations. It measures the size of each state, as larger states will naturally have greater numbers of new plants. Second, it may proxy for location (or 'agglomeration') economies present in concentrations of industry. Finally, the number of existing plants will capture some of the otherwise unobserved characteristics of the states that make them more or less attractive to industry.

3. A model of new plant births

Following Bartik (1988) and McConnell and Schwab (1990) I assume that each new plant has a latent (unobserved) profit function that is dependent on the characteristics of the state in which it locates

$$\hat{\pi}_{ij} = F(w_j, x_j, e_j), \qquad (1)$$

where $\hat{\pi}_{ij}$ are the latent profits that could be earned by plant i in state j, w_j is a vector of state-specific factor prices, x_j is a vector of state-specific fixed factors, and e_j is a measure of the stringency of state j's environmental regulations. If profit-maximizing plant managers consider a number of sites and choose the site at which the plant's profits would be highest, then increases in a state's factor prices or regulatory stringency, or decreases in the amount of infrastructure available, will lower these latent profits and decrease the likelihood of a plant choosing that state. In other words, $\partial \pi_{ij}/\partial w_j < 0$, $\partial \pi_{ij}/\partial x_j > 0$, and $\partial \pi_{ij}/\partial e_j < 0$. McFadden's (1974) conditional logit model can then be used to represent plant location choice econometrically.

To use the conditional logit model, I assume that Eq. (1) can be estimated in log form with a disturbance term following a Weibull distribution, where the profits of firm i, if the firm were to locate in state j, are equal to

$$\pi_{ij} = \beta' z_j + \epsilon_{ij}, \qquad (2)$$

and where $z_j = (w_j, x_j, e_j)$ is a vector of state characteristics. The probability that state k maximizes profits for plant i is then

$$P(ik) = \frac{e^{\beta' z_k}}{\sum_{j=1}^{J} e^{\beta' z_j}}, \qquad (3)$$

where J represents the total number of possible states. Eq. (3) forms the basis for the conditional logit model. In the empirical work that follows, the parameter β is estimated using maximum likelihood.

The strong assumption that the error terms in Eq. (2) are independently and identically distributed Weibull, while convenient analytically, imposes the unfortunate 'independence of irrelevant alternatives' (IIA) restriction on the predicted probabilities. With 48 choices (the contiguous United States), this property could be problematic. There is no reason, for example, to think that a firm's decision not to locate a plant in Oregon is independent of its decision to reject Washington or Idaho. To mitigate this problem, regional dummy variables are included for the four Census regions.[13] To the extent that the error terms are correlated only within regions and not across regions, the regional dummies should reflect this correlation and reduce the IIA problem. However, if the error terms are correlated across states that do not lie in the same region, the model may be misspecified. In the next section I discuss results from the conditional logit model for single-firm plants and for the branch plants of the largest 500 multi-plant manufacturing firms.

4. Empirical results

As a first look at mobility and state characteristics, I used Alexander Grant & Co.'s (1985) index of general manufacturing climates, with the environmental regulatory variable removed.[14] I separated from the census of new manufacturing plants the new branch plants of the largest 500 multi-plant manufacturing firms (ranked by value added). Results from the conditional logit models for all new plants and for new branch plants of large firms are presented in Table 4. The manufacturing climate coefficient is larger and more statistically significant for the branch plants of large firms than for all new plants in general, indicating that the branch plants of large

---

[13] An alternative correction for the IIA assumption that preserves the convenience of the logistic distribution is the 'nested' multinomial logit model. A nested model here would assume that plants first choose a region of the country, and then a state within that region. However, it is difficult to conceive of regional characteristics that affect location choice in ways different from the state characteristics already included. Instead, I follow Bartik (1988) and McConnell and Schwab (1990) and include dummy variables for Census regions.

[14] Alexander Grant & Co. is a consulting firm specializing in manufacturer location decisions. Its 1985 index of general manufacturing climates consists of 22 variables, normalized and then weighted according to responses to a survey of 37 state manufacturers' associations. Their environmental index is aggregate state-wide capital and operating costs of pollution abatement equipment, divided by the dollar value of industrial shipments. Of all the environmental variables explored by this paper, theirs is the only one having a positive relationship with the number of plant births. The problem, I suspect, lies with their inclusion of capital costs. States with many new plant births have high aggregate capital costs for pollution abatement equipment.

Table 4
Conditional logit model of location sensitivity to 'manufacturing climate'

	All new plants[a]	Branch plants of large firms
Manufacturing climate variable	0.0047* (0.0010)	0.0160* (0.0014)
Existing plants	1.04* (0.02)	0.94* (0.02)
Pseudo R^2	0.13	0.11
Log-likelihood	13 008	7120
n	3880	2060

* Statistically significant at 5%.
[a] Random sample.
Standard errors in parentheses.

firms are more sensitive to states' manufacturing climates.[15] It could be that large multi-plant firms have economies of scale in location searches. They have experience with operating in many states and know first-hand the attributes of those states. It may therefore be easier for the branch plants of multi-plant firms to be sensitive to states' business climates. Alternatively, branch plants could simply be more geographically flexible. One might imagine that an entrepreneur opening a single unaffiliated plant would be more likely to do so where he or she resides, while a large multi-plant firm would hire managers to run that plant and would be more flexible in its choice of location. As a consequence, the discussion that follows will focus on the branch plants of large firms, the sample that appears more likely to demonstrate sensitivity to environmental regulations.[16]

Table 5 presents results from the conditional logit model with a full set of state characteristics and using the branch plants of the largest 500 firms.[17] The tax variable is never significant at 5%, although in all but one of the

---

[15] For computational reasons, for the all-plant specification I took a random sample of plants, stratified by state so that the proportion of new plants appearing in each state would remain true to the total (subject to rounding errors necessary to maintain integer quantities of new plants).

[16] To provide further evidence that branch plants of large firms are more sensitive to state characteristics, I ran the conditional logit models for a full set of state characteristics using all new plants (the 'all new plant' analog to Table 5 below). As in Table 4, branch plants of large firms appear to be more sensitive to a variety of state characteristics, especially infrastructure and unionization, than do all new plants.

[17] For computational reasons, I needed to take a random sample of 80% of the 2060 new large-firm branch plants.

Table 5
Industrial location and state characteristics
New branch plants of large firms, conditional logit model

	(1)	(2)	(3)	(4)	(5)	(6)	(7)
Conservation Foundation	−0.006 (0.005)						
FREE Index		−0.016* (0.006)					−0.009** (0.005)
Green Index			−0.014 (0.013)				
Monitoring Employment				−0.130 (0.080)			−0.099 (0.073)
Aggregate Abatement Cost					−0.081 (0.079)		
Industry Abatement Cost						−0.599* (0.278)	−0.501* (0.252)
1-Business tax	1.095 (1.812)	−0.207 (1.841)	1.151 (1.825)	1.191 (1.772)	2.405 (1.808)	2.132 (1.740)	0.797 (1.699)
Wages	−0.085 (0.376)	−0.084 (0.367)	−0.211 (0.365)	−0.035 (0.378)	0.085 (0.458)	0.007 (0.377)	0.122 (0.350)

Table 5 (continued)

	(1)	(2)	(3)	(4)	(5)	(6)	(7)
Unionization	−1.189* (0.397)	−1.391* (0.398)	−1.018* (0.381)	−1.102* (0.385)	−1.065* (0.382)	−0.788* (0.399)	−1.058* (0.377)
Roads	0.390* (0.134)	0.424* (0.136)	0.396* (0.135)	0.333* (0.135)	0.345* (0.135)	0.448* (0.139)	0.364* (0.127)
Energy cost	−0.368 (0.297)	−0.192 (0.305)	−0.349 (0.298)	−0.282 (0.302)	−0.399 (0.297)	−0.236 (0.305)	−0.013 (0.281)
West	0.570* (0.121)	0.572* (0.121)	0.599* (0.127)	0.563* (0.121)	0.527* (0.124)	0.540* (0.122)	0.547* (0.108)
Midwest	0.527* (0.100)	0.661* (0.109)	0.570* (0.105)	0.535* (0.100)	0.485* (0.111)	0.535* (0.100)	0.603* (0.097)
South	0.750* (0.116)	0.768* (0.116)	0.763* (0.116)	0.841* (0.128)	0.772* (0.117)	0.838* (0.123)	0.818* (0.120)
Existing plants	1.032* (0.042)	1.098* (0.048)	1.023* (0.039)	0.965* (0.049)	1.025* (0.041)	1.013* (0.039)	1.028* (0.052)
Log-likelihood	5673	5670	5674	5673	5674	5672	7071
Pseudo R^2	0.1107	0.1113	0.1107	0.1108	0.1107	0.1109	0.1132

$n = 1648$

Standard errors in parentheses.
* Statistically significant at 5%.
** Statistically significant at 10%.

regressions it has the expected positive sign.[18] The average wage of production workers is insignificant. One explanation for this result may be that there are unmeasured and therefore omitted productivity differences between states. If omitted productivity is positively correlated with both wages and states' attractiveness, then it imparts a positive bias on the wage coefficient. I have run these models with several productivity measures included (output per manufacturing worker and education levels) with unsatisfactory results. An alternative explanation for the statistical insignificance of average wages may be that any wage effect is being captured by the unionization variable, which is uniformly negative and significant. The robustness of this result confirms some of the previous work on location choice, for which unionization seems to play an important role (Bartik, 1991; Crandall, 1993). The proxy for infrastructure (road miles per 1000 acres) is consistently positive and significant, and the measure of energy costs is consistently negative and insignificant. The dummy variables for the census regions are all positive and significant, indicating that new plants are opening at markedly lower rates in the Northeast, even controlling for other characteristics of those states.

Finally, the environmental measures appear with uniformly negative coefficients in the conditional logit model. The coefficient on the FREE index is statistically significant at 5%, Monitoring Employment is close to significance at 10%, and Industry Abatement Cost also appears to be significant, although its standard errors are likely to be underestimated.[19] Given the pattern of correlation among these measures of stringency (Table 2), it seems possible that they measure different characteristics of state environmental regulatory regimes that manufacturers care about when making location decisions. To address this possibility, I ran a similar set of regressions including three measures of stringency simultaneously: one qualitative index of state laws, the FREE index; a quantitative measure of enforcement, Monitoring Employment; and one measure of compliance costs, Industry Abatement Cost. The results with all three measures of stringency are presented in column (7) of Table 5. Included together, the FREE Index is negative and significant at 10%, Monitoring Employment is negative but insignificant, and Industry Abatement Cost appears to be significant, with the same caveat regarding its standard errors.

To draw conclusions about these variables beyond their statistical signifi-

---

[18] If business taxes are interpreted as a profits tax, then the left-hand side of Eq. (2) is $\ln(\pi(1-t))$. I thus include $\ln(1-t)$ as an independent variable, and its expected coefficient is positive.

[19] Recall that the Industry Abatement Cost measures are the coefficients on state dummies from the first-stage regression of abatement costs on plant characteristics in Table 2. Therefore the standard errors on Industry Abatement Cost in the second stage, the conditional logit, are understated (Murphy and Topel, 1985).

cance, it is necessary to interpret their magnitudes. The predicted probability of a plant choosing a state under the conditional logit specification is as in Eq. (3). To interpret the size of the coefficient, note that

$$\frac{\partial \ln P(ij)}{\partial z_j} = \hat{\beta}[1 - P(ij)]. \qquad (4)$$

Thus the interpretation of any coefficient depends on the characteristics of the state being analyzed. To place these coefficients in context, Table 6 presents the percentage change in the probability of any one plant locating in a state with average characteristics, resulting from an increase in each of the listed parameters by one standard deviation. For example, the second column suggests that increasing the value of the FREE Index from 30 to 40, while holding all of the other parameters at their averages, would result in a 1.73% drop in the probability that a plant chooses to open in the

Table 6
Interpreting the coefficients of Table 5
The predicted percentage change in the probability of locating in a state with average characteristics as a result of a standard deviation increase in each independent variable

	(1) (%)	(2) (%)	(3) (%)	(4) (%)	(5) (%)	(6) (%)	(7) (%)
Conservation Foundation	−0.56	−	−	−	−	−	−
FREE Index	−	−1.73*	−	−	−	−	−0.86**
Green Index	−	−	−0.59	−	−	−	−
Monitoring Employment	−	−	−	−1.12	−	−	−0.76
Aggregate Abatement Cost	−	−	−	−	−0.89	−	−
Industry Abatement Cost	−	−	−	−	−	−1.21*	−0.94*
1-Business tax	−0.34	0.06	−0.37	−0.36	−0.72	−0.62	−0.21
Wages	−0.14	−0.13	−0.37	−0.06	0.14	0.01	0.18
Unionization	−1.79*	−1.96*	−1.58*	−1.62*	−1.54*	−1.11*	−1.38*
Roads	2.31*	2.34*	2.42*	1.92*	1.96*	2.49*	1.87*
Energy Cost	−1.22	−0.59	−1.19	−0.91	−1.27	−0.73	−0.04
Existing Plants	16.36*	16.22*	16.71*	14.91*	15.64*	15.03*	14.14*

* Underlying coefficient (Table 5) is significant at 5%.
** Underlying coefficient (Table 5) is significant at 10%.

hypothetical average state. Similarly, a one standard deviation change in Industry Abatement Cost, roughly equivalent to a change from Massachusetts to Minnesota, would result in a 1.21% fall in the probability of a new plant opening.[20]

Whether these effects are economically significant is debatable. Given that the average new large-firm branch plant employed 152 production workers in 1987, and that the average state attracted 43 such plants from 1982 to 1987, a 1% decline in the number of new branch plant openings over a five-year period results in the loss of only 65 production jobs. Even if a 1% decline in plant openings applied to all new plants with at least 20 employees, this would would result in the loss of only 305 jobs from the average state over five years. If these are the only costs of increasing environmental standard stringency by one standard deviation, then they are clearly not high.

One explanation for the lack of statistical or economic significance of the environmental stringency coefficients may be that stringent environmental standards merely alter the industrial composition of states without affecting the probability of new plant locations. In other words, while pollution-intensive industries may be deterred from locating in stringent states, clean industries may be attracted to those states for a variety of reasons. Clean industry could be attracted to stringent states by depressed land values, or if labor supply is relatively immobile, by depressed wages. Or, if labor supply is relatively mobile and if workers receive compensating wages for locating in lax (dirty) states, then clean industries could be deterred from locating in those lax states and attracted to clean states. To test this, I ranked the 20 two-digit SIC codes according to total abatement capital expenditures per dollar of investment. These range from essentially zero, for SIC 23 (apparel and other textile products) to over 16% for SIC 29 (petroleum and coal products).[21] The conditional logit model developed above was then run separately for new branch plants of large firms in each SIC code. The coefficients on the environmental variables from those estimations are presented in Table 7.

Very few of the environmental variables in Table 7 have significant and negative coefficients. The nine that do tend to be at the bottom of the table, among the dirtier industries, supporting the industrial composition hypothesis. However two of the five positive and significant coefficients also tend to be among dirtier industries. Nevertheless, it would be wrong to conclude that significant negative signs on the environmental variables in Table 5 are

---

[20] These calculations use the point estimates of each of the coefficients, regardless of their significance.

[21] A similar pattern is obtained if industries are ranked by operating costs per production worker, which range from essentially zero to $26 000 for petroleum and coal.

Table 7
Environmental coefficients by SIC code: Using specification from Table 5

SIC	Pollution intensity (%)	n	Conservation Foundation		FREE Index		Green Index		Monitoring Employment		Aggregate Abatement Cost		Industry Abatement Cost	
			Coeff.	Std. err.	Coeff.	Std. err.	Coeff.	Std. err.	Coeff.	Std. err.	Coeff.	Std. err.	Coeff.	Std. err.
23 Apparel	—	40	0.002	(0.035)	0.036	(0.033)	0.089	(0.088)	0.284	(0.516)	−0.815	(0.553)	−0.424	(2.041)
27 Printing/publishing	0.6	181	−0.018	(0.018)	−0.047*	(0.021)	−0.065	(0.045)	0.164	(0.208)	−0.373	(0.229)	−0.759	(0.864)
35 Machinery	0.7	173	0.006	(0.017)	0.005	(0.018)	0.040	(0.040)	−0.019	(0.275)	−0.272	(0.244)	−0.019	(0.275)
38 Instruments	0.8	133	0.041**	(0.020)	−0.003	(0.024)	0.143**	(0.049)	0.023	(0.288)	−0.148	(0.294)	−1.096	(1.134)
30 Rubber/plastics	1.2	152	−0.030	(0.017)	−0.030	(0.018)	−0.071	(0.047)	0.226	(0.263)	−0.086	(0.259)	−1.547	(0.984)
36 Electronics	1.4	181	0.015	(0.017)	0.029	(0.019)	0.029	(0.042)	−0.365	(0.245)	−0.064	(0.269)	−0.956	(0.955)
22 Textiles	1.6	40	−0.040	(0.049)	−0.059	(0.035)	0.085	(0.164)	−0.065	(0.649)	−0.139	(0.734)	−1.777	(2.961)
24 Lumber	2.0	95	0.051**	(0.022)	0.015	(0.019)	0.002	(0.055)	−0.264	(0.301)	−0.623	(0.336)	−0.875	(1.015)
20 Food	2.7	249	0.000	(0.013)	0.006	(0.015)	−0.006	(0.033)	−0.607*	(0.210)	−0.518*	(0.199)	0.189	(0.662)
25 Furniture/fixtures	2.7	33	−0.065	(0.043)	−0.019	(0.047)	−0.025	(0.108)	−0.443	(0.669)	−0.006	(0.775)	1.047	(2.554)
34 Fabricated metals	3.0	158	−0.004	(0.018)	−0.030	(0.018)	0.018	(0.051)	−0.510	(0.283)	0.483	(0.298)	0.432	(1.033)
32 Stone, clay & glass	3.6	97	−0.005	(0.026)	−0.066*	(0.024)	0.056	(0.057)	−0.174	(0.360)	−0.851*	(0.318)	−3.274*	(1.155)
26 Paper	4.5	79	0.022	(0.026)	−0.025	(0.024)	−0.000	(0.067)	0.263	(0.365)	0.383	(0.422)	0.099	(1.471)
37 Transportation	4.8	149	−0.005	(0.017)	0.007	(0.018)	0.003	(0.045)	0.026	(0.293)	0.256	(0.300)	−0.800	(0.957)
33 Primary metals	7.1	52	−0.028	(0.025)	−0.012	(0.025)	0.006	(0.072)	0.150	(0.449)	−0.597	(0.397)	−1.088	(1.498)
28 Chemicals	7.9	200	−0.036*	(0.016)	−0.033*	(0.017)	−0.014	(0.039)	0.531**	(0.204)	0.549**	(0.219)	0.623	(0.863)
29 Petroleum & coal	16.5	26	−0.034	(0.042)	0.049	(0.051)	−0.012	(0.110)	−0.678	(0.545)	−1.012*	(0.507)	−3.399	(2.100)

'Pollution intensity' is pollution abatement capital expenditures as a percentage of total new capital expenditures, 1986.
* Significant and negative at 5%.
** Significant and positive at 5%.

spurious simply because the more pollution-intensive industries in Table 7 do not have larger or more significantly negative signs than the cleaner industries. The industries in Table 7 are ranked by pollution abatement costs, not geographic flexibility, and it is possible that some of the industries at the bottom of Table 7, such as primary metals (SIC 33), paper (26), and transportation products (37), which show no apparent sensitivity to environmental regulations, are simply not geographically footloose. It is also true that the relevant sample size for some of these industries (for the branch plants of large firms) is probably too small to make broad generalizations.[22]

5. Conclusion

This study makes a systematic attempt to measure the effect of state environmental regulations on new manufacturing plant locations. It uses establishment-level data on location choices and pollution abatement costs, and focuses on a potentially sensitive subset of manufacturers, i.e. new branch plants of large multi-plant firms. Despite this effort, there seems to be little evidence that stringent state environmental regulations deter new plants from opening. Given the conclusion that regulations do not affect plant openings, the natural follow-up question is: Why not? It seems unlikely that environmental compliance costs are too small to weigh into location decisions, especially for the more pollution-intensive industries. On average, the industries studied here spent about 4% of their investment dollars on pollution abatement equipment. Some industries spent more than 5%, and one (petroleum and coal) spent 16% (see Table 7). An alternative explanation is that firms manufacturing products in a variety of jurisdictions find it most cost effective to operate according to the most stringent regulations, eliminating the necessity of designing a different production process for each location. Some argue that even if environmental compliance costs currently differ across states, they are converging to a uniform level. Or, it may simply be that the more pollution-intensive industries also happen to be the least footloose. These explanations lie outside the scope of this paper, but may be fertile ground for future research.

Three general conclusions may be drawn from this project. The first is that the branch plants of large firms appear more sensitive to local conditions, including environmental regulations, than do all plants in

---

[22] In fact, leather products (SIC 31), tobacco manufacturers (21), and miscellaneous industries (39) have been dropped from Table 7 for exactly this reason: too few large-firm branch plants appeared in these industries between 1982 and 1987.

general. Although several proxies for environmental standard stringency appear to have negative effects on the new plant births, these coefficients are significant only for the branch plants of very large firms. Two theories might explain why large-firm branch plants are more sensitive to variations in local environmental stringency. Such firms may have economies of scale in conducting site searches, and such plants may be more footloose than those of independent manufacturers. Either way, the sensitive subset of plants appears to be small.

A second important conclusion comes from examining the location choice model industry by industry. Very few industries have negative and significant coefficients for the environmental stringency variables, and an offsetting few have positive and significant coefficients. While it is difficult to sort the industries that are footloose from those that are not, industries that spend more on pollution abatement do not appear systematically less likely to locate in states with stringent environmental standards. The lack of a sensible pattern across industries provides further evidence against environmental regulations having a deterrent effect on manufacturer locations.

Finally, a third lesson that can be learned here is that care must be taken when interpreting the results of industry-specific studies, or studies that use only one of several possible measures of environmental stringency. It would be easy, for example, to pick any one of a number of the industries in Table 7, such as food products (SIC 20), and perform a study showing that plants in that industry are less likely to locate in states with lots of environmental regulators, as measured by the Monitoring Employment variable. Without comparing that industry with others, and without comparing that measure of stringency with others, such an interpretation would be misleading. Examining plant-level location decisions for many industries and measures of environmental regulatory stringency, the predicted effects of tighter standards are statistically insignificant and economically small, and do not appear to vary sensibly with the pollution intensity of the industry.

Acknowledgements

Support for this project was provided in part by an Environmental Protection Agency Exploratory Research Grant. Special thanks to Robert McGuckin and Robert Bechtold at the Center for Economic Studies at the U.S. Census Bureau. Conversations with Rosanne Altshuler, David Beede, David Bloom, Chris Cavanagh, Sherry Glied, Todd Idson, Leslie Papke, Cecilia Rouse, and John Karl Scholz have been extremely helpful. I am also indebted to Hilary Sigman, Christiano Antonelli, Roger Gordon, and three anonymous referees for thoughtful comments, and to Bill Harbaugh for his invaluable counsel and research assistance.

References

Alexander Grant & Company, 1985, General manufacturing climates of the forty-eight contiguous states (Alexander Grant & Co., Chicago).
Bartik, T.J., 1988, The effects of environmental regulation on business location in the United States, Growth and Change 19, 22–44.
Bartik, T.J., 1991, Who benefits from state and local economic development policies? (Upjohn Institute, Kalamazoo, MI).
Crandall, R.W., 1993, Manufacturing on the move (The Brookings Institution, Washington, DC).
Duerksen, C.J., 1983, Environmental regulation of industrial plant siting (The Conservation Foundation, Washington, DC).
Duffy-Deno, K.T., 1992, Pollution abatement expenditures and regional manufacturing activity, Journal of Regional Science 32, 419–436.
Epping, M.G., 1986, Tradition in transition: The emergence of new categories in plant location, Arkansas Business and Economic Review 19, 16–25.
Friedman, J., D.A. Gerlowski and J. Silberman, 1992, What attracts foreign multinational corporations? Evidence from branch plant location in the United States, Journal of Regional Science 32, 403–418.
Fund for Renewable Energy and the Environment (FREE), 1987, The state of the states (FREE, Washington, DC).
Grossman, G.M. and A.B. Krueger, 1991, Environmental impacts of a North American Free Trade Agreement, Unpublished paper, Woodrow Wilson School, Princeton, NJ.
Hall, B. and M.L. Kerr, 1991, Green index: A state-by-state guide to the nation's environmental health (Island Press, Washington, DC).
Leonard, H.J., 1988, Pollution and the struggle for the world product (Cambridge University Press, Cambridge).
Low, P. and A. Yeats, 1992, Do 'dirty' industries migrate?, in: P. Low, ed., International trade and the environment (The World Bank, Washington, DC).
Lyne, J., 1985, Survey suggests laws on reuse of industrial sites toughening in many states, Site selection handbook (Conway Data Inc., Atlanta, GA).
Lyne, J., 1990, Service taxes, international site selection and the 'green' movement dominate executives' political focus, Site Selection 5, 1134–1138.
McConnell, V.D. and R.M. Schwab, 1990, The impact of environmental regulation on industry location decisions: The motor vehicle industry, Land Economics 66, 67–81.
McFadden, D., 1974, Conditional logit analysis of qualitative choice behavior, in: P. Zarembka, ed., Frontiers in econometrics (Academic Press, New York) 105–142.
Murphy, K.M. and R.H. Topel, 1985, Estimation and inference in two-step econometric models, Journal of Business and Economic Statistics 3, 370–379.
National Governors' Association (NGA) Committee on Energy and Environment, 1982, The state of the states: Management of environmental programs in the 1980s (NGA, Washington, DC).
Schmenner, R., 1982, Making business location decisions (Prentice-Hall, Englewood Cliffs, NJ).
Stafford, H.A., 1985, Environmental protection and industrial location, Annals of the Association of American Geographers 75, 227–240.

Tobey, J.A., 1990, The impact of domestic environmental policies on patterns of world trade: An empirical test, Kyklos 43, 191–209.

Troy, L. and N. Sheflin, 1985, U.S. union sourcebook (Industrial Relations Data and Information Services, West Orange, NJ).

Wheaton, W.C., 1983, Interstate differences in the level of business taxation, National Tax Journal 36, 83–94.

Wintner, L., 1982, Urban plant siting (The Conference Board, New York).

[10]
Effects of Air Quality Regulations on Polluting Industries

Randy Becker
U.S. Bureau of the Census

Vernon Henderson
Brown University

> This paper examines unintended effects of air quality regulation, using plant data for 1963–92. A key regulatory tool since 1978 is the annual designation of county air quality attainment status. Nonattainment status triggers specific equipment requirements, with the severity and enforcement of regulations rising with plant size. The differential in regulation favors attainment areas, reducing births for polluting industries in nonattainment areas by 26–

Support of the National Science Foundation (grants SBR 9422440 and SBR 9730142) is gratefully acknowledged, as well as the Alfred Sloan Foundation through a grant to the National Bureau of Economic Research project on Industrial Technology and Productivity. This work was carried out at the Boston Research Data Center of the U.S. Bureau of the Census, with data provided by the Center for Economic Studies. We thank Arnie Reznek and Joyce Cooper for their help and cooperation. Tim Dunne also provided early advice on the use of the Longitudinal Research Database. We are indebted to Leslie Papke and Jeff Wooldridge for use of their program to calculate robust standard errors in conditional Poisson models. The work has benefited from insightful comments by Arik Levinson, as well as Wayne Gray, Karen Palmer, Gilbert Metcalf, and participants in seminars at British Columbia, Brown, Harvard, Mannheim, Wisconsin, National Bureau of Economic Research, Center for Economic Studies, and Resources for the Future and in presentations at meetings of the American Economic Association, National Tax Association, Regional Science Association International, Western Economic Association, and World Congress of Environmental and Resource Economists. The opinions and conclusions expressed in this paper are those of the authors and do not necessarily represent those of the U.S. Bureau of the Census. All papers are screened to ensure that they do not disclose confidential information.

45 percent. Industries and sectors with bigger plants are affected the most, shifting industrial structure toward less regulated single-plant firms. Large preregulation plants do benefit from grandfathering provisions, but both grandfathering and shifts to small-scale new plants contribute to environmental degradation.

This paper investigates the effects of air quality regulation on firm decisions concerning plant locations, births, sizes, and investment patterns in major polluting industries. The intent of the Clean Air Act (CAA) and its amendments from 1970 on is to have plants limit airborne emissions through investment in "greener" equipment and in cleaner day-to-day operations, thus helping localities meet national air quality standards. While regulation has curbed emissions, it has had other unintended and potentially costly effects on firm decisions.

The key findings in this paper derive from the fact that the specification and application of air quality regulations vary intentionally across space and by plant and firm size, as well as effectively over time. While application is nonuniform in these dimensions, paradoxically, the CAA and its designers did not intend there to be nonuniform effects. Nevertheless, perhaps not surprisingly, nonuniformity of regulations over space and plant sizes has resulted in nonuniform outcomes. In particular, we show that there has been significant relocation of polluting industries from more to less polluted areas to avoid stricter regulation in more polluted areas; there has been relative proliferation of small-scale, less regulated enterprises in some industries, altering industrial structure; and, in regulated areas, the timing of plant investments by new plants has been dramatically altered.

Such effects are costly, moving plants to inferior (more costly, less productive) locations, having plants operate at a less than efficient scale, and altering investment decisions under uncertainty. This does not mean that nonuniformity of regulations is necessarily bad. Nonuniformity conserves on regulatory resources, targeting the biggest polluters in the worst polluted areas. Moreover, for example, relocation of polluting industries to less polluted areas generally means that plants move to areas with lower populations and fewer victims to damage. Quantifying the myriad of welfare costs and gains to regulatory policy is beyond the scope of this paper. Rather, the object is to identify unrecognized key effects of air quality regulation and their potential welfare implications. In the last section of the paper, we explore these implications and comment on alternative regulatory policies.

AIR QUALITY REGULATIONS

We focus on air quality regulation of ground-level, or tropospheric, ozone—a major component of "smog." Ozone, along with fine particulates, is the current target of the U.S. Environmental Protection Agency's (EPA) air quality regulatory activity because it has proved to be the most persistent air pollution problem. Since more stringent standards for ozone were proposed in 1997, understanding regulatory impacts is an even more pressing concern. Ozone forms as a result of emissions of mostly volatile organic compounds (VOC) and nitrogen oxides (NO_x) from various sources and atmospheric conditions such as wind, temperature, and sunlight. Regulation focuses on mobile and stationary industrial sources of VOC and, to some extent, NO_x emissions. This paper will examine the effects of regulation on manufacturing industries that are major VOC (and NO_x) emitters, but not major polluters in other air quality dimensions (so as not to confound findings with regulation of other criterion pollutants).

To analyze regulatory effects, we first discuss the regulatory process as it has evolved (see Environmental Protection Agency 1971, 1972, 1973, 1978a, 1978b, 1992a, 1992b, 1995; Melnick 1983; Liroff 1986; Laws 1992; Waxman 1992) and examine the literature on prior research. That, along with our own interviews of regulators and plant officials and a preliminary look at the data, will lead to a statement of hypotheses.

Formulating and Testing Regulatory Hypotheses

The Regulatory Process

Prior to 1970, air quality regulation was primarily a responsibility of state governments. Disappointed by the states' inactivity, Congress enacted the 1970 amendments to the Clean Air Act, creating the EPA and dramatically increasing the federal government's role. National ambient air quality standards (NAAQSs) were established for the air quality regions of the country for the different criterion pollutants. Each state was required to submit a state implementation plan (SIP), detailing how it intended to bring its nonattainment regions into attainment of NAAQSs. In the early 1970s, states lacked the expertise and resources to implement effectively a regulatory system. Achieving attainment through federal regulation of auto emissions seemed a potential escape clause for state activity. Some states did promulgate control technologies for stationary sources, focused primarily on large plants. However, lawsuits filed over the laxness or stringency of SIPs by environmentalists and industry groups were partially responsible for considerable paralysis in the process. These and other problems led to the 1977 amendments to the CAA.

Under the 1977 amendments, each July every *county* in the United States is officially classified as being either in or out of attainment of the national standards for each of the criterion pollutants.[1] For ozone, the standard has been that the second-highest daily maximum hourly concentration in a year not exceed 0.12 parts per million. (The standard was 0.08 parts per million prior to 1979, and new standards were announced in 1998.) The SIPs were to be revised, detailing specifically how states intended to bring violating counties into attainment by 1987. Federal enforcement was strengthened, with the potential to withhold federal grants on, for example, highway funds or to impose moratoria on new plant construction in recalcitrant states, as well as to impose civil penalties directly on polluters.

In considering the regulatory process, we focus on the (non)attainment status designation of counties and the impact of that designation on technological controls on equipment, the key regulatory instrument. Under federal guidelines, new plants locating in nonattainment counties are subject to the lowest achievable emission rate (LAER), requiring the installation of the cleanest available technology, supposedly regardless of costs. In addition, these plants can be required to purchase pollution offsets from existing plants. In contrast, in attainment areas, only those new plants that are class A polluters are subject to regulation and then only to best available control technology (BACT), which incorporates cost considerations, a weaker standard than LAER. In the 1980s, class A polluters are those with the potential to emit over 100 tons per year of a criterion pollutant. New small plants in attainment areas are exempt from regulation. For existing equipment, in nonattainment areas, plants are subject to reasonably available control technology—usually retrofitting—whereas in attainment areas, existing equipment is not subject to any technological standards. In summary, new and existing plants are each subject to much stricter controls in nonattainment areas, relative to attainment areas, with new small plants in attainment areas subject to no regulations.

To get a sense of how regulations are enforced, we interviewed officials and reviewed files of the Air Quality Division of the Rhode Island Department of Environmental Management (DEM) and interviewed managers and environmental engineers at a few important VOC-emitting plants in Rhode Island. Rhode Island is a nonattainment area. Given the EPA focus and limited regulatory resources in

---

[1] These designations are published each year in the Code of Federal Regulations (Title 40, pt. 81, subsection C).

AIR QUALITY REGULATIONS 383

the early years in Rhode Island, only bigger plants were regulated; typically local regulators did not know either that certain medium- or small-size plants existed or that certain plants were VOC or NO_x emitters. With time the local DEM moved on to medium- and smaller-size plants. Nonetheless, today, annual inspections and enforcement remain focused on big plants, with smaller plants either never inspected or inspected only once or twice a decade. This confers a cost advantage on smaller plants. To confirm these impressions based on Rhode Island, we examined data on U.S. inspections listed by the EPA. These are noted later in table 1, and they indicate a strong positive relationship nationally between size and likelihood of being inspected in the late 1980s and early 1990s.

Our interviews were also instructive about how the regulatory process affects the investment behavior of plants. In the choice of new equipment, there are issues concerning the interpretation of LAER and BACT. Firms engage in a costly negotiation process with officials of the local DEM and sometimes regional EPA, using their own engineers and also making extensive use of consultants. Such negotiations for a major plant can involve almost weekly meetings over, say, a two-year period, with all the required background work. Later, we shall argue that, in setting up new plants or engaging in expansion of existing plants, relative to phased-in investments of the past, now plants in nonattainment areas make investments in bigger lumps (i.e., "all at once," relatively speaking) to avoid repeated negotiations and to ensure consistency of equipment specifications across what would have been different investment phases in the past.

Literature

Of the issues noted above, the literature focuses on plant location. While it seems likely that polluting plants would avoid heavily regulated areas, previous studies have generally concluded that environmental regulation does not affect plant location decisions (see Gray [1996] and Levinson [1996] for a review). Many studies have been conducted at the state level, ignoring significant regulatory differences *within* states. Some lump together disparate polluting and nonpolluting industries in their analyses—such as those that look at "all manufacturing" or two-digit standard industrial classification (SIC) categories of manufacturing. In most studies, the proxies for environmental regulation are not based on the specific regulatory process but are indices of state "green" activity, based on congressional voting records, the existence of environmental laws, and the like. Some studies (e.g., Bartik 1988) focus on just the early confused period of regulation before 1978 or use cross-sectional data or estimation methods (e.g., McConnell and Schwab 1990). The use of these methods is problematic. In locational analysis, we must recognize that counties are in nonattainment because polluting plants have historically viewed them as productive, cost-effective places to locate. If these "favorable" attributes are not controlled for (say, by fixed-effects methods), then coefficients on nonattainment variables will be biased.

Two recent studies that have used county nonattainment status as a proxy for stringent environmental regulation have found some compelling results. Kahn (1994) shows that growth in manufacturing employment has been slower in particulate nonattainment counties. Henderson (1996) looks at the effects of county ozone nonattainment on the *stock* of plants in VOC-emitting industries, finding significant reductions in polluting plants in counties that switch into nonattainment status. However, he looks only at plant stocks *within* the regulatory period (1978–87) and has no information on flows, or births and closings. As we shall see, the birth and death processes are asymmetric, with opposing effects from regulation on stocks in nonattainment counties. An analysis of stocks masks the differing effects of regulation.

This paper builds on the existing literature in several ways. We examine births and location decisions of new plants, distinguishing among (1) different types of industries, (2) bigger and smaller plant sectors of industries, (3) the preregulatory (before 1972) and the regulatory time period, (4) earlier and later years in the regulatory period, and (5) the likely severity of regulations in different nonattainment areas. Besides births, we look at plant closings and decisions concerning size and investment timing, as affected by regulation. Finally, we use detailed plant- and firm-level census data over a 30-year period.

Hypothesized Impacts of Regulation

In deciding whether and when to put a plant into operation or take it out of operation in a county, a firm is acting to maximize net expected present value. On the spatial side, considerations are straightforward. With regulation, equipment costs of locating any new plant in nonattainment areas rose significantly (as a result of LAER); in attainment areas for small plants they remained the same, and for big plants rose more modestly. Thus it became less profitable to start up new polluting plants in nonattainment areas, and there should be a significant increase in the relative number of births in attainment areas. Nonpolluting industries should not experience these effects. The magnitude of this shift for polluting industries will

AIR QUALITY REGULATIONS

depend on the likely severity of regulation in different nonattainment areas.

Given this basic shift to attainment areas, there are four other key, general regulatory effects. First, the timing of the shift to attainment areas varies within and across industries. We divide each industry into two sectors: the "corporate" sector, where plants are owned by multiplant firms, and the "nonaffiliate" sector, where firms are single-plant firms. Corporate plants are much larger, typically 10-fold, and they serve large regional or even international markets with relatively standardized products. The smaller nonaffiliates tend to serve more local markets with special-order products. In general, the fraction of nonaffiliate plants in any industry that qualify as class A polluters is very small (see table 1 below). Across industries, average plant sizes also differ enormously by production process. Since regulators focused on the biggest plants first and then successively incorporated smaller plants in nonattainment areas, we expect the relative shift to attainment areas to occur first for corporate plants and then later for nonaffiliates. Similarly across industries, we expect the shift to occur in bigger-plant industries first.

Second, we expect the cumulative effects of regulation to differ between bigger and smaller plants and perhaps between bigger and smaller firms, where corporate firms are more visible, with deeper pockets. Smaller plants in attainment areas escape regulation altogether, and those in nonattainment areas come under regulation later and perhaps in weaker form. All this confers a competitive advantage on the nonaffiliate sector compared to the corporate sector, potentially allowing the market share of nonaffiliates to expand. The extent of the shift toward nonaffiliate plants will vary across industries according to how important plant scale economies are for an industry and how costly it is to shift production to attainment areas. But there is a subtlety in the process in the early years of regulation. At that time, corporate firms may have held back on establishing new plants in polluting industries to allow the uncertainty over the costs of regulation to be resolved (Pindyck's [1993] "input cost" uncertainty) and to allow for the development of cost-effective green equipment. In contrast, nonaffiliates may have jumped into the industry, especially in nonattainment areas, to explore the possible competitive edge granted them under regulation: to learn about cost and production conditions in attainment areas with no history of the industry and to learn about the extent to which they escape regulation (thus resolving Pindyck's "technical" uncertainty).

Third, regulation should extend the lives of "grandfathered" older plants, especially in nonattainment areas. Existing plants with grandfathered equipment operate temporarily with a cost advantage relative to new plants, which are required to purchase more expensive regulated equipment. Firms may prolong the life of existing plants and delay openings of costly new plants or delay renewals of existing plants. Grandfathering effects could, for example, extend the lives of plants born prior to the onset of regulation in the 1970s and extend the lives of plants born in the early years of regulation, as regulations facing entrants later tighten over time.

Finally, regulation may affect the size and investment patterns of large corporate plants, especially in nonattainment areas. Plants may downsize to reduce regulatory scrutiny or to reduce the investment at risk at any site, in the face of uncertainty about the application of regulations across space. Investment patterns may also be altered. Given negotiation costs and considerations of consistency of equipment specifications, large plants may have higher up-front investments and less phasing in of investments in nonattainment areas. So initial irreversible investments will increase in nonattainment areas, whether or not mature plant sizes in nonattainment versus attainment areas differ.

Industry Choice and Data

To choose a set of industries, we studied EPA publications and documents. From the Sector Notebook Project series (Environmental Protection Agency 1995, exhibit 29), we took the 13 industries that typically emit over 25,000 short tons of VOCs a year. Many of them are also major NO_x emitters, but the EPA focuses on VOCs. From that group we selected the industries in which VOC and NO_x emissions accounted for more than 60 percent of total emissions, including carbon monoxide, sulfur dioxide, and particulates, to isolate industries that are likely to be more the focus of regulation of ozone, as opposed to other criterion pollutants. For these industries, using information in Environmental Protection Agency (1978, 1992*b*), we picked three- or four-digit SIC categories that seemed to be the key contributors to VOCs and the target of EPA attention. These categories are (1) industrial organic chemicals (specifically SIC 2865 and 2869 combined), an industry that actually manufactures VOCs; (2) miscellaneous plastic products (SIC 308), which use VOCs intensively in production; (3) metal cans and barrels (SIC 3411 and 3412 combined), a major "surface coater" using VOCs to deliver paint pigments to surfaces; (4) wood furniture (SIC 2511), another major surface coater; (5) commercial printing, gravure (SIC 2754); and (6) motor vehicles and car bodies (SIC 3711).

In the analysis we focus on the first four of these industries, which account for 6 percent of U.S. manufacturing sales. Commercial printing, gravure is very small before 1970. Since we focus on comparisons of preregulatory versus regulatory years in the paper, we drop this industry. For motor vehicles, we report basic birth results but exclude it from detailed analysis because it has relatively few plants, especially in the corporate sector compared to our other industries. That creates sample size and census disclosure problems for the detailed analysis. We also examine regulatory effects on births for a control group of industries that appear to uniquely have two features relative to other industries. For each industry, expenditures (capital and operating) in the 1991 Pollution Abatement Costs and Expenditures (PACE), Current Industrial Reports, of the U.S. Bureau of the Census, on air pollution control are $100,000 total nationally or less; and the industry is not a major input into polluting industries. Our control group consists of eight industries: all apparel industries, which seem to be below the horizon of the EPA; mattresses and bedsprings (SIC 2515); and leather gloves, mittens, luggage, and handbags (SIC 315–17).

Data

Plant and industry data come from the Longitudinal Research Database (LRD), available through the Center for Economic Studies (CES) of the U.S. Census Bureau. The LRD links data on firms and plants over time. For births and size analyses, we focus on data from the *Census of Manufactures*, conducted every five years (more specifically, 1963, 1967, 1972, 1977, 1982, 1987, and 1992), to comprehensively track plants in the United States. The census data link plants to firms and follow plants over time. The census is intended to be a census of establishments—of physical buildings. Each structure (or set of structures)—a plant—devoted to manufacturing is assigned a permanent plant number (PPN). The plant retains that PPN and is "alive" as long as the building remains active in manufacturing. A birth is a new PPN, involving the construction of a new plant, a reopening of a manufacturing plant that was closed ("boarded up") in the prior census, or a conversion of an establishment from service or residential use to manufacturing use. Relocators, which are generally given new PPNs, are births. Plants switching from one SIC classification to another are not births. There are uncorrected linkage problems in the 1987 and 1992 censuses (only), where corporate mergers or administrative restructuring sometimes generates new PPNs for existing plants. In footnotes we report on results from our attempts to eliminate these false births; such adjustments have negligible effects.

The geographic unit of observation is the county. Since 1978, attainment status is defined by county each year in the Code of Federal Regulations (although some northeastern coastal states classify all counties within a state with the same attainment status). For ozone, generally, a county either is or is not in attainment of primary national air quality standards. There is no secondary standard for ozone. While there is a designation of partial attainment (widely used in classification for particulates and sulfur oxides), for ozone, only a handful of counties are listed as partial attainment; most of them are large California counties with the worst air quality readings in the nation. We treat them as nonattainment counties. For the early 1970s, attainment status is defined nationally for 247 air quality control regions. We do the appropriate mapping of regions to counties, defining counties in "priority 1" regions as nonattainment.

For estimation, we need data on county economic characteristics over time. The CES kindly provided LRD-derived data on county manufacturing employment, wages, and salaries. Combining these data with data on our industries of interest, we can calculate the prevailing hourly wage and total overall employment in manufacturing, *outside* the own industry. Sample size is restricted to counties with data not subject to censoring (for disclosure reasons) for *overall* manufacturing by the Census Bureau. For industrial organic chemicals, for example, that reduces the total county sample size by 9 percent in the birth models. Wages are deflated by the output price index for each of our industries from the National Bureau of Economic Research–CES Manufacturing Industry Database by Eric Bartelsman, Randy Becker, and Wayne Gray (available at http://www.nber.org.), resulting in a real wage in output units. Later in the paper, total value of sales is deflated by the same price deflator. Book value of capital stock for mature plants is deflated using price indices for equipment and structures for the relevant industries (e.g., chemicals and allied products for industrial organic chemicals) from the Bureau of Economic Analysis's "Fixed Reproducible Tangible Wealth in the U.S., 1925–." Book value of machinery and equipment in newborn plants is deflated by the producer price index for machinery inputs to the relevant industry (e.g., for industrial organic chemicals, chemical industry machinery [commodity group 1166-04]).

Industry Background

The four industries we focus on in this paper—industrial organic chemicals, metal containers, plastics, and wood furniture—have experienced different effects of regulation, probably as a result of their

AIR QUALITY REGULATIONS 389

differences in national size and typical plant size and the role of the corporate sector. Industrial organic chemicals and metal containers are more alike in these dimensions than plastics and wood furniture. Some basic numbers are given in table 1 for a sample of time periods. The stock of plants and average employment numbers pertain to the end years in the table (1972, 1982, and 1992). The births (since the prior census) and their corresponding new investment numbers pertain to the same ending years.

From table 1, plastics and wood furniture are bigger industries nationally in terms of employment than industrial organic chemicals and metal containers. And there has been rapid growth in plastics. On the other hand, plant sizes in terms of sales and capital-to-labor ratios are much larger in industrial organic chemicals and metal containers than in plastics and wood furniture. Also, the corporate sector plays a dominant role in industrial organic chemicals and, to some extent, metal containers, compared to plastics and wood furniture. With reference to size differences, we note that plant inspections are much more likely in industrial organic chemicals and metal containers. In terms of our hypotheses concerning big plants and plants in industries in which the corporate sector is more highly regulated than the nonaffiliated sector, we expect these hypotheses to apply more strongly to industrial organic chemicals and metal containers.

Table 1 already sheds light on certain hypotheses discussed earlier. In all industries, the share of "dirty" counties in births drops between the preregulatory (1967–72) era and 1987–92, even though there is no shift in general economic activity out of dirty counties (Henderson 1996). In all industries, capital-to-labor ratios for new plants rise dramatically in the same time frame. In all industries, the share of the corporate sector in births drops in the initial years (1977–82) of regulation; and in wood furniture and metal containers, it stays low. In metal containers, under regulation the corporate sector is hit heavily, with a small fraction of 1963 plants surviving to 1992.

In figure 1 we illustrate the time pattern of the shift in births out of nonattainment, or dirty, counties. The industrial organic chemicals industry, our heaviest polluter, is the prototype. After 1977, with the big increase in regulatory intensity, there is a sharp sustained drop in the share of dirty counties in births, with stocks then starting to drop steadily. Other industries show the big drop from the preregulatory era (1967) to 1992. But the pattern can be noisy, as in the small sample size metal containers industry; or it can show a steady decline throughout rather than a sharp decline after

TABLE 1
SIZE AND COMPOSITION OF INDUSTRIES

	1967–72	1977–82	1987–92
	Industrial Organic Chemicals		
Stock of plants	684	865	898
Corporate	62%	58%	60%
New plants (births)	191	246	204
Corporate	42%	28%	41%
In dirty counties*	70%	57%	59%
Average real value of sales (millions of 1987 dollars):			
Corporate	87	72	95
Nonaffiliates	3.3	2.8	5.3
Average corporate employment	304	264	213
All corporate births[†] (thousands of 1987 dollars): total real value of equipment/total employment	258	406	438
Plants inspected, 1985–92[‡]	...	...	20%
1963 plants surviving to 1992	...	...	56%
	Metal Containers		
Stock of plants	547	564	478
Corporate	76%	71%	65%
New plants (births)	178	135	120
Corporate	60%	39%	38%
In dirty counties*	68%	67%	63%
Average real value of sales (millions of 1987 dollars):			
Corporate	31	32	39
Nonaffiliates	3.0	2.3	3.4
Average corporate employment	179	137	116
All corporate births[†] (thousands of 1987 dollars): total real value of equipment/total employment	96	95	130
Plants inspected, 1985–92[‡]	...	...	27%
1963 plants surviving to 1992	...	...	31%
	Plastics		
Stock of plants	7,608	11,630	13,073
Corporate	26%	25%	28%
New plants (births)	4,082	4,524	4,644
Corporate	21%	17%	19%
In dirty counties*	70%	67%	59%
Average real value of sales (millions of 1987 dollars):			
Corporate	10	9.7	14
Nonaffiliates	1.2	1.4	2.7
Average corporate employment	121	103	112
All corporate births[†] (thousands of 1987 dollars): total real value of equipment/total employment	14	32	48
Plants inspected, 1985–92[‡]	...	...	2.4%
1963 plants surviving to 1992	...	...	54%

TABLE 1 (*Continued*)

	1967–72	1977–82	1987–92
	Wood Furniture		
Stock of plants	2,339	2,600	2,783
Corporate	16%	14%	11%
New plants (births)	1,300	1,318	1,279
Corporate	8.9%	4.6%	4.5%
In dirty counties*	63%	57%	48%
Average real value of sales (millions of 1987 dollars):			
Corporate	13	11	17
Nonaffiliates	1.1	.93	.95
Average corporate employment	231	229	253
All corporate births† (thousands of 1987 dollars): total real value of equipment/total employment	9.5	9.6	14
Plants inspected, 1985–92‡	...	...	6.8%
1963 plants surviving to 1992	...	...	49%

* Counties that are in nonattainment in all of 1978, 1982, and 1987.
† Capital stock numbers here are largely imputed by the Census Bureau.
‡ This ratio is the total number of plants reported in the EPA database (County Point Source Summary [AFP649]) as having at least one inspection from 1985 to 1992 divided by the 1987 stock of plants. For the four industries, the ratios of plants that were class A polluters in that sample for VOC or NO_x emissions relative to the 1987 stock are, respectively, 12 percent, 14 percent, 0.7 percent, and 5.0 percent, and the ratios of class A polluters relative to the 1987 stock of corporate plants are 20 percent, 21 percent, 2.6 percent, and 42 percent.

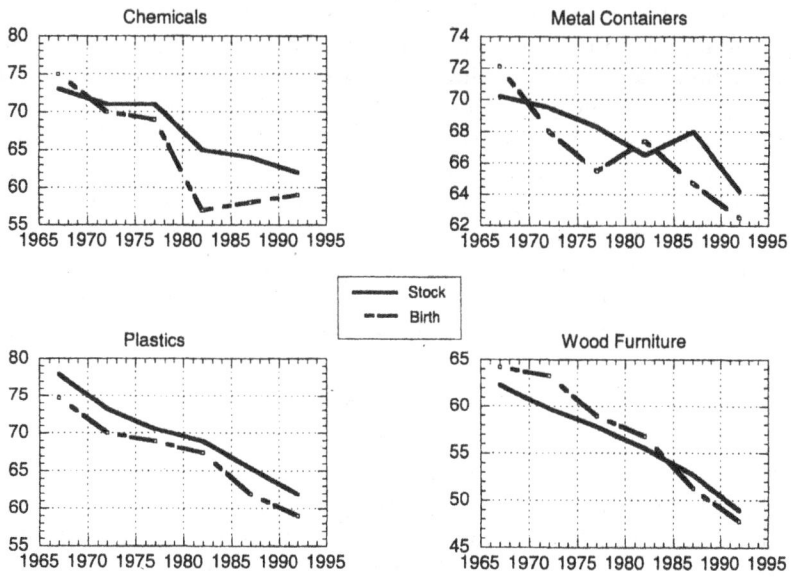

FIG. 1.—"Dirty" counties' percentage share of births and stocks

1977. This suggests that we need to control for economic conditions in dirty versus clean counties to factor out other influences on location patterns besides attainment status. We turn to modeling this next.

Births in Polluting Industries

In this section, we estimate econometric models of births of plants to evaluate our hypotheses concerning the locational shift from nonattainment to attainment areas, the timing of that shift, and relative expansion of the nonaffiliated sector under regulation.

Modeling Births

For the birth process in each county, we adapt the stock model in Henderson, Kuncoro, and Turner (1995) to a flow (gross births) situation. For each separate industry, at a point in time, there is a supply of entrepreneurs in each county who might enter this industry (as opposed to entering other local industries or not starting a new plant). This supply relationship to a county is upward sloping in "births" (gross flows) and "expected net present value (NPV) per plant" space. As one moves up the supply curve, the higher the NPVs, the more local entrepreneurs will enter this industry. The curve may shift outward, say, as county size (e.g., total employment or population) increases. In terms of the opportunities for new plants, there is a corresponding "demand" curve, representing how NPVs per plant change locally with additional births in the industry in the county. The demand curve may be locally upward (local industry external scale economies) or downward (competition in local output markets) sloping. The demand curve shifts up/out as real wages fall, county sizes increase (representing increases in local product demand), or county regulation weakens.

Total births are given by the intersection of the demand and supply curves, in birth-NPV space. This gives a reduced-form equation

$$B_{jt} = B(\mathbf{Y}_{jt}, f_j + e_{jt}), \tag{1}$$

where B_{jt} is births in county j in time t; $\mathbf{Y}_{jt}$ is a vector of county characteristics including attainment status, as well as year dummies; f_j is a county fixed effect of unmeasured time-invariant features of the county affecting births in the industry and is potentially related to the measured county characteristics; and e_{jt} is a contemporaneous independently and identically distributed error term.[2] In general, regularity (i.e., a "stable" intersection of supply and demand) requires the sign of $\partial B_{jt}/\partial Y_{jt}$ to be the same as the sign of the partial derivative of the potential NPVs per plant to be earned (demand curve) with respect to Y_{jt}.[3]

There are three issues concerning this birth model.[4] First is the method of inference for regulatory effects in equation (1). Since we use fixed-effects methods, the "treatment group" includes counties that are designated nonattainment starting in 1978 (and possibly priority 1 in 1972) or switch in later years from attainment to nonattainment status. The "control group" includes all counties historically (1963 up to 1972 or 1978) plus attainment counties in the regulatory era. Inferences are based primarily on how births in nonattainment counties react to the imposition of regulation following 1977, compared to how they react in attainment counties. There is an issue that our sample of industries itself is a regulated group. Accordingly, we examine a control group of eight industries in which there should be no treatment effect of nonattainment status versus attainment status.

The second issue of concern is that this "partial equilibrium" model of county births best fits a situation in which plants are single-plant firms of local entrepreneurs deciding whether to enter this or some other industry locally. In multiplant firms, within an industry,

---

[2] Conditional on controlling for fixed effects that may be spatially correlated, in calculation of standard errors there remains an issue of whether the e_{jt} may be spatially correlated. Henderson (1997) looks at this question in some detail for employment growth for five two-digit capital goods manufacturing industries. In 10 of 11 industry years, controlling for fixed effects, he could not reject the hypothesis that industry-county contemporaneous error terms are uncorrelated within the same metro area for the sample of 317 metro areas.

[3] If $\pi(Y_{jt}, B_{jt}, \delta_{jt})$ is the demand relationship and $\tilde{\pi}(Z_{jt}, B_{jt}, \epsilon_{jt})$ the supply relationship, where Z_{jt} is a subset of Y_{jt}, then $\partial B_{jt}/\partial y_{jt} = (\partial \pi/\partial y_{jt})/[-(\partial \pi/\partial B_{jt}) + (\partial \tilde{\pi}/\partial B_{jt})]$, where the denominator must be positive under regularity. For a common element, such as county scale, $\partial B_{jt}/\partial z_{jt} = [(\partial \pi/\partial z_{jt}) - (\partial \tilde{\pi}/\partial z_{jt})]/[(-\partial \pi/\partial B_{jt}) + (\partial \tilde{\pi}/\partial B_{jt})]$, where we expect $\partial \tilde{\pi}/\partial z_{jt} < 0$.

[4] There is also the issue that NPV opportunities and births are not unrelated to existing stocks (which potential plants take as given). One could condition on existing stocks; but in a panel framework, where stocks evolve through births, that leaves us with prior-period births explaining this-period births (apart from deaths). Alternatively viewed, suppose that we go back to the first period, $t = 0$, in which the industry is in the county. Those births and the initial stock are determined by Y_{j0}, f_j, e_{j0}. In the next period, births are determined by Y_{j1}, f_j, e_{j1} and prior stock, or Y_{j0}, f_j, e_{j0}. As we proceed forward, births in period t are a function of $(\{Y_{j0}, Y_{j1}, \ldots, Y_{jt}\}, f_j, \{e_{j0}, e_{j1}, \ldots, e_{jt}\})$, where the Y_{jt}'s are highly correlated over time and may be strongly affected by the f_j. That is, in panel data set estimation with fixed effects, the f_j essentially control for history and accumulated stocks. In estimation, we report results on eq. (1) as formulated. Including lagged regressors ($Y_{j,t-1}$) results in insignificant coefficients for those regressors.

corporate headquarters may scan the entire U.S. geography to pick a profit-maximizing location in, say, a conditional logit framework. Later in this section we estimate conditional logit models for corporate births and compare results.

The final issue concerns the nature of births in the data. We observe six periods of births (from 1963–67 births to 1987–92 births). The number of births per county typically is small. For example, for U.S. counties that ever have births in industrial organic chemicals from 1963 to 1992, the numbers of counties with 0, 1, 2, 3, . . . , 10 births in 1982 were 263, 123, 19, 5, 2, 1, 0, 1, 0, 0, and 1, respectively. Thus not only are births a discrete number, but in any period there are many zeros. Therefore, a sequence of births for a county over the six periods might be {1, 2, 0, 2, 1, 0}. For counties having births in a year, the median county has one birth in all industries (control and treatment groups) except plastics, where the median is two. A formulation allowing for (a) discreteness, (b) zeros, (c) positive numbers close to one, and (d) consistent estimates with fixed effects is suggested. A version of the Poisson seems a natural choice, and it is conceptually consistent with the county partial equilibrium framework. Results are tested for sensitivity to outliers (industries in which a few counties have very many births compared to most other counties).

Equation (1) is estimated using the conditional Poisson model in Hausman, Hall, and Griliches (1984) (see Anderson [1972] on conditional maximum likelihood), with robust standard errors (Wooldridge [1991] and Papke [1991]; robust to violation of the Poisson assumptions of equality of the mean and variance of the distribution). In the basic Poisson model, the probability of observing B_{jt} births in county j at time t is

$$\text{prob}(B_{jt}) = \frac{e^{-\lambda_{jt}} \lambda_{jt}^{B_{jt}}}{B_{jt}!}, \qquad (2)$$

where λ_{jt} is the Poisson parameter—the expected value of B_{jt}. In the conditional estimator with panel data, a common form for λ_{jt} is

$$\lambda_{jt} = \exp(\mathbf{Y}_{jt}\boldsymbol{\alpha} + f_j), \qquad (3)$$

where $\mathbf{Y}_{jt}$ are our exogenous variables, $\boldsymbol{\alpha}$ is the parameter vector, and f_j is the county fixed effect. The last represents time-invariant unobserved county determinants of birth and introduces some commonality in the conditional means of a county over time.

In estimation, the fixed effect is conditioned out by modeling the event in the likelihood function as the sequence of births in a county over time, conditional on total births for that county over time. Evaluating and rearranging this gives us, as an event in the likelihood function,

$$\text{prob}\left(B_{j1}, B_{j2}, \ldots, B_{jt} \middle| \sum_{t=1}^{T} B_{jt}\right) = \prod_{t=1}^{T} \left[\frac{\exp(Y_{jt}\alpha)}{\sum_{s=1}^{T} \exp(Y_{js}\alpha)}\right]^{B_{jt}} \cdot \frac{\left(\sum_{t=1}^{T} B_{jt}\right)!}{\prod_{t=1}^{T} (B_{jt}!)}, \quad (4)$$

where

$$\text{prob}(B_{j1}, \ldots, B_{jt}) = \frac{\exp\left(-\sum_{t=1}^{T} \lambda_{jt}\right) \prod_{t=1}^{T} \lambda_{jt}^{B_{jt}}}{\prod_{t=1}^{T} (B_{jt}!)},$$

$$\text{prob}\left(\sum_{t=1}^{T} B_{jt}\right) = \frac{\exp\left(-\sum_{t=1}^{T} \lambda_{jt}\right) \left(\sum_{t=1}^{T} \lambda_{jt}\right)^{\sum_{t=1}^{T} B_{jt}}}{\left(\sum_{t=1}^{T} B_{jt}\right)!}.$$

The log likelihood function is globally concave.

Issues in estimating (4) are goodness-of-fit measures and specification tests. For goodness of fit we use an R^2 type measure. Since we cannot predict a county's expected births because f_j's are not estimated, we predict its pattern of births over time, given its total births. In particular,

$$R^2 = 1 - \frac{\sum_{j=1}^{N} \sum_{t=1}^{T} (B_{jt} - E[B_{jt}])^2}{\sum_{j=1}^{N} \sum_{t=1}^{T} (B_{jt} - \bar{B})^2}, \quad (5)$$

where

$$E[B_{jt}] = \left(\sum_{s=1}^{T} B_{js}\right) \cdot \left[\frac{\exp(\mathbf{Y}_{jt}\hat{\boldsymbol{\alpha}})}{\sum_{s=1}^{T} \exp(\mathbf{Y}_{js}\hat{\boldsymbol{\alpha}})}\right].$$

Note that $E[B_{jt}]$ is based on actual total births in j multiplied by the predicted proportion occurring in t. The $\boldsymbol{\alpha}$ coefficients in (4) are consistently estimated as long as the conditional mean is correctly specified and the true distribution is linear exponential, even if it is not Poisson. Wooldridge (1991) devises a Hausman statistic to compare the Poisson estimated parameters with other consistent estimates from nonlinear least squares. In our estimations the χ^2 statistic is sometimes close to the 5 percent critical value, but failure never occurs when we segment the sample into corporate versus nonaffiliate births.

Birth Results

In examining births, we start with our bottom line formulation and result: Plant births drop in nonattainment areas relative to attainment areas as a result of regulation, with the shift depending on the extent to which a county is out of attainment. We present the results, analyze their (large) order of magnitude, and defend them against various possible criticisms. Then we shall turn to more detailed analyses, concerning the timing of the shift to attainment areas between and within industries and the role of the nonaffiliate versus corporate sector.

Basic Results

The main sets of results on the conditional Poisson birth models are all in Appendix tables A1–A4. Births in a county for, say, 1982–87 in the formulation are manufacturing plants in the industry in 1987 that did not exist in manufacturing in 1982. Depending on the industry, over the six waves of births, the number of counties covered ranges from 334 to 1,575 from column 1 of tables A1–A4. Control variables in the model, apart from conditioned-out fixed effects and nonattainment status, are time dummies representing national industry trends and shocks, county manufacturing wages (outside the own industry), and county scale, as measured by all other manufacturing employment in the county. The latter two are base period measures (e.g., 1982 variables for 1982–87 births). Nonattainment status also pertains to the base period, with nonattainment effects

AIR QUALITY REGULATIONS

in column 1 of tables A1–A4 constrained to be the same for 1978, 1982, and 1987 nonattainment status applied to 1977–82, 1982–87, and 1987–92 births (1978 is the first year nonattainment status appears in the Code of Federal Regulations). For the moment, we presume that effective regulation in nonattainment counties starts in 1977–78.

We start with a presentation of results for the control variables. Coefficients in tables A1–A4 may be interpreted as elasticities (given $\lambda_{jt} = \exp[\mathbf{Y}_{jt}\alpha + f_j]$). For the control on county scale, a 1 percent increase in county employment leads to a 0.17–0.46 percent increase in expected births, depending on the industry. For real wages, only for industrial organic chemicals does the coefficient have the expected negative sign and a reasonable degree of significance, with an elasticity of $-.83$. While inclusion or exclusion of a wage variable has no effect on our other results, this disappointing performance of the wage variable is at odds with some other locational studies (e.g., Bartik's [1988] cross-section study). In part, this may be due to the fixed-effects estimation meant to isolate regulatory effects, where there is limited time-series variation in real wages. For example, for 1977–82, the average absolute percentage variation in real wages within counties for industrial organic chemicals is 6.5 percent (vs. 24.4 percent for all other manufacturing employment), whereas cross-sectionally, wages may vary by 100 percent. Also, changes in overall manufacturing wages may crudely measure changes in wages relevant for specific industry subgroups.

Part A of table 2 reports the basic effect of regulation on births in our four industries. Nonattainment status in the regulatory era reduces the expected number of births in a county by 26–45 percent, depending on the industry, with the largest impact occurring for the industry with the largest plant sizes, industrial organic chemicals. Nonattainment status also reduces births in other major VOC industries such as motor vehicles.[5] Magnitudes are not sensitive to dropping anywhere from one to nine outlier (large-birth) counties from each sample.

While the coefficients are large, they are consistent with the raw numbers in table 1 and figure 1 on shifts in birth patterns. For example, for industrial organic chemicals, the coefficient $-.45$ states that, ceteris paribus, nonattainment counties will experience a 45 percent reduction in births, with no change for attainment counties. In

---

[5] Besides motor vehicles (SIC 3711), we also estimated our models for another major apparent VOC emitter (from PACE expenditure data), refrigeration equipment (SIC 3585). For SIC 3711 and 3585, nonattainment status coefficients were, respectively, $-.23^*$ and $-.28^{**}$ (significant at the 10 percent and 5 percent levels, respectively).

TABLE 2

BIRTHS: OVERALL NONATTAINMENT EFFECTS

	Industrial Organic Chemicals	Metal Containers	Plastics	Wood Furniture
	A. Basic Formulation			
Nonattainment status (1978, 1982, 1987)	−.45**	−.27*	−.26**	−.29**
	B. Formulation Allowing for Intensity of Regulation			
Nonattainment:				
County not monitored	−.51**	−.46*	−.19**	−.23**
County monitored	−.93**	−.31	−.61**	−.56**
ln(second-highest daily maximum)—if monitored and nonattainment	−.26	−.03	−.17	−.13
ln(second-highest daily maximum for 1987–92), corporate plants	−1.74**	−.48	−.44**	−1.83**

NOTE.—Covariates in col. 1 of tables A1–A4 are wages, county scale, nonattainment status, and year dummies. Fixed effects are conditioned out.
* Significant at the 10 percent level.
** Significant at the 5 percent level.

1967–72 (preregulation), there were 134 births in "dirty" counties (those in nonattainment throughout 1978, 1982, and 1987) and 57 in "cleaner" counties, so the share of dirty counties is 70 percent. Regulation should reduce, ceteris paribus, the 134 births in dirty counties by 45 percent to 74 births, with births in attainment counties unchanged, so there is a national total of 131 (74 + 57). Thus the expected share of dirty counties in births should drop from 70 percent to 56 percent (74/131). The actual 1987–92 share for dirty counties is 59 percent (see table 1 and fig. 1). Similarly, predicted (vs. actual) shares for metal containers, plastics, and wood furniture are 61 (vs. 63), 63 (vs. 59), and 55 (vs. 48). The differences are not great, and there is no pattern of over- or underprediction. Of course, ceteris paribus does not hold. Not only have relative wages and scale changed, there are also time trends reflected in the time dummies in tables A1–A4; and the reduction in expected births in nonattainment counties may elicit regeneration of the industry to fill national demand. So, for example, between 1967–72 and 1987–92, the time dummy in table A1 predicts that industrial organic chemicals grew by 44 percent, which is roughly consistent with the 56 percent growth from the 131 births predicted above to the 204 actual births in 1987–92.

These large coefficients on nonattainment status make the case that nonattainment counties became less profitable locations following regulation. This conclusion is reinforced if we believe that local governments may have attempted to mitigate the negative effects of nonattainment status by offering potentially offsetting fiscal incentives for newly locating plants. While our estimating equation is reduced-form, if the denominator of the $\partial B_{jt}/\partial y_{jt}$ expression in note 3 equals, say, $\frac{1}{2}$, reflecting a local supply elasticity of new entrepreneurs to the industry of around two, that implies that regulation reduces NPVs by 13–22 percent.[6] Regardless, there seems to be a significant welfare cost as plants shift from more efficient (nonattainment) to less efficient (attainment) counties, to be weighed against environmental gains. To value the extent of welfare losses, one could ask also what magnitudes of environmental costs are suggested by plant input data. Unfortunately, it is generally difficult to get accurate cost data for large samples of newborn plants from the LRD since nonimputed data in the census for items such as capital stock are typically available for only more mature plants, especially before 1987. Nonetheless in an ongoing study (Becker and Henderson 1999), we have estimated average total cost functions for plants in industrial organic chemicals and plastics, with some representation of plants of all ages. The formulation specifies average total costs to be a quadratic function of output, with differential responses by age and attainment status, controlling for time and county fixed effects and county scale and real wages. At plant sizes that minimize average total costs, in industrial organic chemicals, average total costs are higher in nonattainment counties by 17.5 percent for plants 0–4 years of age, by 9.5 percent for plants 5–9 years old, and by 10 percent for plants 10 or more years old. Results for plastics show differentials of 4.5 percent for plants 0–4 years old, 8.5 percent for plants 5–9 years old, and 5.5 percent for older plants. Except for the youngest plants in plastics, calculations are based on sets of coefficients all of which are statistically significant. These cost numbers are in line with our profit function results and consistent with notions of grandfathering, where plants with older equipment escape the increasingly stringent regulations on new equipment, at least until they renew equipment. Cost differentials for nonattainment status are probably understated since cost figures exclude purchased environmental consulting services.

The significant measured effects of regulation on births can be criticized on two grounds: the nonattainment status designation could represent other underlying phenomena, and the (0, 1) measure of regulation in the nonattainment dummy based on equip-

---

[6] We are treating $\pi(\cdot)$ and $\bar{\pi}(\cdot)$ as double log functions. If we assume that, on the demand side, scale or congestion effects are small and the supply of entrepreneurs is fairly elastic, then the inverse elasticities of supply $(\partial \bar{\pi}/\partial B \geq 0)$ and demand $(-\partial \pi/\partial B \gtrless 0)$ will sum to less than $\frac{1}{2}$.

ment regulation is too coarse a measure. We address each of these concerns.

There has been a shift of economic activity from the Northeast and North Central to the West and South. Perhaps nonattainment status in the Northeast, where most counties are nonattainment, is capturing this shift rather than the effects of regulation. However, as Henderson (1996) documents, at the national level, total employment in nonattainment counties grew as fast as or faster than in attainment counties for 1977–87, although nonattainment counties' share of manufacturing employment fell modestly. Our control for county scale measured by total all other manufacturing in and of itself should control for any such regional shifts in economic activity. To check on this, we also examined intraregional shifts in activity to make sure that shifts to attainment counties were occurring in all regions; they are.[7]

Another way to check on whether other phenomena are at work is to examine what happens in a control group of industries. Our control group consists of apparel industries, mattresses, and certain leather products, specifically SIC 231, 232, 2337, 234, 235, 236, 2515, and 315–17. (We selected women's outerwear 2337 from the enormous 233 and avoided the huge catchall 239.) Respective coefficients for these industries are −.09, −.18**, .13, .17, −.32, .03, −.03, and −.16. Of these eight coefficients, only one is significant at any level (at the 5 percent level). For the seven insignificant coefficients, three are close to zero (under 0.1); and of the others, two are positive and three negative. Only one of them is comparable in magnitude to those for our experimental industries, and it is completely insignificant. The significant negative coefficient pertains to men's furnishings (SIC 232), and it presents a very interesting example of the problems in constructing a control group. Men's furnishings heavily utilize elastics and synthetics, from the strongly regulated chemicals industry. While apparel may be below the horizon of the EPA, for men's furnishings, its sister input industries are not. We hope that the point is made: polluting industries experience regulatory effects; nonpolluting ones do not, if they are unconnected through derived demand effects to polluting industries.[8]

---

[7] We illustrate with industrial organic chemicals. For the Northeast, North Central, South, and West, total births changed from 1967–72 to 1987–82 by −13 percent, +16 percent, +3 percent, and +48 percent. The share of dirty counties in births in each of these respective regions between 1967–72 and 1987–92 changed from 89 percent to 85 percent, 70 percent to 42 percent, 51 percent to 49 percent, and 78 percent to 68 percent. Much of the shift to attainment counties occurred in the North Central and West (although we note for the South that dirty counties' share of stocks fell from 53 percent to 46 percent).

[8] There are other difficulties in defining a control group. Industries need to be nonpolluting in all air quality dimensions since nonattainment status across criterion pollutants is correlated. Second, they cannot be "somewhat" clean industries such

AIR QUALITY REGULATIONS

The second issue concerns intensity of regulation and the coarseness of the (0, 1) measure of nonattainment. We cannot measure "intensity" year by year in a way we are comfortable with at the state level, let alone at the county level. We can only infer intensity by arguing that a greater extent of county nonattainment induces greater regulatory activity and, hence, even greater birth reductions. We introduce two measures of regulatory intensity, into the column 1 Poisson models in tables A1–A4. First, we check whether a nonattainment county is currently monitored in the base year (1977, 1982, and 1987), noting that a number of nonattainment counties (especially in the Northeast) are not routinely monitored. Being monitored is an indicator of both degree of nonattainment and general regulatory seriousness for that county. Second, if a nonattainment county is monitored, we interact that status with a measure of its degree of nonattainment. For this measure we use the county's annual air quality reading (for the base year) on which nonattainment status is based—the second-highest daily maximum hourly reading. Being more out of compliance, given that a county is already sufficiently out to warrant monitoring, should induce greater regulatory activity, further reducing births.

In part B of table 2, we report just the attainment status and regulatory variables in this respecified version of column 1 of tables A1–A4. In three of the four cases in which both coefficients are significant, those nonattainment counties that are monitored experience noticeably greater reductions in births than those that are not monitored. Second, given monitoring, the coefficients on the log of the second-highest daily maximum reading are negative, as hypothesized, but never significant. We did break the evaluation up into corporate and nonaffiliate sectors by year (see table 3 below). For the final year, 1987–92, for the corporate sector, effects of the second-highest daily maximum are much stronger. For the four industries, in the last row of table 2, a 1 percent increase in the second-highest daily maximum reading reduces births by 0.44–1.8 percent. In summary, it appears that intensity matters.

Detailed Effects

We now turn to a more detailed analysis of the effects of regulation on births. First, there is the timing of the shift in births from nonattainment to attainment areas. In comparing the corporate and nonaffiliate sectors within industries and in comparing bigger versus

---

as special or general industrial machinery, which are derived demand inputs into polluting industries (for capital goods, SIC 355 and 356, nonattainment status coefficients are negative and significant).

smaller plant industries, we expect the shift to attainment areas to occur later for small plant sectors, since they came under effective regulation later. Second, there are the effects of the competitive edge granted the less regulated nonaffiliate sector in each industry. Details on results are given in columns 2–4 of tables A1–A4. Columns 2–4 both split births in each industry into corporate and nonaffiliate sectors and allow nonattainment effects to vary by year (1978, 1982, and 1987 for 1977–82, 1982–87, and 1987–92 births), as well as allowing for early nonattainment effects in 1972 for 1972–77 births. In part A of table 3, we focus on the differences between nonaffiliates and the corporate sector, general time effects, and the timing of nonattainment effects. We start with timing.

Timing of the shift to attainment counties.—Within each industry, as indicated by the boldfaced pairs of coefficients, the full force of nonattainment status appears to hit the corporate sector a census period before it hits the nonaffiliate sector, with its smaller, less regulated plants. So, for example, the first significant negative coefficient on nonattainment status for corporate industrial organic chemicals appears for 1972–77 births, whereas for nonaffiliates it appears for 1977–82 births. For wood furniture, while nonaffiliates first have a significant negative coefficient in the same time frame (1982–87) as corporate plants, the initial coefficient for nonaffiliates is relatively small absolutely (−.27 vs. −.55) and grows over time (from −.27 to −.45). This time pattern of coefficients across all industries supports the view that large, more visible plants came under regulatory scrutiny earlier than small nonaffiliates.

In terms of timing issues across industries, regulatory effects seem to take hold earlier in industries with bigger plants that are heavier polluters. So, earliest with strong impacts are industrial organic chemicals[9] and then metal containers. Plastics and wood furniture either follow after metal containers or are more phased in. The shift to attainment areas for both nonaffiliates and corporate plants for plastics and wood furniture strengthens over time, to very strong shifts across the board for 1987–92 births.

While shifts to attainment areas strengthen over time for plastics and wood furniture, there is an appearance that, in the corporate sector, effects wane with time for the bigger-plant, more polluting industries, industrial organic chemicals and metals. Measured effects for these two industries in the corporate sector are insignificant for

---

[9] In industrial chemicals, for 1972–77 births, for nonaffiliates it looks as though nonattainment status initially spurs births. That could be an anomaly, or it could be that nonaffiliates moved in to fill the vacuum left by the corporate sector in nonattainment areas, in an era in which nonaffiliates may have not foreseen current or future regulations affecting them.

TABLE 3
BIRTHS: NONATTAINMENT STATUS EFFECTS BY YEAR AND SECTOR

YEAR	INDUSTRIAL ORGANIC CHEMICALS		METAL CONTAINERS		PLASTICS		WOOD FURNITURE	
	Corporate	Nonaffiliated	Corporate	Nonaffiliated	Corporate	Nonaffiliated	Corporate	Nonaffiliated
A. Results from Cols. 3 and 4 of Tables A1–A4								
1972 (for 1972–77 births)	−.49*	.57**	−.16	−.09	−.03	.14**	.03	.02
1978 (for 1977–82 births)	−.29	−.53*	−.66*	.05	−.37**	.05	.05	−.11
1982 (for 1982–87 births)	−.65**	−.60**	.14	−.59*	−.41**	−.18**	−.55**	−.27**
1987 (for 1987–92 births)	−.34	−.25	−.14	−.68**	−.45**	−.35**	−.52*	−.45**
Time dummies:								
1972–77	.10	−.02	−.32	.05	.13	−.01	−.18	.33**
1977–82	.10	.78**	−.15	.13	.12	.04	−.54*	.11
1982–87	.60**	.39*	−.80**	.65**	.39*	.07	−.04	.32**
1987–92	.10	.47*	−.88**	.51**	.24	.22**	−.28	.21**
B. Results from Logit Formulation in the Corporate Sector								
1972	−.46*		−.24		.15***		.02	
1978	−.23		−.64*		−.34***		.07	
1982	−.58**		−.01		−.48***		−.56**	
1987	−.53**		−.10		−.49***		−.50**	

NOTE.—Covariates are wages, county scale, nonattainment status by year, and year dummies. Fixed effects are conditioned out.
* Significant at the 10 percent level.
** Significant at the 5 percent level.
*** Because of computational constraints (the number of county dummy variables), these coefficients are obtained from 11 estimations of 10 percent random samples from plastics data. For 1978, 1982, and 1987, these coefficients are significantly negative at the 10 percent level in four, six, and eight cases, respectively. For 1982 and 1987, the coefficients range from zero to −.89.

1987–92 births. It is possible that effects could wane. For example, green equipment in early regulated industries could become cost efficient and standard everywhere, so the costs and choices of new plants would be less affected by nonattainment status. Nevertheless, we believe that other things are going on. First, for corporate industrial organic chemicals, no waning occurs in logit results discussed below, and for this industry and sector, a logit specification may be more relevant. For metal containers, the corporate sector appears to be decimated by regulation, so that distinguishing between attainment and nonattainment areas beyond 1982 is difficult. That is, in estimation, inferences are being based in later censuses on a total of fewer than 40 corporate births, much less than other industries (in any census).

Potential expansion of nonaffiliates.—Given that nonaffiliate plants are unregulated in attainment areas and less regulated in nonattainment areas, we might expect an expansion of the nonaffiliate relative to the corporate sector. Moreover, as noted earlier, on the basis of Pindyck (1993) type reasoning, in the early years of regulation, corporate firms may delay establishing new plants in polluting industries to allow the uncertainty over the costs of regulation to be resolved, whereas nonaffiliates may jump in the industry to learn about the possible competitive edge granted them under regulation.

What do our results tell us? We base our analysis on the *relative* magnitude of time dummies in the corporate versus nonaffiliate sector within the different industries in part A of table 3. What we are looking for is a postregulation (1972–77 or 1977–82 onward) pattern, where nonaffiliate time dummies exceed those of corporate time dummies, relative to the preregulation base period (1967–72) in the Poisson, indicating more relative births in the nonaffiliate sector. Except for the nationally rapidly growing plastics sector, this appears to be the case. For industrial organic chemicals, metal containers, and wood furniture, in 10 out of 12 cases for 1972–77 onward, the nonaffiliate dummy exceeds the corresponding corporate dummy, in seven cases significantly.[10] Two items stand out in the patterns in part A of table 3.

First, for metal containers, after 1982, births in nonaffiliates jump

[10] This pattern is not weakened if we reestimate the model eliminating potential false (corporate) births in 1987 and 1992. These occur when corporate mergers and restructuring cause new PPNs to be assigned to existing plants. We use industrial organic chemicals as an example. For 1987 and 1992, we relinked a total of 12 false births-deaths, where the exact same plant appeared to be operating despite a new PPN, and dropped seven suspicious cases, eliminating a total of 19 corporate births, or about 10 percent of corporate births. The new table 3 coefficients for nonattainment status and time dummies for industrial organic chemicals are $-.52^*$, $-.34$, $-.76^{**}$, $-.12$; $-.043$, $.12$, $.60^{**}$, $-.34$.

50–65 percent; in the corporate sector, they fall by 80–90 percent. This is the decimation of the corporate sector in metal containers noted earlier in table 1. One could interpret the initial decline in 1977–82 as a corporate response to uncertainty over future costs in the early days of regulation and the later response (after 1982) as a reaction to "bad news" for corporate sector metal containers. After 1982, corporate production in metal containers remains relatively unprofitable compared to the past.

Similar considerations but somewhat different outcomes apply to industrial organic chemicals. In 1972–77 and 1977–82, births are stagnant (actually decline in raw numbers) in the corporate sector. But here the long-term news is good, and 1982–87 births rebound. Also interesting is the situation for nonaffiliates in this industry. The early uncertain regulatory period (1977–82) for nonaffiliates brings an explosion of births—the highest positive time dummy in table 3—and raw numbers jump from 111 nonaffiliate births in 1967–72 to 176 in 1977–82. Many of these births are in attainment counties never having the industry before. The number of clean counties experiencing births rises from 27 in 1972–77 to 64 in 1977–82, before falling back to 46 in 1982–87. This may be small plants experimenting to see how competitive they are operating in attainment counties. Unfortunately, the survival rates of these 1977–82 experimenters are very poor. Only 18 percent of nonaffiliate births in industrial organic chemicals in 1977–82 in attainment counties survive in business five years compared to five-year survival rates for 1967–72 and 1982–87 births of 59 percent and 39 percent. Survival rates for nonaffiliates in nonattainment counties in these years range from 41 to 53 percent. Moreover, average initial investments by nonaffiliates in these attainment counties in 1977–82 are 39 percent of those in nonattainment counties, whereas in other years there is no differential.[11] Presumably the news for nonaffiliate experimenters in industrial organic chemicals was not great; and, after 1982, their share of births is similar to preregulation levels.

Birth Logits

Earlier we noted that the Poisson model of internal county generation of births may not be the best conceptual framework for corpo-

---

[11] On the basis of capital stock numbers from the census (largely imputed) among 1977–82 births, in attainment counties, new plants averaged 1982 capital (machinery and equipment) of $466,000, whereas in nonattainment areas new plants averaged $1,247,000. In 1967–72, births in attainment counties averaged $578,000 in capital (in 1972), which was greater than in nonattainment counties ($407,000). In 1982–87 again the differences in average capital stocks for births in attainment vs. nonattainment counties were small: $6,165,000 vs. $7,038,000, respectively.

rate births. Rather, a conditional logit model may be more applicable, where, conditional on the number of national births, owners of new plants in an industry in each time period survey all counties and pick the profit-maximizing location for the plant. We estimated a maximum likelihood conditional logit model for the plants in the corporate sector of our industries, corresponding to the Poisson model in column 3 of the tables in the Appendix. In each of the six census periods in which this experiment occurs, each birth chooses its best county, with common coefficients on control variables and county dummy variables across the years. We report results on just the key nonattainment variable in logits in part B of table 3 (see Becker [1998] for other results). We find that a switch to nonattainment status reduces the probability that a birth will occur in that county. The magnitudes of coefficients can be compared directly to those in part A of the table. Part A gives a percentage change in expected number of births, whereas part B gives the percentage change in the probability of a typical birth. The two sets of coefficients are similar, with one exception. With conditional logits, in industrial organic chemicals for 1987–92 births, there is no tailing off in the negative nonattainment status effects. Nonattainment status reduces the probability of a birth by 53 percent, comparable to magnitudes in other census periods.

Survival of Births

For the births just described, it would be informative to know about their survival rates. Survival refers to survival of the plant in the county of its birth and in the manufacturing sector. In Becker and Henderson (1997), we examine the five-year survival rates of cohorts of births (survival from first to second census), based on probit estimation. We also estimated more general hazard models and 10-year survival rates. In estimation, it quickly became apparent that survival in the nonaffiliate sector is very noisy and all models had very poor fits in terms of covariates (except plastics, with its huge sample size). This might suggest that unobserved Jovanovic (1982) effects dominate the small-scale sector. So we focused on corporate survivals. In examining corporate survivals, we had sample size problems for all industries but plastics,[12] making it impossible to identify nonattainment effects by year in the corporate sector because of cell size prob-

---

[12] For example, ordinary probit results are problematical, given that unmeasured county attributes affect survivals as well as covariates. So we added county dummy variables to the pooled five waves of five-year survivals for births. Doing so cuts the sample size by 40 percent, eliminating counties in which all births always either survived or died.

lems for industrial organic chemicals, metal containers, and wood furniture. Here we report on just two sets of results: survivals in industrial organic chemicals for all plants (we pooled corporate plants and nonaffiliate plants [which are still noisy but larger in this industry]) and survivals in plastics in the corporate sector.

In table 4, we give point estimates of survival probabilities for a corporate plant in a "typical" county, for different years by nonattainment status, based on the probits in the note to the table. The results for plastics are similar to those in industrial organic chemicals but are less pronounced. First, initial grandfathering effects are apparent, especially in industrial organic chemicals. The survival probability for a typical plant born just before regulation (1967–72) jumps dramatically to .94–.98, compared to a probability of .57 for preregulation (1963–67) births. If a plant got in with cheaper, dirtier equipment just before regulation, it stayed in. Second, for births in the early years of regulation, 1972–77 and 1977–82, a gap develops for survivals in nonattainment versus attainment areas in both plastics and industrial organic chemicals. The relatively low survival rates in attainment areas for those births would be due to their experimental nature. Also, corporate plants born in the early years of regulation could benefit from grandfathering effects as regulations tighten for later births. In the last period (1982–87 births), in the more mature regulatory phase, survival rates for nonattainment and attainment areas again converge, although at higher levels in industrial organic chemicals.

Summary

In all our polluting industries, there has been a relative shift in births from nonattainment to attainment counties, with the magnitude of the shift depending on the extent of nonattainment in a county. Within industries, the shift starts a census period earlier for corporate than for nonaffiliate plants; and, across industries, it appears to start earlier for industries with bigger plant sizes. Overall there is a shift in births from the more regulated corporate to the less regulated nonaffiliate sector in all industries except plastics. The analysis of births, deaths, and survivals does omit an important phenomenon for industrial organic chemicals—switches in and out of the industry, detailed in Becker and Henderson (1997). In general, after regulation, the number of corporate plants switching out of industrial organic chemicals into other manufacturing industries increases dramatically, as does their average size. Sizes of those switching in decline, particularly in later years.

TABLE 4

Survival Probability: Corporate Plants in a Typical County

	Industrial Organic Chemicals	Plastics
Births 1963–67	.57	.51
Births 1967–72:		
Attainment areas	.98**	.57
Nonattainment areas	.94	.57
Births 1972–77:		
Attainment areas	.10	.31**
Nonattainment areas	.71*	.49**
Births 1977–82:		
Attainment areas	.39	.27**
Nonattainment areas	.56	.50**
Births 1982–87:		
Attainment areas	.82	.50
Nonattainment areas	.88	.50

Note.—Estimated probits for industrial organic chemicals ($N = 613$) are (standard errors are in parentheses):

prob(survive) = 2.13 + .394 ln(all other manufacturing employment)
               (3.94) (.321)

    − 3.06 ln(real wage) + .455 corporate dummy
       (1.24)   (.128)

    + 2.05 born 1967–72 − 1.43 born 1972–77
       (.715)   (1.01)

    − .476 born 1977–82 + .737 born 1982–87
       (.635)   (.493)
    − .713 nonattainment 1972 (for 1967–72 births)
       (.547)

    + 1.81 nonattainment 1977 + .466 nonattainment 1982
       (1.02)   (.645)

    + .278 nonattainment 1987 + county dummy variables
       (.434)

For plastics ($N = 3{,}158$):

prob(survive) = .273 − .042 ln(all other manufacturing employment)
               (1.84) (.147)

    + .209 ln(real wage) + .158 born 1967–72
       (.506)   (.192)

    − .510 born 1972–77 − .639 born 1977–82
       (.217)   (.238)

    − .031 born 1982–87 + .0018 nonattainment 1972
       (.216)   (.143)

    + .465 nonattainment 1977 + .678 nonattainment 1982
       (.199)   (.197)

    + .013 nonattainment 1987 + county dummy variables.
       (.156)

* Calculated probability based on a dummy variable significant at the 10 percent level.
** Calculated probability based on a dummy variable significant at the 5 percent level.

AIR QUALITY REGULATIONS 409

Plant Sizes and Timing of Investments

In this section, we look at how plant sizes and investment patterns have changed in the four industries to try to see whether and how regulation has affected plant sizes and investment patterns. We hypothesized that plants may downsize under regulation, for example to reduce regulatory scrutiny that is keyed toward class A polluters. In table 1, we looked at plant production in the corporate sector, measuring size by real sales. In all industries, average corporate real sales per plant rise from 1972 to 1992, so there certainly is no overall downsizing. In three of the four industries, employment per plant does drop, but the table 1 numbers on capital-to-labor ratios for new plants suggest that capital inputs rose, as did sales.

With regard to plant downsizing, the numbers in table 1 could mask possible changes in the age composition of industries. In Becker and Henderson (1997), we explore the question in detail for corporate plants, examining size by age over the years. Only one industry—industrial organic chemicals, which is the largest plant size industry—exhibits the hypothesized size effects, supported by cohort regressions reported on below. When one controls for age, corporate plants born in 1967 before regulation are much larger than plants born later; and 1963 plants with no age controls are even larger than 1967 plants.[13] This suggests plant downsizing among postregulation plants in this particular industry, but we cannot claim that downsizing is a general phenomenon.

Timing of Investments

We hypothesized that new plants in nonattainment areas will undertake larger initial investments than historically or than in attainment counties. Given the costs and structure of environment negotiations in nonattainment counties and perhaps the nature of equipment specification, rather than traditional phasing in, new plants in nonattainment counties do much of their investment up-front, in the beginning. In three of the four industries in the raw data, the ratio of average sales of new plants in dirty relative to clean counties does rise from 1967 to 1992. (For chemicals, plastics, metal containers, and furniture, the pairs of 1967 and 1992 ratios are, respectively,

---

[13] Average real sales for plants 5–9 years old born in 1967, 1972, 1977, 1982, and 1987 are, respectively, $59 million, $45 million, $42 million, $37 million, and $49 million (1987 dollars). For plants 10–14 years old born in 1967, 1972, 1977, and 1982, average real sales are, respectively, $75 million, $46 million, $57 million, and $47 million. Finally, for plants 15–19 years old born in 1967, 1972, and 1977, average real sales are, respectively, $88 million, $49 million, and $57 million.

(1.3, 2.0), (.70, .89), (1.17, .61), and (.32, .87).) However, the ratios are extremely noisy, and econometric analysis is essential to sort out patterns.

To assess the effects of regulation on the timing of new plant investments, we turn to an analysis of differential growth patterns of plant sales between attainment and nonattainment areas. For plants before 1987, we do not have capital stock information in the census; after 1987, equipment and structures cannot be distinguished. We infer investment patterns from sales growth patterns. To assess growth patterns, we look at sizes of all plants by age in each census.

The basic estimating equation explains variation in the logarithm of the real value of plant sales over time, with covariates of county characteristics (log of wages and of all other manufacturing employment), plant characteristics of age and corporate status, nonattainment status information (interacted with age), and then year and county dummies (see below). Nonattainment status interacted with age quantifies the differential growth patterns of plants in nonattainment relative to attainment areas. This formulation imposes common age and nonattainment coefficients for plants of different vintages; below we shall comment on some results of vintage-cohort analyses.

In the current formulation, we distinguish only three age categories (newborn, 5–9 years, and 10+ years), so we can start plant observations in 1972, where all 1963 plants are 10+ years old (almost).[14] To quantify differential growth patterns by attainment status, besides dummy variables for each age category, we have dummy variables for all plants (the effect for new plants) in nonattainment areas, plants 5–9 years in nonattainment areas, and plants 10+ years in nonattainment areas. Then for older plants (10+ years), for example, the net effect of nonattainment status relative to attainment areas is the sum of the nonattainment coefficients for all plants and for plants 10+ years.

There are two issues in estimation. The first concerns the sample. We exclude plants with just administrative records (i.e., plants in existence but whose sales are imputed, not surveyed). Eliminating administrative records leaves virtually all corporate plants but eliminates most smaller plants in the nonaffiliate sector.[15] Consequently,

---

[14] If we added a fourth category, 10–14 years (then 15+ years), we would need either to drop all 1963 plants (since we could not tell whether they were 10–14 or 15+ years) or to start size regressions in 1977, dropping 1972 plants and eliminating a comparison with the preregulation era. Thus the sample covers plants observed in 1972, 1977, 1982, 1987, and 1992 in the census.

[15] For two industries the corporate sample in ordinary least squares (OLS) estimation for 1972–92 is entirely nonadministrative records. The biggest deviator is plastics, with just nine out of 13,324 records being administrative for 1972–92 in the

distinguishing between corporate and nonaffiliate plants is no longer so important; and, more critically, results for corporate versus all plants with nonadministrative records are similar, so we report just on the latter. Second, in estimation we have a choice between OLS, county fixed effects, and plant fixed effects. We choose county fixed effects. It is clear that OLS estimates are problematical. Plant sizes and county characteristics (e.g., wages and nonattainment status) are related to county unobservables. Imposing county fixed effects has little impact on sample size (relative to OLS), excluding only plants in counties in which only one plant ever appears just once. The biggest drop (wood furniture) is 5 percent. Imposing plant fixed effects requires plants to be in the sample two censuses, eliminating all newborn plants in 1992 (a key group) as well as many other newborns in other years. This results in nonrandom percentage drops in sample sizes of 24 percent for industrial organic chemicals, 17 percent for metal containers, 28 percent for plastics, and 43 percent for wood furniture. It appears that results differ between county and plant fixed-effect formulations because of changes in the sample.[16]

The basic results are in table 5. In the estimating equations, because size is contemporaneous, so are covariates. So 1982 size is a function of 1982 county and plant covariates (where 1981 attainment status defines status through July 1982). We briefly comment on the nonregulatory variables. County wage and scale covariates have little impact on plant sizes, indicating that plant scale (vs. local industry scale) is little affected. Age dummies have expected strong effects. Plant sizes increase by 55–75 percent and then by about 100 percent when one moves from a 0–4-year age to a 5–9 and then 10+ age category, respectively. Corporate plant sizes, ceteris paribus, are typically 130 percent larger than noncorporate plants in this restricted sample.

With regard to nonattainment status effects in table 5, except for metal containers, there is a clear pattern. New plants (the "all" category) are significantly larger in nonattainment counties than in attainment counties, by 25–69 percent. That effect then diminishes with age, so that plants 10+ years have a similar size in nonattainment counties. For these plants, for industrial organic chemicals,

---

corporate sector. For all plants, the share of administrative records in all records in census years 1972–92 is 19 percent for industrial organic chemicals, 16 percent for metal containers, 33 percent for plastics, and 48 percent for wood products. These numbers already exclude records with zero sales.

[16] For example, when just the plant fixed-effect sample is used, for county and plant fixed-effect formulations, results are similar; but results with county fixed effects differ between the plant fixed-effect vs. county fixed-effect samples.

TABLE 5

SIZE DETERMINANTS: TOTAL REAL VALUE OF SALES

	Industrial Organic Chemicals	Metal Containers	Plastics	Wood Furniture
ln (all other manufacturing)	−.075	.256*	−.020	−.085
	(.129)	(.149)	(.036)	(.088)
ln (real wage)	−.071	−.576	.040	−.451*
	(.326)	(.402)	(.108)	(.245)
Age 5–9 years	.755**	.643**	.570**	.554**
	(.125)	(.112)	(.023)	(.056)
Age 10+ years	1.41**	1.03**	.950**	1.07**
	(.115)	(.110)	(.022)	(.052)
Dummy corporation	1.34**	1.27**	1.16**	1.30**
	(.079)	(.112)	(.015)	(.050)
Nonattainment, 1981, 1986, 1991:				
All	.685**	−.013	.250**	.482**
	(.175)	(.181)	(.037)	(.080)
Age 5–9 years	−.736*	−.158	−.191**	−.268**
	(.196)	(.211)	(.037)	(.088)
Age 10+ years	−.572**	−.202	−.272**	−.565**
	(.159)	(.173)	(.032)	(.080)
Year dummies:				
1977	−.148	−.097	.035	−.023
	(.148)	(.090)	(.027)	(.049)
1982	−.477**	−.219**	−.079**	−.330**
	(.161)	(.102)	(.032)	(.063)
1987	−.097	−.046	.367**	.073
	(.115)	(.098)	(.032)	(.065)
1992	−.139	.077	.308**	−.109*
	(.122)	(.108)	(.033)	(.066)
Adjusted R^2	.535	.488	.372	.530
Observations	2,858	2,024	32,024	6,046
Counties	319	261	1,321	635

* Significant at the 10 percent level.
** Significant at the 5 percent level.

plastics, and wood furniture, the net effects of nonattainment status for older plants are 11, −2, and −8 percent, respectively. Table 6 breaks out attainment status–age effects by year. Generally effects of 1981 attainment status on 1982 size are not so important, except for wood furniture. Strong effects exist in 1987 and 1992, where, for example, for industrial organic chemicals, new plants in nonattainment counties are 90 percent larger in sales than their counterparts in attainment counties (when we control for observed and unobserved county characteristics). Again with age, the differences appear to evaporate. Effects for metal containers also appear in 1987 and 1992, although positive effects for new plants seem to be outweighed by negative effects with aging.

A concern with these results is the existence of potential false

AIR QUALITY REGULATIONS

TABLE 6
TOTAL REAL SALES: TIME-VARYING NONATTAINMENT STATUS

	Industrial Organic Chemicals	Metal Containers	Plastics	Wood Furniture
1981 nonattainment:				
All	.351	−.453*	.134**	.429**
	(.231)	(.257)	(.052)	(.102)
Age 5–9	−.417	.339	−.124**	−.290**
	(.275)	(.299)	(.054)	(.133)
Age 10+	−.084	.306	−.070	−.595**
	(.211)	(.252)	(.047)	(.112)
1986 nonattainment:				
All	.859**	.241	.423**	.552**
	(.231)	(.252)	(.049)	(.106)
Age 5–9	−.910**	−.684*	−.305**	−.268**
	(.279)	(.365)	(.053)	(.125)
Age 10+	−.784**	−.501**	−.482**	−.577**
	(.222)	(.246)	(.046)	(.118)
1991 nonattainment:				
All	.962**	.330	.219**	.484**
	(.239)	(.287)	(.050)	(.114)
Age 5–9	−.964**	−.387	−.156**	−.246**
	(.321)	(.347)	(.056)	(.141)
Age 10+	−.980**	−.619**	−.283**	−.528**
	(.227)	(.285)	(.047)	(.122)

* Significant at the 10 percent level.
** Significant at the 5 percent level.

births: existing plants that are assigned new PPNs by "mistake" in 1987 and 1992, creating both a false death (old PPN) and birth (new PPN). False births in later years could occur disproportionately among traditional plants in nonattainment areas and involve large existing plants, hence giving the appearance of large births in nonattainment areas. As explained in note 10, for industrial organic chemicals, metal containers, and wood furniture, we went through births by hand to relink obvious false deaths-births and eliminate suspicious cases. We reestimated the size models with the new samples, getting size results very similar to those in tables 5 and 6.[17]

Results in tables 5 and 6 do not allow for vintage-size and vintage-nonattainment-age effects. For nonattainment status, cohort regressions support the results in tables 5 and 6 and do not suggest new

[17] The new sets of table 6 coefficients for these three industries by column are, respectively, (i) .359, −.415, −.097; .755**, −.803**, −.694**; .961**, −.978**, −.941**; (ii) −.395, .301, .255; .178, −.577, −.415*; .175, −.230, −.440*; and (iii) .443**, −.298**, −.612**; .571**, −.276**, −.594**; .503**, −.245*, −.539**.

insights.[18] With respect to vintage-size effects, a cohort specification allows for more specific downsizing patterns. For industrial organic chemicals, these regressions support the notion that plants born in the regulatory era grow to smaller sizes than preregulation plants, as suggested earlier. For example, in cohort regressions, from Becker and Henderson (1997), when plants born in 1967 are 5–9 years old, their sizes exceed those of same-age plants of 1972, 1977, 1982, and 1987 births by 48, 64, 45, and 20 percent, respectively. When they are 10–14 years old, 1967 plants exceed sizes of same-age births for 1972, 1977, and 1982 births by 115, 29, and 29 percent, respectively.

Conclusions and Assessment

The key tool of air quality regulation is stringency of equipment specifications, to limit emissions from production processes. The stringency of regulation has varied over time and space and by plant size, age, and visibility. Officially, stringency varies by space according to nonattainment versus attainment status of counties; it varies by plant size according to the plant's perceived potential to pollute; and it varies by age according to whether the plant is new or already in business. Unofficially, stringency varies by time, given slower implementation for smaller plants; and it varies currently by plant size given regulatory strategies to focus inspections and monitoring on bigger plants. An alternative to the current regulatory regime would be complete uniformity of regulation by space, size, and age. In this section we review our results and discuss the effects of regulation, using complete uniformity as a benchmark of comparison.

In this paper we obtained the following results.

1. Births fall dramatically in nonattainment counties, compared to attainment counties, with the advent of regulation, with effects

[18] Cohort regressions on the logarithm of the real value of sales in census years 1972–92 apart from county covariates and county dummy variables have 42 other dummy variables (with attendant cell size problems), one dummy variable for each census time and birth year (going back to 1963), with a differential dummy for each of them for 1982 and beyond for nonattainment status. For industrial organic chemicals, metal containers, plastics, and wood furniture, respectively, the triplets of the percentages by which average plant sizes for new plants in nonattainment areas exceed those in attainment areas in 1982, 1987, and 1992 are (41, 21, 67), (22, −41, −81), (3, 21, 13), and (55, 34, 57). As before, results for the small sample size metal containers do not correspond to those for the other industries. For new plants in 1982, after 10 years in 1992, the percentage differentials in average plant sizes in nonattainment areas compared to attainment areas are insignificant. Plants in attainment areas catch up to their nonattainment counterparts with age.

increasing with the extent of nonattainment of air quality standards. The shift in birth patterns induces a reallocation of stocks of plants toward attainment areas. Depending on the interpretation of reduced-form coefficients, net present value for a typical new plant in a nonattainment area could fall by 13–22 percent. Those numbers may seem large, but they pertain to just these very heavy polluting industries. The shift in plants has affected air quality. For example, in Henderson (1996), the reduction in stocks of polluting plants in nonattainment areas helps bring those areas into attainment, and the shift of key industries to attainment areas causes air quality degradation there. These are unintended consequences of the Clean Air Act, but not necessarily bad ones. If regulatory policy was uniform across space, there would be no incentive for plants to relocate to attainment areas. That would improve production efficiency, but there would not be a spreading out of pollution. Spreading out of pollution lowers ozone peaks in high-pollution areas and moves pollution to less populous areas. Both may improve overall health.

2. Regulation has spurred births in the small-scale nonaffiliate sector, compared to the corporate sector. However, only in metal containers and wood furniture is there a sustained gain in nonaffiliate births and stocks, resulting in an increase in their market share of plants. To evaluate the cost of this shift, we would need to know the shape of long-run cost functions for these industries, an exercise beyond the scope of this paper. From an environmental point of view, the shift is probably bad. It presumably promotes growth of small, relatively dirty (unregulated) plants.

In the short run, in the early years of regulation, there was a burst of nonaffiliate births with poor survival rates. These births could be viewed as experiments made to learn about (a) the market potential for nonaffiliates, especially in nontraditional attainment areas, and (b) the extent to which small plants would escape regulation in nonattainment areas. Uniform regulation by space and plant size would have stopped both such experimentation and the changes in industrial structure in metal containers and wood furniture.

3. Grandfathering of preregulation plants raises survival rates, limiting "natural" plant turnover and keeping otherwise unprofitable operations in business. It also slows the improvement in air quality, as older, dirtier plants have prolonged lives. A more uniform policy with respect to age would have encouraged retrofitting and other antipollution activities of existing VOC and NO_x emitters much earlier in the regulatory process.

4. Investment or growth patterns of plants appear to be affected by regulation. In particular, relative to attainment areas, new plants

subject to strong regulation in nonattainment areas start off significantly larger (more up-front investment), but over time (within 10 years) their sizes converge to those of plants in attainment areas (with more phased-in investments). This difference across space in growth patterns probably means that investments in nonattainment areas are more cautious (since they involve bigger sunk investments), limiting turnover in those areas, whereas attainment areas attract more risky investments. Again, these are spatial distortions.

Appendix

TABLE A1

BIRTHS: INDUSTRIAL ORGANIC CHEMICALS

	All Births ($N = 415$)		Corporate Births ($N = 212$)	Nonaffiliate Births ($N = 316$)
	(1)	(2)	(3)	(4)
ln(manufacturing employment)	.463**	.466**	.424**	.468**
	(.142)	(.141)	(.214)	(.195)
ln(real wage)	−.834*	−.854*	.306	−1.52**
	(.466)	(.469)	(.736)	(.644)
Nonattainment:				
1978, 1982, 1987	−.450**			
	(.132)			
1972 (for 1972–77 births)		.097	−.487*	.566**
		(.192)	(.271)	(.268)
1978 (for 1977–82 births)		−.456**	−.292	−.532**
		(.192)	(.333)	(.251)
1982 (for 1982–87 births)		−.616**	−.647**	−.603**
		(.187)	(.286)	(.247)
1987 (for 1987–92 births)		−.279	−.340	−.250
		(.192)	(.296)	(.251)
Period:				
1963–67	−.223	−.226	.110	−.454**
	(.138)	(.138)	(.207)	(.176)
1972–77	.166	.105	.104	−.021
	(.217)	(.258)	(.351)	(.375)
1977–82	.551**	.555**	.095	.783**
	(.142)	(.182)	(.301)	(.241)
1982–87	.369**	.483**	.599**	.389*
	(.141)	(.167)	(.257)	(.222)
1987–92	.437**	.334*	.095	.469*
	(.185)	(.199)	(.318)	(.268)
T	6	6	6	6
Pseudo R^2	.615	.615	.450	.453
Robust Hausman statistic	16.77	21.01	11.71	16.46

* Significant at the 10 percent level.
** Significant at the 5 percent level.

TABLE A2
Births: Metal Containers

	All Births (N = 334)		Corporate Births (N = 215)	Nonaffiliate Births (N = 212)
	(1)	(2)	(3)	(4)
ln (manufacturing employment)	.327**	.325**	.576**	.145
	(.161)	(.161)	(.237)	(.223)
ln (real wage)	.278	.266	1.05	.227
	(.663)	(.660)	(1.08)	(.873)
Nonattainment:				
1978, 1982, 1987	−.272*			
	(.165)			
1972 (for 1972–77 births)		−.116	−.159	−.092
		(.187)	(.261)	(.281)
1978 (for 1977–82 births)		−.232	−.658*	.051
		(.268)	(.371)	(.422)
1982 (for 1982–87 births)		−.240	.142	−.590*
		(.232)	(.377)	(.316)
1987 (for 1987–92 births)		−.371*	−.135	−.683**
		(.221)	(.344)	(.291)
Period:				
1963–67	−.387**	−.389**	−.115	−.730**
	(.147)	(.147)	(.183)	(.236)
1972–77	−.216*	−.136	−.316	.054
	(.122)	(.167)	(.231)	(.259)
1977–82	−.035	−.067	−.148	.132
	(.196)	(.260)	(.342)	(.407)
1982–87	−.051	−.074	−.799**	.647**
	(.170)	(.220)	(.344)	(.289)
1987–92	−.247	−.183	−.881**	.512**
	(.167)	(.179)	(.271)	(.259)
T	6	6	6	6
Pseudo R^2	.534	.535	.352	.446
Robust Hausman statistic	8.05	8.53	6.41	9.41

* Significant at the 10 percent level.
** Significant at the 5 percent level.

TABLE A3
BIRTHS: MISCELLANEOUS PLASTICS PRODUCTS

	ALL BIRTHS ($N = 1,575$)		CORPORATE BIRTHS ($N = 1,001$)	NONAFFILIATE BIRTHS ($N = 1,443$)
	(1)	(2)	(3)	(4)
ln(manufacturing employment)	.392**	.399**	.337**	.416**
	(.059)	(.058)	(.076)	(.063)
ln(real wage)	.192	.181	.069	.245
	(.193)	(.195)	(.277)	(.206)
Nonattainment:				
1978, 1982, 1987	−.261**			
	(.047)			
1972 (for 1972–77 births)		.104**	−.034	.142**
		(.039)	(.083)	(.044)
1978 (for 1977–82 births)		−.023	−.366**	.050
		(.049)	(.100)	(.057)
1982 (for 1982–87 births)		−.245**	−.414**	−.184**
		(.057)	(.097)	(.062)
1987 (for 1987–92 births)		−.367**	−.453**	−.351**
		(.065)	(.098)	(.068)
Period:				
1963–67	−.591**	−.593**	−.457**	−.626**
	(.066)	(.066)	(.082)	(.073)
1972–77	.099	.033	.131	−.006
	(.063)	(.072)	(.116)	(.076)
1977–82	.253**	.062	.123	.040
	(.059)	(.061)	(.109)	(.068)
1982–87	.170**	.158**	.385**	.074
	(.067)	(.075)	(.121)	(.080)
1987–92	.165*	.232**	.244*	.218**
	(.096)	(.093)	(.146)	(.097)
T	6	6	6	6
Pseudo R^2	.931	.937	.810	.936
Robust Hausman statistic	15.35	16.54	12.71	17.46

* Significant at the 10 percent level.
** Significant at the 5 percent level.

TABLE A4
BIRTHS: WOOD FURNITURE

	ALL BIRTHS ($N = 1{,}226$)		CORPORATE BIRTHS ($N = 255$)	NONAFFILIATE BIRTHS ($N = 1{,}185$)
	(1)	(2)	(3)	(4)
ln (manufacturing employment)	.173**	.177**	−.071	.184**
	(.060)	(.060)	(.216)	(.061)
ln (real wage)	−.018	−.012	−.649	.033
	(.225)	(.225)	(.822)	(.228)
Nonattainment:				
1978, 1982, 1987	−.289**			
	(.065)			
1972 (for 1972–77 births)		.028	.027	.023
		(.067)	(.278)	(.071)
1978 (for 1977–82 births)		−.095	.050	−.111
		(.084)	(.311)	(.089)
1982 (for 1982–87 births)		−.276**	−.547**	−.267**
		(.089)	(.299)	(.090)
1987 (for 1987–92 births)		−.442**	−.520*	−.445**
		(.082)	(.307)	(.085)
Period:				
1963–67	−.142**	−.141**	−.846**	−.094**
	(.045)	(.045)	(.194)	(.046)
1972–77	.307**	.290**	−.184	.328**
	(.048)	(.068)	(.224)	(.071)
1977–82	.195**	.056	−.542*	.105
	(.075)	(.085)	(.299)	(.090)
1982–87	.304**	.293**	−.040	.323**
	(.081)	(.080)	(.267)	(.081)
1987–92	.094	.172*	−.280	.210**
	(.079)	(.088)	(.297)	(.089)
T	6	6	6	6
Pseudo R^2	.926	.926	.423	.924
Robust Hausman statistic	17.93	17.03	10.41	16.59

* Significant at the 10 percent level.
** Significant at the 5 percent level.

References

Andersen, Erling B. "The Numerical Solution of a Set of Conditional Estimation Equations." *J. Royal Statis. Soc.*, ser. B, 34 (April 1972): 42–54.

Bartik, Timothy J. "The Effects of Environmental Regulation on Business Location in the United States." *Growth and Change* 19 (Summer 1988): 22–44.

Becker, Randy. "The Effects of Environmental Regulation on Firm Behavior." Ph.D. dissertation, Brown Univ., 1998.

Becker, Randy, and Henderson, J. Vernon. "Effects of Air Quality Regulation on Decisions of Firms in Polluting Industries." Working Paper no. 6160. Cambridge, Mass.: NBER, September 1997.

———. "Costs of Air Quality Regulation." Manuscript. Washington: U.S. Bur. Census, Center Econ. Studies, June 1999.

Environmental Protection Agency. "Requirements for Preparation, Adoption, and Submittal of Implementation Plans." *Fed. Register* 36 (August 14, 1971).

———. *Federal Air Quality Control Regions*. Rockville, Md.: Off. Air Programs, 1972.

———. *The National Air Monitoring Program: Air Quality and Emission Trends (Annual Report)*. Research Triangle Park, N.C.: Off. Air Quality Planning and Standards, 1973.

———. *Air Quality Criteria for Ozone and Other Photochemical Oxidants*. Research Triangle Park, N.C.: Environmental Criteria and Assessment Off., 1978. (*a*)

———. *Summary of Group I Control Technique Guideline Documents for Control of Volatile Organic Emissions from Existing Stationary Sources*. Research Triangle Park, N.C.: Off. Air Quality Planning and Standards, 1978. (*b*)

———. *National Air Pollutant Emission Estimates, 1900–1991*. Research Triangle Park, N.C.: Off. Air Quality Planning and Standards, 1992. (*a*)

———. *National Air Quality and Emission Trends Report*. Research Triangle Park, N.C.: Off. Air Quality Planning and Standards, 1992. (*b*)

———. *Sector Notebook Project*. Washington: Off. Compliance, 1995.

Gray, Wayne B. "Does State Environmental Regulation Affect Plant Location?" Manuscript. Worcester, Mass.: Clark Univ., Dept. Econ., 1996.

Hausman, Jerry A.; Hall, Bronwyn H.; and Griliches, Zvi. "Econometric Models for Count Data with an Application to the Patents–R & D Relationship." *Econometrica* 52 (July 1984): 909–38.

Henderson, J. Vernon. "Effects of Air Quality Regulation." *A.E.R.* 86 (September 1996): 789–813.

———. "Externalities and Industrial Development." *J. Urban Econ.* 42 (November 1997): 449–70.

Henderson, J. Vernon: Kuncoro, Ari; and Turner, Matthew. "Industrial Development in Cities." *J.P.E.* 103 (October 1995): 1067–90.

Jovanovic, Boyan. "Selection and the Evolution of Industry." *Econometrica* 50 (May 1982): 649–70.

Kahn, Matthew E. "Regulation's Impact on County Pollution and Manufacturing Growth in the 1980's." Manuscript. New York: Columbia Univ., Dept. Econ., 1994.

Laws, Elliott P. "The Regulation of Stationary Sources." In *Clean Air Law and Regulation*, edited by Timothy A. Vanderver. Washington: Bur. Nat. Affairs, 1992.

Levinson, Arik. "Environmental Regulations and Manufacturers' Location Choices: Evidence from the Census of Manufactures." *J. Public Econ.* 62 (October 1996): 5–29.

Liroff, Richard A. *Reforming Air Pollution Regulation: The Toil and Trouble of EPA's Bubble.* Washington: Conservation Found., 1986.

McConnell, Virginia D., and Schwab, Robert M. "The Impact of Environmental Regulation on Industry Location Decisions: The Motor Vehicle Industry." *Land Econ.* 66 (February 1990): 67–81.

Melnick, R. Shep. *Regulation and the Courts: The Case of the Clean Air Act.* Washington: Brookings Inst., 1983.

Papke, Leslie E. "Interstate Business Tax Differentials and New Firm Location: Evidence from Panel Data." *J. Public Econ.* 45 (June 1991): 47–68.

Pindyck, Robert S. "Investments of Uncertain Cost." *J. Financial Econ.* 34 (August 1993): 53–76.

Waxman, Henry A. "The Clean Air Act of 1990: An Overview of Its History and Policy." In *Clean Air Law and Regulation,* edited by Timothy A. Vanderver. Washington: Bur. Nat. Affairs, 1992.

Wooldridge, Jeffrey M. "Specification Testing and Quasi-Maximum-Likelihood Estimation." *J. Econometrics* 48 (May 1991): 29–55.

Part III
Macroeconomic and General Equilibrium Effects

[11]

Environmental regulation and U.S. economic growth

Dale W. Jorgenson*

and

Peter J. Wilcoxen*

In this article we quantify the costs of pollution controls by reporting the results of simulations of the growth of the U.S. economy with and without regulation. For this purpose, we have constructed a detailed model of the economy that includes the determinants of long-term growth. We have also analyzed the interaction between industries in order to capture the full repercussions of environmental regulations. However, we have not attempted to assess the benefits resulting from a cleaner environment. We find that pollution abatement has emerged as a major claimant on the resources of the U.S. economy. The cost of emission controls is more than 10% of the total cost of government purchases of goods and services.

1. Introduction

■ The most striking economic development in the United States during the postwar period has been the sharp decline in the rate of economic growth during the 1970s and 1980s. Real output grew at an average annual rate of 3.7% during the period 1947–1973. By contrast the growth rate from 1973 to 1985 was only 2.5%, fully 1.2 percentage points lower. Two events coincided with the slowdown—the advent of environmental regulation and the increase of world petroleum prices. In this study we focus on the relationship between pollution abatement costs and economic growth.

We begin with the usual disclaimer in economic studies about the costs of environmental regulation. In this article we quantify the costs of environmental regulation and compare these costs with those of governmentally mandated activities that are financed directly through the government budget. We have not attempted to assess the benefits resulting from a cleaner environment.[1] We have not accounted for consumption benefits resulting from environmental cleanup or production benefits associated with pollution abatement. The

---

* Harvard University.
We are deeply indebted to Mun Sing Ho for his work on the model presented in this article and to Richard Goettle and Edward Hudson for their collaboration on an earlier phase of the research. Barbara Fraumeni, Dackeun Park, and Daniel Slesnick generously provided essential data. We are grateful to Jan Acton, Lawrence Goulder, William Hogan, Robert Stavins, and two anonymous referees for many useful comments on an earlier draft of this article. Needless to say, we alone are responsible for any remaining deficiencies.

[1] The evaluation of environmental benefits is discussed, for example, in Freeman (1985) and Maler (1985).

conclusions of this study cannot be taken to imply that pollution control is too burdensome or, for that matter, insufficiently restrictive.

Pollution control legislation began in earnest in the United States in 1965, when amendments to the Clean Air Act set national automobile emissions standards for the first time. The extent of regulation increased dramatically in 1970 with the passage of the National Environmental Policy Act and amendments to the Clean Air Act. In 1972 the Clean Water Act was passed and revisions to this Act and the Clean Air Act were adopted in 1977.[2] The consequence of this legislation was a large and abrupt shift of economic resources toward pollution abatement.

The possible responses of producers to new environmental regulations fall into three categories—substitution of less polluting inputs for more polluting ones, investment in pollution abatement devices to clean up waste, and changes in production processes to reduce emissions. Switching to cleaner inputs is the least disruptive of these responses, since it does not require a reorganization of the production process. A prime example is the substitution of low-sulfur coal for high-sulfur coal by electric utilities during the 1970s to comply with restrictions on sulfur dioxide emissions. Another important example is the shift from leaded to unleaded fuels for the purpose of cleaning up motor vehicle emissions.

The second response to emissions controls is the use of special devices to treat wastes after they have been generated. This is commonly known as end-of-pipe abatement and is frequently the method of choice for retrofitting existing facilities to meet newly imposed environmental standards. A typical example is the use of electrostatic precipitators to reduce the emission of particulates from combustion. Regulations promulgated in the United States by the Environmental Protection Agency effectively encourage the use of this approach by setting standards for emissions on the basis of the "best available technology."

Process changes involve redesigning production methods to reduce emissions. An example is the introduction of fluidized bed technology for combustion, which results in reduced emissions. Gollop and Roberts (1983) constructed a detailed econometric model of electric utility firms that is based on a cost function that incorporates the impact of environmental regulation on the cost of producing electricity and the rate of productivity growth. They concluded that the annual productivity growth of electric utilities impacted by more restrictive emissions controls declined by .59 percentage points over the period 1974–1979. This was the result of switching technologies to meet new standards for sulfur dioxide emissions.

We analyze the impact of environmental regulation by simulating the long-term growth of the U.S. economy with and without regulation. For this purpose, we have constructed a detailed model of the economy that includes the determinants of long-run growth. Before considering the impact of specific pollution controls, we present an overview of the model in Section 2. We focus attention on features that facilitate the incorporation of changes in environmental policy. We also discuss the dynamics of the response of the economy to new pollution abatement requirements.

In Section 3 we show that pollution abatement has emerged as a major claimant on the resources of the U.S. economy. The long-run cost of environmental regulation is a reduction of 2.59% in the level of the U.S. gross national product. This is more than 10% of the share of total government purchases of goods and services in the national product during the period 1973–1985. Over this period, the annual growth rate of the U.S. economy has been reduced by .191%. This is several times the reduction in growth estimated in previous studies.

Since the stringency of pollution control differs substantially among industries, our model also assesses the impact of environmental regulations on individual industries. We

---

[2] A detailed survey of U.S. environmental policy is presented in Christiansen and Tietenberg (1985).

have analyzed the interactions between industries in order to quantify the full repercussions of these regulations. We find that pollution controls have had their most pronounced effects on the chemicals, coal mining, motor vehicles, and primary processing industries—such as petroleum refining, primary metals, and pulp and paper. For example, we find that the long-run output of the automobile industry has been reduced by 15%, mainly as a consequence of motor vehicle emissions controls.

2. An overview of the model

■ The purpose of our model of the U.S. economy is to analyze the impact of changes in environmental policy by simulating the long-term growth of the economy with and without regulation. We began by dividing the U.S. economy into business, household, government, and rest-of-the-world sectors. Since environmental regulations differ substantially among industries, we subdivided the business sector into the thirty-five industries listed in Table 1. Each industry produces a primary product, and many industries also produce one or more secondary products. Thirty-five commodity groups are represented in our model, each corresponding to the primary product of one of the industries listed in Table 1.

TABLE 1	The Definitions of Industries
Number	Description
1	Agriculture, forestry, and fisheries
2	Metal mining
3	Coal mining
4	Crude petroleum and natural gas
5	Nonmetallic mineral mining
6	Construction
7	Food and kindred products
8	Tobacco manufacturers
9	Textile mill products
10	Apparel and other textile products
11	Lumber and wood products
12	Furniture and fixtures
13	Paper and allied products
14	Printing and publishing
15	Chemicals and allied products
16	Petroleum refining
17	Rubber and plastic products
18	Leather and leather products
19	Stone, clay, and glass products
20	Primary metals
21	Fabricated metal products
22	Machinery, except electrical
23	Electrical machinery
24	Motor vehicles
25	Other transportation equipment
26	Instruments
27	Miscellaneous manufacturing
28	Transportation and warehousing
29	Communication
30	Electric utilities
31	Gas utilities
32	Trade
33	Finance, insurance, and real estate
34	Other services
35	Government enterprises

The total supply of each commodity group is provided by domestic production and imports from the rest of the world. This supply is divided between intermediate and final demands. The intermediate demands are the inputs of the commodity into all thirty-five industries. Final demands include expenditures by the household and government sectors for consumption, purchases by the business and household sectors for investment, and exports to the rest of the world. Each industry utilizes inputs of capital and labor services, and these services are also allocated to final demands. Noncompeting imports, commodities that are not produced domestically, are allocated in the same way as capital and labor services.

To implement our model, we have constructed a consistent annual time series of interindustry transactions tables for the U.S. economy for the period 1947–1985.[3] These tables provide detailed information on production by each of the thirty-five industries in current and constant prices. The quantities of each commodity, including primary factors of production and noncompeting imports, have been allocated to intermediate and final demands using a "use" table. The quantities of all commodities made by each industry are presented in a "make" table. The "use" and "make" tables are presented diagrammatically in Figure 1. Figure 2 provides definitions of the variables that occur in both tables.

▫ **Producer behavior.** The first problem in modelling producer behavior is to represent substitution between inputs. For this purpose, we have constructed econometric models of the demands of each industry for all inputs. We have identified inputs of capital and energy separately, since environmental regulations often require the use of specific types of equipment or restrict the combustion of certain types of fuels. For example, a restriction on sulfur dioxide emissions may require the substitution of low-sulfur for high-sulfur fuel. Similarly, regulations on particulate emissions may necessitate the use of an electrostatic precipitator, which requires additional capital inputs.

The econometric approach to modelling producer behavior is very demanding in terms of data requirements. An alternative approach is to characterize substitution between inputs by calibration from a single data point.[4] For example, almost all applied general equilibrium models employ the assumption of fixed input-output coefficients for intermediate goods, following the specification originated by Johansen (1960).[5] The ratio of the input of each commodity to the output of an industry is calculated from a single use table, like the one presented in Figure 1. However, the possibility of substitution between intermediate goods, such as energy and materials, is ruled out by assumption.

A high degree of substitutability between inputs implies that the cost of environmental regulation is low, while a low degree of substitutability implies high costs of environmental regulation. Although a calibration approach avoids the burden of estimation, it also specifies the nature of substitutability among inputs by assumption rather than relying on empirical

---

[3] The data on interindustry transactions are based on input-output tables for the U.S. constructed by the Bureau of Economic Analysis (1984). The income data came from the U.S. national income and product accounts, also developed by the Bureau of Economic Analysis (1986). The data on capital and labor services are based on those of Jorgenson, Gollop, and Fraumeni (1987). Our data are organized according to an accounting system based on the United Nations (1968) system of national accounts. The details are given in Appendix C in Wilcoxen (1988).

[4] The calibration approach is discussed in Mansur and Whalley (1984). This approach was employed by Borges and Goulder (1984) in a model analyzing the impact of energy prices on U.S. economic growth. The model is based on data for the year 1973. The econometric approach to this problem is reviewed in Jorgenson (1982). Further details on the econometric methodology are presented in Jorgenson (1984).

[5] Forsund and Strom (1976) employed the specification of substitution between commodities introduced by Johansen (1960). The materials balance approach introduced by Kneese, Ayres, and d'Arge (1970) is considered in a general equilibrium setting in Maler (1974). A detailed survey of fixed coefficient input-output models employed in environmental economics is given in Forsund (1985).

FIGURE 1

ORGANIZATION OF THE USE TABLE

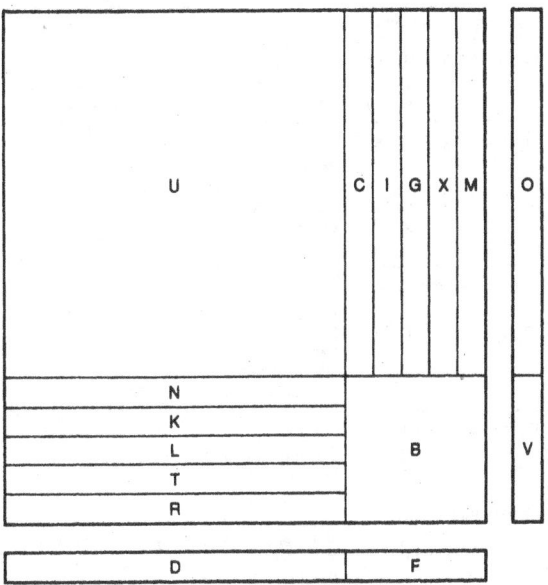

Organization of the Make Table

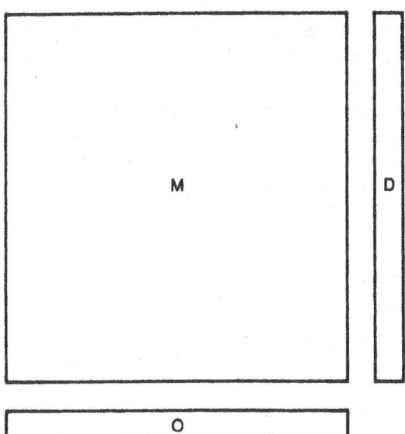

evidence. This defeats the main purpose of modelling the impact of environmental policy. We conclude that empirical evidence on the substitutability of inputs is essential in analyzing the impact of environmental regulations.

The most important mechanisms to control environmental pollution are to induce substitution away from polluting inputs and require pollution abatement. These measures can affect the rate of productivity growth in an industry. If the level of productivity in an industry increases, the price of the output of the industry will fall relative to the prices of its inputs, while a decrease in the industry's productivity level will result in a rise in the

FIGURE 2
MAKE AND USE TABLE VARIABLES

Category	Variable	Description
Industry-commodity flows:		
	U	Commodities *used* by industries (use table)
	M	Commodities *made* by industries (make table)
Final demand columns:		
	C	Personal consumption
	I	Gross private domestic investment
	G	Government spending
	X	Exports
	M	Imports
Value added rows:		
	N	Noncompeting imports
	K	Capital
	L	Labor
	T	Net taxes
	R	Rest of the world
Commodity and Industry output:		
	O	Commodity output
	D	Industry output
Other variables:		
	B	Value added sold directly to final demand
	V	Total value added
	F	Total final demand

price of its output relative to its input prices. Our models of producer behavior endogenize productivity growth by representing the rate of productivity growth in each industry as a function of the prices of all its inputs.[6]

Our econometric models of producer behavior allocate the value of the output of each industry among the inputs of the thirty-five commodity groups, capital services, labor services, and noncompeting imports. Inputs of the thirty-five commodities into each industry are given in the columns labelled U in the use table presented in Figure 1. Inputs of capital services, labor services and noncompeting imports into all industries are given in the rows labelled K, L, and N, respectively. The remaining rows of this table give indirect taxes paid by all industries and inputs of factor services from the rest of the world into these industries.

The sum of all of the entries in each column of the use table is the value of the output of the corresponding industry. This output includes a primary product and, possibly, one or more secondary products. We have modelled the shares of all industries that produce a given commodity in the value of the total domestic production of that commodity as functions of the output prices of these industries. The model uses these value shares to allocate the domestic supply of each commodity among the industries that produce it. This allocation is given in the columns of the make table in Figure 1. Similarly, we have modelled the value shares of imports and domestic production of each commodity and employed these shares in generating the imports of each commodity in the column labelled M in the use table in Figure 1.[7]

---

[6] Our approach to endogenous productivity growth was originated by Jorgenson and Fraumeni (1981). The implementation of a general equilibrium model of production that incorporates both substitution among inputs and endogenous productivity growth is discussed by Jorgenson (1984, 1986). This model has been analyzed in detail by Hogan and Jorgenson (1990).

[7] This approach was originated by Armington (1969).

In our model of the U.S. economy, there is a single stock of capital that is allocated among all sectors, including the household sector. The supply of capital available in each period is the result of past investment. This relationship is represented by an accumulation equation that gives capital at the end of each period as a function of investment during the period and capital at the beginning of the period. This equation is backward-looking and captures the impact of investments in all past periods on the capital available in the current period. We have assumed that capital is perfectly malleable and mobile among sectors, so the price of capital services in each sector is proportional to a single capital service price for the economy as a whole. The value of capital services is equal to capital income.

Our model of producer behavior includes an equation giving the price of capital services in terms of the price of investment goods at the beginning and end of each period, the rate of return to capital for the economy as a whole, the rate of depreciation, and variables describing the tax structure for income from capital. The current price of investment goods incorporates expectations about all future prices of capital services and all future discount rates.[8] Our model of the U.S. economy includes this forward-looking relationship for the price of investment goods in each time period. The price of capital services determined by the model enters into the price of investment goods through the assumption of perfect foresight or rational expectations. Under this assumption, the price of investment goods in every period is based on the expectations of future capital services' prices and discount rates that are fulfilled by the solution of the model.

The final demands for the commodity groups in our model include purchases by the business and household sectors for investment purposes. The final set of behavioral equations in our model of producer behavior is a system of demand functions for investment goods. We have modelled the value shares of all commodities accumulated by the business and household sectors—including producers' and consumers' durables, residential and nonresidential structures, and inventories—as functions of the prices of these commodities. The shares are used to allocate the value of investment goods among commodity groups, as in column I in the use table in Figure 1.

□ **Consumer behavior.** An important objective of environmental regulation is to induce the substitution of nonpolluting products for polluting ones. This substitution can take place within the household sector as well as the business sector. For example, regulations on the exhaust emissions of motor vehicles affect household demands for vehicles and motor fuel. The first problem in modelling consumer behavior is to represent substitution between commodities that are purchased by households. For this purpose, we have constructed an econometric model of the demands for individual commodities by the household sector. As in our models of producer behavior, we have identified purchases of energy and capital services separately, since these commodity groups are directly affected by environmental regulation.[9]

Our model of consumer behavior allocates personal consumption expenditures among the thirty-five commodity groups included in our model of the U.S. economy, capital and labor services, and noncompeting imports. The allocation to individual commodities is given in the column labelled C in the use table in Figure 1. Our model of personal consumption expenditures can be used to represent the behavior of individual households, as in the studies of regulatory policy by Jorgenson and Slesnick (1985). Here, we employ the model to represent aggregate consumer behavior in simulations of the U.S. economy under alternative policies for environmental regulation. For this purpose, we have embeded this

---

[8] Further details are given in Jorgenson (1989).

[9] The econometric methodology employed in our study was originated by Jorgenson, Lau, and Stoker (1982). The econometric model we have employed was constructed by Jorgenson and Slesnick (1987). Further details on the econometric methodology are given in Jorgenson (1984, forthcoming).

model of personal consumption expenditures into a higher-level model that determines consumer choices between labor and leisure and between consumption and saving.

The second stage of our model of the household sector is based on the concept of full consumption, which is composed of goods and services and leisure time. We have simplified the representation of household preferences between goods and leisure by introducing the notion of a representative consumer. In each time period, the representative consumer allocates the value of full consumption between personal consumption expenditures and leisure time.[10] This produces an allocation of the exogenously given time endowment between leisure time and the labor market. Labor market time is allocated between the thirty-five industries represented in the model and final demands for personal consumption expenditures and government consumption. We have assumed that labor is perfectly mobile between sectors, so the price of labor services in each sector is proportional to a single wage rate for the economy as a whole. The value of the time allocated to the labor market equals labor income.

The third and final stage of our model of the household sector is a model of intertemporal consumer behavior. We have described intertemporal preferences by means of a utility function for a representative consumer that depends on levels of full consumption in current and future time periods. The representative consumer maximizes this utility function subject to an intertemporal budget constraint. The budget constraint gives full wealth as the discounted value of current and future full consumption. The necessary conditions for a maximum of the utility function subject to the budget constraint can be expressed in the form of an Euler equation, giving the rate of growth of full consumption as a function of the discount rate and the rate of growth of the price of full consumption.[11]

The Euler equation for full consumption is forward-looking, so the current level of full consumption incorporates expectations about future prices of full consumption and future discount rates. The solution of our model includes this forward-looking relationship for full consumption in each time period. The price of full consumption determined by the model enters full consumption through the assumption of perfect foresight or rational expectations. Under this assumption, full consumption in every period is based on expectations about future prices of full consumption and discount rates that are fulfilled by the solution of the model.

□ **The solution of the model.** We conclude this overview by outlining the solution of our model of the U.S. economy. An intertemporal submodel incorporates backward-looking and forward-looking equations that determine the time paths of the capital stock and full consumption. Given the values of these variables, an intratemporal submodel determines the prices that balance demand and supply in each time period for the thirty-five commodity groups included in the model, capital services, and labor services. These two submodels must be solved simultaneously to obtain a complete solution of the model.

The dynamics of adjustment to changes in evironmental policy are determined by the intertemporal features of our model. For example, investment in equipment for pollution abatement was a very substantial proportion of investment in producers' durable equipment during parts of our sample period, 1947–1985. This type of mandated investment increased the price of investment goods, requiring adjustments of capital service prices and discount

---

[10] The price of leisure time is equal to the market wage rate reduced by the marginal tax rate on labor income, which is the opportunity cost of foregone labor income. The price of personal consumption expenditures is a cost of living index generated from the first stage of our model of consumer behavior. This cost of living index is discussed in Jorgenson and Slesnick (1983).

[11] The Euler equation approach to modelling intertemporal consumer behavior was originated by Hall (1978). Our application of this approach to full consumption follows Jorgenson and Yun (1986).

rates over the whole future time path of the economy. Reductions in investment in capital accumulation reduced the capital available for production in subsequent time periods.

Given the prices of capital and labor services and noncompeting imports, the first step in the solution of the intratemporal model is to determine prices for the outputs of the thirty-five industries represented in the model. Given these prices, the next step is to determine the domestic supply prices for the corresponding commodities. Finally, the domestic supply price for each commodity is combined with the price of imports to determine the total supply price. These commodity prices enter the determination of intermediate demands by industries and final demands by the household, business, government, and rest-of-the-world sectors.

We have described the determination of supply prices for the thirty-five commodity groups included in our model given the prices of capital and labor services and the prices of competing and noncompeting imports. The prices of imports are given exogenously in every time period. The prices of capital and labor services are determined by balancing demand and supply for these services. The supply of capital is determined by previous investments and is taken as given in every period. The exogenously given time endowment of the household sector is allocated between the labor market and leisure time by our model of consumer behavior.

The demand side of the intratemporal model is divided between intermediate and final demands for the thirty-five commodity groups, capital and labor services, and noncompeting imports as presented in the use table in Figure 1. Our models of producer behavior include value shares for inputs of commodities, primary factors of production, and noncompeting imports into each industry. These value shares incorporate income-expenditure identities for the industry, since the total value of output must be equal to the value of the inputs. The value shares determine inputs per unit of output for each industry as functions of the input and output prices. The endogenously determined input-output coefficients in each industry are multiplied by the output of the industry to obtain the input quantities. These quantities are then summed over the thirty-five industries to obtain total intermediate demands.

In our intratemporal model, final demands are divided among personal consumption expenditures, purchases by the business and household sectors for investment purposes, expenditures by the government for public consumption, and exports to the rest of the world. To determine the quantities of the thirty-five commodities for each of these final demand categories, our model of consumer behavior allocates the value of full consumption between the aggregate expenditure on goods and services that make up personal consumption expenditures and the value of leisure time. Given aggregate expenditure, its distribution among households, and commodity prices, this model also allocates personal consumption expenditures among commodity groups, including capital and labor services and noncompeting imports. This allocation determines the quantity of each commodity included in the final demand for personal consumption. These quantities are included in column C in the use table in Figure 1.

While the value of personal consumption expenditures is determined within our model of consumer behavior, the value of gross private domestic investment is driven by private savings. First, the income of the household sector is the sum of incomes from the supply of labor and capital services, interest payments from the government and rest-of-the-world sectors, all net of taxes, and transfers from the government. Savings are equal to income minus personal consumption expenditures minus personal transfers to foreigners and nontax payments to the government. This is the income-expenditure identity of the household sector.

The balance sheet identity of the household sector sets private wealth equal to the sum of the value of the capital stock in the private sector, claims on the government, and claims on the rest of the world. The change in the value of private wealth from period to period is the sum of private savings and the revaluation of wealth as a result of inflation. Private savings plus government savings equals the current account balance of the rest-of-the-world sector plus gross private domestic investment. Within our intratemporal model, the level of investment is determined by savings, since the government deficit and the current account balance are taken to be exogenous. Our model of producer behavior allocates gross private domestic investment among commodity groups. Given the commodity prices, this allocation determines the quantity of each group included in final demand for investment purposes. These quantities are included in column I in the use table in Figure 1.

In order to complete the determination of final demands in our model, we considered purchases by the government and rest-of-the-world sectors. Wherever possible, we have assigned government enterprises to the corresponding industry. For example, we have assigned the Tennessee Valley Authority to electric utilities and municipal transportation systems to transportation services. A separate industrial sector includes the remaining government enterprises, such as the U.S. Postal Service. Demands for commodities by government enterprises have been incorporated into intermediate demands. Purchases by the government sector for public consumption are part of final demands. Similarly, demands for competing and noncompeting imports are determined by our econometric models of producer behavior. Exports to the rest-of-the-world sector are part of final demands.

The final demands for public consumption are determined by the income-expenditure identity for the government sector. Government revenues are generated by exogenously given tax rates applied to appropriate transactions in the business and household sectors. For example, sales tax rates are applied to the values of the outputs of the thirty-five industries to generate sales tax revenues; tariff rates are applied to imports to generate tariff revenues, and income tax rates are applied to incomes from capital and labor services to generate income tax revenues. In addition, property and wealth tax rates are applied to property employed in the business and household sectors and to household sector wealth to generate revenues from property and wealth taxes.

The model of the government sector adds the capital income of government enterprises, determined endogenously, and nontax receipts, given exogenously, to tax revenues to obtain total revenues of the government sector. The model subtracts the government budget surplus (or adds the government budget deficit) from (to) these revenues to obtain government expenditures. The key assumption here is that the government budget surplus (or deficit) is given exogenously. To arrive at government purchases of goods and services, it subtracts interest paid to domestic and foreign holders of government bonds and government transfer payments to domestic and foreign recipients from these expenditures. The shares of individual commodity groups in government purchases are taken to be exogenous. The model determines the quantities of all commodities included in the final demand of the government sector by dividing the values of government purchases by the corresponding commodity price. The resulting quantities are given in column G in the use table in Figure 1.

Our intratemporal model incorporates the income-expenditure identity of the rest-of-the-world sector. The current account surplus of the rest of the world equals the value of exports minus the value of imports plus the interest received on domestic holdings of foreign bonds minus private and government transfers abroad minus the interest on government bonds paid to foreigners. The key assumption of our model of the rest-of-the-world sector is that the current account balance is exogenous, so the exchange rate is endogenous. Exports to the rest of the world are determined by demand equations that depend on world income and on ratios of commodity prices in U.S. currency to the exchange rate. The quantities of exports of all commodities are included in column X in the use table in Figure 1. Exogenously given prices of competing and noncompeting imports in foreign currency are expressed in U.S. currency by multiplying these prices by the exchange rate.

To construct a solution of our model of the U.S. economy, we first require values of all the exogenous variables. These variables have been set equal to their historical values for the sample period, 1947–1985. We have projected all the exogenous variables for the postsample period, 1986–2050, and taken these variables to be constant at their 2050 values through the year 2100. The exogenous variables have been held constant for the period 2050–2100 to allow sufficient time for the endogenous variables determined by the model to converge to their steady-state values.

We require projections of the exogenous components of the income-expenditure identities for government and rest-of-the-world sectors in order to project final demands for public consumption and exports. We have projected a gradual decline in the government deficit to the year 2025. For all later years, this deficit has been set to 4% of the nominal value of the government debt. This has the effect of maintaining a constant ratio of the value of the government debt to the value of the national product at a 4% inflation rate in a steady-state solution to our model.

We have set future prices of import and exports in foreign currency equal to the prices in 1985, the last year of our sample period. Projections of prices in U.S. domestic currency depend on the endogenously determined exchange rate. We have projected that the exogenous current account balance for the rest-of-the-world sector will fall gradually to zero by the year 2000. For later years, we have projected a current account surplus sufficient to produce a stock of net claims on foreigners by the year 2050 that equals the same proportion of national wealth as it did in 1982.

The most important exogenous variables in our model of the U.S. economy are those associated with the U.S. population and the corresponding time endowment. We have projected population by individual year of age, individual year of educational attainment, and sex to the year 2050, using demographic assumptions that result in a maximum population in that year.[12] In projecting future levels of educational attainment, we have assumed that future demographic cohorts will have the same level of attainment as the cohort that reached age 35 in the year 1985. We have transformed our population projection into a projection of the time endowment used in our model of the labor market by assuming that the relative wages have been constant at 1985 levels.

The size of the economy corresponding to the steady state of our model is effectively determined by the time endowment. The capital stock adjusts to this time endowment, while the rate of return depends only on the intertemporal preferences of the household sector. In this sense, the supply of capital is perfectly elastic in the long run. It is useful to contrast the behavior of our model with that of a neoclassical growth model of the Cass-Koopmans type.[13] For example, the rate of return in the stationary solution of our model is independent of environmental policy, just as in a one-sector neoclassical growth model. However, different policies result in different levels of capital intensity—all corresponding to the same rate of return. This is impossible in a one-sector model.

In the short run, the supply of capital in our model is perfectly inelastic, since it is completely determined by past investment. Under our assumption of perfect mobility of capital and labor, changes in environmental policy can affect the distribution of capital and labor supplies among sectors, even in the short run. The transition path for the economy depends on environmental policy. It also depends on the time path of variables that are exogenous to the model. If the initial wealth of the economy is low relative to the time endowment, the rate of return will exceed the stationary rate of return. This will induce the representative consumer to postpone the consumption of goods and leisure into the future,

---

[12] Our breakdown of the U.S. population by age, educational attainment, and sex is based on the system of demographic accounts compiled by Jorgenson and Fraumeni (1989). The population projections are discussed in detail in Appendix B in Wilcoxen (1988).

[13] This model was originated by Cass (1965) and Koopmans (1967). The Cass-Koopmans model has recently been discussed by Lucas (1988) and Romer (1989). Neoclassical growth models with pollution abatement have been presented by Maler (1975) and Uzawa (1975).

so the rate of capital accumulation will be positive. Conversely, if the initial wealth of the economy is sufficiently high relative to the time endowment, the rate of capital accumulation will be negative.

3. The impact of environmental regulation

■ Our next objective is to assess the impact of environmental regulation by projecting the growth of the U.S. economy with and without regulation. The base case for our simulations is a regime with pollution controls in effect. To determine the impact of environmental restrictions on economic activity, we simulate U.S. economic growth in the absence of regulation. We perform separate simulations to assess the impact of pollution control in industry and controls on motor vehicle emissions, which also affect the consumption behavior of households. We then estimate the overall impact of environmental regulation by eliminating both types of pollution control.

Simulations of the U.S. economy in which pollution controls are removed differ from the base case in the steady state, the initial equilibrium, and the transition path between the two. Since the capital stock is endogenous in our model, the new steady state corresponds to the long-run impact of environmental regulation on the U.S. economy. The initial equilibrium with a fixed capital stock gives the short-run impact of a change in environmental policy. Since agents in the model are endowed with perfect foresight, this initial equilibrium reflects changes along the entire time path of future regulatory policy. Finally, the transition path between the initial equilibrium and the steady state traces out the dynamics of the adjustment of the economy to a new policy for environmental regulation.

In presenting the results of our simulatons of U.S. economic growth, we begin by quantifying the impact of pollution controls on production costs. We then incorporate the changes in costs into our model of the U.S. economy. We first consider the impact of environmental regulations on the steady state of the economy. For this purpose, we focus attention on a few key variables. The capital stock determines the production capacity of the economy, since the time endowment is given exogenously. Full consumption is a measure of the goods and services and leisure time available to the household sector. The level of the gross national product is an overall measure of the output of the economy, including private and public consumption, investment, and net exports to the rest of the world. Finally, the exchange rate is an indicator of the international competitiveness of the U.S. economy.

The second step in our analysis of the impact of environmental regulation is to analyze the transition path of the U.S. economy from the initial equilibrium to the new steady state. The time path of the capital stock is the most important indicator of the process of economic adjustment to a change in environmental policy. The price of investment goods is an important determinant of the time path of capital stock, since it incorporates expectations about future prices of capital services and discount rates. The rental price of capital services also reflects the rate of return, which is critical to the allocation of national income between consumption and savings. We employ the time paths of capital stock, the price of investment goods, the price of capital services, and the level of GNP in describing the adjustment process.

□ **Operating costs.** We have used data collected by the Bureau of the Census (Bureau of the Census, various issues, 1973–1983) to estimate investment in pollution abatement equipment and operating costs of pollution control activities for manufacturing industries.[14] The investment data give capital expenditures on pollution abatement equipment in current prices, while the data on operating costs give current outlays attributable to pollution control.

---

[14] A detailed description of the data is given in Appendix D in Wilcoxen (1988).

These are the actual costs reported by the business sector and do not include taxes levied as part of the Superfund program. Taxes amounting to more than a billion dollars a year were placed on the petroleum-refining and chemicals industries in 1981 and the primary metals industry in 1986. These may have had a substantial impact on U.S. economic growth, but we do not examine their consequences in this article.

Figure 3 summarizes the share of pollution abatement in industry costs, the share of individual industries in total abatement costs, and the share of abatement devices in industry investment for the manufacturing industries. Inspection of the first panel shows that pollution control expenses have formed only a small part of total costs for individual industries. The

FIGURE 3

THE IMPACT OF ENVIRONMENTAL REGULATION

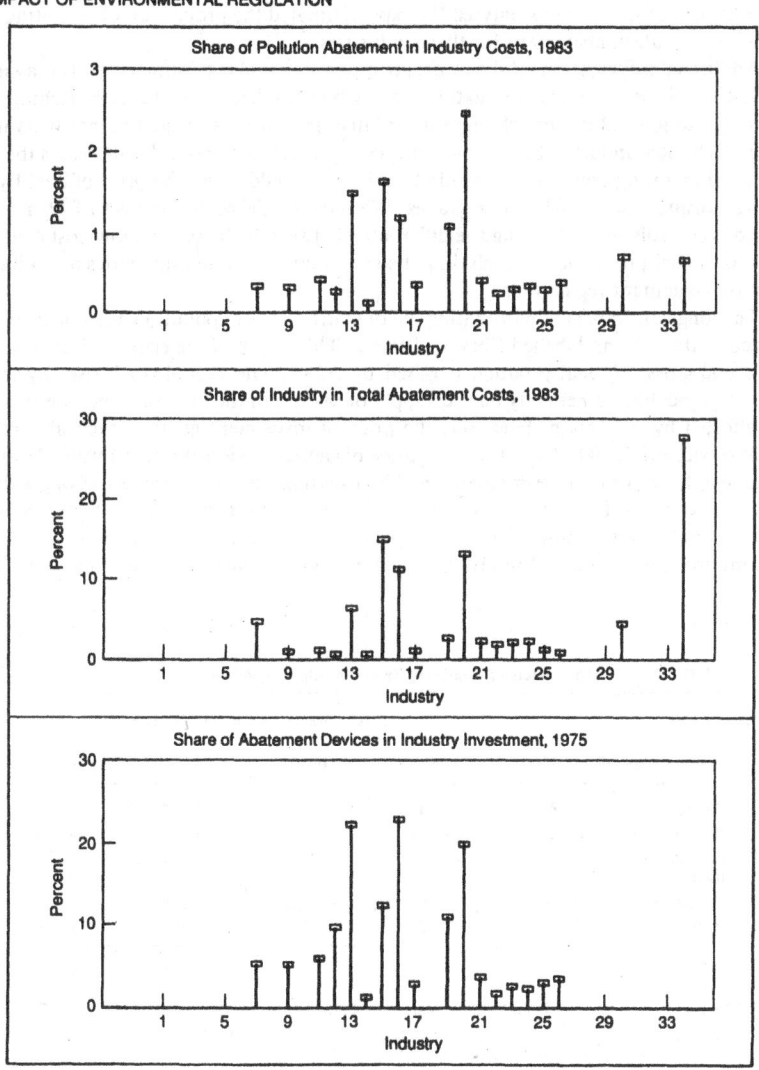

largest share is for the primary metals industry, at slightly more than 2%. The second panel shows that the expenses for pollution abatement have been concentrated in a relatively small number of industries. Three sectors—chemicals, petroleum refining, and primary metals—account for 55% of total spending. The third panel shows that investment in pollution abatement equipment has consumed more than 20% of total investment for paper and pulp, petroleum refining, and primary metals industries.

The first step in eliminating the operating costs of pollution control is to estimate the share of pollution abatement in the total costs of each industry. The 1983 cost shares are a maximum for the period 1973–1983, since pollution controls have increased steadily over the period. We have assumed that shares for the later years have been constant at the 1983 values. Data for industries outside manufacturing were available only for electric utilities and wastewater treatment, which is part of the services industry. For both industries, data on operating costs and investment expenditures for pollution abatement have been compiled by the Bureau of Economic Analysis. We have estimated the proportion of operating costs devoted to pollution abatement for these industries.[15]

Additional information on the impact of environmental regulation on costs is available for electric utilities, namely, the extra costs of burning low-sulfur fuels. Switching from high-sulfur to low-sulfur coal changes the relative proportions of the two products in the output of the coal industry. Since low-sulfur coal is more expensive, this increases the price of coal. Eliminating regulations on sulfur emissions would lower the price of coal by permitting substitution to high-sulfur grades. We have modelled the impact of lifting these emissions controls by subtracting the differential between high-cost and low-cost coal from the costs of coal production.[16] Including the coal industry, twenty industries are subject to pollution abatement regulations.

The long-run impact of eliminating the operating costs of pollution abatement is summarized in the column labelled ENV in Table 2. The output of the economy, as measured by the real gross national product, is raised by .728%. The capital stock rises by .544%. Since our model has a perfectly elastic supply of savings in the long run, the rate of return is unaffected by regulation. However, the price of investment goods, which also reflects capital service prices, falls by .897%. The price of capital services declines by .907%, almost the same as the price of investment goods. The resulting decrease in the prices of goods and services produces a rise in full consumption of .278%. This increase is less than that of the gross national product, since full consumption includes leisure time as well as personal consumption expenditures. Finally, the exchange rate, which gives the domestic cost of

TABLE 2   The Effects of Removing Environmental Regulation

Variable	Percentage Change in the Steady State			
	ENV	INV	MV	ALL
Capital Stock	.544	2.266	1.118	3.792
Price of Investment Goods	−.897	−2.652	−1.323	−4.520
Full Consumption	.278	.489	.282	.975
Real GNP	.728	1.290	.752	2.592
Rental Price of Capital	−.907	−2.730	−1.358	−4.635
Exchange Rate	−.703	−.462	−.392	−1.298

[15] The details are given in Appendix D in Wilcoxen (1988).
[16] The details of our methodology for estimating cost differentials between high-sulfur and low-sulfur coal are given in Appendix D in Wilcoxen (1988).

FIGURE 4

THE EFFECTS OF REMOVING ABATEMENT COSTS ON INDUSTRIES

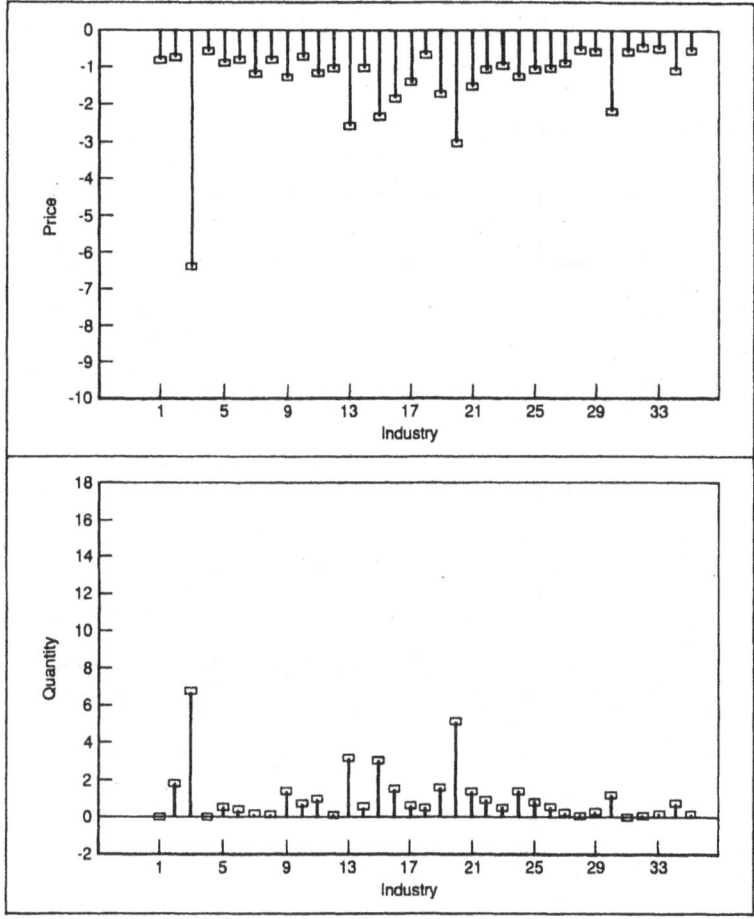

foreign goods, falls slightly, indicating an increase in the international competitiveness of the U.S. economy.[17]

The long-run effects of eliminating operating costs associated with pollution abatement on the prices and outputs of individual industries are shown in Figure 4. The bars in the first panel indicate the percentage change in the steady-state output price of the corresponding industry. The bars in the second panel give the percentage changes in industry output levels. Not surprisingly, the principal beneficiaries of the elimination of operating costs are the most heavily regulated industries. The greatest expansion of output occurs in coal production, since the fuel cost differential between low-sulfur and high-sulfur coal is large relative to the total costs of the coal industry. Turning to manufacturing industries, the primary metals, paper, and chemicals industries have the largest gains in output from the elimination of

---

[17] An alternative analysis of the impact of environmental regulation on U.S. international competitiveness is given in Kalt (1988).

operating costs for pollution abatement. Several other sectors benefit from the removal of operating costs of pollution abatement, but the impact is fairly modest.

We have now summarized the long-run impact of eliminating operating costs associated with pollution controls in industry. Figure 5 presents the dynamics of the process of ad-

FIGURE 5

THE DYNAMIC EFFECTS OF REMOVING ABATEMENT COSTS

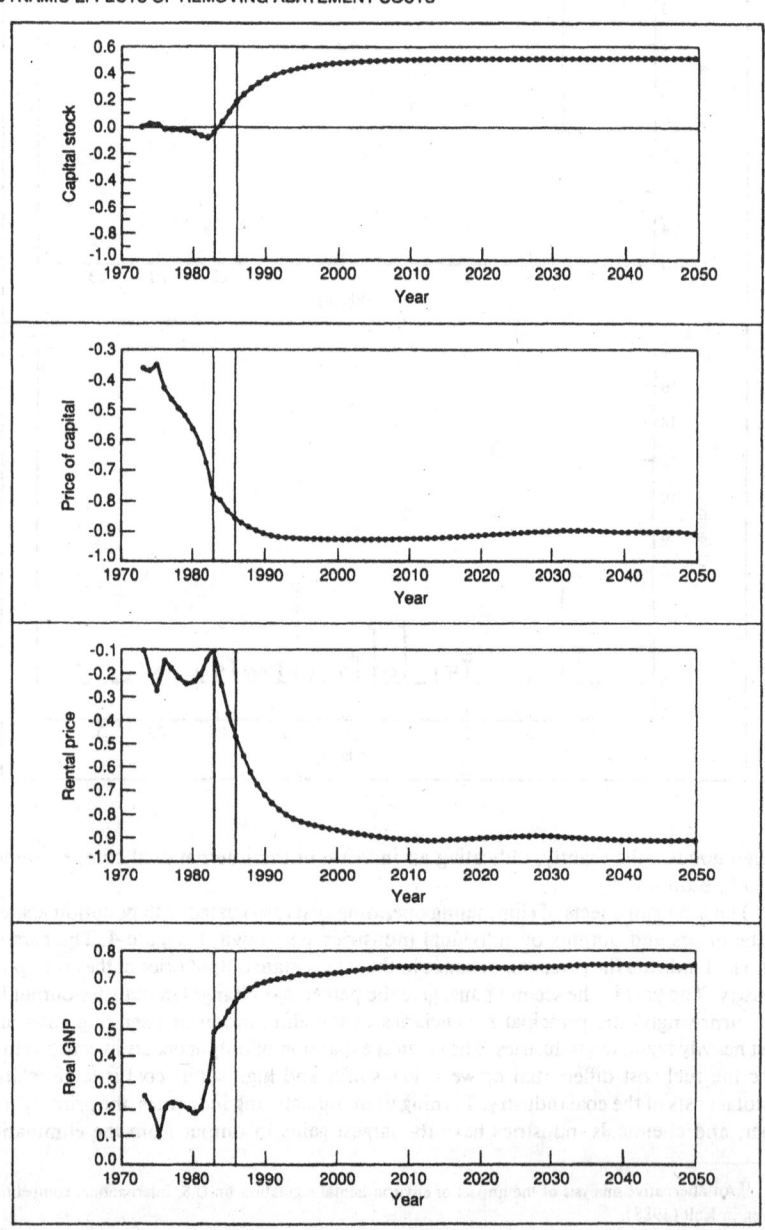

justment to lower costs. After 1973, the price of investment goods falls slowly, reflecting the gradual price decline brought about by the elimination of operating costs associated with increasingly stringent regulations. Lower costs of investment goods tend to increase the rate of return, stimulate savings, and produce more rapid capital accumulation. Additional capital eventually brings down the rental price of capital, lowering costs still further. Finally, the quantity of full consumption rises rapidly to the new steady-state level and remains there.

The transition from the short run to the steady state is relatively slow, requiring almost three decades for the capital stock and the price of capital services to fully adjust to the change in environmental policy. The graph of the capital stock shows that the process of adjustment is not complete until the year 2000. This reflects the nature of our simulation experiment. The regulations are imposed gradually, so their removal is also gradual. On the other hand, full consumption attains its final value more quickly as a consequence of intertemporal optimization by households under perfect foresight. Since income is permanently higher in the future, current consumption rises in anticipation. However, the rise of consumption is dampened by an increase in the rate of return that produces greater investment.

☐ **Investment in pollution control equipment.** The most important impact of environmental regulation for some industries is the imposition of requirements for investment in costly new equipment for pollution abatement. Investment in pollution control devices crowds out investment for capital accumulation, further reducing the rate of economic growth. Our second simulation of U.S. economic growth is designed to assess the impact of investment for pollution control. An examination of the data on investment presented in Figure 3 reveals several striking features. First, the paper, petroleum-refining, and primary metals industries each spent more than 20% of the their total investment on pollution control devices in 1975. Some other sectors were not far behind, and the overall share of this investment in total gross private domestic investment was substantial.

The share of investment for pollution abatement rose to a peak in the early 1970s and then declined substantially. This can be attributed to the fact that much of the early effort in pollution control was directed at reducing emissions from existing sources by retrofitting equipment already in place. The appropriate method for modelling mandatory investment in pollution control requires a distinction between achieving environmental standards for existing sources of emissions and meeting restrictions on new sources of emissions. Environmental regulations increase the cost of new investments, since producers are required to purchase pollution abatement equipment whenever they acquire new investment goods.

We assumed that investment in pollution control equipment provides no benefits to the producer other than satisfying environmental regulations. Accordingly, we simulate mandated investment as an increase in the price of investment goods. Unfortunately, the existing data do not provide a separation between investments required for new and existing facilities. We have assumed that the backlog of investment for retrofitting old sources of emissions had been eliminated by 1983. We simulate the impact of removing environmental regulations on investment by reducing the price of investment goods by the proportion of total investment attributable to pollution control for 1983. This captures the effect of requirements for pollution abatement on investment in new capital goods but does not include the effect of windfall losses to owners of the capital associated with old sources of emissions.

Our method for simulating the impact of investment requirements for pollution control has certain limitations that should be pointed out. First, it relies on the assumption that capital is completely malleable and mobile between sectors. An alternative approach would be to incorporate costs of adjustment into our models of producer behavior. However, this approach would lead to considerable additional complexity in modelling and simulating producer behavior. The long-run impact of environmental regulations would be unaffected by costs of adjustment, since these costs would be zero in the steady state of our model.

The steady-state effects of mandated investment in pollution control devices are given in the column labelled INV in Table 2. The largest change is in the capital stock, which rises by 2.266% as a direct result of the drop in the price of investment goods. In the short run, this price decline pushes up the rate of return, which raises the level of investment. Higher capital accumulation leads to a fall in the rental price of capital services, decreasing the overall price level. The long-run level of full consumption rises by .489%, almost double the increase resulting from eliminating operating costs of pollution abatement. The 1.290% rise in GNP is also nearly twice as large as this increase. The exchange rate appreciates by .462%, indicating an increase in international competitiveness of the U.S. economy.

The effects of eliminating pollution abatement investment on industry output and price levels are shown in Figure 6. These effects stem from the drop in the rental price of capital services. The largest gains in output are for communications, electric utilities, and gas utilities, since these are the most capital intensive industries. While most sectors gain from eliminating investment for pollution control, a few sectors are hurt by this change in

FIGURE 6

THE EFFECTS OF REMOVING ABATEMENT INVESTMENT ON INDUSTRIES

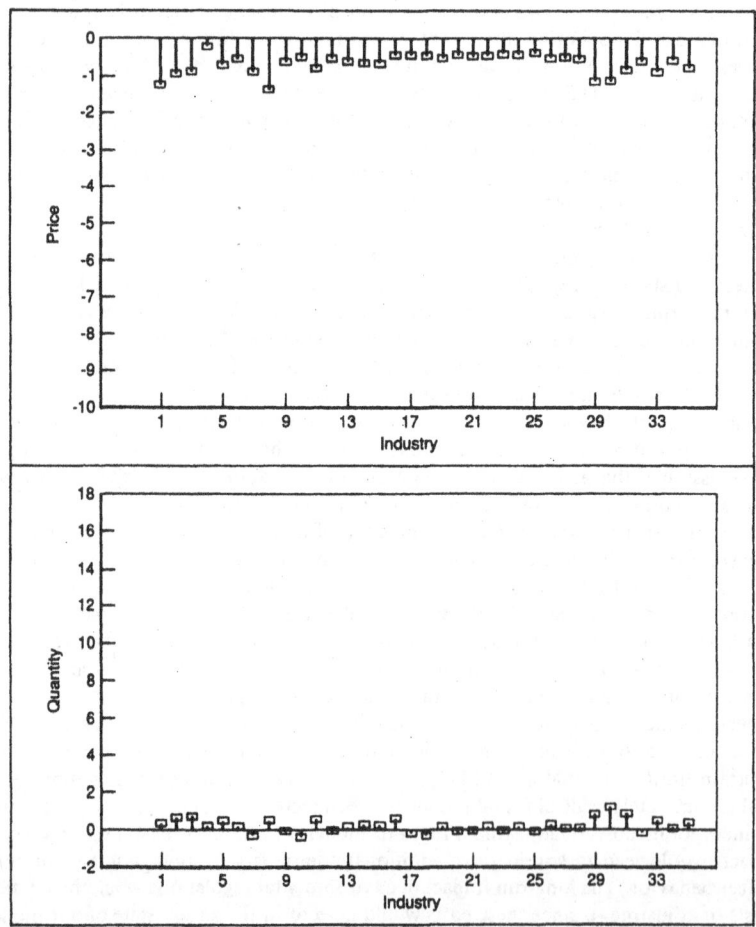

environmental policy. Outputs of food, apparel, rubber and plastic, and leather all decline noticeably. These sectors are among the least capital intensive, so the fall in the rental price of capital services has little effect on the prices of outputs. Buyers of the commodities produced by these industries face higher prices and substitute other commodities in both intermediate and final demand.

The transition path of the U.S. economy after investment requirements for pollution control have been eliminated is summarized in Figure 7. The process of adjustment is markedly different from that of the previous simulation. The capital stock grows immediately and rapidly to its new equilibrium value. This comes about as a consequence of the fall in the price of investment goods. As new capital goods become cheaper, beginning in 1973, the rate of return rises, driving up investment and producing a sharp increase in the capital stock. This explanation is further substantiated by the behavior of full consumption. Initially, consumption drops, and a larger share of income is diverted to investment. Then, as the capital stock rises, so does consumption. The path of the rental price reflects the behavior of the capital stock and drives output prices downward as more capital is accumulated.

□ **Motor vehicle emissions control.** Environmental regulation is not limited to controlling emissions by industries within the business sector. Regulations on motor vehicle emissions affect users of motor vehicles, including households as well as businesses. Motor vehicle regulation is set apart from other forms of environmental control by the fact that the pollution abatement equipment is installed by the manufacturer. Like pollution control in industry, the reduction of motor vehicle exhaust emissions adds to both capital expenditures and operating costs. The catalytic converter is a typical piece of pollution abatement equipment requiring capital expenditures. The premium paid for unleaded gasoline represents an increase in operating costs.

Using data obtained from Kappler and Rutledge (1985), we have estimated the change in motor vehicle prices resulting from emission control regulations. Pollution abatement also imposes additional operating costs on users of motor vehicles. Kappler and Rutledge separated these additional expenses into three components—increased fuel consumption, increased fuel prices, and increased motor vehicle maintenance. We first divided the total cost of pollution abatement equipment between imported and domestic vehicles in proportion to their shares in total supply. We excluded the cost of this equipment from the total cost of domestic production of motor vehicles. Now, we reduce the price of motor vehicles in proportion to the cost of pollution control devices to simulate the impact of eliminating controls on motor vehicle emissions.

The price premium for unleaded motor fuels can be modelled as a change in the cost of the output of the petroleum-refining sector. This is similar to the treatment of the fuel cost differential between high-sulfur and low-sulfur coal used in our simulations of the impact of pollution abatement in industry. Only the costs associated with higher fuel prices are removed in our simulation of U.S. economic growth without motor vehicle emissions controls. Consequently, our results will understate the impact of these controls. To complete the inputs to our simulation of U.S. economic growth in the absence of controls on motor vehicles emissions, we reduce the price of imported motor vehicles in the same proportion as the price of domestic vehicles.

The economic impact of imposing emissions controls on motor vehicles is similar in magnitude to the impact of pollution controls in industry. These results are summarized in the column labelled MV in Table 2. The long-run capital stock rises by 1.118% after the elimination of controls on emissions, while full consumption increases by .282%. Real GNP increases by .752% in the absence of controls. Finally, the exchange rate appreciates by .392%. Almost all of the economic impact is due to decreased motor vehicle prices as a consequence of the absence of emissions controls. Changes in the price of investment goods

FIGURE 7
THE DYNAMIC EFFECTS OF REMOVING ABATEMENT INVESTMENTS

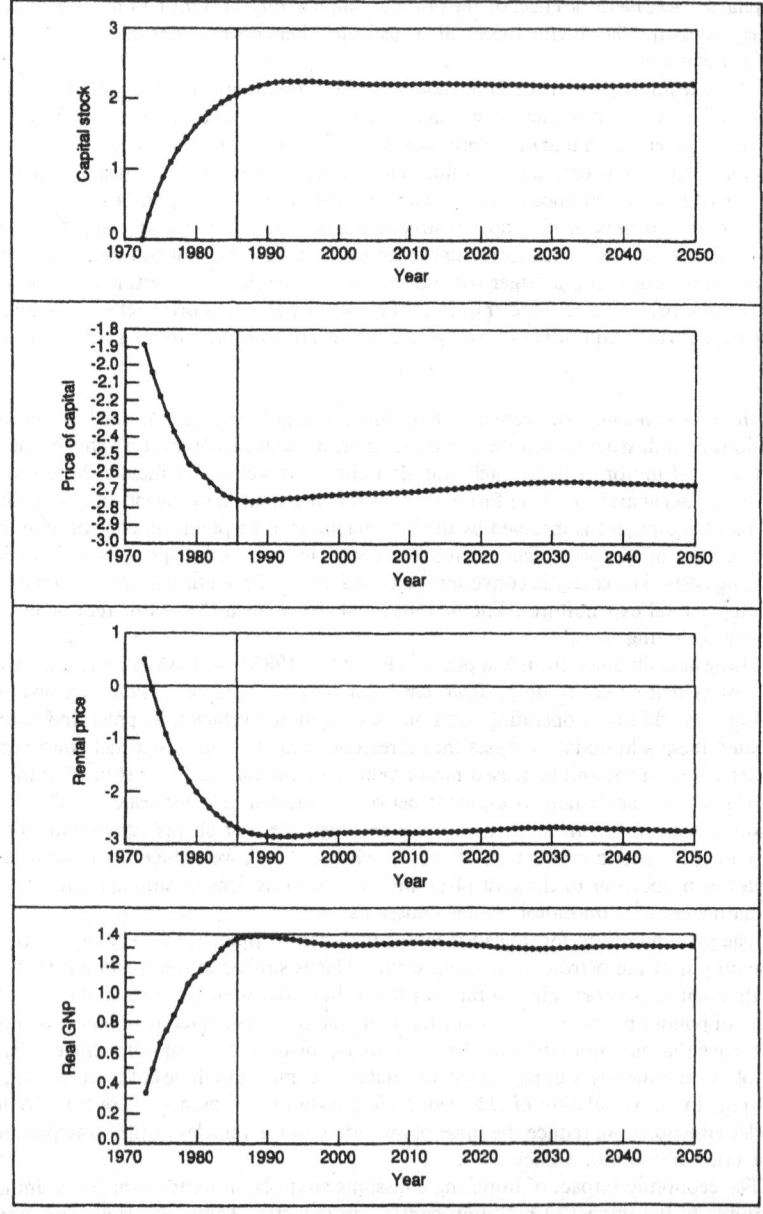

raise the rate of return, leading to large changes in the capital stock. The price of investment goods changes substantially, since motor vehicles make up nearly 15% of new capital goods.

The long-run impact of eliminating motor vehicle emissions controls on the outputs and prices of individual industries is shown in Figure 8. The principal beneficiary of the

FIGURE 8

THE EFFECTS OF REMOVING VEHICLE REGULATION ON INDUSTRIES

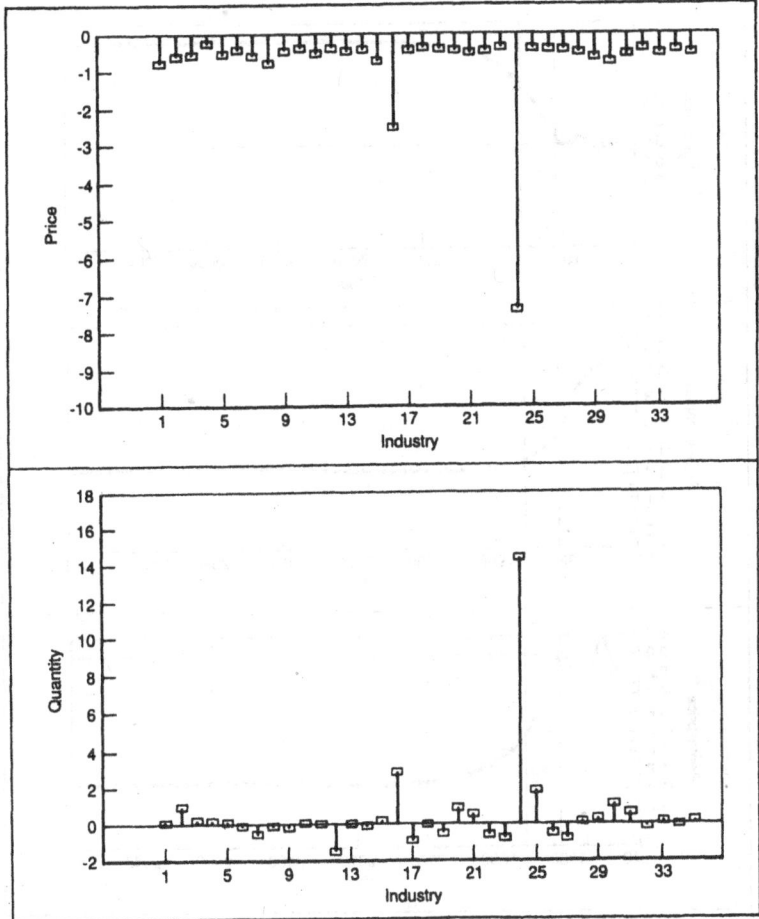

elimination of these regulations is the motor vehicles industry. This is partly due to the fact that the demand for motor vehicles is price elastic. A price change of 7% produces an output change of 14%. Two other industries also benefit significantly from the elimination of environmental controls—petroleum refining and electric utilities. Both gain from the reduction in fuel prices associated with elimination of the fuel price premium.

The process of adjustment to a change in controls on motor vehicle emissions is shown for key variables of the model in Figure 9. The important features of this path are similar to those for the removal of pollution abatement investment in industry. Vehicles are a large part of investment, so lowering their price brings down the cost of new capital goods substantially. This increases the rate of return, stimulates saving, and leads to a surge in investment. Since the change in vehicle prices is largest in later years, however, the effect is more gradual, and the capital stock does not climb as rapidly.

□ **The impact of environmental regulation.** To measure the total impact of eliminating all three costs of environmental regulation—operating costs resulting from pollution abatement

FIGURE 9
THE DYNAMIC EFFECTS OF MOTOR VEHICLE REGULATION

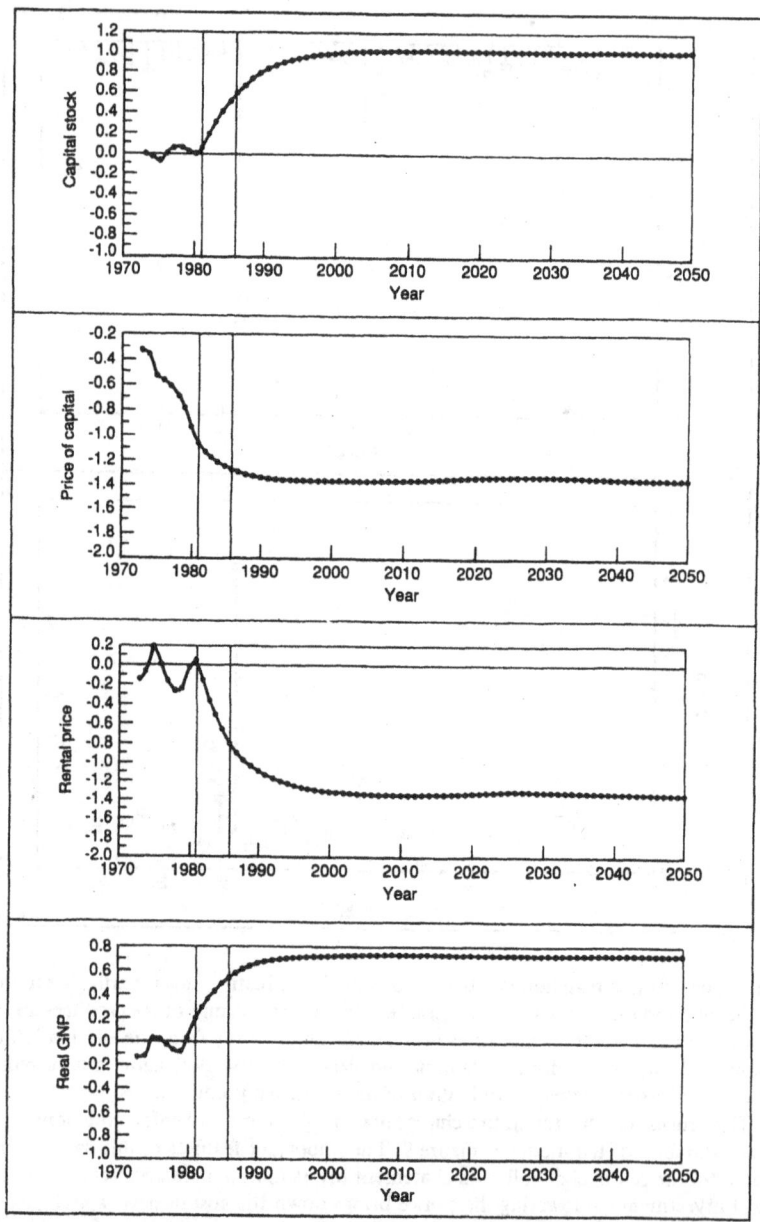

in industry, costs of investments required by industry to meet environmental standards, and costs of emissions controls on motor vehicles—we perform a final simulation. This simulation is not a simple combination of its three components. Operating costs include capital costs, so combining the reductions in operating costs with the elimination of investment requirements would count the cost reductions associated with capital twice. To solve this problem, the capital component is removed from operating costs in the combined simulation. The results of removing all forms of environmental regulation are summarized in the column labelled ALL in Table 2.

The long-run consequences of pollution control for different industries are presented in Figure 10. The sectors hit hardest by environmental regulations are the motor vehicles and coal-mining industries. Primary metals and petroleum refining follow close behind. About half of the remaining industries have increases in output of 1% to 5% after pollution controls are removed. The rest are largely unaffected by environmental regulations. The economy follows the transition path to the new steady state shown in Figure 11. Driven by large changes in the price of investment goods, the capital stock rises sharply. The quantity of full consumption rises at a similar rate, as does real GNP. The adjustment process is dominated by the rapid accumulation of capital and is largely complete within two decades.

FIGURE 10

THE EFFECTS OF REMOVING ALL ENVIRONMENTAL REGULATION ON INDUSTRIES

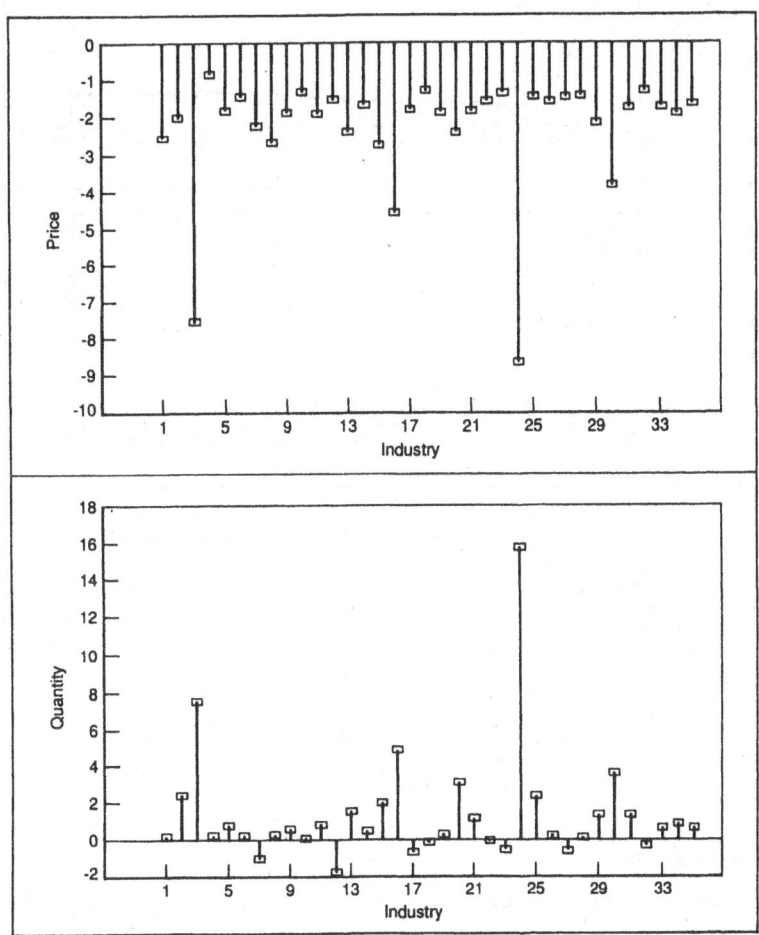

FIGURE 11
THE DYNAMIC EFFECTS OF REMOVING ALL ENVIRONMENTAL REGULATION

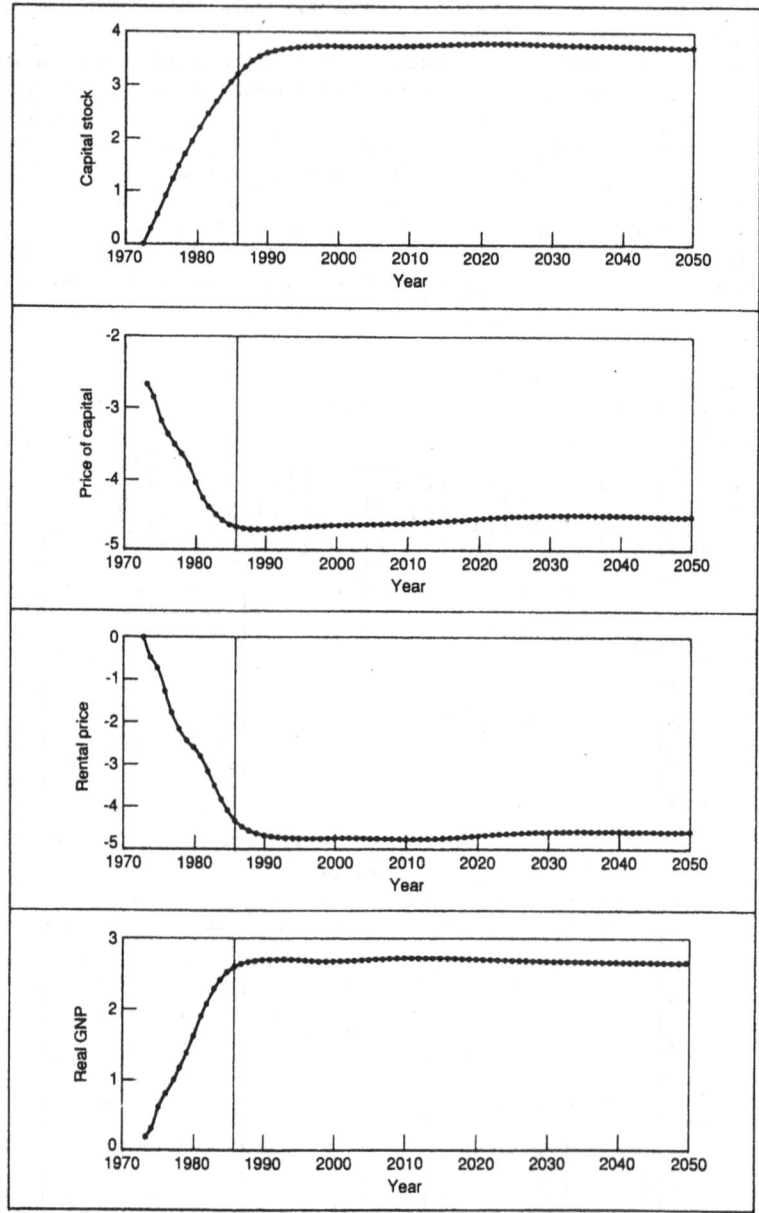

4. Conclusions

■ We can summarize the impact of environmental regulation by analyzing the effects on the growth of GNP over the period 1973–1985. These effects are given in Table 3. Mandated

TABLE 3   Summary of the Effects on Growth over 1974–1985

Simulation	Change in Growth Rate
Operating Costs	.034
Investment	.074
Old Source Investment	.026
Motor Vehicles	.051
All Effects	.191

investment in pollution control equipment has the largest impact, while motor vehicle emissions control is not far behind. The added operating costs due to pollution abatement play a minor role in the growth slowdown. The three types of environmental regulation together are responsible for a drop in GNP growth of .191 percentage points.

A number of studies have attempted to measure the effect of pollution control on productivity and economic growth.[18] For example, Denison (1985) found that the growth rate of the U.S. economy was reduced by only .07 percentage points over the period 1973–1982 due to pollution controls. His estimate is based on an aggregate production function and does not take into account the important differences in environmental restrictions among industries. In addition, Denison did not model the dynamic response of the U.S. economy to pollution controls. Our model incorporates differences among industries in pollution abatement and captures the effect of environmental costs on the rate of capital formation. Accordingly, our estimate of the impact of environmental regulation on U.S. economic growth is several times that reported by Denison.

We can also summarize the impact of higher operating costs associated with environmental regulation on economic growth, using the results given in Table 3. U.S. economic growth would have been .034 percentage points higher during the period 1973–1985 in the absence of the operating costs resulting from environmental regulation. These operating costs had a small but significant effect on long-run output and the rate of growth of the economy in the 1970s and early 1980s. In addition, these costs affected the distribution of economic activity with industries such as primary metals experiencing a considerable drop in output. However, operating costs arising from pollution abatement are not the only effects of environmental regulation.

The impact of pollution abatement investment on the rate of GNP growth during the period 1973–1985 is also given in Table 3. The growth of GNP would have been .074 percentage points higher in the absence of mandated investment in pollution control. Slower productivity growth contributed .015 percentage points to this total, while the rest came from slower growth of the primary factors of production. Mandated investment in pollution control had two effects. First, it lowered the long-run capital stock and reduced long-run consumption. Second, it reduced the rate of capital accumulation in the early years of regulation. This reduced the rate of growth of GNP. The impact of eliminating mandated investment in pollution abatement devices was substantially larger than that of eliminating operating costs.

The dampening effect of investment for pollution control on capital accumulation is exacerbated by the investment required to bring existing sources of emissions into compliance with environmental standards. We have taken the share of investment attributable to new investment goods as the 1983 share. The difference between the actual shares in earlier years

---

[18] A detailed survey of studies of the impact of environmental regulation on productivity and economic growth in the United States is presented in Christiansen and Tietenberg (1985).

and the 1983 share gives the proportion devoted to existing sources of emssions. The data presented in Figure 6 show that this expenditure reached as much as 3% of total investment during the mid-1970s.

We modified our simulation of U.S. economic growth to assess the importance of mandated investment in pollution abatement equipment for existing sources of emissions. For this purpose, we increased the level of investment expenditures for the years 1973 to 1983 by the share attributable to pollution abatement for existing sources. This raises the rate of capital accumulation for the mid-1970s, but there is no long-run effect on economic growth. Eliminating investment in pollution control devices for both new and existing sources raises the average rate of growth for the period 1973–1985 by .100 percentage points. We estimated an increase in the growth rate of .074 percentage points for the investment required for new sources alone, so we can attribute an increase of .026 points to the investment required to bring existing sources into compliance.

Finally, the rate of growth of the U.S. national product over the period 1973–1985 would have been .051 percentage points higher in the absence of motor vehicle emissions controls. This is a surprisingly large effect. It is nearly twice as large as the gain from eliminating mandatory investments for bringing existing sources of emissions into compliance with environmental standards and about half as large as removing all operating costs and all investment requirements for pollution control in industry.

References

ARMINGTON, P.S. "The Geographic Pattern of Trade and the Effects of Price Changes." *IMF Staff Papers*, Vol. 16 (1969), pp. 176–199.

BORGES, A.M. AND GOULDER, L.H. "Decomposing the Impact of Higher Energy Prices on Long-Term Growth." In H.E. Scarf and J.B. Shoven, eds., *Applied General Equilibrium Analysis*. Cambridge: Cambridge University Press, 1984.

BUREAU OF THE CENSUS, U.S. DEPARTMENT OF COMMERCE. *Pollution Abatement Costs and Expenditures*. Washington D.C.: U.S. Department of Commerce, various annual issues, 1973–1983.

BUREAU OF ECONOMIC ANALYSIS, U.S. DEPARTMENT OF COMMERCE. "The Input-Output Structure of the U.S. Economy, 1977." *Survey of Current Business*, Vol. 64 (1984), pp. 42–79.

———. *The National Income and Product Accounts of the United States, 1929–1982: Statistical Tables*. Washington, D.C.: U.S. Department of Commerce, 1986.

CASS, D. "Optimum Growth in an Aggregative Model of Capital Accumulation." *Review of Economic Studies*, Vol. 32 (1965), pp. 233–240.

CHRISTIANSEN, G.B. AND TIETENBERG, T.H. "Distributional and Macroeconomic Aspects of Environmental Policy." In A.V. Kneese and J.L. Sweeney, eds., *Handbook of Natural Resource and Energy Economics*. Vol. 1. Amsterdam: North-Holland, 1985.

DENISON, E.F. *Trends in American Economic Growth, 1929–1982*. Washington, D.C.: The Brookings Institution, 1985.

FORSUND, F.R. "Input-Output Models, National Economic Models, and the Environment." In A.V. Kneese and J.L. Sweeney, eds., *Handbook of Natural Resource and Energy Economics*, Vol. 1. Amsterdam: North-Holland, 1985.

——— AND STROM, S. "The Generation of Residual Flows In Norway: An Input-Output Approach." *Journal of Environmental Economics and Management*, Vol. 3 (1974), pp. 129–141.

FREEMAN, A.M. "Methods for Assessing the Benefits of Environmental Programs." In A.V. Kneese and J.L. Sweeney, eds., *Handbook of Natural Resources and Energy Economics*, Vol. 1. Amsterdam: North-Holland, 1985.

GOLLOP, F.M. AND ROBERTS, M.J. "Environmental Regulations and Productivity Growth: The Case of Fossil-fueled Electric Power Generation." *Journal of Political Economy*, Vol. 91 (1983), pp. 654–673.

HALL, R.E. "Stochastic Implications of the Life Cycle-Permanent Income Hypothesis: Theory and Evidence." *Journal of Political Economy*, Vol. 86 (1978), pp. 971–988.

HOGAN, W.W. AND JORGENSON, D.W. "Productivity Trends and the Costs of Reducing Carbon Dioxide Emissions." *Energy Journal*, Vol. 11 (1990), forthcoming.

JOHANSEN, L. *A Multi-Sectoral Study of Economic Growth*. Amsterdam: North-Holland, 1960.

JORGENSON, D.W. "Econometric and Process Analysis Models for the Analysis of Energy Policy." In R. Amit and M. Avriel, eds., *Perspectives in Resource Policy Modeling: Energy and Minerals*. Cambridge: Ballinger, 1982.

———. "Econometric Methods for Applied General Equilibrium Analysis." In H.E. Scarf and J.B. Shoven, eds., *Applied General Equilibrium Analysis*. Cambridge: Cambridge University Press, 1984.

———. "Econometric Methods for Modelling Producer Behavior." In Z. Griliches and M.D. Intriligator, eds., *Handbook of Econometrics*, Vol. 3. Amsterdam: North-Holland, 1986.

———. "Capital as a Factor of Production." In D.W. Jorgenson and R. Landau, eds., *Technology and Capital Formation*. Cambridge Mass.: MIT Press, 1989.

———. "Aggregate Consumer Behavior and the Measurement of Social Welfare." *Econometrica*, forthcoming.

——— AND FRAUMENI, B.M. "Relative Prices and Technical Change." In E. Berndt and B. Field, eds., *Modeling and Measuring Natural Resource Substitution*. Cambridge Mass.: MIT Press, 1981.

——— AND ———. "The Accumulation of Human and Nonhuman Capital, 1948-1984." In R.E. Lipsey and H.S. Tice, eds., *The Measurement of Saving, Investment, and Wealth*. Chicago: University of Chicago Press, 1989.

——— AND SLESNICK, D.T. "Individual and Social Cost of Living Indexes." In W.E. Diewert and C. Montmarquette, eds., *Price Level Measurement*. Ottawa: Statistics Canada, 1983.

——— AND ———. "General Equilibrium Analysis of Economic Policy." In J. Piggott and J. Whalley, eds., *New Developments in Applied General Equilibrium Analysis*. Cambridge: Cambridge University Press, 1985.

——— AND ———. "Aggregate Consumer Behavior and Household Equivalence Scales." *Journal of Business and Economic Statistics*, Vol. 5 (1987), pp. 219-232.

——— AND YUN, K.-Y. "The Efficiency of Capital Accumulation." *Scandinavian Journal of Economics*, Vol. 88 (1986), pp. 85-107.

———, GOLLOP, F.M., AND FRAUMENI, B.M. *Productivity and U.S. Economic Growth*. Cambridge, Mass.: Harvard University Press, 1987.

———, LAU, L.J., AND STOKER, T.M. "The Transcendental Logarithmic Model of Aggregate Consumer Behavior." In R.L. Basmann and G. Rhodes, eds., *Advances in Econometrics*, Vol. 1. Greenwich: JAI Press, 1982.

KALT, J.P. "The Impact of Domestic Environmental Regulatory Policies on U.S. International Competitiveness." In A.M. Spence and H.A. Hazard, eds., *International Competitiveness*. Cambridge: Ballinger, 1988.

KAPPLER, F.G. AND RUTLEDGE, G.L. "Expenditures for Abating Pollutant Emissions From Motor Vehicles, 1968-84." *Survey of Current Business*, Vol. 65 (1985), pp. 29-35.

KNEESE, A.V., AYRES, R.U., AND D'ARGE, R.C. *Economics and the Environment: A Materials Balance Approach*. Baltimore: Johns Hopkins University Press, 1970.

KOOPMANS, T.C. "Objectives, Constraints, and Outcomes in Optimal Growth." *Econometrica*, Vol. 35 (1967), pp. 1-15.

LUCAS, R.E., JR. "On the Mechanics of Economic Development." *Journal of Monetary Economics*, Vol. 22 (1988), pp. 3-42.

MALER, K.-G. *Environmental Economics, A Theoretical Inquiry*. Baltimore: Johns Hopkins University Press, 1974.

———. "Macroeconomic Aspects of Environmental Policy." In E.S. Mills, ed., *Economic Analysis of Environmental Problems*. New York: Columbia University Press, 1975.

———. "Welfare Economics and the Environment." In A.V. Kneese and J.L. Sweeney, eds., *Handbook of Natural Resource and Energy Economics*, Vol. 1. Amsterdam: North-Holland, 1985.

MANSUR, A. AND WHALLEY, J. "Numerical Specification of Applied General Equilibrium Models: Estimation, Calibration, and Data." In H.E. Scarf and J.B. Shoven, eds., *Applied General Equilibrium Analysis*. Cambridge: Cambridge University Press, 1984.

UNITED NATIONS. *A System of National Accounts*. New York: United Nations, 1968.

ROMER, P.M. "Capital Accumulation in the Theory of Long-Run Growth." In R.J. Barro, ed., *Modern Business Cycle Theory*. Cambridge, Mass.: Harvard University Press, 1989.

UZAWA, H. "Optimal Investment in Social Overhead Capital." In E.S. Mills, ed., *Economic Analysis of Environmental Problems*. New York: Columbia University Press, 1975.

WILCOXEN, P.J. "The Effects of Environmental Regulation and Energy Prices on U.S. Economic Performance." Ph.D. dissertation, Harvard University, 1988.

[12]

Social Cost of Environmental Quality Regulations: A General Equilibrium Analysis

Michael Hazilla
American University

Raymond J. Kopp
Resources for the Future

The use of cost-benefit analysis by federal regulatory agencies has expanded greatly in scope and sophistication. Unfortunately, agencies continue to employ private cost rather than social cost to evaluate environmental quality regulations. Furthermore, general equilibrium impacts and intertemporal effects of regulations are typically not included in the evaluation. In this paper we estimate the social cost of environmental quality regulations mandated by the Clean Air and Clean Water acts. We construct an econometric general equilibrium model of the United States to demonstrate that social cost estimates diverge sharply from private cost estimates. We also demonstrate that general equilibrium impacts are significant and pervasive and that intertemporal effects of the regulations, heretofore ignored, are significant.

I. Introduction

By presidential executive order, federal agencies are required to analyze new regulations, or changes in existing regulations, using benefit-

This research was supported in part by the U.S. Environmental Protection Agency, Office of Air Quality Planning and Standards, under contract no. 68-02-35-82. Although the research described in this article has been funded in part by the U.S. Environmental Protection Agency and the Senate Research Committee of the American University, no official endorsement should be inferred. We acknowledge helpful comments provided by Maureen Cropper, Robert Haveman, Dale Jorgenson, Al McGartland, John Mullahy, Wallace Oates, Sam Peltzman, Paul Portney, and V. Kerry Smith.

cost analysis.[1] Even though it improves on the economic analysis of public policies, the executive order includes neither explicit guidelines for conducting analyses nor precise definitions of benefits and costs. In the absence of formal guidelines, one might conclude that the executive order mandates an interpretation of benefits and costs consistent with applied welfare economics. More specifically, one might infer that benefits and costs are measured on the basis of the compensation principle.[2] Unfortunately, a theoretically precise social cost measure is not used in practice, and current procedures, based on private costs, are subject to errors of unknown magnitude and without basis in modern applied welfare economics.[3] The objective of this paper is to improve on these procedures by using compensating variation welfare measures to evaluate the social cost of environmental quality regulations promulgated under the Clean Air and Clean Water acts.

While federal agencies conducting benefit-cost analyses have, for the most part, employed benefit measures consistent with economic theory, they have inappropriately used private expenditures as a measure of social cost. From a social welfare perspective, the correct theoretical cost measure is the monetized change in social welfare due to reallocation of resources from production of goods and services to pollution abatement activities. If one assumes that social welfare can be measured using a function additive in individual utilities, then social cost is equal to the sum of individual compensating variations. Moreover, under the additivity assumption, a theoretically consistent social cost estimate can be constructed from observable market information.

It is well known that the cost of regulations, as calculated by agencies such as the U.S. Environmental Protection Agency (EPA), is not based on the theoretical concept of social cost. Rather, agencies equate social cost with annualized engineering costs of installed capital and related operating and maintenance expenses. Setting aside

---

[1] For instance, Executive Order 12291, issued by President Ronald Reagan, states that "in promulgating new regulations, reviewing existing regulations, and developing legislative proposals concerning regulation, all agencies, to the extent permitted by law shall adhere to the following requirements: . . . b) Regulatory action shall not be undertaken unless the potential benefits to society for the regulation outweigh the potential costs to society" (*Fed. Register* 46 [February 19, 1981]: 13193–98).

[2] More precisely, benefits are measured using the maximum amount of money individuals would be willing to pay to live in a world with the policy in force rather than not. Conversely, one could assess the cost of the policy as the minimum amount of money necessary to compensate individuals to endure the policy's adverse effects.

[3] Benefits and costs are measured using a money metric of the gains or losses in utility associated with changes in the individual's economic circumstances. It is important to recognize that there is some controversy regarding use of money metric utility (see, e.g., Blackorby and Donaldson 1986).

these theoretical issues, one still finds problems with the use of engineering costs. For example, engineering costs generally do not account for partial equilibrium adjustments, let alone general equilibrium effects. Furthermore, engineering notions of cost are static and do not consider intertemporal regulatory impacts on household and firm decision making.

Some regulatory agencies acknowledge that their cost estimate is inconsistent with benefit measures and that it does not account for dynamic and general equilibrium impacts of regulation. Agencies and many economists believe, however, that engineering cost estimates are suitable proxies for social cost and maintain that dynamic, general equilibrium impacts are insignificant. If this conjecture is valid, then static engineering cost estimates are appropriate for social cost measurement. If, on the other hand, one can demonstrate empirically that engineering estimates are poor proxies for social cost and that dynamic, general equilibrium effects are important, then one can argue that social cost estimates must be based on the precepts of welfare economics and encompass general equilibrium and intertemporal effects.

This paper contrasts static engineering cost estimates, based on private expenditures, with social cost estimates derived from modern applied welfare economics. To estimate the dynamic social cost of environmental quality regulations, we construct an econometric general equilibrium model of the U.S. economy. The model encompasses both static and intertemporal behavioral adjustments. Most important, the general equilibrium model includes an explicit characterization of household utility that is used to assess welfare changes.

The model maintains certain assumptions that the reader should keep in mind when interpreting the results.[4] Like the majority of computable general equilibrium models, the model employed maintains the assumption of perfect competition in all markets. Production is modeled using a single form of malleable capital, and all inputs are assumed mobile. The capital stock is fixed in any given period and augmented at the end of the period by current-period net investment. The household is modeled using myopic expectations and assigned an initial wealth endowment. Transactions costs are assumed to be zero. Prices within the model are measured relative to a wage numeraire. Labor supply is endogenous while population growth is specified exogenously. Finally, as the major intertemporal link, household labor supply determines household income and savings. Household savings determine investment and the capital stock available in the

---

[4] One may, of course, find a model with different assumptions, but those in our model are standard.

next period. Through this intertemporal link, perturbations in the current-period labor market are transmitted to the capital market in the next period.

An outline of the paper follows. A broad review of the legislative basis for the environmental quality regulations is developed in Section II. The EPA estimates of the private cost of compliance with the Clean Air and Clean Water acts are also presented. Section III outlines the general equilibrium model.[5] Section IV describes modeling technology-based regulations, and Section V presents the social cost estimates of regulatory compliance. Concluding remarks are presented in Section VI.

II. Private Costs of Regulation

The majority of environmental regulations, promulgated during the 1970s and early 1980s, have been associated with the Clean Air and Clean Water acts. The 1970 Clean Air Act requires the EPA to establish national ambient air quality standards (NAAQS) for six pollutants.[6] In response to the legislation, the EPA established two regulatory programs. The first focuses on mobile emission sources, while the second concentrates on stationary sources. Each state is required to develop an environmental strategy that ensures that ambient air quality meets the NAAQS standards. This state-level strategy is termed the state implementation plan.

The EPA's responsibility to regulate waterborne pollutants emanates from the Federal Water Pollution Control Act of 1972 and amendments to the Clean Water Act of 1977. The legislation requires the EPA to establish regulations limiting industrial pollutant discharge. Like the Clean Air Act, the water legislation specifies the engineering character of the control technologies. The law initially requires application of "best practicable control technology" currently available but also mandates future implementation of the "best available technology" economically achievable. Similarly, new sources of emissions are regulated under "new source performance standards."[7]

Finally, in addition to the regulatory powers they confer, the Clean Air and Clean Water acts require the EPA to provide Congress with detailed compliance cost estimates. The most recent report, completed in 1983 and encompassing the regulatory framework existing

---

[5] Unfortunately, space limitations do not permit a full and detailed discussion of the model employed in this analysis. A longer version of the present paper and a detailed technical appendix are available on request from the authors.

[6] The six criteria pollutants are particulate matter, sulfur oxides, nitrogen oxides, carbon monoxide, ozone, and lead.

[7] See Portney (1989) for a complete discussion of air and water quality regulations.

in December 1982, forms the basis for our social cost analysis (see U.S. Environmental Protection Agency 1984).

The EPA cost estimates are composed of annualized capital costs of equipment and installation, and direct operating and maintenance expenditures associated with this equipment. These costs pertain only to regulatory actions resulting from the Clean Air and Clean Water acts and exclude voluntary expenditure, or expenditures required by state or local government and other federal laws. Annual 1981 compliance costs reported by the EPA to Congress are displayed by major industries in column 1 of table 1. Total annual cost over the period 1981–90 is reported in column 2 of table 1. The EPA report states that the average annual cost of the regulations in 1981 dollars between 1970 and 1978 was $19 billion, was $40 billion between 1979 and 1981, and will be $58 billion between 1981 and 1990.

In fairness, we note that the EPA does not claim that the estimates reported in table 1 represent social costs, but rather that the estimates are initial private costs of complying with the acts. However, these private cost estimates do not account for general equilibrium cost effects that can be transmitted from a regulated industry to those not directly affected by regulation. The neglect of such secondary effects can understate the private costs.

III. The General Equilibrium Model

Overview

Measuring the social cost of significant and complex regulatory programs, such as the Clean Air and Clean Water acts, requires a modeling structure with particular features. The most important feature is the ability to measure social cost using household willingness to pay rather than measures based on compliance expenditure. This requirement can be satisfied by constructing appropriate demand and supply curves for goods whose prices may be affected and measuring the net change in consumer and producer surplus. Alternatively, one can characterize household preferences with an indirect utility or expenditure function and proceed to monetize the changes in utility due to price and income changes brought about by the regulatory program. If one expects the regulatory program to change several prices and incomes, then measuring the social cost using compensating or equivalent variation measures (derived from expenditure functions) is preferable to using net changes in consumer and producer surplus. The modeling framework adopted follows the work of Jorgenson and Slesnick (1985*a*) and models household preference using a hierarchy of indirect utility functions. Measures of compensating variation may be readily obtained from these functions.

TABLE 1
Estimated Annual Capital and Operating Expenses Associated with Clean Air and Clean Water Acts Regulations (Millions of 1981 Dollars)

Sector	Annual Cost, 1981 (1)	Cumulative Annual Cost, 1981-90 (2)
Energy:		
Coal mining	103	1,189
Oil and gas extraction	576	6,318
Petroleum refining	1,153	12,346
Electric utilities	7,760	99,132
Coal gasification		302
Food processing:		
Feedlots and meat processing	182	2,725
Other food processing	1,389	14,324
Chemicals:		
Basic inorganic chemicals	403	4,008
Organic chemicals	1,019	15,837
Agricultural chemicals	246	3,358
Formulated chemicals	286	2,944
Construction materials	397	4,742
Metals:		
Ore mining and dressing	166	1,657
Iron and steel	1,596	22,223
Aluminum	199	2,348
Copper	416	3,644
Nonferrous metals	243	2,876
Soft goods:		
Pulp and paper	1,173	11,987
Textiles	27	355
Leather and rubber	66	1,022
Manufacturing:		
Electroplating	0	910
Surface coatings	122	2,375
Furniture manufacture	7	70
Lead acid batteries	6	64
Services:		
Dry cleaning	0	467
Hospitals	102	1,668
Photographic processing	2	21
Municipal waste incineration	26	250
Other industrial costs:		
Boilers	2,547	26,599
Incinerators	157	2,488
Government expenditures	16,125	197,013
Mobile sources	6,047	80,554
Total expenditures	42,541	525,816

Source.—U.S. Environmental Protection Agency (1984).

ENVIRONMENTAL QUALITY

Assessing the reasonableness of static partial equilibrium assumptions underlying the use of expenditures as social cost measures also requires a modeling framework that allows for dynamic general equilibrium responses to regulatory programs. The model we develop departs from the static partial equilibrium analyses by drawing on recent developments in econometric general equilibrium models. The model incorporates intertemporal household behavior and is suitable for assessing long-run impacts of regulatory programs on neoclassical economic growth.

The final important modeling feature concerns production. Imposing command and control technological requirements on industries subject to environmental regulation requires a detailed econometric production model. In our model, pollution control regulations can be imposed directly on the technologies. The model we develop contains 36 production sectors. Pollution control impacts are modeled through modification of the derived input demand equations in each sector.[8]

General Framework

To our knowledge, a model possessing the full set of attributes discussed above, which might be used to examine the usefulness of compliance expenditures as proxies for social cost, does not exist. Many computable general equilibrium models exist—some relying on calibration techniques and others based on a full set of econometrically estimated parameters—but in some aspect we have found them deficient.[9] The most popular and sophisticated calibration model is described in Ballard et al. (1985). Calibration models employ input-output matrices to describe derived input demand and constrain, a priori, substitution possibilities. The premier econometric general equilibrium model developed by Hudson and Jorgenson (1974), and extended by Hudson (1981) and Goettle and Hudson (1984), allows

---

[8] Experience with the 36-sector model suggests that a more aggregate sectoral model may have produced similar results. The nine-sector model in Hudson and Jorgenson (1974) comes to mind; however, we have not undertaken a model aggregation to confirm this conjecture. Most of the initial compliance expenditures are borne by the motor vehicle and energy sectors, a small set of industrial boilers, the iron and steel industry, and organic chemicals. Neglecting the other sectors may have little effect on the results. It is important, however, to recognize that large disaggregate models may now be routinely constructed, and thus there is little reason (other than computer time) to employ more aggregate versions.

[9] Many parameters in models of the Shoven and Whalley (1972) type are determined by a method known as "calibration." Such a method employs a single observational vector of endogenous variables to solve for the parameters of the model's behavioral equations consistent with observed values. The econometric approach to general equilibrium model building is discussed in Jorgenson (1984).

for substitution possibilities, intertemporal household behavior, and neoclassical growth, but it models production at a high level of aggregation.[10]

We have selected an econometric general equilibrium approach over one based on calibration methods because substitution and intertemporal dynamics are fundamental components in the evaluation of environmental quality regulations. Nevertheless, while we have utilized the Hudson-Jorgenson framework, we have also econometrically estimated disaggregate production sectors in a manner internally consistent with the remainder of the model.[11] The result is a new model, directly descendant from Hudson and Jorgenson, in which production is characterized econometrically, using "Diewert" flexible functional forms.[12] The sectoral econometric models correspond to two-digit industry groups in the Standard Industrial Classification.

The Structure of Production

Production in the model is disaggregated into 36 producing sectors. With the exception of government services, each sector is algebraically formulated as a hierarchical system of translog cost functions exhibiting constant returns to scale. This system gives rise to competitive derived demand equations for capital and labor, four forms of energy, and 30 intermediate inputs.

The translog system is estimated subject to symmetry, linear homogeneity, monotonicity, and concavity constraints. The symmetry and linear homogeneity parametric restrictions are well known, but imposing monotonicity and concavity constraints is a recent development (see Hazilla and Kopp 1986c). The econometric model is estimated using data from 1958–74 predating the Clean Air and Clean Water acts.[13] While it is possible to estimate the model using post-1974 data, the objective is to characterize the base case economy using the preregulation technologies.

---

[10] The Hudson-Jorgenson (1974) model divides the production side of the economy into nine sectors, but manufacturing activity is represented as one sector.

[11] The Hudson-Jorgenson model is probably the most well known of the numerical general equilibrium models and is described in various publications. Hudson and Jorgenson (1974, 1976) provide the most complete discussions readily available to the interested reader. Complete discussions of the model's inner workings are found in Berndt et al. (1981) and Hudson (1981). Other published sources include Hudson and Jorgenson (1978a, 1978b).

[12] A function $f(x)$ is Diewert flexible if at a point x^* it has enough free parameters so that $f(x^*)$, $\nabla f(x^*)$ (the N-dimensional gradient vector of f evaluated at x^*), and $\nabla^2 f(x^*)$ (the $N \times N$ Hessian matrix of second-order partial derivatives of f) can attain arbitrary values. See Diewert and Wales (1986).

[13] The data are extensively discussed in Hazilla and Kopp (1986b).

ENVIRONMENTAL QUALITY

The Structure of Consumption

The consumption side of the model is drawn from Berndt et al. (1981). The model relies on the notion of a representative household and implies that households share common preferences.[14] These common preferences, described by a set of hierarchical indirect translog utility functions, serve to model both intertemporal and intratemporal household decisions.

The initial intertemporal decision faced by households concerns the choice between present and future consumption. That is, a household must allocate a lifetime wealth endowment between present and future consumption of goods and leisure. Following this choice, the household focuses on two sequential intratemporal decisions. The first is to select the proportions of current-period consumption to take in the form of goods and leisure. This choice determines household labor supply and leisure. The second sequential decision is household allocation of current-period goods consumption among the following commodity groups: energy, durable goods, imported goods, agriculture and construction, manufacturing, commercial and transportation, and other services.[15]

Social Welfare Measures

Social costs of environmental regulations may be measured at any level in the household preference hierarchy from the uppermost intertemporal wealth-consumption decision to the intratemporal decisions regarding commodity consumption. Because household behavioral response is limited, the lower in the hierarchy one performs the measurement, the larger will be the estimates of social cost. Since the

---

[14] The assumption of a representative household may be relaxed by relying on the exact aggregation theorems due to Lau (1977a, 1977b); see also Jorgenson and Slesnick (1985b) and Hazilla and Kopp (1986a). This amendment to the model adds to the computational burden and for that reason is not utilized in the current study. Hazilla and Kopp (1986a), examining a specific environmental regulation but over a shorter time period, utilized the detailed consumer model provided by Jorgenson, Lau, and Stoker (1982) in place of the representative household model. While the latter model permits one to distribute the costs of regulation over demographic groups, it does not produce aggregate social welfare losses significantly different from the representative household model.

[15] The hierarchical indirect utility functions were estimated by Berndt et al. (1981) subject to adding-up, monotonicity, symmetry, and convexity restrictions using techniques attributed to Lau (1974). Although not of direct interest to our discussion, we should point out that the model incorporates a government and foreign-trade sector. The government sector collects taxes on capital and labor income, purchases goods and services (government expenditures), and provides transfer payments to consumers and subsidies to producers. A foreign-trade sector, which serves as an alternative to domestic supply, closes the model.

purpose of this study is to draw sharp contrast between private expenditures and social costs, we measure the welfare cost of environmental regulations using the indirect utility function describing preferences for goods and leisure.[16]

Social welfare is measured using the expenditure function and the Hicksian notion of compensating variation (Hicks 1946). The expenditure function is derived from an econometrically estimated indirect utility function. If we let $e(v, p)$ denote the expenditure function, compensating variation is defined as

$$CV = e(v^0, p^0) - e(v^0, p^1), \quad (1)$$

where CV represents the difference between the minimum expenditure necessary to achieve a utility level v^0, given commodity prices p^1, and the expenditure necessary to maintain v^0 at reference prices p^0. With this definition, a positive value for the compensating variation suggests a welfare gain whereas a negative value implies a welfare loss.[17]

IV. Technology-based Regulations

The Clean Air and Clean Water acts' compliance expenditures may be divided into three categories. The first and largest is private firm expenditures on air and water pollutant abatement equipment. The second category also includes pollution abatement expenditures but pertains to those made by federal, state, and local governments. The last group involves direct consumer expenditures such as increased cost of unleaded gasoline purchases and vehicle inspection fees.

The major portion of compliance cost is borne by stationary sources of air and water pollution, which, in our model, are represented by

---

[16] The goods-leisure indirect utility function lies just below the uppermost portion of the hierarchy describing the decision to consume out of total lifetime endowment. Berndt et al. (1981) estimate the preferences for endowment consumption such that the present period's consumption of endowments depends on time and the price of consumption, while the share out of total endowments depends only on time. Given this simplified view of the intertemporal consumption decision, we have chosen to measure welfare using the more econometrically interesting goods-leisure function. We do recognize that this choice somewhat overstates the welfare loss.

[17] When one is considering the welfare costs of significant government policies such as the Clean Air and Clean Water acts, however, income effects can be significant. Accordingly, to account for an income effect, CV may be calculated using

$$CV^* = e(v^0, p^0) - e(v^0, p^1) + y^1 - y^0$$
$$= y^1 - e(v^0, p^1),$$

where y^0 is the reference period income and y^1 is the postregulation income. The measure of social cost employed in this paper is based on CV^*.

ENVIRONMENTAL QUALITY

the production sectors. In contrast to other forms of regulation, environmental regulations often require producers to employ resources that include the services of specialized capital, operating and maintenance labor, and the purchase of related intermediate inputs. Since input choice is endogenous in a general equilibrium model, representing technology-based regulations is markedly different from the characterization of policies that affect a general equilibrium solely through exogenous economic variables.

Technology-based regulations, the focus of our study, are modeled by specifying four aggregate input qualities—capital (K), labor (L), energy (E), and intermediate materials (M)—needed to comply with the regulations. Under a technology-based regulation, the structure of each production sector is modified to account for increased input usage. To illustrate the technique, consider a production sector whose technology is characterized by constant returns to scale and nonneutral technological change. The technology is represented by the translog cost function

$$\ln c = \alpha_0 + \sum_i \alpha_i \ln p_i + \tfrac{1}{2} \sum_i \sum_j \gamma_{ij} \ln p_i \ln p_j + \ln q \\ + \alpha_t t + \tfrac{1}{2}\gamma_{tt} t^2 + \sum_i \gamma_{ti} t \ln p_i, \quad i, j = K, L, E, M, \quad (2)$$

where ln denotes the natural logarithm of cost (c), input prices (p_i), and output (q); t represents technological change; and α and γ are parameter vectors. In the absence of the environmental regulation, the optimal (sectoral) input demand equations are

$$x_i^* = \frac{\partial c}{\partial p_i} = \frac{c}{p_i}\left(\alpha_i + \sum_j \gamma_{ij} \ln p_j + \gamma_{ti} t\right), \quad (3)$$

where $c = \exp(\ln c)$. If Δ_i represents the increased quantity of the ith input required by the regulation, the demand equations would be modified as

$$\bar{x}_i = x_i^* + \Delta_i, \quad (4)$$

where $\bar{x}_i$ is the postregulation quantity of the ith input demanded.

Using (4), one can integrate back to the cost function

$$c = c(p, q) + \sum_i p_i \Delta_i q, \quad (5)$$

where Δ_i now represents input requirements per unit of output.

A second and somewhat more complicated approach, but one that reduces computational burden, is to embed pollution control expenditures directly into the technology. To illustrate this approach, consider the input demand equations

$$x_i^* = \frac{c}{p_i}\left(\alpha_i + \sum_j \gamma_{ij} \ln p_j + \gamma_{ti}t_i\right) \quad (6)$$

and cost function

$$c = \exp\left(\alpha_0 + \sum_i \alpha_i \ln p_i + \tfrac{1}{2}\sum_i\sum_j \gamma_{ij} \ln p_i \ln p_j + \alpha_t t_c + \tfrac{1}{2}\gamma_{tt}t_c^2 + \sum_i \gamma_{ti}t_i + \ln q\right) \text{ for } i, j = K, L, E, M,$$

where the technology variable (t) is replaced with t_c and t_i ($i = K, L, E,$ and M). Without the regulations, $t = t_c = t_i$ for all i. Under the regulations, t_c and t_i may be used to solve the system

$$\begin{aligned} x_i^* + \Delta_i q &= \frac{\partial c}{\partial p_i}, \\ c + \sum_i p_i \Delta_i q &= \exp c(\mathbf{p}, q, \mathbf{t}), \end{aligned} \quad (7)$$

where $\mathbf{p} = [p_K, p_L, p_E, p_M]$ denotes the input price vector and the technology vector is $[t_c, t_K, t_L, t_E, t_M]$.

The second approach is employed in this study since it yields tractable demand equations. One should note that even though the technology terms are altered in this approach, biases and rate of technological progress are unchanged. Most important, however, imposing regulation does not affect theoretical properties of the cost functions.

There are two additional features of modeling technology-based regulation that are important for interpreting the social cost estimates. First, within a general equilibrium framework, the social cost of increased government expenditures to finance, for example, expenditures on municipal sewage treatment plants, can be significant. An exogenously imposed fixed deficit rule is used to account for increased taxes necessary to finance the expenditures. Arguably, it may be more realistic to finance these expenditures with an increased deficit, but, for expediency, we have forgone this added complexity.

Second, we have modeled the impact of regulations on consumer expenditures by taking into account that the majority of consumer expenditures associated with the acts result from regulations affecting mobile sources (private vehicles). These expenditures take the form of increased vehicle operating and maintenance expenses. Although one could incorporate operating and maintenance expenses within the appropriate consumer commodity group in the model, the source

ENVIRONMENTAL QUALITY

TABLE 2

Annual Social Cost and EPA Compliance Cost Estimates of the Clean Air and Clean Water Acts (Billions of Current Dollars)

Year	Social Cost	EPA Compliance Cost
1975	6.8	14.1
1981	28.3	42.5
1985	70.6	56.0
1990	203.0	78.6
1981–90	977.0	648.0

of expenditure information does not distinguish these expenses from the costs of control technologies (see U.S. Environmental Protection Agency 1984). Accordingly, incremental vehicle expenditures, required by control technologies, have been aggregated into the vehicle purchase price.

V. Estimates of Social Cost

Estimates of the social cost of environmental regulations are based on general equilibrium price and income vectors derived from two simulations. The first, termed the base case simulation, pertains to the period 1970–90. The base case simulation uses both historical values (1970–85) and Data Resources Incorporated forecasts (1986–90) for the exogenous variables. The second simulation, termed the regulatory scenario, uses the same exogenous variables but introduces regulation on the production technologies using the second method described in Section IV.

The estimates of social cost based on measures of compensating variation are displayed in table 2. The general equilibrium model estimate of the social cost of federal air and water pollution control regulations in 1981 was approximately $28 billion. This may be directly compared to the EPA's $42.5 billion engineering cost estimate. These results imply that a 1981 benefit-cost analysis of the regulations based on the EPA estimates would understate the net benefits of the Clean Air and Clean Water acts by $14.5 billion.

The advantage of a general equilibrium analysis is its ability to capture the complexity of economic adjustments that are intractable within an analytical framework. Unfortunately, this feature adds to the difficulty of interpreting the results since one cannot explicitly formulate the adjustment path. In the current context, the divergence between cost estimates is due in large part to a demand-driven decrease in control costs and the substitution effect.

The significance of the demand effect is best demonstrated by considering the electric generating sector. This sector incurs the largest private-sector control costs, the largest increase in customer prices, and the largest decline in demand (produced output declines by 13 percent). In equilibrium, the 13 percent decline in demand implies a decreased need for generating capacity and a complementary decline in regulatory compliance expenditures. Though not as pronounced, the same demand phenomenon is observed in the petroleum refining, food processing, chemicals, iron and steel, and pulp and paper sectors. Since the EPA methodology does not take into account the effect of changes in demand on compliance expenditures, it overstates these expenditures.

The significant decline in electricity demand is also indicative of both producer and consumer substitution. The ability of the economy to substitute "clean" goods (lower polluting) for "dirty" goods (higher polluting) gives rise to a significant difference between private expenditures and social costs. This substitution may be readily seen by examining the labor-leisure portion of the consumer model in which welfare costs are estimated.

The 1981 equilibria show that while household expenditure on goods and services is $43.6 billion less under the regulation scenario, household leisure consumption also increases by $14.6 billion (measured in postregulation prices). Admittedly, this is only an approximate measure of compensating variation, but the difference between the decline in consumption and increased leisure ($28 billion) provides a reasonable estimate and serves to highlight the labor-leisure consumer response.

While the 1981 social cost estimate is significantly lower than the EPA estimate, one cannot conclude that social costs are always less than comparable estimates based on private expenditures. Economists have long recognized that governmental regulations have significant dynamic impacts.[18] For example, the EPA estimates that federal air and water pollution control costs are $525.8 billion (1981 dollars) between 1981 and 1990. If we uniformly distribute these expenditures over the 10-year interval and then convert to nominal dollars (using the personal consumption expenditure price index in the model), the total nominal pollution control cost is approximately $648 billion. By contrast, the general equilibrium social cost estimate is $977 billion. Very few policymakers have recognized that social costs

---

[18] In addition to the effect on investment, capital accumulation, and labor supply, regulation may also induce subtle changes that affect sectoral productivity and technological change. Productivity effects due to input prices are captured by the nonneutral treatment of technological change in the translog cost function.

TABLE 3
PERCENTAGE CHANGE IN SELECTED MACRO VARIABLES BETWEEN BASE AND SCENARIO

Macro Variable	1981	1990
Real consumption	−2.68	−6.53
Real growth private domestic investment	−4.15	−8.35
Real gross national product	−2.43	−5.85
Real private domestic capital stock	−2.02	−5.96
Real household labor supply	−.84	−1.18
Current value of gross national product	−.25	−.14
Price index for consumer goods	2.05	6.29
Government revenue from taxes on capital	5.02	12.50
Government revenue from taxes on labor	5.57	12.80

can exceed private expenditures, but it is a direct result of household behavior in which leisure is substituted for consumption.

It is useful to examine some indicators of macroeconomic activity in the base case and regulatory scenarios before discussing the intuition behind leisure-consumption substitution. For comparative purposes, we recount the EPA cost estimate and the macroeconomic discussion. The U.S. EPA 1984 executive summary states that "the 1981 annualized cost of pollution control due to federal regulations was estimated to be $42.3 billion or about one percent of GNP in 1981. The cumulative cost from 1970 to 1978 was $171 billion and the projected cost over the period 1981 to 1990 is estimated at $525.8 billion" (p. 3). The report concludes that consumer prices in 1981 were 3.3 percent higher than they would have been without federal pollution control regulations and that GNP was marginally lower (less than 1 percent).

Table 3 displays percentage changes in selected macro variables between the base case and regulatory scenario for 1981 and 1990. On the basis of the general equilibrium model regulation scenario simulations, consumer prices are found to be only 2 percent higher in 1981 but 6 percent higher in 1990. While the effect on current-dollar GNP is negligible, real GNP is about 2 percent lower in 1981 and 6 percent lower in 1990. The magnitude of the price increase in 1981 is approximately the same in both simulations. In contrast, significantly larger price increases in 1990 under the regulatory scenario suggest that the dynamic consequences of regulation, not addressed in the EPA report, are important.

Consider changes in levels of investment, capital stock, and labor supply brought about by the regulations, reported in table 3. The factor underlying the decrease is the household labor supply decision. In this case, since the relative price of consumption to leisure has increased, labor supply declines under the postregulation scenario.

TABLE 4

CHANGES IN SECTORAL VARIABLES BETWEEN BASE AND IMPACT SCENARIOS (Evaluated in 1990)

Sector	Percentage Change in Output Price	Percentage Change in Output Quantity	Percentage Change in Employment
Agriculture, forestry, and fisheries	6.11	−5.67	−3.78
Metal mining	5.02	−4.72	−.48
Coal mining	5.95	−3.38	1.54
Crude petroleum and natural gas	22.65	−15.28	.00
Nonmetallic mining and quarrying	5.88	−5.86	−3.92
Construction	2.98	−4.48	−1.58
Food and kindred products	7.38	−6.66	−4.79
Tobacco manufactures	5.33	−4.86	−.53
Textile mill products	5.49	−4.74	−4.22
Apparel and other fabricated textile products	3.36	−3.92	−1.67
Lumber and wood products except furniture	5.02	−5.59	−3.91
Furniture and fixtures	3.21	−4.32	−3.22
Paper and allied products	9.64	−7.12	−.94

Printing, publishing, and allied products	3.80	−3.91	−.97
Chemicals and allied products	11.33	−8.88	−2.95
Petroleum refining and allied industries	8.64	−5.12	.23
Rubber and miscellaneous plastic products	6.88	−5.60	−1.47
Leather and leather products	3.75	−4.29	−2.31
Stone, clay, and glass products	5.53	−5.07	−.89
Primary metal products	15.51	−10.51	−1.71
Fabricated metal products	7.31	−6.41	−1.42
Machinery excluding electrical	3.98	−4.04	−.52
Electrical machinery	5.52	−5.01	−3.89
Motor vehicles and equipment	36.63	−19.73	7.68
Transportation equipment and ordnance	3.42	−4.16	−3.29
Instruments	4.32	−3.69	−1.91
Miscellaneous manufacturing	5.42	−5.19	−2.97
Transportation and warehousing	3.08	−2.41	−.49
Communications	2.73	−3.53	−.60
Electrical utilities	44.41	−28.95	1.99
Gas utilities	8.85	−5.73	1.60
Wholesale and retail trade	3.39	−3.49	1.10
Finance, insurance, and real estate	5.12	−4.97	−2.64
Other services	3.27	−3.26	−1.57

Reduced labor supply also induces a decline in income and saving. The decline in saving causes investment to fall and, with it, capital stock growth. While supplied labor hours and capital availability increase over time under the regulatory scenario, both increase at a diminished rate. Consequently, household real income declines and aggregate economic growth is retarded.[19]

As noted above, in our model, the macroeconomic impacts of environmental regulations are the result of microeconomic decisions, largely dominated by household behavior. An equally important set of decisions are, however, also made by production sectors in the economy. The impact of producer decisions is displayed in table 4. We summarize the effect of producer decisions by reporting the percentage change in output price and quantity and employment between the base case and the regulatory scenario. The production sectors most severely affected by the regulations are electric utilities, motor vehicles, crude petroleum and natural gas, primary metals, and chemicals and allied products. In these sectors, environmental regulation induced output price increases that exceed 10 percent (44 percent in electric utilities) and an output decline that ranges between 8 and 28 percent in 1990. All industries experienced declines in labor productivity, and some sectors experienced declines in employment. These impacts can also be substantial; for example, employment falls 7.6 percent in the motor vehicle sector.

Sectoral regulatory impacts reported in table 4 highlight a point often made by economists but largely ignored by regulators: regulations affecting production sectors that supply important intermediate products can have significant secondary impacts. Table 4 reveals that while pollution control investments were required in only 13 sectors, the cost of production increased, and output and labor productivity fell, in *all* production sectors. A good example of the magnitude of the secondary effects is found in the finance, insurance, and real estate sector of the economy. The finance sector was not required to invest in pollution abatement equipment and obviously did not incur higher operating costs as a *direct* consequence of the Clean Air and Clean Water acts. Thus, under the EPA cost methodology, the sector would bear no regulatory cost. But on the basis of the general equilibrium analysis, the cost of production in the finance sector is 2 percent higher in 1981 as a result of indirect impacts of the regulation—more

---

[19] Unfortunately, there is no macro policy fix to this problem. The economy is already fully employed in the postregulation world, and the prices are "correct" in the sense that there exist no noncompetitive distortions. The problem arises from the fact that real wages have fallen and households have adjusted accordingly.

specifically, higher factor prices. Higher production costs represent another private cost to the sector and are another source of error in the EPA cost estimate.

VI. Conclusions

Applied welfare economics can play a central role in policy evaluation. Empirical work in applied policy analysis must be guided by theoretically precise measures of social cost and dynamic general equilibrium considerations. The issuance of several presidential executive orders over the past decade appears to give applied welfare economics a formal position in the analysis of government regulatory policy. Unfortunately, the lack of specificity in the orders, regarding the definition of costs, has allowed federal agencies to continue equating the cost of regulation with private expenditures in an assessment of regulatory impacts. Many economists believe that private expenditures are suitable proxies for the social cost. Our findings demonstrate that private expenditures are poor measures of social cost.

In addition to highlighting the divergence between private compliance expenditures and social costs, the analysis serves to reinforce a frequent conjecture about the effects of regulation on the economy. Specifically, regulations affect intertemporal microeconomic decisions and cause social cost to increase over time. Failure to quantify and account for these intertemporal phenomena in a benefit-cost analysis will likely lead to errors of unknown magnitude. On the basis of our findings of significant intertemporal impacts, currently practiced methods are unacceptable.

It is difficult to overemphasize the importance of approaching policy analysis from a general equilibrium perspective. This emphasis is reinforced by our finding that while only a subset of the industries are directly affected under the regulation scenarios, all production sectors in the model ultimately bear the burden of regulations. This finding suggests that even expenditure-based estimates of costs would be inaccurately estimated.

Although perhaps obvious, one final point deserves mention. Our attention has focused on costs associated with environmental quality regulations. Any normative judgment about the desirability of the regulations depends on comparing appropriately measured costs with corresponding benefits. While benefits have generally been measured using an appropriate willingness-to-pay criterion, an intertemporal general equilibrium approach to benefit estimation might show similar divergences from reported results based on static partial equilibrium analysis.

References

Ballard, Charles L.; Fullerton, Don; Shoven, John B.; and Whalley, John. *A General Equilibrium Model for Tax Policy Evaluation*. Chicago: Univ. Chicago Press (for NBER), 1985.

Berndt, Ernst R.; Fraumeni, Barbara M.; Hudson, Edward A.; Jorgenson, Dale W.; and Stoker, Thomas M. "Econometrics and Data of the 9 Sector Dynamic General Equilibrium Model." Final report to the Macroeconomic Analysis Division, Energy Information Administration. Vol. 3. Washington: Dept. Energy, 1981.

Blackorby, Charles, and Donaldson, D. "Money Metric Utility: A Harmless Normalization?" Discussion Paper no. 86-09. Vancouver: Univ. British Columbia, Dept. Econ., 1986.

Diewert, W. E., and Wales, Terence J. "Semiflexible Functional Forms." Discussion paper. Vancouver: Univ. British Columbia, Dept. Econ., 1986.

Goettle, Richard J., IV, and Hudson, Edward A. "Final Report on the Dynamic General Equilibrium Model." Report. Washington: Emergency Management Agency, February 1984.

Hazilla, Michael, and Kopp, Raymond J. "The Social Cost of Alternative Ambient Air Quality Standards for Total Suspended Particulates: A General Equilibrium Analysis." Final report. Research Triangle Park, N.C.: Office of Air Quality Planning and Standards, U.S. Environmental Protection Agency, 1986. (a)

———. "Systematic Effects of Capital Service Price Definition on Perceptions of Input Substitution." *J. Bus. and Econ. Statis.* 4 (April 1986): 209–24. (b)

———. "Testing for Separable Functional Structure Using Temporary Equilibrium Models." *J. Econometrics* 33 (October/November 1986): 119–41. (c)

Hicks, John R. *Value and Capital: An Inquiry into Some Fundamental Principles of Economic Theory*. 2d ed. Oxford: Clarendon, 1946.

Hudson, Edward A. "The 9 Sector Dynamic General Equilibrium Model: Specification and Structure." Final report to the Macroeconomic Analysis Division, Energy Information Administration. Vol. 2. Washington: Dept. Energy, 1981.

Hudson, Edward A., and Jorgenson, Dale W. "U.S. Energy Policy and Economic Growth, 1975–2000." *Bell J. Econ. and Management Sci.* 5 (Autumn 1974): 461–514.

———. "Tax Policy and Energy Conservation." In *Econometric Studies of U.S. Energy Policy*, edited by Dale W. Jorgenson. Amsterdam: North-Holland, 1976.

———. "The Economic Impact of Policies to Reduce U.S. Energy Growth." *Resources and Energy* 1 (November 1978): 205–29. (a)

———. "Energy Prices and the U.S. Economy, 1972–1976." *Natural Resources J.* 18 (October 1978): 877–97. (b)

Jorgenson, Dale W. "Econometric Methods for Applied General Equilibrium Analysis." In *Applied General Equilibrium Analysis*, edited by Herbert E. Scarf and John B. Shoven. Cambridge: Cambridge Univ. Press, 1984.

Jorgenson, Dale W.; Lau, Lawrence J.; and Stoker, Thomas M. "The Transcendental Logarithmic Model of Aggregate Consumer Behavior." In *Advances in Econometrics*, vol. 1, edited by R. L. Basmann and George F. Rhodes, Jr. Greenwich, Conn.: JAI, 1982.

Jorgenson, Dale W., and Slesnick, Daniel T. "Efficiency versus Equity in Natural Gas Price Regulation." *J. Econometrics* 30 (October/November 1985): 301–16. (a)

———. "General Equilibrium Analysis of Economic Policy." Paper presented at the Econometric Society Fifth World Congress, Cambridge, Mass., August 1985.
Lau, Lawrence J. "Econometrics of Monotonicity, Convexity and Quasi-Convexity." Technical Report no. 123. Stanford, Calif.: Stanford Univ., Inst. Math. Studies Soc. Sci., 1974.
———. "Complete Systems of Consumer Demand Functions through Duality." In *Frontiers of Quantitative Economics*, vol. 3A, edited by Michael D. Intriligator. Amsterdam: North-Holland, 1977.
———. "Existence Conditions for Aggregate Demand Functions." Technical Report no. 248. Stanford, Calif.: Stanford Univ., Inst. Math. Studies Soc. Sci., 1977 (rev. February 1980).
Portney, Paul R. *Environmental Regulation in the U.S.: Public Policies and Their Consequences*. Washington: Resources for the Future, 1989.
Shoven, John B., and Whalley, John. "A General Equilibrium Calculation of the Effects of Differential Taxation of Income from Capital in the U.S." *J. Public Econ.* 1 (November 1972): 281.
U.S. Environmental Protection Agency. "Final Report: The Cost of Clean Air and Water: Report to Congress 1984." Washington: U.S. Environmental Protection Agency, May 1984.

Part IV
Trade and Competitiveness

[13]

Economic growth, international competitiveness and environmental protection: R & D and innovation strategies with the WARM model*

Carlo Carraro[a,c], Marzio Galeotti[b,c]

[a]*Department of Economics, University of Venice, Ca'Foscari, 30123 Venice, Italy*
[b]*University of Bergamo, Piazza Rosate 2, 24129 Bergamo, Italy*
[c]*FEEM, Corso Magenta 63, 20123 Milan, Italy*

Abstract

It is often argued that policies designed to protect the environment may harm economic growth. Moreover, if introduced unilaterally by a given country, they may reduce the competitiveness of domestic firms. These arguments are generally based on the assumption that environmental protection has to be achieved through the introduction of emission charges (e.g. a carbon tax). However, three issues need to be raised: first, the tax is not the only policy instrument—and is not the most efficient one—that can be used to reduce polluting emissions; secondly, even when a tax policy is implemented, it is important to assess the feedback effects induced by recycling the tax revenue; thirdly, and most importantly, the role of technical progress cannot be neglected. Therefore, there may exist a policy mix that provides firms with the correct incentives to adopt energy-saving technologies and to invest in environment-friendly R & D. The first two issues have partly been explored both in the theoretical and empirical literature. The third issue, i.e. the role of incentives to technical progress, still lacks adequate quantitative assessment. This is why a new model has been developed which endogenizes technical progress and its effects and feedbacks on economic, energy and environmental variables. Using WARM, an econometric general equilibrium model for the European Union and for each member country, this paper

---

* Paper prepared for the 1995 LBS/IFORS Joint International Symposium on Energy Models for Policy and Planning, London, 18-20 July 1995. The research described in this paper has been completed at GRETA by Michele Botteon, Giorgio Brunello, Maria de Paoli, Paola Fasulo, Gianpiero Gallo, Massimo Gallo, Marzio Galeotti, Nicola Rossi, Pierantonio Rosso and Domenico Sartore. Helpful comments have been provided by Terry Barker, Jim Poterba, Domenico Siniscalco, Pierre Valette and John Whalley. Financial support from DGXII and FEEM is gratefully acknowledged.

presents simulation results up to 2015 of the effects of some industrial–environmental policies which are aimed at protecting the environment without necessarily damaging competitiveness and economic growth. The results show that policies that stimulate environmental R & D, technological innovation and diffusion may provide firms with the correct incentives to avoid damaging the environment, while preserving their competitiveness in the market. Moreover, such a policy, based both on R & D subsidies and on innovation incentives, may not worsen the public-sector budget balance, as a result of the positive effects on economic growth.

JEL classification: H21; O33; Q32; Q43; Q48

Keywords: Environment; Fiscal reforms; Innovation; Sustainable development

1. Introduction

Although the theoretical literature has proposed several policy tools to deal with environmental problems, most empirical investigations have focused on energy taxation as the main (sometimes unique) instrument to control polluting emissions. The reason is quite simple: taxation is one of the few incentive-based policy variables that can be used to protect the environment. More importantly, emission charges may raise relevant tax revenues, which could be used to cut the high levels of distortionary taxation that exist in industrialized countries. In this way, it would be possible to achieve a cleaner environment and a less distortionary tax system, with obvious beneficial effects on the economy in the case in which the two objectives can actually be achieved.[1]

However, some criticisms have been raised against environmental taxation. In addition to the usual ones, which often refer to the loss of competitiveness that arises in countries which unilaterally adopt such a policy measure, and which call for international coordination of environmental charges, new critical remarks have recently been proposed. On the grounds of efficiency, emission permits have been shown to improve on emission charges when agents' intertemporal decisions (particularly on innovation) cannot be neglected (Laffont and Tirole, 1994). Moreover, when more than one externality has to be accounted for (such as in oligopoly, or in the presence of R & D spillovers), environmental taxation must be combined with other policy instruments to achieve the social optimum (Carraro et al., 1996). Similarly, information asymmetries (such as in non-point source pollution prob-

---

[1] However, many doubts have been raised concerning the possibility of achieving both goals. For example, Zimmermann (1993) suggests that it would be more efficient to use tradeable permits to achieve the environmental goal, and a revenue tax to fund public spending which stimulates economic recovery. Bovenberg and de Mooij (1994) and Parry (1994) present a theoretical analysis that supports the conclusion that energy taxation might exacerbate rather than reduce pre-existing tax distortions. Similar arguments are proposed by Bovenberg and Goulder (1993) and Schoeb (1994).

lems) ask for policy interventions that are far more complex than environmental taxation (Dosi and Graham-Tomasi, 1994).

More importantly, it has been suggested that the environmental benefit (pollution control) provided by environmental taxation would be too costly (in terms of lower economic growth)[2] and/or that the tax rate necessary to stabilize emissions would be too high to be economically and politically acceptable.[3] This is why environmental economists often claim the existence of the so-called 'environment–growth' trade-off, even if recent contributions on the 'double (or triple) dividend hypothesis'[4] seem to suggest that environmental protection could be achieved without harming economic growth and employment, whenever the revenue raised by the environmental tax is properly recycled. However, the most recent theoretical and empirical contributions on this issue[5] seem to provide evidence that recycling the environmental tax is unlikely to boost employment and economic growth, even if the economic costs of the tax are much lower than those proposed in the earlier literature (IPCC, 1990; Burniaux et al., 1992; DRI, 1992; Karadeloglou, 1992) which did not consider the effects of tax recycling.

A different approach is often proposed in the engineering literature, which recognizes that technical progress is the main way through which relevant emission reductions can actually be achieved. There is no doubt that technical progress may bring the economic system to growth paths where the environment is not harmed. This is not only a theoretical proposition but is supported by several endogenous growth studies (Michel, 1993; Verdier, 1995). This is also suggested by empirical bottom-up analysis in which the potential for energy-saving technological improvements is shown to be very high (Johansson and Swisher, 1993; Wilson and Swisher, 1993; Carraro et al., 1994). Other evidence which stresses the importance of environmentally friendly technical progress to stabilize emissions in the long run is given by Holtz-Eakin and Selden (1992), Baldwin (1995) and Grossman (1995).

The above remarks lead to the following questions. Is the tax the appropriate instrument to protect the environment? If the most effective tool for cutting polluting emissions is technical progress, then is there a policy instrument that can help to accelerate the adoption of cleaner technologies and to foster energy-saving R & D? Can the tax and the related tax revenue be directed to foster technological innovation?

The tax is certainly a candidate to be such an instrument. However, recent analyses have shown that environmental taxes or emission permits are likely to be suboptimal instruments for achieving an adequate level of technological innovation.[6] For example, Laffont and Tirole (1994) show that, in a dynamic framework,

---

[2] A survey of the economic costs of environmental taxes is given by Grubb et al. (1993).
[3] This point was stressed in Voyoukas' opening speech at the LBS/IFORS conference on energy models for policy and planning, London, 18–20 July 1995, where this paper was also presented.
[4] See Grubb et al. (1993) and Denis and Koopman (1994) for a survey.
[5] A survey of the theoretical literature is given by Bovenberg (1997). Some recent empirical results are provided by Bovenberg and Goulder (1993), Brunello (1996) and Carraro et al. (1997).
[6] A detailed discussion of this statement is provided by Carraro and Siniscalco (1994) and by Carraro et al. (1994).

taxes or permits can lead firms to overinvest in environmental innovation, in order to by-pass the fiscal burden, so reducing social welfare. However, for an endogenous growth model, Musu (1994) shows that emission charges alone are unable to induce firms to account for the positive R & D externalities that would lead to the appropriate investment in innovation; hence, firms tend to underinvest. A similar conclusion is attained by Carraro and Topa (1995), using an industrial organization model of dynamic innovation. The paper shows that firms tend to delay innovation, rather than to underinvest, when the only policy instrument is environmental or energy taxation.

However, there are two other strands of economic literature that ought to be considered. First, the theory of industrial organization has proposed R & D incentives and innovation subsidies as the main policy instruments to accelerate the dynamics of technical progress. Secondly, several microeconomic studies have shown how policy decisions directed to reduce the fixed costs of R & D and investment are more likely to induce firms to develop or adopt new, energy-saving technologies (Johansson and Swisher, 1993; Boetti and Botteon, 1994).

Therefore, in this paper, we try to follow this second route. Instead of assessing the effect of an environmental tax, we focus on technological innovation, by simulating the effects of two policies designed to foster firms' R & D activity and their adoption of 'cleaner', 'best available' technologies.

To address all the above issues and to quantify the answers to the above questions, a new model had to be developed. The reason is that, when modelling the effects of technological progress on greenhouse gas emissions, it is not sufficient to compare the energy efficiencies of different technologies (as in the bottom-up approach). It is instead necessary to assess the incentives that the market provides for the adoption of environment-friendly technologies, and the impact that policy decisions, taken by one country or internationally coordinated, can have on firms' innovation strategies.

The model which has enabled us to capture these economic effects is a newly developed general equilibrium econometric model of the European economy, called the WARM (world assessment of resource management) model, with which different policies to accelerate technical progress have been simulated. This paper presents the results of some of these simulations, and compares the relative efficiency of alternative energy–environmental policies.

In particular, we compare the effects of two policy options: (1) first, the usual policy strategy, in which the government subsidizes the development of new, industry-wide and firm-specific energy-saving technologies; (2) the second policy concerns the adoption of available energy-saving technologies, when the firm commits to improving the energy–environmental quality of its capital stock and receives a subsidy for the necessary investment.

The paper is organized as follows. Section 2 surveys the main developments of the econometrics of technical progress, and shows the theoretical advances provided by the WARM model. Section 3 describes the other main features of the WARM model. Section 4 presents the simulations performed with the model, and summarizes the main achievements and the effects of the proposed environmental–energy policies. Finally, Section 5 discusses directions for future research.

2. Modelling technical progress in economic–environmental models

Economists and engineers agree on two relevant issues: first, the different ways in which technological progress has been modelled in those quantitative models that have so far been used to assess the costs of mitigating greenhouse gases are responsible for their highly different results; secondly, it is through technology changes and innovations that environmental protection can more quickly and efficiently be achieved.

Despite the convincing arguments offered to support the above statements (Carraro and Siniscalco, 1994), technical change and innovation are not satisfactorily modelled in most economic–environmental models. In particular, technical progress often has an exogenous representation. Hence, we have the need for a new generation of environmental–economic models which endogenize the linkages between economic variables (policy variables, in particular) and technical progress.

Before presenting some possible ways of integrating a model description of the working of an economic system with a better representation of the decision process that leads firms to innovate, let us review the technology features of existing models.

In most top-down models, technical progress is represented by an exogenous deterministic trend, or by exogenous changes in one of the production function parameters (the autonomous energy efficiency improvement (AEEI)). In bottom-up models, the shift from the technology currently in use to a different, already available and less polluting technology is kept exogenous, i.e. the process that leads to such a decision is not endogenized; moreover, the type and number of technologies among which each firm can choose are also exogenous, i.e. the role of R & D activity is not endogenized. In addition to making the assessment of the costs of environmental policies unreliable, the exogeneity of technical progress is inconsistent with modelling and predictions provided by economic theory.[7]

Therefore, let us briefly review how recent econometric and computable general equilibrium (CGE) models have attempted to solve the 'exogeneity impasse' on technical progress.

As stated above, most top-down models have so far introduced an exogenous time trend as a proxy for technical change. With respect to this approach, the model of Jorgenson and Wilcoxen (1990) presents the most interesting contribution. They assume a translog unit cost function that contains terms in which the input prices interact with the time trend. Therefore, the firms' cost trends depend on input prices and on the time trend. Finally, technical progress influences input demands, without interacting with any other variable. The authors show how such a trend—in addition to prices—affects the rate of total factor productivity. As a consequence, policy decisions that affect relative prices determine an endogenous

---

[7] This issue is surveyed by Echia and Mariotti (1994). Theoretical models of environmental innovation are provided by Downing and White (1986), Milliman and Prince (1989), Carraro and Topa (1995) and Carraro and Soubeyran (1996).

change in total factor productivity. In this way, the proposal by Jorgenson and Wilcoxen partially endogenizes technical progress.

A more satisfactory treatment of technical progress in recent applied general equilibrium (AGE)/CGE models relying on the concept of vintage capital can be found in Conrad and Henseler-Unger (1986) and Conrad and Ehrlich (1993). A similar approach has been followed in the OECD's GREEN model. Here, the substitution possibilities are more feasible with the most recent capital vintages. Thus, adjusting to relative price shocks depends not only on the elasticity of substitution but also on the capital replacement rate. This is a novelty with respect to previous CGE modelling approaches, because the technical change shows its effects on the firms' cost structure through a parametrization of each vintage's cost functions. Another vintage model has been proposed by Carlevaro et al. (1992).

Models that use the idea of capital vintages have some drawbacks too, because they do not provide a precise evaluation of the mechanisms with which markets and agents act to modify the existing technologies towards energy-saving and environmental potentials. As an example, the model of Carlevaro et al. (1992) uses technical coefficients that define, say, the energy/capital ratio, which are endogenous but depend only on the future trend of energy prices. Similarly to the technical–economic models, this approach does not explicitly take into account the economic profitability of the new technologies: the existence of a new, less polluting technology does not imply that it will be adopted by firms.

There are two other ideas, on which econometricians are currently working, that could constitute another step towards the endogenization of technical progress. The first proposal is a direct extension of the usual econometric approach, which consists of adding a deterministic exogenous trend to the equations that describe factor demand, including energy, investments, prices, etc. In the new approach (Boone et al., 1992), technical progress is still represented by a variable which is added to the main equations of the model. However, this variable is no longer a deterministic function of time. It is instead a stochastic function of time, in which other economic effects are also accounted for. However, the relationship between the indicator of technical progress and other economic variables is purely stochastic, i.e. it is not derived from explicit assumptions on firms' R & D and innovation strategies.

Another proposal (Carraro, 1994; Carraro and Galeotti, 1994a,b) attempts to provide a more explicit description of the economic mechanism through which economic variables affect technical progress. The basic idea is that technical progress cannot be observed and that it can be inferred observing the dynamics of other variables.[8] However, the focus is now on the capital stock. It is assumed that

---

[8] More technically, we propose to adopt a latent variable structural equation model which uses data on total expenditures from research from public and private sources; on imports of patents, and on business cycle indicators as cause variables for the latent technological variable. The latent variable approach extracts information from indicators and cause variables, while being able to avoid using them as exact representations of technological change. The goal is to minimize measurement errors, so also minimizing the inconsistency of the estimation procedure.

the capital stock can be decomposed into two parts: the energy-saving or environment-friendly capital stock and the energy-consuming or polluting part. Each year, a new vintage of the capital stock becomes operational. In this way, new capital is added to the two components. The characteristics of this new capital depend on a number of economic variables which affect firms' decisions of installing energy-saving capital. The ratio between the two types of capital constitutes our indicator of technical progress.

Let k_t be the capital stock and k_e and k_p the environment-friendly and polluting stocks respectively. By definition, $k_t = k_e + k_p$, which implies

$$g_k = g_p + (g_e - g_p)(k_e/k_t) \tag{1}$$

where g_k, g_p and g_e are the growth rates of the overall, polluting and environment-friendly capital stocks respectively. Suppose that

$$g_e - g_p = f(x)/(k_e/k_t) + \varepsilon \tag{2}$$

where $f(x)$ is the capital growth rate in the long run, when all technological possibilities to reduce energy consumption have been implemented, i.e. when $k_t = k_e$ and $g_p = 0$; x is a set of explanatory variables and ε is a stochastic error. The implicit assumption here is that, when the stock of polluting capital is high, the rate of growth of the environment-friendly capital is greater than the rate of growth of the polluting capital; the difference decreases as k_e approaches k_t. Finally, the following equation defines the dynamics of the polluting component of the capital stock:

$$g_p = h(W, \nu) \tag{3}$$

Here, W is a set of explanatory variables and ν is a stochastic error term. In particular, the explanatory variables include R & D spending, output demand, factor prices and the number of imported patents. All else equal, it is likely that more R & D spending increases the technological possibilities of the economic system, so inducing investment in environment-friendly capital, which replaces investment in polluting capital. Similarly, higher energy prices may induce firms to reduce investment in energy-consuming technologies.

The amount of R & D carried out by firms is an endogenous variable of the model. We relate it to the total output demand (assuming a unitary elasticity in the long run), relative factor prices and policy variables. These include environmental taxation (via energy prices) and innovation subsidies (via publicly funded R & D expenditures).

Eqs. (1)–(3) and the set of equations which endogenize R & D expenditure, factor prices and output demand define the structure of the latent variable model. Because g_p and g_e are not observable, they must be estimated by filtering the information contained in the observable variables. To achieve this, let us rewrite Eqs. (1)–(3) in a state space form as

$$g_k = Hs + \varepsilon \tag{4}$$

$$s = Fs(-1) + \nu \qquad (5)$$

where s is the state space vector which contains the unobservable variable g_p and the parameter vectors β and δ associated with the variable vectors x and W respectively. More precisely, we have

$$H = [1 \; x \; 0], \qquad s = \begin{bmatrix} g_p \\ \beta \\ \delta \end{bmatrix}, \qquad F = \begin{bmatrix} m & 0 & W \\ 0 & 1 & 0 \\ 0 & 0 & 1 \end{bmatrix}$$

The matrix H is called the output matrix, while the matrix F is the transition matrix of the state space form of the model that contains the parameters, which captures the adjustment speed m of the components of the capital stock, the variable vector W and the zeros and ones necessary to reproduce the identities concerning all the time-invariant coefficients. The error terms ε and ν are assumed to be normally distributed and serially uncorrelated.

The state space form of Eqs. (4) and (5) has been estimated using the square root Kalman and information filters described by Carraro (1988). The covariance matrix of the error terms ε and ν has been estimated using the maximum-likelihood method. The initial values for the state vector have been estimated using the generalized least-squares (GLS) procedure proposed by Carraro (1985). The results of our estimates of the state space transition matrix F, the output matrix H and the state vector s (in particular, the vector δ) show that the filtering procedure which we use to decompose the capital stock yields homogenous results across different EU countries.

For example, the parameters of the vector δ that reflect the impact on the growth rate of the polluting capital stock g_p induced by domestic R & D expenditures and by imported patents are negative and about -0.022 and -0.021 in all EU countries (the EU averages are -0.0226 and -0.0217). Moreover, the impact of output growth on the same growth rate g_p ranges from 0.209 to 0.210 in all EU countries. Some differences can be found in the speed of adjustment coefficient m of the composition of the capital stock to the desired value (the only unknown parameter in the matrix F), and in the autonomous change of the growth rate of the polluting capital stock (the constant in the vector x).

The speed of adjustment ranges from 0.726 in France to 0.924 in Denmark and Ireland. The EU average is 0.768. The autonomous change of the growth rate of the polluting capital stock is greater (in absolute value) in Greece, Spain and Irelande, i.e. in the less-developed European countries (the values in these countries are -0.0082, -0.0044 and -0.0082 respectively). This implies that, in less-developed countries, the polluting capital stock is replaced more quickly than occurs in developed countries. By contrast, because more developed countries have already implemented a large number of best available technologies, the substitution between the two components of the capital stock takes place more slowly in such countries (the best examples are Germany and the UK, where the parameter values for the autonomous change are -0.0017 and -0.0012 respectively).

The small cross-country differences in the parameters of the vector δ show that the dynamics of the components of the capital stock tend to be spatially homogeneous in the long run. There are structural differences across EU economies (captured by the autonomous change parameter) and medium-run differences captured by the different speeds of adjustment to the long-run equilibrium.

Notice that, as expected, domestic R & D and imported patents reduce the growth rate of the polluting capital stock, which is therefore replaced by environment-friendly capital. By contrast, when output grows, both types of capital stock grow. Finally, the speed of adjustment is quite high in all countries, showing little sluggishness in environmental innovation.

Given the above results, the dynamics of the two time series k_e and k_p has been reconstructed (notice that the method is similar to that used to decompose a time series into cyclical and seasonal components (Harvey, 1987)). Then an indicator of technical change, it is interpreted here as an indicator of the environmental quality of the capital stock, and is provided by the ratio $T = k_e/k_p$. The average growth rate of this indicator is fairly low in the EU developed countries (about 2% in Germany, France and Italy, and slightly lower in the UK), whereas it is much higher in the less-developed countries (from 9% in Ireland to 30% in Greece). In all countries, the growth rate of the technical progress indicator becomes lower as the country grows (because the model objective is to capture the implementation of best available technologies in the short and medium terms).

The dynamics of k_e/k_p generally affect the decision rules of all the agents in the model: not only do they affect the firms' input and output decisions, as previously shown, but they also influence households' choices, especially those pertaining to the consumption of energy sources (see below). Moreover, the dynamics of technical change concerns total private capital stock, and not only the component used as a production input by firms. Note that an important implication of our treatment of environment–technical change is that it is a diffuse phenomenon. In fact, the technological indicator is an argument of the behavioural equations concerning the demand for inputs and the supply of outputs (via marginal costs). In particular, this is the case for the manufacturing firms. Thus, over time, an increasing amount of environment-friendly capital is used in production, which translates into an improvement of the production process and, in turn, of the quality of goods and services supplied. To the extent that these goods and services are purchased by the other firms and by households, the process of endogenous technical change affects all sectors of the economy (and the rest of the World as well).

The modelling structure just (briefly) described belongs to the European module of the macroeconometric global WARM model, the general features of which will be briefly described in the next section.

3. Other main features of the WARM model

The WARM model is a new generation model which incorporates most of the requirements previously indicated (Cline, 1992) as being desirable for an economic–energy–environmental model. In particular, imperfectly competitive markets, international trade flows, the structure of energy markets and the role of technical progress are explicitly modelled.

3.1. General features

The WARM model is an annual econometric model estimated for the 12 EU countries (as well as for the EU as a whole) over the period 1978–89. Because its modelling strategy focuses on agents' behaviour, the WARM model in not a traditional market-based macroeconometric model. It is instead more similar to carefully designed AGE/CGE models. However, because it is econometrically estimated, it is not subject to the constraints in terms of flexible parametrizations and quantitative information basis of the behavioural relationships placed by calibration on AGE/CGE models. Finally, because it is not a multicountry interlinked model, it has the ability to integrate differences from a common European denominator within a unified coherent framework. The WARM model exploits panel data econometric techniques that, on the one hand, conveniently increase the size of the sample and, on the other hand, allow the specification of each structural parameter of the estimated behavioural relationships for each country in terms of the deviation from the corresponding EU macro-region parameter.[9]

The WARM model has been econometrically estimated for the period 1978–89; the data come from official sources—mainly the OECD and EUROSTAT. When necessary, they have been integrated with information obtained from each country's official national account statistics.

Given the main intended uses of the model, special efforts are made in describing the production, consumption and exchange of energy resources. According to Cline (1992), to analyze properly the economic implications of CO_2 emissions, a model should allow for substitution possibilities among fossil fuels; substitution among fossil and non-fossil fuels; substitution among energy and other inputs; and, finally, product substitution in the consumption mix. According to Edmonds (1992), such a model should further allow for the multiplicity of economic activities (agriculture, industry, transportation and energy production) which generate emissions to different degrees and account for the greenhouse gases other than carbon dioxide.

The model described here takes into account the above aspects within the limits imposed by data availability. In particular, we distinguish four types of production activity carried out by representative firms operating in each European country. The manufacturing firm is involved in the production and distribution of non-agricultural, non-energy outputs that consist of durables, non-durables and ser-

---

[9] An accurate description of the WARM model is given by Carraro and Galeotti (1994b). The endogenization of technical progress and its role in the model is assessed by Carraro (1994) and Botteon et al. (1994).

vices.[10] The factors used are the services from labour, capital, energy and a non-energy intermediate input. The demand for this intermediate good results from the aggregation of agricultural products and imported (durable and non-durable) goods and services. The energy aggregate is made up of electricity and fossil fuels. These fuels in turn are comprised of coal, gas and petroleum products (divided into products for industrial use and for transportation). Electricity is supplied by the electricity firm, which uses capital, labour and energy sources as inputs. This firm also directly imports electricity from abroad to be distributed nationwide. The fossil fuel transformation firm (or 'energy firm' for short) supplies and distributes non-electric energy sources to all other firms and to households, combining primary factors along with imported fuels. Finally, the agricultural output is entirely supplied to the manufacturing sector by an agricultural firm which combines capital, labour, land and energy.

3.2. Input demands and output supplies

Firms are run by managers who act in the best interest of their owners. Owners and managers are part of the household sector. We decompose the set of decisions made by firms into three different conceptual stages. First, given the amounts of outputs and capital stock, the cost-minimizing levels of variable inputs are determined. Through appropriate assumptions about the technology, this problem is formulated as a multi-stage decision process and yields sets of interrelated input demands. Next, variable profits are maximized by selecting the optimal output levels: this process generates a set of inverse supply relationships or price functions. Finally, the optimal investment decisions are taken by the firm in such a way that total long-run profits are maximized.

The technological relationship which, at each point in time, constrains producers' choices is embodied in a variable cost function that allows for multi-output production. To achieve the highest level of disaggregation permitted by the data, the manufacturing firm is assumed to produce three distinct outputs (durables, non-durables and services), while the energy firm separately supplies outputs of coal, oil products and gas. The remaining firms of the model produce a single output. In addition to variable input prices, output levels and quasi-fixed input stocks, the variable cost function (Lau, 1976) depends on an index of the composition of the capital stock: as explained in the previous section, changes in this indicator represent energy-saving technological improvements which induce outward shifts of the production isoquant over time. The variable cost function is parametrized as a modified generalized Leontief flexible functional form.[11] The application of Shephard's lemma yields the system of demand functions for variable inputs.

A maintained assumption regarding the firm's production structure is that of a homothetically separable technology—a feature shared by many econometric and

---

[10] This firm carries out economic activities which go beyond manufacturing in the strict sense. We term it 'manufacturing' for the sake of brevity.
[11] See Morrison (1988) for a similar specification.

AGE models. With it, we can achieve relevant simplifications in the design of the input decision process: these choices proceed along several stages where the optimal mix within homogeneous groups of inputs is found and the aggregate input quantities, to be used in higher stages of the decision tree, are formed.

Turning now to the output supply side, on the basis of the assumed generalized Leontief cost function, we can compute a marginal cost function for each output produced. To obtain the firm's supply relationships, we need to make specific assumptions about the nature of output markets. In the model, we assume that, in general, imperfect competition prevails. While we note that the perfect competition hypothesis may be sustained in the case of (very) long-run analyses, we can think of entry barriers which do not vanish in the medium term as the rationale for imperfect competition in our model. Moreover, from the European experience, it is apparent that labour markets are far from competitive. Finally, in the WARM model, some activities are non-competitive by construction: for instance, this is the case of the electricity and energy firms which are the sole domestic suppliers of their output.

To describe the price formation process, we assume that firms are price-makers and apply a mark-up pricing rule. In the current version of the model, the price mark-up is assumed to be constant and time invariant. While we deem this assumption as acceptable for a medium-term model, where cyclical movements in price-cost margins ought not to be quantitatively important, there is no doubt that it represents an important simplification when it comes to explaining the determinants of margins in terms of demand elasticities and strategic firm behaviour.

In a second stage, producers supply their outputs to different customers according to a price-discriminating strategy. Given the price function for each type of output, the price charged to each customer is chained to the corresponding output price by means of a proportionality factor.[12] Note that the joint estimation in the model of these price functions, together with the corresponding output demand relationships that originate from the other sectors, ensure that market-clearing conditions are enforced. Finally, notice that outputs are expressed at factor cost, so that the corresponding prices are net of (net) indirect taxes. These tax rates are introduced when specifying the demand price for each product.

3.3. Household behaviour

The basic behavioural assumption that characterizes households' decisions is the maximization of the life cycle utility, subject to a budget constraint that equates expenditures to available resources. These are given by labour income, profits distributed by firms and the return on financial wealth. In the model, financial wealth essentially takes the form of government bonds. The utility of a household is a function of leisure and overall consumption: however, for convenience, we

---

[12] This proportionality coefficient is again treated as a constant parameter. As an alternative to price discrimination, we can think of this coefficient as a fixed transaction cost (for distribution, transportation, etc.).

assume that the utility function is separable in the two arguments, so that we can treat consumption choices independently from labour-supply decisions.

Consumption decisions take place in a sequential way. First, resources are intertemporally allocated, so that current and future consumption (savings) are determined. At a second stage, intratemporal consumption decisions are taken. In a manner analogous to the production sector, we have here a multi-stage decision process, with each stage generating systems of consumer demands for homogeneous groups of goods and services. Finally, the model describes how savings are allocated between the acquisition of durable consumption goods, residential buildings and financial assets.

3.4. Labour demand and wage bargaining

A distinctive feature of the WARM model is the assumed structure of the labour market, which is not competitive but segmented. In particular, we distinguish between a primary sector for all production activities, including the public sector and excluding agriculture, where wages and employment are the outcomes of a bargaining process between unions and firms' managers. Specifically, the manufacturing firm plays a role of leadership and pattern-setter for the other firms (and for the government), while both agricultural employment and unemployment have a residual role.

The institutional set-up of the European countries is such that a role of unions is more relevant than elsewhere. We think of the union as an agent who aggregates the preferences of those who participate in the labour market and who use their bargaining power to obtain a wage above the competitive level. The presence of unions provides the rationale for involuntary unemployment, which was a typical phenomenon of European economies in the 1980s.[13] Bargaining is a sequential process: at first, unions and representatives of the manufacturing firm agree on the wage rate; subsequently, the other firms and the government set their wages on the basis of differentials which depend on the union bargaining power as well as on general and sector-specific economic conditions (Dobson, 1994). In contrast, there are no unions in the secondary labour market (i.e. agriculture) and wages are determined according to an arbitrage condition relative to the unemployment status.

The description of the functioning of the labour markets in the WARM model can be completed by noting that, given the wages, employment is determined by the labour demand equations derived from the cost minimization process described in Section 3.2 (see Section 3.5 for the government's demand for labour). Given an exogenous temporal profile of the labour force, mainly driven by demographic factors, the rate of unemployment is determined residually.

---

[13] The efficiency wages hypothesis provides an alternative rationale for the existence of involuntary unemployment. However, this theoretical option appears to be ill suited for the European experience, because it is based on the idea that the wage rate is set to a level unilaterally decided by the firm (Blanchard and Fisher, 1989).

3.5. The government

A noticeable feature of the WARM model is the endogenization of government behaviour. The fundamental assumption here is that the government's strategies can be endogenized as functions of the economic policy goals, i.e. is through a set of reaction functions.

The government undertakes four main activities. The first is the production of a public good (public spending) using inputs from labour, fixed capital and a composite intermediate material good. This activity is formally represented by a variable Cobb-Douglas cost function which, via Shephard's lemma, yields the demand for public employment and for materials. Both demand equations depend on factor prices, and are conditional on a given level of output and on the stock of public capital.

The second economic activity is public investment. The stock of public capital depends on past investment. However, unlike the behaviour of the other agents, we do not base the optimal investment decision on the government's variable cost function via the envelope condition. We instead make the assumption that public investment is one of the government's control variables used to smooth business cycle fluctuations. It follows that public investment is endogenized through a reaction function which responds to changes in three factors: the cost of investment (as represented by variable input prices and the user cost of public capital); the cost of funds available for financing investment expenditures (as represented by the change in the degree of fiscal pressure, as well as in the interest payments on public debt); the economic policy targets (captured by the rate of change in total employment).

The production and investment activities undertaken by the public agent are subject to the usual budget constraint, by which expenditures are financed by indirect and direct tax revenues and by issues of government bonds. The items of the budget currently endogenized in the model are the revenues from direct income taxation, the interest payments on the stock of public debt outstanding, the amount of pensions paid to households, and the social security contributions that arise from households and firms. The other two activities of the government, therefore, are the regulation of the level of business activity through appropriate fiscal and expenditure policies, and the redistribution of income.

Looking now at the sources of public funds, the starting point is that taxation serves the dual purpose of pursuing efficiency (such as to correct externalities) and income redistribution. Indirect fiscal revenues are calculated by applying the effective tax rate and excise rate, respectively, to the value of output consumed and to the volume of goods and services consumed. On adding the revenues from each taxable basis, we obtain the overall fiscal revenue. The model accounts for 11 different VAT rates and 19 different excise rates. The revenues from direct taxation are computed on the basis of a single, time-varying tax rate applied to total income.[14] The tax rate is endogenous and determined by a reaction function

---

[14] We do not distinguish between taxes on households and taxes on firms.

that depends on the rate of inflation (to account for fiscal drag phenomena), the amount of public good supplied (public spending to be financed) and the Maastricht goals (debt-to-GDP ratio and budget-deficit-to-GDP ratio, to account for the government's efforts in meeting the requirements for eligibility to the EMU).

Turning now to the uses of public funds, we endogenize the nominal rate of interest on public debt. Given the exogenous amount of existing debt, we again treat the interest rate as a control variable, which depends via a reaction function on the rate of inflation, the trade balance and the growth rate of public debt (to capture the risk premium demanded by investors in high debt countries). The amount of pensions paid by the government is related to the number of persons over 65 relative to the toal population, to the average personal income and to the distribution of income between wages and profits. Social contributions (as a share of total labour costs) depend on the real wages, the inflation rate and the average pension perceived by individuals. There is a final item, i.e. government subsidies paid to firms, which is kept as exogenous in the model. We use this variable for simulation purposes, with the aim of analyzing the effects of policies designed to stimulate technological innovation, export activity, etc.

3.6. Foreign sector

The model adopts a production-theoretic view of international trade flows. In fact, households cannot make direct purchases from abroad, and all flows of goods and services go through the production sector (especially the manufacturing firm), which performs repackaging, distribution and similar activities.[15] Viewing imports as an input to the production process, this approach allows an integrated treatment of trade flows, in that exports are viewed as an output of the same production process (Kohli, 1991).

The model is characterized by a precise specialization in the import–export activity of firms. The agricultural firm can sell its output to domestic and to foreign markets. The manufacturing firm is the only agent that trades manufactured goods and services internationally. Imported electricity is only handled by the corresponding firm and this is also the case for other energy sources for the corresponding firm.

Import decisions are reached through a two-stage allocation process. The procedure is the same as that previously described for generic inputs: on the basis of

---

[15] An important remark concerns the primary factors of production and their international mobility. The demand for labour generated by the firms and by the government matches the households' labour supply. Thus, the labour market is a national market and this input is internationally immobile. No migration flows are present in the model, because of the paucity of the necessary data. As far as capital is concerned, there is only one type of durable good which is demanded by households (consumer durables) or by firms (investment goods). Capital is a partly mobile input, in the following sense. While durable goods, including capital goods, can be traded internationally, once in place owing to the firms' investment activity, they become perfectly immobile. As already clarified, financial capital flows are not explicitly modelled.

relative prices, the total import demand for each good and service is determined. Next, the aggregate price of a good being bought by the domestic firm from abroad is viewed as a unit cost function. Shephard's lemma then yields the demand function of that good by the importing country from each selling country. Analytical tractability for a problem that involves many goods and many countries at the same time suggested the use of Cobb–Douglas unit cost functions.

On the export side, we follow the approach already mentioned, when describing the behaviour of producers. The price of a good produced by country i and sold to country j is a constant fraction of the production price of the same good. The simple representation of trade flows just described is sufficient for describing the structure of bilateral exchanges of goods, services and energy sources among the EU12 countries, as well as the rest of the World.

3.7. Emissions

The role of the environmental module in the WARM model lies in assessing the impact of the economic activities on the environment. This task is performed by measuring the amount of harmful emissions.[16] A series of technical coefficients provide the amount of emissions generated by the various forms of economic activity specified by the model. The attention is centred on the following pollutants: sulphur oxide (SO_x), nitrogen oxide (NO_x), particulate matter, carbon monoxide (CO) and volatile organic components. These pollutants are largely related to the use of fossil fuels in the various production and consumptin activities. Moreover, fossil fuels are the most relevant anthropogenic source of CO_2 emissions, which are largely responsible for the 'greenhouse' phenomenon.

The model disaggregation across economic activities (i.e. economic agents) and across energy sources allows precise assessment of the individual contributions to the overall emissions.

4. Effects of innovation policies on environment, competitiveness and growth

Having presented the main features of the WARM model, with particular emphasis on the endogenization of technical progress, as explained in Section 2, we now present the results of the simulation experiments designed to quantify the effects of R & D and innovation subsidies on the main macroeconomic variables (growth, employment, emissions and trade balance). We recall that our main objective is to check whether there exists an environmental policy not based on

---

[16] The current version of the model does not incorporate a full-blown analysis of the environmental impact of the economic activity. In particular, the model lacks a description of the feedbacks from the environment on to the behaviour of the economic agents through households' welfare and firms' cost-benefit analysis. However, there is indirect feedback via the government's reaction functions (say, if polluting emissions increase, then energy tax rates can be raised).

emission charges which can attain the objective of reducing polluting emissions without harming economic growth and domestic firms' competitiveness.

To carry out our proposed simulation experiments, a number of exogenous variables have to be projected up to 2015. These are all the demographic variables; prices of imported energy sources; export flows to non-European countries of durables, non-durables goods and services; prices of these goods and services in the non-European countries; the exchange rates; and, finally, some items of the government current account, such as public expenditures and subsidies. The baseline scenario is based on World Bank data sources.

We carried out four simulation experiments over the time-horizon spanning from 1995 to 2015, and the results have been compared with those obtained in the baseline scenario. In particular, two policy strategies have been simulated: first, the government aims at developing new energy-saving technologies, such that it provides firms with incentives to carry out some R & D investments which may yield a substantial change of the environmental quality of the capital stock; secondly, the government subsidizes the adoption of available energy-improving technologies, such that the firm commits to improving the energy–environmental quality of its capital stock and receives a subsidy for the necessary investment. For both innovation policies, the effects of two financing strategies have been explored: in the first case, the subsidy is financed by increasing direct taxation, whereas, in the second case, the financing comes from indirect taxation.

Each fiscal reform is assumed to be introduced in 1995 and to be maintained through the year 2015. The R & D and the investment subsidies exponentially decline over time with the inflation rate (because they are kept constant in nominal terms).

Let us provide a more detailed description of the above simulation experiments.

R & D policy

In the case in which the government's policy concerns the development of new energy-saving or environment-friendly technologies, we assume the following.

(1) Firms commit to increasing the amount of R & D that they carry out; because no time series on environmental R & D were available, we assume that the total amount of R & D is increased.
(2) Each government sets the level of the subsidy as functions of engineering information on the existing characteristics of the capital stock, and of its perception of the consumers' willingness to pay for the environment. To homogenize policy simulations across countries, we assume that voters are ready to accept a subsidy to environmental innovation equal to 0.5% of GDP in each country. To give a rough idea of the figures involved, a 0.5% of GDP subsidy approximately corresponds (in 1995) to the CEC carbon tax of about 19 ECUs per ton of CO_2.
(3) Governments finance the R & D policy either by increasing income taxes or by increasing indirect taxation.

(4) The model endogenizes the effects of firms' R & D on the structure of the capital stock, i.e. other things being equal, an increase in R & D reduces investments in polluting capital stock and increases investments in energy-saving or environment-friendly capital stock.

Innovation policy

In the case in which firms commit to the adoption of best available technologies, we assume the following.

(1) The investment in new vintages of the capital stock concerns either new plants or plants that have become obsolete, i.e. we assume a net increase in the energy-saving or environment-friendly capital stock equal to the subsidy.
(2) To compare the outcomes of the R & D policy with those of the innovation policy, we assume again that each government spends for increasing firms' energy-saving investments a sum that corresponds to 0.5% of GDP; as in the previous case, this sum is kept constant in nominal terms throughout the simulation period.
(3) Given the amount of money to be transferred to firms, each government decides the tax policy which is necessary to finance the subsidy (either an indirect or a revenue tax).

Notice that the primary effect of all the policy scenarios is to modify the growth rate of technical progress, which implies that the ratio between the environment-friendly capital stock and the polluting stock increases; according to the model specification, this increase feeds back into all factor demands and production prices, so affecting investment, imports, exports, consumption, employment, etc. In particular, our aim is to verify whether the proposed policy reforms can achieve a reduction in CO_2 emissions, an improvement in firms' competitiveness, an increase in employment and a higher GDP growth rate.

The results of the four simulations are summarized in the Tables in Appendix A. These tables concern six EU countries (Germany, France, the UK, Italy, The Netherlands and Belgium) and show the change with respect to the baseline scenario of the main economic variables under discussion: GDP, trade balance, employment, CO_2 emissions, and the energy-environmental quality of the capital stock. To compare the long-run cumulated effects of the different policy scenarios, we computed the time series of the cumulated differences with respect to the baseline of the above five basic variables. The 2005 and 2015 levels of these cumulated differences are reported in the tables. Leaving the reader with the task of a detailed analysis of our results, we summarize here their main implications.

Let us consider first economic growth. In all countries, either one or both policy strategies provide a stimulus to economic growth. It seems that the innovation policy has a greater positive impact in the short run, because it affects directly the aggregate demand. However, there are cases (The Netherlands and Italy) in which the R & D policy seems to be more effective, even in the short run. By contrast, in

France, R & D subsidies are slightly more effective in the long run. In the other countries, the higher final GDP level is obtained by introducing the innovation policy. The way of financing the necessary government expenditure is relevant in

Table A1
Belgium

		GDP	TB	CO_2	Empl.	KeQ
Percentage difference in cumulated values						
S1-B	2005	0.31	−2.39	−0.77	−0.14	2.49
	2015	0.12	0.11	−1.82	−0.42	4.14
S2-B	2005	0.45	−2.23	−0.65	0.01	2.49
	2015	0.03	3.56	−1.80	−0.28	4.14
S3-B	2005	−0.16	0.95	−1.48	−0.54	3.69
	2015	−0.62	12.29	−3.67	−1.17	5.32
S4-B	2005	−0.03	1.11	−1.35	−0.39	3.68
	2015	−0.70	15.72	−3.63	−1.02	5.32
Absolute difference in cumulated values						
S1-B	2005	3646	−3368	−2.92	−0.07	0.04
	2015	2952	137	−11.63	−0.35	0.11
S2-B	2005	5260	−3137	−2.44	0.01	0.04
	2015	702	4402	−11.47	−0.23	0.11
S3-B	2005	−1921	1336	−5.59	−0.25	0.07
	2015	−15600	15217	−23.39	−0.98	0.14
S4-B	2005	−299	1571	−5.11	−0.18	0.07
	2015	−17814	19465	−23.17	−0.85	0.14

Table A2
France

		GDP	TB	CO_2	Empl.	KeQ
Percentage difference in cumulated values						
S1-B	2005	0.29	−12.65	−0.78	−0.10	2.72
	2015	0.21	−7.25	−1.71	−0.05	4.59
S2-B	2005	0.71	−12.03	−0.54	0.05	2.70
	2015	0.65	−7.01	−1.35	0.15	4.54
S3-B	2005	−0.13	−4.15	−1.38	−0.22	2.89
	2015	0.29	−1.00	−2.50	−0.30	4.23
S4-B	2005	0.30	−3.56	−1.15	−0.07	2.87
	2015	0.74	−0.80	−2.15	−0.11	4.21
Absolute difference in cumulated values						
S1-B	2005	25834	−61400.1	−10.87	−0.36	0.05
	2015	40778	−132719	−42.49	−0.30	0.13
S2-B	2005	64421	−58383.9	−7.62	0.18	0.05
	2015	126492	−128236	−33.70	0.92	0.13
S3-B	2005	−11761	−20130.7	−19.29	−0.78	0.05
	2015	56348	−18380.3	−62.35	−1.92	0.12
S4-B	2005	27495	−17279.3	−16.04	−0.24	0.05
	2015	143972	−14640.9	−53.62	−0.69	0.12

France, Germany, The Netherlands and the UK, where revenue taxation is to be preferred (at least as far as economic growth is concerned).

The effects on employment are more straightforward. Whether positive or negative, the impact of the R & D and innovation policies on employment is likely to be negligible. The cumulated per cent change is always very small, indicating that technological innovation designed to reduce energy consumption in not likely to be labour intensive. This result is confirmed by the microeconomic, bottom-up analysis carried out by Boetti and Botteon (1994).

Is the economic expansion induced by the R & D and innovation policies harmful to the environment? In other words, do emissions increase? The answer is negative. In all countries, and for all policy strategies, emissions are reduced. This can be explained by the introduction of environment-friendly, energy-saving technologies, which improves the capital stock quality and reduces the emission output ratio. The simulation results show that this technical progress effect is greater than the growth effect previously described. Notice that this conclusion also seems to be consistent with the cross-section analyses carried out by Holtz-Eaken and Selden (1992), Baldwin (1995) and Grossman (1995), which show a decreasing emission rate as per-capita GDP increases. Finally, notice that, in the long run, the best results in terms of emission reduction are obtained by the R & D policy financed through indirect taxes. Hence, indirect taxation could be preferred on the grounds of environmental efficiency.

As far as competitiveness is concerned, in Belgium and The Netherlands, the trade balance improves with both policy strategies; in Germany, Italy and the UK, it improves when the R & D policy is implemented; whereas in France, the trade

Table A3
Germany

		GDP	TB	CO_2	Empl.	KeQ
Percentage difference in cumulated values						
S1-B	2005	0.16	−12.02	−0.14	−0.09	2.73
	2015	0.51	−11.70	−0.10	0.01	4.66
S2-B	2005	0.43	−10.89	−0.01	0.02	2.72
	2015	0.74	−10.17	0.02	0.14	4.66
S3-B	2015	−0.29	−0.57	−0.46	−0.22	2.23
	2015	−0.05	3.41	−1.01	−0.32	3.04
S4-B	2005	−0.03	0.78	−0.34	−0.11	2.22
	2015	0.17	5.34	−0.91	−0.20	3.03
Absolute difference in cumulated values						
S1-B	2005	14 249	−64 506	−4.19	−0.36	0.05
	2015	94 398	−235 316	−6.23	0.06	0.11
S2-B	2005	38 154	−58 444	−0.33	0.08	0.05
	2005	137 016	−204 682	0.97	1.00	0.11
S3-B	2005	−25 413	−3050	−13.82	−0.87	0.04
	2015	−9118	68 635	−61.42	−2.35	0.07
S4-B	2005	−2741	4164	−10.20	−0.43	0.04
	2015	31 580	107 364	−55.79	−1.42	0.07

Table A4
Italy

		GDP	TB	CO_2	Empl.	KeQ
Percentage difference in cumulated values						
S1-B	2005	0.22	−16.47	−0.29	0.00	3.45
	2015	0.77	−2.80	−0.49	−0.22	6.53
S2-B	2005	0.38	−13.20	−0.17	−0.03	3.44
	2015	0.97	−0.32	−0.48	−0.23	6.52
S3-B	2005	0.36	−7.70	−0.68	−0.20	4.66
	2015	1.37	1.40	−1.06	−0.49	6.88
S4-B	2005	0.52	−4.48	−0.56	−0.23	4.65
	2015	1.56	3.89	−1.07	−0.50	6.89
Absolute difference in cumulated values						
S1-B	2005	13 285	−24 958	−4.00	0.00	0.06
	2015	96 126	−33 905	−13.11	−1.13	0.13
S2-B	2005	22 727	−20 006	−2.35	−0.10	0.05
	2015	120 631	−3878	−13.03	−1.20	0.13
S3-B	2005	21 479	−11 666	−9.45	−0.60	0.07
	2015	170 427	16 943	−28.67	−2.54	0.13
S4-B	2005	31 233	−6792	−7.80	−0.70	0.07
	2015	195 086	46 999	−28.85	−2.61	0.13

balance worsens. Hence, in all countries except France, the R & D policy also seems to provide an increased competitiveness of the domestic economy relative to the foreign economies. This confirms the intuition that energy-saving technical progress also provides a higher economic efficiency, so yielding cost reductions that increase firms' competitiveness. The way of financing the policy seems to have a significant impact on the trade balance only in Italy, where income taxation should be preferred to indirect taxes.

Finally, let us consider the energy-environmental quality of the capital stock. The improvement in this variable, which captures the energy efficiency of the economic system, is generally large with both policy strategies. However, in the long run, the best results are achieved by the R & D policy, which provides a direct stimulus to technical progress, as well as an indirect stimulus through higher economic activity and international competitiveness. The use of income rather than indirect taxation to finance the government's policy seems to have no differential effect on the growth rate of technical progress.

Given the long time-horizon of our policy simulations, the reader may wonder how sensitive are the above results to the model estimated coefficients. The complex structure of the model (about 10 000 equations) and the large number of parameters do not allow us to perform a detailed and generalized sensitivity analysis. However, because this paper focuses on the role of technical progress, we performed the sensitivity analysis by changing the values of the coefficients in the submodel designed to capture the dynamics of the two components of the capital

Table A5
The Netherlands

		GDP	TB	CO_2	Empl.	KeQ
Percentage difference in cumulated values						
S1-B	2005	−0.44	−4.21	−0.41	−0.29	2.42
	2015	−0.71	0.71	−1.40	−0.64	4.07
S2-B	2005	−0.02	−3.02	−0.32	0.03	2.42
	2015	−0.23	0.81	−1.23	−0.32	4.05
S3-B	2005	−0.35	0.52	−0.99	−0.58	3.23
	2015	−0.14	5.27	−2.66	−1.32	4.63
S4-B	2005	0.07	1.83	−0.90	−0.26	3.23
	2015	0.35	5.39	−2.51	−1.00	4.64
Absolute difference in cumulated values						
S1-B	2005	−8305	−13 816	−2.69	−0.19	0.05
	2015	−28 567	6005	−17.05	−0.73	0.11
S2-B	2005	−361	−9897	−2.09	0.02	0.05
	2015	−9335	6908	−15.06	−0.36	0.11
S3-B	2005	−6697	1710	−6.53	−0.38	0.07
	2015	−5798	44 724	−32.53	−1.51	0.13
S4-B	2005	1412	6006	−5.95	−0.17	0.07
	2015	14 090	45 675	−30.62	−1.14	0.13

Table A6
The UK

		GDP	TB	CO_2	Empl.	KeQ
Percentage difference in cumulated values						
S1-B	2005	0.26	−8.09	0.30	0.12	3.22
	2015	0.44	−14.99	0.85	0.12	5.53
S2-B	2005	0.38	−7.86	0.39	0.14	3.20
	2015	0.27	−11.75	0.69	0.04	5.54
S3-B	2005	−0.46	9.57	−0.36	−0.42	2.24
	2015	−0.49	24.46	−0.94	−0.87	2.30
S4-B	2005	−0.33	9.78	−0.26	−0.39	2.23
	2015	−0.65	26.88	−1.10	−0.95	2.27
Absolute difference in cumulated values						
S1-B	2005	14 402	−19 580	6.94	0.39	0.03
	2015	54 285	−58 098	43.44	0.86	0.06
S2-B	2005	21 654	−19 035	8.99	0.48	0.03
	2015	33 262	−45 518	35.49	0.31	0.06
S3-B	2005	−26 039	23 179	−8.28	−1.40	0.02
	2015	−59 842	94 779	−48.01	−6.25	0.03
S4-B	2005	−18 650	23 668	−6.14	−1.31	0.02
	2015	−80 596	104 173	−56.13	−6.81	0.03

stock. In particular, we modified the autonomous growth rate of technical progress (the constant in the function $f(x)$) and the parameter vector δ. These changes modify the growth path of most variables in the baseline scenario, but no significant change could be observed in the differences between the simulated values for the different policy options and the baseline. This seems to confirm that the theoretical mechanisms embodied in the model are robust to parameter changes. This also further supports our results on the effectiveness of technical progress to control pollution without harming economic growth and competitiveness.

5. Conclusions

The recent political and theoretical debate on environmental policy has focused on the costs rather than on the benefits to policies to control greenhouse gas emissions. This has led many economists to consider how the revenue that arises from the introduction of environmental taxation can be recycled to reduce the economic cost of environmental policy (with the possible recycling of the tax, the idea of using the tax revenue to stimulate labour demand, so increasing employment, has received the greatest attention).

In this paper, we have taken a different attitude. The starting point has been how to achieve the environmental benefit in the most efficient way, rather than at the lowest cost. Because the main suggestion from the theoretical and empirical (bottom-up) literature is that technical progress and environmental innovation are the best tools to control emissions, this paper has focused on two economic instruments to induce innovation and the adoption of environment-friendly technologies. The first instrument is a set of incentives to foster energy-saving R & D. The second instrument, is a subsidy for energy-saving innovation (the adoption of best available technologies). These two policy strategies are financed through direct or through indirect taxation.

This paper has presented the results of the simulations of this type of emission control strategies for six European countries (Belgium, France, Germany, Italy, The Netherlands and the UK). The model used for carrying out the policy simulations is the WARM model—a new model for Europe and for each single European country—which is aimed at embedding both the advantages of calibrated general equilibrium models, and the benefits of dynamic, econometrically estimated macro-models.

The conclusions that can be derived from our simulation experiments can be summarized as follows: R & D or innovation subsidies designed to stimulate technical progress can achieve the goal of environmental protection, and the goal of higher economic growth and improved competitiveness. Moreover, the effects on employment, whether positive or negative, are negligible.

The question of which specific policy instrument should be used cannot find a general answer. Whether the R & D incentive strategy or the investment subsidy has to be implemented depends on the country-specific economic structure and on the weight given to the different economic objectives.

Finally, the way of financing incentives for innovation and R & D (either direct or indirect taxes) only slightly affects the policy outcomes:

(1) income taxation may be preferred as far as economic efficiency is concerned (it provides greater positive effects on growth and competitiveness);
(2) indirect taxation may be preferred in terms of environmental efficiency;
(3) the impact of the financing strategies on technical progress is negligible.

Therefore, our results support a new approach to environmental protection, in which emission control is not inconsistent with economic growth. Within this approach, environmental problems are analyzed and solved jointly with other policy issues, such as economic growth and employment. As a consequence, the resulting policy prescriptions enable the policy-maker to achieve several goals and to harmonize the effects of different policy tools.

A final remark is necessary. The results presented in this paper should not be used against the proposal of introducing emission charges (such as a carbon tax). Instead, they call for a more general policy strategy in which several instruments are used to control emissions. In particular, as often stressed by bottom-up analyses, these instruments should be directed to foster technical progress and to increase the adoption of energy-saving technologies.

Appendix A

Simulations

The index i-B in Tables A1–A6 indicates that the figures reported are the difference between the simulated variable in simulation i and the same variable in the baseline scenario. Moreover, simulation 1 concerns the innovation policy, in which the government subsidizes the investment in best available technologies, financed by an indirect tax. Simulation 2 concerns the innovation policy financed by an income tax. Simulation 3 concerns the R & D policy, in which the government subsidizes firms' R & D activity, financed by an indirect tax. Simulation 4 concerns the R & D policy financed by an income tax.

Variables

GDP	GDP at 1980 prices (change with respect to baseline scenario; million ECUs)
TB	foreign trade surplus at 1980 prices (change with respect to baseline scenario; million ECUs)
Empl	total employment (change with respect to baseline scenario; millions)
CO_2	CO_2 emissions from fossil fuel combustions (change with respect to baseline scenario; million tons)
KEQ	indicator of the energy–environmental quality of the capital stock (change with respect to baseline scenario; index).

References

Baldwin, R., 1995. Does sustainability require growth? In: Goldin, I., Winter, A. (Eds.), The Economics of Sustainable Development. Cambridge University Press, Cambridge.

Blanchard, O., Fisher, S., 1989. Lectures on Macroeconomics. MIT Press, Cambridge, MA.

Boetti, M., Botteon, M., 1994. Environmental policy and the choice of the best available technology: an empirical assessment. CEC-DGXII JOULE II Research Programme, GRETA, Venice, Italy.

Boone, L., Hall, S., Kemball-Cook, D., 1992. Endogenous technical progress in fossil fuel demand. Mimeo, Centre for Economic Forecasting, London Business School.

Botteon, M., Carraro, C., Galeotti, M., 1994. Advances in the econometric modelling of environment-economy linkages. Paper presented at the 50th IIPF Congress, Harvard University, Cambridge, MA.

Bovenberg, L., 1997. Environmental policy, distortionary labour taxation and employment: pollution taxes and the double dividend. In: Carraro, C., Siniscalco, D., (Eds.), New Directions in the Economic Theory of the Environment. Cambridge University Press, Cambridge, MA.

Bovenberg, L., Goulder, L., 1993. Integrating environmental and distortionary taxes: general equilibrium analysis. Paper presented at the Conference on Market Approaches to Environmental Protection, Stanford University, Stanford, CA.

Bovenberg, L., de Mooij, R., 1994. Environmental levies and distortionary taxation. American Economic Review (September), 1085-1089.

Brunello, G., 1996. Labour market institutions and the double dividend. In: Carraro, C., Siniscalco, D. (Eds.), Environmental Fiscal Reform and Unemployment. Kluwer, Dordrecht.

Burniaux, J.M., Martin, J.P., Nicoletti, G., Oliveira Martins, J., 1992. The costs of reducing CO_2 emissions: evidence from GREEN. Working Paper 115, OECD Economics and Statistics Department.

Carlevaro, F., Garbely, M., Muller, T., 1992. Vers une modélisation en équilibre général des mesures de politique énergétique en Suisse. Serie de Publications du CUEPE 49, Université de Genève.

Carraro, C., 1985. New methods for macroeconomic policy analysis. Unpublished Ph.D. Dissertation, Princeton University, Princeton, NJ.

Carraro, C., 1988. Square root Kalman algorithms in econometrics. Computers Science in Economics and Management 1, 28-36.

Carraro, C., 1994. Modelling technological progress in top-down models. Paper prepared for the Meeting of the IPCC Working Group III, Milan.

Carraro, C., Galeotti, M., 1994a. Endogenous technical progress and emission control: policy experiments with the WARM model. Paper presented at the Advanced Research Workshop on the Economics of Atmospheric Pollution, Wageningen.

Carraro, C., Galeotti, M., 1994b. WARM (World Assessment of Resource Management): Technical Report, GRETA, Venice.

Carraro, C., Siniscalco, D., 1994. Environmental policy re-considered: the role of technological innovation. European Economic Review 38, 545-554.

Carraro, C., Soubeyran, A., 1996. Environmental taxation, market-share, and profits in oligopoly. In Carraro, C., Katsoulacos, Y., Xepapadeas, A. (Eds.) Environmental Policy and Market Structure. Kluwer, Dordrecht.

Carraro, C., Topa, G., 1995. Taxation and environmental innovation. In: Carraro, C., Filar, J. (Eds.), Control and Game-theoretic Models of the Environment. Birckauser, Boston, MA.

Carraro, C., Galeotti, M., Gallo, M., 1997. Environmental taxation and unemployment: some evidence on the double-dividend hypothesis in Europe. Journal of Public Economics, 62/1-2, 141-181.

Carraro, C., Lanza, A., Tudini, A., 1994. Technological change, technology transfers and the negotiation of international environmental agreements. Environmental Economic Affairs 6, 203-222.

Carraro, C., Katsoulacos, Y., Xepapadeas, A., (Eds.), 1996. *Environmental Policy and Market Structure*. Kluwer, Dordrecht.

Cline, W.R., 1992. The Economics of Global Warming. Institute for International Economics, Washington, DC.

Conrad, K., Ehrlich, M., 1993. The impact of embodied and disembodied technical progress on productivity gaps — an applied general equilibrium analysis for Germany and Spain. Journal of Productivity Analysis 4, 317–335.

Conrad, K., Henseler-Unger, I., 1986. Applied general equilibrium modeling for long-term energy policy in Germany. Journal of Policy Modeling 8, 531–549.

Data Resources Inc. (DRI), 1992. Impact of a package of EC measures to control CO_2 emissions on European industry. Report for the Commission of the European Communities, DGXI.

Denis, C., Koopman, G.J., 1994. Differential treatment of sectors and energy products in the design of a CO_2 energy tax. Paper presented at the FEEM Conference on Environmental Taxation, Revenue Recycling and Unemployment, Milan.

Dobson, A., 1994. Multifirm unions and the incentive to adopt pattern bargaining in oligopoly. European Economic Review 38, 87–100.

Dosi, C., Graham-Tomasi, T., 1994. Non-point Source Pollution Regulation: Issues and Analysis. Kluwer, Dordrecht.

Downing, P.B., White, L.J., 1986. Innovation in pollution control. Journal of Environmental Economics and Management 13, 18–29.

Echia, G., Mariotti, G., 1994. Innovation and environmental policy: a survey. FEEM Discussion Paper 44.94, Milan.

Edmonds, J.A., 1992. Long term modelling of the links between economics, technical progress, and environment: evolution of approaches and new trends. Mimeo, Pacific Northwest Laboratory, Washington, DC.

Grossman, G., 1995. Pollution and growth: what do we know? In: Goldin, L., Winters, A. (Eds.), The Economics of Sustainable Development. Cambridge University Press, Cambridge.

Grubb, M., Edmonds, J., ten Brink, P., Morrison, M., 1993. The costs of limiting fossil-fuel CO_2 emissions. Annual Review of Energy and Environment 18, 397–478.

Harvey, A.C., 1987. Applications of the Kalman filter in econometrics. In Bewley, T.F. (Ed.), Advances in Econometrics. Cambridge University Press, Cambridge.

Holtz-Eakin, T., Selden, T., 1992. Stoking the fires? CO_2 emissions and growth. NBER Working Paper 4248, Cambridge, MA.

IPCC, 1990. Potential impact of climate change. Working Group 2 Final Report, WMO-UNEP, Geneva.

Johansson, T.B., Swisher J.N., 1993. Perspectives on bottom-up analysis of costs of carbon dioxide emissions reductions. OECD/IAE Conference on the Economics of Climate Change, Paris.

Jorgenson, D.W., Wilcoxen, P.J., 1990. Intertemporal general equilibrium modelling of U.S. environmental regulation. Journal of Policy Modeling 12, 7 15–744.

Karadeloglou, P., 1992. Energy tax versus carbon tax: a quantitative macro-economic analysis with the HERMES-MIDAS models. European Economy, Special Edition no. 1, CEC-DGII, Brussels.

Kohli, U., 1991. Technology, Duality, and Foreign Trade. Harvester Wheatsheaf, Hemel Hempstead.

Laffont, J.J., Tirole J., 1994. Pollution permits and compliance strategies. FEEM Discussion Paper 43.94, Milan.

Lau, L.J., 1976. A characterization of the normalized restricted profit function. Journal of Economic Theory 12, 131–183.

Michel, P., 1993. Pollution and growth towards the ecological paradise. FEEM Discussion Paper 80.93, Milan.

Milliman, S.R., Prince R., 1989. Firm incentives to promote technological change in pollution control. Journal of Environmental Economics and Management 17, 247–265.

Morrison, C.J., 1988. Quasi-fixed inputs in U.S. and Japanese manufacturing: a generalized Leontief restricted cost function approach. Review of Economics and Statistics LXX, 275–287.

Musu, I., 1994. On sustainable endogenous growth. FEEM Discussion paper 11.94, Milan.

Parry, I., 1994. Pollution taxes and revenue recycling. Paper presented at the FEEM Conference on Environmental Taxation, Revenue Recycling and Unemployment, Milan.

Schoeb, R., 1994. Environmental taxes on exhaustible resources. Paper presented at the Advanced Research Workshop on the Economics of Atmospheric Pollution, Wageningen.

Verdier, T., 1995. Environmental pollution and endogenous growth. In: Carraro, C., Filar, J., (Eds.), Game-theoretic Models of the Environment. Birckauser, New York.

Wilson, D., Swisher, J., 1993. Top-down versus bottom-up analyses of the cost of mitigating global warming. Energy Policy 21, 249–262.

Zimmermann, H., 1993. The revenue effect of environmental charges. Mimeo, University of Marburg.

[14]

Do Stringent Environmental Regulations Reduce the International Competitiveness of Environmentally Sensitive Goods? A Global Perspective

XINPENG XU *
The Australian National University, Canberra, Australia

Summary. — In this paper I examine whether stringent environmental standards reduce the international competitiveness of environmentally sensitive industries using a comprehensive dataset of trade flows of environmentally sensitive goods (ESGs) disaggregated at the four-digit level of the Standard International Trade Classification. The data relate 1965–95 and cover 34 countries, accounting for nearly 80% of world exports of ESGs in 1995. I find that export performance of ESGs for most countries remained unchanged between the 1960s and 1990s, despite the introduction of stringent environmental standards in most developed countries in the 1970s and 1980s. © 1999 Elsevier Science Ltd. All rights reserved.

1. INTRODUCTION

Widespread concerns have been expressed recently about the relationship between international competitiveness of environmentally sensitive goods (ESGs, hereafter) and environmental regulations.[1] Does free trade with countries with lower environmental standards lead to a shift of production activity from home countries with higher environmental standards to foreign countries? Will countries with higher standards be forced to lower their standards if capital and jobs also migrate to exploit lower environmental standards abroad (the so-called race to the bottom)?[2] Is it really the case that countries with lower environmental regulations increase their competitiveness in the production of ESGs? This last question receives considerable attention whenever countries are in the process of passing new pollution control measures.

This paper seeks to examine whether the pattern of export performance of ESGs has undergone systematic changes due to the introduction of stringent environmental standards in most developed countries in the 1970s and the 1980s. More precisely, I seek to examine whether countries with high export performance in ESGs in the 1960s shifted to countries with low export performance in ESGs in the 1990s. A comprehensive dataset of trade flows of ESGs disaggregated to the four-digit level of the Standard International Trade Classification (SITC) is employed. The data relate to 1965–95 for 34 reporter countries. These 34 reporter countries include 25 OECD countries and some developing economies in East Asia and accounted for nearly 80% of world exports of ESGs in 1995. Given these disaggregated trade data and the coverage of the reporter countries, I believe that this can provide us with a full picture of the changing trade patterns of ESGs. The important empirical finding is that export performance of ESGs for most countries remained intact between the 1960s and the 1990s, despite the introduction of stringent environmental standards in most of the developed countries in the 1970s and 1980s.

---

* This paper is part of my Ph.D. thesis defended at the Australian National University. I am indebted to my supervisors, Peter Drysdale, Kali Kalirajan, Ben Smith, Neil Vousden, for their continuous guidance and advice. I am grateful to Peter Warr, Chandra P. Athukorala, Ligang Song, Weiguo Lu, seminar participants at the Australian National University, and one anonymous referee for their constructive comments and suggestions. The usual disclaimers apply. Final revision accepted: 22 December 1998.

I first look at the export performance of each ESG for each of the reporter countries in the initial year 1965, the first year in which data are available, and compare it with that in the end year 1995. Those countries which exported more than world average of ESGs, namely, had a revealed comparative advantage [RCA] index[3] greater than one in 1965 achieved the same level of performance in 1995. Looking more closely at the year-to-year path of the RCA index of ESGs, I found that those commodities with either one or two years' high export performance (RCA index greater than one) and those commodities with either 30 or 31 years' high export performance accounted for a large proportion of the exports of ESGs for most countries. Time-series patterns for the changing export performance of ESGs for some countries that claim to have higher environmental standards did not reveal a significant reduction in exports in the 1970s and 1980s. The results are quite robust in terms of both the weighted and the unweighted version of this trade pattern. This suggests that the pattern of export performance of ESGs did not undergo systematic change despite the introduction of stringent environmental standards in most developed countries in the 1970s and 1980s.

The following section reviews briefly the established literature. Section 3 provides a brief definition of ESGs and its relevant trade categories in terms of Standard International Trade Classification; The dataset and methodology used in this study are discussed in section 4. Section 5 reports the results. Section 6 examines the robustness of the results and the final section presents a conclusion.

2. LITERATURE

As surveyed by Levinson (1996), the literature on trade and the environment has evolved in two waves. The first wave of research peaked during the late 1970s and seems to have been inspired by the introduction of stringent environmental regulations in developed countries since the early 1970s. The second wave occured in the 1990s, mainly motivated by the debate over international trade agreements such as North American Free Trade Agreement (NAFTA) and the Uruguay Round of the General Agreement on Tariffs and Trade (GATT).

The relationship between stringent environmental regulations and international competitiveness[4] has been addressed in the following ways. The first is the so-called race to the bottom effect.[5] If free trade occurs between countries with different environmental standards, countries with higher environmental standards will be forced by their domestic interest groups to lower their standards to ensure the survival of their environmentally sensitive industries. Therefore, there will be a tendency toward a "race to the bottom" when trade among these countries is liberalized. This concern mainly emanates from those countries with higher environmental standards.

The second is the so-called pollution haven hypothesis (Walter and Ugelow, 1979; Walter, 1982). If free trade occurs between countries with different environmental standards, countries with lower environmental standards will tend over time to develop a comparative advantage[6] in environmentally sensitive industries which will result in "havens" for the world's dirty industries (Cropper and Oates, 1992).

The third concern is whether increasingly stringent domestic environmental regulations will reduce the international competitiveness of environmentally sensitive industries. In a recent study, Porter and Linde (1995) argue that the relationship between environmental regulations and international competitiveness can be "complementary" rather than "mutually exclusive" since "properly designed environmental standards can trigger innovation that may partially or more than fully offset the costs of complying with them." Palmer, Oates and Portney (1995) criticize this view and argue that there is always a trade-off between environmental regulations and international competitiveness.

At the heart of all these concerns is the impact of environmental standards on the industrial competitiveness. The existing empirical literature provides a mixed picture of the relationship between environmental regulations and industrial competitiveness. For example, Low and Yeats (1992) show that developing countries gained a comparative advantage in ESGs at a greater rate than developed countries. Robison (1988) found that the abatement content of US imports has risen more rapidly than the abatement content of exports as US environmental standards have become more stringent than those in the rest of the world. Kalt (1988) shows that domestic environmental regulation appears to have a negative effect on industries trade performance. All these studies found some evidence suggesting that stringent environmental standards have a negative effect on industrial competitiveness. By contrast, Leonard (1988) found little evidence that pollution control measures have exerted a systematic effect on international trade and investment by conducting a large case study of trade and foreign investment flows for several key industries and countries.

Tobey (1990) sets up a Heckscher-Ohlin-Vanek (HOV) multifactor, multicommodity model. Using 1975 data for 23 countries, Tobey regresses the net exports of five different industries which are classified as pollution intensive on the stocks of productive factors, including the environment. The environment variable Tobey uses is the stringency of environmental regulations, varying from 1 to 7, acting as the proxy for the stock of the environment. A country with more stringent regulations is assumed to have a lower environment stock than other countries. He found no evidence that the introduction of environmental control measures has caused trade patterns to deviate from the HOV predictions.

Grossman and Krueger (1993) investigate empirically the environmental impacts of NAFTA. They regress 1987 US imports from Mexico (relative to total US shipments) in 135 industries on factor shares which reflect the factor intensity of each industry. Environment intensity is approximated by the ratio of pollution abatement costs to total value added in that US industry. Grossman and Krueger find that the traditional determinants of trade and investment patterns are significant, but that the alleged competitive advantages created by lax pollution controls in Mexico play no substantial role in motivating trade and investment flows.

One shortcoming of the existing literature is that the changing pattern of export performance of ESGs over time is seldom explored. This leads to an incomplete picture of the impact of environmental standards on industrial competitiveness. Low and Yeats (1992) first took up this issue but they put too much emphasis on one particular industry (Iron and Steel Pipes and Tubes, SITC 678) and, when looking at the ESGs groups, they only look at the overall performance of two groups of countries, namely developed countries and developing countries. The study also only looks at the beginning (late 1960s) and end years (late 1980s). All this might result in an incomplete picture of the changing pattern of export performance of ESGs over time. Sorsa (1994) also looks at this issue but at a more aggregated level.

In this paper, I try to avoid the above shortcomings by using a comprehensive dataset and by examining the data from a number of different perspectives. The aim is to provide a full picture of the changing pattern of export performance of ESGs over time.

3. DEFINITION OF ENVIRONMENTALLY SENSITIVE GOODS

There is no uniformly agreed-upon definition of environmentally sensitive goods. Two approaches have been used to identify environmentally sensitive goods in the received literature.[7] The conventional approach has been to identify ESG sectors as those that have incurred high levels of abatement expenditure per unit of output in the United States and other OECD economies (see, for example, Robison, 1988; Tobey, 1990 and Low and Yeats, 1992). The second approach is to select sectors which rank high on actual emissions intensity (emissions per unit of output) in the United States (see for example, Mani and Wheeler, 1997). I adopt the conventional approach in this study. Both approaches however come up with similar environmentally sensitive sectors. Five sectors have typically emerged as leading candidates for environmentally sensitive sectors: iron and steel, nonferrous metals, industrial chemicals, pulp and paper, and nonmetallic products.

As defined in Low and Yeats (1992), environmentally sensitive goods includes all four-digit products in SITC 67 (iron and steel), SITC 68 (nonferrous metals) and SITC 69 (metal manufactures n.e.s.). Also included are all four-digit products in pulp and waste paper (251); organic chemicals (512); inorganic chemicals (513, 514); radioactive material (515); coal, petroleum chemicals (521); manufactured fertilizers (561); paper and paperboard (641); paper articles (642); veneers, plywood (631); wood manufactures n.e.s. (632); petroleum products (332); agricultural chemicals (599); and cement (661).[8] These industries incurred pollution abatement and control expenditures of approximately 1% or more of the value of their total sales (1988). The highest expenditure:output ratio in 1988 was just over 3% (cement) and the weighted average for all US industry was 0.54%.

4. DATA AND METHODOLOGY

This study uses a comprehensive dataset of annual trade flows (exports and imports) of ESGs disaggregated at the four-digit level of the Standard International Trade Classification from 1965-95 for 34 reporter countries.[9] These 34 reporter countries accounted for nearly 80% of world exports (and trade) of ESGs in 1995. They include 25 of the 29 OECD countries[10] as of May 1997, and major East Asian developing economies. There are 134 ESG commodities at the four-digit level. ESGs at the four-digit level include: chemical phosphatic fertiliser (SITC code 5612), newsprint paper (SITC code 6411), cement (SITC code 6612) and iron, steel wire products (SITC code 6731). There are 286,905 observations in total.

As is well known and discussed by Gagnon and Rose (1995),[11] the value of international trade flows has increased substantially in the last 40 years. This is partly a result of inflation, partly a result of real economic growth and partly a result of the increasing importance of trade relative to total output. In particular, a macroeconomic imbalance may result in substantial changes in net exports.

To abstract these effects from our data, the export revealed comparative advantage ($XRCA$) index is used in this analysis. This $XRCA$ index, introduced by Balassa 1989 in 1965, is defined as a country's share in the exports of a particular commodity divided by the share of that particular commodity in the world exports of manufactured goods, as follows:

$$XRCA_i^k = \left(\frac{X_{iw}^k}{X_{iw}^{ll}}\right) \div \left(\frac{X_{ww}^k}{X_{ww}^{ll}}\right), \qquad (1)$$

where $XRCA_i^k$ gives country i's export revealed comparative advantage in industry k, X stands for exports, subscript w stands for world, subscript k represents industry k, and subscript l stands for total exports. This index has some limitations. It might not "reveal" the comparative advantage of a particular commodity especially when domestic or international distortions are present. As discussed in another paper by Balassa in 1987, however, other indices have their own disadvantages. For example, the net export index used by Balassa (1989) has the practical disadvantage of being affected by the idiosyncrasies of national import protection; in the case of intermediate products, net exports are influenced by demand for the purpose of further transformation in export production. Ballance, Forstner and Murray, 1987 discuss the RCA index and find that, while cardinal measures of different RCA indices are highly inconsistent, both ordinal and dichotomous, and especially dichotomous measures generate consistent results.[12] For the purposes of this study, I am interested only in the changing pattern of comparative advantage which can be viewed as dichotomous measures. The choice of this index serves the purpose of this study. Drysdale and Garnaut (1982) and Drysdale (1988) also provide extensive discussion of this and other related indices.

This $XRCA$ index works reasonably well in terms of the above-mentioned data issue. Since it is an index, the inflation effect can be removed if it is an across-the-board increase in the prices of all commodities. By dividing exports of a particular commodity category by total manufactured exports, this index also takes into account macroeconomic trade balance effects. For instance, a 1% growth in exports spread uniformly across all goods (for example, when domestic savings are greater than domestic investment) will not affect the level of this index. Furthermore, by dividing a country's export sectoral share of a particular commodity category by the same sectoral share in the world exports of manufactured goods, a general increase or decrease in world exports of a particular commodity (growth effect) will not change the level of this index either. This is particularly useful since the share of ESGs exports to total exports has declined from 21.7% in 1965 to 16.9% in 1995 (Table 1).

For reasons that will shortly become clear, a normalization is used for the commodity trade share. This measures the relative importance of a particular commodity trade share in the trade of total ESGs at a particular point in time, as follows:

$$S_{it} = \frac{1}{2}\left(\frac{X_{it}}{X_{et}} + \frac{M_{it}}{M_{et}}\right) 100, \qquad (2)$$

where i refers to a particular commodity category within ESGs, t refers to a point in time and e indicates total ESGs. The sum of any time period over all ESGs is 100, and S_{it} is a percentage measure.

This dataset will be analyzed from the following four perspectives. Changes in the dichotomous measures of the $XRCA$ index between the beginning and the ending period of the sample will be examined first. We would like to see by what percentage the export flows of ESGs change in 1995 compared with those in

Table 1. *Exports of ESGs and their importance in world trade: cross section and time series*

	Europe OECD (18) countries [a]	North America [b]	Oceania [c]	Northeast Asia [d]	Southeast Asia [e]	Other	World
Market shares of total exports by region (%)							
1965	45.1	20.8	2.3	6.7	2.5	22.7	100
1975	43.8	17.0	1.7	9.3	2.5	25.6	100
1985	42.4	17.5	1.6	15.6	3.8	19.1	100
1995	43.7	17.3	1.3	19.4	6.6	11.6	100
Shares of ESGs to total exports (%)							
1965	24.4	20.3	9.2	23.1	18.1	18.8	21.7
1975	24.5	17.2	15.1	23.6	17.8	16.1	20.7
1985	23.5	16.3	17.6	13.4	19.1	22.9	20.3
1995	18.7	16.5	20.2	11.3	11.9	22.6	16.9
Market shares of ESG exports by region (%)							
1965	50.6	19.5	1.0	7.1	2.1	19.7	100
1975	52.0	14.1	1.3	10.6	2.1	19.9	100
1985	49.1	14.1	1.4	10.3	3.6	21.6	100
1995	48.4	16.9	1.6	13.0	4.7	15.5	100

[a] Europe OECD includes 18 of the 22 European OECD countries (Finland, Greece, Ireland, the Netherlands, Poland, Sweden, the United Kingdom, Austria, France, Italy, Belgium, Luxemburg, Portugal, Switzerland, Denmark, Germany, Norway and Spain) but not Hungary, Turkey, Czech Republic and Iceland, as of May 1997.
[b] North America refers to the United States, Canada and Mexico.
[c] Oceania includes Australia, New Zealand and Papua New Guinea.
[d] Northeast Asia includes Japan, Korea, Taiwan, China and Hong Kong.
[e] Southeast Asia includes Thailand, Malaysia, the Philippines, Indonesia and Singapore.
Source: Author's calculations on the basis of the United Nations COMTRADE database from International Economic Data Bank, Australian National University.

1965 for each of the reporter countries. One would expect that those commodities with a high export performance at the beginning of the sample period will become less competitive at the end of the sample period if the claim that stringent environmental standards reduce "international competitiveness" holds.

A second and more rigorous statistical test of the association between the 1965 series and the 1995 series is performed to determine whether there is any association between export performance of ESGs in the beginning and end years. Although a few tests for association are available, I choose Kendall's tau-b[13] which ranks the $XRCA$ index for each year and calculates the test statistic based on the number of concordant and discordant pairs of observations. Kendall's tau-b is similar to a gamma test but has the advantage that it also takes tied pairs into account (that is, pairs of observations that have equal values of X or equal values of Y).[14]

As a third step in this analysis, histograms for each reporter country based on the number of years each reporter country has "revealed comparative advantage" (or "specialization") with an $XRCA$ greater than one are used to look at the ESG export performance in the intervening years. Of course, there are two different ways to look at this. The first counts the number of commodities that fall into each of the zero and 31-year frequencies and reports this as a percentage of the total number of commodities. The other takes the normalized trade share of each commodity in a particular year (1990 in this exercise) as the weight, and reports this percentage. The latter is generally supposed to convey more information. As an alternative way to look at this issue, however, the former will be discussed in the section on robustness. One might expect there to be many fluctuations of these histograms indicating that many ESGs have changed their export performance position if environmental standards have significant effects on trade flows of ESGs.

Fourth, to provide an alternative perspective to look at the export performance of ESGs in the intervening years, a time-series pattern of export performance of ESGs is calculated. The indicator we used here is the percentage trade share of those ESGs that indicated a "specialization" in total ESGs trade for each year and each country. Since a dichotomous measure can be assigned to each commodity at a particular point in time, the normalized trade share of those commodities (within the ESG group) is summed to provide a percentage share of the normalized trade of all ESGs. If the above histogram does not convey sufficient information about the locus of the changing share of one country's competitive ESGs, this time-series pattern then offers a unique picture to look at the export performance of ESGs for a selected country over time. This indicator therefore can be expressed as

$$C_{it} = \left\{ \sum^{k} S_{it}^{k} | XRCA_{it}^{k} \geq 1 \right\}, \qquad (3)$$

where C_{it} is the competitive indicator for country i at time t. k denotes commodity (ESGs). S_{it} denotes shares of commodity k in country i's total trade at time t.

5. RESULTS

Table 2 shows the breakdown of dichotomous measures of the $XRCA$ index between the beginning (1965) and the end of the period (1995). This is the weighted version of the breakdown of the $XRCA$ index during 1965–95.

"N" stands for "nonspecialization" where the $XRCA$ index is less than one while "S" refers to "specialization" where the $XRCA$ index greater than one. It is a dichotomous measure in the sense that each commodity at a particular point in time is either in the position of "S" or "N". "1965N" therefore represents percentage of normalized trade flows of ESGs that were not specialized in 1965. While "1965S" represents those commodities that had "revealed comparative advantage" in 1965. The same logic applies to both "1995N" and "1995S". "1965N–95N" indicates percentage of normalized trade flows of ESGs that were not specialized in 1965 remained so in 1995. "1965N–95S" indicates percentage of normalized trade flows of ESGs that were not specialized in 1965 becomes specialized in 1995. Similarly, "1965S–95N" indicates percentage of normalized trade flows of ESGs that were specialized in 1965 became not specialized in 1995. "1965S–95S" indicates percentage of normalized trade flows of ESGs that were specialized in 1965 remained so in 1995.

Since this is the weighted version (using commodity shares in the ESG group in 1990 as the weight) of the $XRCA$ dichotomy, the number in the tables represents the percentage of trade flows rather than the percentage of the number of commodities. These trade flow percentages of ESGs should sum to 100 at any given point in time. For example, numbers in columns 6 and 7 sum to 100 for each country. So do numbers in columns 8 and 9.

For example, in the case of Australia, 49.2% of the normalized trade flows of ESGs were in a position of "nonspecialization" while 50.8% of the normalized trade flows of ESGs were in a position of "specialization" in 1965. Among the 49.2% of the normalized trade flows of ESGs which were in a position of "nonspecialization" in 1965, 38.1% remains in a position of "nonspecialization" in 1995 while 11.1% switch to a position of "specialization".

If the claim that stringent environmental standards hurt those countries with higher environmental standards (mostly developed countries) and benefit those countries with lower environmental standards (mostly developing countries) is to hold, one would expect there to be a significant downturn in the export performance of ESGs across countries. In other words, the export performance of the ESGs of developing countries would increase while that of developed countries would decrease. There is however, one striking feature revealed in this table. That is trade volumes that move from a "specialization" position to a "nonspecialization" position account for no more than 15% of the ESG trade volumes for the majority countries except for China, France, Japan, Norway and Singapore, whose percentage is about 20.[15]

Further, taking into account those trade volumes that move from a position of "nonspecialization" to a position of "specialization", one can see that these trade volumes always exceed trade volumes that move from a "specialization" position to a "nonspecialization" position with the exceptions of Japan, Norway and China.[16] Even in the case of Japan, Norway and China, this difference is very small, 9.57%, 5.95% and 9.01%, respectively. It becomes clear that the pattern of export performance of ESGs is quite persistent in the sample period. Those commodities which did not display much "revealed comparative advantage" at the beginning of the sample period tend to remain in a position of "nonspecial-

Table 2. *Export performance of ESGs: 1965 versus 1995*

Country	1965N-95N	1965N-95S	1965S-95N	1965S-95S	1965N	1965S	1995N	1995S	Kendall's tau-b	p-value	No. of ESGs
Australia	38.1	11.1	10.1	40.7	49.2	50.8	48.2	51.9	0.27	0.0001	133
Austria	20.0	17.1	12.2	50.7	37.1	63.0	32.2	67.8	0.34	0.0001	133
Belgium-Luxembourg	18.8	32.0	6.8	42.4	50.8	49.2	25.6	74.4	0.39	0.0001	134
Brazil	25.8	46.8	1.6	25.9	72.5	27.5	27.3	72.7	0.25	0.0001	130
Canada	31.2	23.3	5.8	39.8	54.5	45.6	37.0	63.1	0.29	0.0001	125
Chile	42.9	12.4	0.0	44.6	55.4	44.6	43.0	57.0	0.27	0.0001	129
China	57.0	8.4	17.4	17.1	65.4	34.6	74.4	25.6	0.15	0.0100	134
Denmark	38.6	19.4	7.5	34.5	58.0	42.0	46.1	53.9	0.40	0.0001	134
Finland	31.2	20.6	2.7	45.6	51.8	48.2	33.8	66.2	0.30	0.0001	132
France	26.7	22.5	19.3	31.5	49.2	50.8	46.0	54.0	0.15	0.0128	133
Greece	45.1	26.9	7.7	20.4	72.0	28.0	52.7	47.3	0.24	0.0002	128
Hong Kong	59.1	17.9	4.0	17.5	77.0	21.5	63.1	35.4	0.50	0.0001	106
Indonesia	45.5	49.8	1.9	2.8	95.3	4.7	47.4	52.6	0.20	0.0050	128
Ireland	37.7	46.8	9.1	6.4	84.5	15.5	46.8	53.2	0.21	0.0020	132
Italy	41.7	14.6	10.8	32.9	56.3	43.7	52.5	47.5	0.38	0.0001	134
Japan	52.4	8.1	17.7	21.8	60.5	39.5	70.1	29.9	0.31	0.0001	134
Korea	40.6	42.1	8.2	9.1	82.7	17.3	48.8	51.2	0.26	0.0001	133
Malaysia	56.4	20.6	3.5	19.5	77.0	23.0	59.9	40.1	0.38	0.0001	133
Mexico	46.3	15.8	15.8	22.2	62.0	38.0	62.0	38.0	0.28	0.0001	134
Netherlands	22.1	16.4	0.9	60.7	38.4	61.6	23.0	77.0	0.40	0.0001	133
New Zealand	31.2	45.2	0.3	23.3	76.4	23.6	31.5	68.5	0.44	0.0001	131
Norway	26.5	15.3	21.2	37.0	41.8	58.2	47.7	52.3	0.23	0.0001	131
Philippines	62.5	23.3	10.0	4.3	85.8	14.2	72.5	27.5	0.22	0.0027	124
Poland	18.6	31.1	13.1	37.2	49.7	50.3	31.7	68.3	0.20	0.0005	134
Portugal	52.5	25.8	3.2	18.5	78.3	21.7	55.7	44.3	0.37	0.0001	133
Singapore	60.4	16.8	17.8	5.0	77.2	22.8	78.2	21.8	0.15	0.0123	131
Spain	42.8	40.0	7.6	9.6	82.8	17.2	50.4	49.6	0.21	0.0005	134
Sweden	28.4	17.1	6.0	48.5	45.5	54.5	34.4	65.6	0.50	0.0001	132
Switzerland	37.9	21.5	0.5	40.2	59.3	40.7	38.4	61.6	0.49	0.0001	133
Taiwan	45.9	37.7	14.3	2.1	83.6	16.4	60.1	39.9	0.13	0.0337	134
Thailand	67.9	19.9	1.7	10.4	87.9	12.1	69.6	30.4	0.38	0.0001	131
United Kingdom	42.5	31.6	5.3	20.6	74.2	25.9	47.8	52.2	0.39	0.0001	134
United States	41.4	14.2	14.3	30.1	55.6	44.4	55.8	44.2	0.39	0.0001	134
Venezuela	27.9	67.7	1.8	2.2	95.7	4.0	29.8	69.9	0.04	0.5800	130

Source: Author's calculations on the basis of the United Nations COMTRADE database from International Economic Data Bank, Australian National University.

ization", while those commodities which had a "revealed comparative advantage" at the beginning of the sample period remain in a position of "specialization".

Two exceptions, Brazil and Venezuela, require more attention. The pattern of ESG export performance in these two countries changed dramatically over 1965–95. In Brazil, 72.5% of the normalized trade flows of ESGs were in a position of "nonspecialization" while 27.5% of the normalized trade flows of ESGs were in a position of "specialization" in 1965. In 1995, 72.7% of the normalized trade flows of ESGs were in a position of "specialization" while 27.3% of the normalized trade flows of ESGs were in a position of "nonspecializa-tion". In the case of Venezuela, 95.7% of the normalized trade flows of ESGs were in a position of "nonspecialization" while 4.0% of the normalized trade flows of ESGs were in a position of "specialization" in 1965. In 1995, 69.9% of the normalized trade flows of ESGs were in a position of "specialization" while only 29.8% of the normalized trade flows of ESGs were in a position of "nonspecialization".

Measures of association using Kendall's tau-b test statistic also convey the economic message that there is a strong association between the export performance of ESGs over 1965–95. The p-value shows that the null hypothesis that the two series are distributed independently can be rejected at a significance level of 1% for most countries except China (1.02%), France (1.28%), Singapore (1.23%), Taiwan (3.37%) and Venezuela (58.1%). This result is presented for each country in Table 2. Note that Kendall's tau-b ranges from −1 to +1 and the nominator is the difference between twice the number of concordances and twice the number of disconcordances. If this difference is not very large, Kendall's tau-b coefficient can be very low. This does not necessarily mean that the correlation between the two series is weak.

This table and their statistical tests suggest that those commodities with a high export performance at the beginning of the sample period remain competitive at the end of the sample period for most countries.

Figure 1 provides a histogram of *years in "specialization"* for selected country that claim to have higher environmental standards. The data are first classified by reporter and commodity. The number of *years in "specialization"* is then counted for each commodity. Since there are 31 years of observations in total, a subgroup that was in *"specialization"* for each of the 31 years then is put to the extreme right of the histogram while a subgroup that was not in *"specialization"* for each of the 31 years is put to the extreme left of the histogram. These are the weighted versions of the histogram in the sense that it is the normalized trade volume rather than the number of commodities that is put into each cell.

If stringent environmental standards do have a significant impact on the international competitiveness of ESGs, one would expect that many goods will not be in consistent "specialization" or "nonspecialization". For most countries, one can see a bimodal breakdown of the composition of trade in ESGs, especially for OECD countries, indicating that most trade in ESGs is accounted for by goods in consistent "specialization" or "nonspecialization".

For developing countries, one can see the same results with the exceptions of Brazil, Mexico, Philippines and Venezuela. Overall, these histograms also reveal that export performance of ESGs for most countries is quite persistent. As these histograms do not consider the sequencing of export performance of ESGs, an alternative way to look at the ESG export performance in the intervening years is necessary.

Figure 2 shows the time-series pattern of the share of the normalized trade volume of those ESGs with the *XRCA* index greater than one as to total ESG trade for some selected countries that claim to have higher environmental standards. This simple figure reveals a more striking result. The share of the normalized trade volume of those ESGs with an *XRCA* index greater than one as to total ESGs trade did not decrease over time for most countries, except Japan.

If the sample period is then divided into two subperiods, before and after the end of the 1980s, for Japan and the United States, one can see that after a slow decrease in competitiveness of ESGs in the first period, there was a stark increase in competitiveness of ESGs in the second period. This is an interesting story that

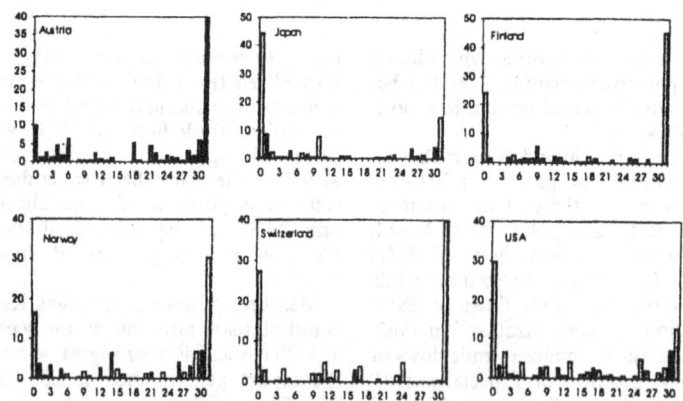

Figure 1. *Histograms of years in "specialization" of ESGs for selected countries, 1965–95.*

A GLOBAL PERSPECTIVE

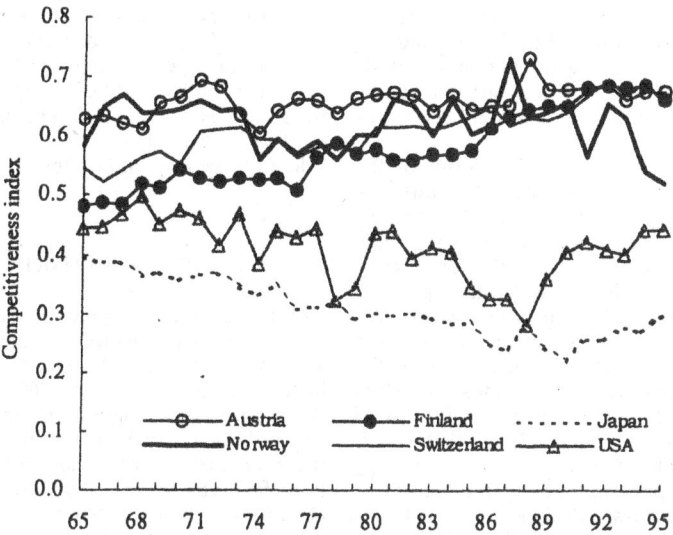

Figure 2. *Time-series pattern of the overall competitiveness indices of ESGs for selected countries, 1965–95.*

requires more theoretical explanation along with an examination of the overall export performance of ESGs over time.

The above analysis suggests that the export performance of ESGs is persistent throughout the sample period despite the introduction of stringent environmental standards by the industrialized countries two decades ago. The claim that higher environmental standards reduce the "international competitiveness" of ESGs cannot be justified in the light of the available data.

6. ROBUSTNESS

The dataset used in this study is comprehensive in the sense that it covers nearly 80% of the world exports of ESGs. It is important to test the robustness of the results to determine the extent to which the results are affected by the way we look at these data.

As a check on the robustness of my findings, the data are smoothed using a three-year average in order to reduce the influence of any irregular variations in a particular year. Two period averages, 1965–67 and 1993–95, have been chosen as representative of the 1960s and the 1990s. A similar breakdown of Tables is then calculated both for the weighted and the unweighted trade volume of each country. The finding that trade volumes that move from a position of "specialization" to a position of "nonspecialization" account for no more than 15% of the ESG trade volumes for the majority of countries is even more starkly apparent. France, with 19.3% previously, had a 13.09% downturn in this three-year average version. The maximum percentage downturn is 18.97% (Singapore) in this version compared with 21.20% (for Norway, which recorded 17.09% in the three-year average) in the previous version.

Unweighted versions of tables are also calculated for each of the countries and the findings remain unchanged. Those commodities that move from a position of "specialization" to a position of "nonspecialization" account for a small proportion of the ESG trade (less than 20%) for the majority of countries.

To check the robustness of these results using the dichotomous measure, I take an approach suggested by Gagnon and Rose (1995) and Carolan, Singh and Talati (1996). To eliminate small deviations from one in the *XRCA* index, ESGs are classified into categories: (a) those with a value of *XRCA* greater than one standard deviation above one, "specialization"; (b) those with a value of *XRCA* index within a standard deviation of one, "balance"; (c) those with a value of *XRCA* index at least one standard deviation below one, "nonspecialization"; where the standard deviation is computed for each commodity's *XRCA* time series. This categorization is then applied to the first and last years of the data. Using the normalized trade volume computed earlier as the weight, we obtain the weighted "standardized" version of Tables.

The result shows that the majority of the ESGs commodities that have the status of "specialization", "balance", or "nonspecialization" in the first year remain in the same position in the last year for all the countries of interest. Those ESGs that switch their position from "specialization" in the first year to "balance" or "nonspecialization" in the last year again account for no more than 15% of the total ESG trade volume for most countries except Japan, Mexico, France and Poland. If one takes account of those ESGs that switch their positions from "balance" in the beginning year to "nonspecialization" in the final year, the ESGs that show a decline in their competitiveness still account for less than 15% for the majority of the countries except Japan, Mexico, France, Poland, Norway and China, which have a reduction of around 20%. This result is quite consistent with the result obtained from the simple dichotomous measures of Tables.

Another check on the robustness of this finding is to calculate the unweighted version of histogram of *years in "specialization"* for each country. Instead of the normalized trade volume that corresponds to the cells they belong to in the histogram, the number of commodities is used in the calculation of cell entry. The results also show a bimodality for most countries.

One caveat is in order. While the *XRCA* index can be distorted by domestic or international protection, international protection may be more significant than domestic protection for exports of ESGs. In either case, this distortion would underestimate the *XRCA* index especially for developed countries whose average tariff levels are relatively lower than those of developing countries. This will lead to an underestimation of the percentage share of those commodities with a downturn from a position of "specialization" to "nonspecialization."

If one looks at the changing pattern of those trade volumes that move from "nonspecialization" to "specialization," however, these trade volumes always exceed trade volumes that move from "specialization" to "nonspecialization" for the majority of the countries except for Japan, Norway and China, as discussed in the fifth section. This finding can thus be considered to be even more robust.

7. CONCLUSION

In this paper, I examine whether the pattern of export performance of environmentally sensitive goods underwent systematic changes in the period between the 1960s to the 1990s. A comprehensive dataset of trade flows of ESGs disaggregated to the four-digit level of the Standard International Trade Classification, for 1965–95 for 34 reporter countries is employed. These 34 reporter countries accounted for nearly 80% of world exports of ESGs in 1995. It is therefore to be expected that this analysis will provide a full picture of the changing performance of ESGs over time. Two different means to break down the export performance data of ESGs, using a histogram and time series pattern, have been employed to examine the pattern of export performance of ESGs between the beginning (1965) and end year (1995), as well as in the intervening years.

The important empirical finding is that the export performance of ESGs for most countries remained unchanged between the 1960s and the 1990s despite the introduction of stringent environmental standards in most of the developed countries in the 1970s and the 1980s. This result suggests that the claim that higher environmental standards reduce the "international competitiveness" of ESGs cannot be justified easily, at least on the basis of this examination of the data.

Since the relationship between environmental standards and international competitiveness has been treated as mutually exclusive theoretically (Pethig, 1976; McGuire, 1982; Palmer, Oates and Portney, 1995), the persistence of ESG export performance deserves closer scrutiny.

NOTES

1. See Anderson and Blackhurst (1992), Dean (1992) and Low and Yeats (1992).

2. See Bhagwati and Hudec (1996).

3. See section 3 for the definition of the RCA index.

4. The concept of 'international competitiveness' in this paper is loosely defined as refering to the industry level. See Warr (1994) for a discussion of this concept.

5. For an excellent discussion of this issue, see Bhagwati and Hudec (1996). See also Anderson and Blackhurst (1992).

6. See Warr (1994) for a comparison of the concepts of "comparative advantage" and "competitiveness".

7. See Mani and Wheeler (1997).

8. Low and Yeats (1992). Tobey (1990) used a similar definition of environmentally sensitive goods.

9. I focus on the SITC four-digit level rather than five-digit level because data for some commodities stop at the four-digit level without any further disaggregation. The data used in this study are taken from the United Nations trade database from International Economic Databank, the Australian National University.

10. Except Hungary, Czech Republic, Turkey and Iceland.

11. Gagnon and Rose (1995) used similar methodology to test product cycle theory.

12. See Ballance, Forstner and Murray (1987 for detailed discussion of alternative RCA indices.

13. The formula for Kendall's tau-b is as follows: tau-b $= (P-Q)/((w_r w_c)^{1/2})$, where $P = \sum_i \sum_j n_{ij} A_{ij}$ (twice the number of concordances), $Q = \sum_i \sum_j n_{ij} D_{ij}$ (twice the number of disconcordances), $A_{ij} = \sum_{k>i} \sum_{l>j} n_{kl} + \sum_{k<i} \sum_{l<j} n_{kl}$, $D_{ij} = \sum_{k>i} \sum_{l<j} n_{kl} + \sum_{k<i} \sum_{l>j} n_{kl}$, $w_r = n^2 - \sum_i n_i^2$ and $w_c = n^2 - \sum_j n_j^2$. See Kendall and Stuart (1979).

14. The Spearman correlation test statistic does not take tied pairs into account.

15. Mexico is on the margin, i.e. 15.75%.

16. The United States is on the margin with 14.34% to 14.16%.

REFERENCES

Anderson, K. and Blackhurst, R. (1992) *The Greening of World Trade Issues*. University of Michigan Press, Ann Arbor.

Balassa, B. (1989) Comparative advantage, trade policy and economic development: introduction–an autobiographical essay. In *Comparative Advantage, Trade Policy and Economic Development*, ed. Bela Balassa, pp. xv–xxv. University Press, New York.

Ballance, R. H., Forstner, H. and Murray, T. (1987) Consistency tests of alternative measures of comparative advantage. *Review of Economics and Statistics* **69** (1), 157–161.

Bhagwati, J. and Hudec, R. (1996) *Fair Trade and Harmonization: Prerequisites for Free Trade?* MIT Press, Cambridge and London.

Carolan, T., Singh, N. and Talati, C. (1996) The composition of U.S.–East Asia trade and changing comparative advantage, mimeo, University of California at Santa Cruz.

Cropper, M. L. and Oates, W. E. (1992) Environmental economics: A survey. *Journal of Economic Literature* **30** (2), 675–740.

Dean, J. M. (1992) Trade and the environment: a survey of the literature. In *International Trade And The Environment*, ed. P. Low, pp. 15–28, World Bank Discussion Papers, no. 159. World Bank, Washington, DC.

Drysdale, P. (1988) *International Economic Pluralism: Economic Policy in East Asia and the Pacific*. Allen & Unwin, Sydney, Australia.

Drysdale, P. and Garnaut, R. (1982) Trade intensities and the analysis of bilateral trade flows in a many-country world. *Hitotsubashi Journal of Economics* **22** (2), 62–84.

Gagnon, J. E. and Rose, A. K. (1995) Dynamic persistence of industry trade balances: how pervasive is the product cycle. *Oxford Economic Papers* **47** (2), 229–248.

Grossman, G. M. and Krueger, A. B. (1993). Environmental impacts of a North American Free Trade Agreement. In *The U.S.–Mexico Free Trade Aggreement*, ed. P. Garber. MIT Press, Cambridge, MA.

Kalt, J. P. (1988) The impact of domestic environmental regulatory policies on US international competitiveness. In *International Competitiveness*, ed. A. M. Spence and H. A. Hazard, pp. 221–62. Harper and Row, Ballinger, Cambridge, MA.

Kendall, M. and Stuart, A. (1979) *The Advanced Theory of Statistics*. Charles Griffin & Company Limited, London.

Leonard, H. J. (1988) *Pollution and the Struggle for the World Product*. Cambridge University Press, Cambridge.

Levinson, A. (1996) Environmental regulations and industry location: international and domestic evidence. In *Fair Trade and Harmonization: Prerequisites for Free Trade?* Vol. 1, eds. J. Bhagwati and R. Hudec, pp. 429–458. MIT Press, Cambridge and London.

Low, P. and Yeats, A. (1992) Do "dirty" industries migrate? In *International Trade and the Environment*, ed. P. Low, pp. 89–103, World Bank Discussion Papers, NO. 159, World Bank, Washington, DC.

Mani, M., Wheeler, D. (1997) In search of pollution havens? Dirty industry in the world economy, 1960–1995. World Bank Policy Research Working Paper, World Bank, Washington, DC.

McGuire, M. C. (1982), Regulation, factor rewards, and international trade. *Journal of Public Economics* 17 (3), 335–54.

Pethig, R. (1976). Pollution, welfare, and environmental policy in the theory of comparative advantage. *Journal of Environmental Economics and Management* 2, 160–169.

Palmer, K., Oates, W. E. and Portney, P. R. (1995) Tightening environmental standards: the benefit–cost or the no-cost paradigm? *Journal of Economic Perspectives* 9 (4), 119–132.

Porter, M. E. and Linde, C. (1995) Toward a new conception of the environment–competitiveness relationship. *Journal of Economic Perspectives* 9 (4), 97–118.

Robison, H. D. (1988) Industrial pollution abatement: The impact on balance of trade. *Canadian Journal of Economics* 21 (1), 187–199.

Sorsa, P. (1994) Competitveness and environmental standards: Some exploratory results. World Bank Policy Research Working Paper 1249, World Bank, Washington, DC.

Tobey, J. A. (1990) The effects of domestic environmental policies on patterns of world trade: An empirical test. *Kyklos* 43 (2), 191–209.

Walter, I. (1982) Environmentally induced industrial relocation in developing countries. In *Environment and Trade*, ed. J. Seymour, J. Rubin and T. R. Graham, pp. 67–101. Allanheld, Osmun, and Co., Totowa, NJ.

Walter, I. and Ugelow, J. (1979) Environmental policies in developing countries. *Ambio* 8 (2, 3), 102–109.

Warr, P. G. (1994) Comparative and competitive advantage. *Asian Pacific Economic Literature* 8 (2), 1–14.

[15]

Industrial pollution abatement: the impact on balance of trade

H. DAVID ROBISON Louisiana Tech University

Abstract. This paper uses an ex-post partial-equilibrium framework to measure the impact of marginal changes in industrial pollution abatement costs on the U.S. balance of trade in general, and balance of trade with Canada in particular. The impacts are found to be negative for most industries, growing with trade volume, and small relative to domestic consumption. In addition, some evidence is found that pollution control programs have changed the U.S. comparative advantage such that more high-abatement-cost goods are imported and more low-abatement-cost goods are exported.

La réduction de la pollution industrielle: l'impact sur la balance commerciale. Ce mémoire utilise un cadre d'analyse d'équilibre partiel ex-post pour calibrer l'impact de changements à la marge dans les coûts de la réduction de la pollution industrielle sur la balance commerciale des Etats-Unis et en particulier sur la balance commerciale avec le Canada. Il appert que les impacts sont négatifs pour la plupart des industries, qu'ils croissent avec la taille des flux commerciaux, et qu'ils sont petits relativement à la consommation domestique. De plus, il semble que les programmes de lutte à la pollution ont transformé l'avantage comparatif des Etats-Unis de telle manière qu'on importe davantage de biens pour lesquels les coûts de réduction de la pollution sont élevés et qu'on exporte davantage de biens pour lesquels ces coûts sont bas.

Although economists agree that, by raising the prices of domestically produced products, pollution abatement expenditures alter a country's comparative advantage and trading pattern, no formal measurement of the impact has been made. This paper attempts to measure on an ex post basis the impact of marginal changes in industrial pollution abatement on U.S. balance of trade in general, and balance of trade with Canada as a special case. More specifically, Baumol and Oates's (1975) theoretical work on the trade impacts of industrial

I would like to thank Wallace Oates, Clopper Almon, Matt Hyle, Ralph Monaco, Margaret McCarthy, and Don Meyer for their helpful comments on earlier drafts. I would also like to thank Douglas Nyhus and Lorraine Sullivan of the INFORUM staff for their assistance with some of the data work.

pollution abatement is extended from a two final-good model to a seventy-eight sector model with all interindustry effects considered. Using this extended model, measurements of the trade impacts of marginal increases in abatement expenditures are made for each sector. These measurements are an upper bound to potential impacts on the balance of trade because all mitigating variables such as improved terms of trade, offsetting governmental policies, and adjustments in exchange rates are ignored. The results for 1977 range from $-0.1 through $-80.9 to $-566.6 million for transportation services, electric utilities, and ferrous metals, respectively.

In addition, this paper uses Walter's (1973) concept of the abatement content of trade to test the proposition, discussed by Baumol and Oates among others,[1] that undertaking pollution abatement will reduce the abating country's comparative advantage in producing high-abatement-cost goods and improve the comparative advantage in low-abatement-cost goods. Results indicate that the abatement content of imports has grown more rapidly than that of exports, thus supporting this proposition.

Baumol and Oates define and discuss the conditions by which increased industrial abatement costs can improve or hurt a country's balance of trade in a two-country, two-good world.[2] No intermediate product flows are considered in the Baumol-Oates world, which would be sufficient if most abatement costs were incurred in producing final goods. However, most industrial pollution abatement (IPA) costs occur at basic levels of production, requiring the incorporation of interindustry effects, as is done in this study.

Measuring the price changes caused by IPA is a straightforward application of input-output analysis as discussed in Leontieff (1970) and performed in Walter (1973), Pasurka (1984), and Robison (1985). The Robison method for measuring the price change is used in the current study.

A general-equilibrium framework, including an input-output table, would seem the appropriate approach for this type of study. D'Arge (1971), Mutti and Richardson (1977), Evans (1973), and two commercial economic consulting firms[3] provide 'general equilibrium' based forecasting studies designed to examine the impact of IPA on the macro economy and trade. There are, however, at least two problems with each of these studies. First, because the studies use ex-ante forecasting, they must assume or estimate abatement costs. Second, assumptions are made as to how the abatement costs are allocated between return to capital, labour, etc. in order to run the forecasting routines.[4]

---

1 See D'Arge (1971), Mutti and Richardson (1977), and Magee and Ford (1972) for additional discussions.
2 A less general approach to this issue can be found in Magee and Ford (1972).
3 These forecasts are discussed in Portney (1981).
4 A third problem, argued by Dorfman (1973) in response to Evans (1973) but not treated in the current study, is that there will never be a true general-equilibrium model until pollution emitted by all sources is included in the production functions of all industries. Given this point, a partial equilibrium framework is the only alternative.

By choosing an ex post partial-equilibrium approach, these problems are avoided.

MODEL FRAMEWORK

The Baumol and Oates work derives the balance of trade conditions for a two-good two-country world. In doing so, one good has pollution associated with its production, while the other does not. In this simple world only direct abatement costs affect prices and trade. Here more general conditions are derived for the seventy-eight industries of the INFORUM interindustry macro model.

The balance of trade is obtained by

$$BT = \sum_{i=1}^{78} (P_i EX_i - P_i IM_i), \qquad (1)$$

where

BT = balance of trade

P_i = US domestic price of good i

EX_i = US exports for sector i

IM_i = US imports for sector i

$i = 1, 2, 3, \ldots, 78$.

If environmental regulations affect the price of products produced by industry j, the change in the balance of trade is found by

$$\partial BT/\partial P_j = \sum_{i=1}^{78} [(\partial P_i/\partial P_j) EX_i + P_i (\partial EX_i/\partial P_j)$$
$$- (\partial P_i/\partial P_j) IM_i - P_i (\partial IM_i/\partial P_j)]. \qquad (2)$$

Note:

$$(\partial EX_i/\partial P_j) = (\partial EX_i/\partial P_i)(\partial P_i/\partial P_j), \qquad (3)$$

and

$$(\partial IM_i/\partial P_j) = (\partial IM_i/\partial P_i)(\partial P_i/\partial P_j), \qquad (4)$$

substituting (3) and (4) into (2) and rewriting:

$$\partial BT/\partial P_j = \sum_{i=1}^{78} [(1 + \eta_i E) EX_i(\% \Delta P_i/\% \Delta P_j)(P_i/P_j)$$
$$- (1 + \eta_i I) IM_i (\% \Delta P_i/\% \Delta P_j)(P_i/P_j)]. \qquad (5)$$

where

$\eta_i E$ = export own price elasticity for industry i

$\eta_i I$ = import own price elasticity for industry i.

In equation (5) the ratios of the percentage change in price of good i to the percentage change in price of good j are the terms through which the interindustry impacts are felt. These terms are the j, ith coefficient in the total requirements matrix.[5] Thus, exports of industry i are indirectly affected by a change in the price of good j.

The abatement induced price increase for industry j can increase or decrease export revenues depending on the export price elasticities, export volume, the coefficients of the jth row of the total requirements matrix, and industry prices. The impact of a change in the price of industry j on the export revenues of each industry i is found by multiplying exports of i times the j, ith element of the total requirements matrix times the price ratio times one plus $\eta_i E$. Revenues will rise, remain constant, or fall if $\eta_i E$ is greater than, equal to, or less that -1, respectively.

The dollar value of imports will rise for two reasons. First, with a higher domestic price more goods will be imported. Second, higher domestic prices will permit foreign producers to charge higher prices for the larger quantity they are shipping to the United States. Obviously, the lower the import price elasticity is, the smaller the impact on the balance of trade.

In order for an abatement cost induced change in the price of industry j to have a positive net effect on the balance of trade, the export impact must be positive and greater than the import impact. While not the case in the current study, this condition might occur if the import and export price elasticities for all sectors were small in absolute value. It might also occur if the United States exports several times more of product j than it imports (a strong net exporter), with low export and import price elasticities.

The assumption of full-cost pass-through into prices is reasonable in the long run. Alternate assumptions and their implications are discussed in detail in Lake, Hanneman, and Oster (1979), but a summary is warranted. Greater than full-cost pass-through is possible in oligopolistic industries. This non-competitive behaviour has the effect of encouraging more foreign firms to compete for domestic markets than would simple cost pass-through. Conversely, foreign firms would be discouraged from competing in U.S. markets by price increases smaller than cost increases, as might occur in highly competitive

---

[5] This simple result comes from the input-output price determination equation: $p = pA + v$, where: p = vector of 78 sector prices; v = vector of 78 sector value added; A = 78 by 78 input-output coefficient matrix. Solving this equation for prices: $p = (I - A)^{-1}v$. A change in industrial pollution abatement for a sector changes the value added for that sector and prices of all sectors according to the coefficients of the total requirements matrix, $(I - A)^{-1}$.

industries. Use of the full-cost pass-through assumption helps ensure that the estimates are, in fact, upper bounds.

Most studies using input-output to measure price changes caused by environmental regulations simply multiply the abatement cost vector by the standard total requirements matrix (see, e.g., Pasurka, 1984; Mutti and Richardson, 1977; Walter, 1973). This approach misses a small portion of abatement costs, those implicit in capital goods used in the production process. To account for these additional costs, a 'capital-included' total requirements matrix is formed following the method described in Robison (1985). The general procedure is to add to the standard coefficient 'A' matrix a capital flows coefficient, or 'B' matrix that has been scaled so that the columns sum to the depreciation to output ratio of that industry. Given this modified A matrix, called A^*, the capital-included total requirements matrix is formed $(I - A^*)^{-1}$. Each j, i element of the total requirements shows the percentage price increase for industry i caused by a one percent increase in the price of input j.

DATA

All economic data and the estimated import and export price elasticities are provided by the INFORUM project.[6] A discussion of the general form of the merchandise import and export equations can be found in Almon, et al. (1974), while modifications, recent estimation results, and the non-merchandise equations are described in the INFORUM staff paper (1986).[7]

Abatement costs for each firm are defined as including only the costs of abating pollution generated by the firm, not the cost of abatement equipment built into the goods the firm produces. For example, the costs of abatement equipment built in U.S. automobiles are classified as being incurred by the auto's purchaser, not the producer.

The abatement data for the manufacturing sectors are taken from *Pollution Abatement Costs and Expenditures* for 1973, 1977, and 1983 (1976, 1979, 1984). No annual operating cost data are available for the non-manufacturing sectors. Capital expenditures on abatement equipment are, however, available for non-manufacturing in *The Survey of Current Business* (1984, 1978, 1980). Operating costs are approximated by assuming that the ratio of capital expenditures for abatement equipment to annual operating costs is the same for non-manufacturing as for manufacturing.[8]

[6] INFORUM is the Interindustry Forecasting Project of The University of Maryland.
[7] The general forms of the merchandise trade equations are $M_t = (a + bD_t)P_t^\eta$ and $E_t = (a + bF_t)P_t^\eta$ where: M_t = imports in domestic-port prices; D_t = domestic demand for the product; P_t = the effective ratio of the foreign price to the domestic price; η = the price elasticity; E_t = exports; F_t = foreign demand index. The non-merchandise equations are too sector specific to present a general form. See Almon (1974) and INFORUM staff (1986) for details.
[8] More detailed information about the data is available from the author upon request.

TABLE 1

Average abatement content of U.S. trade (1.00 Means 1 cent per dollar)

	1973	1977	1982
Total U.S. imports	0.428	0.628	0.993
Total U.S. exports	0.372	0.538	0.715
Total U.S. output	0.499	0.692	0.927
Ratio of import content to export content	1.151	1.167	1.389
U.S. imports from Canada[a]	0.652	0.971	1.512
U.S. exports to Canada[a]	0.586	0.893	1.319
Ratio of import content to export content	1.113	1.087	1.146

a U.S.-Canada trade data is available only for the merchandise sectors. For this reason, the results are not directly comparable to the total trade figures.

RESULTS

The two major findings of this study are much as expected. First, there is some evidence that U.S. pollution control programs have changed the U.S. comparative advantage such that more high-abatement-cost goods will be imported and more low-abatement-cost goods exported. Second, the impact on the U.S. balance of trade of marginal changes in IPA is negative for most industries, growing with trade volume, and small relative to domestic consumption.

Table 1 presents the average abatement content of U.S. total and U.S.-Canadian trade for the years 1973, 1977, and 1982 as well as the average abatement content of U.S. output.[9] No detailed abatement data are available for countries (including Canada) for which similar input output tables are available. Hence, what is reported as abatement content of imports is, in fact, the abatement content of the goods had they been produced in the United States. Because of this data restriction, a rise in the abatement content of imports relative to exports indicates that the United States is importing goods with high U.S. abatement costs.

While the level of abatement costs implicit in both imports and exports rose rapidly over the period, they rose relatively more quickly for total imports than total exports. Relative shifts can be seen by looking at the ratio of import to export abatement content, which rose from 1.17 to 1.39 between 1977 and 1982. The rise in the abatement content ratio clearly indicates a shift towards importing goods with high U.S. abatement costs. Further evidence of a shift in comparative advantage is found in comparing the abatement content of U.S. exports, imports, and output. Over the 1973 to 1982 period the abatement costs implicit in U.S. exports and output grew proportionately. The abatement content of imports grew more quickly, rising above that of output in 1982.

9 A 1972 input-output table is used for the 1973 computations. The 1977 input-output table is also used for the 1982 computations, given that no 1982 table is available.

Thus, in 1982, the average dollar's worth of imports had more abatement costs implicit in it than the average dollar's worth of u.s. output. Stated another way, if the United States had produced the goods it imported, the average abatement content of u.s. output would have been higher.

Table 1 shows virtually no change in the abatement content ratio for u.s.-Canadian trade, thus implying no major shift in trading pattern. Given Canada's adoption of environmental quality regulations, this result is not surprising. In total trade, rising u.s. abatement costs increased the price differential for some products relative to countries with little or no environmental regulation and induced a change in the trading pattern. Canada, by adopting environmental regulations, prevented the price differential and corresponding shift in trading pattern from occurring. The Canadian results also suggest that the trading pattern shift is stronger for all other countries than in indicated in table 1. No shift is apparent for trade with Canada, which accounts for approximately 15 per cent of all u.s. trade. Thus, to get the total trade shift of table 1, the change in trading patterns with all other countries must be greater than the average indicated.

Table 2 presents the results of equation (5) for selected sectors under the assumption that additional abatement costs raised the sectoral price by 1 per cent. Thus, the value of -245.1 for the agricultural products sector indicates that, if additional abatement costs raised the price of agricultural products holding everything else constant, the u.s. balance of trade would have been reduced by at most $245.1 million. Of the $245.1 million impact, $95.8 million is attributed to reduced agricultural exports and increased agricultural imports, while the remainder is the result of indirect effects of agricultural prices on other sectoral prices.

As can be seen in table 2, the direct impacts are large relative to indirect impacts in most manufacturing sectors such as food and tobacco, ferrous metals, and motor vehicles. The indirect effects are relatively large for service sectors such as gas utilities, retail trade, and business services. The importance of the indirect effects is best exemplified by electrical utilities (sector 56), which has large abatement costs but a small trade volume. A 1 per cent increase in the price of electrical utilities would have only a $-1.5 million direct impact on the balance of trade, yet an $-80.9 million total impact.

Table 2 and appendix tables A1 and A2 strongly support most economists' intuitive position that higher abatement costs will reduce the u.s. balance of trade. The only sectors with positive impacts on the trade balance are coal mining (1973 and 1982 for all trade, and all years for trade with Canada), transportation services (1973 for all trade), and special industry machinery (1973 and 1982 for trade with Canada). All three sectors have low export and import elasticities, and the United States is a strong exporter of coal and transportation services. In trade with Canada, the United States is a strong net exporter of special industry machinery, whereas in total trade the United States is a net importer.

TABLE 2
Impacts on U.S. balance of trade for 1 per cent price increases (in millions of 1977 dollars)

	Total U.S.		U.S.-Canadian		Total U.S. domestic consumption
	Direct impact	Total impact	Direct impact	Total impact	
1 Agriculture	−95.8	−245.1	−52.3	−71.9	133,273.
2 Iron ore mining	−12.8	−41.0	−7.4	−12.7	3,567.
4 Coal mining	22.1	−6.3	8.1	2.1	16,701.
6 Crude petroleum	−316.4	−434.5	−16.7	−36.0	64,920.
9 Food and tobacco	−249.4	−285.8	−17.3	−28.2	210,733.
13 Paper	−111.0	−180.0	−75.4	−86.0	52,294.
15 Agricultural fertilizers	−5.6	−25.2	−8.3	−13.7	10,523.
16 Other chemicals	−132.5	−314.6	−26.9	−63.3	99,808.
17 Petroleum refining	−82.0	−201.5	−5.2	−32.3	104,290.
20 Plastic products	−24.3	−78.6	−6.1	−16.2	24,206.
24 Stone, clay & glass	−46.5	−83.1	−5.6	−12.9	35,462.
25 Ferrous metals	−376.4	−566.5	−54.5	−106.7	71,719.
26 Copper	−28.2	−64.4	−4.9	−14.0	9,300.
27 Other nonferrous metals	−76.0	−172.5	−26.8	−47.4	35,033.
28 Metal products	−91.4	−219.8	−22.1	−54.8	86,228.
29 Engines & turbines	−13.3	−28.9	−9.1	−13.4	9,454.
32 Metalworking machinery	−15.3	−42.3	−1.6	−7.4	13,734.
33 Special industry machinery	4.9	−4.5	2.9	1.1	7,547.
35 Computers	−29.5	−34.4	−6.6	−7.5	10,424.
40 Household appliances	−20.1	−22.7	−1.2	−1.8	10,728.
42 TV, radio & phonographs	−50.9	−52.5	−4.0	−4.6	9,492.
43 Motor vehicles	−285.5	−330.2	−119.2	−126.5	128,208.
54 Transportation services	3.3	−0.1	a	−0.5	2,025.
55 Communication services	−7.5	−50.4	a	−7.9	60,105.
56 Electrical utilities	−1.5	−80.9	a	−17.2	63,568.
57 Gas utilities	−3.0	−62.0	a	−13.4	46,708.
60 Retail trade	−0.4	−11.2	a	−2.0	194,613.
61 Eating & drinking places	0.0	−33.4	a	−6.5	87,819.
62 Finance & insurance	−9.0	−57.0	a	−9.5	127,952.
66 Business services	−17.7	−210.9	a	−37.1	161,049.

a No direct effects can be measured, owing to data limitations.

Relative to domestic consumption of the respective sector, the impacts on the balance of trade are quite small, with a range of 0.006 per cent (retail trade) to 0.8 per cent (ferrous metals). When measured as a percentage of total U.S. trade (exports plus imports) of individual sectors, the impacts range from −0.12 per cent (special industry machinery) to −7.08 per cent (copper) for the

TABLE 3

Total impact of industrial pollution abatement on trade (in millions of 1977 dollars)

	1973	1977	1982
Total trade			
U.S. export impact	−133.5	−258.8	−426.3
U.S. import impact	−1,247.9	−2,133.5	−3,978.9
Total trade impact	−1,381.4	−2,392.3	−4,405.3
Total U.S. trade volume	256,405.0	354,895.0	453,825.0
U.S.-Canadian trade			
Export impact	−33.7	−63.2	−64.0
Import impact	−303.7	−480.8	−786.0
Total trade impact	−337.4	−544.0	−850.0
U.S.-Canadian trade volume	48,467.0	53,413.0	51,733.0

merchandise sectors, with an average of −2.69 per cent. For trade with Canada, the impacts range from 0.2 (coal mining) to −8.9 (petroleum refining) per cent, with an average of −2.53 per cent.

Table 2 also provides a measure of a side benefit derived from the U.S. governmental policy of paying a large portion of farmers' abatement costs. If this program held agricultural prices down by 1 per cent, the 1977 U.S. balance of trade was improved by $245.1 million.

Little can be said about the growth in the effects shown in tables A1 and A2. Although additional abatement costs will have an impact on trade patterns, other influences such as macro-economic policies and influences of changing exchange rates make it impossible to determine exactly what portion of the shifts can be attributed to increased abatement costs.

Table 3 presents estimates of the total impact of IPA on the balance of trade under the assumption that the INFORUM import and export price elasticities hold for the full price change. In addition, all general equilibrium mitigating effects that might occur through changes in income or exchange rates are ignored. Therefore, these estimates should be the maximum potential effects. Given these caveats, the net reduction in the balance of trade for 1977 is $2,392.3 million for all trade and $544 million for trade with Canada. These figures are 0.67 and 1.02 per cent of the respective trade volumes.

The total impacts found in this study are above those forecasted in Evans (1973) and the Chase Econometrics (1981) studies but below those in the Data Resources Study (1981). The most striking difference between the current study and previous work is the growth in the size of IPA's impact over time. This study finds the impact grew by 218.9 per cent in constant dollars between 1973 and 1982, compared with a high of 28 per cent (the Data Resources study) among the other studies. The tremendous difference may in part be due to general equilibrium effects in the forecasting studies, but it is likely that these studies mis-estimated both the size of IPA costs and the length of the adjustment period.

CONCLUDING REMARKS

By providing a framework for examining the impact industrial pollution abatement has on the U.S. balance of trade, this paper has moved one step towards a more accurate assessment of U.S. environmental policy. General conditions for positive and negative impacts are derived in an interindustry framework under the assumption of full cost pass-through. This framework establishes an upper bound for the impact by explicitly ignoring all offsetting general-equilibrium effects such as changes in exchange rates. The statistical results indicate that marginal changes in IPA will reduce the U.S. balance of trade for all but a few industries. In addition, empirical support is found for the proposition that IPA is inducing changes in the U.S. comparative advantage such that the abatement content of imported goods is rising relative to that of exported goods.

The implications of this work for U.S. policy makers are fairly obvious. First, marginal changes in abatement costs, such as those resulting from the recent acid-rain talks with Canada, will result in a reduction in the U.S. balance of trade. Second, the inefficiency of the current regulatory system contributes substantially to the impact on the balance of trade. A 1982 Government Accounting Office report (1982) suggests that, if a more efficient regulatory scheme were used, air pollution abatement costs could be reduced 40 to 90 per cent, which would in turn improve the U.S. balance of trade. Finally, the adoption of similar environmental regulations by other countries will reduce the impact on the trade balance, although high-abatement-cost industries are likely to move to countries that do not adopt an environmental policy.

REFERENCES

Almon, Clopper Jr, Margaret Buckler, Lawrence Horwitz, and Thomas Reimbold (1974) *1985: Interindustry Forecasts of the American Economy* (Lexington, MA: Lexington Books)

Baumol, William J. and Wallace E. Oates (1975) *The Theory of Environmental Policy* (New Jersey: Prentice-Hall Inc.)

D'Arge, Ralph C. (1971) 'International Trade, Domestic Income, and Environmental Controls: Some Empirical Estimates.' In *Managing the Environment* edited by Allen V. Kneese, Sidney E. Rolfe, and Joseph W. Harned (New York: Praeger Publishers)

Dorfman, Robert (1973) Discussion of presented papers. *American Economic Review* 63, 253–6

Evans, Michael K. (1973) 'A forecasting model applied to pollution control costs.' *American Economic Review* 63, 244–52
INFORUM Staff (1986) 'The INFORUM models: a closer look.' INFORUM Research Report No. 75
Lake, Elizabeth E., William M. Hanneman, and Sharon M. Oster (1979) *Who Pays for Clean Water? The Distribution of Water Pollution Control Costs* (Boulder, CO: Westview Press)
Leontief, Wassily (1970) 'Environmental repercussions and the economic structure: an input-output approach.' *The Review of Economics and Statistics* 52, 262–71
Magee, Stephen P. and William F. Ford (1972) 'Environmental pollution, the terms of trade and the balance of payments.' *Kyklos* 25, 101–18
Mutti, John H. and David J. Richardson (1977) 'International competitive displacement from environmental control: the quantitative gains from methodological refinement.' *Journal of Environmental Economics and Management* 4, 135–52
Pasurka, Carl A. (1984) 'The short-run impact of environmental protection costs on U.S. product prices.' *Journal of Environmental Economics and Management* 11, 380–90
Portney, Paul R. (1981) 'The macro-economic impacts of federal environmental regulation.' In Henry M. Peskin, Paul R. Portney, and Allen V. Kneese, eds, *Environmental Regulation and the U.S. Economy* (Baltimore: Johns Hopkins University Press)
Robison, H. David (1985) 'Who pays for industrial pollution abatement?' *Review of Economics and Statistics* 67, 702–6
Russo, William J. and Gary L. Rutledge (1984) 'Plant and equipment expenditures by business for pollution abatement, 1983 and planned 1984.' *Survey of Current Business* 64, 31–4
Rutledge, Gary L., F.J. Dreiling, and B.C. Dunlap (1978) 'Capital Expenditures by Business for Pollution Abatement 1973–7 and Planned 1978.' *Survey of Current Business* 58, 33–8
Rutledge, Gary L. and Betsy O'Connor (1980) 'Capital expenditures by business for pollution abatement, 1977, 1978, and planned 1979.' *Survey of Current Business* 60, 19–22
U.S. Bureau of the Census (1976) *Pollution Abatement Costs and Expenditures 1973* (Washington, D.C.: U.S. Government Printing Office)
U.S. Bureau of the Census (1979) *Pollution Abatement Costs and Expenditures 1977* (Washington, D.C.: U.S. Government Printing Office)
U.S. Bureau of the Census (1984) *Pollution Abatement Costs and Expenditures 1982* (Washington, D.C.: U.S. Government Printing Office)
U.S. General Accounting Office (1982) *A Market Approach to Air Pollution Control Could Reduce Compliance Costs Without Jeopardizing Clean Air Goals* (Washington, D.C.: U.S. Government Printing Office)
Walter, Ingo (1973) 'The pollution content of American trade.' *Western Economic Journal* 11, 61–70

APPENDIX

TABLE A1

Impacts on U.S. balance of trade for 1 per cent price increases (in millions of 1977 dollars)

	1973	1977	1982
1 Agriculture	−258.3	−245.1	−295.0
2 Iron ore mining	−27.4	−41.0	−41.5
4 Coal mining	4.6	−6.3	5.8
6 Crude petroleum	−225.0	−434.5	−469.7
9 Food and tobacco	−249.4	−285.8	−319.7
13 Paper	−151.6	−180.0	−221.8
15 Agricultural fertilizers	−8.4	−25.2	−25.7
16 Other chemicals	−210.5	−314.6	−445.7
17 Petroleum refining	−149.3	−201.5	−335.3
20 Plastic products	−43.5	−78.6	−111.3
24 Stone, clay & glass	−74.1	−83.1	−108.7
25 Ferrous metals	−429.2	−566.5	−651.1
26 Copper	−65.9	−64.4	−78.0
27 Other nonferrous metals	−127.1	−172.5	−251.1
28 Metal products	−167.7	−219.8	−284.3
29 Engines & turbines	−22.0	−28.9	−46.3
32 Metalworking machinery	−33.0	−42.3	−71.8
33 Special industry machinery	−6.9	−4.5	−32.3
35 Computers	−29.4	−34.4	−97.2
40 Household appliances	−17.7	−22.7	−27.0
42 TV, radio & phonographs	−47.0	−52.5	−70.1
43 Motor vehicles	−269.0	−330.2	−438.9
54 Transportation services	0.7	−0.1	−1.8
55 Communication services	−47.7	−50.4	−65.1
56 Electrical utilities	−43.1	−80.9	−126.9
57 Gas utilities	−25.9	−62.0	−108.6
60 Retail trade	−10.0	−11.2	−13.0
61 Eating & drinking places	−29.4	−33.4	−50.1
62 Finance & insurance	−60.8	−57.0	−72.7
66 Business services	−173.2	−210.9	−284.7

TABLE A2

Impacts on U.S. balance of trade with Canada for 1 per cent price increases (in millions of 1977 dollars)

	1973	1977	1982
1 Agriculture	−76.6	−71.9	−82.3
2 Iron ore mining	−8.4	−12.7	−11.9
4 Coal mining	3.1	2.1	0.8
6 Crude petroleum	−49.1	−36.0	−58.1
9 Food and tobacco	−26.8	−28.2	−31.1
13 Paper	−78.2	−86.0	−90.7
15 Agricultural fertilizers	−7.1	−13.7	−13.0
16 Other chemicals	−47.2	−63.3	−86.3
17 Petroleum refining	−23.5	−32.3	−56.0
20 Plastic products	−11.6	−16.2	−18.1
24 Stone, clay & glass	−12.8	−12.9	−13.4
25 Ferrous metals	−78.7	−106.7	−104.4
26 Copper	−19.8	−14.0	−13.6
27 Other nonferrous metals	−45.5	−47.4	−50.0
28 Metal products	−45.1	−54.8	−60.8
29 Engines & turbines	−11.1	−13.4	−10.6
32 Metalworking machinery	−7.0	−7.4	−8.9
33 Special industry machinery	1.2	1.1	−0.4
35 Computers	−6.5	−7.5	−7.6
40 Household appliances	−1.7	−1.8	−2.1
42 TV, radio & phonographs	−4.3	−4.6	−5.6
43 Motor vehicles	−96.3	−126.5	−136.1
54 Transportation services[a]	−0.3	−0.5	−0.7
55 Communication services[a]	−9.2	−7.9	−8.2
56 Electrical utilities[a]	−10.2	−17.2	−22.6
57 Gas utilities[a]	−5.3	−13.4	−20.5
60 Retail trade[a]	−2.3	−2.0	−2.1
61 Eating & drinking places[a]	−6.8	−6.5	−7.8
62 Finance & insurance[a]	−11.9	−9.5	−10.1
66 Business services[a]	−35.9	−37.1	−42.8

[a] Includes only the indirect impacts on merchandise sectors due to data limitations.

Part V
Miscellaneous Effects

Plant Closures

[16]

Enforcement of Pollution Regulations in a Declining Industry[1]

MARY E. DEILY

Department of Economics, Rauch Business Center 37, Lehigh University, Bethlehem, Pennsylvania 18015

AND

WAYNE B. GRAY

Department of Economics, Clark University, 950 Main St., Worcester, Massachusetts 01610

Received October 30, 1990; revised April 1, 1991

A regulatory agency enforcing compliance in a declining industry might recognize that certain plants would close rather than comply, imposing large costs on the local community. Data on EPA enforcement activity in the U.S. steel industry are examined for evidence of this with a two-equation model linking EPA enforcement decisions and firms' plant-closing decisions. The results indicate that the EPA directed fewer enforcement actions toward plants with a high predicted probability of closing and plants that were major employers in their community; also, plants predicted to face relatively heavy enforcement were more likely to close. © 1991 Academic Press, Inc.

I. INTRODUCTION

Previous research has established that pollution-control legislation and regulations favor struggling industries and slower-growing regions. The government's sensitivity to politically awkward trade-offs between pollution control and jobs reveals itself in special deals stretching out the compliance schedules of individual industries, in regulations biased against new sources, and in congressional voting patterns on policies like PSD (prevention of significant deterioration) (Crandall [4]; Pashigian [25]).[2] Given this history, it seems likely that the potential political costs of pollution control have also influenced regulators' enforcement decisions.

This paper presents the first empirical study of the EPA's enforcement activity at the plant level. We examine the EPA's enforcement actions at U.S. steel plants during the years 1977–1986 for evidence that enforcement was responsive to the possible economic disruption from plant closings.[3] During this period, the EPA faced the problem of enforcing new, higher air quality standards on an industry that was a major polluter, but that was also undergoing severe contraction. We

---

[1]Part of this research was completed while Mary E. Deily was a Visiting Scholar at the Federal Reserve Bank of Cleveland. Financial support was also provided by National Science Foundation grant SES-8921277.

[2]Also, see Eberts and Fogarty [9] for an estimate of the differences in the productivity cost of pollution regulation across regions.

[3]We use "EPA" in this paper to refer to both the individual state pollution agencies and the federal agency. Much of the enforcement is actually done by the state agencies, under EPA supervision.

estimate a simultaneous system of EPA enforcement decisions and firms' plant-closing decisions to test the hypothesis that the EPA directed less enforcement activity toward plants that were likely to close, or that were located where a closing would generate higher-than-average adjustment costs.

We model the regulator as wishing to reduce steel industry air pollution while at the same time avoiding the political costs of even appearing to be the deciding factor in a firm's plant-closing decision. Thus the expected political cost of enforcement depends on the probability that a plant will close and on the amount of local disruption that will occur if the plant does close. Firms, in turn, must decide which plants to close during the contraction, and they include a prediction of future enforcement activity by the EPA in their assessments of future plant profits.

We estimate our two-equation model using data on 49 plants, which together represented virtually all the capacity of the U.S. integrated steel industry in 1976.[4] While restricting our study to plants from a single industry reduces our sample size, it allows us to eliminate the possible effects of inter-industry variation, arising, for example, from technology or pollution control costs, that would be difficult to control.

The steel industry has several characteristics that make it an appropriate test case. First, the industry produces a great deal of pollution, forcing the EPA to take some action toward it.[5] Second, steel plants employ large amounts of workers, increasing the potential for large local adjustment costs. Third, the industry contracted sharply during the test period: of the 49 plants in our sample, 21 closed by 1987. Studying an industry undergoing such very sharp contraction increases the likelihood of observing EPA sensitivity to potential adjustment costs.

We discuss the model of EPA enforcement and firms' plant-closing decisions in Section II. In Section III we review the estimation procedures used and describe the specification. The results are discussed in Section IV, and Section V is the conclusion.

II. MODEL

Assume that new anti-pollution legislation tightening air quality standards is enacted. Assume further that one of the major polluters is an industry that is contracting because of declining demand. We first discuss the EPA enforcement decision in this situation, and then the firms' plant-closing decisions.

The Enforcement Decision

We use a model of regulatory behavior in which the regulator allocates enforcement resources so as to maximize net political support (Stigler [30]; Peltzman

---

[4]The steel industry can be roughly split into integrated firms and minimill firms. Unless otherwise stated, all references to the steel industry are references to the integrated firms.

[5]"The iron and steel industry... may be responsible for as much as 10 percent of all particulate air emissions...." "How Federal Policies Affect the Steel Industry: A Special Study," p. 43, Congressional Budget Office, U.S. Govt. Printing Office, Washington, DC (February 1987).

[26]).[6] We single out two main sources of political reaction to EPA activity. The first is the general public, which we assume would prefer reduced levels of pollution. Thus, other things equal, the regulator will attempt to reduce as much pollution as possible per unit of regulatory resource expended by directing more enforcement toward plants emitting higher levels of pollution.

The public's perceived benefit from pollution reduction may vary from place to place, however, depending on local conditions: we expect that support for reducing pollution will be greater in more heavily polluted areas. We thus predict more enforcement activity toward plants emitting more pollution, and toward plants in more polluted areas, ceteris paribus.[7]

As the benefits of pollution reduction are diffused across a largely unorganized general public, we expect that opposition to regulatory enforcement arising from smaller groups facing the possibility of sharp losses may have a stronger impact on enforcement decisions. One such potential loser is the firm: bringing a plant into compliance with regulations may impose costs in extra investment, increased operating costs, and reduced productivity.[8]

Given a set schedule of fines, a firm has more incentive to resist agency enforcement efforts the greater the cost is of bringing a plant into compliance. In the limit in which either the fines in the case of non-compliance or the costs of bringing the plant into full compliance reduce the present value of the plant below zero, the firm would shut down the plant rather than comply. The agency might thus find itself using scarce resources to enforce a compliance that could be very costly in terms of political support. We therefore predict that less enforcement activity will be directed toward plants requiring greater firm expenditures to bring into compliance in a declining industry, since inducing compliance has a higher expected cost in agency resources and in possible loss of political support.[9]

The second source of opposition to agency activity is employees and other local citizens that are threatened by a plant-closing. When plants close workers become unemployed and the local community loses income. In some cases local govern-

---

[6]Regulators could in principle have set less stringent standards for marginal plants (driven by the same goal of maximizing net political support). Fewer enforcement actions toward such plants might then reflect differences in initial standards, rather than in enforcement behavior. However, conversations with regulatory officials indicate that the State Implementation Plans developed in the 1970s did not include such accommodations for marginal plants. Since then, plant-specific exceptions have generally involved delays in required compliance dates rather than relaxation of the standards themselves.

[7]The benefits from enforcement would also be affected by the plant's compliance status, and firms' compliance decisions may well be affected by expected enforcement. In an earlier version of this paper (Deily and Gray [7]) we attempted to study steel firm compliance separately by including a third equation for this decision, in the manner of Bartel and Thomas [2]. We were unsuccessful, however, due to poor data on compliance status.

[8]See Crandall [4] and Gollup and Roberts [13]. See also Gray ([15, 16]) for evidence that industries facing heavy enforcement tended to have lower productivity growth.

[9]Such an outcome is not necessarily inefficient: as previous authors have noted, the net social benefit of pollution control is maximized if the EPA enforces regulations so as to equalize marginal abatement costs. See Gollup and Roberts [14], and the citations listed therein. However, an alternative possibility is that the regulatory agency is using a more sophisticated dynamic strategy that induces greater compliance by all firms by specifically concentrating on firms that do not comply, casting them into "purgatory," where they would receive more inspections and higher fines, and from whence they could escape only with continual compliance (Scholz [28]; Harrington [18]).

ments must reduce provision of such services as police and fire.[10] The political costs of having regulatory enforcement behavior cause, or even appear to cause, a plant to shut down may induce regulators to direct their enforcement toward plants for which the probability of closing, and the adjustment cost if closing occurs, are lower. Further, aside from the purely political considerations, it may be more efficient to avoid spending resources to enforce compliance at a plant that is likely to close, since time is likely to take care of the problem.

In summary, the regulatory agency enforces compliance across plants in a declining industry so as to reduce pollution at minimal political cost. The agency receives general political support for reducing pollution levels, but will enforce regulations less rigorously when the cost of bringing a plant into compliance is very high, or when a plant is in danger of closing anyway, particularly if adjustment costs for local communities associated with a plant-closing would be high.

The Plant-Closing Decision

Several recent articles have examined the factors that determine which plants exit from a contracting industry. Theoretical work has focused on examining strategic behavior among oligopolists in a declining industry (Ghemawat and Nalebuff [11, 12]; Reynolds [27]; Whinston [33]). Industry studies have analyzed the effect of plant characteristics and of firm size or diversification on exit from contracting industries (Franklin [10]; Harrigan [17]; Deily [6]; Lieberman [23]; Baden-Fuller [1]).

Firms in a declining industry minimize their losses by closing plants with the lowest expected long-run net revenues. Net revenues depend on a plant's production costs and the competition that it faces. A plant with an older capital stock is more likely to be closed than a plant with a newer capital stock, ceteris paribus, simply because major re-investment decisions should arise in the older plant first (Stigler [29]). (This effect will be exaggerated, of course, if newer capital is more efficient.) Thus, plants with the lowest expected revenue, the highest expected production costs, and the oldest capital should be the most likely to close.

Government efforts to control pollution may affect the pattern of exit from the industry in two ways. First, the costs of complying with pollution regulations may vary across plants. These costs include capital expenditures for pollution control equipment or for retrofitting current capital, operating costs of pollution equipment, and any lost productivity of the original capital due to pollution control efforts. The higher the cost, the lower the plant's expected net revenues, and the more likely it is to close.

Second, the expected compliance cost depends on the level of enforcement that a firm expects to encounter at each plant. Other things equal, plants expected to face more enforcement pressure will need to spend more for pollution control. Plants facing more expected enforcement activity will have lower expected net revenues because of higher expected compliance costs; such plants are more likely to close. Thus, variation in enforcement levels also may affect the pattern of exit.

---

[10]"When Bethlehem Steel decided to shut its Lackawanna, N.Y., plant, idling 7300, Lackawanna authorities began planning layoffs of fire and police and other government workers: half the municipal budget came from Bethlehem's $6 million in taxes." David Nyhan, "Crisis in Steel and for a Way of Life," *Boston Globe*, page 1 and ff., 1/30/83.

In summary, firms minimize their losses by closing plants with the lowest expected net revenues, the oldest capital, and the highest expected compliance costs. Firms are more likely to close plants where more enforcement is expected to occur, since enforcement is likely to raise compliance costs.

III. ECONOMETRICS AND SPECIFICATION

Our model has two endogenous variables: EPA enforcement at a plant and the plant-closing decision of the firm. These decisions are linked in our model because enforcement at a plant depends on the expected probability that the owning-firm will close the plant, and because the probability of a plant-closing depends on the expected cost of compliance at the plant, determined in part by the expected level of enforcement.

We estimate the system using a two-stage, instrumental variables method, instead of a more efficient full-information maximum likelihood estimator, because the enforcement equation has a continuous dependent variable and is estimated with panel data, while the plant-closing equation has a dichotomous dependent variable and is estimated with cross-section data. We use the first-stage equations to generate predicted values for each decision, and then use the predicted values as instruments in the second-stage (structural) equations.

In the first-stage estimations, the plant-closing probabilities are estimated using a logit model, while an ordinary regression model is used for the enforcement decision. All equations include a number of variables that are fixed for each plant: its location, product mix and size, the age of its capital in 1976, the amount of emissions it produces, and the cost of bringing the plant into full compliance. All equations also include the plant's employment relative to the size of its local labor market, which is measured in 1976 for the cross-sectional equations, and annually for the panel. The enforcement equation also includes year dummies and local unemployment rates.[11]

One final adjustment is required to generate a full set of instruments for the second-stage equations. The information about enforcement over time must be compressed into a single number for the cross-section (plant-closing) estimation. But when a firm decides to close a plant, no more enforcement is directed toward that plant, potentially skewing the enforcement measure in the plant-closing equation. Therefore, we use the estimated enforcement equation to predict enforcement in all years for every plant. We then sum the 11 years of predicted enforcement for each plant, including those that close during the sample period.

The first-stage estimations, and the additional adjustments, yield the instruments: PCLOSE, the predicted probability of closing, and PLENFSUM, the sum of predicted enforcement activity over the whole sample period. We now discuss the structural equations in which these variables are used.

---

[11]The area unemployment rate is not included in the other equation because it varies substantially during the sample (so the 1976 value would not pick up cross sectional differences) and may be affected if the plant is closed during the period (so the average unemployment during the sample might not be exogenous).

Enforcement

We use the specification for the enforcement equation,

$$\text{LENF}_{i,t} = f(\text{LEMIT}_i,\ \text{ATTAIN}_i,\ \text{PCLOSE}_i,\ \text{LRELEMP}_{i,t},\ \text{CNTYU}_{i,t},$$
$$\text{COMPCAP}_i,\ 10\ \text{YEAR dummies},\ 14\ \text{STATE dummies}), \quad (1)$$

where i indexes plants and t indexes time. The dependent variable, LENF, is the log of the number of enforcement actions directed toward the plant each year by agencies regulating air pollution. Agency actions range from letters and phone calls to inspections and enforcement orders.[12]

The first two variables, LEMIT and ATTAIN, are measures of the potential for pollution damage represented by a plant. LEMIT, the log of the annual tons of pollutants emitted by a plant (an average of 1981 and 1985 values), is included to control for variation across plants in their pollution production. For each plant, emissions of three major pollutants, particulates, sulfur dioxide, and nitrogen oxides, were summed to get a single measure of the pollution potential of the plant.[13]

The variable ATTAIN is a dummy variable indicating that the plant is located in an area that is meeting its air-quality standards. Assuming that the EPA wishes to maintain general public support by reducing pollution enough to meet air-quality standards, it will do so most efficiently by allocating enforcement resources toward plants producing greater amounts of pollution in areas that have not attained minimal air-quality standards. Thus, we expect the coefficient on LEMIT to be positive, and that of ATTAIN to be negative.

We use four variables to measure the cost of the compliance that enforcement is designed to produce. The first, the variable COMPCAP, is an estimate of the total expenditure (per ton of plant capacity) needed to bring a plant into full compliance.[14] Since higher compliance costs will be associated with a lower payoff in reduced pollution per enforcement resource expended (due to greater firm resistance), and may also involve political costs, the coefficient of this variable is expected to be negative.

The other three variables model the potential local adjustment costs that are the focus of this paper: PCLOSE is the predicted probability that the plant will close

---

[12] Since we lack systematic information about the relative importance of these actions, all are included and each receives equal weight. We obtain similar results if only "serious actions" (inspections, penalties, and enforcement orders, which represent 49% of total actions) are counted.

[13] We summed the pollutants because we had no measure of the relative damage caused by each pollutant, and because the pollutants were of similar magnitudes. Further, emissions of the three pollutants are highly correlated. Including the three pollutants together in the equation results in three positive coefficients (as expected) with only one coefficient significant; estimating the equation using only one pollutant at a time results in a significant positive coefficient in all three cases.

[14] We do not know what pollution control expenditures had already been undertaken at the plant, so COMPCAP does not measure incremental compliance costs. Rather, we use estimates in Temple, Barker and Sloane, Inc. [31] of the total national expenditures necessary to bring each piece of steel equipment into compliance with air pollution regulations. Dividing these totals by national capacities of each type of equipment provides a national average cost for bringing each type of equipment into compliance. Total costs for individual plants were then calculated by aggregating the appropriate compliance costs according to the equipment present in the plant, weighted by the capacity of that equipment.

sometime during the sample period, indicating whether the plant is "near the borderline" of being closed; LRELEMP is the log of the ratio of employment at the plant to employment in the local labor market; and CNTYU, the local area unemployment rate, captures the difficulty that laid-off workers might have in finding their next job. All three variables are expected to have negative coefficients.

Finally, the enforcement effort directed toward a particular plant depends on the total amount of enforcement being carried out (or at least, being recorded) during each year in each state.[15] Equation (1) controls for variation in regulation over time and across states with YEAR and STATE dummies. But with only 45 plants in 15 states, the state dummies greatly reduce the explanatory power of the other plant-specific variables. As an alternative, we re-estimate Eq. (1), replacing the STATE dummies with a single variable, LSTATEAV, which measures the total enforcement done in a state during a year. In addition to preserving degrees of freedom, this formulation has the advantage of picking up changes in enforcement within each state over time as well as controlling for variation across states.

Plant Closing

We base our model of steel firms' plant-closing decisions on the estimations reported in Deily [6]. In that work, the probability of exit is determined by a set of plant characteristics only; owning-firm characteristics appear to have been relatively unimportant in this industry. Further, since the individual characteristics of steel plants were quite stable over time, they are measured just once (at the start of the contraction), and the plant-closing probabilities are then estimated from the resulting cross-section data set. The model correctly predicts whether or not a plant survived the decline in over 80% of the cases.

We use an augmented version of this model in the current paper that includes the effect of regulatory enforcement. The following specification is employed,

$$\text{CLOSE}_i = f(\text{COAST}_i, \text{SHAPES}_i, \text{LCAPNEW}_i, \text{LCAP}_i, \text{COMPCAP}_i, \text{PLENFSUM}_i), \quad (2)$$

where i indexes plants. The dependent variable, CLOSE, is dichotomous, equal to one for those plants that closed by the end of 1987, and zero for those that remained open.

The first two variables are proxies for a plant's expected long-run revenues, based on the competition faced by the plant. COAST is a dummy variable indicating plants that are located on the coast, facing more import competition. SHAPES measures the percentage of a plant's product mix composed of plates, structural shapes and pilings, and bars and bar shapes. Plants producing these products face a relatively larger decrease in demand because minimills (a competing source of supply) produce some of the products, while others are made for industries that were themselves undergoing contraction (e.g., railroads). The coefficients of both variables should be positive.

---

[15] The amount of enforcement carried out varies from year to year as enforcement budgets change, from state to state due to differing state policies, and within states over time as state policies evolve.

The variable LCAPNEW, the percentage of a plant's capacity that is new, controls for variation among plants in age of capital stock. LCAP, the annual steel producing capacity of the plant, controls for scale economies in steel production. The coefficients of both variables should be negative.

The final two variables are related to the costs the plant will face in complying with EPA regulations. COMPCAP, the cost of fully complying with pollution regulations, controls for variation in potential expenditures for pollution control. PLENFSUM, the sum of predicted logs of enforcement for the plant, measures the pressure to comply that the plant is expected to face. The coefficients on COMPCAP and PLENFSUM should be positive.

IV. RESULTS

Table I presents the means and variances of the data used for each independent variable, for the two dependent variables of the first-stage estimations, and for the two instruments PCLOSE and PLENFSUM.

TABLE I
Means and Standard Deviations[a]

Variable	Enforcement ($N = 412$)	Plant-closing ($N = 49$)
ATTAIN	0.17	—
	(0.38)	
CNTYU	8.92	—
	(3.50)	
COAST	0.11	0.14
	(0.31)	(0.35)
COMPCAP	26.04	25.55
	(8.55)	(9.01)
LCAP	1.05	0.93
	(0.59)	(0.69)
LCAPNEW	3.49	3.25
	(0.98)	(1.26)
LEMIT	9.00	8.89
	(1.19)	(1.21)
LRELEMP	−3.55	−3.62
	(1.67)	(1.74)
LSTATEAV	0.59	—
	(0.31)	
PCLOSE∗CNTYU	2.87	—
	(2.68)	
SHAPES	0.32	0.36
	(0.32)	(0.34)
CLOSE	—	0.43
		(0.50)
LENF	2.05	—
	(1.34)	
PCLOSE	0.34	—
	(0.29)	
PLENFSUM	—	22.84
		(5.92)

[a] Variables beginning with the letter L are in logs.

TABLE II
First-Stage Estimations[a]

	Dependent variable	
	LENF[b]	CLOSE
INTERCEPT	−1.57**	−6.06
	(0.75)	(5.49)
COAST	−0.12	0.94
	(0.19)	(1.20)
SHAPES	0.27	2.68*
	(0.18)	(1.37)
LCAP	0.53**	−2.54**
	(0.12)	(1.12)
LCAPNEW	0.15**	−0.49
	(0.06)	(0.32)
CNTYU	0.17**	—
	(0.02)	
ATTAIN	−0.14	—
	(0.15)	
LEMIT	0.13*	1.11*
	(0.07)	(0.65)
LRELEMP	−0.14**	−0.27
	(0.04)	(0.28)
COMPCAP	0.004	−0.09
	(0.007)	(0.05)
Adj R-squ	0.43	—
F statistic	17.07	—
LL	—	−21.70
Correct predictions	—	82%
N	412	49

[a] Standard errors are in parentheses.
[b] Estimated equation included 10 year dummies.
*Significant at the 10% level, 2-tail test.
**Significant at the 5% level, 2-tail test.

The results of the first-stage estimations are shown in Table II. The enforcement equation does well, with several significant variables explaining over 43% of the variance in (the log of) enforcement actions. The plant-closing equation also does well, with several variables contributing to predict correctly 82% of the plant closing decisions.

The second-stage equations are presented in Tables III and IV. In general, the interactions between the decisions are as expected, although some of the exogenous variables offer significant surprises. We first discuss the enforcement equation estimations reported in Table III. The estimation in column 1 includes 14 state dummies to control for variation in state-level regulatory behavior, while the estimation in column 2 replaces the dummies with the variable LSTATEAV. The estimations are quite similar, but we prefer the more parsimonious Model 2, and refer to its results in the following discussion.

Turning to the main thesis of the paper, we find evidence that enforcement behavior is indeed influenced by potential adjustment costs to local communities. The coefficient of PCLOSE is negative and significant; enforcement activity drops

TABLE III
Second-Stage Estimations: Enforcement[a]

	Dependent variable: LENF		
	(1)[b]	(2)[c]	(3)[c]
INTERCEPT	−2.06**	−2.40**	−2.56**
	(0.81)	(0.65)	(0.63)
PCLOSE	−0.74**	−0.65**	1.58**
	(0.29)	(0.20)	(0.54)
LRELEMP	−0.14**	−0.19**	−0.15**
	(0.05)	(0.04)	(0.04)
CNTYU	0.13**	0.17**	0.24**
	(0.03)	(0.02)	(0.03)
PCLOSE*CNTYU	—	—	−0.25**
			(0.06)
LEMIT	0.33**	0.28**	0.25**
	(0.07)	(0.05)	(0.05)
ATTAIN	−0.05	−0.25*	−0.25*
	(0.18)	(0.14)	(0.14)
COMPCAP	−0.01	−0.006	−0.001
	(0.01)	(0.007)	(0.007)
LSTATEAV	—	1.00**	0.77**
		(0.25)	(0.25)
Adj R-squ	0.46	0.42	0.45
F statistic	12.61	18.51	19.38
N	412	412	412

[a] Standard errors are in parentheses.
[b] Estimated equation included 10 year dummies and 14 state dummies.
[c] Estimated equation included 10 year dummies.
*Significant at the 10% level, 2-tail test.
**Significant at the 5% level, 2-tail test.

by 6.5% for each 10 percentage-point increase in the probability of closing. The coefficient of the variable LRELEMP is also negative and significant, indicating that a 10% increase in employment size relative to the community work force decreases enforcement actions by 1.9%. However, the estimated coefficient of the third adjustment-cost variable, CNTYU, is positive and significant. This indicates that plants in high-unemployment counties receive *more* enforcement actions rather than fewer.

We investigate this unexpected result by adding an interaction term, PCLOSE*CNTYU, to the enforcement equation, and re-estimating (column 3). The coefficient on the interacted term is negative and significant, while the coefficient of PCLOSE becomes positive and significant. These results indicate that the tendency for marginal plants to face less enforcement (seen in column 2) is concentrated in counties with high unemployment. Regulators seem to be "skewing" their enforcement more in these counties than in others, with greater enforcement on average, but much less for the plants that are in danger of closing.

Note that this is *not* a reflection of inter-state differences, since variables are included to control for that variation. Rather, enforcement levels are varying for different counties in the same state. This could be due to unmeasured variation in

TABLE IV
Second-Stage Estimation: Plant-Closing[a]

		Marginal effects[b]	
Dependent variable: CLOSE		COAST = 0	COAST = 1
INTERCEPT	−0.87	—	—
	(2.69)		
PLENFSUM	0.40**	0.086	0.019
	(0.16)		
COAST	3.72**	—	—
	(1.74)		
SHAPES	3.09**	0.669	0.145
	(1.48)		
LCAP	−4.23**	−0.917	−0.199
	(1.50)		
LCAPNEW	−1.07**	−0.232	−0.050
	(0.43)		
COMPCAP	−0.10*	−0.022	−0.005
	(0.06)		
LL	−19.27		
Correct predictions	88%		
N	49		

[a] Standard errors are in parentheses.
[b] Calculated at sample means.
* Significant at the 10% level, 2-tail test.
** Significant at the 5% level, 2-tail test.

the benefits from reducing emissions. To the extent that high-unemployment areas tend to be more populous or more polluted, the benefits from reducing emissions in such areas may be greater.[16]

The other variables in the enforcement equation hold few surprises. The coefficient on LEMIT is positive and always significant, indicating that a plant producing 10% more emissions will receive 2.8% more enforcement activity. The coefficient of ATTAIN is negative as expected, though only significant at the 10% level. It indicates that plants located in areas that attained mandated levels of air quality experienced, on average, 22% fewer enforcement actions each year.

The coefficient of COMPCAP is negative as expected but insignificant, perhaps indicating that regulators do not pay much attention to variation in abatement costs across plants. LSTATEAV's coefficient is significant, and close to one, indicating it measures overall shifts in enforcement affecting all plants proportionally.

Estimation results for the plant-closing equation are presented in column 1 of Table IV; columns 2 and 3 present the corresponding marginal effects of each variable on the probability of closing, column 2 for inland plants and column 3 for

---

[16] One might think that the concentration of steel plants in a few high-unemployment states is also part of the answer, but note that including state dummies or state unemployment rates does not affect the result.

coastal plants. Since 86% of the plants were located inland, we concentrate on the results in columns 1 and 2.

The estimated coefficient on PLENFSUM, which is positive and significant, indicates that firms are more likely to close plants that are expected to face more enforcement in the future. A 12% increase in expected enforcement increases the probability of closing by 1 percentage point. As expected, the estimated coefficients of the plant-characteristics variables indicate that small, old, coastal plants producing bars and structural shapes are significantly more likely to close. The one unexpected result is the negative and marginally significant coefficient on compliance costs, which suggests that firms were less likely to close plants that cost more to bring into compliance.[17]

V. CONCLUSIONS AND FUTURE WORK

The evidence presented here indicates that air-pollution regulators generally allocate their enforcement activity as if they want to avoid causing local adjustment costs. Plants that were "large" in their local labor market encountered less enforcement pressure. On average, plants with a higher probability of closing also experienced less enforcement pressure. However, plants in high unemployment counties are found, unaccountably, to face greater enforcement.

This pattern of enforcement, with stronger plants bearing more of the costs, reinforces previous work indicating that the regulatory burden has been heavier in faster growing, high-employment regions. However, since we include controls for state-level enforcement, our results are not based on regional differences, but on plant-specific differences in the probability of closing. Thus, for two plants in the same state, the plant with the greater risk of closing faces less enforcement, ceteris paribus.

Our results also show that firms' plant-closing decisions during this period of drastic industry decline were influenced by the enforcement activity of regulators. Plants predicted to face more enforcement were more likely to close. This provides further support for the sensitivity of regulators to the probability of a plant's closing.

We plan to extend this research along a number of lines. First, we can test whether our results hold in another regulatory area by looking at OSHA's enforcement activity in these same steel plants. Second, we plan to look at similar data for other declining industries, to see if enforcement is sensitive to their economic conditions. Finally, we will examine firms' responses to enforcement on a company-wide basis, looking at compliance decisions as well as plant-closing decisions, to test whether these decisions are interrelated across plants within a company and how the decisions are related to the economic health of the firm. Insight into these matters will add to our understanding of the complex relationship between regulatory and firm decision-making.

---

[17]This may come from the use of total rather than incremental compliance costs, or from problems with data quality. Alternatively, it may reflect a technological coincidence. Large plants producing flat-rolled products were most likely to survive, but these plants also generally operated their own coke ovens, and coke ovens represented the largest single compliance expenditure for steel plants (over 40% of the total compliance costs faced by the industry (Temple, Barker and Sloane, Inc. [31])).

APPENDIX: DATA

The sample is the 48 steelmaking plants owned by the integrated producers listed by the Institute for Iron and Steel Studies (IISS) [20], plus the Portsmouth, Ohio, plant of Cyclops. (Small electric-arc based plants and plants producing mainly specialty steels are excluded.) The EPA data sets we use have the plant as the unit of observation and list each plant's name, street address, city, county, state, and industry. We used this information to find the records belonging to the plants in our sample.

The enforcement data are from the EPA's Compliance Data System (CDS). We use the CDS from early 1983 and the CDS from early 1987; the 1983 data are needed because plants are eventually removed from the CDS after they close. Only 3 of the 49 plants are not found on either data set (2 closed in 1977 and the third in 1978). The plants in our sample faced a total of 9316 enforcement actions during the period 1977–1986.

Data on plant closings are from Hogan [19], corporate reports, and phone calls to companies. A plant closed if its steel-making furnaces were shut down; three plants that experienced capacity reductions of over 65% were also counted as closed plants. In all, 21 of 49 plants (43%) closed.

Emissions data are from the EPA's National Emissions Data System (NEDS). As with the CDS, we use two versions of the NEDS, the end-of-year tapes from 1981 and 1985. Data from NEDS include the amount of a plant's emissions of five major pollutants; the three we use (particulates, sulfur dioxide, and nitrogen oxides) were regularly present for steel plants.

The two NEDS tapes, plus emissions data on the pollutants contained in the two CDS data sets, gave us three or four possible measures of plant-level emissions for each pollutant for most plants. (No emissions data were available for two plants; they were assigned the predicted value from a regression of log(total emissions) on log(capacity), log(employment), log(new capital) and a dummy for electric-arc furnaces, which produce much less pollution.) We used the median of the available values for each pollutant (the figures varied substantially across the four data sets) which gave us three measures of emissions at each plant.

The 1986 CDS indicates whether a plant is in an Air Quality Control Region that is attaining its standards for each of the major air pollutants. We say that a plant is located in an "attainment" area if the area is attaining the standards for any of the three pollutants. In our sample, only seven plants were located in an attainment area.

The cost of full compliance is calculated for each plant using estimates from Temple, Barker and Sloane, Inc. [31] of the total cost to the industry of bringing each major piece of equipment into full compliance by 1984. For each type of equipment, we took the total expected capital cost through 1985 and divided it by the gross capacity expected to exist in 1985 to get a cost per unit annual capacity.

Data on the actual equipment in each plant and on the equipment's capacity (both as near to 1976 as was possible) are from Deily [5], IISS [22], annual reports, and various issues of "Directory of Iron and Steel Works of the U.S. and Canada" [8] and of Cordero and Serjeantson [3]. The cost of full compliance for a plant was calculated as the cost (per ton of capacity) of bringing each particular type of equipment into compliance, times the equipment's capacity, summed over the different types of equipment in each plant. This sum, divided by plant capacity in

1976, is our estimate of the cost of bringing the plant into compliance, in 1980 dollars per ton of plant capacity. (The costs of operating the equipment are not included, but are highly correlated with the capital costs.)

Average state-level enforcement rates were calculated from the CDS data as the total number of enforcement actions in the state, minus the number of enforcement actions directed toward the particular plant, divided by the number of all other plants on the CDS for that state.

Information on the local labor market is from the Bureau of Labor Statistic publication "Employment and Unemployment in States and Local Areas" [32], in annual editions from 1976–1986. Labor market tightness is measured by the unemployment rate in the county where the plant is located. The size of the local labor market is measured by the number of people employed in the county.

Data on employment at the plant is from the 1975–1976, 1979–1980, and 1981–1982 issues of "Marketing Economics, Key Plants" [24]. We assigned the numbers in an issue to the first year of the issue (i.e., 1975, 1979, and 1981), and interpolated the remaining years of the sample, with the 1981 value used for 1981–1986.

Coastal plants were those located on or near the East, West, or Gulf coasts. The SHAPES variable is the percentage of a plant's hot-rolled capacity used to produce plates, structural shapes and pilings, and bars and bar shapes. The data are from the 1962 issue of Cordero and Serjeantson [3]. A plant's size is its annual raw-steel capacity in 1976 (IISS [20, 21]).

The percentage of new (post-1959) capacity in each of four major departments (coke-making, blast furnace, steel furnace, and primary rolling/continuous casting) was calculated, and the sum was divided by the number of these departments a plant contained. Thus, the figure is the percentage of each plant that is "new," adjusted for the number of departments located at the plant and for the amount of replacement within a department. The necessary data on investments made at each plant and on the capacity of each department in a plant are from Deily [5], IISS [22], annual reports, and various issues of "Directory of Iron and Steel Works of the U.S. and Canada" [8] and of Cordero and Serjeantson [3].

REFERENCES

1. C. W. F. Baden-Fuller, Exit from declining industries and the case of steel castings, *Econom. J.* **99**, 949–961 (1989).
2. A. P. Bartel and L. G. Thomas, Direct and indirect effects of regulations: A new look at OSHA's impact, *J. Law Econom.* **28**, 1–25 (1985).
3. R. Cordero and R. Serjeantson (Eds.), "Iron and Steel Works of the World," Metal Bulletin Books, Ltd., New York (various years).
4. R. W. Crandall, "Controlling Industrial Pollution," Brookings Institution, Washington, DC (1983).
5. M. E. Deily, Investment activity and the exit decision, *Rev. Econom. Statist.* **70**, 595–602 (1988).
6. M. E. Deily, "The Impact of Firm Characteristics on Plant-Closing Decisions," Federal Reserve Bank of Cleveland Working Paper No. 8803 (1988).
7. M. E. Deily and W. B. Gray, "Enforcement of Pollution Regulations in a Declining Industry," Federal Reserve Bank of Cleveland Working Paper No. 8912 (1989).
8. "Directory of Iron and Steel Works of the U.S. and Canada," American Iron and Steel Institute, Washington, DC (various years).
9. R. W. Eberts and M. S. Fogarty, The differential effects of federal regulations on regional productivity, Federal Reserve Bank of Cleveland Mimeo (1987).

10. P. J. Franklin, Some observations on exit from the motor insurance industry, 1966–1972, *J. Ind. Econom.* **22**, 299–313 (1974).
11. P. Ghemawat and B. Nalebuff, Exit, *Rand J. Econom.* **16**, 184–194 (1985).
12. P. Ghemawat and B. Nalebuff, The devolution of declining industries, *Quart. J. Econom.* **105**, 167–186 (1990).
13. F. M. Gollup and M. J. Roberts, Environmental regulations and productivity growth: The case of fossil-fueled electric power generation, *J. Polit. Econom.* **91**, 654–674 (1983).
14. F. M. Gollup and M. J. Roberts, Cost-minimizing regulation of sulfur emissions: Regional gains in electric power, *Rev. Econom. Statist.* **67**, 81–90 (1985).
15. W. B. Gray, "Productivity versus OSHA and EPA Regulations," UMI Research Press, Ann Arbor, MI (1986).
16. W. B. Gray, The cost of regulation: OSHA, EPA, and the productivity slowdown, *Amer. Econom. Rev.* **77**, 998–1006 (1987).
17. K. R. Harrigan, "Strategies for Declining Businesses," Lexington Books, Lexington, MA (1980).
18. W. Harrington, Enforcement leverage when penalties are restricted, *J. Public Econom.* **37**, 29–53 (1988).
19. W. T. Hogan, SJ, "Minimills and Integrated Mills: A Comparison of Steelmaking in the United States," Lexington Books, Lexington, MA (1987).
20. Institute for Iron and Steel Studies, "IISS Commentary: Special Reports I," Institute for Iron and Steel Studies, Greenbrook, NJ (1977).
21. Institute for Iron and Steel Studies, "Steel Plants U.S.A.: Raw Steelmaking Capacities, 1960 and 1973–1980," Institute for Iron and Steel Studies, Greenbrook, NJ (1979).
22. Institute for Iron and Steel Studies, "Steel Industry in Brief: Databook, U.S.A. 1983," Institute for Iron and Steel Studies, Greenbrook, NJ (1983).
23. M. B. Lieberman, Exit from declining industries: "Shakeout" or "stakeout"?, *Rand J. Econom.* **21**, 538–554 (1990).
24. Marketing Economics Institute, "Marketing Economics, Key Plants," Marketing Economics Institute, New York (various issues).
25. B. P. Pashigian, Environmental regulation: Whose self-interests are being protected?, *Econom. Inquiry* **23**, 551–584 (1985).
26. S. Peltzman, Toward a more general theory of regulation, *J. Law Econom.* **19**, 211–240 (1976).
27. S. S. Reynolds, Plant closings and exit behavior in declining industries, *Economica* **55**, 493–503 (1988).
28. J. T. Scholz, Cooperation, deterrence, and the ecology of regulatory enforcement, *Law & Society Rev.* **18**, 179–224 (1984).
29. G. J. Stigler, "The Theory of Price," 3rd ed., MacMillan Co., New York (1966).
30. G. J. Stigler, The theory of economic regulation, *Bell J. Econom. Management Sci.* **2**, 3–21 (1971).
31. Temple, Barker and Sloane, Inc., "An Economic Analysis of Final Effluent Limitations Guidelines, New Source Performance Standards, and Pretreatment Standards for the Iron and Steel Manufacturing Point Source Category," NTIS PB82231291, Environmental Protection Agency, Washington, DC (May 1982).
32. United States Bureau of Labor Statistics, "Employment and Unemployment in States and Local Areas," U.S. Govt. Printing Office, Washington, DC (various issues).
33. M. D. Whinston, Exit with multiplant firms, *Rand J. Econom.* **9**, 74–94 (1988).

Investment

[17]

ENVIRONMENTAL REGULATION, INVESTMENT TIMING, AND TECHNOLOGY CHOICE*

Wayne B. Gray† and Ronald J. Shadbegian‡

We test whether environmental regulation affects investment decisions, using Census data for individual paper mills. New mills in states with strict environmental regulations choose cleaner production technologies, with differences in air and water pollution regulation also influencing technology choice. Examining investment allocation across existing plants, we find that abatement and productive investment tend to be scheduled together. However, plants with high abatement investment over the entire period spend significantly less on productive capital. This seems to reflect both environmental investment 'crowding out' productive investment within a plant, and firms shifting investment towards plants facing less stringent abatement requirements.

I. INTRODUCTION

ENVIRONMENTAL regulation in the US has changed dramatically over the past thirty years. In the 1960s and before, environmental regulation was done by state and local agencies, usually without much active enforcement. With the establishment of the Environmental Protection Agency in the early 1970s, and the passage of the Clean Water and Clean Air Acts, the federal government took the lead role in regulation. Still, state agencies are heavily involved in setting standards for individual plants and enforcing those standards, backed now by the more serious penalties in the federal statutes. Therefore, differences across states in regulatory stringency could play a role in investment decisions.

---

*Financial support from the National Science Foundation (SBR-9410059) and the NBER Project on Industrial Technology and Productivity, funded by the Alfred P. Sloan Foundation, is gratefully acknowledged. We are also grateful to the many people in the paper industry who allowed us to visit their plants and shared their knowledge of the industry with us. Capable research assistance was provided by Zahid Hafeez. Helpful comments came from Ernst Berndt, Martin Feldstein, Adam Jaffe, Severin Borenstein, an anonymous referee, and participants in the 1996 NBER Summer Institute on Public Economics. Some of this research was carried out at the Census Bureau's Boston Research Data Center. All papers are screened to ensure that they do not disclose confidential Census information. Any opinions expressed are those of the authors and not the Census Bureau or NBER. Any remaining errors or omissions are also ours.

†Authors' affiliation: Wayne B. Gray, Department of Economics, Clark University, 950 Main St, Worcester, MA 01610-1477, USA and NBER.
email: wgray@clarku.edu

‡Ronald J. Shadbegian, Department of Economics, University of Massachusetts at Dartmouth, Old Westport Road, North Dartmouth, MA 02747, USA.
email: rshadbegian@umassd.edu

Much of the existing research on the impact of environmental regulation examines its impact on productivity. This research has tended to find a significant, though not always overwhelmingly large, connection between regulation and productivity.[1] There has also been some work on the connection between environmental regulation and plant openings and closings. An analysis of steel plant closing decisions (Deily and Gray [1991]) found that steel mills facing more air pollution enforcement were more likely to be closed. A state-level analysis of new plant openings (Gray [1997]) also indicated a significant negative relationship between a state's environmental regulation and the number of new plants opened in the state, though other studies (e.g. Bartik [1988]) have found smaller impacts. Thus we have some indication that environmental regulation may influence business decisions such as investment, but that such influences are likely to be small.

Our research tests for an impact of environmental regulation on a broad range of investment decisions. We consider three possible impacts. First, a new plant's choice of production technology may be influenced by differences in the pollution characteristics of these technologies. Second, a firm's allocation of capital investment across existing plants may be influenced by differences in the environmental stringency faced by the plants. Third, a plant's investment in pollution abatement equipment may influence the timing and amount of investment in production equipment at the plant. If environmental regulation greatly affects profitability, it could influence all of these investment decisions.

We have chosen to study the pulp and paper industry for a variety of reasons. The industry is a major polluter, with both air and water pollution concerns, and spends more on pollution abatement than most other manufacturing industries. Paper mills employ a variety of production technologies, which differ substantially in the pollution generated. Finally, we had already studied the industry using plant-level Census data, finding a significant impact of pollution abatement costs on productivity (Gray and Shadbegian [1995]).

Our basic investment data come from the Census Bureau's Longitudinal Research Database. We have annual investment data for 116 paper mills from the Annual Survey of Manufactures, beginning in 1972. Starting in 1979 we also have annual information on pollution abatement investment at 68 of the 116 plants, so we can examine the relationship between productive and pollution abatement investment. We use an industry publication (the *Lockwood Directory*) to identify the production technology used at a sample of 227 plants for the technology choice analysis.

---

[1] Studies with industry-level data include Barbera and McConnell [1986] and Gray [1986, 1987]; plant-level data studies include Gollop and Roberts [1983] and Gray and Shadbegian [1995].

We find a significant connection between a plant's technology and state-level measures of regulatory stringency. New mills in states with strict environmental regulations are less likely to employ the most polluting technologies (those which involve pulping processes starting with raw wood). When we disaggregate the regulatory stringency by type of pollution, we find the expected results (though not always significant): the technology which emits the most air pollution is less commonly used in states with greater air pollution stringency, while the technology emitting more water pollution is less commonly used in states with greater water pollution stringency.

We find small impacts, not always significant, of state regulatory stringency and plant technology on annual investment spending at existing plants. However, we find significant relationships between a plant's productive (non-abatement) investment spending and the amount and timing of pollution abatement investment. Investment tends to be lumpy, with pollution abatement and productive investment projects occurring simultaneously. This is consistent with paper mills having high fixed costs for shutting down during renovations. However, productive investment is significantly lower in plants which do more pollution abatement investment over the period, with $1 of abatement investment associated with $1.88 lower productive investment. Since this estimate includes firm dummies, it could reflect both environmental investment crowding out productive investment within a plant, and firms shifting investment towards plants facing less stringent abatement requirements. Estimates placing less weight on within-firm reallocation of investment indicate approximate dollar-for-dollar ($0.99) crowding out of productive investment.

Section II describes the paper industry in more detail, including the reasons why different production technologies could be differentially affected by regulation. Section III sketches brief econometric models of the impact of regulation on technology choice and investment. Section IV describes the data used for the analysis. Section V presents the results, with concluding remarks in Section VI.

II. PAPER INDUSTRY INVESTMENT AND ENVIRONMENTAL REGULATION

What facts about the paper industry are relevant for a study of environmental regulation, technology choice, and investment?[2] First, even though all paper mills belong to the same industry, they use many different production technologies. Paper-making begins with a fiber source such as trees, wood chips, recycled cardboard, or waste paper. Plants beginning

---

[2] The following discussion of the paper industry is based upon visits to several paper mills and conversations with people in the paper industry.

© Blackwell Publishers Ltd. 1998.

with raw wood use a variety of pulping processes (mechanical, chemical, or a combination) to separate out the wood fibers. The resulting mixture of fiber and water is either deposited onto a rapidly-moving wire mesh (the fourdrinier process), or layered onto rotating drums (the cylinder process) before passing through a series of dryers to remove water and create a continuous sheet of paper.

Second, these differences in production technology have important environmental consequences, especially in the pulping process (the paper-drying process requires substantial energy, but there are fewer differences across plants). Kraft (sulfate) pulping, using chemicals which are recycled, is most common among plants starting with raw wood. The older sulfite process uses less expensive chemicals which were once flushed directly into the river, generating more water pollution. Mechanical pulpers (like giant blenders) can also be used to separate the fibers, reducing water pollution but increasing air pollution from large power boilers. Plants using recycled cardboard or paper as inputs generate much less pollution. Inks and other contaminants can make it difficult to produce top-grade white recycled paper, but deinking processes have improved in recent years, encouraged by paper recycling programs.

Third, it can be difficult or impossible for older mills to make major changes in their production process to meet environmental regulations. Some older plants were built directly over a river, with floor openings that allowed spills to flow 'conveniently' into the water for disposal; containing such spills is now a top priority. Installing oxygen delignification to reduce the need for chlorine bleaching increases the flow to a recovery boiler by 3 percent, requiring the plant to cut output by 3 percent or spend tens of millions of dollars on a new, slightly larger recovery boiler. This fixity of the production process may make existing plants less desirable targets for investment.

Fourth, there are sizable differences across states in the stringency of environmental regulation. Federal EPA rules provide the framework for regulation, but state regulators have substantial discretion when making plant-level decisions, such as where to direct enforcement activity, and how strict (or slow) to make the permit application process. States may choose to be stricter due to having greater political support for environmental protection. States may also be forced to increase their stringency if they have more serious pollution problems. The EPA explicitly requires stricter controls on both new and existing plants in areas that fail to meet air quality standards. Water pollution regulations designed to protect stream quality can also impose tighter controls where water quality is poorer. Thus both political pressures and pollution problems could lead to differences in regulatory stringency.

Fifth, environmental regulation may affect both large and small investment projects. Smaller projects are generally funded out of a capital budget for the plant, with plant managers reporting that legally required environmental projects 'crowd out' productivity-improving projects. Regulatory stringency could also affect the allocation of investment across plants, especially for larger projects involving the firm choosing between different locations. Paper industry people report that delays and uncertainty in the regulatory permitting process are a major barrier to new investments.

Finally, paper mills are highly capital intensive, making it costly to shut down operations in order to renovate the plant. If possible, plants try to schedule several investment projects at the same time to minimize downtime. This may induce a positive correlation between high abatement investment and other investment in annual data, which may make it difficult to find evidence of crowding out.

III. MODELS OF TECHNOLOGY CHANGE AND INVESTMENT

Consider a model of technology choice. Suppose that a company is planning to build plant i (in a particular state at a particular time). The firm can choose from a set of J available technologies. Each technology j has an associated profitability (Π_{ij}) which depends on a set of k regulatory factors R_{ik} and m other observable plant- or state-specific factors X_{im}, along with unobserved plant-technology-specific influences (ϵ_{ij}). The firm chooses the most profitable technology out of the set, leading to a multinomial logit model:

$$\Pi_{i1} = f\left(\sum_k \beta_{r1k} R_{ik} + \sum_m \beta_{x1m} X_{im} + \epsilon_{i1}\right)$$

(1) ...

$$\Pi_{iJ} = f\left(\sum_k \beta_{rJk} R_{ik} + \sum_m \beta_{xJm} X_{im} + \epsilon_{iJ}\right)$$

choose n if $\Pi_{in} \geq \Pi_{ij}$ for $j = 1, \ldots, J$.

Since different paper-making technologies produce different types of pollution, state differences in regulatory stringency across pollution media (e.g. being especially strict on air pollution but lax on water pollution) could influence technology choice, and would be included in R. The overall level of environmental stringency might also be relevant, especially for the choice between pulping and recycled technologies. Other state-specific control variables X include energy prices, likely to affect the more energy-intensive mechanical pulping process, the availability of commercial timber, affecting all of the pulping methods, and population density, affecting recycled paper processes through the relative availability of wastepaper. We also control for the plant's product mix.

We should note some possible concerns with this model. First, there could be different sets of technologies available at different times, which would complicate the selection process. As it happens, all of the technologies considered here were in use by 1960, which is when our dataset on technology choice begins.[3] Second, the profitability being compared in equation (1) is in principle the expected profitability over the plant's lifetime, so expectations about future R and X values at the plant enter the equation. There is a high degree of persistence in cross-state regulatory differences, so current regulatory values should capture most of the available information about future regulation.[4]

Turning to the allocation of investment at existing plants, we take advantage of the neoclassical investment model developed by Jorgenson [1963]. Assuming a Cobb–Douglas production function with elasticity of output with respect to capital of g, the plant's desired amount of capital stock K^* is related to nominal output (pQ) and the user cost of capital (c) by:

$$(2) \qquad K^* = g \cdot \frac{pQ}{c}.$$

Here the cost of capital incorporates information about the tax treatment of profits and investment expenditures, as well as the price of new capital goods and interest rates. Following Jorgenson, we assume that plants adjust their capital stocks to reflect deviations from the desired optimum value, so investment flows are closely connected changes in the desired capital stock. Since major investments can take two years or more to implement, lagged values of (pQ/c) enter the estimation.[5] Our investment measures are gross rather than net of depreciation, so we also need to account for replacement investment, assumed proportional to the prior-period capital stock at the plant i, $K_{i,t-1}$. Finally, the error term is assumed to follow a first-order autoregressive process, resulting in the following equation:

---

[3] There is technological change associated with each technique over time, but the broad categories we will be considering – kraft, sulfite (and other chemical methods), mechanical, and recycled – were all widely available by 1960. In a broader time frame, recycled is the oldest (the earliest US paper mills used recycled rags), sulfite and mechanical are also relatively old, and kraft is somewhat newer, while the use of recycled inputs to produce high-quality white paper, by 'deinking' wastepaper, is the newest technology of all.

[4] Gray [1995] examines different measures of regulatory stringency, finding that differences across states were fairly stable over time. We did test models (results available on the JIE editorial web page) which included population growth rates as well as population density, as a test for the importance of expected future population density. The coefficients on population growth were insignificant, though their signs were consistent with the signs on current population density (suggesting they might be capturing a bit of future expectations). The other coefficients in the model were similar to those reported here.

[5] Most of the investment literature works with quarterly investment data while ours is annual, so we use 2 lagged years of pQ/c (rather than 8 lagged quarters).

© Blackwell Publishers Ltd. 1998.

$$(3) \quad I_{it} = \sum_k \gamma_k X_{itk} + \sum_m \beta_m (pQ/c)_{i,t-m} + \delta K_{i,t-1} + u_{it}$$

where $u_{it} = pu_{i,t-1} + e_{it}$.

The k plant-specific explanatory variables (X_{itk}) include regulatory measures (state stringency and plant abatement investment) along with the plant's production technology and product mix. Some models include firm dummies, measuring the importance of reallocating investment across plants within the same firm. Plant dummies are also tried, although this eliminates cross-sectional variables such as technology and product mix from the model.

In addition to the neoclassical investment model we considered two alternatives. In Gray and Shadbegian [1997] we relied on the pattern of past investments at a plant to predict future investment, following Cooper, et al. [1995]. We also tried a cash flow model (see Bischoff [1971]), where firms are constrained by capital market imperfections from borrowing; firms with higher cash flow can self-finance more investment. All three investment models give similar results for the impact of regulation, particularly for the plant-specific pollution abatement investment variables.[6]

IV. DATA AND ECONOMETRIC ISSUES

The investment data for the project come from the Longitudinal Research Database (LRD) containing information from the Annual Survey of Manufacturers (ASM), linked together for individual plants over time (for a more detailed description of the LRD data, see McGuckin and Pascoe [1988]). In earlier work examining the impact of regulation on productivity (Gray and Shadbegian [1995]) we prepared a dataset of 116 paper industry plants with continuous ASM data over the 1972–1990 period, and we use the same sample of plants here. Our dependent variable is *INVEST*: total annual capital investment spending, including purchases of new and used plant and equipment. Our capital stock measure K is constructed for each plant using the perpetual inventory method, based on gross book value in an initial year and the plant's annual investment flows. To calculate pQ/c in equation (3) we use the plant's nominal shipments (pQ), divided by a measure of the paper industry's user cost of capital (c) from the Federal Reserve Board's Capital Stock Database. The impact of the tax treatment of investment, as well as interest rates and the price of investment goods, is included in c (Jorgenson [1963]).

---

[6] Adding cash flow measures to the neoclassical model gives positive (but insignificant) coefficients: plants owned by firms with high cash flow do more investment. Results for these alternative models are available on the JIE editorial web page.

© Blackwell Publishers Ltd. 1998.

We combine LRD data with two other plant-level data sources: the *Lockwood Directory* and the Pollution Abatement Costs and Expenditures survey. First, the *Lockwood Directory*, is an annual listing of pulp and paper mills. We examine *Lockwood* directories from several different years to see when each plant first appeared, indicating the approximate vintage of the plant. For the analysis of technology choice we concentrate on 227 plants that opened after 1960, and create a dummy *BORN7195* to indicate plants which first appeared after 1970. The *Lockwood Directory* includes information on the production technology being used at each mill (whether the mill uses raw wood or recycled inputs, and how the raw wood is pulped), and the products produced at the plant. The technology and product information is also used in the analysis of investment data, linked to the LRD data using plant name and address information.

Our final plant-level data source is the Pollution Abatement Costs and Expenditures (PACE) survey, conducted annually by the Census Bureau. The PACE questionnaire is sent to a subset of firms in the Annual Survey of Manufactures, oversampling high-pollution plants such as paper mills. Part of our investment analysis requires plants to have complete PACE data. Since only a subset of plants complete the PACE survey each year and these plants change over time, our sample shrinks from 116 plants to 68 plants with complete pollution abatement investment data from 1979–1990.[7]

In addition to the plant-level data, we use several state-level explanatory variables. The *Statistical Abstract* provides *POPDEN* (thousands of people per square mile), *ENERGY* (energy price per million *BTU* in thousands of 1982 dollars), and *FOREST* (timber availability in million cubic feet of softwood growing stock per square mile of land area). Overall regulatory stringency is measured by *VOTE* (the League of Conservation Voters' pro-environment voting score for the state's Congressional delegation, supplemented by our own voting measure for the 1960s taken from data in the *Congressional Record*). *VOTE* was found to be significantly related to manufacturing plant location decisions in Gray [1997].

Measuring differences in air and water pollution stringency across states is difficult, especially capturing changes over time. Ringquist [1993] (pp. 106 and 158) provides cross-sectional measures of the strength of each state's air and water pollution control programs for the late 1980s. We create time-varying stringency indices, *REGAIR* and *REGWATER*,

---

[7] The PACE survey was not done in 1987. We imputed values for PACE investment in 1987 based on the plant's total investment in that year, in order to maintain a complete panel for estimating the autoregressive portion of the investment model. All our models include year dummies, which should help reduce any bias in the estimated coefficients (the most likely bias would be towards zero, understating the impact of abatement investment on productive investment).

© Blackwell Publishers Ltd. 1998.

ENVIRONMENTAL REGULATION, INVESTMENT AND TECHNOLOGY 243

regressing Ringquist's air and water stringency measures on the 1987 values for Z, a vector of state characteristics. We then generate 'predicted values' for the index in earlier years, using the values of the Z variables in those years.[8] The Z vector for both models includes *VOTE* (described above), the membership rate in several major conservation organizations, and the percent voting Democratic in the latest Congressional elections, all designed to capture differences in political support for regulatory stringency.

The other factors identified in Section II as determinants of regulatory stringency are pollution problems. Each Z vector includes an index of the severity of that medium's pollution problems for air or water in the state, taken from the *Green Index* (Hall and Kerr [1991]). Regulations are likely to be stricter where pollution problems are more severe, and the pollution measures are needed to provide a distinction between *REGAIR* and *REGWATER* when they are used together in the technology choice analysis.[9] It's possible that pollution problems and stringency are both driven by other forces, but it's not obvious which way the bias would go. Greater environmental awareness could lead a state to be both stricter and cleaner, but this would suggest a negative relationship between pollution problems and stringency. Instead, we find a positive connection between pollution problems and regulatory stringency, indicating that pollution problems result in stricter enforcement.

V. ESTIMATION RESULTS

We begin with the analysis of technology choice. We have technology information for a total of 686 plants, but include only the 227 plants which began operations after 1960, when plants were more likely to face some environmental regulation. We assign the plants to five technology categories: kraft, sulfite (including other chemical and semichemical pulping methods), mechanical, deinking, and 'other'. The 'other' category includes mills that do not do their own pulping, but either purchase pulp from others or use recycled inputs, and tend to be smaller and less sophisticated, producing lower-quality products. The means and standard deviations of the variables used in the analysis are presented in Table I.

---

[8] The first-stage regressions explain about 30% of the variation in air pollution stringency, and 25% of the variation in water pollution stringency across states. The resulting stringency measures do impart some time-series variation, but they remain predominantly cross-sectional (80% or more of the total variation in *REGAIR* and *REGWATER*). The detailed results are available at the JIE editorial web page.

[9] Other regulatory measures were considered, from the *Green Index* and other sources. The results (available on the JIE editorial web page) were similar to those presented here, although occasionally one differed (for example, one alternative index of state water pollution problems showed a positive, rather than negative, impact on choosing sulfite pulping).

© Blackwell Publishers Ltd. 1998.

TABLE 1
TECHNOLOGY CHOICE DATASET
SUMMARY STATISTICS
MEAN (STD DEV)
(227 POST-1960 PLANTS)

TECHNOLOGY		
0.203	KRAFT	kraft
0.057	SULF	sulphite/semichemical
0.132	MECH	mechanical
0.057	DEINK	deinking
0.551	other/recycled	<base group in multinomial logit>
PRODUCT		
0.137	FINE	fine/office/writing/specialty
0.128	TISSUE	tissue/napkin/towel
0.260	BOX	boxboard/corrugated/chipboard/linerboard
0.525	other	<base group, includes plants with missing data>

BORN7195	0.498	(0.501)	1970 <plant birth<=1995
VOTE	44.960	(19.290)	Congressional voting pro-environment
REGAIR	5.142	(1.409)	index of air pollution stringency
REGWATER	7.884	(1.331)	index of water pollution stringency
POPDEN	0.018	(0.083)	state population density (1000/sq mi)
ENERGY	0.515	(1.765)	state energy prices ($/MBTU)
FOREST	20.132	(21.426)	Commercially available softwood

Sources:
Lockwood Directory: *TECHNOLOGY, PRODUCT, BORN7195.*
League of Conservation Voters: *VOTE.*
Statistical Abstract: *POPDEN, ENERGY, FOREST.*
Regression-based indices: *REGAIR, REGWATER.*

Table II shows the results of a multinomial logit analysis of technology choice, with the 'other' category being the base group. Population density and energy prices have no significant impact on technology choice. Not surprisingly, plants with pulping processes are more likely in states with more commercial forests. Deinking plants are more common among plants born after 1970 (though not significantly so), presumably encouraged by policies to promote paper recycling. The product mix at the plant is significantly connected to technology choice.[10] However, dropping product mix doesn't affect the regulatory coefficients significantly (results available on JIE editorial web page).

Plants in states with greater regulatory stringency, as measured by *VOTE*, are significantly less likely to incorporate a pulping process. A one standard deviation increase in *VOTE* is associated with a 7.5 percentage point lower probability of choosing kraft pulping, 2.0 percentage points for sulfite, and 5.2 percentage points for mechanical. This corresponds to a

---

[10] The missing coefficients (—) in Tables II and III correspond to cases where no new plants producing that product with that technology opened after 1960.

TABLE II
TECHNOLOGY CHOICE
SINGLE REGULATORY STRINGENCY MEASURE
PRODUCT CONTROLS
MULTINOMIAL LOGIT
($N = 227$)

Choice:	KRAFT	SULF	MECH	DEINK
CONSTANT	0.310	−2.486**	0.596	−2.913***
	(0.59)	(1.10)	(0.65)	(1.10)
VOTE	−0.042***	−0.041**	−0.046***	0.002
	(0.01)	(0.02)	(0.01)	(0.02)
POPDEN	−7.215	−19.55	−1.643	1.535
	(13.07)	(30.47)	(5.53)	(10.02)
FOREST	0.036***	0.056***	0.037***	−0.008
	(0.01)	(0.01)	(0.01)	(0.02)
ENERGY	0.268	0.582	0.302	−0.004
	(0.33)	(0.63)	(0.20)	(0.31)
FINE	0.450	0.689	−0.851	—
	(0.63)	(1.27)	(0.87)	
TISSUE	−2.925**	—	−3.161***	1.013
	(1.17)		(1.18)	(0.64)
BOX	0.843*	1.869**	−0.683	—
	(0.44)	(0.75)	(0.59)	
BORN7195	−0.781*	−0.111	−1.032**	1.143
	(0.42)	(0.70)	(0.51)	(0.74)
LOG-L	−227.307			

Standard errors in parentheses.
*** = significant at 1% level
** = significant at 5% level
* = significant at 10% level
— = In these cases there were no post-1960 plants producing this product with this technology, so the estimated coefficient is a large negative number (and the standard error is not defined).

reduction of one-third in the number of plants choosing each technology.

Table III replaces the single regulatory stringency measure, *VOTE*, with *REGAIR* and *REGWATER*. We find that, as expected, mechanical pulping is less likely in states with greater air pollution stringency, while sulfite pulping is less likely in states with greater water pollution stringency. A one standard deviation increase in *REGAIR* is associated with an 8.8 percentage point reduction in the probability of choosing mechanical pulping. The comparable figure for *REGWATER* and sulfite pulping is 2.3 percentage points. The coefficients on other variables are similar to those in Table II.

We next turn to the analysis of the investment decision, with means and standard deviations presented in Table IV. Our model includes measures of lagged pQ/c and lagged capital stock, as called for in the

TABLE III
TECHNOLOGY CHOICE
MULTIPLE REGULATORY STRINGENCY MEASURES
PRODUCT CONTROLS
MULTINOMIAL LOGIT
($N = 227$)

Choice:	KRAFT	SULF	MECH	DEINK
CONSTANT	6.173***	−0.197	4.903***	−5.282**
	(1.39)	(2.37)	(1.53)	(2.60)
REGAIR	−0.254	0.230	−0.781***	0.002
	(0.26)	(0.43)	(0.30)	(0.40)
REGWATER	−0.881***	−0.685*	−0.311	0.300
	(0.25)	(0.39)	(0.27)	(0.41)
POPDEN	−4.009	−24.00	−0.328	0.335
	(8.19)	(33.57)	(4.94)	(11.14)
FOREST	0.043***	0.068***	0.026*	−0.011
	(0.01)	(0.02)	(0.01)	(0.02)
ENERGY	0.216	0.682	0.258	0.031
	(0.25)	(0.69)	(0.20)	(0.34)
FINE	0.761	0.597	−0.594	—
	(0.68)	(1.26)	0.88	
TISSUE	−3.137***	—	−3.434***	1.132*
	(1.17)		(1.17)	(0.66)
BOX	0.847*	2.040***	−0.745	—
	(0.48)	(0.76)	(0.62)	
BORN7195	−0.414	−0.290	−0.488	1.166
	(0.48)	(0.73)	(0.55)	(0.76)
LOG-L	−210.527			

Standard errors in parentheses.
*** = significant at 1% level
** = significant at 5% level
* = significant at 10% level
— = In these cases there were no post-1960 plants producing this product with this technology, so the estimated coefficient is a large negative number (and the standard error is not defined).

neoclassical investment model. We use two samples of plants in this analysis. The full sample of 116 plants is used for the basic analysis, examining whether technology, product mix, or state regulatory stringency affects annual investment. The PACE subsample of 68 plants is used to analyze the effect of pollution abatement investment on other investment.

Table V presents the results, with the basic neoclassical investment model (column 1) explaining about one-third of the variation in investment spending. There is a strongly positive autoregressive component, indicating that plants doing a sizable investment in one year are likely to have high investment in the following year. The coefficients on pQ/c_{t-1} and K_{t-1} are both positive as expected, though not always significant.

TABLE IV
INVESTMENT DATASET
MEAN (STD DEV)

	Full Sample (116 plants)		PACE Subsample (68 plants)	
Number of Obs	1392		816	
INVEST	5 979	(10 725)		
PRODINV			6 149	(10 325)
pQ/c_{t-1}	12 556	(8 990)	14 905	(8 967)
pQ/c_{t-2}	12 477	(8 853)	14 847	(8 813)
K_{t-1}	51 578	(48 692)	62 753	(49 067)
ABATEYEAR			0.254	(0.435)
ABATEAVG			0.100	(0.108)
VOTE	59.45	(15.9)	57.86	(15.7)
Technology Dummies <not given exactly, due to disclosure issues>				
KRAFT	0.4		0.5	
SULF	< 0.1		< 0.1	
MECH	< 0.1		< 0.1	
DEINK	< 0.1		< 0.1	
KRAFT*VOTE	21.7	(27.1)	24.6	(28.0)
SULF*VOTE	5.1	(17.5)	7.7	(21.1)
MECH*VOTE	5.7	(18.6)	6.7	(19.8)
DEINK*VOTE	5.7	(18.7)	2.9	(13.6)

Product Dummies <not given, due to disclosure issues>
FINE
TISSUE
BOX
NEWS <newsprint – not included in the technology choice runs because few newsprint mills opened during the post-1960 period >

Variable Definitions and Sources

Longitudinal Research Database, Census Bureau
    INVEST = investment (plant & equipment), in $000s (1982$)
    pQ/c_{t-1} = nominal shipments/user cost of capital, lagged 1 year
    pQ/c_{t-2} = nominal shipments/user cost of capital, lagged 2 years
    K_{t-1} = real capital stock in $000s (1982$), lagged 1 year

Pollution Abatement Cost Survey, Census Bureau
    ABATEYEAR = if pollution abatement investment >= $500 000 in year
    ABATEAVG = (pollution abatement investment)/(total investment), averaged over the entire sample period

League of Conservation Voters
    VOTE = Congress voting pro-environment

Lockwood Directory
    KRAFT = 1 if kraft mill
    SULF = 1 if sulfite or semi-chemical mill
    MECH = 1 if mechanical mill
    DEINK = 1 if deinking mill
    <base group = other/recycled>

TABLE V
INVESTMENT MODELS
TOTAL INVESTMENT SPENDING
(FULL SAMPLE, $N = 1392$)

	(1)	(2)	(3)	(4)	(5)	(6)
VOTE		−46.19*	−35.33	−37.41	−47.18*	−6.769
		(25.79)	(26.34)	(44.11)	(26.14)	(36.12)
pQ/c_{t-1}	0.241*	0.236*	0.234*	0.240*	0.229*	0.083
	(0.13)	(0.13)	(0.13)	(0.13)	(0.13)	(0.13)
pQ/c_{t-2}	0.078	0.074	0.067	0.060	0.075	−0.105
	(0.13)	(0.13)	(0.13)	(0.13)	(0.13)	(0.13)
K_{t-1}	0.040**	0.036**	0.020	0.020	0.036**	−0.160***
	(0.02)	(0.02)	(0.02)	(0.02)	(0.02)	(0.03)
Technology:						
KRAFT			3 285**	3 532		
			(1 346)	(3 576)		
SULF			765	1 807		
			(1 963)	(11 120)		
MECH			728	−4 019		
			(1 992)	(8 223)		
DEINK			1 132	−2 561		
			(1 887)	(11 800)		
KRAFT*VOTE				−4.038		
				(54.18)		
SULF*VOTE				−16.164		
				(172.1)		
MECH*VOTE				71.937		
				(120.5)		
DEINK*VOTE				57.153		
				(180.00)		
Product:						
BOX					1 628	
					(1 624)	
FINE					−85	
					(1 139)	
NEWS					−603	
					(2 179)	
TISSUE					1 009	
					(1 425)	

TABLE V (continued)

	(1)	(2)	(3)	(4)	(5)	(6)
Year:						
1980	529 (1021)	637 (1020)	653 (1020)	644 (1023)	646 (1022)	947 (1002)
1981	730 (1186)	856 (1187)	899 (1186)	852 (1190)	867 (1188)	1559 (1138)
1982	−221 (1242)	174 (1261)	185 (1260)	124 (1272)	197 (1263)	1336 (1216)
1983	2242* (1252)	−1831 (1273)	−1809 (1272)	−1832 (1276)	−1816 (1275)	−516 (1226)
1984	−810 (1275)	−351 (1301)	−340 (1299)	−346 (1305)	−357 (1304)	442 (1236)
1985	990 (1283)	1302 (1296)	1327 (1294)	1344 (1298)	1295 (1298)	1876 (1205)
1986	470 (1305)	717 (1312)	747 (1310)	772 (1314)	700 (1315)	966 (1211)
1987	853 (1337)	1325 (1363)	1327 (1361)	1297 (1367)	1329 (1366)	1165 (1253)
1988	2085 (1325)	2555* (1351)	2547* (1349)	2512* (1354)	2554* (1354)	2182* (1247)
1989	3590*** (1312)	4154*** (1348)	4134*** (1347)	4116*** (1351)	4176*** (1351)	4014*** (1251)
1990	2474** (1110)	3057*** (1155)	3070*** (1155)	3053*** (1160)	3091*** (1158)	3761*** (1086)
FIRM	X	X	X	X	X	
PLANT						X
AR(1)	0.338*** (0.03)	0.342*** (0.03)	0.341*** (0.03)	0.341*** (0.03)	0.341*** (0.03)	0.280*** (0.03)
R^2	0.342	0.343	0.347	0.347	0.344	0.419

Standard errors in parentheses.

*** = significant at 1% level
** = significant at 5% level
* = significant at 10% level

Technology dummies are more powerful than product dummies in explaining investment, with kraft mills receiving more investment, but neither set of dummies is jointly significant. The pattern of year dummies is consistent across the different models, with less investment around 1983 and more investment in 1989 and 1990, corresponding to cyclical changes in paper industry demand. Finally, we included plant dummies (model 6), resulting in a fixed-effects estimate.

State regulatory stringency, as measured by *VOTE*, has a consistently negative sign, indicating lower investment spending in more stringent states. Its effect is never more than marginally significant, and loses that significance when technology dummies are included. The magnitude of the coefficients are relatively large: a one standard deviation increase in *VOTE* is associated with a $734 000 reduction in investment, a 12.3 percent reduction when evaluated at the mean level of investment. Interacting the plant's technology with *VOTE* doesn't indicate significant differences in regulatory impact across different technologies.

In our subsample of 68 plants with complete PACE information, we measure two aspects of pollution abatement investment. *ABATEYEAR* reflects the timing of abatement investment, identifying those years with more than $500 000 of abatement investment at the plant. *ABATEAVG* is a cross-sectional variable, dividing the plant's abatement investment over the entire period by its total investment over the period.[11] This reflects the extent to which the plant's investment spending had to be directed towards pollution abatement. We also modify the dependent variable *INVEST* by subtracting off abatement investment, so that it represents only 'productive' investment, *PRODINV*.

Tables VI and VII present the results for the PACE subsample. The basic investment variables have similar coefficients to the full-sample results in Table V, both in sign and significance. Both plant-specific measures of pollution abatement investment are significant, whether included separately or together. Years with high pollution abatement investment (*ABATEYEAR*) tend to have significantly higher 'productive' investment. This probably reflects the high cost of closing a paper mill for renovations, leading to a bunching of investment spending throughout the plant. It also indicates the need for caution when estimating the impact of abatement investment on productive investment (a simple regression of productive investment on abatement investment would tend to find a positive association).

---

[11] Dividing by *INVEST* might be expected to induce a negative coefficient on *ABATEAVG*, through endogeneity bias (positive shocks to *INVEST* being negative shocks to *ABATEAVG*). We did Hausman tests for each of the equations. The instrument set included the other explanatory variables in the investment analysis. We also included a set of factors expected to reflect regulatory stringency and hence to influence pollution abatement investment: state air pollution enforcement activity, overall state pollution levels, and the plant's non-capital pollution abatement expenditures as a share of its total costs. We found no evidence for endogeneity: the 'residual' *ABATEAVG* value was never significant, with its *t*-ratio usually below 1.

TABLE VI
INVESTMENT MODELS
PRODUCTIVE INVESTMENT SPENDING
(PACE Subsample, $N = 816$)

	(1)	(2)	(3)	(4)	(5)	(6)
ABATEAVG	−17 164**		−19 080***	−9 880**		−11 315***
	(6 797)		(6 740)	(3 897)		(3 855)
ABATEYEAR		2 087**	2 375***		2 069**	2 427***
		(861)	(863)		(829)	(833)
pQ/c_{t-1}	0.308***	0.299*	0.286*	0.413***	0.397***	0.388***
	(0.16)	(0.16)	(0.16)	(0.15)	(0.15)	(0.14)
pQ/c_{t-2}	−0.001	−0.060	−0.015	−0.032	−0.047	−0.046
	(0.15)	(0.15)	(0.15)	(0.15)	(0.15)	(0.15)
K_{t-1}	0.056**	0.042*	0.050**	0.029*	0.024	0.028*
	(0.02)	(0.02)	(0.02)	(0.02)	(0.02)	(0.02)
FIRM	X	X	X			
AR(1)	0.243***	0.228***	0.232***	0.284***	0.274***	0.270***
	(0.03)	(0.03)	(0.03)	(0.03)	(0.03)	(0.03)
R^2	0.307	0.307	0.314	0.271	0.271	0.278

All regressions included year dummies (coefficients available on JIE editorial web page).

Standard errors in parentheses.

*** = significant at 1% level
** = significant at 5% level
* = significant at 10% level

Abatement intensity, *ABATEAVG*, is negatively associated with spending on productive investment. Consider what the magnitude of the *ABATEAVG* coefficient means, using model 1 from Table VI, with a coefficient of −17 164. An increase in *ABATEAVG* from 0.10 (the sample mean) to 0.11 would result in a decrease of productive investment of $171 640. A detailed calculation,[12] shows that this could be accomplished by an increase of

---

[12] The crowding out calculation is as follows.
i. Productive investment must be 9 times abatement investment, since *ABATEAVG* starts at 0.100 = abatement/(abatement + productive). Let Q be initial abatement investment.
ii. Let c be the drop in productive investment and x be the increase in abatement investment which results in a new value of *ABATEAVG* equal to 0.11.
iii. The new value of *ABATEAVG* is $(Q + x)/(Q + x + 9Q − c) = 0.11$
iv. Solving for x we get $x = (0.1Q − 0.11c)/0.89$
v. For $Q = 1000$ (a round number comparable to values found in data) and $c = 171.64$ (the regression coefficient, multiplied by the increase in *ABATEAVG* of 0.01), we get $x = 91.15$. Smaller x values would correspond to smaller increases in abatement investment needed to achieve a given increase in *ABATEAVG* (and greater crowding out).
vi. Since the reduction in productive investment (171.64) exceeds the increase in abatement investment (91.15), we get more than 100 percent crowding out (in this case, 188 percent).

© Blackwell Publishers Ltd. 1998.

abatement investment of about $90 000. The decrease in productive investment is larger than the increase in abatement investment, so we have more than 100 percent crowding out (188 percent). A two standard error confidence interval would range between 33 percent and 414 percent.

Do these results reflect crowding out within a plant, or shifts in investment across plants within a firm? The magnitude of the effect gives one piece of evidence: pure 'crowding out' could not reduce productive investment by more than 100 percent. Another clue comes from similar regressions using total investment as the dependent variable, rather than productive investment. These find a significant negative coefficient on *ABATEAVG*, confirming that productive investment falls by more than the increase in abatement investment.[13] Finally, models 1–3 include firm dummies, so that all variables are measured as deviations from the firm mean. In particular, the negative *ABATEAVG* coefficient indicates that plants with above-average abatement investment *within their firm* have lower-than-average productive investment within their firm. These results tend to rely relatively heavily on a within-firm reallocation of investment across plants.

Comparable models (4–6) without firm dummies find substantially smaller coefficients on *ABATEAVG*. This is consistent with there being a sizable within-firm shifting of investment towards low-abatement-cost plants. Comparing model 4 with model 1, we find that the measure of 'crowding out' falls from 188 percent to 99 percent. Therefore nearly half of the estimated *ABATEAVG* coefficient in model 1 could be attributed to within-firm reallocation. Although distinguishing between these two effects is difficult, in any event the results provide evidence against the view that environmental regulations induce firms to upgrade their productive capital stock more rapidly, expanding total investment.

Table VII presents the results of adding technology and product variables to the model, along with the state-level regulatory variable, *VOTE*. The coefficients on *ABATEAVG* and *ABATEYEAR* are, if anything, a bit larger than in Table VI. These models include firm dummies and thus reflect both within-plant crowding out and across-plant reallocation of investment. Comparable models without firm dummies find substantially smaller coefficients on *ABATEAVG* (−11 529, −12 345, −12 546, and −10 044 corresponding to models 2–5). The *VOTE* coefficients are similar to those found in Table V, though usually insignificant. As before, technology and product dummies show neither a significant impact on investment spending nor a significant interaction with *VOTE*.

---

[13] Regression results available on JIE editorial web page.

TABLE VII
INVESTMENT MODELS
PRODUCTIVE INVESTMENT SPENDING
(PACE SUBSAMPLE, $N = 816$)

	(1)	(2)	(3)	(4)	(5)	(6)
ABATEAVG		−18 214*** (6 810)	−19 426*** (7 195)	−20 539*** (7 342)	−18 910*** (6 883)	
ABATEYEAR		2 360*** (862)	2 303*** (864)	2 339*** (866)	2 353*** (865)	1 764** (863)
VOTE	−59.26* (34.12)	−50.10 (33.89)	−47.76 (34.16)	21.633 (71.00)	−60.81* (34.94)	−18.99 (51.35)
pQ/c_{t-1}	0.309** (0.16)	0.281* (0.15)	0.280* (0.16)	0.293* (0.16)	0.290* (0.16)	0.214 (0.16)
pQ/c_{t-2}	−0.055 (0.15)	−0.027 (0.15)	−0.036 (0.15)	−0.034 (0.16)	−0.010 (0.16)	−0.219 (0.16)
K_{t-1}	0.044* (0.02)	0.046** (0.02)	0.034 (0.03)	0.037 (0.03)	0.036 (0.02)	−0.247*** (0.05)
Technology:						
KRAFT			1 440 (1 765)	6 918 (4 875)		
SULF			715 (2 460)	4 862 (12 160)		
MECH			−1 789 (2 530)	−3 786 (10 870)		
DEINK			−681 (3 255)	−3 713 (23 050)		
KRAFT*VOTE				−95.726 (78.84)		
SULF*VOTE				−69.510 (190.3)		
MRCH*VOTE				24.216 (162.7)		
DEINK*VOTE				42.499 (351.0)		
Product:						
BOX					1 969 (2 906)	
FINE					2 353 (1 634)	
NEWS					−3 979 (3 873)	
TISSUE					−369 (1 890)	

TABLE VII (continued)

	(1)	(2)	(3)	(4)	(5)	(6)
FIRM	X	X	X	X	X	
PLANT						X
AR(1)	0.245***	0.238***	0.240***	0.239***	0.238***	0.235***
	(0.03)	(0.03)	(0.03)	(0.03)	(0.03)	(0.03)
R^2	0.304	0.316	0.318	0.320	0.321	0.373

All regressions included year dummies.

Standard errors in parentheses.

*** = significant at 1% level
** = significant at 5% level
* = significant at 10% level

VI. CONCLUSIONS

This paper examines the impact of environmental regulation on two aspects of the investment decision for paper mills: the specific production technology installed in a new mill, and annual investment spending at existing mills. We find that new plants in more stringent states are less likely to incorporate the dirtier production technologies. Looking at different types of pollution, we find that mechanical pulping, which generates more air pollution, is less likely in states with stricter air regulations. Sulfite pulping, the most water pollution intensive, is less likely in states with stricter water regulation. The magnitudes of these impacts are sizable, with a one standard deviation increase in stringency reducing the probability of choosing a pulping technology by several percentage points.

We find a small impact of state regulatory stringency on a plant's investment spending, though not very strong. The weakness of these results may reflect a tendency for existing plants to be kept operating, especially since older plants are often exempt from newer regulations.

We find more significant connections between pollution abatement investment and productive (non-abatement) investment. First, pollution abatement and productive investments tend to happen in the same years, consistent with the high cost of shutting down a paper mill for renovations. Second, plants with relatively high pollution abatement capital expenditures over the period invest less in productive capital. The reduction in productive investment is greater than the increase in abatement investment, leading to lower total investment at high abatement cost plants. The magnitude of this impact is quite large, suggesting that a dollar of pollution abatement investment reduces productive investment by $1.88 at that plant. This seems to reflect both environmental investment

© Blackwell Publishers Ltd. 1998.

crowding out productive investment within a plant, and firms shifting investment towards plants facing less stringent abatement requirements. Estimates placing less weight on within-firm reallocation of investment indicate approximate dollar-for-dollar ($0.99) crowding out of productive investment.

ACCEPTED DECEMBER 1997

REFERENCES

Barbera, A. J. and McConnell, V. D., 1986, 'Effects of Pollution Control on Industry Productivity: a Factor Demand Approach', *Journal of Industrial Economics*, 35, pp. 161–172.
Bartik, T. J., 1988, 'The Effects of Environmental Regulation on Business Location in the United States,' *Growth and Change*, pp. 22–44.
Bischoff, C. W., 1971, 'Business Investment in the 1970's: A Comparison of Models', Brookings Papers on Economic Activity, 1, pp. 13–58.
Cooper, R., Haltiwanger, J. and Power, L., 1995, 'Machine Replacement and the Business Cycle: Lumps and Bumps', Working Paper 5260, National Bureau of Economic Research, Cambridge, Mass.
Deily, M. E. and Gray, W. B., 1991, 'Enforcement of Pollution Regulations in a Declining Industry', *Journal of Environmental Economics and Management*, 21, pp. 260–274.
Gollop, F. M. and Roberts, M. J., 1983, 'Environmental Regulations and Productivity Growth: the Case of Fossil-fueled Electric Power Generation', *Journal of Political Economy*, 91, pp. 654–674.
Gray, W. B., 1987, 'The Cost of Regulation: OSHA, EPA and the Productivity Slowdown', *American Economic Review*, 77, pp. 998–1006.
Gray, W. B., 1986, 'Productivity versus OSHA and EPA Regulations' (UMI Research Press, Ann Arbor).
Gray, W. B., 1995, 'How and Why do States Differ in Environmental Regulation?', mimeo April 1995.
Gray, W. B., 1997, 'Manufacturing Plant Location: Does State Pollution Regulation Matter?' Working Paper 5880, National Bureau of Economic Research, Cambridge, Mass.
Gray, W. B. and Shadbegian, R. J., 1995, 'Pollution Abatement Costs, Regulation, and Plant-Level Productivity', Working Paper 4994, National Bureau of Economic Research, Cambridge, Mass.
Gray, W. B. and Shadbegian, R. J., 1997, 'Environmental Regulation, Investment Timing, and Technology Choice', Working Paper 6036, National Bureau of Economic Research, Cambridge, Mass.
Hall, B. and Kerr, M. L., 1991, *Green Index: A State-by-State Guide to the Nation's Environmental Health* (Island Press, Washington).
Jorgenson, D. W., 1963, 'Capital Theory and Investment Behavior', *American Economic Review*, 53, pp. 247–259.
Lockwood-Post Pulp and Paper Directory, Miller-Freeman Publishing Company, San Francisco, CA.
McGuckin, R. H. and Pascoe, G. A., 1988, 'The Longitudinal Research Database: Status and Research Possibilities', *Survey of Current Business*, November.

Ringquist, E. J., 1993, *Environmental Protection at the State Level: Politics and Progress in Controlling Pollution*, (M. E. Sharpe, New York).

US Bureau of the Census, 'Pollution Abatement Costs and Expenditures', MA-200 (GPO, Washington).

US Bureau of the Census, *Statistical Abstract of the United States* (GPO, Washington).

Capital Turnover

[18]

DIFFERENTIAL ENVIRONMENTAL REGULATION: EFFECTS ON ELECTRIC UTILITY CAPITAL TURNOVER AND EMISSIONS

Randy A. Nelson, Tom Tietenberg, and Michael R. Donihue*

Abstract—This paper tests the hypothesis that differential regulations reduced the rate of capital turnover in the electric utility industry, resulting in increased emissions of sulfur dioxide. Based on a sample of forty-four privately owned electric utilities operating over the period 1969-83, our results indicate that (i) regulation increased the age of capital by an average of 3.29 years (24.6%), (ii) increases in the age of capital have no statistically significant impact on emissions, and (iii) in the absence of regulation emissions would have increased by 3.79 tons per million kWhs (34.6%).

I. Introduction

In controlling air pollution in the United States the brunt of environmental regulation has been borne by new sources. Applying the most stringent controls on new sources raises their cost, relative to the chief alternative, operating existing sources longer. This regulatory bias towards new sources increases the attractiveness of older capital relative to new capital, thus reducing the rate of capital turnover. Because new plants are typically thought to be cleaner than old plants, capital turnover normally produces emission reductions. More stringent regulation on new sources will mean that each new source would pollute less than otherwise, but it will also slow down the introduction of new sources. The former means a reduction in emissions, but the latter means an increase. Which effect dominates is an empirical question.

The effect of differential regulation on the rate of turnover in the automotive fleet in the United States has been documented by Gruenspecht (1982). In response to the higher cost of emissions control devices on new cars, owners held onto old automobiles longer. Since new cars were substantially cleaner than older cars, emission reductions were delayed. In effect, this shift in fleet composition was equivalent to a setback of three to four years in the timetable for reducing emissions.[1] The impact of differential regulation appears to be significant for stationary sources as well. In a study of the electric utility industry, Joskow and Rose (1985) report that the installation of environmental control equipment increased the construction cost of coal-burning generating plants by approximately 20%, an estimate within the range of 14%-62% reported by Faltmayer (1979), Bain (1986), Prewitt (1988) and Willenbrock and Thomas (1980). In addition, Weaver (1975) and Gordon (1990) report a 25%-50% increase in the work force of generating plants that installed scrubbers. Ackerman and Hassler (1981) report that the incentive to continue operating older plants in the Midwest significantly increased emissions. Maloney and Brady (1988) investigate the consequences of restrictions on emissions trading in conjunction with the environmentally-induced increase in the cost of new generating plants. Using state-level data they conclude that environmental regulations increased the average age of generating plants by approximately four years, resulting in a 27% increase in emissions.

Received for publication November 7, 1990. Revision accepted for publication January 6, 1992.
*Colby College.
We are indebted to four anonymous referees and the participants at the Association of Environmental Economists meetings in Washington, D.C. in 1990 for helpful comments and suggestions, to Chuck Lakin for help in obtaining the necessary data, and to the Robert N. Anthony Fund at Colby College for financial assistance.

---

[1] See Crandall et al. (1986, p. 96).

This paper reexamines the relationship between environmental regulation and capital turnover, and the effect this relationship has had on emission reductions in the electric utility industry. Using a pooled database of 44 electric utilities over the 1969–1983 time period, a simultaneous three-equation system is estimated to determine (1) the impact of regulation on the age of capital, (2) the impact of regulation and age on emissions, and (3) the effect of emissions on regulation. Our results suggest that imposing more stringent controls on new sources does retard capital turnover, but that the increased age of capital does not have a significant impact on emissions. In addition, simulations indicate that emissions would have increased by 34.6%, on average, in the absence of regulation.

II. Environmental Regulations and the Age of Capital

The 1970 Clean Air Act (CAA) led to the establishment of National Ambient Air Quality Standards (NAAQS) for the United States.[2] By 1975 it had become apparent that, despite major gains in air quality, many areas had not met and would not meet the NAAQS by statutory deadlines. Therefore, in the 1977 Amendments to the CAA, areas not meeting the original deadlines were designated as nonattainment areas. Following the 1977 Amendments, newly constructed large pollution sources, or large sources undergoing major modifications, could only obtain operating permits in nonattainment areas if emissions were limited to the lowest achievable rate (LAER), defined as the lowest emission rate in any state implementation plan. Existing sources in nonattainment areas were required only to meet standards based upon the less-stringent Reasonably Available Control Technologies. New pollution sources in attainment areas were also held to higher standards than existing sources. In addition, the EPA defined uniform national emission standards, known as the New Source Performance Standards (NSPS), for major new emission sources. New sources and sources undergoing major modifications are also required to undergo the "New Source Review Process," a time-consuming and expensive permitting process.

An emissions trading program was adopted in the mid-1970s in an effort to inject more flexibility into the manner in which the clean air objectives were met. Under emissions trading, sources are encouraged to change the mix of control technologies envisioned in the standards as long as air quality is improved or at least not adversely affected by the change.[3] Central to the emissions trading program is the emissions reduction credit (ERC). Should any source control an emission point to a higher degree than necessary to fulfill its legal obligations, it can apply to the control authority for certification of the excess control as an ERC. In addition, an offset policy was established to allow new or expanding sources to commence operations in a nonattainment area provided they acquire sufficient ERCs from existing sources.[4] By buying the ERCs, new sources, in effect, finance emission controls undertaken by existing sources. Finally, netting was permitted, whereby sources undergoing modification or review can escape the burden of a new source review if the net increase in plant-wide emissions is deemed to be insignificant.[5]

Restrictions in the emissions trading program limited its ability to mitigate the new source bias. Authorities chose to grandfather the operating permits of existing plants, while requiring new plants to purchase or otherwise obtain ERCs in order to operate. In addition, the offset policy requires new sources to acquire more ERCs from existing sources than necessary to compensate for its own emissions. In essence a disproportionate share of the burden of improving air quality was transferred to new sources. Furthermore, ERCs cannot be used to meet either the NSPS or LAER standards. Firms are thus required to install prescribed control equipment, increasing the relative cost of compliance for new sources.

III. Model Specification and Data

Any attempt to quantify the magnitude of the new source bias must take into consideration (i) the effect of regulation on the age of capital, (ii) the impact of the age of capital on emissions, and (iii) the effect of emissions on the extent of regulation. To accommodate the obvious feedback effects, a three-equation model was specified and estimated using three-stage least squares.

The specification of the age equation is based on a model presented by Smith and Basala (1981), who investigate the impact of environmental regulations on the age of capital. Their model indicates that the age of capital (Age) is a function of changes in input prices and demand, and the degree of regulatory intensity. Since the construction of a new plant may take up to ten years, the appropriate lags must be taken into consideration. The age equation is specified as

$$Age = f(Demandr, PFr, Wr, PKr, Demandr2, PFr2, Wr2, PKr2, Regulation, Nuclear, Genpct, ROR). \quad (1)$$

---

[2] The existing primary and secondary standards can be found in the Code of Federal Regulations, Vol. 40, Parts 50.4, 50.6, 50.8, 50.9, 50.11, and 50.12 (1989).

[3] For a general discussion of emissions trading see Tietenberg (1985); for a detailed study of emissions trading in the electric utility industry, see Raufer and Feldman (1987).

[4] For an evaluation of the offset program, see Dudeck and Palmisano (1988, pp. 217–256).

[5] For an evaluation of the netting program, see Hahn and Hester (1989, pp. 132–136).

The variables *Demandr*, *PFr*, *Wr*, and *PKr* represent the average growth rate over the last five years ($t - 5$ to t) of demand, the price of fuel, wages, and the price of capital, respectively. *Demandr2*, *PFr2*, *Wr2*, and *PKr2* represent the average growth rates of these variables from $t - 10$ to $t - 5$ (the five-year period starting ten years prior to t and ending five years prior to t). The coefficients of *Demandr*, *PFr*, *Wr*, *Demandr2*, *Pfr2*, and *Wr2* are all expected to be negative, while the coefficients of *Pkr*, *Pkr2*, and *Regulation* are expected to be positive.[6] To account for non-fossil fuel steam generation the variables *Nuclear* (the ratio of nuclear to total capacity) and *Genpct* (the percentage of total sales generated by the utility) are also included in the equation. Firms with extensive nuclear facilities would have reduced demand for steam generating facilities, implying that the coefficient of nuclear should be positive. Firms that produce, instead of purchase, power will have greater demand for new steam generating capacity, implying that the coefficient of *Genpct* should be negative. The earned rate of return (*ROR*) is included in the equation to account for the effects of rate of return regulation. Firms with higher *ROR*s should more easily be able to finance new construction, implying a negative coefficient for this variable.

The level of sulfur-dioxide emissions per kilowatt-hour is assumed to be a function of the firm's fuel mix, the average age of the firm's steam-electric generating capacity, other operating characteristics, and the extent of regulation. The emissions equation is specified as

$$Emissions = f(Coal, Oil, Age, CU, Q, Regulation). \quad (2)$$

Coal and *Oil* represent the percentage of total BTUs obtained from these two fuels. Since the sulfur content of both coal and oil is greater than that of the omitted fuel, natural gas, the coefficients of these variables should be positive. Assuming that older plants have higher emissions rates than newer plants, the *Age* coefficient is expected to be positive. A disproportionate share of emissions occur during start up, implying that utilities with higher rates of capacity utilization should emit less sulfur dioxide per kilowatt-hour; the coefficient of *CU*, which measures the rate of capacity utilization, is thus expected to be negative. The output variable, *Q*, is included to allow for possible scale effects in the production of emissions; the sign of the coefficient for *Q* is indeterminate. The coefficient for the regulatory variable is expected to be negative.

The intensity of regulation faced by a given firm is assumed to be a function of the firm's emissions, and various aspects of the population of the state in which the firm operates. The regulation equation is given by

$$Regulation = f(Emissions, Income, Popul, Educ, Popage). \quad (3)$$

Assuming that regulators react to higher emissions by increasing the stringency of enforcement, the coefficient of *Emissions* should be positive.[7] *Income* represents the average per capita income for the state in which the utility is located. Since environmental quality is presumed to have a high income elasticity of demand, the coefficient of *Income* should be positive. *Popul* is the population per square mile for the state where the utility is located. The greater damage caused by emissions in areas with high population densities should generate more political support for regulation, implying a positive coefficient. The variable *Educ* is an index of educational attainment for the state where the utility is located. Since the demand for environmental quality presumably rises with the level of education, the coefficient for this variable is expected to be positive. Finally, the *Popage* variable represents the percentage of the population under seventeen years of age and over sixty-five. Since children and older people are more sensitive to the effects of pollution, increases in *Popage* should increase the demand for regulation, implying a positive coefficient.

The model was estimated using data from a sample of forty-four privately-owned electric utilities operating over the period 1969–83. Firm-specific emissions rates were computed using the data sources and procedures detailed in Gollop and Roberts (1983). The *Age* variable was computed as the current year minus the average date of installation of a firm's steam generating capacity; the construction of this variable is discussed in detail in Nelson (1984). Other variable definitions and data sources are contained in a data appendix available upon request.

Utilities face a variety of environmental regulations, many of which directly affect their emissions rate or their incentive to invest in new generating facilities. To capture these effects several proxies were employed to represent the degree of regulatory intensity. To allow a comparison with the results presented by Maloney and Brady (1988), the enforcement expenditures of the state air quality management agency are used as one regulatory variable. These expenditures were normalized by the number of electric utilities, and the number of steam-electric generating plants in a state to form

---

[6] Growing environmental awareness throughout the 1970s and 1980s, as reflected in the NIMBY (not in my backyard) attitude, may also be responsible for the increased age of capital. Many environmental groups were successful in delaying or halting construction of electric generating plants. The coefficient of *Regulation* may be biased upwards if the regulatory variable is correlated with this effect.

[7] It could be argued that regulation is a function of past, and not current emissions. A test of the null hypothesis that current emissions are uncorrelated with the error term in the regulation equation was rejected at the 5% level using a Hausman specification test.

the regulatory variables *RS*1, and *RS*2, respectively. Data for these variables are available for the period 1969–80.

In previous studies of the impact of environmental regulations on the electric utility industry, Gollop and Roberts (1983) employ a regulatory variable that measures the severity of emissions constraints on utility operations, while Fuller (1987) constructed an enforcement variable based on a frontier index of comparative enforcement stringency relative to the best practice level. Both regulatory variables were designed primarily to capture the emissions reductions resulting from a switch from high-sulfur to low-sulfur fuels. In an effort to more directly measure the impact of environmental regulations on the cost of new generating plants two alternative regulatory proxies are employed in this study. The first, *RF*1, represents the value of the firm's air pollution control facilities per KW of capacity, while *RF*2 represents the value of the total (air, water, noise, and esthetic) pollution control facilities per KW of capacity. Data for *RF*1 and *RF*2 are available for the period 1976–83. In an effort to differentiate between firms located in nonattainment and attainment areas, a second regulatory variable, *SOR*, defined as the percentage of a firm's steam generating capacity located in a (sulfur dioxide) nonattainment area, was included in each equation.

IV. Empirical Results

Four different versions of the model, one for each of the regulatory variables, were estimated using three-stage least squares. A fixed effects model was employed to control for the omission of variables that are constant over time for a given firm and correlated with the other explanatory variables. The null hypothesis that the estimated coefficients of the firm dummy variables equal zero was rejected at the 1% significance level using a Wald test. The estimated parameters are presented in table 1.

The estimated parameters of the age equation generally conform to our a priori expectations. The age of fossil-fueled plants decreases as firms reduce their nuclear capacity, increase their dependence on purchased power, or construct new plants to meet growing demand. Increases in the price of fuel and capital reduce the average age in the *RS*1 and *RS*2 equations, but not in the *RF*1 and *RF*2 equations. Firms in nonattainment areas have newer plants in the state-level regulatory variable regressions; this variable is insignificant in the firm-level regulatory regressions. Contrary to our expectations, increases in the *ROR* are associated with increases in age.

The coefficients of the regulatory variables are positive and statistically significant at the 5% significance level or better in every case, implying that increases in regulatory intensity lead firms to delay the construction of new steam-generating plants. Based on the estimated coefficients and the mean level of the regulatory variable in various years, increases in state environmental expenditures per firm increased the average age of capital by 0.63 years (4.92%) in 1969, 2.75 years (20.58%) in 1976, and 4.26 years (28.36%) in 1980; the corresponding estimates for *RS*2 are 0.77 years (6.03%), 3.36 years (24.92%), and 4.68 years (32.14%), respectively. In 1976, 1980, and 1983 expenditures on air pollution control facilities increased the average age by 0.39 years (2.96%), 1.06 years (7.45%), and 1.31 years (8.53%), respectively; the corresponding estimates for *RF*2 are 1.51 years (11.64%), 3.16 years (22.38%), and 3.64 years (24.17%). Maloney and Brady (1988, p. 222, table 6) report an average elasticity of age with respect to regulation of 0.084; the average elasticity implied by this study is 0.155. Their estimated increase in age between the ten states with the highest levels of regulation and the remaining forty states was approximately 4 years, or 24.6%. The mean increase in age between the average level of regulation in 1980 and no regulation in this study is 3.29 years, or 22.64%.

The results for the emissions equation reported in table 1 generally conform to our a priori expectations, although emissions appear to be independent of output and capacity utilization. The estimated coefficient of the *Age* variable is statistically insignificant at the 5% confidence level using a two-tailed asymptotic *t*-test in every regression.[8] The indirect effect of regulation on emissions, as transmitted by the age effect, may be evaluated as the product of the *Regulation* coefficient from the age equation and the *Age* coefficient from the *Emissions* equation. This term is insignificant at the 5% level in every case.

The insignificant *Age* coefficient in the emissions equation appears to contradict Maloney and Brady's (1988, p. 222) claim that "regulation has induced delay in the retirement of capital and that this delay has been detrimental to the improvement of the environment." A closer examination of their results, however, indicates (table 5, p. 221) that the *Age* variable in their emissions equation is statistically significant at the 5% level using a two-tailed *t*-test in only one of their eight regressions. In addition, the indirect effect of regulation on emissions is significant at the 5% level in only three of their eight regressions. Taken together, the two sets of results offer little support for the hypothesis that the regulatory-induced increase in the age of generating plants has significantly increased emissions in the electric utility industry.

One possible explanation for the lack of a significant relationship between age and emissions is reported by Joskow and Schmalense (1985), who examine the per-

---

[8] The addition of an Age^2 variable to the emissions equation does not alter our finding that emissions are independent of age.

TABLE 1.—THREE STAGE LEAST SQUARES ESTIMATES

| | Age Equation | | | | | Emissions Equation | | | |
| | Regulatory Variable | | | | | Regulatory Variable | | | |
Variable	RF1	RF2	RS1	RS2	Variable	RF1	RF2	RS1	RS2
Nuclear	6.490	2.612	8.463	6.268	Coal	0.0079	0.0053	0.0129	0.0100
	(2.31)	(3.13)	(5.58)	(4.48)		(4.17)	(3.42)	(5.99)	(5.01)
Genpct	−3.901	−2.762	−3.855	−3.317	Oil	0.0055	0.0032	0.0091	0.0060
	(3.40)	(2.23)	(4.68)	(3.67)		(3.60)	(2.26)	(4.40)	(3.64)
ROR	0.266	0.220	0.260	0.230	Age	0.265E-3	0.157E-3	−0.248E-3	−0.286E-4
	(3.00)	(2.56)	(2.99)	(2.65)		(1.89)	(0.98)	(1.66)	(0.21)
Demandr	−13.08	−7.741	−9.609	−12.25	CU	−0.0262	−0.0228	0.0105	−0.0325
	(2.72)	(1.60)	(2.45)	(3.15)		(1.27)	(1.16)	(0.60)	(1.97)
PFr	0.881	1.397	−4.786	−5.041	Q	0.629E-6	0.347E-6	−0.353E-6	0.493E-6
	(0.43)	(0.69)	(3.68)	(3.53)		(1.02)	(0.61)	(0.52)	(0.83)
PKr	4.409	3.251	−1.614	0.353	Regulation	−0.0011	−0.0005	−0.349E-3	−0.222E-2
	(1.33)	(0.99)	(0.42)	(0.09)		(5.07)	(3.33)	(5.11)	(7.53)
Wr	−5.330	−12.06	1.411	−2.663	SOR	0.0659	−0.0130	0.3446	0.5125
	(0.70)	(1.56)	(0.20)	(0.32)		(1.58)	(0.36)	(3.94)	(5.53)
Demandr2	−9.094	−1.615	−21.06	−22.77	Intercept	0.0049	0.0077	0.0036	0.0052
	(1.86)	(0.31)	(4.98)	(4.83)		(1.81)	(3.15)	(1.03)	(1.60)
PFr2	0.095	−0.0914	−7.776	−6.224		Regulation Equation			
	(0.05)	(0.47)	(3.98)	(3.31)					
PKr2	0.444	2.785	−7.663	−7.604	Emissions	32.85	−353.9	−461.8	−147.3
	(0.09)	(0.56)	(3.12)	(2.90)		(0.31)	(2.28)	(1.74)	(2.77)
Wr2	−1.070	−11.30	3.912	−6.582	Income	−0.1447	−0.0455	0.240	0.0333
	(0.10)	(1.08)	(0.36)	(0.55)		(2.35)	(0.52)	(0.95)	(0.77)
Regulation	0.3785	0.5698	0.320	1.578	Popul	−40.23	43.52	156.5	34.10
	(2.49)	(5.27)	(6.65)	(3.74)		(1.54)	(1.19)	(1.94)	(2.37)
SOR	−24.36	−46.97	−268.4	−325.3	Educ	30.67	38.80	46.13	11.98
	(0.69)	(1.37)	(4.81)	(3.15)		(6.89)	(6.07)	(1.93)	(2.74)
Intercept	11.98	10.88	18.66	18.07	Popage	14.71	−1.759	44.34	15.13
	(6.00)	(5.37)	(11.73)	(11.23)		(1.42)	(0.12)	(0.69)	(1.26)
					SOR	113.50	83.37	945.9	229.9
						(5.39)	(2.60)	(7.70)	(8.73)
					Intercept	−11.80	−11.96	−189.1	−42.99
						(1.75)	(1.28)	(2.25)	(2.59)

Note: Values in parentheses are asympototic *t*-statistics.

formance characteristics of coal-burning generating units built in the U.S. over the period 1960–80. They conclude that the gross heat rate (GHR) (the number of BTU's of fuel required to generate a KWH of electricity), after falling steadily until the mid-1960s, stabilized in the 1970s and in some units actually increased. If emissions are related to fuel efficiency, and the GHR for units built in the late 1960s and 1970s is equivalent to the GHR of older units, then the link between emissions and age would have broken down in the 1970s.

The coefficient for the regulatory variable is negative and significant at the 1% level in all four models, indicating that tighter regulation reduces sulfur emissions. Based on the estimated coefficients and the mean values of the regulatory variables in various years, emissions would have increased by 0.999 tons per million KWH (8.27%) in 1976, 2.722 tons (24.85%) in 1980, and 3.384 tons (31.43%) in 1983 in the absence of any air pollution control facilities; the corresponding estimates for *RF*2 are 0.968 tons (8.93%), 2.026 tons (20.15%), and 2.332 tons (23.29%). If state environmental control expenditures per firm had been reduced to zero, emissions would have increased by 0.839 tons per million KWH (6.44%) in 1969, 3.69 tons (31.80%) in 1976, and 5.709 tons (53.82%) in 1980; the corresponding estimates for *RS*2 are 1.108 tons (8.09%), 4.817 tons (42.72%), and 6.715 tons (61.58%). Averaging over all four regulatory variables, emissions would have increased by 3.788 tons per million KWH (34.60%) in 1980 in the absence of any environmental controls.

The estimates of the regulation equation presented in table 1 indicate that regulatory expenditures are higher in nonattainment areas, and in states with high education levels. Contrary to expectations, average per capita income, population density, and the percentage of the population under the age of seventeen or over sixty-five generally have no impact on regulatory expenditures. Finally, in two of the four equations the regulatory variable is negative and statistically significant, indicating lower regulatory expenditures in high pollution areas.

V. Conclusions

This study has examined the impact of environmental regulations on capital turnover and emissions of sulfur dioxide in the electric utility industry. Based on a sample of forty-four privately-owned utilities operating over the period 1969-83, our results indicate that environmental regulations increased the average age of fossil-fueled steam generating plants by an average of 3.29 years, or 22.64%. This figure is slightly below the approximately four year increase in age, or 24.6%, reported by Maloney and Brady (1988) using state-level data. Furthermore, our results indicate that the regulatory-induced increase in the age of capital had no statistically significant impact on sulfur dioxide emissions rates. Contrary to their claim, this result is in fact consistent with the statistical results presented in Maloney and Brady (table 5, p. 221), in which the age coefficient in their emissions equation is statistically significant at the 5% level (using a two-tailed t-test) in only one of eight regressions. Finally, our results indicate that sulfur emissions would have increased by an average of 3.79 tons per million KWHs (34.60%) in 1980 in the absence of regulation. This finding is in contrast to the results presented in Maloney and Brady, who found that environmental regulations had no statistically significant impact on sulfur emissions.

Evidence for the automotive industry indicates that differential environmental regulations increased the average age of capital, and that the increased age has resulted in increased emissions.[9] The statistical results presented in this study and by Maloney and Brady (1983) support the first conclusion, but not the second, for the electric utility industry. One important extension of this analysis would be to determine whether the results for this industry apply to other stationary sources as well, or are the result of stagnation in the average heat rate and technical change for electric utilities reported by Joskow (1987).

REFERENCES

Ackerman, Bruce A., and William T. Hasler, *Clean Air/Dirty Coal* (New Haven, CT: Yale University Press, 1981).
Bain, Edward C., "Scrubber Scrapper," *Fortune* (April 14, 1986), 63-64.
Crandall, Robert W., Howard K. Gruenspecht, Theodore E.

[9] See Gruenspecht (1982) or Crandall et al. (1986).

Keeler, and Lester B. Lave, *Regulating the Automobile* (Washington, D.C.: The Brookings Institution, 1986).
Dudek, Daniel J., and John Palmisano, "Emissions Trading: Why Is this Thoroughbred Hobbled?" *Columbia Journal of Environmental Law* 13 (1988), 217-56.
Faltermayer, Edmund, "Nuclear Power after Three-Mile Island," *Fortune* (May 7, 1979), 115-122.
Fuller, Dan A., "Compliance, Avoidance, and Evasion: Emissions Control Under Imperfect Enforcement in Steam-Electric Generation," *Rand Journal of Economics* 18 (Spring 1987), 124-137.
Gollop, Frank M., and Mark J. Roberts, "Environmental Regulations and Productivity Growth: The Case of Fossil-Fueled Electric Power Generation," *Journal of Political Economy* 91 (June 1983), 654-674.
Gordon, Robert J., *The Measurement of Durable Goods Prices* (Chicago: University of Chicago Press, 1990).
Gruenspecht, Howard K., "Differentiated Regulation: The Case of Auto Emission Standards," *The American Economic Review* 72 (May 1982), 328-331.
Hahn Robert W., and Gordon L. Hester, "Where Did All the Markets Go? An Analysis of EPA's Emission Trading Program," *Yale Journal of Regulation* 6 (Winter 1989), 109-153.
Joskow, Paul L., "Productivity Growth and Technical Change in the Generation of Electricity," *Energy Journal* 8 (1987), 17-38.
Jowkow, Paul L., and Nancy Rose, "The Effects of Technological Change, Experience, and Environmental Regulation on the Construction Cost of Coal-Burning Generating Units," *The Rand Journal of Economics* 16 (Spring 1985), 1-27.
Joskow, Paul L., and Richard Schmalensee, "The Performance of Coal-Burning Electric Generating Units in the U.S.: 1960-1980," Working Paper No. 379, Department of Economics, MIT (July 1985).
Maloney, Michael, and Gordon L. Brady, "Capital Turnover and Marketable Property Rights," *The Journal of Law and Economics* 31 (Apr. 1988), 203-226.
Nelson, Randy A., "Regulation, Capital Vintage, and Technical Change in the Electric Utility Industry," this REVIEW 56 (Feb. 1984), 59-69.
Prewitt, Edward, "Cleaning up the King of Kilowatts," *Fortune* (June 6, 1988), 180.
Raufer, Roger K., and Stephen L. Feldman, *Acid Rain and Emissions Trading: Implementing a Market Approach to Pollution* (Totowa, NJ: Rowman & Littlefield, 1987).
Smith, Vincent H., and Allen C. Basala, "The Economic and Environmental Impacts of New Source Performance Standards," Department of Economics, North Carolina State University (1981).
Tietenberg, Tom, *Emissions Trading: An Exercise in Reforming Pollution Policy* (Washington, D.C.: Resources for the Future, 1985).
Weaver, Paul H., "Behind the Great Scrubber Fracas," *Fortune* (Feb. 1975), 106-114.
Willenbrock, Jack H., and H. Randolph Thomas, *Planning, Engineering, and Construction of Electric Power Generation Plants* (New York: John Wiley and Sons, 1980).

improve air
[19]
THE EFFECT OF ENVIRONMENTAL REGULATION ON OPTIMAL PLANT SIZE AND FACTOR SHARES*

B. PETER PASHIGIAN
University of Chicago

I. Introduction

THE regulation of environmental conditions by the federal government began in earnest in 1970. With the passage of the 1970 Clean Air Act, the federal government inaugurated a comprehensive program to improve air and then water quality by establishing minimum ambient standards, by promulgating new source performance standards, and by limiting the deterioration of air quality in clean air areas. The federal government's role in the regulation of environmental conditions is not completely clear: many economists would argue that it is to correct interstate and regional externalities caused by the mobility of airborne emissions and water discharges. This assessment is widely shared but may have been reached somewhat prematurely. The effects of environmental regulation are scarcely known, and no comprehensive assessment can be contemplated at this stage. While the legislation clearly focuses on the need for an improvement in public health, experience with other government regulatory programs suggests the stated goals and the actual effects are not one and the same. The enforcement of regulations often has effects not readily apparent from a reading of the legislation. An essential first step in the process of understanding the reasons for environmental regulation is a careful catalog of the actual effects of environmental regulation.

While the externality hypothesis may be helpful in explaining the role of the federal government, it does not seem capable of explaining some

---

* This research was supported by the Graduate School of Business, and the Center for the Study of the Economy and the State, at the University of Chicago. Helpful comments were received from Yale Brozen, Phil Graves, Gregg Jarrell, Sam Peltzman, Rodney Smith, and George Stigler. I am responsible for remaining errors. James Rasulo collected the data, performed the calculations and served as an able research assistant.

features of environmental regulation, for example, the use of technology-forcing abatement methods and the special restrictive regulations applied to clean air areas. For an understanding of these features, it may be helpful to consider the important role played by special interest groups in shaping the legislation and the regulations. Testimony at congressional hearings and votes cast on environmental bills reveal fundamental conflicts between developed and developing areas of the country, between urban areas and underdeveloped rural areas, between environmental and industry groups, and between low- and high-sulfur coal producers.[1] Much less attention has been focused on the intraindustry conflicts between firms and plants caused by environmental regulation. Environmental regulations can be drawn to favor one group of producers in an industry over another group and to redistribute intraindustry rents.[2] If the minimum optimal size of plant increases because of economies of scale in compliance, then larger plants may benefit more than smaller plants. On the other hand, smaller plants can benefit from regulations if larger plants are subject to more stringent regulation.[3] The twin objectives of this paper are

---

[1] Peter Navarro suggests the 1977 Clean Air Amendments represented a victory for the eastern industrial / coal producers / environmental coalition and reversed the loss suffered by eastern groups with the passage of the 1970 Clean Air Act; Peter Navarro, The Politics of Air Pollution, 59 Pub. Interest 36 (1980). The forced use of scrubbers and high-sulfur coal has been described by Bruce Ackerman & William Hassler in Clean Air/Dirty Coal (1981). B. Peter Pashigian has examined the regional and urban-rural conflict over the policy of preventing significant deterioration (PSD) of air quality in clean-air areas and suggests that PSD policy allows environmental improvements in northern cities with a smaller loss of factors to rural areas and less developed regions; B. Peter Pashigian, Environmental Protection: Whose Self-Interests Are Being Protected? (Working Paper No. 022, Univ. Chicago, Center for the Study of the Economy and the State, 1982).

[2] The running conflict between western low-sulfur coal producers and eastern high-sulfur coal producers often surfaces in environmental legislation and in the setting of regulatory standards.

[3] An interesting study of the effect of compliance costs on plant costs was presented by Robert Leone & John Jackson in The Political Economy of Federal Regulatory Activity: The Case of Water Pollution Controls, in Studies in Public Regulation 231 (Gary Fromm ed. 1981). The authors examined the differential effect on plant costs because of compliance in the tissue paper segment of the pulp and paper industry. Economic impact statements sometimes include predictions of the effects of a proposed standard on the costs of selected idealized plants. These statements have limited objectives and only examine the effect of the single standard. A comprehensive study of the combined effects of all standards applicable to an industry was never attempted. A comprehensive tabulation of the effects of different government regulatory programs on size of firm or plant has not been compiled. Milton Kafogles has suggested there are economies of scale in compliance but that small firms benefit from less stringent enforcement; Milton Kafogles, Mandated Costs: Impact on Small Business, in Economic Effects of Government-Mandated Costs 111 (Robert Lanzillotte ed. 1978). George Neumann and Jon Nelson argue the enforcement of the Coal Mine Health and Safety Act of 1969 reduced the competition from small mines and benefited the larger mines;

to measure the effects of environmental regulation on the size distribution of plants and on the distribution of factor shares. Section II reviews the possible effects of environmental regulation on the costs of different-size plants, the distribution of industry output by plant size, and the shares of output distributed to capital and labor. The methodology of testing for the effects of environmental regulation is presented in Section III. In Section IV the economic characteristics of the twenty industries with highest per unit pollution abatement costs are compared with those of the twenty industries with the lowest per unit pollution abatement costs. Section V focuses on a much larger sample of four-digit industries and estimates the effect of environmental regulation on the number of plants in an industry, the mean size of plant, and capital's share of output. In Section VI a variant of the survivorship method is employed to determine if the size distribution of plants in the high pollution cost industries changed more under regulation than the size distribution of plants in the low pollution cost industries. The paper ends with a brief summary and a discussion of why large firms will be less vocal opponents of environmental regulation than are small firms.

II. The Effect of Environmental Regulation on Plant Size and Factor Shares

Environmental regulation will change the size distribution of plants if compliance costs change the optimal plant size or the range of optimum sizes. If the long-run industry supply curve is horizontal, no long-run rents can exist. If the firm's long-run average cost curve is flat over a range of output, small and large plants can coexist in the industry. Suppose there are some economies of scale in compliance and the minimum optimal plant size is larger with compliance than without. Mandated cost increases will raise the market share of large plants because small plants will either withdraw from the industry or become large plants. Regulation raises the average size of plant. In the long run, no rents can be earned by the surviving plants. Rents could be earned by the surviving plants only if the regulations imposed still higher per unit compliance costs on new entrants and if demand increased subsequently.

George R. Neumann & Jon P. Nelson, Safety Regulation and Firm Size: Effects of the Coal Mine Health and Safety Act of 1969, 25 J. Law & Econ. 183 (1982). Large companies benefited from the flammability standard applied to mattresses. See Peter Linneman, The Effects of Consumer Safety Standards: The 1973 Mattress Flammability Standard, 23 J. Law & Econ. 461 (1980). The entry of small regional airlines and truckers with deregulation suggests small firms were harmed because of government regulation.

Regulation could benefit small plants (firms) at the expense of large plants (firms) if small plants (firms) were politically important and obtained exemptions or were subject to less stringent enforcement.[4] If small plants are treated less harshly, regulation will increase the market share of small plants as large plants leave the industry or shrink in size. Here again, the surviving plants in the industry earn no rents in the long run unless the regulations impose still higher per unit compliance costs on new plants and demand increases.

When the long run average cost is flat over a range of outputs, a mandated cost increase that reduces the market share of small plants implies that regulation has increased the minimum optimal size of plant. Unfortunately, this is not a general conclusion. When there are external diseconomies, the combined market share of small companies may decline with compliance even though the per unit cost of compliance is the same for all plants or firms. For example, let there be just two types of plants in an industry, small and large. The supply curve of each group has a positive slope because of external diseconomies but the supply elasticities need not be equal. Suppose compliance with regulation raises the marginal cost curve of each type of plant and shifts the supply curve of each group to the left.[5] The effect on the combined market share of small plants depends on (1) the percentage shift in the supply curve (at a given price) for each group and (2) the elasticity of supply of each group. The interested reader is referred to Appendix A for the formal results. Consider the following illustrations. Suppose the regulations cause the supply curves of each group to shift to the left by the same percentage. The reduced supply at the original equilibrium price causes the equilibrium price to rise. The combined market share of small plants will decline if the elasticity of

---

[4] The regulatory agency will allocate resources toward investigating larger plants since there is a fixed cost associated with each investigation.

[5] Two studies in the same spirit are Elisabeth Landes, The Effect of State Maximum-Hour Laws on the Employment of Women in 1920, 87 J. Pol. Econ. 476 (1980); and Howard P. Marvel, Factory Regulation: A Reinterpretation of Early English Experience, 20 J. Law & Econ. 379 (1977). Landes examined the effect of hours restrictions for female workers on wage rates and employment. Marvel analyzes how the regulation of child labor lowered the supply curve of small water-powered mills. In each paper regulation reduces the supply curve of one group of suppliers and necessarily raises the rents earned by the unaffected sector of the industry. Environmental regulation has some similar and some dissimilar features. Compliance with environmental regulation shifts the supply curves of all suppliers to the left but not necessarily by equal amounts. This effect could lower the rents earned by all surviving suppliers. On the other hand environmental regulation imposes more stringent standards on new entrants and could raise the rents of existing suppliers by raising the cost of entry. A recent analysis of the effects of different forms of emission regulations and of new source performance standards is by Donald Dewees, Instrument Choice in Environmental Policy, 21 Econ. Inquiry 53 (1983).

supply of small plants is less than the elasticity of supply of large plants. Now consider the case where there are no economies of scale in compliance. The per unit and marginal cost rise by the same *absolute* amount for both small and large plants, the supply curve of small plants will usually decrease by a larger percentage amount because small plants as a group often supply less than 50 percent of output. Here again, the combined market share of small plants must decline if the supply elasticity of small plants does not exceed the supply elasticity of large plants. In this case the small plants' market share falls even though there are no economies of scale in compliance. Inferring the presence of economies of scale in compliance simply from the changes in market share is subject to errors without knowledge of the elasticities of supply of the small and large plants.

Changes in market shares can be caused by variables other than regulation. Distinguishing changes in share caused by regulation from those caused by other factors is always difficult. One important exogenous change, the change in energy prices, deserves special consideration. Energy prices rose sharply during the period of more stringent environmental regulation. The rise in energy prices increased the cost of production for both small and large plants in an industry. If large plants use energy (and capital) more intensively and if the rise in the price of energy causes the supply curve of large plants to shift to the left by a larger percentage, the rise in energy prices would cause the market share of large plants to decline as long as the supply elasticity of large plants does not exceed the supply elasticity of small plants.[6] So, the rise in energy prices may have increased the combined market share of the smaller, less energy intensive, less capital intensive plants. If so, a rise in the large plants' market share during this period of both higher energy prices and more stringent environmental regulation would indicate that the effects of environmental regulation had more than offset the effects of higher energy prices on market share. On the other hand, a fall in the large plants' market share could be due to the rise in energy prices, which more than offsets the rise in share caused by compliance with environmental regulation.

---

[6] The controversy over the complementarity of energy and capital has not been resolved. Most of the empirical studies treat the industry as the unit of analysis and have not investigated how the elasticity of substitution varies by plant or firm size. The time-series studies appear to support the complementarity hypothesis while cross-sectional and cross-country studies suggest the two factors are substitutes. For a recent summary, see James Griffin, The Energy-Capital Complementarity Controversy: A Progress Report on Reconciliation Attempts, in Modeling and Measuring Natural Resource Substitution 70 (Ernst Berndt & Barry Field eds. 1981).

Environmental regulation may have changed not only the distribution of market shares but also the distribution of factor shares between labor and capital. First, technology-forcing features of environmental regulations can favor more capital intensive methods for reducing or treating emissions. Second, policies that delay entry or that raise the cost for new or enlarged plants, such as a policy of prevention of significant deterioration, can increase the rents of existing plants. Third, mandated compliance costs can cause short-run losses. When new plants are subject to more stringent regulations, prices must rise by a larger amount before these new plants will be constructed and existing plants obtain higher rents than otherwise if market demand increases. The first and second effects represent moderate- to long-term effects of environmental regulation and raise capital's share of industry output (value added). If compliance with environmental regulation has had a major long-term effect on industry output, then capital's share of value added should have increased in the industries most affected by environmental regulation.

III. Methodology for Measuring the Effects of Regulation

Environmental regulation has had a very uneven impact on manufacturing industries. A small number of industries have incurred relatively high per unit compliance costs, while many industries have been barely affected. For example, gross annual pollution abatement costs have averaged about 9 percent of industry value added in the primary copper industry. Other four-digit industries in paper; chemical; stone, clay, and glass; petroleum; and primary metals have incurred smaller but still sizable per unit compliance costs.

The uneven industrial impact of environmental regulation is a blessing for the researcher, though a bane for subject industries. By selecting and then grouping industries with very high or with very low per unit compliance costs, a "high abatement cost" and a "low abatement cost" control portfolio of industries can be formed. The difference between the mean per unit compliance cost of the two groups of industries will be large by design so the effects of compliance should be detectable, providing they exist. Changes in the size distribution of plants in each industry have been studied from 1958 to 1972, the preregulatory period, and then from 1972 to 1977, the regulatory period. These dates were selected because census data are used. This method will detect any systematic shifts in the size distribution for industries in each group prior to regulation and any change during regulation. If there is a pervasive economy-wide trend toward large or smaller plants, this trend will be detected through changes in the size distribution of plants in both the control group and the high cost

TABLE 1
ENERGY INTENSITY BY SIZE OF COMPANY, 1975
(Manufacturing Sector)

Size of Company (Employees)	British Thermal Unit per Employee (Millions of BTUs) (1)	Total Cost of Purchased Electricity and Fuels/Value of Shipments (2)	Total Cost of Purchased Electricity and Fuels/Value of Shipments − Cost of Materials (3)
1– 19	224	.015	.034
20– 99	202	.014	.029
100–259	288	.016	.036
250–499	328	.017	.038
500 or more	917	.024	.059
Total	696	.022	.052

SOURCE.—Unpublished tables supplied by Bureau of Census.

group. Effects due to environmental regulation will be detected by observing larger changes during the regulatory period in the "high-cost" group of industries than in the "low-cost" group and during the regulatory period compared with the preregulatory period.

As mentioned above, real energy prices rose during the regulatory period and may have caused the size distribution of plants and the number of plants to change. In some industries larger plants appear to be both more energy and more capital intensive. Unfortunately, the only relevant data are from a special study and are limited to companies, not plants. Table 1 shows larger manufacturing companies produced more BTUs per employee in 1975 and incurred higher total energy costs relative to shipments and value added. Part of the increase in relative energy cost is due to changing industrial mix with increasing company size. Table 2 shows relative energy cost by two-digit industry but just for companies with less than or more than 250 employees. In twelve of the twenty industries large companies use energy more intensively. However, larger companies use energy more intensively in paper, chemicals, and primary metals industries, three of the four two-digit industries with relatively high pollution abatement costs. In these industries a rise in energy prices will induce a shift toward small companies that use more labor intensive methods of production if capital and energy are complements.

Because environmental regulations are often applied to industrial processes and are applicable to plants, the appropriate unit of analysis appears to be the plant and not the firm. For this reason, this study uses the

TABLE 2
Cost of Purchased Fuels and Electric Energy as a Percentage of Value of Shipments, 1975

Industry	Companies with Fewer than 250 Employees (1)	Companies with More than 250 Employees (2)	Column 1/ Column 2 (3)
20. Food	1.07	1.08	.99
21. Tobacco	.86	.60	1.43
22. Textile	2.32	2.85	.81
23. Apparel	.61	.68	.90
24. Lumber	2.32	2.09	1.11
25. Furniture	.97	1.22	.80
26. Paper	1.94	5.65	.34
27. Printing	.92	.76	1.21
28. Chemicals	1.76	5.08	.35
29. Petroleum	2.71	2.45	1.11
30. Rubber	2.07	2.40	.86
31. Leather	1.13	.96	1.18
32. Stone, clay, and glass	3.60	8.12	.44
33. Primary metals	3.17	5.82	.54
34. Fabricated metals	1.42	1.41	1.01
35. Machinery	1.05	.95	1.11
36. Electrical machinery	1.01	1.12	.90
37. Transportation	.93	.88	1.06
38. Instruments	.75	.92	.82
39. Miscellaneous	.93	1.10	.85
All manufacturing	1.47	2.40	.61

SOURCE.—Unpublished tables supplied by Bureau of Census.

plant-size distribution data as reported in the census of manufacturers. Gross pollution abatement operating costs have been collected and published by the Bureau of Census at the four-digit industry level since 1973. About 19,000 manufacturing plants are surveyed annually. Respondents report payments to governments for public sewage use, solid waste collection and disposal, depreciation, labor, equipment leasing and materials and supplies. Four-digit industries can be ranked by the rates of pollution abatement operating costs to value added.[7] The weighted average of gross pollution abatement operating cost per thousand dollars of value added (hereafter PACVA) for 1974, 1975 and 1977 was calculated for each eligible four-digit industry.[8] PACVA measures the importance of pollution

---

[7] Pollution abatement cost data are not available by four-digit industry and by size of plant.

[8] Miscellaneous industries were excluded as well as a few industries without information.

abatement costs relative to industry output as measured by industry value added.[9]

IV. High and Low Pollution Abatement Cost Industries

The twenty industries with the highest and the twenty industries with the lowest values of PACVA are identified in Table 3 along with the value of PACVA.[10] The high pollution abatement cost industries are often found in paper; chemical; petroleum; stone, clay, and glass; and primary metals while the low pollution abatement cost industries are often found in the printing and machinery industries. The average value of PACVA for the high-cost group is more than seventy times the average value of PACVA for the low-cost group. The average value of PACVA for a sample of 319 four-digit industries was .74 percent. This large sample includes all four-digit industries after miscellaneous industries and industries with abnormally large changes in the number of plants between 1972 and 1977 due to census reclassification of plants among industries were excluded.

Table 4 presents some descriptive statistics for the two groups and for the sample of 319 manufacturing industries. The high-cost group has fewer but larger establishments (rows 1 and 3). These industries are more capital intensive (row 4), as measured by one minus the ratio of payrolls to value added, and more fuel intensive (row 6), as measured by the ratio of fuels purchased to value added; and use electricity more intensively (row 5), as measured by the ratio of purchased electricity to value added. To summarize, industries with relatively high pollution abatement costs have fewer and larger plants and are high energy and capital users compared with the representative manufacturing industry. Table 4 highlights the different experiences of the two groups of industries from 1972 to 1977. In the high-cost group the mean number of plants declined (row 7) even while mean industry value added grew by 84.6 percent (row 9) in this group compared with a growth of 59.8 percent in manufacturing and only 64.1 percent in the low-cost group. Consequently, the mean percentage change in plant size (row 8)—value added per plant—rose more in the high-cost group (105.9) than in manufacturing (51.3) or in the low-cost

---

[9] Pollution abatement operating costs as a fraction of industry shipments were also calculated and found to be highly correlated with pollution abatement costs divided by value added. The fraction of PACVA attributable to the federal regulatory program is unknown. If only a small fraction results from the federal program or if there are serious measurement errors in PACVA, then PACVA will not be an important or significant determinant of changes in the size distribution of plants or in the distribution of factor shares.

[10] Each of the industries must also have had reasonably consistent industry definitions from 1958 to 1977 to be included. The reason for this requirement is explained below.

TABLE 3
TWENTY INDUSTRIES WITH HIGHEST AND TWENTY INDUSTRIES WITH LOWEST PERCENTAGE OF POLLUTION ABATEMENT COSTS TO VALUES ADDED (PACVA)

Twenty Highest-Cost Industries			Twenty Lowest-Cost Industries		
Industry	SIC Number	PACVA	Industry	SIC Number	PACVA
1. Primary copper	3331	8.72	1. Lace goods	2292	.00
2. Primary zinc	3333	7.14	2. Periodicals	2721	.02
3. Petroleum refining	2911	5.87	3. Miscellaneous publishing	2741	.02
4. Electrometallurgical products	3313	5.75	4. Typesetting	2791	.04
5. Inorganic pigment	2816	5.58	5. Book publishing	2731	.05
6. Primary lead	3332	5.42	6. Special dies, tools, and jigs	3544	.06
7. Pulp mills	2611	4.74	7. Industrial patterns	3565	.06
8. Lime	3274	4.74	8. Newspapers	2711	.06
9. Phosphatic fertilizers	2874	4.71	9. Jewelry, precious metals	3911	.06
10. Explosives	2892	4.68	10. Hoists, cranes, and monorails	3536	.06
11. Carbon black	2895	4.65	11. Industrial furnaces and ovens	3567	.07
12. Hydraulic cement	3241	4.55	12. Set-up paperboard boxes	2652	.07
13. Paperboard mills	2631	4.27	13. Blankbooks and looseleaf binders	2782	.08
14. Cyclic crudes and intermediates	2865	4.02	14. Jewelers' materials and lapidary	3915	.08
15. Paper mills excl. bldg. paper	2621	3.63	15. Women's handbags and purses	3171	.08
16. Minerals, ground or treated	3295	3.38	16. Signs and advertising displays	3993	.08
17. Primary aluminum	3334	3.13	17. Luggage	3161	.09
18. Blast furnaces and steel mills	3312	2.99	18. Conveyers and conveying equipment	3535	.09
19. Mineral wool	3296	2.76	19. Fabricated structural metal	3441	.09
20. Wet corn milling	2046	2.73	20. Fabricated pipe and fittings	3498	.09
Average		4.67	Average		.06
SD		1.49	SD		.03

SOURCES.—U.S. Bureau of Census, Census of Manufactures (various issues); US Bureau of Census, Annual Survey (various issues); US Bureau of Census, Pollution Abatement Costs and Expenditures (Industrial Reports No. MA-200, 1974–78).

TABLE 4

MEAN AND STANDARD DEVIATION FOR SELECTED VARIABLES: HIGH-COST GROUP, ALL INDUSTRIES, AND LOW-COST GROUP

Variable	Twenty Industries with Relatively High Abatement Costs	All Industries ($N = 319$)	Twenty Industries with Relatively Low Abatement Costs
1. Number of establishments, 1977	154 (153)	754 (1,635)	1,934 (2,342)
2. Industry value Added, 1977	2,542 (4,406)	1,396 (2,060)	1,536 (2,174)
3. Value added per establishment, 1977	16.67 (15.28)	4.95 (8.80)	.93 (.57)
4. Total payroll to value added, 1977	.338 (.117)	.427 (.106)	.478 (.103)
5. Purchased electricity to value added, 1977	.102 (.111)	.029 (.043)	.010 (.004)
6. Fuels consumed to value added, 1977	.176 (.129)	.036 (.062)	.007 (.011)
7. Percentage change in number of establishments 1972–77	−5.9 (23.8)	7.5 (19.9)	13.6 (19.6)
8. Percentage change in value added per establishment 1972–77	105.9 (75.1)	51.3 (41.6)	44.7 (16.7)
9. Percentage change in industry value added 1972–77	84.6 (57.2)	59.8 (42.6)	64.1 (32.6)
10. Percentage change in industry payroll to value added, 1972–77	−12.2 (18.1)	−6.9 (11.2)	−9.4 (7.9)

SOURCES.—See Table 3.
NOTE.—SD in brackets.

group (75.1). In some ways these are puzzling changes. The high abatement cost industries were actually growing more rapidly as measured by the larger percentage increases in value added. Yet they experienced an absolute decline in the number of plants. Growth in industry output is usually accompanied by a growth in the number of plants. Some other factors must have caused the decline in the mean number of plants per industry in the high-cost group of industries. The high- and low-cost industries differ in one other interesting regard. The high-cost group became less labor intensive from 1972 to 1977 than did the low-cost group. The ratio of payrolls to value added fell by 12.2 percent (row 10) for the high-cost group, by 9.4 percent for the low-cost group, and by 6.9 percent for the large sample. Under environmental regulation labor's share of product fell relatively more and capital's share consequently grew more in the high abatement cost industries.

V. Causes of the Change in the Number of Plants, Size of Plant, and Factor Shares

Environmental regulation is one of several prime suspect causes for these unusual changes. The 1972–77 period was an unusual one not only because of the shock of high energy prices but also because of several new regulatory programs. Another program that might have had a large effect on the manufacturing sector was the occupational and safety regulatory program. The full sample of 319 industries was employed to identify the effect of (1) each of these two regulatory programs, environmental and occupational health and safety; (2) the rise in energy costs; and (3) the growth in size of market. These independent variables were used to explain the *change* from 1972 to 1977 in (1) the log of the number of plants, (2) the log of value added per plant, (3) the log of payrolls to value added. The definitions of the dependent and independent variable are presented in Table 5.

Regression results in Table 6 indicate compliance with environmental regulation did cause a decline in labor's share of value added and in the number of plants per industry as well as an increase in plant size. In contrast, the effects of the OSHA variables are weaker and less often statistically significant.[11] Environmental regulation appears to have had

---

[11] The insignificant and erratic effects attributed to OSHA may arise from defective proxy measures for compliance costs caused by OSHA. The absence of compliance-cost data motivated the use of data on penalties imposed and resources devoted to inspections. The link between inspection probabilities and expected penalties and compliance costs incurred is not a simple one. So, the limitations of the proxy measures used in the paper may be responsible for the insignificant results attributed to OSHA. However, enforcement of

TABLE 5
DEFINITION OF VARIABLES

Dependent variables:
DLN_7 — Difference between logs of number of plants in 1977 and 1972
DLS_7 — Difference between logs of value added per establishment in 1977 and 1972
DLL_7 — Difference between logs of payroll divided by value added in 1977 and 1972 (this variable is also used as an independent variable in some regressions)

Independent variables:
Change in absolute size of market:
$DLVA_7$ — Difference between logs of industry value added in 1977 and 1972

Government regulation:
Environmental:
$LPACVA_7$ — Log of gross pollution abatement annual costs to industry value added (selected years 1974–78)

Occupational health and safety:
$LPENVA_7$ — Log of average annual penalties for all violations per dollar of industry value added, 1973–77
$LPENPT_7$ — Log of average annual penalties for all violations per plant, 1973–77
$LAVIN_7$ — Log of average annual number of inspections per plant, 1973–77

Change in relative energy costs:
$DLEN_7$ — Difference between logs of cost of purchased electricity and fuels consumed divided by industry value added in 1977 and 1972

TABLE 6

CHANGE IN LABOR'S SHARE OF VALUE ADDED, NUMBER OF PLANTS AND PLANT SIZE, 1972–77

	Dependent Variable		
Independent Variable	Change in Labor Share (DLL_7)	Change in Establishments (DLN_7)	Change in Plant Size (DLS_7)
Constant	−.362 (9.8)	−.372 (5.4)	−.297 (4.3)	.888 (10.8)	.509 (6.2)
Change in market size ($DLVA_7$)	...	.336 (8.3)	.425 (9.3)	...	...
Environmental regulation ($LPACVA_7$)	−.023 (4.2)	−.045 (5.0)	−.038 (4.2)	.068 (5.6)	.040 (3.6)
OSHA regulation ($LPENVA_7$)	.0081 (2.9)	.0015 (.3)	.0016 (.4)	.0032 (.6)	.0098 (1.9)
OSHA regulation ($LAVIN_7$)	−.011 (1.8)	...	...	...	...
Change in energy costs ($DLEN_7$)	.283 (11.4)	.053 (1.2)	−.028 (.6)	−.305 (5.4)	−.011 (.2)
Change in labor share (DLL_7)	...	...	.412 (3.9)	...	−1.086 (9.6)
R^2 (adjusted)	.287	.224	.256	.123	.320
SD of residuals	.101	.170	.166	.231	.203

NOTE.—*t*-statistics in parentheses; $N = 319$.

larger and more systematic effects on the size structure of plants and the distribution of factor shares than has the regulation of occupational safety.[12] The effects of a rise in relative energy costs are opposite to the effects of compliance with environmental regulation. Industries with larger increases in relative energy costs experienced a rise in labor's share of value added, a decline in plant size, and no effect on the number of plants in the industry.[13]

These results confirm the suspicion that environmental regulation was the more important program and that compliance was responsible for the differential changes observed during the 1972–77 period. These changes could be a mere continuation of past changes, or the effects attributed to environmental regulation could result from a left-out variable that happens to correlate with environmental regulation. If PACVA is correlated with a left-out variable, then similar findings should be obtained when the regressions are repeated for some period before 1970. If, on the other hand, the effects attributed to PACVA are really due to compliance with environmental regulation, either the coefficient of PACVA will not differ from zero in the regression for the preregulatory period or the difference between the coefficients of PACVA in the preregulatory and regulatory periods will be statistically significant.

Let the regression equation for the 1972–77 period be

$$Y_7 = \alpha_0 + \alpha_1 x_7 + \alpha_2 LPACVA_7 + \eta_7, \tag{1}$$

where x_7 can be thought of as a vector of independent variables other than $LPACVA_7$ and η_7 is a disturbance term. The same regression will be run for 1963–67, the preregulatory period, where the dependent and independent variables except the regulatory variables are measured from 1963 to 1967. The regulatory variables take on the values measured during the 1970s.

$$Y_6 = \beta_0 + \beta_1 x_6 + \beta_2 LPACVA_7 + v_6. \tag{2}$$

OSHA has yielded modest penalties per plant. From 1973 to 1977 the average penalty assessed per manufacturing plant was $38 and inspection hours at each manufacturing plant were five hours per year. Other students of the OSHA program have recorded similar findings, see Kip Viscusi, The Impact of Occupational Safety and Health Regulation, 10 Bell J. Econ. 117 (1979).

[12] Similar results were obtained when substitute measures for the enforcement of OSHA were used. Among the substitutes employed were total inspection hours per plant and serious violations per plant.

[13] A rise in relative energy costs raises product prices and reduces the size of market and the number of plants. In addition, a rise in relative energy costs could reduce the optimal plant size and thereby increase the number of plants. The net effect of a rise in relative energy costs on the number of plants is therefore ambiguous.

The first difference of this equation is

$$Y_7 - Y_6 = \gamma_0 + \alpha_1 x_7 - \beta_1 x_6 + (\alpha_2 - \beta_2) LPACVA_7 + \eta_7 - \nu_6, \quad (3)$$

or

$$Y_7 - Y_6 = \gamma_0 - \gamma_1(x_7 - x_6) + (\alpha_2 - \beta_2) LPACVA_7 + \eta_7 - \nu_6 \quad (4)$$

if $\alpha_1 = \beta_1$, where $\gamma_1 = \alpha_1 = \beta_1$. If $LPACVA_7$ is capturing the effects of environmental regulation, then β_2 will be zero and the coefficient of $LPACVA_7$ in the difference regression (equation 4) will equal α_2. If $LPACVA_7$ is measuring the effect of a left-out variable, then α_2 and β_2 measure the effect of the left-out variable and α_2 should equal β_2. Under this interpretation, the estimated coefficient of $LPACVA_7$ in equation 4 will not be significantly different from zero. This discussion assumes the correlation between PACVA and the left-out variable does not change over time.

A sample of 220 industries with reasonably uniform industry definitions between 1962 and 1977 was selected for study. Regression results for equation 4 are presented in Table 7. The regression coefficients for $LPACVA_7$ are all statistically significant and different from zero. These results indicate $LPACVA_7$ had a different effect on each dependent variable during the regulatory period than during the preregulatory period. The size of the estimated coefficients for $LPACVA_7$ in Tables 6 and 7 indicates $LPACVA_7$ had an insignificant effect on DLL_6 and on DLN_6 but a significant effect on DLS_6. These results indicate $LPACVA$ had a significantly different effect on each of the three independent variables during the seventies than it had during the sixties.

The OSHA regulatory variables perform somewhat better in the difference regressions, but the coefficient estimates at times are of borderline significance. The only other major finding is the insignificant effect of $DLL_7 - DLL_6$ on $DLN_7 - DLN_6$.

Overall, these results reinforce the conclusions reached earlier. Compliance with environmental regulation during the 1970s has raised capital's share of output, reduced the number of establishments per industry, and raised the average plant size. The results indicate the environmental regulation program is not a benign and inconsequential one but has had a significant effect on plant structure. Compliance has favored large plants relative to small plants and raised capital intensity.

VI. Changes in the Size Distribution of Plants in the High and Low Abatement Cost Groups

The twenty industries in the high-cost and low-cost groups, and with consistent industry definitions from 1958 to 1977, were studied more

TABLE 7
DIFFERENCE REGRESSIONS

INDEPENDENT VARIABLE	DEPENDENT VARIABLES			
	$DLL_7 - DLL_6$	$DLVA_7 - DLVA_6$	$DLN_7 - DLN_6$	$DLS_7 - DLS_6$
Constant	−.315	−.336	−.228	−.333	.855	.593
	(6.8)	(7.1)	(2.2)	(3.9)	(8.4)	(5.7)
$DLVA_7 - DLVA_6$	...	...	.236	.251	...	...
			(4.3)	(3.9)		
Environmental regulation ($LPACVA_7$)	−.025	−.026	−.051	−.059	.108	.087
	(3.4)	(3.6)	(4.1)	(5.0)	(7.2)	(6.0)
OSHA regulation ($LPENVA_7$)	...	.0078	...	−.009	...	...
		(1.8)		(1.5)		
OSHA regulation ($LPENPT_7$)	...	...	−.029	...	.008	.012
			(2.4)		(.9)	(1.6)
$DLEN_7 - DLEN_6$	.268	.274	.028	.017	−.259	−.054
	(9.2)	(9.4)	(.6)	(.3)	(4.3)	(.8)
DLL_7	...	...	...	.060	...	−.763
				(.5)		(5.9)
R^2 (adjusted)	.278	.286	.173	.157	.230	.335
SD of residuals	.132	.131	.194	.196	.267	.248

NOTE.—t-statistics in parenthesis; $N = 220$.

TABLE 8
MEAN PERCENTAGE CHANGE IN THE COEFFICIENT OF VARIATION

Period	High Abatement Cost Industries	Low Abatement Cost Industries
1958–72	4.77	−2.69
	(22.8)	(20.5)
1972–77	−7.68	2.73
	(20.5)	(12.78)

NOTE.—Standard deviation of the percentage change in coefficient of variation in parentheses.

closely. The purpose of this smaller-scale investigation was to determine if larger changes in the size distribution were experienced during the regulatory period in the high abatement cost industries than in the low abatement cost industries.

The distribution of plants by employment size for each of the forty industries was tabulated for each census year from 1958 to 1977. A useful way of summarizing the changes in these distributions during the preregulatory and regulatory periods is to compute the percentage change in the coefficient of variation (standard deviation divided by the mean) from 1958 to 1972 and from 1972 to 1977. Then, a grand mean of these percentage changes was calculated for each group and for each period (reported in Table 8). The mean value of the coefficients of variation decreased in the high group during the regulatory period after rising during the 1958–72 period. To test for significant differences between the two groups during the preregulatory and regulatory periods, the percentage change in the coefficient of variation from 1958 to 1972 or from 1972 to 1977 for the ith industry $(CCV)_{it}$ was regressed on three dummy variables. R_{it} is a dummy variable equal to one if the industry is a high pollution-abatement cost industry *and* the period is 1972–77; T_{it} equals one during the regulatory period for all industries and is zero otherwise; I_i equals one if the observation is for the coefficient of variation of the ith industry. The coefficient of R_{it} measures the difference between the mean percentage change in the coefficient of variation of the high- and the low-cost groups during the regulatory period. The coefficient of T_{it} measures any general effect that may have raised or lowered the coefficients of variation in all industries during the regulatory period. The regression equation had the form

$$CCV_{it} = \alpha_0 + \alpha_1 R_{it} + \alpha_2 T_{it} + \sum_{i=1}^{i=39} \beta_i I_i + \eta_{it}, \quad (5)$$

$i = 1, \ldots, 40; t = 1958$–72 or 1972–77. Regression results are presented in Table 9. There is considerable variation in CCV_{it}, so the estimated

TABLE 9
Effects of Compliance on the Coefficient of Variation ($N = 80$)

Independent Variable	CCV (1)	CCV (2)	CCV (3)
Constant	1.604	1.039	−.109
	(.6)	(.3)	(.1)
Dummy, high-cost pollution industry	−9.28	−10.41	−12.71
	(1.8)	(1.7)	(2.6)
Time dummy		1.69	
		(.3)	
Industry dummy variables:			
Phosphatic fertilizer			21.74
			(1.6)
Explosives			25.19
			(1.9)
Primary zinc			21.94
			(1.7)
Blast furnaces			33.88
			(2.6)
R^2 (adjusted)	.030	.098	.142
SD of residuals	19.47	19.58	18.30

coefficients are sometimes lacking in precision. Still, the percentage change in the coefficient of variation in the high-cost industries decreased during the regulatory period. The coefficient of the time dummy for 1972–77 is insignificant, so there was no general reduction in the coefficient of variation in both the high- and low-cost industries in the latter period. In column 3, dummy industry variables for selected industries with systematic larger increases in the coefficient of variation during both periods are included. The results of these tests suggest the variance of the size distribution of plants in the high pollution cost industries decreased relative to mean plant size during the regulatory period. These decreases were caused primarily by the elimination of small plants. Environmental regulation has had more damaging effects on the survival properties of small plants.

A second way of examining the effect of environmental regulation on small plants is to determine just what happened to the market share of small plants both before and after environmental regulation began. The survivorship analysis begins in 1958.[14] The size distribution of plants in each industry was divided into three size classes: small, medium, and large. In the base year, 1958, the size class boundaries were selected so that 25 percent of plants were in the small size class, 50 percent in the

---

[14] George J. Stigler, The Economies of Scale, 1 J. Law & Econ. 54 (1958).

medium, and 25 percent in the large. The employment size class boundaries in each industry were determined by interpolation and are presented in Appendix B. The class boundaries naturally differ from industry to industry but remain stationary at their 1958 limits in all subsequent years. The central question is whether there were any trends over time in the market shares of each size plant and, if so, how these trends were affected by compliance with environmental regulation. Table 10 shows the mean percentage of plants in each class from 1958 to 1977 for the high and low abatement cost groups. In the high abatement cost industries the mean market share of plants in the small size class rose from 25 percent in 1958 to 30.2 percent by 1972.[15] The mean of the annual growth rates in market share of plants from 1958 to 1972 in the small class was .81 percent per year for the high cost industries.[16] Small plants in these industries were gaining share prior to environmental regulation. Much of this increase came from the share of plants in the medium size class. The growth in the share of small plants during the preregulatory period in the high abatement cost industries was not matched by the small plants in the low-cost industries. Over the same period the mean share in these industries barely changed. The mean of the annual growth rate of market share was .02 percent per year. It is significant that small plants were entering and competing successfully with other plants in industries that were to become high abatement cost industries. This significance is highlighted by the events that unfolded during the regulatory period. The rise in market share of plants in the small size class was not only terminated but reversed. By 1977 the mean share of plants in the small class had dropped back to 25 percent, the initial market share in 1958. This decline did not simply reflect a general decline in the market share of small plants throughout the manufacturing sector. In the low abatement cost industries the mean market share of plants in the small class *rose* from 25.5 percent in 1972 to 27.4 percent in 1977 or by 1.43 percent per year. This increase in market share was due to factors other than environmental

---

[15] The sensitivity of the results was checked by defining class boundaries so that 15 percent of industry value added was supplied by plants in both the small and large size classes. This value-added method of determining class boundaries produced substantially different class boundaries. The qualitative effects of environmental regulation on the size distribution of plants were similar to those described below. The value-added share of plants in the large size increased while the share of value added of plants in the small and medium size classes decreased.

[16] g_{it} is the annual growth rate in market share in the small (large) class of the ith industry, during pre or regulatory periods and is determined by

$$S_{i72} = (1 + g_{ijt})^{14} S_{i58}$$
$$S_{i77} = (1 + g_{ijt})_5 S_{i72},$$

where S_{it} is the share of the small (large) size class in the ith industry.

TABLE 10
CHANGES IN THE MARKET SHARE OF PLANTS BY SIZE, 1958–77

	Twenty High Abatement Cost Industries			Twenty Low Abatement Cost Industries		
	Small	Medium	Large	Small	Medium	Large
1. Market share of plants (%):						
1958	25.0	50.0	25.0	25.0	50.0	25.0
1963	27.5	47.6	25.1	27.1	47.8	25.1
	(6.0)	(5.0)	(4.3)	(6.6)	(4.8)	(3.9)
1967	29.5	45.3	25.2	26.6	45.1	28.3
	(8.7)	(5.9)	(9.2)	(5.7)	(4.6)	(5.3)
1972	30.2	42.8	26.9	25.5	47.0	27.5
	(11.9)	(7.6)	(7.7)	(6.4)	(4.6)	(5.6)
1977	25.0	45.4	29.7	27.4	46.1	26.6
	(12.9)	(9.1)	(10.1)	(6.7)	(4.9)	(5.2)
2. Mean of the annual percentage change in market share:						
1958–72	.81	−1.00	.12	.02	−.46	.55
	(3.1)	(1.3)	(2.7)	(1.6)	(.7)	(1.6)
1972–77	−3.51	1.22	1.32	1.43	−.30	−.55
	(11.1)	(4.7)	(7.2)	(3.1)	(1.5)	(2.5)
3. Number of industries in each size class with decreases in market share:						
1958–72	7	16	8	11	15	7
1972–77	12	10	6	6	9	13

NOTE.—Standard deviation in parentheses; market shares may not add to 100 because of rounding.

regulation, for example, the increase in the price of energy or changes in technology. These other factors lowered the optimal size of plant in the low abatement cost industries. Panel 3 shows the number of industries where the market share declined for each size class. Between 1958 and 1972 the market share of plants in the small class dropped in seven of twenty industries in the high abatement cost group and in eleven of the twenty industries in the low abatement cost group. Under environmental regulation the pattern reverses. The market share in the small class falls in twelve of the high abatement cost industries and in only six of the low abatement cost industries. The mean market share of plants in the medium and large size classes increases under regulation in the high abatement cost industries. In review, this evidence also suggests environmental regulation is responsible for the decline in the market share of plants in the small class and the corresponding increases in the medium and large classes.

The effect of environmental regulation on the average annual growth rate of the market share of plants was estimated for both small and large plants.[17] For each of these two classes, the following equation was estimated by ordinary least squares:

$$g_{it} = \alpha_0 + \alpha_1 R_{it} + \alpha_2 T_{it} + \sum_{i=1}^{i=39} \beta_i I_i + \eta_{it}, \qquad (6)$$

$i = 1, \ldots, 40$; $t = 1958\text{–}72$ or $1972\text{–}77$; g_{it} = annual growth rate of market share of plants of the small (large) size class in the ith industry from 1958–72 or from 1972–77. R_{it} is a dummy variable equal to one if the industry is a high pollution cost industry during the regulatory period and zero otherwise. T_{it} is equal to one during the regulatory period for all industries. I_i equals one if the observation is for the growth rate of the ith industry. The coefficient of R_{it} measures the difference between the mean annual growth rates of high and low pollution cost industries during the regulatory period. The coefficient T_{it} captures any general economy-wide shift that raised or lowered the growth rate of all small (large) plants during the regulatory period. The coefficient of each industry dummy captures any industry effect that raised or lowered the growth rate of small (or large) plants over the entire period from 1958 to 1977. There are eighty growth rate observations in each regression, two for each of the forty industries.

[17] Once the market shares in the three size classes in 1958 and 1972 are known, as well as growth rates between 1958 and 1972 for any two of the three classes, the growth rate of the third class can be inferred. The regression analysis was limited to explaining the growth rates in the small and large classes. The residuals in the small-plant equations are assumed to be independent of the residual in the large-plant equation.

Regression results are presented in Table 11. In the high-cost industries, the growth rate in the market share of small plants declined significantly while the growth rate in market share of large plants increased during the regulatory period.[18] Only a small proportion of the variance in growth rates is explained and the precision of some of the coefficient estimates is low. The pollution abatement dummy and the time dummy tend to be correlated, so it is difficult to disentangle the effect of pollution abatement from the effect of the period on the growth rate. Generally, the coefficients of the time variable are not statistically significant. A few of the industry coefficients proved to be statistically significant. The most important determinant of whether the market share of small plants declined from 1972 to 1977 was whether the small plants were members of a high abatement cost industry.

How much lower is the market share of small plants because of environmental regulation? The coefficients in columns 1 and 2 and in columns 4 and 5 of Table 11 can be used to predict the annual growth rate in market share of small and of large plants in the high-cost industries in the absence of environmental regulation. The predicted growth rate in the market share of small plants is .74 percent per year (using the estimates in column 1) or 1.435 percent per year (using the estimates in column 2) in the absence of environmental regulation.[19] Therefore, the predicted mean market share of small plants would have increased to 31.3 percent or 32.4 percent in 1977 from 30.2 in 1972.[20] The difference between the predicted and actual shares by size class is shown in panel 3 of Table 12. Small plants have lost share while large plants have gained share because of compliance with environmental regulation. Table 12 indicates the long-term trend toward smaller plant size in the high abatement cost industries would have persisted through 1977. Compliance with environmental regulation appears to be the principal reason for the trend reversal in the high abatement cost industries.

VII. Conclusions

Compliance with environmental laws has not only reduced the number of plants in the affected industries but has placed a greater burden on small than on large plants. Small plants have found it more difficult to

---

[18] Since dummy variables are the only explanatory variables, the R^2 are comparatively small.

[19] The growth-rate estimate of .74 appears suspect since the rise in the price of energy would have raised the small plants' growth rate from 1972 to 1977 compared with the growth rate during the 1958–72 interval.

[20] The predicted market share of the medium-size plants equals 100 less the sum of the predicted shares of the small and large plants.

TABLE 11
DETERMINANTS OF THE ANNUAL GROWTH RATE OF MARKET SHARE

VARIABLE	SMALL PLANTS			LARGE PLANTS		
	(1)	(2)	(3)	(4)	(5)	(6)
Constant	.740	.393	.843	.040	.335	.483
	(1.0)	(.4)	(1.0)	(.1)	(.5)	(.8)
Pollution abatement dummy (D)	−4.245	−4.940	−4.040	1.280	1.869	2.165
	(2.8)	(2.6)	(2.4)	(1.2)	(1.5)	(1.9)
Time dummy (T)		1.042	.592		−.884	−1.032
		(.6)	(.4)		(.8)	(1.1)
Industry dummy variables:						
Lime			−17.989			8.446
			(4.7)			(3.3)
Cyclic crudes						−8.504
						(3.3)
Phosphatic fertilizers						−5.864
						(2.3)
R^2 (Adjusted)	.077	.070	.220	.006	.001	.248
SD	5.97	6.00	5.31	4.07	4.08	3.54

NOTE.—$N = 80$; t-statistics in brackets.

TABLE 12
ACTUAL AND PREDICTED MARKET SHARES IN THE ABSENCE OF
ENVIRONMENTAL REGULATION (%)

	SIZE OF PLANT		
	Small	Medium	Large
1. Actual mean market share in high pollution cost industries (%):			
a) 1958	25.0	50.0	25.0
b) 1972	30.2	42.8	26.9
c) 1977	25.0	45.4	29.7
2. Predicted mean market share in 1977:			
a) Using coefficients in columns 1 and 4, Table 11	31.3	41.7	27.0
b) Using coefficients in columns 2 and 5, Table 11	32.4	41.1	26.2
3. Difference between actual and predicted market share, 1977:*			
a) Using coefficients in columns 1 and 4, Table 11	−6.3 (21)	3.7 (9)	2.7 (10)
b) Using coefficients in columns 2 and 5, Table 11	−7.4 (25)	4.0 (9)	3.5 (12)

*Number in brackets represents the absolute value of the difference between actual and predicted share divided by 1972 share.

compete and survive with larger plants under environmental regulation. Besides redistributing within-industry market shares, environmental regulation has increased the use of capital relative to labor. An intriguing though unanswered question is whether the rise in capital's share of output is due solely to an increase in capital intensity or also to a rise in the rate of return earned on capital for the surviving plants.[21]

This paper has focused on the effects of environmental regulation on the number and size structure of plants. A compelling reason for this orientation is that plant, not company, emissions and discharges are regulated. Because there is a positive correlation between plant size and company size, there is every reason to believe that the effect of environmental regulation on the market share of small plants will be similar to the effect of environmental regulation on the market share of small companies. Some preliminary results suggest that small companies have been harmed relatively more than large companies.

The effects of any regulatory program must be known if the fundamental reasons for support of and opposition to the program are to be under-

---

[21] For a study which suggests companies gained from the cotton dust standard, see Michael T. Maloney & Robert E. McCormick, A Positive Theory of Environmental Quality Regulation, 25 J. Law & Econ. 99 (1982).

stood. This paper has documented the effects on the manufacturing sector of environmental regulation. Effects on the public utility and mining industries deserve study as well. While the analysis of effects is incomplete, the temptation to speculate from effects to causes is difficult to resist. The owners of small plants cannot be included among the beneficiaries of environmental regulation. The disproportionate burden placed on small plants in the high abatement cost industries may have been an unintended effect of environmental regulation or anticipated, recognized, and accepted by the supporters of the current federal program. If these effects were unintended or an oversight, and no organized interest group has benefited from this regulatory oversight, then small business groups would have exerted political pressure for legislative change or for changes in enforcement by the Environmental Protection Agency. The comparative inactivity of Congress and the EPA suggests that environmental groups and/or larger companies would have effectively opposed any move by the EPA to give special consideration to small companies or plants. If this interpretation is close to the truth, one can expect a continuation of past policy as long as the political capital of environmental groups and larger companies remains intact.[22] While both large and small companies may have suffered losses from environmental regulation, the available evidence suggests that small business has suffered relatively more and should be the more vocal opponent of environmental regulation.

The position of the larger companies in the affected industries toward environmental regulation remains a matter of speculation. On the one hand, environmental regulation imposes higher costs of production, higher prices, and lower output. On the other hand, the evidence suggests that environmental regulation not only terminated but reversed the erosion of the market share due to the entry and success of small plants. The net effect on the rents earned by large companies is unclear. A study of the effect of environmental regulation on the rate of return earned by large and small companies in the affected industries would help resolve this ambiguity.

APPENDIX A

The formal results described in the paper are presented here. The purpose of the analysis is to show how the market share of small plants is changed by stringent regulation that raises the costs of production of both large and small plants.

---

[22] The Regulatory Flexibility Act was passed by Congress and became effective on January 1, 1981. The Act is supposed to give special consideration to small "entities." How small will be interpreted; how the Act is to be administered will be of considerable interest and indicate an increase in the political strength of small business. However, passage of the Act indicates the declining political capital of environmental groups and of large firms.

Assume there are just two types of plants, small and large. Let $Q = D(P)$ be the market demand curve where P is market price. $L(P, \alpha)$ is the supply curve of all large plants in the industry where α is a parameter that is determined by the regulatory authorities and shifts the supply curve. Regulations reduce the quantity supplied by large firms (by raising each firm's average and marginal cost) and higher prices raise the quantity supplied by large plants, so $L_\alpha < 0$ and $L_p > 0$. $S(P, \alpha)$ is the supply curve of all small plants in the industry. In equilibrium,

$$D(P) - L(P, \alpha) - S(P, \alpha) = 0. \tag{A1}$$

An increase in regulatory stringency raises marginal costs and raises the equilibrium price because the quantity supplied by both large and small plants decreases.

$$\frac{dP}{d\alpha} = \frac{P(L_\alpha + S_\alpha)}{D(\eta - k_L \eta_L - k_s \eta_s)} > 0, \tag{A2}$$

where η is the price elasticity, k_L is the share of industry output supplied by large plants, η_L is the supply elasticity of large plants' output, k_s is the share of industry output supplied by small plants, and η_s is the supply elasticity of small plants' output. The change in the market share of small plants' output caused by more stringent regulation is

$$\frac{d(k_s)}{d\alpha} = \frac{D k_s k_L}{(\eta - k_L \eta_L - k_s \eta_s)} \left[(-\eta + \eta_s)\left(\frac{L_\alpha}{L}\right) + (\eta - \eta_L)\left(\frac{S_\alpha}{S}\right) \right]. \tag{A3}$$

Because $\eta - k_L \eta_L - k_s \eta_s < 0$, the small plants' market share will rise (fall) only if the expression in the square brackets is negative (positive), which requires

$$\frac{\eta - \eta_s}{\eta - \eta_L} \stackrel{>}{<} \frac{S_\alpha/S}{L_\alpha/L}. \tag{A4}$$

S_α/S and L_α/L represent the percentage shifts in the small (and large) plants' supply curve due to more stringent regulations. If the small plants' supply curve shifts by a larger percentage because of regulation, then the right side of (A4) is greater than one and the small plants' share must decline as long as $\eta_L > \eta_s$.

If there are no economies of scale in compliance, then per unit costs rise by the same absolute amount for both small and large plants. The small plants' supply will decline by a larger percentage as long as small plants' share of the market is less than 50 percent. If $\eta_L \leq \eta_s$, small plants' share falls even though there are no economies of scale in compliance.

The market share of small plants can change for reasons other than changes in regulatory stringency. For example, an increase in the size of market will reduce the small plants' share if $\eta_L \geq \eta_s$. On the other hand, stable market shares during a period of industry growth would indicate that supply elasticities do not differ; α could also be interpreted as a price of a factor of production, such as the price of energy. A rise in the price of energy raises the per unit cost of production for both large and small plants in an industry. Suppose larger plants use energy more intensively and a rise in the price of energy shifts the supply curve of large plants by a larger percentage amount: then the market share of small plants will rise if $\eta_L \leq \eta_s$. A rise in the price of energy will increase the small plants' share of the market if the large plants' supply curve shifts proportionally more and if the supply elasticity of large plants does not exceed the supply elasticity of small plants.

APPENDIX B

Size Class Limits for Small and Large Plants

Industry	Upper Boundary of Smallest Size Class	Lower Boundary of Largest Size Class
High abatement cost industries:		
1. Primary copper	167	699
2. Primary zinc	212	715
3. Petroleum refining	15	287
4. Electrometallurgical products	81	365
5. Inorganic pigments	8	95
6. Primary lead	133	382
7. Pulp mills	29	394
8. Lime	5	72
9. Phosphatic fertilizer	16	61
10. Explosives	19	250
11. Carbon black	34	143
12. Hydraulic cement	131	339
13. Paperboard mills	71	250
14. Cyclic crude	15	137
15. Paper mills	66	484
16. Minerals, ground or treated	38	174
17. Primary aluminum	5	23
18. Blast furnaces and steel mills	500	1,255
19. Mineral wool	146	2,124
20. Wet corn milling	7	90
Mean	85	417
SD	116	497
Low abatement cost industries:		
1. Lace goods	2	14
2. Periodicals	6	45
3. Miscellaneous publishing	2	32
4. Typesetting	2	11
5. Book publishing	2	10
6. Special dies, tools, and jigs	2	17
7. Industrial patterns	2	23
8. Newspapers	3	15
9. Jewelry, precious metals	2	8
10. Hoists, cranes, and monorails	2	6
11. Industrial furnaces and ovens	2	11
12. Set-up paperboard boxes	17	100
13. Blankbooks and looseleaf binders	15	51
14. Jewelers, materials and lapidary	3	75
15. Women's handbags and purses	2	6
16. Signs and advertising displays	4	43
17. Luggage	3	36
18. Conveyors	6	42
19. Fabricated structural metal	7	54
20. Fabricated pipes and fittings	4	35
Mean	4	32
SD	4	25

Part VI
The Porter Hypothesis

[20]

Toward a New Conception of the Environment-Competitiveness Relationship

Michael E. Porter and Claas van der Linde

The relationship between environmental goals and industrial competitiveness has normally been thought of as involving a tradeoff between social benefits and private costs. The issue was how to balance society's desire for environmental protection with the economic burden on industry. Framed this way, environmental improvement becomes a kind of arm-wrestling match. One side pushes for tougher standards; the other side tries to beat the standards back.

Our central message is that the environment-competitiveness debate has been framed incorrectly. The notion of an inevitable struggle between ecology and the economy grows out of a static view of environmental regulation, in which technology, products, processes and customer needs are all fixed. In this static world, where firms have already made their cost-minimizing choices, environmental regulation inevitably raises costs and will tend to reduce the market share of domestic companies on global markets.

However, the paradigm defining competitiveness has been shifting, particularly in the last 20 to 30 years, away from this static model. The new paradigm of international competitiveness is a dynamic one, based on innovation. A body of research first published in *The Competitive Advantage of Nations* has begun to address these changes (Porter, 1990). Competitiveness at the industry level arises from superior productivity, either in terms of lower costs than rivals or the ability to offer products

■ *Michael E. Porter is the C. Roland Christensen Professor of Business Administration, Harvard Business School, Boston, Massachusetts. Claas van der Linde is on the faculty of the International Management Research Institute of St. Gallen University, St. Gallen, Switzerland.*

with superior value that justify a premium price.[1] Detailed case studies of hundreds of industries, based in dozens of countries, reveal that internationally competitive companies are not those with the cheapest inputs or the largest scale, but those with the capacity to improve and innovate continually. (We use the term innovation broadly, to include a product's or service's design, the segments it serves, how it is produced, how it is marketed and how it is supported.) Competitive advantage, then, rests not on static efficiency nor on optimizing within fixed constraints, but on the capacity for innovation and improvement that shift the constraints.

This paradigm of dynamic competitiveness raises an intriguing possibility: in this paper, we will argue that properly designed environmental standards can trigger innovation that may partially or more than fully offset the costs of complying with them. Such "innovation offsets," as we call them, can not only lower the net cost of meeting environmental regulations, but can even lead to absolute advantages over firms in foreign countries not subject to similar regulations. Innovation offsets will be common because reducing pollution is often coincident with improving the productivity with which resources are used. In short, firms can actually benefit from properly crafted environmental regulations that are more stringent (or are imposed earlier) than those faced by their competitors in other countries. By stimulating innovation, strict environmental regulations can actually enhance competitiveness.

There is a legitimate and continuing controversy over the social benefits of specific environmental standards, and there is a huge benefit-cost literature. Some believe that the risks of pollution have been overstated; others fear the reverse. Our focus here is not on the social benefits of environmental regulation, but on the private costs. Our argument is that whatever the level of social benefits, these costs are far higher than they need to be. The policy focus should, then, be on relaxing the tradeoff between competitiveness and the environment rather than accepting it as a given.

The Link from Regulation to Promoting Innovation

It is sometimes argued that companies must, by the very notion of profit seeking, be pursuing all profitable innovations. In the metaphor economists often cite, $10 bills will never be found on the ground because someone would have already picked them up. In this view, if complying with environmental regulation can be profitable, in the sense that a company can more than offset the cost of compliance, then why is such regulation necessary?

---

[1] At the industry level, the meaning of competitiveness is clear. At the level of a state or nation, however, the notion of competitiveness is less clear because no nation or state is, or can be, competitive in everything. The proper definition of competitiveness at the aggregate level is the average *productivity* of industry or the value created per unit of labor and per dollar of capital invested. Productivity depends on both the quality and features of products (which determine their value) and the efficiency with which they are produced.

Michael E. Porter and Claas van der Linde   99

The possibility that regulation might act as a spur to innovation arises because the world does not fit the Panglossian belief that firms always make optimal choices. This will hold true only in a static optimization framework where information is perfect and profitable opportunities for innovation have already been discovered, so that profit-seeking firms need only choose their approach. Of course, this does not describe reality. Instead, the actual process of dynamic competition is characterized by changing technological opportunities coupled with highly incomplete information, organizational inertia and control problems reflecting the difficulty of aligning individual, group and corporate incentives. Companies have numerous avenues for technological improvement, and limited attention.

Actual experience with energy-saving investments illustrates that in the real world, $10 bills are waiting to be picked up. As one example, consider the "Green Lights" program of the Environmental Protection Agency. Firms volunteering to participate in this program pledge to scrutinize every avenue of electrical energy consumption. In return, they receive advice on efficient lighting, heating and cooling operations. When the EPA collected data on energy-saving lighting upgrades reported by companies as part of the Green Lights program, it showed that nearly 80 percent of the projects had paybacks of two years or less (DeCanio, 1993). Yet only after companies became part of the program, and benefitted from information and cajoling from the EPA, were these highly profitable projects carried out. This paper will present numerous other examples of where environmental innovation produces net benefits for private companies.[2]

We are currently in a transitional phase of industrial history where companies are still inexperienced in dealing creatively with environmental issues. The environment has not been a principal area of corporate or technological emphasis, and knowledge about environmental impacts is still rudimentary in many firms and industries, elevating uncertainty about innovation benefits. Customers are also unaware of the costs of resource inefficiency in the packaging they discard, the scrap value they forego and the disposal costs they bear. Rather than attempting to innovate in every direction at once, firms in fact make choices based on how they perceive their competitive situation and the world around them. In such a world, regulation can be an important influence on the direction of innovation, either for better or for worse. Properly crafted environmental regulation can serve at least six purposes.

First, regulation signals companies about likely resource inefficiencies and potential technological improvements. Companies are still inexperienced in measuring their discharges, understanding the full costs of incomplete utilization of resources and toxicity, and conceiving new approaches to minimize discharges or

---

[2] Of course, there are many nonenvironmental examples of where industry has been extremely slow to pick up available $10 bills by choosing new approaches. For example, total quality management programs only came to the United States and Europe decades after they had been widely diffused in Japan; and only after Japanese firms had devastated U.S. and European competitors in the marketplace. The analogy between searching for product quality and for environmental protection is explored later in this paper.

eliminate hazardous substances. Regulation rivets attention on this area of potential innovation.[3]

Second, regulation focused on information gathering can achieve major benefits by raising corporate awareness. For example, Toxics Release Inventories, which are published annually as part of the 1986 Superfund reauthorization, require more than 20,000 manufacturing plants to report their releases of some 320 toxic chemicals. Such information gathering often leads to environmental improvement without mandating pollution reductions, sometimes even at lower costs.

Third, regulation reduces the uncertainty that investments to address the environment will be valuable. Greater certainty encourages investment in any area.

Fourth, regulation creates pressure that motivates innovation and progress. Our broader research on competitiveness highlights the important role of outside pressure in the innovation process, to overcome organizational inertia, foster creative thinking and mitigate agency problems. Economists are used to the argument that pressure for innovation can come from strong competitors, demanding customers or rising prices of raw materials; we are arguing that properly crafted regulation can also provide such pressure.

Fifth, regulation levels the transitional playing field. During the transition period to innovation-based solutions, regulation ensures that one company cannot opportunistically gain position by avoiding environmental investments. Regulations provide a buffer until new technologies become proven and learning effects reduce their costs.

Sixth, regulation is needed in the case of incomplete offsets. We readily admit that innovation cannot always completely offset the cost of compliance, especially in the short term before learning can reduce the cost of innovation-based solutions. In such cases, regulation will be necessary to improve environmental quality.

Stringent regulation can actually produce greater innovation and innovation offsets than lax regulation. Relatively lax regulation can be dealt with incrementally and without innovation, and often with "end-of-pipe" or secondary treatment solutions. More stringent regulation, however, focuses greater company attention on discharges and emissions, and compliance requires more fundamental solutions, like reconfiguring products and processes. While the cost of compliance may rise with stringency, then, the potential for innovation offsets may rise even faster. Thus the *net* cost of compliance can fall with stringency and may even turn into a net benefit.

How Innovation Offsets Occur

Innovation in response to environmental regulation can take two broad forms. The first is that companies simply get smarter about how to deal with pollution

---

[3] Regulation also raises the likelihood that product and process in general will incorporate environmental improvements.

once it occurs, including the processing of toxic materials and emissions, how to reduce the amount of toxic or harmful material generated (or convert it into salable forms) and how to improve secondary treatment. Molten Metal Technology, of Waltham, Massachusetts, for example, has developed a catalytic extraction process to process many types of hazardous waste efficiently and effectively. This sort of innovation reduces the cost of compliance with pollution control, but changes nothing else.

The second form of innovation addresses environmental impacts while simultaneously improving the affected product itself and/or related processes. In some cases, these "innovation offsets" can exceed the costs of compliance. This second sort of innovation is central to our claim that environmental regulation can actually increase industrial competitiveness.

Innovation offsets can be broadly divided into product offsets and process offsets. Product offsets occur when environmental regulation produces not just less pollution, but also creates better-performing or higher-quality products, safer products, lower product costs (perhaps from material substitution or less packaging), products with higher resale or scrap value (because of ease in recycling or disassembly) or lower costs of product disposal for users. Process offsets occur when environmental regulation not only leads to reduced pollution, but also results in higher resource productivity such as higher process yields, less downtime through more careful monitoring and maintenance, materials savings (due to substitution, reuse or recycling of production inputs), better utilization of by-products, lower energy consumption during the production process, reduced material storage and handling costs, conversion of waste into valuable forms, reduced waste disposal costs or safer workplace conditions. These offsets are frequently related, so that achieving one can lead to the realization of several others.

As yet, no broad tabulation exists of innovation offsets. Most of the work done in this area involves case studies, because case studies are the only vehicle currently available to measure compliance costs and both direct and indirect innovation benefits. This journal is not the place for a comprehensive listing of available case studies. However, offering some examples should help the reader to understand how common and plausible such effects are.

Innovation to comply with environmental regulation often improves product performance or quality. In 1990, for instance, Raytheon found itself required (by the Montreal Protocol and the U.S. Clean Air Act) to eliminate ozone-depleting chlorofluorocarbons (CFCs) used for cleaning printed electronic circuit boards after the soldering process. Scientists at Raytheon initially thought that complete elimination of CFCs would be impossible. However, they eventually adopted a new semiaqueous, terpene-based cleaning agent that could be reused. The new method proved to result in an increase in average product quality, which had occasionally been compromised by the old CFC-based cleaning agent, as well as lower operating costs (Raytheon, 1991, 1993). It would not have been adopted in the absence of environmental regulation mandating the phase-out of CFCs. Another example is the move by the Robbins Company (a jewelry company based in Attleboro,

Massachusetts) to a closed-loop, zero-discharge system for handling the water used in plating (Berube, Nash, Maxwell and Ehrenfeld, 1992). Robbins was facing closure due to violation of its existing discharge permits. The water produced by purification through filtering and ion exchange in the new closed-loop system was 40 times cleaner than city water and led to higher-quality plating and fewer rejects. The result was enhanced competitiveness.

Environmental regulations may also reduce product costs by showing how to eliminate costly materials, reduce unnecessary packaging or simplify designs. Hitachi responded to a 1991 Japanese recycling law by redesigning products to reduce disassembly time. In the process, the number of parts in a washing machine fell 16 percent, and the number of parts on a vacuum cleaner fell 30 percent. In this way, moves to redesign products for better recyclability can lead to fewer components and thus easier assembly.

Environmental standards can also lead to innovation that reduces disposal costs (or boost scrap or resale value) for the user. For instance, regulation that requires recyclability of products can lead to designs that allow valuable materials to be recovered more easily after disposal of the product. Either the customer or the manufacturer who takes back used products reaps greater value.

These have all been examples of product offsets, but process offsets are common as well. Process changes to reduce emissions frequently result in increases in product yields. At Ciba-Geigy's dyestuff plant in New Jersey, the need to meet new environmental standards caused the firm to reexamine its wastewater streams. Two changes in its production process—replacing iron with a different chemical conversion agent that did not result in the formation of solid iron sludge and process changes that eliminated the release of potentially toxic product into the wastewater stream—not only boosted yield by 40 percent but also eliminated wastes, resulting in annual cost savings of $740,000 (Dorfman, Muir and Miller, 1992).[4]

Similarly, 3M discovered that in producing adhesives in batches that were transferred to storage tanks, one bad batch could spoil the entire contents of a tank. The result was wasted raw materials and high costs of hazardous waste disposal. 3M developed a new technique to run quality tests more rapidly on new batches. The new technique allowed 3M to reduce hazardous wastes by 10 tons per year at almost no cost, yielding an annual savings of more than $200,000 (Sheridan, 1992).

Solving environmental problems can also yield benefits in terms of reduced downtime. Many chemical production processes at DuPont, for example, require start-up time to stabilize and bring output within specifications, resulting in an initial period during which only scrap and waste is produced. Installing higher-quality monitoring equipment has allowed DuPont to reduce production interruptions and the associated wasteful production start-ups, thus reducing waste generation as well as downtime (Parkinson, 1990).

---

[4] We should note that this plant was ultimately closed. However, the example described here does illustrate the role of regulatory pressure in process innovation.

Regulation can trigger innovation offsets through substitution of less costly materials or better utilization of materials in the process. For example, 3M faced new regulations that will force many solvent users in paper, plastic and metal coatings to reduce its solvent emissions 90 percent by 1995 (Boroughs and Carpenter, 1991). The company responded by avoiding the use of solvents altogether and developing coating products with safer, water-based solutions. At another 3M plant, a change from a solvent-based to a water-based carrier, used for coating tablets, eliminated 24 tons per year of air emissions. The $60,000 investment saved $180,000 in unneeded pollution control equipment and created annual savings of $15,000 in solvent purchases (Parkinson, 1990). Similarly, when federal and state regulations required that Dow Chemical close certain evaporation ponds used for storing and evaporating wastewater resulting from scrubbing hydrochloric gas with caustic soda, Dow redesigned its production process. By first scrubbing the hydrochloric acid with water and then caustic soda, Dow was able to eliminate the need for evaporation ponds, reduce its use of caustic soda, and capture a portion of the waste stream for reuse as a raw material in other parts of the plant. This process change cost $250,000 to implement. It reduced caustic waste by 6,000 tons per year and hydrochloric acid waste by 80 tons per year, for a savings of $2.4 million per year (Dorfman, Muir and Miller, 1992).

The Robbins Company's jewelry-plating system illustrates similar benefits. In moving to the closed-loop system that purified and recycled water, Robbins saved over $115,000 per year in water, chemicals, disposal costs, and lab fees and reduced water usage from 500,000 gallons per week to 500 gallons per week. The capital cost of the new system, which completely eliminated the waste, was $220,000, compared to about $500,000 for a wastewater treatment facility that would have brought Robbins' discharge into compliance only with current regulations.

At the Tobyhanna Army Depot, for instance, improvements in sandblasting, cleaning, plating and painting operations reduced hazardous waste generation by 82 percent between 1985 and 1992. That reduction saved the depot over $550,000 in disposal costs, and $400,000 in material purchasing and handling costs (PR Newswire, 1993).

Innovation offsets can also be derived by converting waste into more valuable forms. The Robbins Company recovered valuable precious metals in its zero discharge plating system. At Rhone-Poulenc's nylon plant in Chalampe, France, diacids (by-products that had been produced by an adipic acid process) used to be separated and incinerated. Rhone-Poulenc invested Fr 76 million and installed new equipment to recover and sell them as dye and tanning additives or coagulation agents, resulting in annual revenues of about Fr 20.1 million. In the United States, similar by-products from a Monsanto Chemical Company plant in Pensacola, Florida, are sold to utility companies who use them to accelerate sulfur dioxide removal during flue gas desulfurization (Basta and Vagi, 1988).

A few studies of innovation offsets do go beyond individual cases and offer some broader-based data. One of the most extensive studies is by INFORM, an environmental research organization. INFORM investigated activities to prevent waste generation—so-called source reduction activities—at 29 chemical plants in California, Ohio and New Jersey (Dorfman, Muir and Miller, 1992). Of the 181 source-reduction activities identified in this study, only one was found to have resulted in a net cost increase. Of the 70 activities for which the study was able to document changes in product yield, 68 reported yield increases; the average yield increase for the 20 initiatives with specific available data was 7 percent. These innovation offsets were achieved with surprisingly low investments and very short payback periods. One-quarter of the 48 initiatives with detailed capital cost information required no capital investment at all; of the 38 initiatives with payback period data, nearly two-thirds were shown to have recouped their initial investments in six months or less. The annual savings per dollar spent on source reduction averaged $3.49 for the 27 activities for which this information could be calculated. The study also investigated the motivating factors behind the plant's source-reduction activities. Significantly, it found that waste disposal costs were the most often cited, followed by environmental regulation.

To build a broader base of studies on innovation offsets to environmental regulation, we have been collaborating with the Management Institute for Environment and Business on a series of international case studies, sponsored by the EPA, of industries and entire sectors significantly affected by environmental regulation. Sectors studied include pulp and paper, paint and coatings, electronics manufacturing, refrigerators, dry cell batteries and printing inks (Bonifant and Ratcliffe, 1994; Bonifant 1994a,b; van der Linde, 1995a,b,c). Some examples from that effort have already been described here.

A solid body of case study evidence, then, demonstrates that innovation offsets to environmental regulation are common.[5] Even with a generally hostile regulatory climate, which is not designed to encourage such innovation, these offsets can sometimes exceed the cost of compliance. We expect that such examples will proliferate as companies and regulators become more sophisticated and shed old mindsets.

Early-Mover Advantage in International Markets

World demand is moving rapidly in the direction of valuing low-pollution and energy-efficient products, not to mention more resource-efficient products with higher resale or scrap value. Many companies are using innovation to command price premiums for "green" products and open up new market segments. For example, Germany enacted recycling standards earlier than in most other

---

[5] Of course, a list of case examples, however long, does not prove that companies can always innovate or substitute for careful empirical testing in a large cross-section of industries. Given our current ability to capture the true costs and often multifaceted benefits of regulatory-induced innovation, reliance on the weight of case study evidence is necessary. As we discuss elsewhere, there is no countervailing set of case studies that shows that innovation offsets are unlikely or impossible.

countries, which gave German firms an early-mover advantage in developing less packaging-intensive products, which have been warmly received in the marketplace. Scandinavian pulp and paper producers have been leaders in introducing new environmentally friendly production processes, and thus Scandinavian pulp and paper equipment suppliers such as Kamyr and Sunds have made major gains internationally in selling innovative bleaching equipment. In the United States, a parallel example is the development by Cummins Engine of low-emissions diesel engines for trucks, buses and other applications in response to U.S. environmental regulations. Its new competence is allowing the firm to gain international market share.

Clearly, this argument only works to the extent that national environmental standards anticipate and are consistent with international trends in environmental protection, rather than break with them. Creating expertise in cleaning up abandoned hazardous waste sites, as the U.S. Superfund law has done, does little to benefit U.S. suppliers if no other country adopts comparable toxic waste cleanup requirements. But when a competitive edge is attained, especially because a company's home market is sophisticated and demanding in a way that pressures the company to further innovation, the economic gains can be lasting.

Answering Defenders of the Traditional Model

Our argument that strict environmental regulation can be fully consistent with competitiveness was originally put forward in a short *Scientific American* essay (Porter, 1991; see also van der Linde, 1993). This essay received far more scrutiny than we expected. It has been warmly received by many, especially in the business community. But it has also had its share of critics, especially among economists (Jaffe, Peterson, Portney and Stavins, 1993, 1994; Oates, Palmer and Portney, 1993; Palmer and Simpson, 1993; Simpson, 1993; Schmalensee, 1993).

One criticism is that while innovation offsets are theoretically possible, they are likely to be rare or small in practice. We disagree. Pollution is the emission or discharge of a (harmful) substance or energy form into the environment. Fundamentally, it is a manifestation of economic waste and involves unnecessary, inefficient or incomplete utilization of resources, or resources not used to generate their highest value. In many cases, emissions are a sign of inefficiency and force a firm to perform non-value-creating activities such as handling, storage and disposal. Within the company itself, the costs of poor resource utilization are most obvious in incomplete material utilization, but are also manifested in poor process control, which generates unnecessary stored material, waste and defects. There are many other hidden costs of resource inefficiencies later in the life cycle of the product. Packaging discarded by distributors or customers, for example, wastes resources and adds costs. Customers bear additional costs when they use polluting products or products that waste energy. Resources are also wasted when customers discard products embodying unused materials or when they bear the costs of product disposal.[6]

As the many examples discussed earlier suggest, the opportunity to reduce cost by diminishing pollution should thus be the rule, not the exception. Highly toxic materials such as heavy metals or solvents are often expensive and hard to handle, and reducing their use makes sense from several points of view. More broadly, efforts to reduce pollution and maximize profits share the same basic principles, including the efficient use of inputs, substitution of less expensive materials and the minimization of unneeded activities.[7]

A corollary to this observation is that scrap or waste or emissions can carry important information about flaws in product design or the production process. A recent study of process changes in 10 printed circuit board manufacturers, for example, found that 13 of 33 major changes were initiated by pollution control personnel. Of these, 12 resulted in cost reduction, eight in quality improvements and five in extension of production capabilities (King, 1994).

Environmental improvement efforts have traditionally overlooked the systems cost of resource inefficiency. Improvement efforts have focused on *pollution control* through better identification, processing and disposal of discharges or waste, an inherently costly approach. In recent years, more advanced companies and regulators have embraced the concept of *pollution prevention*, sometimes called source reduction, which uses material substitution, closed-loop processes and the like to limit pollution before it occurs.

But although pollution prevention is an important step in the right direction, ultimately companies and regulators must learn to frame environmental improvement in terms of *resource productivity*, or the efficiency and effectiveness with which companies and their customers use resources.[8] Improving resource productivity within companies goes beyond eliminating pollution (and the cost of dealing with it) to lowering true economic cost and raising the true economic value of products. At the level of resource productivity, environmental improvement and competitiveness come together. The imperative for resource productivity rests on the private costs that companies bear because of pollution, not on mitigating pollution's social costs. In addressing these private costs, it highlights the opportunity costs of pollution—wasted resources, wasted efforts and diminished product value to the customer—not its actual costs.

---

[6] At its core, then, pollution is a result of an intermediate state of technology or management methods. Apparent exceptions to the resource productivity thesis often prove the rule by highlighting the role of technology. Paper made with recycled fiber was once greatly inferior, but new de-inking and other technologies have made its quality better and better. Apparent tradeoffs between energy efficiency and emissions rest on incomplete combustion.

[7] Schmalensee (1993) counters that NO_x emissions often result from thermodynamically efficient combustion. But surely this is an anomaly, not the rule, and may represent an intermediate level of efficiency.

[8] One of the pioneering efforts to see environmental improvement this way is Joel Makower's (1993) book, *The E-Factor: The Bottom-Line Approach to Environmentally Responsible Business*.

This view of pollution as unproductive resource utilization suggests a helpful analogy between environmental protection and product quality measured by defects. Companies used to promote quality by conducting careful inspections during the production process, and then by creating a service organization to correct the quality problems that turned up in the field. This approach has proven misguided. Instead, the most cost-effective way to improve quality is to build it into the entire process, which includes design, purchased components, process technology, shipping and handling techniques and so forth. This method dramatically reduces inspection, rework and the need for a large service organization. (It also leads to the oft-quoted phrase, "quality is free.") Similarly, there is reason to believe that companies can enjoy substantial innovation offsets by improving resource productivity throughout the value chain instead of through dealing with the manifestations of inefficiency like emissions and discharges.

Indeed, corporate total quality management programs have strong potential also to reduce pollution and lead to innovation offsets.[9] Dow Chemical, for example, has explicitly identified the link between quality improvement and environmental performance, by using statistical process control to reduce the variance in processes and lower waste (Sheridan, 1992).

A second criticism of our hypothesis is to point to the studies finding high costs of compliance with environmental regulation, as evidence that there is a fixed tradeoff between regulation and competitiveness. But these studies are far from definitive.

Estimates of regulatory compliance costs prior to enactment of a new rule typically exceed the actual costs. In part, this is because such estimates are often self-reported by industries who oppose the rule, which creates a tendency to inflation. A prime example of this type of thinking was a statement by Lee Iacocca, then vice president at the Ford Motor Company, during the debate on the 1970 Clean Air Act. Iacocca warned that compliance with the new regulations would require huge price increases for automobiles, force U.S. automobile production to a halt after January 1, 1975, and "do irreparable damage to the U.S. economy" (Smith, 1992). The 1970 Clean Air Act was subsequently enacted, and Iacocca's predictions turned out to be wrong. Similar dire predictions were made during the 1990 Clean Air Act debate; industry analysts predicted that burdens on the U.S. industry would exceed $100 billion. Of course, the reality has proven to be far less dramatic. In one study in the pulp and paper sector, actual costs of compliance were $4.00 to $5.50 per ton compared to original industry estimates of $16.40 (Bonson, McCubbin and Sprague, 1988).

Early estimates of compliance cost also tend to be exaggerated because they assume no innovation. Early cost estimates for dealing with regulations concerning emission of volatile compounds released during paint application held everything

---

[9] A case study of pollution prevention in a large multinational firm showed those units with strong total quality management programs in place usually undertake more effective pollution prevention efforts than units with less commitment to total quality management. See Rappaport (1992), cited in U.S. Congress, Office of Technology Assessment (1994).

else constant, assuming only the addition of a hood to capture the fumes from paint lines. Innovation that improved the paint's transfer efficiency subsequently allowed not only the reduction of fumes but also paint usage. Further innovation in waterborne paint formulations without any VOC-releasing solvents made it possible to eliminate the need for capturing and treating the fumes altogether (Bonifant, 1994b). Similarly, early estimates of the costs of complying with a 1991 federal clean air regulation calling for a 98 percent reduction in atmospheric emissions of benzene from tar-storage tanks used by coal tar distillers initially assumed that tar-storage tanks would have to be covered by costly gas blankets. While many distillers opposed the regulations, Pittsburgh-based Aristech Chemical, a major distiller of coal tar, subsequently developed an innovative way to remove benzene from tar in the first processing step, thereby eliminating the need for the gas blanket and resulting in a saving of $3.3 million instead of a cost increase (PR Newswire, 1993).

Prices in the new market for trading allowances to emit SO_2 provide another vivid example. At the time the law was passed, analysts projected that the marginal cost of SO_2 controls (and, therefore, the price of an emission allowance) would be on the order of $300 to $600 (or more) per ton in Phase I and up to $1000 or more in Phase II. Actual Phase I allowance prices have turned out to be in the $170 to $250 range, and recent trades are heading lower, with Phase II estimates only slightly higher (after adjusting for the time value of money). In case after case, the differences between initial predictions and actual outcomes—especially after industry has had time to learn and innovate—are striking.

Econometric studies showing that environmental regulation raises costs and harms competitiveness are subject to bias, because net compliance costs are overestimated by assuming away innovation benefits. Jorgenson and Wilcoxen (1990), for example, explicitly state that they did not attempt to assess public or private benefits. Other often-cited studies that solely focus on costs, leaving out benefits, are Hazilla and Kopp (1990) and Gray (1987). By largely assuming away innovation effects, how could economic studies reach any other conclusion than they do?

Internationally competitive industries seem to be much better able to innovate in response to environmental regulation than industries that were uncompetitive to begin with, but no study measuring the effects of environmental regulation on industry competitiveness has taken initial competitiveness into account. In a study by Kalt (1988), for instance, the sectors where high environmental costs were associated with negative trade performance were ones such as ferrous metal mining, nonferrous mining, chemical and fertilizer manufacturing, primary iron and steel and primary nonferrous metals, industries where the United States suffers from dwindling raw material deposits, very high relative electricity costs, heavily subsidized foreign competitors and other disadvantages that have rendered them uncompetitive quite apart from environmental costs.[10] Other sectors identified by Kalt

---

[10] It should be observed that a strong correlation between environmental costs and industry competitiveness does not necessarily indicate causality. Omitting environmental benefits from regulation, and

as having incurred very high environmental costs can actually be interpreted as supporting our hypothesis. Chemicals, plastics and synthetics, fabric, yarn and thread, miscellaneous textiles, leather tanning, paints and allied products, and paperboard containers all had high environmental costs but displayed positive trade performance.

A number of studies have failed to find that stringent environmental regulation hurts industrial competitiveness. Meyer (1992, 1993) tested and refuted the hypothesis that U.S. states with stringent environmental policies experience weak economic growth. Leonard (1988) was unable to demonstrate statistically significant offshore movements by U.S. firms in pollution-intensive industries. Wheeler and Mody (1992) failed to find that environmental regulation affected the foreign investment decisions of U.S. firms. Repetto (1995) found that industries heavily affected by environmental regulations experienced slighter reductions in their share of world exports than did the entire American industry from 1970 to 1990. Using U.S. Bureau of Census Data of more than 200,000 large manufacturing establishments, the study also found that plants with poor environmental records are generally not more profitable than cleaner ones in the same industry, even controlling for their age, size and technology. Jaffe, Peterson, Portney and Stavins (1993) recently surveyed more than 100 studies and concluded there is little evidence to support the view that U.S. environmental regulation had a large adverse effect on competitiveness.

Of course, these studies offer no proof for our hypothesis, either. But it is striking that so many studies find that even the poorly designed environmental laws presently in effect have little adverse effect on competitiveness. After all, traditional approaches to regulation have surely worked to stifle potential innovation offsets and imposed unnecessarily high costs of compliance on industry (as we will discuss in greater detail in the next section). Thus, studies using actual compliance costs to regulation are heavily biased toward finding that such regulation has a substantial cost.[11] In no way do such studies measure the potential of well-crafted environmental regulations to stimulate competitiveness.

A third criticism of our thesis is that even if regulation fosters innovation, it will harm competitiveness by crowding out other potentially more productive investments or avenues for innovation. Given incomplete information, the limited

---

reporting obvious (end-of-pipe) costs but not more difficult to identify or quantify innovation benefits can actually obscure a reverse causal relationship: industries that were uncompetitive in the first place may well be less able to innovate in response to environmental pressures, and thus be prone to end-of-pipe solutions whose costs are easily measured. In contrast, competitive industries capable of addressing environmental problems in innovative ways may report a lower compliance cost.

[11] Gray and Shadbegian (1993), another often-mentioned study, suffers from several of the problems discussed here. The article uses industry-reported compliance costs and does not control for plant technology vintage or the extent of other productivity-enhancing investments at the plant. High compliance costs may well have been borne in old, inefficient plants where firms opted for secondary treatment rather than innovation. Moreover, U.S. producers may well have been disadvantaged in innovating given the nature of the U.S. regulatory process—this seems clearly to have been the case in pulp and paper, one of the industries studied by the Management Institute for Environment and Business (MEB).

attention many companies have devoted to environmental innovations and the inherent linkage between pollution and resource productivity described earlier, it certainly is not obvious that this line of innovation has been so thoroughly explored that the marginal benefits of further investment would be low. The high returns evident in the studies we have cited support this view. Moreover, environmental investments represent only a small percentage of overall investment in all but a very few industries.[12]

A final counterargument, more caricature than criticism, is that we are asserting that any strict environmental regulation will inevitably lead to innovation and competitiveness. Of course, this is not our position. Instead, we believe that if regulations are properly crafted and companies are attuned to the possibilities, then innovation to minimize and even offset the cost of compliance is likely in many circumstances.

Designing Environmental Regulation to Encourage Innovation

If environmental standards are to foster the innovation offsets that arise from new technologies and approaches to production, they should adhere to three principles. First, they must create the maximum opportunity for innovation, leaving the approach to innovation to industry and not the standard-setting agency. Second, regulations should foster continuous improvement, rather than locking in any particular technology. Third, the regulatory process should leave as little room as possible for uncertainty at every stage. Evaluated by these principles, it is clear that U.S. environmental regulations have often been crafted in a way that deters innovative solutions, or even renders them impossible. Environmental laws and regulations need to take three substantial steps: phrasing environmental rules as goals that can be met in flexible ways; encouraging innovation to reach and exceed those goals; and administering the system in a coordinated way.

Clear Goals, Flexible Approaches

Environmental regulation should focus on outcomes, not technologies.[13] Past regulations have often prescribed particular remediation technologies—like catalysts or scrubbers to address air pollution—rather than encouraging innovative approaches. American environmental law emphasized phrases like "best available technology," or "best available control technology." But legislating as if one par-

---

[12] In paints and coatings, for example, environmental investments were 3.3 percent of total capital investment in 1989. According to Department of Commerce (1991) data (self-reported by industry), capital spending for pollution control and abatement outside of the chemical, pulp and paper, petroleum and coal, and primary metal sectors made up just 3.15 percent of total capital spending in 1991.

[13] There will always be instances of extremely hazardous pollution requiring immediate action, where imposing a specific technology by command and control may be the best or only viable solution. However, such methods should be seen as a last resort.

ticular technology is always the "best" almost guarantees that innovation will not occur.

Regulations should encourage product and process changes to better utilize resources and avoid pollution early, rather than mandating end-of-pipe or secondary treatment, which is almost always more costly. For regulators, this poses a question of where to impose regulations in the chain of production from raw materials, equipment, the producer of the end product, to the consumer (Porter, 1985). Regulators must consider the technological capabilities and resources available at each stage, because it affects the likelihood that innovation will occur. With that in mind, the governing principle should be to regulate as late in the production chain as practical, which will normally allow more flexibility for innovation there and in upstream stages.

The EPA should move beyond the single medium (air, water and so on) as the principal way of thinking about the environment, toward total discharges or total impact.[14] It should reorganize around affected industry clusters (including suppliers and related industries) to better understand a cluster's products, technologies and total set of environmental problems. This will foster fundamental rather than piecemeal solutions.[15]

Seeding and Spreading Environmental Innovations

Where possible, regulations should include the use of market incentives, including pollution taxes, deposit-refund schemes and tradable permits.[16] Such approaches often allow considerable flexibility, reinforce resource productivity, and also create incentives for ongoing innovation. Mandating outcomes by setting emission levels, while preferable to choosing a particular technology, still fails to provide incentives for continued and ongoing innovation and will tend to freeze a status quo until new regulations appear. In contrast, market incentives can encourage the introduction of technologies that exceed current standards.

The EPA should also promote an increased use of preemptive standards by industry, which appear to be an effective way of dealing with environmental

---

[14] A first step in this direction is the EPA's recent adjustment of the timing of its air rule for the pulp and paper industry so that it will coincide with the rule for water, allowing industry to see the dual impact of the rules and innovate accordingly.

[15] The EPA's regulatory cluster team concept, under which a team from relevant EPA offices approaches particular problems for a broader viewpoint, is a first step in this direction. Note, however, that of the 17 cluster groups formed, only four were organized around specific industries (petroleum refining, oil and gas production, pulp and paper, printing), while the remaining 13 focused on specific chemicals or types of pollution (U.S. Congress, Office of Technology Assessment, 1994).

[16] Pollution taxes can be implemented as effluent charges on the quantity of pollution discharges, as user charges for public treatment facilities, or as product charges based on the potential pollution of a product. In a deposit-refund system, such product charges may be rebated if a product user disposes of it properly (for example, by returning a lead battery for recycling rather than sending it to a landfill). Under a tradable permit system, like that included in the recent Clean Air Act Amendments, a maximum amount of pollution is set, and rights equal to that cap are distributed to firms. Firms must hold enough rights to cover their emissions; firms with excess rights can sell them to firms who are short.

regulation. Preemptive standards, agreed to with EPA oversight to avoid collusion, can be set and met by industry to avoid government standards that might go further or be more restrictive on innovation. They are not only less costly, but allow faster change and leave the initiative for innovation with industry.

The EPA should play a major role in collecting and disseminating information on innovation offsets and their consequences, both here and in other countries. Limited knowledge about opportunities for innovation is a major constraint on company behavior. A good start can be the "clearinghouse" of information on source-reduction approaches that EPA was directed to establish by the Pollution Prevention Act (PPA) of 1990. The Green Lights and Toxics Release Inventories described at the start of this paper are other programs that involve collecting and spreading information. Yet another important initiative is the EPA program to compare emissions rates at different companies, creating methodologies to measure the full internal costs of pollution and ways of exchanging best practices and learning on innovative technologies.

Regulatory approaches can also function by helping create demand pressure for environmental innovation. One example is the prestigious German "Blue Angel" eco-label, introduced by the German government in 1977, which can be displayed only by products meeting very strict environmental criteria. One of the label's biggest success stories has been in oil and gas heating appliances: the energy efficiency of these appliances improved significantly when the label was introduced, and emissions of sulfur dioxide, carbon monoxide and nitrogen oxides were reduced by more than 30 percent.

Another point of leverage on the demand side is to harness the role of government as a demanding buyer of environmental solutions and environmentally friendly products. While there are benefits of government procurement of products such as recycled paper and retreaded tires, the far more leveraged role is in buying specialized environmental equipment and services.[17] One useful change would be to alter the current practice of requiring bidders in competitive bid processes for government projects to only bid with "proven" technologies, a practice sure to hinder innovation.

The EPA can employ demonstration projects to stimulate and seed innovative new technologies, working through universities and industry associations. A good example is the project to develop and demonstrate technologies for super-efficient refrigerators, which was conducted by the EPA and researchers in government, academia and the private sector (United States Environmental Protection Agency, 1992). An estimated $1.7 billion was spent in 1992 by the federal government on environmental technology R&D, but only $70 million was directed toward research on pollution prevention (U.S. Congress, Office of Technology Assessment, 1994).

Incentives for innovation must also be built into the regulatory process itself. The current permitting system under Title V of the Clean Air Act Amendments, to

---

[17] See Marron (1994) for a demonstration of the modest productivity gains likely from government procurement of standard items, although in a static model.

choose a negative example, requires firms seeking to change or expand their production process in a way that might impact air quality to revise their permit extensively, *no matter how little the potential effect on air quality may be*. This not only deters innovation, but drains the resources of regulators away from timely action on significant matters. On the positive side, the state of Massachusetts has initiated a program to waive permits in some circumstances, or promise an immediate permit, if a company takes a zero-discharge approach.

A final priority is new forums for settling regulatory issues that minimize litigation. Potential litigation creates enormous uncertainty; actual litigation burns resources. Mandatory arbitration, or rigid arbitration steps before litigation is allowed, would benefit innovation. There is also a need to rethink certain liability issues. While adequate safeguards must be provided against companies that recklessly harm citizens, there is a pressing need for liability standards that more clearly recognize the countervailing health and safety benefits of innovations that lower or eliminate the discharge of harmful pollutants.

Regulatory Coordination

Coordination of environmental regulation can be improved in at least three ways: between industry and regulators, between regulators at different levels and places in government, and between U.S. regulators and their international counterparts.

In setting environmental standards and regulatory processes to encourage innovation, substantive industry participation in setting standards is needed right from the beginning, as is common in many European countries. An appropriate regulatory process is one in which regulations themselves are clear, who must meet them is clear, and industry accepts the regulations and begins innovating to address them, rather than spending years attempting to delay or relax them. In our current system, by the time standards are finally settled and clarified, it is often too late to address them fundamentally, making secondary treatment the only alternative. We need to evolve toward a regulatory regime in which the EPA and other regulators make a commitment that standards will be in place for, say, five years, so that industry is motivated to innovate rather than adopt incremental solutions.

Different parts and levels of government must coordinate and organize themselves so that companies are not forced to deal with multiple parties with inconsistent desires and approaches. As a matter of regulatory structure, the EPA's proposed new Innovative Technology Council, being set up to advocate the development of new technology in every field of environmental policy, is a step in the right direction. Another unit in the EPA should be responsible for continued reengineering of the process of regulation to reduce uncertainty and minimize costs. Also, an explicit strategy is needed to coordinate and harmonize federal and state activities.[18]

---

[18] The cluster-based approach to regulation discussed earlier should also help eliminate the practice of sending multiple EPA inspectors to the same plant who do not talk to one another, make conflicting

A final issue of coordination involves the relationship between U.S. environmental regulations and those in other countries. U.S. regulations should be in sync with regulations in other countries and, ideally, be slightly ahead of them. This will minimize possible competitive disadvantages relative to foreign competitors who are not yet subject to the standard, while at the same time maximizing export potential in the pollution control sector. Standards that lead world developments provide domestic firms with opportunities to create valuable early-mover advantages. However, standards should not be too far ahead of, or too different in character from, those that are likely to apply to foreign competitors, for this would lead industry to innovate in the wrong directions.

Critics may note, with some basis, that U.S. regulators may not be able to project better than firms what type of regulations, and resultant demands for environmental products and services, will develop in other nations. However, regulators would seem to possess greater resources and information than firms for understanding the path of regulation in other countries. Moreover, U.S. regulations influence the type and stringency of regulations in other nations, and as such help define demand in other world markets.

Imperatives for Companies

Of course, the regulatory reforms described here also seek to change how companies view environmental issues.[19] Companies must start to recognize the environment as a competitive opportunity—not as an annoying cost or a postponable threat. Yet many companies are ill-prepared to carry out a strategy of environmental innovation that produces sizable compensating offsets.

For starters, companies must improve their measurement and assessment methods to detect environmental costs and benefits.[20] Too often, relevant information is simply lacking. Typical is the case of a large producer of organic chemicals that retained a consulting firm to explore opportunities for reducing waste. The client thought it had 40 waste streams, but a careful audit revealed that 497 different

---

demands and waste time and resources. The potential savings from cluster- and multimedia-oriented permitting and inspection programs appear to be substantial. During a pilot multimedia testing program called the Blackstone Project, the Massachusetts Department of Environmental Protection found that multimedia inspections required 50 percent less time than conventional inspections—which at that time accounted for nearly one-fourth of the department's operating budget (Roy and Dillard, 1990).

[19] For a more detailed perspective on changing company mindsets about competitiveness and environmentalism, see Porter and van der Linde (1995) in the *Harvard Business Review*.

[20] Accounting methods that are currently being discussed in this context include "full cost accounting," which attempts to assign all costs to specific products or processes, and "total cost accounting," which goes a step further and attempts both to allocate costs more specifically and to include cost items beyond traditional concerns, such as indirect or hidden costs (like compliance costs, insurance, on-site waste management, operation of pollution control and future liability) and less tangible benefits (like revenue from enhanced company image). See White, Becker and Goldstein (1991), cited in U.S. Congress, Office of Technology Assessment (1994).

waste streams were actually present (Parkinson, 1990). Few companies analyze the true cost of toxicity, waste, discharges and the second-order impacts of waste and discharges on other activities. Fewer still look beyond the out-of-pocket costs of dealing with pollution to investigate the opportunity costs of the wasted resources or foregone productivity. How much money is going up the smokestack? What percentage of inputs are wasted? Many companies do not even track environmental spending carefully, or subject it to evaluation techniques typical for "normal" investments.

Once environmental costs are measured and understood, the next step is to create a presumption for innovation-based solutions. Discharges, scrap and emissions should be analyzed for insights about beneficial product design or process changes. Approaches based on treatment or handling of discharges should be accepted only after being sent back several times for reconsideration. The responsibility for environmental issues should not be delegated to lawyers or outside consultants except in the adversarial regulatory process, or even to internal specialists removed from the line organization, residing in legal, government or environmental affairs departments. Instead, environmental strategies must become a general management issue if the sorts of process and product redesigns needed for true innovation are to even be considered, much less be proposed and implemented.

Conclusion

We have found that economists as a group are resistant to the notion that even well-designed environmental regulations might lead to improved competitiveness. This hesitancy strikes us as somewhat peculiar, given that in other contexts, economists are extremely willing to argue that technological change has overcome predictions of severe, broadly defined environmental costs. A static model (among other flaws) has been behind many dire predictions of economic disaster and human catastrophe: from the predictions of Thomas Malthus that population would inevitably outstrip food supply; to the *Limits of Growth* (Meadows and Meadows, 1972), which predicted the depletion of the world's natural resources; to *The Population Bomb* (Ehrlich, 1968), which predicted that a quarter of the world's population would starve to death between 1973 and 1983. As economists are often eager to point out, these models failed because they did not appreciate the power of innovations in technology to change old assumptions about resource availability and utilization.

Moreover, the static mindset that environmentalism is inevitably costly has created a self-fulfilling gridlock, where both regulators and industry battle over every inch of territory. The process has spawned an industry of litigators and consultants, driving up costs and draining resources away from real solutions. It has been reported that four out of five EPA decisions are currently challenged in court (Clay, 1993, cited in U.S. Congress, Office of Technology Assessment, 1994). A study by the Rand Institute for Civil Justice found that 88 percent of the money paid out between 1986 and 1989 by insurers on Superfund claims went to pay for legal and administrative costs, while only 12 percent were used for actual site cleanups (Acton and Dixon, 1992).

The United States and other countries need an entirely new way of thinking about the relationship between environment and industrial competitiveness—one closer to the reality of modern competition. The focus should be on relaxing the environment-competitiveness tradeoff rather than accepting and, worse yet, steepening it. The orientation should shift from pollution control to resource productivity. We believe that no lasting success can come from policies that promise that environmentalism will triumph over industry, nor from policies that promise that industry will triumph over environmentalism. Instead, success must involve innovation-based solutions that promote both environmentalism and industrial competitiveness.

■ *The authors are grateful to Alan Auerbach, Ben Bonifant, Daniel C. Esty, Ridgway M. Hall, Jr., Donald B. Marron, Jan Rivkin, Nicolaj Siggelkow, R. David Simpson and Timothy Taylor for extensive valuable editorial suggestions. We are also grateful to Reed Hundt for ongoing discussions that have greatly benefitted our thinking.*

References

Acton, Jan Paul, and Lloyd S. Dixon, *Superfund and Transaction Costs: The Experiences of Insurers and Very Large Industrial Firms.* Santa Monica: Rand Institute for Civil Justice, 1992.

Amoco Corporation and United States Environmental Protection Agency, "Amoco-U.S. EPA Pollution Prevention Project: Yorktown, Virginia, Project Summary," Chicago and Washington, D.C., 1992.

Basta, Nicholas, and David Vagi, "A Casebook of Successful Waste Reduction Projects," *Chemical Engineering,* August 15, 1988, 95:11, 37.

Berube, M., J. Nash, J. Maxwell, and J. Ehrenfeld, "From Pollution Control to Zero Discharge: How the Robbins Company Overcame the Obstacles," *Pollution Prevention Review,* Spring 1992, 2:2, 189–207.

Bonifant, B., "Competitive Implications of Environmental Regulation in the Electronics Manufacturing Industry," Management Institute for Environment and Business, Washington, D.C., 1994a.

Bonifant, B., "Competitive Implications of Environmental Regulation in the Paint and Coatings Industry," Management Institute for Environment and Business, Washington, D.C., 1994b.

Bonifant, B., and I. Ratcliffe, "Competitive Implications of Environmental Regulation in the Pulp and Paper Industry," Management Institute for Environment and Business, Washington, D.C., 1994.

Bonson, N. C., Neil McCubbin, and John B. Sprague, "Kraft Mill Effluents in Ontario." Report prepared for the Technical Advisory Committee, Pulp and Paper Sector of MISA, Ontario Ministry of the Environment, Toronto, Ontario, Canada, March 29, 1988, Section 6, p. 166.

Boroughs, D. L., and B. Carpenter, "Helping the Planet and the Economy," *U.S. News & World Report,* March 25, 1991, *110:*11, 46.

Clay, Don, "New Environmentalist: A Cooperative Strategy," *Forum for Applied Research and Public Policy,* Spring 1993, *8,* 125–28.

DeCanio, Stephen J., "Why Do Profitable Energy-Saving Investment Projects Languish?" Paper presented at the Second International Research Conference of the Greening of Industry Network, Cambridge, Mass., 1993.

Department of Commerce, "Pollution Abatement Costs and Expenditures," Washington, D.C., 1991.

Dorfman, Mark H., Warren R. Muir, and Catherine G. Miller, *Environmental Dividends: Cutting More Chemical Wastes*. New York: INFORM, 1992.

Ehrlich, Paul, *The Population Bomb*. New York: Ballantine Books, 1968.

Freeman, A. Myrick, III, "Methods for Assessing the Benefits of Environmental Programs." In Kneese, A. V., and J. L. Sweeney, eds., *Handbook of Natural Resource and Energy Economics*. Vol. 1. Amsterdam: North-Holland, 1985, pp. 223–70.

Gray, Wayne B., "The Cost of Regulation: OSHA, EPA, and the Productivity Slowdown," *American Economic Review*, 1987, 77:5, 998–1006.

Gray, Wayne B., and Ronald J. Shadbegian, "Environmental Regulation and Productivity at the Plant Level," discussion paper, U.S. Department of Commerce, Center for Economic Studies, Washington, D.C., 1993.

Hartwell, R. V., and L. Bergkamp, "Eco-Labelling in Europe: New Market-Related Environmental Risks?," *BNA International Environment Daily*, Special Report, Oct. 20, 1992.

Hazilla, Michael, and Raymond J. Kopp, "Social Cost of Environmental Quality Regulations: A General Equilibrium Analysis," *Journal of Political Economy*, 1990, 98:4, 853–73.

Jaffe, Adam B., S. Peterson, Paul Portney, and Robert N. Stavins, "Environmental Regulations and the Competitiveness of U.S. Industry," Economics Resource Group, Cambridge, Mass., 1993.

Jaffe, Adam B., S. Peterson, Paul Portney, and Robert N. Stavins, "Environmental Regulation and International Competitiveness: What Does the Evidence Tell Us," draft, January 13, 1994.

Jorgenson, Dale W., and Peter J. Wilcoxen, "Environmental Regulation and U.S. Economic Growth," *Rand Journal of Economics*, Summer 1990, 21:2, 314–40.

Kalt, Joseph P., "The Impact of Domestic Environmental Regulatory Policies on U.S. International Competitiveness." In Spence, A. M., and H. Hazard, eds., *International Competitiveness*, Cambridge, Mass: Harper and Row, Ballinger, 1988, pp. 221–62.

King, A., "Improved Manufacturing Resulting from Learning-From-Waste: Causes, Importance, and Enabling Conditions," working paper, Stern School of Business, New York University, 1994.

Leonard, H. Jeffrey, *Pollution and the Struggle for World Product*. Cambridge, U.K.: Cambridge University Press, 1988.

Makower, Joel, *The E-Factor: The Bottom-Line Approach to Environmentally Responsible Business*. New York: Times Books, 1993.

Marron, Donald B., "Buying Green: Government Procurement as an Instrument of Environmental Policy," mimeo, Massachusetts Institute of Technology, 1994.

Massachusetts Department of Environmental Protection, Daniel S. Greenbaum, Commissioner, interview, Boston, August 8, 1993.

Meadows, Donella H., and Dennis L. Meadows, *The Limits of Growth*. New York: New American Library, 1972.

Meyer, Stephen M., *Environmentalism and Economic Prosperity: Testing the Environmental Impact Hypothesis*. Cambridge, Mass.: Massachusetts Institute of Technology, 1992.

Meyer, Stephen M., *Environmentalism and Economic Prosperity: An Update*. Cambridge, Mass.: Massachusetts Institute of Technology, 1993.

National Paint and Coatings Association, *Improving the Superfund: Correcting a National Public Policy Disaster*. Washington, D.C., 1992.

Palmer, Karen L., and Ralph David Simpson, "Environmental Policy as Industrial Policy," *Resources*, Summer 1993, *112*, 17–21.

Parkinson, Gerald, "Reducing Wastes Can Be Cost-Effective," *Chemical Engineering*, July 1990, 97:7, 30.

Porter, Michael E., *Competitive Advantage: Creating and Sustaining Superior Performance*. New York: Free Press, 1985.

Porter, Michael E., *The Competitive Advantage of Nations*. New York: Free Press, 1990.

Porter, Michael E., "America's Green Strategy," *Scientific American*, April 1991, 264, 168.

Porter, Michael E., and Claas van der Linde, "Green and Competitive: Breaking the Stalemate," *Harvard Business Review*, September-October 1995.

PR Newswire, "Winners Announced for Governor's Waste Minimization Awards," January 21, 1993, State and Regional News Section.

Oates, Wallace, Karen L. Palmer, and Paul Portney, "Environmental Regulation and International Competitiveness: Thinking About the Porter Hypothesis," Resources for the Future Working Paper 94-02, 1993.

Rappaport, Ann, "Development and Transfer of Pollution Prevention Technology Within a Multinational Corporation," dissertation, Department of Civil Engineering, Tufts University, May 1992.

Raytheon Inc., "Alternate Cleaning Technology." Technical Report Phase II. January-October 1991.

Raytheon Inc., J. R. Pasquariello, Vice President Environmental Quality; Kenneth J. Tierney, Director Environmental and Energy Conservation; Frank A. Marino, Senior Corporate Environmental Specialist; interview, Lexington, Mass., April 4, 1993.

Repetto, Robert, "Jobs, Competitiveness, and Environmental Regulation: What are the Real Issues?," Washington, D.C.: World Resources Institute, 1995.

Roy, M., and L. A. Dillard, "Toxics Use in Massachusetts: The Blackstone Project," *Journal of Air and Waste Management Association*, October 1990, *40*:10, 1368–71.

Schmalensee, Richard, "The Costs of Environmental Regulation." Massachusetts Institute of Technology, Center for Energy and Environmental Policy Research Working Paper 93-015, 1993.

Sheridan, J. H., "Attacking Wastes and Saving Money ... Some of the Time," *Industry Week*, February 17, 1992, *241*:4, 43.

Simpson, Ralph David, "Taxing Variable Cost: Environmental Regulation as Industrial Policy." Resources for the Future Working Paper ENR93-12, 1993.

Smith, Zachary A, *The Environmental Policy Paradox*. Englewood Cliffs, N.J.: Prentice Hall, 1992.

United States Environmental Protection Agency, "Multiple Pathways to Super Efficient Refrigerators," Washington, D.C., 1992.

U.S. Congress, Office of Technology Assessment, "Industry, Technology, and the Environment: Competitive Challenges and Business Opportunities," OTA-ITE-586, Washington, D.C., 1994.

van der Linde, Claas, "The Micro-Economic Implications of Environmental Regulation: A Preliminary Framework." In *Environmental Policies and Industrial Competitiveness*. Paris: Organization of Economic Co-Operation and Development, 1993, pp. 69–77.

van der Linde, Claas, "Competitive Implications of Environmental Regulation in the Cell Battery Industry," Hochschule St. Gallen, St. Gallen, forthcoming 1995a.

van der Linde, Claas, "Competitive Implications of Environmental Regulation in the Printing Ink Industry," Hochschule St. Gallen, St. Gallen, forthcoming 1995b.

van der Linde, Claas, "Competitive Implications of Environmental Regulation in the Refrigerator Industry," Hochschule St. Gallen, St. Gallen, forthcoming 1995c.

Wheeler, David, and Ashoka Mody, "International Investment Location Decisions: The Case of U.S. Firms," *Journal of International Economics*, August 1992, *33*, 57–76.

White, A. L., M. Becker, and J. Goldstein, "Alternative Approaches to the Financial Evaluation of Industrial Pollution Prevention Investments," prepared for the New Jersey Department of Environmental Protection, Division of Science and Research, November 1991.

[21]

Tightening Environmental Standards: The Benefit-Cost or the No-Cost Paradigm?

Karen Palmer, Wallace E. Oates, and Paul R. Portney

Michael Porter and Claas van der Linde have written a paper that is interesting and, to us at least, somewhat astonishing. It is a defense of environmental regulation—indeed, an invitation to more stringent regulation—that makes essentially no reference to the *social* benefits of such regulation. This approach contrasts starkly with the methods that economists and other policy analysts have traditionally used when assessing environmental or other regulatory programs.

The traditional approach consists of comparing the beneficial effects of regulation with the costs that must be borne to secure these benefits. For environmental regulation, the social benefits include the reductions in morbidity or premature mortality that can accompany cleaner air, the enhanced recreational opportunities that can result from water-quality improvements, the increased land values that might attend the cleanup of a hazardous waste site, the enhanced vitality of aquatic ecosystems that might follow reductions in agricultural pesticide use or any of the other potentially significant benefits associated with tighter standards. From this benefit-cost approach emerges the standard tradeoff discussed in virtually every economics textbook.

Porter and van der Linde deny the validity of this approach to the analysis of environmental regulation, claiming it to be an artifact of what they see as a "static mindset." In their view, economists have failed to appreciate the capacity of

■ *Karen Palmer is a Fellow at Resources for the Future, Washington, D.C. (e-mail: palmer@rff.org). Wallace E. Oates is Professor of Economics, University of Maryland, College Park, Maryland, and University Fellow, Resources for the Future, Washington, D.C. (oates@econ.umd.edu). Paul R. Portney is Vice President, Resources for the Future, Washington, D.C. (portney@rff.org).*

stringent environmental regulations to induce innovation, and this failure has led them to a fundamental misrepresentation of the problem of environmental regulation. There is no tradeoff, Porter and van der Linde suggest; instead, environmental protection, properly pursued, often presents a free or even a paid lunch. As they put it, there are lots of $10 bills lying around waiting to be picked up.

We take strong issue with their view. If this were simply a matter of intellectual sparring, it would be inconsequential outside academe. But their view has found a ready audience in some parts of the policymaking community. For example, Vice President Gore (1992, p. 342) writes that "3M, in its Pollution Prevention Pays program, has reported significant profit improvement as a direct result of its increased attention to shutting off all the causes of pollution it could find." If environmental regulations are essentially costless (or even carry a negative cost!), then it is unnecessary to justify and measure with care the presumed social benefits of environmental programs. Stringent environmental measures (of the right kind) are good for business as well as the environment; in the Washington parlance, we have ourselves a "win-win situation." Not surprisingly, this view has also been warmly received by environmentalists and by regulators eager to avoid being seen as imposing unwanted costs on businesses or lower levels of government. At a time of burgeoning interest in Congress in the economic justification for federal regulations, Porter and van der Linde suggest the cost of environmental regulation may be negligible or even nonexistent.

To clarify the points that are in dispute, we should state at the outset that we agree with Porter and van der Linde on a number of matters. First, we share their enthusiasm for a heavier reliance on incentive-based regulation in lieu of command-and-control. Early returns suggest, for example, that tradable permits for sulfur dioxide emissions will reduce the cost of the 1990 acid rain control program by at least 50 percent when measured against the most likely command-and-control alternative (Burtraw, 1995; U.S. General Accounting Office, 1994; Rico, 1995). Second, we agree that early estimates of regulatory compliance costs are likely to be biased upward because of unforeseen technological advances in pollution control or prevention. Third, we accept that providing information, such as in EPA's "Green Lights" program (through which the agency provides technical assistance concerning energy-efficient lighting), may well help disseminate new technologies. Fourth, we acknowledge that regulations have sometimes led to the discovery of cost-saving or quality-improving innovation; in other words, we do *not* believe that firms are ever-vigilantly perched on their efficiency frontiers.

On this last point, however, we do not find Porter and van der Linde at all convincing concerning the pervasiveness of inefficiencies. The major empirical evidence that they advance in support of their position is a series of case studies. With literally hundreds of thousands of firms subject to environmental regulation in the United States alone, it would be hard *not* to find instances where regulation has seemingly worked to a polluting firm's advantage. But collecting cases where this has happened in no way establishes a general presumption in favor of this outcome. It would be an easy matter for us to assemble a matching list where firms have found their costs increased and profits reduced as a result of (even enlightened) environmental regulations, not to mention cases where regulation has pushed firms over the brink into bankruptcy.

What is needed, we believe, is a more systematic approach to the issue. Following a general observation to put things in context, we begin with a model in which increasing the stringency of incentive-based environmental regulations *must* result in reduced profits for the firm. This model is incomplete in various ways, but it provides a useful baseline for the succeeding discussion. From this baseline, we can then explore the sorts of changes in the model that could produce the result that regulation leads to higher profits—the outcome that Porter and van der Linde seem to suggest is the norm. We are then in a better position to assess the evidence and the weight of their case.

Innovation and Environmental Regulation: An Observation

Porter and van der Linde accuse mainstream environmental economics, with its "static mindset," of having neglected innovation. This charge is puzzling. For several decades now, environmental economists have made their case for incentive-based policy instruments (such as effluent charges or tradable emission permits) precisely by emphasizing the incentives that these measures provide for innovation in abatement technology (Kneese and Bower, 1968, p. 139). Virtually every standard textbook in environmental economics makes the point that incentive-based approaches are perhaps more attractive for reasons of dynamic efficiency than for their ability to minimize the costs of attaining environmental standards at any particular point in time. A substantial literature has developed in recent years that explores the effects of various policy instruments on research and development decisions concerning abatement technology, a literature on which we shall draw in this discussion.[1]

What distinguishes the Porter and van der Linde perspective from neoclassical environmental economics is *not* the "static mindset" of the latter. It is two other presumptions. First, they see a private sector that systematically overlooks profitable opportunities for innovation.[2] Second, and equally important, they envision a regulatory authority that is in a position to correct this "market failure."[3] With properly designed measures, regulators can set in motion innovative activities through which

---

[1] The reader interested in exploring this literature might begin with Magat (1978), Downing and White (1986), Malueg (1989), Milliman and Prince (1989), Parry (1992), Biglaiser and Horowitz (1995) and Simpson (1995).

[2] This, incidentally, seems a rather odd and sad commentary on the private sector to be coming from one of the country's eminent business professors and consultants.

[3] This "market failure," incidentally, is quite different in character from the usual public goods argument that private firms underinvest in research and development because they will have difficulty appropriating enough of the social benefits. What Porter and van der Linde have in mind is a failure of private decision makers to respond to *private* profit opportunities.

firms can realize these overlooked opportunities. Their vision thus suggests a new role for regulatory activity in bringing about dynamic efficiency: enlightened regulators provide the needed incentives for cost-saving and quality-improving innovations that competition apparently fails to provide. Regulators can, as Porter and van der Linde put it, help firms "to overcome organizational inertia and to foster creative thinking," thereby increasing their profits.[4] We find this view hard to swallow, and suspect that most regulated firms would share our difficulty.

Environmental Regulation and Competitiveness: A Proposition

Drawing on some of the early literature on innovation in abatement technology, we now present a model in which even incentive-based environmental regulation results in reduced profits for the regulated firm. The model essentially formalizes the basic point that the addition (or tightening) of constraints on a firm's set of choices cannot be expected to result in an increased level of profits. Readers uninterested in the analytics may wish to skip to the next section.

We emphasize that this model is static in character and fails to address the inherent uncertainty in research and development (R&D) decisions. In this sense, it is subject to precisely the sort of criticism that Porter and van der Linde level in their paper. However, for the same reason, it provides a useful point of entry into the issue. The model is premised on the assumption that the polluting firm maximizes profits and operates in a perfectly competitive market; the firm takes competitors' outputs and R&D expenditures as given and also takes any regulations as exogenously determined. Given these assumptions, the model does not allow for any sort of strategic interaction. The possible effects of relaxing these assumptions and allowing game-theoretic strategic interactions among firms, or between the polluting firm and the regulator, will be discussed in the next section of this paper.

Figure 1 depicts the polluting firm's options. The horizontal axis shows the "abatement level," so that the reduction in pollution increases as one moves from left to right. The vertical axis is measured in dollars, which means that one can graph both the firm's cost of various levels of pollution abatement and compare those costs with market-oriented effluent charges imposed by environmental regulators. The MAC curve (without a star) is the firm's present "marginal abatement cost" function; it indicates the marginal cost incurred by the firm to reduce pollution by an additional unit. The upward slope of the curve implies that the marginal cost of reducing pollution is rising.

---

[4] It is unclear whether Porter and van der Linde view this expanded role for regulation as a general proposition, or whether it is limited to environmental regulation. They appear to suggest the latter when they contend that as waste emissions into the environment, "[Pollution] is a manifestation of economic waste and involves unnecessary, inefficient or incomplete utilization of resources. . . ." This we also find puzzling. Whether it is efficient to recycle wastes, to discharge them into the environment or to adopt an entirely new technology that employs fewer polluting inputs depends on the costs (meaning, of course, the full social costs) of the various alternatives.

Figure 1
The Incentive to Innovate under an Emission Fee

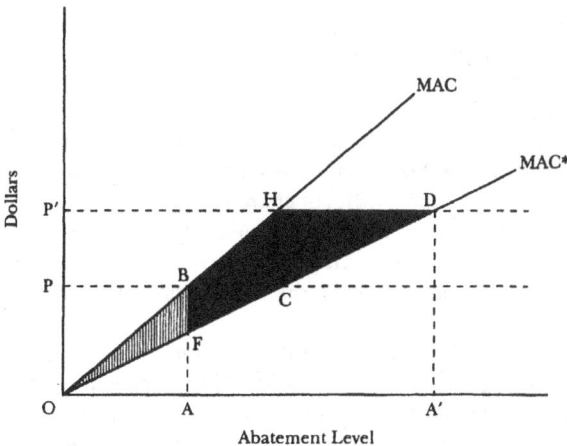

Let us now assume that the firm could, if it chooses, reduce its marginal abatement cost function from the curve MAC to MAC*. Notice that with MAC*, a given marginal expenditure has a greater effect on pollution abatement than it would have with MAC. However, to move from MAC to MAC*, the firm must spend money to research and develop new pollution abatement technology. To simplify the problem, we will assume that the R&D expenditure necessary to move from MAC to MAC* is known completely—there is no risk or uncertainty.

This model will presume market-oriented regulators who use effluent charges to encourage pollution abatement. As long as a profit-maximizing firm can abate pollution itself for less than the effluent charge, it will choose to do so. However, after the point where the cost of abating pollution exceeds the effluent charge, the firm will prefer to pay the charge. Let us assume that the firm is initially confronted by an effluent charge of P. It chooses its profit-maximizing level of abatement activity, A, corresponding to the point B, where marginal abatement cost equals the effluent charge.

If the firm has been operating at abatement level A, an implication is that the (annualized) cost of the R&D effort to reduce MAC to MAC* must exceed the gains to the firm. The R&D investment in additional pollution-abatement technology won't pay off; thus outcome B must produce more profits for the firm than does the attainable point C. Figure 1 also depicts the gains to the polluting firm from undertaking the R&D effort, which can be divided into two parts. The source of the first part is that the earlier level of abatement activity becomes cheaper; the amount of gain here is given by the triangle OFB. The second part comes from the new technology. The company will choose to abate a greater amount of pollution and thus avoid paying the pollution charge on that additional pollution; the gain here is the triangle BCF.

The total gains to the polluting firm from innovation would thus be the area bounded by OFCB. Since the firm has not chosen this option, it must be that the cost of the R&D program that would move the firm from MAC to MAC* exceeds the area of the profit that would be gained, OFCB.

Now, assume that the environmental authority introduces a new, more stringent market-oriented environmental standard, taking the form of an increase in the effluent fee to P'. Without further assumptions, one cannot say whether the firm will respond to the higher effluent charge by sticking with the old technology and ending up at H or by investing in the new one and ending up at D.[5] But we will prove that both H and D generate lower profits than B. Therefore, it will be unambiguously true in this model that the higher effluent standard reduces profits for the firm.

It is straightforward to show that if the firm sticks with its old technology, the higher effluent charge must reduce its profits. In this case, the firm moves from B to H, and while this higher level of pollution abatement may be better for society, the firm is unambiguously worse off. It is paying the same amount to abate pollution up to B as it was before. Between B and H, it is paying more to abate pollution than under the previous, lower effluent charge. And above H, it is paying the higher effluent charge rather than the previously lower one.[6]

It is only a bit trickier to demonstrate that profits at D, where the firm faces a higher effluent charge with the new technology, must be lower than profits at B, where the firm chose to face the lower effluent charge with its existing technology. Notice first that along the MAC* frontier, profits at choice D (given the higher effluent charge) must be lower than profits at point C, given the lower previous effluent charge. As already explained, if technology is constant, the higher effluent charge unambiguously reduces profits. But the basis of this model was that at the

---

[5] What are some of the factors determining whether the firm chooses to respond to a higher effluent charge by investing in new technology? Overall, of course, the question is whether the cost-savings from the new technology exceed the R&D expenditures. Recent work offers some further insights. Ulph (1994) shows that an increase in an emission tax rate may increase a firm's incentive to engage in environmental R&D, but is likely to decrease its incentive to engage in R&D of a general unit-cost-reducing nature, leading to an ambiguous effect on overall R&D expenditures and on the firm's costs. Simpson (1995) suggests that when R&D is both cost reducing and emission reducing, the incentive effects of an increase in the emissions tax for R&D are lower the more R&D reduces marginal cost and the more competitive are rival firms.

[6] This is an application of a more general principle that for a given technology, profit is decreasing in input prices. In the environmental economics literature, waste emissions are typically treated as an input (along with labor, capital and so on) in the production function. This is reasonable, since attempts to cut back on waste emissions will involve the diversion of other inputs to abatement activities, thereby reducing the availability of these other inputs for the production of goods. Reductions in emissions, in short, result in reduced output. Moreover, given the reasonable assumption of rising marginal abatement costs, it makes sense to assume the usual curvature properties so that we can legitimately construct isoquants in emissions and another input and treat them in the usual way. In this framework, the emissions fee becomes simply the price of an input called "waste emissions."

lower effluent charge, the firm didn't find it worthwhile to invest in the new technology; that is, profits were lower at C than at B. By transitivity, if profits at B exceed C, and profits at C exceed D, then it must be true that the higher effluent charge reduces profits for the firm, even if it adopts a new technology.

Thus, in this model of innovation in abatement technology, an increase in the stringency of environmental regulations unambiguously makes the polluting firm worse off. Even if the firm can invest and adopt a new, more efficient abatement technology, if that technology wasn't worth investing in before, its benefits won't be enough to raise the company's profits after the environmental standards are raised, either.

This leads us naturally to ask how one might amend the simple model to alter this basic result. We point out that simply making the model dynamic and/or introducing uncertainty will not overturn this result. It is straightforward to show that our basic proposition likewise applies to a firm that maximizes the expected present value of future profits. What elements, then, are missing from this simplified model that could give rise to an *increase* in profits following the imposition of tighter standards?

We can identify two such elements of potential importance. One possibility is strategic behavior, perhaps involving interactions between polluting firms, or between these firms and the regulating agency, or between regulatory agencies in different countries. The second possibility (the one emphasized by Porter and van der Linde) is the existence of opportunities for profitable innovation in the production of the firm's output that for some reason have been overlooked and that would be realized in the wake of new and tougher environmental regulations. The next two sections take up these extensions to the basic model and present some of the relevant empirical evidence.

Strategic Interaction Among Polluters and Regulators

In the basic model, the polluting firm was operating in a competitive environment, taking as given both the behavior of competing firms and the standards set by the regulator. One important line of extension of the analysis is the introduction of strategic interaction among the various participants. There is some recent and ongoing work along these lines. For example, Barrett (1994) has explored a series of models in which regulators and polluting firms behave strategically. He finds that, in the spirit of the Porter–van der Linde thesis, there are indeed cases in which the government can actually improve the international competitive position of domestic exporters by imposing environmental standards upon them. One such case occurs if each firm takes the price of its competitor as fixed and then competes by setting its own profit-maximizing price. If the government sets a strong emission standard—by which Barrett means a standard beyond the point where the marginal benefits of pollution control equal marginal abatement costs—the domestic firm's marginal cost, and therefore its price, will rise. Recognizing that the domestic firm must charge a higher price to comply with the new standard, foreign competitors raise their prices without fear of retaliation. However, an increase in the foreign price raises demand for the output of the domestic firm with a resulting increase in its profits. This result holds when the domestic industry is an oligopoly as well as when it is a monopoly competing in an oligopolistic international market. It *may* also hold under Cournot competition—where each firm takes the quantity produced by its competitors as given and competes by altering the quantity it produces—if the domestic industry is an oligopoly, although this need not be the case.

In general, however, this result is not robust to other changes in the nature of the strategic behavior. For instance, if the domestic firm is a monopolist in its home country and the domestic and foreign firm are Cournot competitors, then the home government can improve the domestic firm's competitive position by reducing its environmental standards below the efficient level. Kennedy (1994) obtains a similar finding in a model with Cournot competition.

In another treatment of the issue, Simpson and Bradford (1996) develop a strategic trade model that explicitly includes R&D expenditures by firms. In this model, firms behave strategically both in setting levels of spending on R&D and in selecting output levels. The government regulates pollution through an emission fee. Simpson and Bradford find that for certain specifications of the cost and demand functions, increasing the emission fee can increase domestic R&D investment, reduce foreign R&D spending and increase domestic welfare (composed of domestic profits plus pollution fee revenues). However, they note that slight variations in the form of the cost function can reverse these results. Ulph (1994) surveys a number of recent papers that explicitly incorporate strategic R&D investment behavior by firms. This body of work indicates that the effect of environmental regulation on R&D is ambiguous and that even in the cases where higher emissions standards lead to higher domestic R&D spending, governments may still be better off selecting a lower-than-social-cost emission tax rate to shift profits from foreign firms to domestic firms.

Overall, this literature suggests that while it is possible to get results like those that Porter and van der Linde suggest are the norm from models that incorporate strategic behavior, such results are special cases. In many instances, these same strategic trade models suggest that the domestic authority should employ *weak* environmental regulations to promote international competitiveness. Moreover, as Barrett (1994) and Simpson and Bradford (1996) suggest, there are typically other sorts of measures that are more effective at improving international competitiveness than strategic environmental regulatory policy. This bottom line does not deny the Porter–van der Linde argument entirely; certain kinds of strategic models can produce outcomes of the type they describe. But it does seem to us that strategic models are unlikely to establish anything close to a general presumption that stringent environmental measures will enhance competitiveness. In addition, such strategic behavior is not what Porter and van der Linde have in mind. We turn to their basic contention now.

Regulation and "Offsets"

Their claim is that technologies exist of which the firm is unaware until prodded into discovering them by stringent environmental regulations. They go on to contend that such regulation will spur firms to innovate and that the newly discovered technologies will generally offset, or more than offset, the costs of pollution abatement or prevention. Our response takes two very different tacks.

First, we spoke with the vice presidents or corporate directors for environmental protection at Dow, 3M, Ciba-Geigy and Monsanto—all firms mentioned by Porter and van der Linde in their discussion of innovation or process offsets. While each manager acknowledged that in certain instances a particular regulatory requirement may have cost less than had been expected, or perhaps even paid for itself, each also said quite emphatically that, on the whole, environmental regulation amounted to a significant *net* cost to his company.

We have little doubt about the general applicability of this conclusion. Fortunately, we need not confine ourselves to speculation and anecdotes about the pervasiveness or the significance of pollution or innovation offsets. There are data available on this matter, and they indicate that such offsets pale in comparison to expenditures for pollution abatement and control.

Each year the Environmental Economics Division of the Commerce Department's Bureau of Economic Analysis (BEA) makes estimates of pollution abatement and control expenditures in the United States. One source for these estimates are Bureau of the Census surveys of manufacturing establishments, state and local governments, electric utilities, petroleum refiners and mining operations. Other information is gathered on federal government expenditures on pollution control, the cost of solid waste disposal, individual spending for motor vehicle pollution control equipment and operating costs and other environmental spending, as well. In 1992, according to BEA, pollution abatement and control expenditures in the United States came to $102 billion (Rutledge and Vogan, 1994, p. 47).

In addition to estimates of environmental spending, BEA also estimates the magnitude of the "offsets" that Porter and van der Linde claim are so pervasive. In fact, the Census Bureau survey of manufacturers (upon which BEA relies for most of its information about offsets) specifically asks respondents to report "cost offsets," which are defined in such a way as seemingly to encompass both the "product" and "process" offsets that Porter and van der Linde describe (U.S. Commerce Department, 1994).[7] For 1992, BEA estimates that cost offsets for the

---

[7] It is worth including one of the examples from the Census Bureau survey to illustrate how closely the survey conforms to the Porter and van der Linde vision of offsets. The survey (U.S. Commerce Department, 1994, p. A-11) contains the following wording: "A manufacturer installs a closed loop recovery system in the production process so as to prevent the dumping of the chemicals into the water system. Since the closed loop recovery system recaptures and reuses the chemicals in the production process, it reduces expenses for chemicals. The pollution abatement portion of the capital expenditure pertaining to the closed loop recovery system is reported in Item 7 [the section of the survey where new capital

U.S. amounted to $1.7 billion, less than 2 percent of estimated environmental expenditures. This implies *net* spending for environmental protection in excess of $100 billion in 1992.

Net spending on protecting the environment may be greater than that, however, because there is reason to believe that the BEA estimates of environmental costs are on the low side. According to the Environmental Protection Agency (1990), the total cost associated with federal environmental regulation in the United States in 1992 was $135 billion.[8] EPA's estimates differ from those of BEA for a variety of reasons, some of which are difficult to discern. But some of the difference is due to the fact that EPA counts certain expenditures that BEA ignores (like those associated with measures to improve indoor air quality); because EPA apparently includes some opportunity costs in addition to out-of-pocket expenditures; and because the two agencies use different approaches occasionally even when focusing on the same category of pollution control. Some of the additional costs the EPA includes may give rise to their own offsets, but it is unlikely they will increase in proportion to these added costs. This is especially true where the difference between EPA's estimates and BEA's estimates involve imputed or opportunity costs.

One possible criticism of these estimates of offsets is that certain kinds of offsets in response to more stringent environmental regulation are not easily reportable on the Census Bureau survey form, and hence do not find their way into the Census or BEA estimates. For instance, a manufacturing firm that dropped a product line altogether because it wished to avoid environmental regulations, and entered what instead turned out to be a more profitable product line, would be hard-pressed to report this as an "offset" according to the definition provided in the Census Bureau survey. But even if one doubled or tripled or even quadrupled the estimated offsets that are reported by Census and included in BEA's estimates, the total offsets would be less than $10 billion per year, leaving net annual environmental compliance costs in the range of $100 billion or more.

It is impossible to escape the conclusion that the U.S. devotes significant resources, *net of cost savings*, to environmental protection each year. Moreover, we reach this conclusion without making reference to the work of either Jorgenson and Wilcoxen (1990) or Hazilla and Kopp (1990), both of whom showed that the social costs of environmental regulation are *greater* when viewed in a dynamic general equilibrium context than in a static, partial equilibrium setting, because of the manner in which environmental regulations depress "productive" investment and

---

expenditures are reported]. The operating expenses to maintain the system are reported in Item 3 [the analogous section for operating costs]. The value of recovered chemicals is reported as a cost offset." This example matches perfectly the example of the Robbins Company given by Porter and van der Linde, hence suggesting a close connection between the "offsets" described by Porter and van der Linde and the BEA estimates of offsets based on the Census Bureau survey.

[8] To this must be added the costs of additional control measures introduced by states (like California) that have, in some instances, gone beyond the federal statutes. We know of no estimates of these additional costs, but they may be substantial.

the consequent reduction in the rate of economic growth. Porter and van der Linde deny the validity of this work on the grounds that it fails to factor offsets into account. Since these offsets appear to be quite small—based on both the reports of those who make environmental investments, as well as on hard data—this is hardly a liability of the general equilibrium approach.

One more word about offsets. Suppose that every single dollar a firm spent on pollution control or prevention was matched by a dollar of savings in the form of product or process offsets described by Porter and van der Linde. Would it then be the case that environmental regulation is free? Of course not. The sacrifice would be measured by other opportunities foregone. Firms can and do invest in changing the size and skill mix of their labor force, in their capital base, in the sources and term structure of their financing, their research and development strategies and other things, as well. Each of these investments is expected to do more than return one dollar for each dollar spent—typically firms must project returns that exceed a "hurdle rate" of 20 percent or more before undertaking an investment. Thus, even if environmental compliance produced offsets on a dollar-for-dollar basis—rather than one dollar for every 50 spent, as the data suggest—the foregone return on invested capital would still be a significant cost of regulation.

The International Setting

The original question prompting this debate concerned the impact of environmental regulations on the competitiveness of U.S. industry in the international arena. In a much shorter essay that appeared several years ago in *Scientific American*, Porter (1991) argued that the perverse command-and-control character of most U.S. regulation has seriously handicapped American firms in competition with foreign rivals. Making the case (with which we enthusiastically agree) for incentive-based policy measures, Porter argued that U.S. firms were losing out to competition from German and Japanese companies, which benefit from more enlightened regulatory regimes.[9]

However, we believe the truth of the matter is rather different. It is not the case that other countries, including Germany or Japan, have made better use of incentive-based approaches than the United States. While other countries appear to have put in place regulatory programs that are less adversarial (and therefore less time consuming) than certain U.S. programs, most environmental regulation in Europe looks every bit as proscriptive as does the U.S. version. In fact, visitors from OECD and developing countries pour through Washington on a regular basis, trying to learn about the sulfur dioxide trading program put in place here five years ago.

---

[9] For a more detailed treatment of these particular issues, see our response (Oates et al., 1993) to the Porter (1991) paper.

Moreover, it is not clear that environmental regulation is harming the competitiveness of U.S. firms. In fact, Porter and van der Linde acknowledge as much, citing Jaffe et al. (1995, p. 157), who conclude in their survey paper that "overall, there is relatively little evidence to support the hypothesis that environmental regulations have had a large adverse effect on competitiveness, however that elusive term is defined."

This finding is important, but it has little to do with innovation offsets. As Jaffe et al. (1995) point out, there are several reasons why the relative stringency of U.S. environmental regulation to date has not been found to have adverse effects on competitiveness. First, for all but the most heavily polluting industries, the cost of complying with federal environmental regulations is a small fraction of total costs, sufficiently small (in most instances) to be swamped by international differentials in labor and material costs, capital costs, swings in exchange rates and so on. Second, although U.S. environmental regulations are arguably the most stringent in the world, the *differentials* between U.S. standards and those of our major industrialized trading partners are not very great, especially for air and water pollution control. Third, U.S. firms (as well as other multinationals) appear inclined to build modern, state-of-the-art facilities abroad, irrespective of the stringency of environmental statutes in the host country. Thus, even a significant difference in environmental standards between, say, the United States and a developing country will mean little to firms not willing to take advantage of lax standards.[10]

This is not to say that cost differentials stemming from international variations in environmental regulations are nonexistent. But as Jaffe et al. (1995, p. 159) conclude, these differentials "pose insufficient threats to U.S. industrial competitiveness to justify substantial cutbacks in domestic environmental regulations." More basically, the case for redesigning environmental programs to make more effective use of market incentives has little to do with international competitiveness; it's a much more straightforward issue of getting environmental value for the expenditures of social resources.

Conclusion

The underlying message from Porter and van der Linde about environmental regulation is not to worry, because it really won't be all that expensive. But it will. Annual U.S. expenditures for environmental protection, net of any offsets, cur-

---

[10] The rationale for this behavior appears to be two-fold. First, there is a widespread perception that tighter environmental regulations in the developing countries are inevitable, and that it is less expensive to invest initially in state-of-the-art abatement technology than it will be to retrofit later. Second, the aftermath of certain disasters, notably the Union Carbide catastrophe in Bhopal, India, has made management aware of the dangers inherent in the adoption of less than state-of-the-art control technologies in developing countries.

rently are at least $100 billion, and probably considerably more. From *society's* standpoint, with the benefits of a cleaner environment figured into the balance, every dime of this money may be well spent; the literature is replete with examples of environmental programs that pass a benefit-cost test. But a comparison of the benefits and costs is exactly how one should determine the economic attractiveness of specific programs—not on the false premise of cost-free controls.

■ *We are grateful for helpful comments on earlier drafts to Albert McGartland, Richard Schmalensee and the editors of this journal. We wish to thank the Environmental Protection Agency, the National Science Foundation and the Sloan Foundation for support that made this work possible.*

References

Barrett, Scott, "Strategic Environmental Policy and International Trade," *Journal of Public Economics*, 1994, 54:3, 325–38.

Biglaiser, Gary, and John K. Horowitz, "Pollution Regulation and Incentives for Pollution-Control Research," *Journal of Economics and Management Strategy*, Winter 1995, 3, 663–840.

Burtraw, Dallas, "Efficiency Sans Allowance Trades?: Evaluating the SO2 Emission Trading Program to Date." Resources for the Future Discussion Paper No. 95-30, 1995.

Downing, Paul B., and Lawrence J. White, "Innovation in Pollution Control," *Journal of Environmental Economics and Management*, March 1986, 13, 18–29.

Gore, Albert, *Earth in the Balance*. Boston: Houghton Mifflin Co., 1992.

Hazilla, Michael, and Raymond Kopp, "Social Cost of Environmental Quality Regulations: A General Equilibrium Analysis," *Journal of Political Economy*, August 1990, 98, 853–73.

Jaffe, Adam B., Steven R. Peterson, Paul R. Portney, and Robert N. Stavins, "Environmental Regulations and the Competitiveness of U.S. Manufacturing: What Does the Evidence Tell Us?," *Journal of Economic Literature*, March 1995, 33, 132–63.

Jorgenson, Dale W., and Peter J. Wilcoxen, "Environmental Regulation and U.S. Economic Growth," *Rand Journal of Economics*, Summer 1990, 21, 314–40.

Kennedy, Peter, "Equilibrium Pollution Taxes in Open Economies with Imperfect Competition," *Journal of Environmental Economics and Management*, July 1994, 27, 49–63.

Kneese, Allen V., and Blair T. Bower, *Managing Water Quality: Economics, Technology, Institutions*. Baltimore, Md.: Johns Hopkins University Press, 1968.

Magat, Wesley A., "Pollution Control and Technological Advance: A Dynamic Model of the Firm," *Journal of Environmental Economics and Management*, March 1978, 5, 1–25.

Malueg, David A., "Emission Credit Trading and the Incentive to Adopt New Pollution Abatement Technology," *Journal of Environmental Economics and Management*, January 1989, 16, 52–7.

Milliman, Scott R., and Raymond Prince, "Firm Incentives to Promote Technological Change in Pollution Control," *Journal of Environmental Economics and Management*, November 1989, 17, 247–65.

Oates, Wallace E., Karen Palmer, and Paul R. Portney, "Environmental Regulation and International Competitiveness: Thinking About the Porter Hypothesis." Resources for the Future Discussion Paper No. 94–02, 1993.

Parry, Ian, "Environmental R&D and the Choice Between Pigouvian Taxes and Marketable Emissions Permits," unpublished Ph.D. dissertation, University of Chicago, 1992.

Porter, Michael E., "America's Green Strategy," *Scientific American*, April 1991, 264, 168.

Rico, Renee, "The U.S. Allowance Trading System for Sulfer Dioxide: An Update on Market Experience," *Energy and Resource Economics*, March 1995, 5:2, 115–29.

Rutledge, Gary L., and Christine R. Vogan, "Pollution Abatement and Control Expenditures, 1972–92," *Survey of Current Business*, May 1994, 74, 36–49.

Simpson, David, "Environmental Policy, Innovation and Competitive Advantage." Resources for the Future Discussion Paper No. 95-12, 1995.

Simpson, David, and Robert L. Bradford, "Taxing Variable Cost: Environmental Regulation as Industrial Policy," *Journal of Environmental Economics and Management*, forthcoming 1996.

Ulph, Alistair, "Environmental Policy and International Trade: A Survey of Recent Economic Analysis," Milan, Italy: Nota di Lavoro 53.94, Fondazione Eni Enrico Mattei, 1994.

U.S. Department of Commerce (Bureau of the Census), "Pollution Abatement Costs and Expenditures, 1993," Current Industrial Reports; MA200(93)-1, Washington, D.C.: U.S. Government Printing Office, 1994.

U.S. Environmental Protection Agency, *Environmental Investments: The Cost of a Clean Environment.* Washington, D.C.: U.S. Environmental Protection Agency, 1990.

U.S. General Accounting Office, "Allowance Trading Offers an Opportunity to Reduce Emissions at Less Cost," document, GAO/RCED-95-30, 1994.

Name Index

Ackerman, Bruce A. 377
Acton, Jan P. 432
Anderson, Erling B. 194
Anderson jr, Robert J. xxviii

Baden-Fuller, C.W.F. 338
Bain, Edward C. 377
Balassa, B. 308
Baldwin, R. 279, 296
Ballard, Charles L. 259
Barbera, Anthony J. xviii, 66, 114
Barrett, Scott 441
Bartel, Ann P. xxvi
Bartelson, Eric 188
Bartik, Timothy J. xx, 129–51, 156, 157, 165, 183, 197, 354
Basta, Nicholas 419
Baumol, William J. 317, 318, 319
Beamer, William H. 69
Becker, Randy A. xix, xx, xxv, xxviii, 179–221
Berman, Eli xix, xxvii
Berndt, Ernst R. xvi, 104, 261
Berube, M. 418
Bischoff, C.W. 359
Boetti, M. 280, 296
Bonifant, B. 420
Bonson, N.C. 423
Boone, L. 282
Boroughs, D.L. 419
Botteon, M. 280, 296
Bovenberg, A. Lans xxii
Bower, Blair T. 437
Bradford, Robert L. 442
Brady, Gordon L. 377, 379, 380, 382
Brännlund, Runar xix, 113–27
Bui, Linda xix, xxvii
Burniaux, J.M. 279
Burtraw, Dallas 436

Carlevaro, F. 282
Carlson, Curtis xxviii
Carolan, T. 313
Carpenter, B. 419
Carraro, Carlo xxiii, xxiv, 277–303
Cass, D. 235
Christainsen, Gregory B. xvi, xvii, 27–32, 33, 98
Christensen, Laurits R. 50

Clark, Kim B. 70
Clay, Don 431
Cline, W.R. 285, 286
Conrad, Klaus xvi, xvii, xviii, 97–111, 282
Cooper, R. 359
Cordero, R. 347, 348
Crandall, Robert W. xx, 28, 33, 98, 155, 156, 160, 170, 335
Cropper, M.L. 306

D'Arge, Ralph C. 318
Dasgupta, Partha 99, 100
Davis, Harold 16
Deaton, A.S. 117, 119
DeCanio, Stephen J. 415
Deily, Mary E. xxiv, 335–49, 354
de Mooij, Ruud xxii
Denison, Edward F. xiv, xv, xvi, xvii, 3–26, 28, 33, 66, 97, 249
Diewerts, W.E. 58
Dixon, Lloyd S. 432
Dobson, A. 289
Donihue, Michael R. xxv, xxviii, 377–82
Dorfman, Mark H. 418, 419, 420
Dosi, C. 279
Drysdale, P. 308
Duerksen, C.J. 154, 158
Duffy-Deno, K.T. 155

Edmonds, J.A. 286
Ehrenfeld, J. 418
Ehrlich, M. 282
Ehrlich, Paul 431
Ellerman, A. Denny xxviii
Evans, Michael K. 318, 325

Faltmayer, Edmund 377
Färe, Rolf xix, 113–27
Ford, D. 97
Franklin, P.J. 338
Fraumeni, Barbara M. 44, 54
Freeman, A. Myrick xiii
Friedman, J. 156, 157, 160

Gagnon, J.E. 308, 313
Galeotti, Marzio xxiii, xxiv, 277–303
Garnaut, R. 308

Geweke, John 30
Ghemawat, P. 338
Goettle, Richard J. 259
Gollop, Frank M. 29, xix, xxviii, 33, 43–63, 66, 98, 114, 226, 379, 380
Gordon, Robert J. 377
Gore, Al 436
Graham-Tomasi, T. 279
Gray, Wayne B. xvi, xvii, xviii, xix, xxiv, xxvii, 33–41, 65–95, 183, 188, 335–49, 353–74
Griliches, Zvi xviii, 194
Grosskopf, Shawna xix, 113–27
Grossman, G.M. 155, 279, 296, 307
Gruenspecht, Howard K. xxv, 377

Hall, Bronwyn H. 160, 194, 361
Hanneman, William M. 320
Hanson, James S. 69
Harper, Michael J. xvii, 97
Harrigan, K.R. 338
Hassler, William T. 377
Hausman, Jerry A. 39, 194, 196
Haveman, Robert H. xvi, xvii, 27–32, 33
Hazilla, Michael xxi, 253–75, 425, 444
Henderson, Vernon J. xix, xx, xxv, xxviii, 179–221
Henseler-Unger, I. 282
Hetemäki, L. 114
Hicks, John R. 262
Hoerger, Fred 69
Holtz-Eakin, T. 279, 296
Hudson, Edward A. 259, 260

Iacocca, Lee 423

Jaffe, Adam B. xxiv, xxviii, 421, 425, 446
Johansen, L. 228
Johansson, T.B. 279, 280
Jorgenson, Dale W. xx, 35, 44, 50, 54, 225–51, 257, 259, 260, 281, 282, 358, 424, 444
Joskow, Paul L. 377, 380, 382
Jovanovic, Boyan 206

Kahn, Matthew E. 184
Kalt, Joseph P. 98, 306, 425
Kappler, Frederick G. 104, 243
Karadeloglou, P. 279
Kendall, M. 309, 312
Kennedy, Peter 442
Kerr, M.L. 160, 361
King, A. 422
Kneese, Allen V. 437
Kohli, U. 291
Koopmans, T.C. 235
Kopp, Raymond J. xxi, 253–73, 425, 444

Krueger, A.B. 155, 307
Kuncoro, Ari 192
Kunze, Kent xvii, 97

Laffont, J.J. 278, 279
Lake, Elizabeth E. 320
Lau, Lawrence J. 54, 101, 287
Laws, Elliott P. 181
Leonard, H. Jeffrey 155, 307, 425
Leontief, Wassily 97, 318
Lerman, S. 135
Levinson, Arik xx, 153–77, 183, 306
Liebenstein, Harvey 70
Lieberman, M.B. 338
Liljas, B. 114, 124
Liroff, Richard A. 181
Low, P. 155, 306, 307
Lyne, J. 158

McConnell, Virginia D. xviii, 66, 114, 156, 157, 163, 165, 184
McCubbin, Neil 423
McFadden, D. 134, 135, 156, 165
McGuckin, R.H. 359
McGuire, M.C. 314
McGuire, Therese 145
Mairesse, Jacques xviii
Maloney, Michael 377, 379, 380, 382
Mani, Muthukumara xxiii
Markusen, James R. xix
Maxwell, J. 418
Meadows, Dennis L. 431
Meadows, Donella H. 431
Meese, Richard 30
Melnick, R.S. 181
Meyer, Stephen M. 425
Meyers, J.G. 98
Michel, P. 279
Miller, Catherine G. 418, 419, 420
Mody, Ashoka 425
Morgenstern, Richard D. xviii, xxvii
Morrison, Catherine J. xvi, xvii, 97–111
Muir, Warren R. 418, 419, 420
Musu, I. 280
Mutti, John H. 318, 321

Nakamura, L. 98
Nalebuff, B. 338
Nash, J. 418
Navarro, Peter xx
Nelson, Randy A. xxv, xxviii, 377–82
Newman, Robert 133, 145
Nordhaus, William O. 29
Norsworthy, J.R. xvii, 33, 97

Oates, Wallace E. xxii, xxvi, xxvii, 306, 314, 317, 318, 319, 435–48
Oster, Sharon M. 320

Palmer, Karen L. xxii, xxiv, xxvi, xxvii, 306, 314, 421, 435–48
Papke, Leslie E. 194
Parkinson, Gerald 418, 431
Parry, Ian W.H. xxii
Pascoe, G.A. 359
Pashigian, B. Peter xxv, 335, 383–410
Pasurka, Carl A. 318, 321
Peltzman, S. 336
Peterson, S. 421
Pethig, R. 314
Pindyck, Robert S. 185, 204
Pittman, R.W. 97, 114
Plaut, Thomas 133
Pluta, Joseph 133
Porter, Michael E. xxvi, 66, 71, 306, 413–34, 435–8 *passim*, 441–3 *passim*, 445–6 *passim*
Portney, Paul R. xxii, xxvi, xxvii, 306, 314, 421, 425, 435–48
Prewitt, Edward 377

Radcliffe, I. 420
Reid, Robert O. xxviii
Repetto, Robert 425
Reynolds, S.S. 338
Richardson, David J. 318, 321
Rico, Renee 436
Rinquist, E.J. 360
Roberts, Mark J. xix, xxviii, 33, 43–63, 66, 98, 114, 226, 379, 380
Robinson, D.H. 97
Robison, H. David xxiii, 306, 307, 317–29
Rose, A.K. 307, 313
Rose, Nancy 377
Rutledge, Gary L. 104, 243, 443

Scherer, Frank M. xvii
Schmalensee, Richard 380, 421
Schmenner, Roger 130, 133, 134
Schwab, R.M. 156, 157, 163, 165, 184
Selden, T. 279, 296
Serjeantson, R. 347, 348
Seskin, Eugene P. xxviii
Shadbegian, Ronald J. xviii, xix, xxiv, xxvii, 65–95, 353–74
Sheridan, J.H. 418, 423
Siegel, Robin 29
Simpson, David 442
Simpson, Ralph D. 421

Singh, N. 313
Siniscalco, D. 281
Slesnick, D.T. 231, 257
Smith, Zachary A. 423
Solow, Robert M. xv
Sorsa, P. 307
Sprague, John B. 423
Stavins, Robert N. 421, 425
Stigler, G.J. 336, 338
Sullivan, Dennis 133, 145
Swisher, J.N. 279, 280

Talati, C. 313
Thomas, H. Randolph 377
Thomas, Lacy G. xxvi
Tietenberg, Tom xxv, xxviii, 377
Tirole, J. 278, 279
Tobey, J.A. 155, 307
Topa, G. 280
Turner, Matthew 192

Ugelow, J. 306
Ulph, Alistair 442
Unger, Rolf 104

Vagi, David 419
van der Linde, Claas xxvi, 306, 413–34, 435–8 *passim*, 441–3 *passim*, 445–6 *passim*
Verdier, T. 279
Viscusi, W. Kip 69
Vogan, Christine R. 443

Walter, Ingo 306, 318, 321
Walter, J. 97
Wastel, Dieter xviii
Wasylenko, Michael 145
Watkins, G.C. 104
Waxman, Henry A. 181
Weaver, Paul H. 377
Weidenbaum, Murray L. 18
Wheaton, W.C. 163
Wheeler, David xxiii, 425
Whinston, M.D. 338
Wilcoxen, Peter J. xx, 225–51, 281, 282, 424, 444
Willenbrock, Jack H. 377
Wilson, D. 279
Wood, David O. xvi, 104
Wooldridge, Jeffrey M. 194, 196

Xu, Xinpeng xxiii, 306–16

Yeats, A. 155, 306, 307